The Christmas Encyclopedia

The Christmas Encyclopedia

by William D. Crump

McFarland & Company, Inc., Publishers
Jefferson, North Carolina, and London

Frontispiece: Engraving from the 1880s after a work by an artist identified as "Minthrop." From Charles Wesley, *Hark! The Herald Angels Sing* (New York: Dutton, 1889).

Illustration research and selection by Linda Campbell Franklin

To the Lord of Christmas

Library of Congress Cataloguing-in-Publication Data

Crump, William D., 1949–
    The Christmas encyclopedia / by William D. Crump.
      p.   cm.
    Includes bibliographical references and index.
    ISBN 0-7864-1034-5 (illustrated case binding : 50# alkaline paper) ∞
    1. Christmas—Encyclopedias.   I. Title.
GT4985.C74   2001
394.2663'03 — dc21
                                           2001044440

British Library cataloguing data are available

Front cover art © 2001 Eyewire

Manufactured in the United States of America

McFarland & Company, Inc., Publishers
  Box 611, Jefferson, North Carolina 28640
    www.mcfarlandpub.com

Contents

Acknowledgments

I extend grateful appreciation to the following individuals and institutions for contributing valuable information or assistance in the preparation of this manuscript: American Society of Composers, Authors and Publishers (ASCAP), for granting permission to reproduce its list of the "Top 25 Holiday Songs of the [20th] Century"; Jennifer Anthony, Visiting Assistant Professor, Music Library, University of Illinois at Urbana-Champaign; Josip Barlek, Professor and Higher Curator, Ethnographic Museum, Zagreb, Croatia; John Whit Curtis, for his assistance with the entry "Beautiful Star of Bethlehem"; Diane deBlois, Public Affairs Office, Canadian Consulate General, Atlanta, Georgia; Father Krikor Maksoudian, Director, Krikor and Clara Zohrab Information Center, Diocese of the Armenian Church of America, New York City; Institute of Ethnology and Folklore, Zagreb, Croatia, which provided the hardcover book *Christmas in Croatia*; Peter McInally, British Information Services, New York City; Linet Mavesere, Curator of Ethnography, Zimbabwe Museum of Human Sciences, Zimbabwe, Africa; Creighton Pencheon, Ag Director of Culture in the Ministry of Culture, Youth and Sports, Basseterre, St. Kitts, West Indies; Julie Crump Pugh; Ronnie Pugh, Country Music Foundation, Nashville, Tennessee; Richard Starbuck, Director, Archives of the Moravian Church in America, Southern Province, Winston-Salem, North Carolina.

Grateful appreciation is also extended to Ms. Linda Campbell Franklin for illustration research.

I also would like to thank the following foreign embassies in Washington, D.C., for providing summaries of Christmas traditions and customs in their respective countries: Austria, Barbados, Brazil, Bulgaria (Philip Dimitrov, Ambassador), Colombia (Assad Jater, Cultural Attaché), Czech Republic, Denmark (Sarah L. Rothmann, Information Officer), Ecuador (Jorge Saade-Scaff, Cultural and Press Attaché), Ethiopia, Fiji (Lele Vosailagi), Finland, France, Greece, Guyana (Annette Carter-Harris, Executive Officer), Iceland, Indonesia (Puspita Sariwati), Ireland, Italy, Japan, Latvia (Sandija Macane), Lebanon (Wajdi Najjar), Lithuania, Netherlands, Norway, Poland, Sierra Leone (J. G. Caulker, First Secretary), Sweden, Switzerland (C. Cadem), Ukraine (Irene Datsenko, Librarian), Venezuela (Karl Krispin, Cultural Attaché).

Preface

The search for "Christmas Past and Present" began in 1994, when my family made a three-hour audio cassette tape as a holiday project. We collected the best renditions of sacred and secular carols that we could find, recited carol poems, and attempted to sing a few ourselves. We also wanted to include short background sketches about the carols, while the finale would include a segment that detailed the origins of popular Christmas symbols and traditions. Of course we, like so many other families, had blindly carried on these traditions year after year without knowing exactly why we did, and it was time to change that. So off I headed to the library.

I managed to compile sufficient facts to complete the family project. Gleaning them, however, was an education in itself.

To say that the subject of Christmas is vast is a gross understatement. It is astronomical. After all, from the manger to the space age, we have 2,000 years of holiday history, music, traditions, personages, stories, legends, and symbols with which to contend, and all on an international level. Out of all this subject matter, most Christmas books concentrate on just a few facts or themes, requiring persons with more than a passing interest, or Christmas "addicts" like myself, to peruse scores of volumes and other media in order to receive a comprehensive Christmas education. A similar scenario exists when one enters the world of Christmas on the Internet.

It is not difficult to imagine that the average reader (with a passing interest but with no desire to wade through multiple tomes) would most likely shy away from such a formidable holiday arsenal. How, then, could readers become better acquainted with the complete "who, what, when, where, why, and how" of Christmas, and have it all wrapped up in a single, convenient package?

This volume was conceived with just this goal in mind. From a multitude of Christmas sources (reference texts, novels, children's books, poems, anecdotes, short stories, magazine reprints, songbooks, record and compact disc liner notes, videocassettes, and the Internet), this book concisely compiles and reviews essential and fanciful subjects which provide a solid foundation for understanding and appreciating the holiday from every aspect. However, had I attempted to include every facet of Christmas that has ever appeared in print or in the entertainment media since the foundation of Christmas itself, there would have been no end to this book. Therefore the entries herein are those which have remained Christmas treasures through popular association and usage over decades and sometimes centuries.

This volume contains more than 340 entries, the bulk of which place strong emphasis on Christmas as depicted in the popular media. Among the subjects of the entries are individual carols and songs, motion pictures, non-animated television specials, animated cartoons, Christmas episodes of television series, literary subjects, and celebrations around the world. Also covered are familiar aspects of the holiday such as biblical and secular events which have shaped Christmas in history; St. Nicholas, Santa Claus, and other mythical spirits who bring gifts; and symbols such as the Yule log, Christmas tree, holly, ivy, and mistletoe.

Because not every country celebrates Christmas, I have included entries for those nations and regions in which Christianity has been most influential. Some foreign countries stand as individual entries, whereas others are grouped together under larger headings (including for example "Africa," "Baltic States," "Central America," and "South America") because of their geographic proximity or their similar customs. I also include the phrase for "Merry Christmas" in the official or principal language of each country.

In a few instances, the principal text for a custom common to a group of countries may appear as a separate entry with appropriate cross-referencing. For example the entry *Las Posadas* ("The Lodgings") discusses a popular custom found in many Latin American countries.

Whereas traditions may evolve over the centuries, the discussions concentrate on customs currently in vogue. It is not the purpose of this book to render detailed accounts and histories of archaic customs long abandoned, except where they have significantly impacted current practices.

Entries appear alphabetically throughout with extensive cross-referencing. Terms not found as cross-references may be accessible through the index. In general, foreign words appear as principal headings or cross-references only when they name a major custom, event, or item. When incidental foreign words appear within the body of an entry but do not form a part of the heading itself, they are listed only in the index.

Entries for motion pictures, television specials, and cartoons include production credits (principal actors, year released, writers, producers, directors, production companies, video companies, color format, running times) if such are available. Not all film titles appear on video, titles may appear on alternate or additional video labels than those cited herein, and studios may withdraw previously released titles from the video market at any time. Therefore the designation "Video N/A" notes that either a video version does not yet exist or that specific video information was simply unavailable at this writing. All videos cited are in VHS format, and the designation "B & W" indicates that a film is photographed in black and white.

References are listed at the end of this work and include books, periodicals, sound recordings, and Internet sources.

I received considerable information from foreign embassies in Washington, D.C., and directly from some sources overseas regarding international Christmas customs. Most of these sources provided either photocopied material or firsthand accounts that had been written by the embassy staff, ambassador, or some other authority. All identifiable media sources from this collection are listed with the references.

All biblical quotations are taken from the King James version.

A

Account of a Visit from St. Nicholas
See **A Visit from St. Nicholas**

Adeste Fideles
See **O Come, All Ye Faithful**

Advent

Derived from the Latin *adventus* ("coming"), the four-week period prior to Christmas Day observed chiefly by the Roman Catholic, Lutheran, Anglican, and Episcopal churches; in short, by the Western or Roman Church. Advent commences on the Sunday nearest November 30 (St. Andrew the Apostle's Day) and terminates on Christmas Eve. It is a time in which believers are to undergo spiritual cleansing and sometimes fasting in preparation for the Feast of the Nativity, or Christmas.

Although legend holds that an Advent season originated with the Apostle Peter in the first century, the exact time when Advent was first introduced into the Church remains obscure. Early evidence vaguely referring to an Advent period includes the Acts of the Synod of Saragossa (year 380), the writings of St. Maximus, Bishop of Turin (415–466), and those of St. Caesarius, Bishop of Arles (502–542); and documents of the Synod of Lerida, Spain (542), and the Council of Tours, France (567). The Synod of Macon in Gaul (581) specified the period from November 11 to Christmas Day, while homilies of Pope St. Gregory the Great (590–604) only included a sermon for a second Advent Sunday. By 650 in Spain, Advent spanned the five Sundays before Christmas Day, but Pope St. Gregory VII (1073–1085) reduced these to four Sundays instead, and this number has remained constant since then.

While Advent probably was well established by the sixth century in the Western Church, no evidence for its observance in the Orthodox, or Eastern, Church appeared until the eighth century. Even then, instead of joyous anticipation, a mood similar to Easter Lent prevailed, for the Orthodox pre–Christmas period consisted of fasting and abstinence for forty days, from November 15 to Christmas Day, which commemorated Christ's fast of forty days in the wilderness. Today, except for the fast, there is no special Advent liturgy in the Orthodox Church. Advent begins the ecclesiastical year in the Eastern and Western churches.

Much symbolism surrounds Advent. Each of its four Sundays represents one of the four great "comings" of Christ: the first, His coming in the flesh; the second, His coming into the hearts of all who believe in Him; the third, His coming at the hour of death to the faithful; the fourth, His coming at the final judgment. Advent colors are blue, symbolic of the Virgin Mary's robe, and purple, symbolic of penance and cleansing.

Advent wreaths and candles adorn churches and homes alike. Attributed to Martin Luther (1483–1546), a German priest who initiated the Protestant Reformation, Advent wreaths are fashioned from various species of evergreen branches and are either hung from the ceiling or used as table centerpieces. Affixed to the wreath are four candles, each one representing an Advent Sunday. Three candles are purple (for penance) and one is pink (for the coming joy), although some wreaths sport all red candles (symbolic of Christ's blood) or all white candles (symbolic of Christ's purity). The evergreen wreath itself, forming a never-ending circle, symbolizes the promise of eternal life through Christ.

Churches and families successively light one candle on the first Advent Sunday, two the following Sunday, and so on, starting with the purple candles and ending with the pink candle on the fourth Sunday, when all the candles burn. Each lighting provides families with an opportunity to convene for quiet devotions. On Christmas Day, a large red candle can be added, representing Christ.

A variation on this theme is the single Advent candle with the numbers 1 through 25 stamped into the wax. The candle is lit on December 1, allowed to burn down to the number 1, then extinguished. The process is repeated daily, allowing the candle to burn to the corresponding day until Christmas Day.

In some areas of Europe, it is customary for someone named John or Joan to light the Advent wreath, for the Gospel of John describes Christ as the Light of the World, symbolized by the burning candles. The custom may also stem from a legend stating that John the Baptist first beheld a halo around Christ following His baptism.

Designed especially for children, Advent calendars and Advent houses portray behind little flaps sacred or secular holiday themes for each day from December 1 through December 25. On opening each flap, children may find a Bible verse or character, a winter scene, or a small toy or money. On Christmas Day, the final flap reveals either the Nativity scene with the Holy Family or Santa and his reindeer.

During the Advent season, churches additionally observe the feast days of certain saints or other religious events as described below. Although a nation's opening date for its "Christmas season" may not always coincide with the commencement of Advent, the date is usually found among the following:

• ST. ANDREW'S DAY (November 30). One of Christ's twelve apostles, St. Andrew by tradition received martyrdom through crucifixion on an X-shaped cross (now known as St. Andrew's Cross) on the Island of Patmos. He is a patron saint of Scotland and Russia.

• ST. BARBARA'S DAY (December 4). Legend holds that the third-century martyr St. Barbara converted to Christianity after her father, desiring to protect her from the world, confined her to a tower in what is now Izmit (formerly Nicomedia), Turkey. Subsequently beheading her for her faith, the father was struck and killed by lightning, for which St. Barbara became associated with storms. She is the patron saint of artillery. Although the Roman Catholic Church dropped St. Barbara from the church calendar in 1969, there remains a tradition throughout Europe, whereby girls place cherry tree branches ("Barbara branches") in water indoors on this day. If buds bloom by Christmas Eve, the girls will wed within the new year.

• ST. NICHOLAS'S DAY (December 6). This holiday honoring the fourth-century archbishop of Myra (now Demre), Turkey, is celebrated widely throughout Europe. It is probably the most popular of Advent feast days and is detailed further in a separate entry. *See also* **Saint Nicholas Day**.

• FEAST OF THE IMMACULATE CONCEPTION (December 8). This feast, commemorating the belief that the Virgin Mary was born without original sin, opens the Christmas season in many Latin American countries and is detailed in a separate entry. *See also* **Feast of the Immaculate Conception**.

• ST. LUCIA'S DAY (December 13). Legend states that St. Lucia, a native of Syracuse on the island of Sicily, was martyred in 304 for her Christian faith, having been stabbed in the throat. By the fifth century, she is said to have saved Syracuse from famine and to have brought food to Christians hiding in catacombs to escape persecution. To avoid a suitor, she plucked out her eyes and gave them to him, after which the Virgin restored her eyesight; thus artists have rendered her as a maiden wounded in the throat and carrying a knife with two eyes on a tray. St. Lucia is particularly noted for brilliant light radiating from her face, which stems from *lux* (light), the Latin derivative of her name.

Prior to the adoption of the Gregorian calendar in the sixteenth century, St. Lucia's Day fell on the winter solstice, which poses a factor in her association with light, and her day Christianized a day formerly associated with the pagan Germanic goddess Berchta (also variously known as Perchta, Bertha, Hertha, Holda, and others). While some ethnologists associate her as goddess of the home, spinning, and children, others equate her with death. Thus, in various regions of the Balkans, the child-eating witch *Lutzelfrau* ironically appears on St. Lucia Eve with gifts for children. Other pre–Christian witches bearing gifts have included "Black Lucia" and "Grandma Luca" (from "Lucia"), the latter a Croatian being who scorched the fingers of naughty children and punished girls who had not learned to crochet.

An old superstition also stated that sitting on a stool whose construction commenced on St. Lucia's Day and ended on Christmas Eve enabled one to see witches. Other traditions forbade women from conducting some household chores on this day, and girls practiced divination rituals regarding future marriage. Elsewhere, St. Lucia brings gifts to children on the eve of her feast day.

Lucia Day is especially noted for opening the Christmas season in Sweden, and Lucia is the patron saint of Syracuse, Milan, sight, tailors, and blacksmiths. *See also* **Sweden.**

• ST. THOMAS'S DAY (December 21). The Anglican Church still observes this date, the Roman Catholics having moved the date to July 3. According to legend, after the three Wise Men left Bethlehem, their journeys took them to India, where many years later St. Thomas the Apostle, having established himself as an evangelist in that region, converted them to Christianity. In another story from India, St. Thomas took a large sum of money, for which he was to have erected a king's palace, and distributed it among the poor. This latter legend led to the old British custom of "Thomasing" or begging from door to door on December 21, a custom that prevailed from the eighteenth to the early twentieth centuries. *See also* **Great Britain.**

Africa

Because vast areas of this continent remain unsettled, Christmas customs are observed chiefly in a few countries where Christianity has been introduced (as opposed to Islam), principally by European missionaries. Hence, the customs reflect those of the missionaries' home countries as well as native culture. Several traditions are common among the Christians on this continent: attendance at Christmas church services (even if these are the only services attended during the year), which may continue for several hours; the acquisition of new clothes, which parents and children wear at Christmas services; the giving of simple gifts; and feasting with family and

fellow members of one's village. The following paragraphs summarize more specific customs for several countries.

• EGYPT. About 10 percent of the people in this predominantly Muslim nation embrace Christianity; most of these belong to the Coptic Orthodox Church, a body that dates to the fifth century. This church observes Christmas on January 7, which corresponds to the Coptic month of *Khiahk*, or December 25 on the Julian calendar ("Christmas Old Style"). To commemorate Christ's suffering in the wilderness for forty days after His baptism, Christmas is preceded by a forty-day fast with abstinence from meat and dairy products. Christmas Eve includes Midnight masses, the chief of which is celebrated in Alexandria by the Coptic Pope. Following services, people usually observe an early morning breakfast of bread, rice, garlic, and boiled meat. On Christmas Day, the wealthy distribute *zalabya* (doughnuts), *bouri* (mullet fish), and candles to the poor, the latter gift symbolizing the light which illuminated the scene of the Nativity. Christmas is a time for visiting relatives and friends, with the serving of *kahk* (sweet biscuits marked with a cross). "Merry Christmas" in Egypt is: *Idah Saidan Wa Sanah Jadidah* (Arabic). *See also* **Christmas Old Style, Christmas New Style.**

• ETHIOPIA. St. Frumentius brought Christianity to what formerly was known as the Kingdom of Aksum early in the fourth century. Some 50 percent of the population remains Christian, primarily in the North, and belongs to the Ethiopian Orthodox Church. Closely related to the Coptic Church of Egypt (see above), the Ethiopian Church also observes *Genna* (Christmas) on January 7 and *Timkat* ("Baptism," Epiphany) on January 19. Because *Genna* actually refers to a national game similar to field hockey that is played only on Christmas Day, the name has become synonymous with Christmas itself. Christmas dinner may consist of *injera* (flat, sourdough bread) and *dorowat* (chicken stew).

The most elaborate religious rites occur on the eve of *Timkat*, as a procession of worshippers follows priests bearing a *tabot* (ark), a replica of the biblical Ark of the Covenant, to a nearby body of water where celebrations take place all night amid feasting and dancing. On

Timkat morning, priests bless the water by immersing a cross, after which celebrants often wash themselves to receive the blessing. The ark replicas derive from legends stating that the St. Mary of Zion Church in the city of Aksum presently enshrines the actual Ark of the Covenant, presumed to have been lost when the ancient Israelites were taken into Babylonian captivity. The shrine is well guarded, and entry is prohibited. At this time, people make pilgrimages to twelve monolithic churches hewn from solid, volcanic rock in the city of Lalibela. Legends contend that King Lalibela in the twelfth century enlisted the help of angels to build these structures, which stand in two groups on either side of the Jordan River.

Children traditionally receive simple gifts such as clothing only on *Timkat*, and a favorite sport is *feres gugs*, which resembles the jousting matches of medieval Europe. "Merry Christmas" in Ethiopia is: *Melkam Yelidet Beaal* (Amharic, the official language). *See also* **Epiphany.**

• GHANA. Some 60 percent of Ghana's people are Christian, 16 percent are Muslim, and over 20 percent follow traditional beliefs. Christmas dinner often consists of fowl, pork, goat, or sheep, along with rice, *fufu* (yam paste), fruits, and soup consisting of eggs and meat, okra, or beans. Festivities continue for eight days with processions of street bands and dancers; groups of children carol from house to house and traditionally receive gifts from the residents. Families usually decorate a fruit tree with colored paper ornaments, and folklore holds that Father Christmas, a variant of Santa Claus, emerges from the jungles with gifts for the children. "Merry Christmas" is said in English, the official language; also *Afishapa* (Akan language).

• KENYA. About 66 percent of the population is Christian, 6 percent Muslim, and the remainder of the people follow traditional African religions. Christmas dinner includes *nyama choma* (roasted meat), often goat, along with *chapatis* (flat bread). Carolers make their rounds from house to house on Christmas Eve, and the monetary gifts received are donated to local churches. "Merry Christmas" in Kenya is: *Krismas njema na heri za mwaka mpya* (Swahili, a principal language of many).

• REPUBLIC OF SOUTH AFRICA. South Africans are principally (about 80 percent) Christian Protestants. Falling during the summer, Christmas is celebrated with outdoor activities, including "Carols by Candlelight," a custom originating in Australia. Other customs reflect those of Dutch (now termed Afrikaners or Boers) and English settlers, such as children hanging up their stockings in anticipation of a visit by Father Christmas, pantomimes, and Boxing Day. Many native Africans observe a week-long carnival in costumes with gifts, singing, dancing, and feasting. "Merry Christmas" is said in the two official languages, English and *Geseende Kerfees* (Afrikaans), and in a number of other African tongues, such as *Sinifesela ukhisimusi omuhle nonyaka omusha onempumelelo* (Zulu). *See also* **Australia; Boxing Day; Great Britain; Low Countries** (THE NETHERLANDS).

• SIERRA LEONE. Some 10 percent of the people are Christian, 30 percent follow traditional African beliefs, and 30 percent are Muslim. Christmas traditions merge with those of traditional religions. In Freetown, the capital, festivities commence two to three weeks prior to Christmas, during which time bands tour the streets, collecting donations. Children accompany adults who are masked as devils, the latter of whom perform dances for profit. Popular devils consist of the *Fairy*, which resembles a fairy; the *Jobai*, noted for its small head and flamboyant spinning; and the *Congoli* or *Gogoli* with its large head. Sending Christmas cards is also popular, and festivities continue into the New Year. "Merry Christmas" is said in English, the official language.

• UGANDA. About 75 percent of the population is Christian, 16 percent Muslim. Because the usual diet consists of a starch with stewed vegetables, meat is important for Christmas. Therefore Christmas dinner consists of beef or chicken with *matoke* (mashed and cooked banana, served with groundnut sauce). Although no gifts are exchanged as such, men customarily purchase new dresses for their wives at this time. "Merry Christmas" is said in English, the official language; also as *Webale Krismasi* (Rutooro language).

• ZIMBABWE. The population of this former British colony of Rhodesia consists of 25 percent Christians; the majority of the remainder are Synchretics, with a minority following traditional African religions. A key feature of the latter is the worship of family ancestors. Regardless of religious affiliation, families come together at Christmastime, and urban dwellers return to their ancestral homes as well as pay visits to rural relatives. Making such travel convenient, most businesses close for three weeks during the Christmas–New Year season.

Synchretics, who mix Christianity with traditional religions, combine elements of both beliefs into Christmas celebrations, which include Christian sermons, followed by dancing and singing to drums and horns, slaughtering cattle to appease the ancestors, and feasting upon the beef. There is much carousing and visiting between Synchretic households and villages, where drinking and brawling constitute the principal festivities.

Non–Christians choose Christmas Day as a special time to give thanks to, and seek guidance from, the spirits of their ancestors, while the Christian minority celebrates in typical British fashion with roast turkey and Father Christmas, who leaves gifts in a stocking or under the Christmas tree (*see* **Great Britain**).

Soliciting gifts from one's relatives on Christmas Day is a most proper and universal custom which expresses kinship and family ties. A related custom states that, should any two people meet, the first to ask for "Christmas" (implying a gift) will be the recipient of a gift from the other; a person may seek gifts in this manner from as many people as possible, but not twice from the same person. Such a custom is virtually identical to the "Christmas gif'!" which slaves commonly practiced in America's Old South (*see* **United States**). Because the government stresses that people's resources should be shared especially during the holidays, each city hosts a "Mayor's Christmas Cheer Fund," in which the rich are urged to give to the poor. "Merry Christmas" is said in English, the official language.

Ah, Bleak and Chill
See **Alfred Burt Carols**

The Alan Brady Show Presents
See **The Dick Van Dyke Show**

Alfred Burt Carols

Designation applied to fifteen carols, the music for which was composed by the American Alfred S. Burt (1920–1954), published collectively in 1954. The titles include "Ah, Bleak and Chill"; "All on a Christmas Morning"; "Carol of the Mother"; "Caroling, Caroling"; "Christ in the Stranger's Guise"; "Christmas Cometh Caroling"; "Come, Dear Children"; "Jesu Parvule"; "Nigh Bethlehem"; "O Hearken Ye"; "Some Children See Him"; "The Star Carol"; "This Is Christmas"; "We'll Dress the House"; and "What Are the Signs?" Burt's father, Bates G. Burt, and Wihla Hutson contributed the lyrics. As a composer, Alfred Burt is obscure, having died at the age of 33.

With the exception of four, the Alfred Burt Carols also remain rather obscure, although one may find them in selected medley performances. One of the first recordings of note for three of these carols was by country artist Tennessee Ernie Ford, who included "The Star Carol," "O Hearken Ye," and "Some Children See Him" in his 1958 Gold Record–winning Capitol album, *The Star Carol*, which made the *Billboard* charts in 1958, 1959, and during most of the 1960s. These three carols, along with "Caroling, Caroling," which is now reputed to be the best-known of the carols, have acquired the most popularity.

An All Dogs Christmas Carol
See **A Christmas Carol** (Film and Television Versions)

All I Want for Christmas Is My Two Front Teeth

American novelty song composed by Pennsylvania native Don Gardner in 1946. Although the song was first introduced on Perry Como's radio show by an obscure singing group, "The Satisfiers," it did not achieve national fame until 1948, when a recording by Spike Jones and His City Slickers on the RCA Victor label made it the top Christmas song that year. There, George Rock portrayed a child longing for his lost teeth so that he could wish everyone Merry Christmas without lisping. Don Gardner produced no other pieces that remain familiar today.

All My Heart This Night Rejoices

("Fröhlich soll mein Herze springen"). German carol, the lyrics of which are considered to be the most familiar work of Lutheran minister Paul Gerhardt (1607–1676). A popular hymn writer, Gerhardt produced 132 hymns, publishing "All My Heart" in 1653. His poem has enjoyed several musical settings, most notably that of 1666 by composer and compatriot Johann Ebeling, who contributed scores to 120 of Gerhardt's lyrics. Horatio Parker, chairman of Yale University's music department in the United States, provided another setting (1894). Great Britain's Catherine Winkworth (1827–1878), a respected translation specialist, contributed the most widely sung English version of the lyrics.

Consisting of fifteen verses, "All My Heart" is a joyful proclamation of the Gospel of Christ with references to the Nativity interspersed. It rings a message of hope for the weary and wretched of spirit that Christ removes all sin, and that in Him, death is only the beginning of a far better life.

All on a Christmas Morning

See **Alfred Burt Carols**

Alvin's Christmas Carol

See **A Christmas Carol** (FILM AND TELEVISION VERSIONS)

Amahl and the Night Visitors

Opera in one act, the first opera written for television, with music and libretto by Italian-born composer and conductor Gian Carlo Menotti. The NBC Opera Company presented the premiere performance from New York City on Christmas Eve, 1951, starring Chet Allen as Amahl and Rosemary Kuhlman as his mother. Other cast members included Andrew McKinley (Kaspar), David Aiken (Melchior), Leon Lishner (Balthazar), Frank Monachino (The Page), and the Chorus of Shepherds and Villagers. Thomas Schippers conducted the orchestra and chorus.

Amahl, a poverty-stricken, crippled boy who hobbles on a crutch, lives with his widowed mother in the mountains of Italy. Traveling to Bethlehem, the "Visitors"—the three Wise Men and their page—stop by, seeking shelter for the night, and are welcomed into Amahl's house.

As the Wise Men unveil the importance of their mission, Amahl desperately wishes that he could also give as precious a gift to the Christ Child as the Wise Men's gold, frankincense, and myrrh. His mother, on the other hand, is envious of the gold. She steals a portion later that night, but the page apprehends her in the act. Though she pleads that she desperately needs the gold to feed her child, she repents and returns it, and the Wise Men forgive her. She wishes that she could also send a gift to the Christ Child, whereupon Amahl offers to the Wise Men his only possession, his little crutch. In so doing, he is miraculously healed and is able to run like other children. He then accompanies the Wise Men to Bethlehem.

After 1951, Bill McIver played Amahl for a number of seasons on the air, while Kuhlman continued as the mother. *Amahl* received its first stage performances in 1952 at Indiana University, Bloomington, and simultaneously in New York City. In 1953 the *Hallmark Hall of Fame* presented *Amahl* as the first sponsored television show in color. NBC remade the opera in 1978, with Robert Sapolsky as Amahl, Teresa Stratus as the mother, and Giorgio Tozzi, Nico Castel, and Willard White as the Wise Men.

An American Christmas Carol

See **A Christmas Carol** (FILM AND TELEVISION VERSIONS)

The Andy Griffith Show

Popular television situation comedy series that aired on the CBS network from 1960 to 1968.

Of the 249 episodes which comprised *The Andy Griffith Show*, only one featured a Christmas theme. Titled simply "Christmas Story," it aired on December 19, 1960, during the series' first year. The scene is Christmas Eve at the Mayberry courthouse. Reviewing the mail, Andy and Barney enjoy a Christmas card from the Hubacher brothers, which reads, "Merry Christmas from state prison." Barney also receives a card from an old flame, Hilda Mae, which reads, "Merry Christmas, Barney Parney

Poo." Operating on a penal honor system, Andy releases his stock of prisoners for the holiday on their word that they will return to finish their sentences on the day after Christmas. Suddenly in bursts the old, cantankerous merchant, Ben Weaver (Will Wright), dragging in Sam Muggins (Sam Edwards) on a charge of selling bootleg whiskey. Andy certainly has no desire to arrest anyone on Christmas Eve, of all times, and tries to delay everything until the holidays are over. "Christmas? Ha!" is Ben's Scrooge-like reply to Andy's plea for clemency.

Although Andy has no choice but to lock up Sam, he decides that Sam will have a Christmas despite the circumstances. Together with Aunt Bee and druggist Ellie Walker (Elinor Donahue), the lawmen and Opie all throw a Christmas party at the jail for Sam, his wife Bess (Margaret Kerry), and their two children, Effie and Billy. The festivities include decorated Christmas trees for the office and Sam's cell, courtesy of Barney, who dons a Santa suit; an Andy-Ellie duet of "Away in a Manger" with Andy accompanying on guitar; and a turkey dinner with eggnog, courtesy of Aunt Bee. When Ben returns to see the merriment at hand and denounces the scene, Andy cleverly replies that not only was it necessary to arrest the rest of Sam's family as accessories in crime, but that he was also compelled to deputize Aunt Bee, Ellie, and Opie to guard the "desperate" prisoners.

Foiled at every turn, Ben strangely commits a series of misdemeanors himself, but Andy remains compassionate, letting Ben go unpunished. When Ben hauls off a sidewalk bench, Andy lets him keep it as a Christmas present, and Ellie even pays Ben's two-dollar fine in another mishap. Only when he discovers that Ben has fallen off a crate while peering into the jail does Andy realize Ben's utter loneliness and desire to spend Christmas with others. "Arrested" for disturbing the peace, Ben returns with a large suitcase, which Barney immediately searches. To Ben's "incredulity," it contains roller skates, which he gives to Opie; a baseball mitt for Billy; a doll for Effie; perfume for Ellie; a sewing basket for Aunt Bee; and wrapped gifts for the others. As the episode closes, everyone sings "Deck the Halls," and Aunt Bee serves Ben a hearty Christmas dinner.

"Christmas Story" was written by David Adler and directed by Bob Sweeney, who directed eighty episodes of *The Andy Griffith Show*.

The Angel of Pennsylvania Avenue

(1996). Made-for-television drama set during the Depression in 1931. Because work is scarce, Angus Feagan (Robert Urich) leaves his home in Detroit, Michigan, at Christmastime to seek work in Kansas City, Missouri, while his family remains behind. When a riot erupts, he is jailed for a crime he did not commit.

Believing that President Herbert Hoover can work miracles, Angus's three children, Bernice (Tegan Moss), Lilly (Brittney Irvin), and six-year-old Jack (Alexander Pollock), set out for Washington, D.C., hoping to see the president on behalf of their father. They hop trains, hitch rides, and meet several interesting people along the way, including Box Car Louie (Tom Heaton), a pleasant hobo who provides shelter and guidance in the wild, and Andy Handy (Matthew Walker), a traveling puppeteer. When the children need bus fare for the final stage of their journey, Lilly stands on a park bench and sings Christmas carols, while the others pass the hat. Meanwhile Annie Feagan (Diana Scarwid) pursues her children, hitching a ride from kind-hearted strangers like Ray Needles (Alfred Humphreys) and others.

With help from a crowd loitering outside the White House, who create a diversion, the children manage to slip into the mansion and, after dodging the guards, Bernice plunges into Hoover's quarters and pleads dearly for her father. With assurance that Hoover (played by Thomas Peacocke) will do all that he can for Angus, Annie and her children happily return home to prepare for Christmas. Angus's call, however, with news that he will probably remain for another year in prison, shatters their dreams, and Bernice finds it most difficult to attend Christmas Eve services a few days later. But as the children's choir sings "O Come, All Ye Faithful," in walks Angus, a free man, to a splendid Christmas reunion.

With Frank Turner, Don S. Davis, Camille Mitchell. Written by Michael De Guzman, Rider McDowell. Produced by Tom Rowe, Lisa Towers. Directed by Robert Ellis Miller. Video N/A.

Angels and Shepherds

Traditional carol, the music of which arose during the seventeenth or eighteenth century from the Bohemian region of the former Czechoslovakia. Although the original text, beginning as "Nesem vám noviny," reflected a nonpastoral theme, the carol achieved popularity when the German composer Karl Riedel (1827–1888) coupled the original melody with text adapted from Bohemian shepherd songs that comprised Nativity folk dramas of that region. Riedel published his version as "Kommet, ihr Hirten" ("Come, You Shepherds") in the collection *Altböhmische Gesänge* (Leipzig, 1870). Other English translations include "Come, All Ye Shepherds," "From Bethl'em's City," and "Hear What Great News We Bring."

The title "Angels and Shepherds" is derived from Riedel's three-verse text, in which the angelic host first bid the shepherds and others to follow them to the manger. With the second verse, the shepherds joyfully respond with a desire to hurry to Bethlehem to publish abroad all that they witness there, while the third verse summarizes the glad tidings of "Peace on earth" to all.

Angels, from the Realms of Glory

English carol, lyrics composed by James Montgomery (1771–1854). Initially a social activist, Montgomery edited the *Sheffield Iris* (formerly the *Sheffield Register*) for 31 years, during which time he published anti-government sentiments for which he was occasionally jailed. He left the *Iris* in 1825 and devoted his latter days to composing some 400 hymns and adapting many others.

Inspired by the older, familiar French carol, "Les anges dans nos campagnes" ("Angels We Have Heard on High"), Montgomery published one of his most famous hymns, "Angels, from the Realms of Glory," in the *Iris* on Christmas Eve, 1816. Well received throughout England, it appeared in hymnals and broadsheets from 1819 onward and was sung exclusively, and not surprisingly, to the tune of "Les anges" for some fifty years following its initial publication.

The most prominent of several other musical settings arrived with the publication in 1866 of "Regent Square," which the blind London organist Henry Smart composed for *Psalms and Hymns for Divine Worship*, a Presbyterian hymnal. Today the "Regent Square" tune has found a more compatible match with Montgomery's lyrics in the United States. The English, still preferring the tune of "Les anges," reserve Smart's melody for the hymn "Light's Abode, Celestial Salem."

See also **Angels We Have Heard on High**.

Angels' Mass

See **Christmas Masses**

Angels We Have Heard on High

("Les anges dans nos campagnes"). French traditional carol thought to have arisen during the eighteenth century in Lorraine or Provence. The complete anonymity of its origins has prompted several speculations, particularly regarding the Latin refrain, "Gloria in excelsis Deo" (Glory to God in the Highest). One source mentions that in the year 129, Telesphorus, Bishop of Rome, commissioned a Christmas carol, a line of which became the refrain for "Angels." In another, French shepherds, calling the "Gloria" to each other from hilltops on Christmas Eve, supposedly used a traditional tune (possibly from a late medieval Latin chorale) that is identical to the refrain of "Angels." These speculations imply that, because the text consists of two languages, the carol must be derived from two sources. This reasoning cannot always apply, as "The Boar's Head Carol" illustrates: of unquestionably English origin throughout, it is peppered with Latin phrases (*see* **The Boar's Head Carol**).

Whatever the source, music authorities feel that the style of the original eight-stanza text and music dates "Angels" to more modern times. Its earliest known printing lies in Louis Lambillotte's collection *Choix de cantiques sur des airs nouveaux*, published in Paris, 1842. Prior to that time, "Angels" was known in England, at least in 1816, for it was the basis for James Montgomery's "Angels, from the Realms of Glory," published that year (*see* **Angels, from the Realms of Glory**).

Many different English-language translations exist, the first by James Chadwick, Catholic bishop of Newcastle and Hexam, which appeared in *The Holy Family Hymns* of London, 1860. The four-stanza text most often sung today was adapted from Chadwick by Newcastle composer Henri Hémy, who included it in *The Crown of Jesus Music* of 1864.

Annabelle's Wish

(1997). Made-for-video animated cartoon, based on a short story by Dan Henderson. Wishes and miracles fill the holidays in this tale of Annabelle, a calf born on Christmas Eve at Charles Baker's farm in the rural community of Twobridge, Tennessee. Charles, a widower, is also raising Billy, his grandson, an orphan who suddenly went mute after Charles rescued him from a barn fire some years ago.

As midnight approaches, the farm animals anticipate the arrival of Santa, who annually bestows upon them the secret gift of speech for Christmas Day only. It's Annabelle's first encounter with Santa and his flying reindeer, and the latter impress her so much that she is determined to fly some day as they do. Annabelle, Billy's Christmas gift that year, reveals the animals' secret when she automatically says, "Bless you!" after Billy sneezes, but he gladly keeps the secret under his hat. When she expresses her fondest wish to be a reindeer and fly, Billy ties two small branches to her head to simulate antlers. She and Billy become quite close, and joining them in their winter capers is Billy's good friend Emily.

Beautifully chromolithographed, embossed diecut "scraps" mostly made in Germany were sold by the billions in America, Canada and England in the 1870s and 1880s. This one is 2¼" high and shows baby Jesus holding a Christmas rose, while the angels' banner proclaims, "Gloria in excelsis Deo" (Glory to God in the highest)— a refrain popularized by the Christmas carol "Angels We Have Heard on High."

Amid such wholesome surroundings, trouble and heartache must inevitably fall. While the three are out sledding on Christmas Day, Billy and Annabelle lose control and crash through neighbor Gus Holder's fence. Holder and his boys, Bucky and Buster, Scrooges of sorts, loathe Christmas and seize every opportunity to tease Billy about his handicap. To cover the damages, Holder lays claim to Annabelle, since Charles has no ready cash. Rather than see Billy without his calf, Charles sells a beautiful music box that had belonged to Billy's late mother, and Annabelle is returned.

Life is again peaceful until Christmas Eve of the following year, when Billy's rich, lonely, and spiteful Aunt Agnes arrives with a court order granting her guardianship over Billy until such time as he can speak. While Billy prepares his belongings, the animals tow Agnes's car into a pond, forcing her to spend the night on the farm. Once again Santa greets the animals at midnight, but this time Annabelle whispers a special request, since she's been a good little calf all year. On Christmas morning, Billy opens a small box from Santa containing dust. Spilling it on himself, he is able to speak (nullifying the court order), for it is the magic dust of speech which Santa sprinkles on the animals. Annabelle's wish was to give Billy her gift of speech forever, and by so doing, she will never speak again. Holder, learning the sacrifice Charles made to pay for his fence, pops over with his boys, apologizes for being a poor neighbor, and returns the music box.

Years pass. Billy and Emily are now married and still live on the farm. Late one Christmas Eve, Billy follows an aged Annabelle out into a pasture, where she collapses. Suddenly Santa appears and transforms Annabelle into a lovely, talking reindeer that leads the team into the Christmas sky. Annabelle receives her fondest wish at last.

Narrated by Randy Travis. Voices: Jay Johnson, Jerry Van Dyke, Jim Varney, Rue McClanahan, Cloris Leachman, Aria Noelle Curzon, James Lafferty, Charlie Cronin, Jennifer Darling, Clancy Brown, Stu Rosen, Jerry Houser, Brian Cummings, Kaye E. Kuter, Kath Soucie, Hari Oziol, Randy Travis. Musical score by Steve Dorff. Lyrics by Steve Dorff, John Bettis, Randy Travis. Vocals by Randy Travis, Alison Krauss, Beth Nielson Chapman, Michael McGinnis. Written by John Bettis, Ken Blackwell, John Couch, *et al*. Story by Dan Henderson. Produced by Barbara Dunn-Leonard. Directed by Roy Wilson. Running time, 54 min. Hallmark Home Entertainment Video.

In 1998 the Motion Picture Sound Editors, United States, nominated this picture for the Golden Reel Award for Best Sound Editing.

Ralph Edwards Films, the production company for *Annabelle's Wish*, dedicated this picture to the Make-A-Wish Foundation, an organization which seeks to fulfill wishes of terminally ill children, and vowed to grant the wishes of 100 children through the Foundation's 82 organizations across the country.

Argentina

See **South America**

Armenia

Sources vary somewhat regarding the person or persons who introduced Christianity into Armenia. Two of Christ's apostles, Bartholomew and Thaddeus, are said to have first preached there, whereas other sources credit St. Gregory the Illuminator (257?–337?), the patron saint of Armenia, with establishing Christianity there in the year 301. In any event, Armenia became the first nation to embrace Christianity, which led to the Armenian Ortho-

dox Church, the principal faith in that country. Most Armenian churches observe Christ's Theophany (Epiphany in the Western Church), which includes His Nativity and Baptism, all on January 6 by the Gregorian calendar, the exception being the church in Jerusalem, which still adheres to the older, Julian calendar. January 6 on that calendar corresponds to January 19 on the Gregorian calendar.

• HISNAK ("fifty days"), the Advent season, extends for a period of fifty days prior to January 6, with one week of strict fasting prior to the commencement of Advent. Strict fasting includes abstinence not only from milk and all animal products, but also from liturgical commemoration of saints. The Saturday of that week commemorates St. Nicholas along with St. Gregory the Wonderworker and Bishop Myron of Crete, and the Saturday preceding the third Sunday of Advent again commemorates St. Nicholas. Another week of fasting follows the third Advent Sunday, and the Saturday of that week commemorates St. James of Nisibis, said to be the nephew of St. Gregory the Illuminator. The following saints' days, all movable, follow the fourth Advent Sunday: King David; St. James, Brother of Jesus; St. Stephen; Peter the Apostle; and the "Sons of Thunder" (St. James the Apostle and St. John the Evangelist, sons of Zebedee).

Considered a holiday period during which no work is done, the final week of strict fasting from December 31 to January 6 closes Advent and precedes the Feast of Theophany, during which time *Kaghand* (New Year's) is observed on January 1 with gift exchanges, feasting within the limitations of "fast," and visitations. In some regions, children receive their gifts by gathering on rooftops and letting down handkerchiefs, into which parents place treats. Although a strict fast is in force, one of these last seven days is a floating day which commemorates all of the following saints: Basil, Gregory of Nyssa, Pope Sylvester I of Rome, and Ephrem the Syrian.

Strictly a religious observation, the Feast of Theophany begins late in the afternoon of January 5, a day termed *Chragaloyts* ("lighting the lamps"), for the church lamps are filled with wax and new wicks. Following Vespers, numerous readings from the Old Testament, and celebration of a solemn Mass, the clergy form a procession around the church and line up in the nave to sing "Great Mystery," a Nativity hymn about the Incarnation, based on a homily by St. Gregory the Wonderworker. Following a reading from Luke 2:8–14, the congregation is blessed and dismissed. The Feast continues on January 6 with the Holy Offices of the Night Vigil, Matins, and another solemn Mass. Following this is the ritual of "Blessing the Water," wherein the priest places a cross and pours Holy Crism (consecrated oil, symbolic of the Holy Spirit) into a large basin of water. Members of the congregation then take small quantities of the water home with them to anoint the sick. Most Armenians receive Holy Communion either on January 5 or 6. The Feast of Theophany extends for eight days until January 13, during which period there is neither fasting nor commemoration of saints, and people engage in family reunions and greet one another with "Christ is born and is revealed." The response: "These are great tidings to you and to us." The eighth day is dedicated to the Circumcision of the Lord.

Because of the political and social upheavals in the last two centuries, the customs and cuisine once specific to various Armenian cities have largely disappeared.

"Merry Christmas" in Armenia is *Shenoraavor Nor Dari.*

See also **Christmas Old Style, Christmas New Style; Epiphany.**

As I Sat on a Sunny Bank
See **I Saw Three Ships**

As Joseph Was A-Walking
See **The Cherry Tree Carol**

As with Gladness Men of Old
English carol, the lyrics of which were written on January 6 (Epiphany), 1859, by William Chatterton Dix (1837–1898), a poet, hymn writer, and manager of a marine insurance company in Bristol. The day was significant, for Dix, ill in bed at the time, was reading the Gospel of Matthew's account of the Wise Men's visit to the stable, which inspired the lyrics about their mission and journey. Dix also wrote the lyrics to another well-known carol, "What Child Is This?"

The musical setting for "As with Gladness" is an adaptation of a selection from "Treuer Heiland," a German chorale of uncertain authorship that was published in 1838 in a collection edited by organist Conrad Kocher, also perhaps the composer. William H. Monk undertook the adaptation and paired Dix's lyrics with this melody and published them together in *Hymns Ancient and Modern*, edited by William Clowes (London, 1861). Perhaps better known as the setting for the hymn "For the Beauty of the Earth," the Kocher tune ultimately acquired the alternate name of "Dix"; ironically, Dix was never fond of the music.

See also **Epiphany; What Child Is This?**

ASCAP List of Christmas Songs
The repertory of music whose rights are held by the American Society of Composers, Authors and Publishers (ASCAP) includes a number of popular Christmas songs that were composed during the twentieth century. In December of 1998, the Society published a list of its 25 most frequently performed holiday numbers of that century. Here is that list, which is reproduced with the permission of the American Society of Composers, Authors and Publishers (ASCAP), copyright 2000 ASCAP:

1. "White Christmas" by Irving Berlin. 2. "Santa Claus Is Coming to Town" by J. Fred Coots and Haven Gillespie. 3. "The Christmas Song (Chestnuts Roasting on an Open Fire)" by Mel Torme and Robert Wells. 4. "Winter Wonderland" by Felix Bernard and Richard B. Smith. 5. "Rudolph, the Red-Nosed Reindeer" by Johnny Marks. 6. "Sleigh Ride" by Leroy Anderson and Mitchell Parish. 7. "Have Yourself a Merry Little Christmas" by Ralph Blane and Hugh Martin. 8. "Silver Bells" by Jay Livingston and Ray Evans. 9. "Let It Snow! Let It Snow! Let It Snow!" by Sammy Cahn and Jule Styne. 10. "Little Drummer Boy" by Katherine K. Davis, Henry V. Onorati, and Harry Simeone. 11. "Jingle Bell Rock" by Joseph Carleton Beal and James Ross Boothe. 12. "I'll Be Home for Christmas" by Walter Kent, Kim Gannon, and Buck Ram. 13. "Frosty the Snowman" by Steve Nelson and Walter E. Rollins. 14. "Blue Christmas" by Billy Hayes and Jay W. Johnson. 15. "Carol of the Bells" by Peter J. Wilhousky and M. Leontovich. 16. "It's Beginning to Look

a Lot Like Christmas" by Meredith Willson. 17. "Here Comes Santa Claus (Right Down Santa Claus Lane)" by Gene Autry and Oakley Haldeman. 18. "(There's No Place Like) Home for the Holidays" by Bob Allen and Al Stillman. 19. "Rockin' Around the Christmas Tree" by Johnny Marks. 20. "I Saw Mommy Kissing Santa Claus" by Tommie Connor. 21. "We Need a Little Christmas" by Jerry Herman. 22. "The Christmas Waltz" by Sammy Cahn and Jule Styne. 23. "The Chipmunk Song (Christmas Don't Be Late)" by Ross Bagdasarian (David Seville). 24. "Feliz Navidad" by Jose Feliciano. 25. "A Holly Jolly Christmas" by Johnny Marks. Each of these songs is discussed further as a separate entry.

Asia and the South Pacific

With the exception of the Philippines, where Roman Catholicism predominates, most of the countries in this part of the world are non–Christian, and Christmas as a religious holiday is not widely observed. Rather, it is more commonly a secular season occupied with gift exchanges, family reunions, and westernized customs (Christmas trees, Christmas cards, pageants and plays, and the like); despite the secular bent of the holiday, western religious customs are also in evidence (Nativity Scenes, carols, Midnight Mass). The following paragraphs describe those Christmas customs that can be identified in several countries. Christmas in the Philippines is discussed as a separate entry.

• CHINA. For *Sheng Dan Jieh* (Holy Birth Festival), homes are decorated with paper lanterns, and fireworks greet the Nativity. Christmas trees (known as "Trees of Light," decorated with paper ornaments) and Santa Claus (known as *Dun Che Lao Ren*, "Christmas Old Man," or *Lan Khoong-Khoong*, "Nice Old Father") are familiar to the nation's one percent Christian population. Hong Kong celebrates *Ta Chiu*, a festival of peace, in which Taoists invoke their gods, and Christians pay homage to patron saints. This festival closes with the burning of a paper horse to which the names of all villagers are attached. It is believed that in this burning their names will arise to heaven. The principal festival is Chinese New Year, termed the "Spring Festival," which is held near the end of January. There, amid fireworks displays, children receive new clothes and toys, and ancestors are worshipped. "Merry Christmas" in China is: *Gun Tso Sun Tan'Gung Haw Sun* (Cantonese) or *Kung His Hsin Nien Bing Chu Shen Tan* (Mandarin).

• FIJI ISLANDS. The population of this former British colony consists of approximately equal numbers of native Fijians and Eastern Indians, of whom 53 percent are Christians (Methodists and Roman Catholics), 38 percent are Hindus, and 8 percent are Muslims. People of all regions, including those living in urban areas, return to their native villages and extended families for the holidays. Numerous cows and pigs are slaughtered and roasted in an earthen oven known as *lovo* for the Christmas feasting, which is held after early morning church services on Christmas Day. Gift-giving and a mythical being who brings gifts to children are not traditional. "Merry Christmas" is *Me nomu na marau ni Siga-ni-Sucu* (Bahasa, the most commonly spoken of more than 100 languages in Indonesia).

• INDIA. Customs parallel those of Great Britain, which formerly occupied the country. Festivities include children dancing to the music of drums, tambourines, cymbals, and colored sticks. A unique symbol of esteem is the lemon, offered to convey wishes of long life and prosperity. For those living in the plains, Christmas trees are constructed of straw, twigs, and mud, with paper decorations and candles. People in the mountainous regions may cut real evergreen trees. Banana and mango trees often receive decorations, and homes may be decorated with mango leaves. In the North, the aboriginal Bhils engage in all-night caroling during Christmas week, and in the South, citizens often place lighted clay oil lamps on their rooftops and along the walls outside. Christmas services often extend up to three hours. One way of saying "Merry Christmas" in India is: *Shub Naya Baras* (Hindi, one of 1,600 dialects in India).

• INDONESIA. The population is of mixed Malaysian descent; over 85 percent of Indonesians are Muslims, with Protestants constituting the Christian minority. The Christmas season extends from Christmas Eve until the second week of January, and customs reflect

350 years of Dutch occupation (since the early seventeenth century). Thus, traditions are not markedly different from those in the United States, except that Santa Claus (Dutch *Sinterklaas*) in many areas still brings the Christmas gifts on December 5, the eve of St. Nicholas Day. During the second week of December, many of the shopping malls and hotels sponsor events in which children may have lunch with Santa and be photographed with him. The Christmas dinner often features a blend of Indonesian, European, and Chinese foods, including assorted soups, stir-fry vegetables, chicken, beef, seafood, and pork (Muslims abstain from pork). "Merry Christmas" is: *Selamat Hari Natal* (Bahasa, the official language and the most widely spoken of more than 100 languages in Indonesia). *See also* **Saint Nicholas Day.**

 • JAPAN. The prevailing religions are Shintoism and Buddhism, with only 1 percent of the population professing Christianity. Yet since the end of World War II, with the influx of western customs, Japan has adopted *Kurisumasu* (Christmas) strictly as a festive work day. Families send Christmas cards and erect plastic Christmas trees decorated with origami figures, particularly swans, while children exchange origami "birds of peace." Christmas Eve parties, held either in hotels, restaurants, or at home, are fashionable, with chicken as a popular dish. A popular dessert provided on a large scale by confectioners is *Kurisumasu Keiki* (Christmas cake), which is similar to a western birthday cake. Bearing candles, a Santa figure, and a Christmas greeting, such cakes are served only on Christmas Eve and are deemed worthless thereafter; hence, the term "Christmas cake" alternately refers to any woman unwed by the age of twenty-five. Other sites for Christmas Eve entertainment include Tokyo Disneyland, any of the urban leisure parks, and overnight cruises.

Children receive gifts from Santa, known either as *Santa Kurosu* or *Hoteiosho*. Because he always knows children's behavior, he is believed to have eyes in the back of his head.

Sometime during December, most organizations provide year-end bonuses and sponsor a *bonenkai* ("forget the year party") as an expression of thanks to employees for their services.

In the custom of *seibo* ("year's end"), people present gifts to their social superiors and to those from whom they have received favors during the year (an identical custom, *chugen*, is observed at midyear). Polite etiquette requires personal delivery of the gifts.

Shogatsu (term for the first month of the year as well as the New Year holidays, December 31 through January 3) constitutes the most important of Japan's national holidays. Near year's end, houses are thoroughly cleaned, and a *shimenawa* (sacred straw rope) with *shide* (dangling white paper strips) is hung over the front door to greet the *toshigami* (harvest god of the new year) and to repel evil. This god is said to reside in a *kadomatsu* (arrangement of pine boughs—symbol of longevity—and bamboo), one of which is placed on each side of the entrance. The main room of the house features a *toshidana* ("year shelf"), an altar on which is placed a *kagamimochi* (offering to the gods consisting of *mochi* [rice cakes], *sake* [rice wine], and fruit). On *Omisoka* (New Year's Eve), rural families may still practice *mochitsuki* ("rice cake pounding"), the ancient art of forming rice cakes by pounding glutinous rice. Rice cakes, along with *toshikoshi soba* ("year-crossing noodles"), *zoni* (rice cake soup with vegetables), and *toso* (spiced rice wine), are traditional New Year's dishes; the long noodles symbolize hope for a lengthy family fortune. Because Buddhists believe that 108 earthly desires plague mankind, temple bells ring 108 times at midnight, a custom known as *joya no kane*, to encourage people to purge themselves of these evils at the new year.

On *Ganjitsu* (New Year's Day), families congregate, and the emperor offers prayers for the nation. On January 2 and 3, the visitation extends to friends and business associates. During this season, parents and relatives present children with *otoshidama* (spending money), and families observe *hatsumode* (first visit of the year to shrines and temples) to pray for a rich harvest in the new year. One is expected to send *nengajo* (New Year's cards, government-issued postcards printed with lottery numbers) to all relatives, friends, and business customers. The Japanese postal service collects and holds all cards that were mailed by Christmas and delivers them *en masse* on New Year's Day.

Traditional New Year's games include *sugoroku* (variant of Parcheesi), *karuta* (card games), *hanetsuki* (badminton with shuttlecock and battledore), and *takoage* (kite flying). In rural areas, costumed dancers repel evil by performing a *harukoma mai* (pony dance) or a *shishi mai* (lion dance).

"Merry Christmas" is *Meri Kurisumasu*.

• PAKISTAN. The Christian minority in this predominantly Islamic nation observes *Bara Din* ("Big Day," Christmas) in typical westernized fashion. In addition, December 25 is the birthday anniversary of the founder of Pakistan, Quaidi-Azam Mohammed Ali Jinnah, and is a national holiday. "Merry Christmas" in Pakistan is *Nave sal di mubaraka* (Punjabi) or *Naya Saal Mubarak Ho* (Urdu).

• SRI LANKA. Christmas Eve combines Christian and pagan observances, with bonfires, drums, and devil dances. The Christmas tree is known as the Tree of Life and is decorated with colored paper ornaments. "Merry Christmas" is *Suba nath thalak Vewa* (Sinhalese).

Auld Lang Syne

("Old Long Ago"). Scottish folk tune of dismissal, the sentiments of which are now popularly associated with the celebration of the New Year. It was brought to prominence by Robert Burns (1759–1796), considered to be the national poet of Scotland, who claimed that he discovered "Auld Lang Syne" from an old man's singing and that it had never been in print. To the original three verses, Burns added two of his own in similar Scottish dialect, one beginning with "We twa hae run about the braes," the other with "We twa hae paidl'd in the burn," and sent them to a colleague, James Johnson, a music engraver in Edinburgh and a collector of Scottish folk songs. Having solicited Burns's assistance in acquiring such pieces, Johnson published *The Scots Musical Museum* between 1787 and 1803, a collection of six volumes for which Burns acted as editor until his death in 1796, and to which he contributed some 160 songs of his own. Burns's version of "Auld Lang Syne" first appeared in the fifth volume of the *Museum* some six months after his death. Johnson initially hesitated to publish it because the melody (not the melody familiar today) had appeared previously in the same collection to lyrics written by another poet, Allan Ramsay (1686–1758), beginning with "Should auld acquaintance be forgot, / Tho' they return with scars?" That same melody originally used for Ramsay's and Burns's lyrics had first been published in a separate collection, *Original Scotch Tunes* (1700).

The lyrics for "Auld Lang Syne" derive from several sources. One is a folk ballad of 1568, "Auld Kyndnes Foryett." Another is a poem by Sir Robert Ayton (1570–1638), published in *Choice Collection of Scots Poems* (1711), which begins, "Should auld acquaintance be forgot, / And never thought upon." A third possibility is a late seventeenth-century street song containing the following refrain, "On old long syne. / On old long syne, my jo, / On old long syne: / That thou canst never once reflect / On old long syne." There are others in like vein.

The familiar tune paired with "Auld Lang Syne" today was selected by George Thomson, a music enthusiast and Burns contemporary, who occupied himself in finding suitable musical settings for Scotch folk verses. Considered to be a common Scots country dance, this tune was variously named "The Miller's Wedding" in *Scots Reels* (1759) or "The Miller's Daughter" in *Strathspey Reels* (1780), among other versions and titles. Thomson published Burns's lyrics (by then Burns had substituted "my dear" for "my jo" in the refrain) with the present tune in *Select Scottish Airs* (1799).

On the American scene, the band Guy Lombardo and His Royal Canadians popularized "Auld Lang Syne" when they first played it on their New Year's Eve radio broadcast of 1929. It established the work not only as Lombardo's signature song but also as the theme for rejoicing in the coming new year.

Using the same melody but fashioning lyrics that combined Christmas with the New Year sentiment, Frank Military and Mann Curtis produced "Christmas Auld Lang Syne" in 1960, which teen idol Bobby Darin successfully introduced in a recording for the Atco label that year. Formerly associated with Dean Martin and Frank Sinatra, Military is not known for any other major hits. Curtis' other contributions, however, include lyrics for "The Story of a Starry Night" (1941) and "Let It Be Me" (1955), among others.

Australia

Christmas traditions on this continent stem principally from British occupation (beginning with the continent's use as a penal colony) dating to the eighteenth century. Australia observed its first Christmas in 1788 in Sydney, its first settlement, with Arthur Phillip as governor. Because of the season, Phillip commuted the flogging sentence of one Michael Dennison, convicted of having stolen a pound of flour, from the customary 200 lashes to only 150. Today, an Australian Christmas includes a variety of traditions from the influx of immigrants from Northern Europe, Italy, Greece, Spain, France, the Middle East, Asia, and North and South America.

Christmas arrives at the beginning of summer vacation, and, amid figures of Santa and Father Christmas clad in shorts and T-shirts, a picnic atmosphere with water sports activities at the beaches prevails, for the majority of Australia's citizens reside along the coast. According to local tradition, Swag Man, a figure akin to Santa and probably derived from a personage in aboriginal folklore, lives under Uluru in the Northern Territory (Ayers Rock, largest monolith in the world) and emerges at Christmastime with his dingoes to deliver gifts. Children, however, write letters to Santa or Father Christmas, and gifts are exchanged as in Great Britain.

Although Christmas trees may consist of cuttings from the native eucalyptus or gum trees, many Australians prefer artificial trees decorated either with western ornaments or natural elements such as seed pods, gum nuts, or berries. As in the West, decorated Christmas trees are found in all public places, and Sydney's Queen Victoria Shopping Center boasts the largest artificial tree in the southern hemisphere, standing at a height of three stories. Other holiday decorations include the native Christmas bell or Christmas bush.

Initially, the Christmas dinner, a formal affair held indoors where temperatures often exceeded one hundred degrees Fahrenheit, consisted of the traditional British fare of roast turkey with dressing, plum pudding, and other heavy dishes. By the end of the nineteenth century, however, Australians along the coast abandoned this tradition for Christmas at the seaside, or at least outdoors with a buffet, and a menu of cold meats or seafood, salads, fruit, ice cream, fruit cake, chocolates, and perhaps even the traditional mince pie or plum pudding. The latter is still served with items such as a coin, ring, or thimble inside, and folklore holds that whoever finds these items will come into, respectively, wealth, marriage, or spinsterhood in the coming year. Australia also holds the world's record (1987) for the largest plum pudding, weighing some 3,000 pounds and commercially cooked in Kensington, Victoria. Another favorite dessert is *pavlova*, a dish of whipped cream and fruit served in a meringue shell. Christmas meals also include the British "crackers," "poppers," or "bonbons," all terms for party favors wrapped in hollow tubes which make a popping sound when opened.

Traditions unique to Australia include "Carols by Candlelight," large, community-wide singing festivals held in public parks, such as the one held on Christmas Eve at Melbourne's Myer Music Bowl. Although the custom is said to have originated in 1865, when Cornish miners from Moonta in Southern Australia gathered on Christmas Eve to sing carols by the light of candles attached to their hats, the modern "Carols by Candlelight" premiered in 1937 at Melbourne's Alexandria Gardens. Norman Banks, a local radio personality at the time, organized the event because he was touched by those who suffered loneliness at Christmastime, especially the elderly. The largest of these events, "Carols in the Domain," is always held on the last Saturday before Christmas at Sydney's Royal Botanic Gardens. "Carols" are broadcast on radio and television throughout Southeast Asia and New Zealand, and the proceeds of the broadcasts are donated to charity. Other notable festivities in coastal cities include Queensland's "Christmas Lantern Festival," a week-long carnival before Christmas with parades, fireworks, and ornate lantern displays; and Sydney's "Twelve Days of Christmas at Darling Harbor," held twelve days before Christmas and featuring a number of cultural events.

An isolated life exists for those living on ranches in Australia's interior ("bush," or "outback"), where hundreds of miles may lie between them and the nearest village. Yet family members strive to return home for Christmas, and Santa manages to appear via small aircraft or railroad car. For some forty years, the "Tea and Sugar Train" ran a 1,050-mile course in the Nullarbor Plain between Adelaide, South Australia, and Kalgoorlie in Western Australia. The train serviced the railroad camps along the route, and at Christmastime, Santa, decked out in red, brought gifts to some one thousand children in the 1960s. Today most of those camps are closed, and only Cook camp remains.

Boxing Day, December 26, is a national holiday given almost entirely to sporting events or games of skill around the country. The most famous of these is the 630-mile yacht race from Sydney to Holbart, the capital of the island of Tasmania, which features entries from not only Australia and New Zealand, but also Great Britain, Japan, and the United States.

See also **Boxing Day; Great Britain.**

Austria

French missionaries first brought Christianity to Austria in the sixth century when they established the first monastery at Passau on the Danube River. Principally a Roman Catholic nation, Austria observes many Christmas customs quite similar to those of neighboring Germany.

The Christmas season begins with Advent, which features Christmas markets and multiple displays of *Krippen* (Nativity scenes) in churches and public places. A noted *Krippe* resides at Steyr in Upper Austria, extant since 1579. The crypt at St. Peter's, Vienna, also hosts an exhibit of Nativity scenes, where the Society of the Friends of the Nativity Scene encourages new designs.

Households cut branches from cherry trees and place them in water on December 4, St. Barbara's Day. Termed "Barbara branches," these sprigs honor St. Barbara, a third-century Turkish martyr. According to legend, a single person whose Barbara branch blooms by Christmas Day will marry in the coming year. To celebrate St. Barbara's Day, miners from Matzen in Lower Austria have organized an *Erdölpfarre* ("Petroleum Parish") on the first Sunday of Advent since 1950 with a mass, band concerts, and other ceremonies.

On December 5, the eve of St. Nicholas Day, a hideous, fur-clad personification of Satan, known variously by the names *Krampus, Knecht Ruprecht, Pelznickel,* and others, accompanies St. Nicholas for the ecclesiastical quizzing of children, distribution of gifts, and administration of punishment to the naughty. Village squares may sport one or more people dressed as this devil, at whom children delight in throwing snowballs. Another tradition is Nicholas plays, often known by the name of the demon who accompanies St. Nicholas, such as *Klaubaufgehen* (after *Klaubauf*) at Matrei in Tyrol and *Bartel-Lauf* (from *Bartel*) at Oberdrauberg in Carinthia. Another masked figure, *Thomasnikolo* ("Tom Nicholas"), is peculiar to Gams of Styria and appears only on December 21, the old feast day of St. Thomas.

The second Thursday of Advent is devoted to *Wildes Gjaid* ("Wild Hunt") in Salzburg, in which men don masks portraying creatures of folk legends. This custom recalls the belief, prevalent throughout Europe from the ninth to the fourteenth centuries, that spirits of the dead flew about in midwinter, especially during the twelve days of Christmas, to increase the fertility of the fields. Other Advent customs include the "Walk Through Advent," an attraction presented on each of the four Advent Sundays in Salzburg, featuring music, recitations, and Nativity plays. Another featured Nativity folk play is the one held every four years at Bad Ischl in Upper Austria.

Christmas carols are not usually heard as such until Christmas Eve, when groups "showing the Christ Child" may carry a manger from house to house while singing carols. The Christmas tree, sporting real candles, is usually not erected and decorated until this time, after which a bell rings in the home to signal that the *Christkindl* (little Christ Child)—or more specifically His winged messenger, depicted as a small, winged girl—has deposited the gifts under the tree. It is she to whom children write letters outlining their Christmas wishes. They place these letters on windowsills, hoping that the letters will vanish overnight, for then the

Christ Child will grant their wishes. Since 1950, a town of Christkindl has sponsored the official *Postamt Christkindl* (Christmas Post Office), where children may receive a reply postmarked with the traditional stamp showing the Holy Family under the Star of the East.

Other Christmas Eve customs include *Turmblasen* (brass ensembles playing Christmas chorales from church towers), and the *Herbergsuchen* ("Searching for Shelter"), a custom similar to the Latin American *Las Posadas*, in which groups reenact the Holy Couple's search for shelter in Bethlehem and which terminates with *Mitternachtsmette* (Midnight Mass).

The Christmas dinner usually features carp, and holiday baked items often feature *Hetzenbrot* (fruit bread), *Lebkuchen* (gingerbread), *Hussarenkraperl* (Hussar jam-and-almond cookies), *Vanillekipferl* (vanilla crescents), *Kokobusserl* (coconut kisses), and *Zimtsterne* (cinnamon stars), among others.

On St. Stephen's Day (December 26, "Second Christmas Day"), families make traditional visits to friends and relatives. Holy Innocents Day (December 28) is marked with children "beating" their comrades and relatives with sticks to bring luck for the coming year, a custom known in Carinthia, Styria, and Burgenland as *Frish- und G'Sundschlagen* ("Beating to Wellness and Good Health").

On New Year's Eve (St. Sylvester's Day), men dress as an old, hideous creature of pagan origin, the mistletoe-clad Sylvester (renamed after the fourth-century Pope St. Sylvester I), and seek to kiss maidens who chance to walk under evergreen sprigs. At midnight, Sylvester is driven out with the new year. Vienna traditionally stages a production of Johann Strauss's operetta *Die Fledermaus* on New Year's Eve, and instead of singing "Auld Lang Syne" at midnight, the Viennese dance to Strauss's "Blue Danube Waltz." Since the eighteenth century, the Vienna Philharmonic Orchestra has held a performance every New Year's Day, which is now broadcast worldwide.

Epiphany features men dressed as the Three Kings who ride about on horseback. *Sternsinger* ("star singers"), bearing illuminated, revolving stars on poles, parade about while singing the traditional "Song of the Three Kings." Masked figures or mummers include *Glöckler* of Upper Austria, groups wearing elaborate, illuminated headdresses, who race down hillsides and deliver good luck by knocking on doors. A similar group, the *Perchten*, runs near Salzburg. Attired in tall hats, animal masks, and ornate headdresses, they are accompanied by transvestite men, leaping and dancing about. The quality of their dancing supposedly determines the fate and bounty of the village for the new year. Stilt-dancers also bring good luck, and masked *Tresterer* are dancers whose movements mimic threshing. These mummings recall the ancient conflicts between the life of summer and the death of winter, of fertility versus impotence.

"Merry Christmas" in Austria is spoken in German: *Fröehliche Weihnachten*.

See also **Advent; Germany; Mistletoe; Silent Night.**

Ave Maria

("Hail Mary"). Title applied to a number of musical pieces in honor of the Virgin Mary, the two most prominent of which were written by Austrian composer Franz Schubert (1797–1828) and French composer Charles Gounod (1818–1893).

Schubert, who wrote over 600 songs, composed his "Ave Maria" in 1825, originally with verses from "The Lady of the Lake," a poem written in 1810 by English author Sir Walter Scott (1771–1832). In that poem, the heroine is forced into an unwanted marriage and appeals to the Virgin Mary for help. Later, the music was adapted to the Latin text of the Roman Catholic prayer to the Virgin, better known as the "Hail Mary," based on the angel Gabriel's annunciation to Mary that she is to be the mother of Jesus (Luke 1:26–28). The first performance in 1825 featured Schubert with his favorite vocalist, Johann Michael Vogl.

Gounod — also known for his operas *Faust* and *Romeo and Juliet*, among other works — originally published his melody in 1853 as an instrumental piece, "Meditation on the First Prelude of S. Bach." It consisted of an original, counterpoint melody superimposed on the opening C-major prelude of *The Well-Tempered Clavier*, a collection which German composer Johann Sebastian Bach had published in

1722. Gounod treated the Bach prelude as background harmony for his own melody, leaving Bach's subtly changing arpeggios intact, and scored his hybrid piece for violin, piano, and organ. Although some verses and a soprano part were added later, the Bach-Gounod setting, as it is now known, was adapted to the Roman Catholic prayer, "Hail Mary," in 1859.

Away in a Manger

American carol, erroneously attributed to Martin Luther, the German priest of the Middle Ages who initiated the Protestant Reformation, and to an obscure Carl Mueller, to whom there is no other connection. The first two of its three anonymous verses appeared in *Little Children's Book for Schools and Families* (Philadelphia, 1885), authorized by the General Council of the Evangelical Lutheran Church of North America. The third verse (sometimes attributed, without substantiation, to a John T. McFarland) was first published in another Lutheran collection, *Gabriel's Vineyard Songs* (edited by Charles H. Gabriel, Louisville, Kentucky, 1892). In between these two publications, the carol's appearance in *Dainty Songs for Little Lads and Lasses, for Use in the Kindergarten, School and Home* (Cincinnati, 1897), edited by James R. Murray (1841–1905), initiated the confusion about Martin Luther. There, Murray included the heading "Luther's Cradle Hymn (Composed by Martin Luther for his children, and still sung by German mothers to their little ones)." He signed this setting with his initials and included "Music by J. R. M." in a subsequent publication a year later. Whether Murray genuinely believed that Luther had written the words or whether he merely used Luther's name for publicity, the carol quickly became popular, perpetuating the Luther myth for some sixty years. According to research published in 1945 by Richard S. Hill from the Library of Congress, however, the words to the first two verses originated as an anonymous poem taken from a series of American Lutheran children's dramatic presentations, which honored the four-hundredth anniversary of Luther's birthday in 1883. This settled the Luther issue.

The carol has been sung to some forty different musical settings, the most popular of which in America is that composed by James Murray. Two other notable settings are those by Americans Jonathan E. Spilman in 1836 (also the setting for Robert Burns's poem "Flow Gently, Sweet Afton") and William J. Kirkpatrick in 1895 (more popular in England), the latter of whom also supplied the music for hymns such as "Tis So Sweet to Trust in Jesus" and "We Have Heard the Joyful Sound."

B

B.C.: A Special Christmas

(1984). Made-for-television animated cartoon, based on the popular comic strip *B.C.*, created by Johnny Hart. Cavemen Peter and Wiley devise a money-making scheme by creating the legend of a man who delivers presents to everyone once a year. When people accept the legend, they will give gifts, which Peter and Wiley will sell to their friends in the name of this man, who will be called "Santa Claus." A tree will be his symbol, and he will fly in a reindeer sleigh. Since the two cavemen will sell "X" amount of merchandise to the "masses," the holiday will be known as "Xmas." But during the planning, the true Santa makes his visit on December 24, and the legend becomes a reality.

Voices: Bob Elliott, Ray Goulding, Barbara Hamilton, Henry Ramer, Keith Hampshire, John Stocker, Melleny Brown. Written by Johnny Hart. Produced and directed by Vlad Goetzelman. A Cinera Production in Association with Hardlake Animated Pictures and Field Enterprises. Nelson Entertainment/ Embassy Home Entertainment. Color. Half-hour.

Babar and Father Christmas

Classic children's book by French author Jean de Brunhoff, published posthumously in 1940. In this tale set in the Elephants' country, Zephir the monkey has discovered that on Christmas Eve, Father Christmas brings toys to all the children in Man's country. Receiving no reply after he and his friends, elephant children Arthur, Pom, Flora, and Alexander, write letters inviting Father Christmas to visit them also, Elephant King Babar decides to find Father Christmas and extend a personal invitation.

Babar's trek carries him to Europe, where he learns that Father Christmas lives in Bohemia on a mountain near "Prjmneswe." Accompanied by Duck, a little dog who tracks Father Christmas's scent on a doll, Babar easily overcomes a group of mountain dwarfs bent on preventing their access to Father Christmas's secret cave. A sudden storm forces the two to burrow into what seems to be a snow bank but in reality is a chimney, and they fall into Father Christmas's parlor. When he politely declines Babar's request on the basis of weariness and pressures of schedule, Babar invites Father Christmas to take a vacation in the Elephants' tropical clime, to which he agrees. They all return in Father Christmas's flying machine, which bears the initials "PN 1" for *Père Noël* 1 (Father Christmas 1).

As Christmas Eve approaches and Father Christmas prepares for his rounds, he commissions Babar to deliver the gifts to the residents of the Elephant country. He provides Babar not only with a Santa suit that enables him to fly, but also with a magic bag that always remains filled with toys. Thus Babar brings Christmas to his land, and Father Christmas promises to return each year.

De Brunhoff's son, Laurent, narrated a made-for-television animated cartoon adaptation of this story (1986), which featured the voices of Jim Bradford, Rick Jones, Kemp Edwards, Kai Engstad, Rock LaFortune, Derek Diorio, Louise Villenueve, Les Lye, Courtney Carroll, Brahm Olzynko, Noel Council, Bridgitte Robinson. Vocals: John Brough, Teresa Dunn, Geri Childs, Craig Kennedy. Written by Gerry Capelle, Laurent de Brunhoff, and Merilyn Read. Based on the book by Jean de Brunhoff. Produced by Alison Clayton. Directed by Gerry Capelle. An Atkinson Film Arts and MTR Ottawa Production. Hi-Tops Video. Color. Half-hour.

Jean de Brunhoff (1899–1937), originally a painter, based a series of children's books on stories told by his mother, who had created an elephant character for her children. Jean later named the elephant Babar. His first book, *The Story of Babar* (1931), included illustrations by the author with text in cursive handwriting. Following Jean's death in 1937, Laurent supplied the colors to the drawings in his father's unfinished works and eventually published his own *Babar* books, beginning with *Babar and That Rascal Arthur* (1946).

Babes in Toyland

Operetta written in 1903 with musical score by the Irish-American composer Victor Herbert (1859–1924) and lyrics by Brooklyn native Glen MacDonough (1870–1924). The production was principally a musical revue with a minimal story line revolving around Mother Goose nursery rhymes and storybook characters: Two children, Alan and Jane, escape from their miserly uncle to the fantasy world of Toyland via the garden of Contrary Mary ("Mary, Mary, quite contrary..."). Highlights of the operetta, which saw nearly 200 stage performances, include an elaborate Christmas pageant and the songs "Toyland" (vocal) and "March of the Toys" (instrumental).

Babes in Toyland is now best remembered through its motion picture versions. Although childhood fantasy, and not Christmas as such, is the central theme of these productions, it is this fantasy that makes the story especially appealing at Christmas, when the season turns most people into children again for a few days.

In 1934, producer Hal Roach (of the *Our Gang Comedies*) created a different and more substantial story line for a film that would feature the renowned comedy team of Stan Laurel and Oliver Hardy. Laurel preferred a more fanciful approach, however, and that is what viewers see today. The Laurel and Hardy film incorporated a large segment of Herbert's score as background music with several vocal solos, time constraints precluding the other numbers. Two songs, "Go to Sleep, Slumber Deep" and "Castle in Spain," which had been cut from the original operetta, appeared in the 1934 film. Two additional songs from "outside" sources, "Who's Afraid of the Big Bad Wolf?" and "Rock-a-Bye Baby," were the creations of Walt Disney Studios (for the Three Little Pigs) and Effie I. Canning, respectively. In addition to the title *Babes in Toyland*, this film is known as *Laurel and Hardy in Toyland*, *March of the Wooden Soldiers*, *Wooden Soldiers*, and *Revenge Is Sweet*.

In the film, Mother Goose (Virginia Karns) introduces the principal nursery rhyme and storybook characters depicted in Toyland: "Little Bo-Peep"; "Tom-Tom, the Piper's Son"; "The Little Old Lady Who Lived in a Shoe"; "Hi Diddle Diddle, the Cat and the Fiddle"; "The Three Little Pigs"; "Little Miss Muffet"; "Rock-a-Bye Baby"; "Mary, Mary Quite Contrary"; "Little Jack Horner"; "Jack and Jill"; and "Little Red Riding Hood."

When Widow Peep (Florence Roberts), proprietor of a boarding shoe-house, defaults on her mortgage payment to Silas Barnaby (Henry Brandon, credited as Henry Kleinbach), this "meanest man in town" offers to cancel the mortgage if her daughter, Little Bo-Peep (Charlotte Henry), will marry him. Knowing that Bo-Peep is engaged to Tom-Tom (Felix Knight), boarders Stannie Dum and Ollie Dee (Laurel and Hardy, their characters parodies of Tweedle Dum and Tweedle Dee), attempt to steal the mortgage. With Ollie hidden in a large gift box, Stannie carts him to Barnaby's house, admonishing Barnaby not to open the box until Christmas, which is five months away. The plan almost works until Stannie calls out, "Good night, Ollie," and Ollie answers. Charged with burglary, Dum and Dee are sentenced by Old King Cole (Kewpie Morgan) to be dunked and exiled to Bogeyland, but Bo-Peep intervenes and consents to wed Barnaby, who drops the charges. Determined to foil Barnaby, Ollie gives the bride away and destroys the mortgage papers as Barnaby lifts the veil, only to find that his

"bride" is Stannie in drag. With no mortgage and no bride, Barnaby seeks revenge by kidnapping one of the three little pigs and planting the evidence (fiddle, hat, and some sausage links) in Tom-Tom's house. Framed, Tom-Tom is thrown into Bogeyland for "pig-napping." When Ollie discovers that the sausage is beef instead of pork, he and Stannie rescue the pig from Barnaby's cellar, and Toyland pursues Barnaby, who escapes through a secret passage into Bogeyland. Summoning all the bogeymen (hideous, half-human monsters), Barnaby and his troupe storm into Toyland, where a battle of good versus evil rages. After Stannie and Ollie rescue Tom-Tom, victory is assured when they activate 100 six-foot-tall mechanical toy soldiers, who rout the villains out of the city forever.

A particularly memorable comedy routine features Stannie and the game of Pee-Wee. Stannie has used up his and Ollie's savings to buy Pee-Wees, short, round, wooden pieces tapered on both ends. Placing a Pee-Wee on the ground and striking one end with a stick pops it into the air; then Stannie bats it like a conventional baseball, and it comes back to him like a boomerang. The game proves most useful for knocking Barnaby in the head. In another routine, Stannie and Ollie, employees at the Toyland Toy Factory, have misinterpreted Santa's order for 600 toy soldiers, each one foot high. Instead, the factory makes 100 mechanical soldiers, each six feet high. A demonstration of their working functions leaves the factory in shambles, and the boys are fired on the spot. Of course it is these six-foot soldiers who later save the day.

With William Burress, Alice Cook, Alice Dahl, Pete Gordon, Ferdinand Munier, Angelo Rossito. Released as *March of the Wooden Soldiers*. Written by Frank Butler and Nick Grinde. Produced by Hal Roach. Directed by Gus Meins and Charles Rogers. Hal Roach Studios and Metro-Goldwyn-Mayer. The Samuel Goldwyn Company and Goodtimes Home Video. B & W. 77 min.

There have been several remakes of *Babes in Toyland*, as follows:

A 1960 made-for-television version starred Paul Ford, Shirley Temple, Jonathan Winters. Production and video N/A.

The Walt Disney Company produced its motion picture version in 1961, starring Ray Bolger, Tommy Sands, Annette Funicello, Ed Wynn, Tommy Kirk, Kevin Corcoran. It received 1962 Academy Award nominations for Best Scoring of a Musical Picture and Best Color Costume Design. Written by Lowell S. Hawley, Ward Kimball, Joe Rinaldi. Produced by Walt Disney. Directed by Jack Donohue. Walt Disney Home Video. Color. 106 min.

A 1986 made-for-television movie under the same title featured Drew Barrymore, Richard Mulligan, Eileen Brennan, Keanu Reeves, Pat Morita. Written by Paul Zindel. Produced by Tony Ford, Neil T. Maffeo. Directed by Clive Donner. The Finnegan/Pinchuk Company in Association with Bavarian Atelier GmbH. Orion Home Video. Color. 96 min.

A 1997 animated cartoon version included the voices of Charles Nelson Reilly, Lacey Chabert, Joseph Ashton, Raphael Sbarge, Catherine Cavadini, Christopher Plummer, Susan Silo, Bronson Pinchot, James Belushi, Lindsay Schnebly. Cavadini and Plummer received 1998 Academy Award nominations for Outstanding Achievement in Voice Acting in an Animated Feature. Written by John Loy. Produced by Paul Sabella, Jonathan Dern, Kelly Ward, Mark Young. Directed by Charles Grosvenor, Toby Bluth, Paul Sabella. Metro-Goldwyn-Mayer. MGM/UA Home Video. Color. 74 min.

Baboushka
See **Russia**

A Baby in the Cradle
See **He Smiles Within His Cradle**

Baby Jesus, in a Manger
See **Infant Holy, Infant Lowly**

A Baby Lies in the Cradle
See **He Smiles Within His Cradle**

Bagpipers' Carol
See **Carol of the Bagpipers**

Bah, Humbug! The Story of Charles Dickens' "A Christmas Carol"
See **A Christmas Carol** (FILM AND TELE-VISION VERSION)

Bahamas
See **West Indies**

Baltic States (Estonia, Latvia, Lithuania)

These nations have enjoyed Christmas since the thirteenth century, when German Crusaders brought Christianity to this region. While Estonia and Latvia primarily adhere to the Lutheran Church, Lithuania remains predominantly Roman Catholic. Although specific Christmas traditions differ within the three nations, they share a mixture of Christian beliefs with those of agrarian rites and superstitions from ancient pagan winter solstice festivals, and they also share typical Advent customs. During the period from 1940 to 1991, Soviet occupation suppressed Christmas celebrations and established a secular season by substituting "Grandfather Frost" for St. Nicholas as the bearer of gifts and by transferring the winter festival to New Year's Day. Once again independent, these three nations have reinstated their former traditions, which the following paragraphs summarize.

• ESTONIA. Although the *Joulud* (Christmas) season extends from Advent to Epiphany, the principal holidays occur between Christmas Eve and the two days following Christmas. In southern Estonia, Christmas is known as *Talvistepuha* ("Winter Holiday"). Santa Claus and Christmas trees are well known, the latter adopted from local German culture during the mid-nineteenth century. Trees, often fir, are decorated with small toys, sweets, and candles. Other traditions include "Little Christmas" observances borrowed from Scandinavians, which consist of office parties during early Advent; bringing home Christmas straw, symbolic of the manger; making Christmas crowns in the likenesses of church chandeliers (the custom was brought from Finland through Swedish descendants living on the island of Vormsi); bathing in a sauna on Christmas Eve prior to any festivities; dressing children in new clothes for Christmas Eve services; and the annual Christmas Eve declaration of "Christmas Peace" by the Estonian president, a tradition practiced since the seventeeth century.

Seven to twelve different meals are served on Christmas Eve (abundant food symbolizes bounty for the coming year), and the menu traditionally consists of pork with sauerkraut, "white" and "blood" sausage, Christmas barrow (bread), ale, and mead. Livestock receive portions of the meal, the remainder of which must stand on the table overnight for the benefit of the spirits of family ancestors, and a fire must also burn throughout Christmas Eve night to dispel evil (a custom deriving from winter solstice festivals).

Following Christmas Eve church services, families adorn graves of family members with lighted candles, a custom that also once symbolized a national protest against the Communist regime. Christmas Day is spent with immediate family, while the remaining holidays are given to outside visitations.

"Merry Christmas" in Estonia is *Roomsaid Joulupuhi.*

• LATVIA. *Ziemassvetki* ("Winter Festival," Christmas) extends for four days, symbolized by the Brothers Ziemassvetki, four mythical, celestial beings of undifferentiated form who are believed to bring prosperity and gifts. Tradition also celebrates this time as the birth of *Dievs* (God). In addition to Christmas trees, homes are decorated with sun symbols made from straw, which are hung from the ceiling and corners, along with birds' feathers and dried flowers.

As the festival commences, families pull an oak log around the exterior of the house during the day in the belief that all the year's evil is transferred to the log. Then the log is burned that night amid a chorus of carols to cleanse the house and fields from the evil trapped therein. This ritual also stems from ancient rites which supposedly aided the sun's ascent at the winter solstice. The festival includes much singing and dancing as *kekatnieki*, throngs of people costumed as wolves, bears, or other animals, walk about frightening away evil spirits in rural areas and performing plays and skits. Other groups consist of *kaladnieces*, roving bands of female carolers, who receive treats and gifts from homes serenaded, and *Iekatas*, costumed singers who also set fire to tires and roll them down hills as symbols of the "burning wheel" of the winter solstice. A favorite costume is "Death" (white head scarf, flour on the face, and black circles under the

eyes), which wards off its namesake. Urban regions are more likely to sport a Father Christmas figure.

The principal feast occurs on Christmas Eve with a menu often consisting of smoked pig's head and all manner of pork products, grey beans for maturity and strength, peas to shed fewer tears, *piragi* (dumplings stuffed with bacon and ham) for sunny days, breads, baked apples, and beer. The more one eats, it is believed, the healthier one will become, and those men who consume the greatest quantity of sausages are considered to be the strongest.

"Merry Christmas" is *Priecigus Ziemassvetkus.*

• LITHUANIA. The principal season, extending from Advent to Epiphany, is dominated by the rituals of *Kucios* (the same word denotes "Christmas Eve" and "Christmas Eve supper"), which commences when the first star of the evening, believed to be the Star of Bethlehem, is sighted. The meal begins with unleavened communion wafers, variously known as *plotkeles*, *paplotelis*, *plokstainelis*, or *Dievo pyragai* (God's cakes), that are stamped with Nativity scenes. As family members exchange portions of wafer with ritual greetings, each person attempts to break off a piece larger than what remains behind, for a larger piece portends a successful new year. In contrast, he whose piece is smaller has his luck broken. Apples on the table also commemorate December 24 as the feast day of Adam and Eve. The lady of the house slices an apple and presents the first piece to her husband, symbolic of Eve offering the forbidden fruit to Adam as detailed in the Book of Genesis, after which she distributes the remaining slices to those at the table. Symbolic of the manger, hay or straw lies beneath the white tablecloth. The table has been decorated with candles and fir boughs, and the communion wafers, one for each person present, have been arranged on a plate at center table.

Meat is no longer forbidden, yet to observe strict *Kucios* tradition is to serve twelve meatless courses, symbolic of Christ's twelve apostles. The menu may include herring and other fish, *slizikai* (small, hard biscuits served with poppy seeds and honey sauce or milk), *kisielius* (cranberry pudding), dried fruit compote, mushroom soup, potatoes, assorted dried or pickled vegetables, sauerkraut, bread, and assorted cakes. Drinks include water or juice but never alcohol or other stimulants. Some regions may feature *kucia*, a most traditional dish of bygone days, which consists of a mixture of cooked grains served with honey and boiled water.

Anyone who does not at least taste each course is said to risk death within the coming year; a similar fate awaits the person who does not participate in the breaking of the wafer.

Fir twigs and myrtle adorn the seats at the table, and a vacant place, marked with a chair, a plate with a burning candle, but no eating utensils, is set for any deceased family member. Any food remaining is left on the table overnight for the spirits of deceased family members who are believed to return overnight, and no one leaves the table until all have eaten and the auguries have been read (see subentry below, "Superstitions"), lest death befall him.

Decorating Christmas trees and other secular aspects of Christmas such as gift giving came into vogue in Lithuania at the turn of the twentieth century; prior to that time, Christmas was observed as a strictly religious holiday. The most distinctively Lithuanian Christmas tree ornaments are fashioned either from real wheat or rye straw or plastic drinking straws into elaborate mobiles of innumerable sizes and shapes. Some ornaments are created from colored eggshells, paper, pastry, apples, pine cones, and nuts, but these are usually omitted when straw ornaments are utilized. If a tree decorated with straw ornaments is to be illuminated, custom dictates using only yellow lights, which enhance the straw shapes in ways not possible with multi-colored lights. Straw may also form the principal element of wayside shrines adorning country roads. The Christmas tree is decorated on Christmas Eve prior to *Kucios*, and gifts are opened after the auguries and a period of caroling around the family tree.

With the coming of independence, Santa Claus has returned to Lithuania in the form of *Kaledu Senelis* (Grandfather Christmas), who arrives on Christmas Eve demanding a "price" from children in exchange for gifts. To that end, children sing carols, recite poems, dance, or play instruments for his amusement. Fol-

lowing these festivities, Christmas Eve concludes with *Piemeneliu Misos* ("Shepherd's Mass"), which is held either at midnight or at dawn on Christmas Day. Families attend church services and visit friends on Christmas Day.

New Year's Eve recalls the atmosphere of Christmas Eve with another family dinner and a repetition of auguries, and young people masquerade about in costumes of animals or as the "Old Year" and "New Year." On Epiphany, families write "K. M. B.," the initials of the three Wise Men — Kaspar, Melchior, and Balthazar — on their doors along with signs of the cross, and young people masquerade as the Wise Men.

"Merry Christmas" in Lithuania is *Linksmu Kaledu*.

• SUPERSTITIONS. According to folklore, by no means unique to the Baltic States, the future may be revealed on Christmas Eve and New Year's Day, for whatever transpires on these two days will impact the coming new year. Because the number of superstitions is almost without limit, only a few are cited here. For example, many stars clustered together forecast a good year. If there is snow on Christmas Day, Easter will be green, and *vice versa*. A clear New Year's Day that brings good news or frost covering the trees predicts a bountiful year; snow, rain, or thick fog on New Year's Day predicts disaster. To become wealthy, carry a black cat around a church, eat as many grey peas as possible, or eat nine times before midnight on Christmas Eve.

A girl may seek glimpses of her future mate through several rituals. If she pours hot lead into a glass of water, the shape of the mass will reveal his occupation. After Christmas Eve supper, if a girl sweeps the floor and tosses the refuse at a crossroads, the next dog that barks determines the direction from which her husband will come; one variation calls for the girl merely to stand outside and howl like a dog, then listen for a bark. The length and shape of a straw pulled randomly beneath the tablecloth or a piece of wood pulled from a woodpile predicts a future spouse's physical appearance. (For one already married, a fat or thin straw or piece of wood forecasts abundance or poverty, respectively, in the coming year.) If a girl tosses her shoe backward toward a door and the toe points to the door, she will wed in the coming year; if the toe points away, she will remain single that year. If a girl can count any batch of items evenly by twos, she will wed in the new year. In one elaborate ritual, a girl writes the name of a different boy on each of twelve slips of paper, folds them in half, then distributes them around the edge of a bowl of water. She places a small, lighted candle in half of a nutshell and floats this on the water. The name at which the "boat" stops reveals the name of her future husband.

If the first person to visit the home on New Year's Day is a man, the entire year will be plentiful; the opposite if the visitor is a woman.

See also **Advent**; **Epiphany**.

Barbados
See **West Indies**

The Bear Who Slept Through Christmas

Children's book published in 1980 by John Barrett, also adapted for television as an animated cartoon. Ted E. Bear dreams of being the first bear to find Christmas, with all of its gifts and music, said holiday rumored to be supervised by a man wearing a red suit and white beard. When Ted is fired from his job at Organic Honeyworks for daydreaming, he sets out for the city in quest of Christmas. He investigates a toy store with dazzling gifts and surveys a church whose choir certainly provides the beautiful music, but, to his dismay, Christmas is not there.

By chance Ted meets the red-suited, white-bearded man, who advises that Christmas can only be found in the heart and offers an address where Ted can fulfill his wish. The address is an ordinary house, to which Ted easily gains access, and there he finds only a Christmas tree, a few gifts, and no music. Falling asleep under the tree, he awakens in the morning to find a happy little girl cuddling him closely to her, overjoyed that Santa brought him as her Christmas gift. Ted has found Christmas, for, as Santa said, Christmas is a way of giving, of sharing, and of loving.

The 1983 television animated cartoon featured the voices of Tom Smothers, Barbara Fel-

don, Arte Johnson, Robert Holt, Kelly Lange, Michael Bell, Casey Kasem, Caryn Paperny. There followed a series of Ted E. Bear storybook adventures. A Sed-bar Production in Association with DePatie-Freleng Enterprises. Color. Half-hour. Video N/A.

Other books by John Barrett include *Christmas Comes to Monster Island* (1981), *Easter Bear* (1981), *The Great Bear Scare* (1981), and *Ted E. Bear Rescues Santa Claus* (1985).

The Bears' Christmas
See **The Berenstain Bears**

Beautiful Star of Bethlehem

Popular American Southern Gospel carol, the lyrics of which were written by Robert Fisher Boyce (1887–1968), a rural dairy farmer who resided in the Big Springs community south of Murfreesboro, Tennessee. Claiming to have received inspiration from God, Boyce penned the lyrics in his barn during the summer of 1938 and then provided a musical setting with assistance from a daughter, Nannie Lou Taylor. Afterwards, Boyce attended so-called "singing schools" sponsored by the James D. Vaughan Publishing Company of Lawrenceburg, Tennessee, a firm which promoted the sale of hymnals and gospel music by offering courses in music notation. Aside from the merits of the carol itself, Boyce's subsequent service as an instructor for these courses probably contributed to the publication of "Beautiful Star," which Vaughan first published in their 1940 song book, *Beautiful Praise*, and later in their *Favorite Radio Songs*. Although Boyce is considered to be the sole lyricist, printed arrangements have included the name of Adger M. Pace, an editor for Vaughan at the time.

Boyce's creation, an allegory in which the Star of Bethlehem serves to light the path to salvation through Christ, was originally intended as a simple hymn to be sung throughout the year, yet its popular appeal over time through the country, gospel, and bluegrass genres has associated it far more with the Christmas season. The John Daniel Quartet first recorded "Beautiful Star" in Nashville on their Daniel label with John "Whit" Curtis as arranger and sole accompanist, probably around Christmas of 1953 or 1954. Two recordings have been proposed as "definitive" versions:

one by the Stanley Brothers in their album *Hymns from the Cross* (King Records, 1964) and one by Ralph Stanley and the Clinch Mountain Boys in their album *Clinch Mountain Gospel* (Rebel Records, 1977). Other notable recordings featuring "Beautiful Star" include the Jimmie Davis album *Highway to Heaven* (Decca, 1964); the Emmylou Harris album *Light of the Stable* (Warner Bros., 1981); and the Judds album *Christmas Time with the Judds* (RCA/Curb, 1987). The Judds also performed "Beautiful Star" at the White House during a Bob Hope television special.

Robert Boyce had been writing songs since the age of 24, yet only one other title is known, "Safe in His Love," his first work, which was published by the A.J. Showalter Company.

Behold a Branch Is Growing
See **Lo, How a Rose E'er Blooming**

Belgium
See **The Low Countries**

Belize
See **Central America**

Ben-Hur: A Tale of the Christ

Highly acclaimed American novel and best-known work of Lewis (Lew) Wallace, published in 1880. Although this historical novel, most often remembered for its spectacular chariot race, does not typically fall into the Christmas literary repertoire, its Book First, designed as an extended prologue, beautifully expands upon the Nativity story as presented in the Gospels of Matthew and Luke. Here, riding white camels, the three Wise Men, Melchior of India, Gaspar of Greece, and Balthazar of Egypt, rendezvous in the Arabian Desert on December 25 in the year 747 of Rome to commence their search for the Christ. Arriving in Bethlehem twelve days later (Epiphany), they find a cave wherein the Babe lies in a manger not of wood, but of stone. An epigraph also cites lines from English poet John Milton's "On the Morning of Christ's Nativity."

Initially an agnostic, Lew Wallace (1827–

"In order to properly appreciate the movie, you should read the book first," advises this 1915 Sears Roebuck catalog plug for Ben-Hur. The famed chariot race gets the starring role.

1905), a noted American Civil War general and literary genius, set out to write a book that would destroy Christianity. For two years he conducted research in the best libraries of America and Europe. While writing the second chapter of this would-be book, all his research abruptly ceased when, reviewing all the accumulated evidence, he was overwhelmed with a sudden conviction of Christ as the Son of God. Wallace found himself on his knees pouring forth his faith, a faith which later enabled him to write *Ben-Hur*. His other novels include *The Fair God* (1873) and *The Prince of India* (1893). *See also* **On the Morning of Christ's Nativity; Nativity.**

The Berenstain Bears

Large, popular American series of books for young children written and illustrated by the award-winning husband-and-wife cartoonists, Stan and Jan Berenstain. To date the Berenstains' bear family has appeared in more than 100 titles, three of which are Christmas titles:

The Berenstain Bears: The Bears' Christmas (1970). Papa Bear attempts to show Brother how to use the sled, skates, and skis that Santa brought. A 1989 animated version of the same title included three stories: "The Bears' Christmas"; "Inside, Outside, Upside Down"; and "The Bike Lesson." Sony Wonder Video. Color.

The Berenstain Bears' Christmas Tree (1980), based on the 1979 animated television special of the same title. Planning to find and cut down the perfect Christmas tree, Papa Bear, at first thinking of his own Christmas interests, soon realizes that many animals have set up housekeeping in these trees. Because he spares them and because Grizzly Gus's Christmas tree lot is sold out, the same forest animals surprise Papa by decorating the exterior of his house. Animated version narrated by Ron McLarty. Voices: Ron McLarty, Pat Lysinger, Jonathan Lewis, Gabriela Glatzer. Written by Stan and Jan Berenstain. Produced by Buzz Potamkin. Directed by Mordicai Gerstein. A Cates Brothers Company Production in Association with Perpetual Motion Pictures. Kids Classics Home Video. Color. Half-hour.

The Berenstain Bears Meet Santa Bear (1984). At first wanting every toy they see on Saturday morning television, the cubs learn that the spirit of Christmas lies in giving, not receiving.

The Berenstain Bears' Christmas Tree
See The Berenstain Bears

The Berenstain Bears Meet Santa Bear
See The Berenstain Bears

The Best Christmas
See The Waltons

The Best Christmas Pageant Ever
Children's book written by Barbara Robinson, published in 1972. An abbreviated version appeared in *McCall's Magazine* as "The Christmas Pageant."

For years, the annual Sunday school Christmas pageant has featured the same songs, the same cast (Alice Wendleken always portrays Mary), and the same script. The children certainly loath it, and nobody really enjoys attending such an ordeal.

This year, however, everything is different when the Herdmans arrive. Incorrigible school bullies, forever pulling pranks (like blowing up Mr. Shoemaker's tool shed with a chemistry set), and totally unfamiliar with the Christmas story, the abominable Herdman children — Ralph, Imogene, Leroy, Claude, Ollie, and Gladys — crash the Christmas pageant rehearsal and take over the lead roles by intimidating the other children, including Alice. Latch-key children because their father has deserted them and their mother works double shift at the shoe factory, the Herdmans acquire an interest in Sunday school and thence the pageant through Charlie, a school mate who deceives them with notions of receiving delicious refreshments there.

With Mrs. Armstrong out of commission with a broken leg, Charlie's mother assumes the role of pageant director, which includes familiarizing the Herdmans with the Nativity. As she reads from Luke and Matthew, surprisingly they ask innumerable questions about the characters' roles. They are appalled that a pregnant Mary must reside in a "barn," and they take much interest in King Herod, whom Imogene especially wants to punish because he sought to kill Baby Jesus. The Herdmans also decide that more "decent" gifts than gold, frankincense, and myrrh must be sought for the pageant.

On pageant night, the congregation, deliciously anticipating Herdman mayhem, turns out in droves to see Imogene as Mary; Ralph as Joseph; Leroy, Claude, and Ollie as Wise Men; and little Gladys as the Angel of the Lord. The production at first includes the usual minor miscues, but the atmosphere changes as Mary enters, burping a baby doll; the Angel addresses the shepherds with, "Hey! Unto you a child is born!"; and the Wise Men lay a large ham (from the Herdmans' Christmas food basket) before the manger. And as everyone sings a final "Silent Night," the magnitude of Christmas overwhelms Imogene, who begins weeping. This best-ever pageant transforms the ragamuffins and the congregation alike: the former are more sedate, docile, and perhaps more considerate of others afterwards; the latter more clearly sees the human side of the Nativity — impoverished parents facing hardships while bringing a new life into the world.

A 1983 American-Canadian adaptation of the story for television starred Loretta Swit, Anthony Holland, Jackson Davies, David Alexander, Fairuza Balk, Ocean Hellman, Teri Dean, Beau Heaton, Megan Hunt, Jason Micus, Shane Punt, and Glen Reid. Written by Barbara Robinson. Produced and directed by George Schaefer. Schaefer-Karpf Productions in Association with Comworld Productions. Regency Home Video. Color. 48 min.

The story has also been adapted for the stage.

A native of Portsmouth, Ohio, Barbara Robinson has written a number of children's books, among them *Across from Indian Shore* (1962), *The Fattest Bear in the First Grade* (1969), *Temporary Times, Temporary Places* (1982), and *The Best School Year Ever* (1994). Her short stories have appeared in women's magazines, and she currently resides in Berwyn, Pennsylvania.

Bewitched

Popular Emmy Award–winning television situation comedy series of 254 episodes that ran on the ABC network from 1964 to 1972. *Bewitched* revolved around the zany "mixed marriage" of mortal Darrin Stephens (Dick York, 1964–69, and Dick Sargent, 1969–72) and his wife, Samantha (Elizabeth Montgomery), a beautiful, immortal witch. The Stephenses enjoyed Christmas in four December episodes:

A Vision of Sugar Plums (1964). Visiting the local orphanage on Christmas Eve, the Stephenses have arranged for six-year-old Michael (Billy Mumy), a disturbed little boy who cares nothing for Christmas or Santa, to share the holiday with them in their home. Their neighbors, Abner and Gladys Kravitz (George Tobias and Alice Pearce), take home seven-year-old Tommy (Kevin Tate), a firm believer in Santa. When all else fails to raise Michael's spirits, including Darrin's posing as Santa, Samantha confesses that she is a witch and zaps herself into a black costume with pointed hat. Determined to convince the boy that Santa is real, she whisks the boy and Darrin as well off to the North Pole on her broomstick to see St. Nick himself, one of Samantha's personal friends. Amid the toys and elves, Michael is more than convinced, and the sen-

timental philosophy of Santa (Cecil Kellaway), that the real happiness of Christmas lies in giving, hits home. Encouraged to select a gift, Michael chooses a toy fire truck, which he gives to Tommy the next morning. He also presents a toolbox, a most promising sign, to the Johnsons (Bill Dailey and Gerry Johnson), a couple who had unsatisfactorily adopted him twice before and who have stopped by with Mrs. Grange (Sara Seegar) from the orphanage to try again. This episode was rerun in December 1965. Written by Herman Groves. Produced by Danny Arnold. Directed by Alan Rafkin. This half-hour, B & W episode is included in the video collection *A Bewitched Christmas*. Screen Gems and Columbia Pictures Television. Columbia Tristar Home Video.

Humbug Not to Be Spoken Here (1967), a parody on the Dickens classic *A Christmas Carol*. Darrin and his boss, Larry Tate (David White), are anxious to have the Mortimer Soup Company as a client of their advertising firm, but Mr. Mortimer (Charles Lane), a Scrooge at heart, tries Darrin's patience by demanding a business meeting on Christmas Eve. Over Mortimer's objections, Darrin leaves by mid-evening to buy a Christmas tree and spend time with Samantha and daughter Tabitha (Erin Murphy). Dropping in on the happy Stephens family with Larry, an enraged Mortimer cancels the account. Later that evening, Samantha, dressed in glittering red, surprises a sleeping Mortimer by confessing that she's a witch and transports him to see the real Santa via her red-and-white striped broomstick. After joining Santa (Don Beddoe) on his worldwide rounds, Sam and Mortimer watch Mortimer's butler Hawkins (Martin Ashe) making merry with his wife and child at home. When Mortimer wonders why the financially strapped butler is so happy, Sam asks Mortimer if wealth has really made him happy. On Christmas morning, Mortimer, a changed man, drops by to apologize and brings a gift box of Mortimer Instant Soups. Seeing Samantha plus Tabitha's new "Susie-Bruisie" doll (he had seen the same doll at the North Pole), Mortimer wonders if his trip was real or just a dream, and Sam invites him to spend Christmas with them. With Rosalyn Burbage. Written by Lila Garrett and Bernie Kahn. Produced and directed by

William Asher. This half-hour, color episode is included in the video collection *A Bewitched Christmas*. Screen Gems and Columbia Pictures Television. Columbia Tristar Home Video.

Santa Comes to Visit and Stays and Stays (1969). Two days before Christmas, Sam enlists Cousin Esmeralda (Alice Ghostley) to babysit while she goes shopping. Esmeralda's magic often backfires; in this episode, when she sneezes, creatures appear. Following sneezes that conjure up first a goat then two seals, a third sneeze zaps up Santa himself (Ronald Long). Ordinarily, the creatures vanish over time, but Santa remains far too long, and now Christmas Eve is at hand. Because he has much work remaining, Samantha twitches up the elves, whom Santa supervises in doubletime toymaking in her living room. When Sam zaps the sleigh and reindeer onto her front lawn, neighbor Abner Kravitz (George Tobias) believes that the Stephenses have done a remarkable job of exterior decorating. Larry, having had a few drinks, arrives just as Santa takes to the skies, but passes off the "hallucination" as a case of mild inebriation. With Dick Sargent, Erin Murphy, and Sandra Gould. Written by Ed Jurist. Produced by William Asher. Directed by Richard Michaels. This half-hour, color episode is included in the video collection *A Bewitched Christmas II*. Screen Gems and Columbia Pictures Television. Columbia Tristar Home Video.

Sisters at Heart (1970). This was Elizabeth Montgomery's favorite episode. The story was written by Marcella Saunders's tenth-grade English class, fifth period, at Thomas Jefferson High School, an inner-city school in Los Angeles, with assistance from *Bewitched* writer Barbara Avedon. Originally, the story line centered around true kinship being based on spirit and not skin color, but Avedon took a further step and suggested building that theme around Christmas. The episode won the Governor's Award at the 1971 Emmy Awards ceremony.

Tabitha (Erin Murphy) wishes that she and her African-American friend Lisa Wilson (Venetta Rogers) could be real sisters, but feels that their different skin colors prevent that. To make them both look alike, Tabitha zaps white spots on Lisa and black spots on herself, a spell

that seemingly cannot be reversed. Meanwhile, Mr. Brockway (Parley Baer), a million-dollar client of the McMann-Tate advertising firm, while checking up on Darrin, forms the erroneous opinion that Tabitha and Lisa are products of an interracial marriage and makes excuses to have Darrin removed from the account. Unaware of Brockway's bigotry, Larry feels that if Darrin hosts the office Christmas party at his home and invites Brockway, the account can be saved. Lisa's parents arrive, for her father, Keith (Don Marshall), is a McMann-Tate agent, and Samantha frantically searches for a spell to remove children's spots. According to Dr. Bombay (Bernard Fox), the supernatural physician, only Tabitha can remove the spots, and only if she truly wishes for them to leave. The spell is reversed after Samantha convinces Tabitha that she and Lisa can always be friends in spirit, despite their different races. Seeing Darrin conversing with Lisa's mother, Dorothy (Janee Michelle), Brockway assumes that she is Darrin's wife until Samantha appears, to Brockway's relief. The scene reveals his racist reasons for wanting Darrin removed, an irate Larry cancels the account, and Samantha teaches Brockway a lesson by forcing him to see himself and all of his friends as black. On Christmas morning, a more sober Brockway returns to apologize to the Stephenses and the visiting Wilsons, and Sam invites him to Christmas dinner. Additional writing by William Asher. Produced and directed by William Asher. This half-hour, color episode is included in the video collection *A Bewitched Christmas II*. Screen Gems and Columbia Pictures Television. Columbia Tristar Home Video.

Birth of Christ
See **Christmas Day; Nativity**

The Birthday of a King
American carol written around 1890 by Brooklyn native William Harold Neidlinger (1863–1924). A choral conductor, singing teacher, and organist, Neidlinger principally composed songs for children in such collections as *Earth, Sky and Air in Song* and *Little Folks' Song Book*. His 1896 work *Small Songs for Small Singers* was a popular book for kindergartens.

Probably his most famous song is "The Birthday of a King."

Consisting of two verses, the simple lyrics recall that a holy light shone over the place where the Child lay in Bethlehem, and that from a humble manger, a holy way was led to God. In the refrain, angels sing a birthday song to Jesus in the form of an "Alleluia."

The Bishop's Wife ✗

(1947). Motion picture comedy-romance, based on the 1928 novel of the same title by Robert Nathan.

Too preoccupied at Christmastime with raising funds for a new cathedral in New York, Bishop Henry Brougham (David Niven) neglects his wife Julia (Loretta Young), young daughter Debbie (Karolyn Grimes), and even St. Timothy's Church, where he was formerly the rector. The church's largest patron, a demanding Mrs. Agnes Hamilton (Gladys Cooper), has pledged one million dollars toward the cathedral, provided that it be built as a shrine to her late husband. Henry, torn over this ethical and spiritual dilemma, prays for guidance, whereupon the angel Dudley (Cary Grant) appears in answer and poses as Henry's assistant.

Dudley, however, takes more interest in Julia's happiness and well-being, which includes lunching with her at Michele's, buying her a hat she's always wanted, and ice skating with her in the park — in short, being a substitute Henry. A jealous Henry finally confronts Dudley and affirms his love for his wife, at which point Dudley's work is finished. Departing, he leaves no memory of his visit behind.

Dudley's encounter with several other people on Christmas Eve changes their lives for the better. Old Professor Wutheridge (Monty Woolley) receives the inspiration to write a long-overdue history of Rome; the cabby Sylvester (James Gleason) develops more faith in humanity; and Mrs. Hamilton diverts her millions to causes more desperate than the erecting of cathedrals. Leaving, Dudley also touches an unwitting St. Timothy's congregation through Henry's Christmas Eve message, which Dudley has altered. On the subject of Christmas stockings, the message calls for filling Jesus' stocking with loving kindness, warm hearts, and a stretched out hand of tolerance, all the shining gifts that make "peace on earth."

Nominated for five Academy Awards, including Best Picture, Best Director, Best Film Editing, and Best Music Scoring, *The Bishop's Wife* received only the award for Best Sound.

With Elsa Lanchester and The Mitchell Boychoir. Written by Robert E. Sherwood and Leonardo Bercovici. Produced by Samuel Goldwyn. Directed by Henry Koster. The Samuel Goldwyn Company. HBO Home Video. B & W. 109 min.

Several interesting behind-the-scenes anecdotes are notable. Originally, Cary Grant was cast as the bishop and David Niven as Dudley, with William Seiter directing. After several weeks of filming, producer Samuel Goldwyn reversed Grant's and Niven's roles, and brought in Henry Koster to replace Seiter as director. Loretta Young was the third choice for Julia, after Teresa Wright and Jean Arthur rejected the role. Once, when Grant complained that a wintertime picture should display frost on the windows, a scene was delayed while the stage crew added that extra little touch. Grant's and Young's vain insistence on having only their right profiles filmed prompted a sarcastic Goldwyn to ask if they would be willing to work for half salary.

Child actors Karolyn Grimes (Debbie Brougham here) and Bobby Anderson (boy in the snowball fight here) also starred in another Christmas classic, *It's a Wonderful Life*. There, Karolyn played George Bailey's daughter Zuzu, and Bobby played a young George Bailey.

The Bishop's Wife was the first American film to be selected for a screening by the Royal Family at England's Royal Command Performances for movies, begun in 1946.

A remake in 1996, *The Preacher's Wife*, featured virtually an all–African American cast, with Denzel Washington, Whitney Houston, and Courtney B. Vance. In 1997, this picture was nominated for an Academy Award for Best Music, and also nominated for Image Awards: Outstanding Motion Picture, Outstanding Supporting Actress (Loretta Devine, Jennifer Lewis), Outstanding Youth Actor (Justin Pierre Edmund). It won the Image Award for Outstanding Lead Actress (Whitney Houston). In 1998 it received a Blockbuster Entertainment Award nomination for Favorite Soundtrack.

Written by Nat Mauldin, Allan Scott, Todd Graff. Produced by Samuel Goldwyn, Jr. Directed by Penny Marshall. The Samuel Goldwyn Company and Touchstone Pictures. Touchstone Video. Color. 124 min.

Blackadder's Christmas Carol
See **A Christmas Carol** (FILM AND TELEVISION VERSIONS)

Blessed Be That Maid Marie
English traditional carol, the modernized lyrics of which are derived from a fifteenth-century manuscript of carols which resides in the British Library in London. The Reverend George R. Woodward (1838–1934), the Anglican priest who adapted the text, sought artistic worth in church music over the Victorian styles at the turn of the century. He also composed original hymn lyrics in the style of the sixteenth or seventeenth century, then selected appropriate melodies from that era to fit his lyrics. In fact, it is thought that, of the five verses that comprise "Blessed Be That Maid Marie," verse three is Woodward's alone. He was responsible for many of the reforms in *The English Hymnal* (1906) and compiled three collections, *Songs of Syon* (1904), *An Italian Carol Book* (1920), and *The Cowley Carol Book* (1901, 1919, for the Fathers at Cowley, Oxford), the latter three in collaboration with Cambridge musician Charles Wood (1866–1926). "Blessed Be That Maid Marie" first appeared in both editions of *The Cowley Carol Book*. Wood provided the musical setting, a folk tune originally titled "Staines Morris," which first appeared in a lute book by a William Ballet (c. 1600).

The macaronic verses (a mixture of vernacular English with Latin) recall that because God, present before time began, was born in time as the Son of Man in a manger, was serenaded by angels, and was visited by kings, we should make merry on this fest. While verses 2–5 each contain one Latin line (the others being English), the refrain is entirely Latin: "Eya! Ihesus hodie / Natus est de Virgine" ("Rejoice! Jesus today is born of a Virgin").

Blessing of the Waters
See **Epiphany**

The Blessings of Mary
See **The Seven Joys of Mary**

Blowing in the Yule
Christmas Eve tradition found in Germany, Austria, and portions of Scandinavia, whereby brass ensembles herald the coming of Christmas by playing chorales from church towers. The custom derives from the pagan belief that loud noises created during winter solstice festivals dispelled the spirits of darkness. *See also* **Winter Solstice; Yule.**

Blue Christmas
Popular American song written in 1948 by Billy Hayes and Jay Johnson, the only Christmas piece of the eight tunes upon which the two collaborated. "Blue Christmas" centers on the "blue" or melancholy spirits evoked when one must spend the holidays without the person he loves. Initial recordings by various artists failed to generate a hit, until country singer Ernest Tubb recorded his version on the Decca label in 1949 with a vocal group, the Beasley Sisters. His record competed for the number one spot on the pop charts of 1949 with two by Gene Autry, "Rudolph, the Red-Nosed Reindeer" and "Here Comes Santa Claus," and together these three hits helped to establish the country Christmas tradition. Other "Blue Christmas" recordings making the charts in 1949 included those by Russ Morgan (Decca) and Hugo Winterhalter and His Orchestra (Columbia). In 1964, Elvis Presley's rendition (RCA), briefly achieving the number one position that year and again in 1973 on the *Billboard Christmas Singles* chart, sold over a million copies, and continued to make the pop charts each year in between.

Of the 25 most frequently performed Christmas songs of the twentieth century listed by the American Society of Composers, Authors and Publishers (ASCAP), "Blue Christmas" is ranked number 14.

Other tunes by Hayes and Johnson include "House Warmin'," "How Now Brown Cow," "Little Wedding Bells," "Peaceful," "Pizza Polka" (with Harry Simeone), "There's a Cute Little Pig," and "Whittlin'" (with Lionel Taylor).

The Boar's Head Carol
Title applied to several English carols which accompanied the traditional ceremony of serving a wild boar's head at Christmas feasts during the Middle Ages. This tradition

probably derived from pagan Scandinavian winter solstice festivals, at which a wild boar was sacrificed to Freya, Norse goddess of fertility, who was symbolized as riding across the heavens on a golden boar. Another possible derivation included the annual slaughtering of pigs and other livestock in late fall as an alternative to witnessing their starvation during heavy winter snows.

The custom is still observed annually, most notably at Queen's College, Oxford, where the carol adopted for the ceremony has become the most familiar of the boar's head carols. The anonymous text, thought to date from the fifteenth century, is taken from Jan van Wynkyn de Worde's *Christmasse Carolles* (London, 1521), the oldest surviving collection of printed Christmas carols; its tune, also anonymous, derives from at least the eighteenth century. Its macaronic lyrics (mixture of Latin with vernacular English) call for all to make merry at the feast with song and praises to the Lord. Latin comprises not only the last line of each of the three verses but the entire refrain as well. Originally the refrain read, "Caput apri defero / Reddens laudes Domino, / laudes Domino, laudes Domino, Domino" ("I bring in the boar's head, / Giving thanks to the Lord, / thanks to the Lord, thanks to the Lord, to the Lord"), but in 1901, the music of the refrain was rewritten and its text shortened to eliminate the repeated "laudes Domino."

The circumstances under which Queen's College instituted a boar's head ceremony are a matter of amusing legend. Allegedly, a wild boar threatened a young student of the college as he perused a book containing the works of Aristotle while walking in Shotover Woods on Christmas Day. Exclaiming, "Graecum est!" (Latin, "It is Greek [to me]!"), the boy saved himself by ramming Aristotle down the boar's throat and choking it, then served the animal to the student body with elaborate festivities that evening. The special reference to Aristotle supposedly implies that, even in the Middle Ages, the Greek philosopher was as unpalatable as he is today.

Since the fourteenth century, a trumpet

"Be glad, both more and less/For this hath ordained our steward,/To cheer you all this Christmas—/The boar's head, and mustard!" reads a stanza of a verse in "A Boy King's Christmas," a story from Our Young Folks: An Illustrated Magazine for Boys and Girls *(Boston: Ticknor and Fields, 1868).*

fanfare has announced the ceremony at Queen's, after which the Provost and Fellows of the College assume their places. Following grace, the procession enters: first the solo singer, then the choir walking backwards, facing three chefs who bear the boar's head (actually that of a suckling pig, for wild boars became extinct in England during the seventeenth century) on a silver platter, which is flanked by torch bearers. Garnished with bay and rosemary, as the carol dictates, the head sports a crown and flags, the mouth an orange. The procession advances only during the refrains and pauses for the verses, at the conclusion of which the Provost distributes the garnishments to the choir and the orange to the soloist.

Whereas "The Boar's Head Carol" of Queen's College is actually more convivial than religious, the opposite is true for another and lesser known of these carols, "The Exeter Boar's Head Carol." Written by Richard Smert, rector of Plymtree in Devon from 1435 to 1477 and vicar choral of Exeter Cathedral from 1428 to 1466, this carol is quite unique in that it reveres the boar's head as a symbol of Christ.

Bolivia

See **South America**

Boxing Day

Falling on December 26, Boxing Day is a legal holiday in those countries forming the Commonwealth of Nations, especially Australia, Canada, and Great Britain. It is also known as Second Christmas Day and, in the Roman Catholic Church, as St. Stephen's Day, which honors Stephen, the first Christian martyr.

Boxing Day, which became a public holiday through an act of Parliament in 1871, derives its name from an English tradition dating to the Middle Ages, when churches opened their alms boxes, or Christmas boxes, on this day and distributed funds to the poor. This practice had evolved by the seventeenth century into members of the working class seeking gratuities from those to whom they had rendered services during the past year, and the tips received became known as "boxes."

This custom of boxing fell into decline by the nineteenth century, principally because the increasing number of tradespeople soliciting "boxes" had become quite burdensome. This did not prevent generous employers, however, from voluntarily bestowing monetary gifts upon their employees in the spirit of the season, which formed the basis for the Christmas bonuses that were more prevalent during the late nineteenth century. By the end of the twentieth century, Christmas bonuses had declined but not completely vanished.

From the eighteenth century or earlier, the British Isles and France observed "Hunting the Wren" on St. Stephen's Day, a custom that survives in modified form in Ireland. Boxing Day currently is a day for recreation, with pageants, plays, pantomimes, and sporting events, for example.

See also **Great Britain; Hunting the Wren; Ireland.**

Boy-Bishop

Ecclesiastical office originating in Europe during the Middle Ages, instituted in 844 by Pope Gregory IV and observed particularly in England. As a tribute to St. Nicholas, the fourth-century bishop of Myra and patron saint of children, on St. Nicholas Day (December 6), one boy was elected by his peers from the local church or monastery school to serve in the full capacity of a bishop until Holy Innocents Day (December 28), a memorial to those children (innocents) massacred in Bethlehem by Herod the Great (Matthew 2:1–18). Arrayed in official vestments and mitre, the Boy-Bishop assumed all responsibilities of the Church and toured his parish blessing people as his comrades followed in priests' robes. Should he die in office, he was buried with full ecclesiastical honors. In England, at the cathedral in Salisbury and at Lulworth Castle, are remains of two boys, both believed to have died as Boy-Bishops.

A Boy-Bishop, from an unnamed parish, as depicted in William Hone's Ancient Mysteries Described *(London: 1823).*

In other parts of Europe by the eleventh century, Holy Innocents Day had also become a feast for students and choirboys, and the holiday, including the role of the Boy-Bishop, had degenerated to an atmosphere of secular revelry. Because several other riotous holidays were observed between Christmas and Epiphany (January 6), these festivals were collectively termed the Feast of Fools. The Council of Basle finally abolished the Boy-Bishop in 1431 on the European continent, but in England the custom survived until the reign of Elizabeth I.

See also **Feast of Fools; Holy Innocents Day; Nativity; Saint Nicholas Day.**

A Boy Is Born in Bethlehem

("Puer natus in Bethlehem"). Traditional, medieval Latin carol, one from a host of such carols that has managed to retain some popularity through the centuries. Believed to have originated in Bohemia, its earliest written sources include a processional from a Bohemian Benedictine nunnery that dates to 1320 and a late thirteenth-century antiphonary from Bobbio, Italy. Although these earlier settings consisted of only three verses, additional stanzas accumulated over the centuries, *The Hereford Breviary* (1505) showing ten and the *Piae Cantiones* (Greifswald, 1582) with fourteen, four verses of the latter having been contributed by a Hermann Bonn (1504–1548), a hymn translator and pupil of Martin Luther.

From the sixteenth century on, "A Boy Is Born in Bethlehem" enjoyed numerous harmonizations, notably by German composers Michael Praetorius (1571–1621) in his 1607 and 1609 volumes of *Musae Sioniae* and J. S. Bach (1685–1750) in his Epiphany Cantata *Sie werden aus Saba alle kommen* (BWV 65). Organ chorale preludes based on the carol are also the works of Bach (*Orgelbüchlein*, BWV 603); Bach's cousin, Johann Walther (1684–1748); and the Dane Dietrich Buxtehude (1637–1707).

A Boy's Thanksgiving Day

See **Over the River and Through the Woods**

The Brady Bunch

Popular family television situation comedy series of 117 episodes which aired on the ABC network from 1969 to 1974. The principal characters included Mike and Carol Brady (Robert Reed and Florence Henderson); their children, Greg (Barry Williams), Peter (Christopher Knight), Bobby (Mike Lookinland), Marcia (Maureen McCormick), Jan (Eve Plumb), and Cindy (Susan Olsen); and their housekeeper, Alice Nelson (Ann B. Davis).

The original series featured only one holiday episode, "The Voice of Christmas," which aired during the first year in December 1969. As the Bradys launch into Christmas Eve, Carol develops laryngitis and will be unable to sing a solo in church the next day. Alice soaks a towel in a revolting home remedy of mustard, camphor, vinegar, and pepper and places this around Carol's neck with faith that it will cure her. When Cindy visits a department store Santa (Hal Smith), her only wish is that he restore her mother's voice, and Santa agrees to the cure. Mike cautions Cindy not to expect miracles, but her faith in Santa cannot be shattered. The other children, however, are prepared to postpone Christmas until Carol regains her voice. Later that night, Mike awakens to hear Carol humming "O Come, All Ye Faithful" in her sleep. With her voice restored, she delivers a beautiful rendition of the same carol in church as planned. Cindy writes a note of thanks to Santa, and Mike enjoys renewed faith in Christmas miracles.

The next celebration of Christmas with the Brady family occurred in 1988 with *A Very Brady Christmas*, the third highest-rated television movie for that year. The movie features the original cast, except for Cindy, played here by Jennifer Runyon. After twenty years, Mike and Carol are now alone, for their children are grown and have moved away. The two independently plan to give each other vacations to Greece and Japan as Christmas presents, but their coincidental meeting at the same travel agency puts this idea on hold. Alice appears on their doorstep, her husband Sam the butcher having left her, and the Bradys take her in. As Mike and Carol reminisce about vacations, the scene flashes back to the episode "A-Camping We Will Go" (November 1969), in which the girls frightened the boys into believing that a bear was outside their tent. This gives Carol the idea to have all the Brady children and their families return home for a Christmas reunion.

The children agree to come, but Mike and Carol are unaware that bits of humbug surround the children's personal lives. Wally Logan (Jerry Houser), Marcia's husband, has just lost his job as salesman for Tyler Toys; Jan, an architect like her father, and her husband, Phillip Covington III (Ron Kuhlman), a university professor, are separating; Peter's boss, Valerie Thomas (Carol Huston), is more than romantically interested in him, which disturbs macho Peter; Bobby has dropped out of graduate school to race cars; and Cindy, about to graduate from college and feeling that her parents are ordering her home, would rather have gone on a skiing trip with her friends. The problem for Greg, now a physician, is that his nurse wife Nora (Caryn Richman) wishes to spend Christmas with her parents while Greg and little son Kevin (Zachary Bostron) go on to the Bradys.

Although Christmas Eve sees the brood arriving amid mirth and joy, Carol senses that all is not well. Soon, however, Jan and Phillip have patched up their differences. On Christmas Day, Mike, tipped off by Wally's boy Mickey (G. W. Lee), introduces Wally to neighbor Leonard Prescott (F. J. O'Neil) of Prescott Toys, who hires him as a new salesman. During Christmas dinner, the other Brady children openly confess their secrets or problems, and Peter and Valerie simultaneously propose to each other. Mike is called away to a construction site on which he was formerly the architect (he resigned because the client had declined his added safety recommendations), where a cave-in has trapped two security guards. Mike goes in to rescue the guards, but after the guards escape, the site collapses, now trapping Mike.

As the Bradys wait, Cindy exhorts Carol to have faith. The scene flashes back to the earlier Christmas episode when Carol lost her voice. First Carol, then Cindy, then all the Bradys begin singing "O Come, All Ye Faithful," after which Mike emerges from the ruins, shaken but unharmed. Back home, Sam the butcher (Lewis Arquette) appears dressed as Santa and begs Alice to take him back.

With Jaclyn Bernstein and Phillip Richard Allen. Written by Sherwood Schwartz, Lloyd J. Schwartz. Produced by Lloyd J. Schwartz, Barry Berg. Directed by Peter Baldwin. The Sherwood Schwartz Company in Association with Paramount Pictures Television. Paramount Video. Color. 94 min.

Brazil
See **South America**

Br'er Rabbit's Christmas Carol
See **A Christmas Carol** (FILM AND TELEVISION VERSIONS)

Brightest and Best of the Sons of the Morning

English carol for Epiphany, the lyrics of which were first published in the *Christian Observer* (1811) by Reginald Heber (1783–1826), a hymnwriter and Anglican vicar of Hodnet, Shropshire, who in 1823 became bishop of Calcutta, India. Also known under the shorter title "Brightest and Best," the carol appeared in William Caldwell's collection, *Union Harmony or Family Musician* (Maryville, Tennessee, 1837), with the title "Star in the East," based on a line in the first verse. Heber originally wrote four verses filled with high imagery and repeated the first verse as a fifth. An additional, anonymous verse was added at some point, incongruous with the others because of its reference to Christmas rather than Epiphany. In *The New Oxford Book of Carols*, this altered carol is titled "Hail the Blest Morn!" with the rogue verse shifted to the fore, Heber's first verse as the refrain, and the remaining verses as 2–4.

The lyrics have been paired with some twenty different musical settings, several from the American South, such as those harmonized by William Walker in *The Southern Harmony* (Spartanburg, South Carolina, 1835) and by William Caldwell above. Another setting derives from a tune written in 1892 by James P. Harding (1850–1911), a London civil service clerk and church organist. No particular setting, however, has gained popularity over the others.

Other well-known hymns by Heber include "Holy, Holy, Holy" and "From Greenland's Icy Mountains."

Bring a Torch, Jeannette, Isabella

("Un flambeau, Jeannette, Isabelle"). Provençal traditional carol believed to date to the seventeenth century and possibly earlier.

Two facts are well established: that Émile Blémont's modern French translation of the text, beginning as "Un flambeau," first appeared in Julien Tiersot's *Noëls Français* (1901); and that Edward Cuthbert Nunn (1868–1914), an Englishman, provided the most popular English version. Other descriptions regarding the carol's origin vary. For example, the music is said to date from a lively *ritournelle* of the fourteenth century, and the text and music are said to have first appeared together in a Christmas collection, *Cantiques de Première Advenement de Jésus-Christ* (1553). *The New Oxford Book of Carols*, on the other hand, makes no mention of this latter collection, implying instead that Blémont based his translation on a Provençal carol first published in a collection by Nicolas Saboly (1699). Furthermore, the *Oxford Book* attributes the tune as the drinking-song creation of French composer Marc-Antoine Charpentier (1645–1704). Although the specific identities of "Jeannette" and "Isabella" are also lacking, their names may have influenced the French artist Georges de La Tour's painting of the Nativity, which depicts two maids observing at a distance.

Bugs Bunny's Looney Christmas Tales

(1979). Made-for-television collection of three new animated, holiday cartoon "shorts" from Friz Freleng and Chuck Jones, directors of the animation department at Warner Bros. Studios. These shorts use the famous Warner Bros. characters popular since the late 1930s in theatrical shorts, including Bugs Bunny, Elmer Fudd and Porky Pig.

Bugs Bunny's Christmas Carol, abbreviated spoof of the Dickens classic, with Yosemite Sam as Scrooge, Porky Pig as Bob Cratchit, and Tweety Bird as Tiny Tim. Trickster Bugs pulls slapstick gags on Scrooge, then poses as the "Ghost of Christmas" and threatens to take him to see the man with the red suit in the nether regions (not Santa), whereupon Scrooge reforms.

In *Freeze Frame*, Wile E. Coyote attempts to nab Roadrunner by chasing him into the mountains, for, according to *Everything You Ever Wanted to Know About Roadrunners but Were Afraid to Ask*, snow is a roadrunner's nemesis. As usual, every ploy used by Coyote backfires.

Fright Before Christmas. The Tazmanian Devil, escaping from an aircraft over the North Pole on Christmas Eve, parachutes into Santa's suit drying on a clothes line and hijacks the reindeer sleigh. Entering Bugs's home via the chimney, Taz wreaks havoc and finally floats into the sky after swallowing a gift from Bugs, a life raft that inflates on consumption.

Written by Friz Freleng, John Dunn, Chuck Jones, Tony Benedict. Produced and directed by Friz Freleng, Chuck Jones. A DePatie-Freleng Enterprises and Chuck Jones Enterprises Production in Association with Warner Bros. Television. Warner Home Video. Color. Half-hour.

Bulgaria

This nation has celebrated Christmas since 865, when Boris I (ruled 852–889), the Khan, accepted Christianity upon yielding to pressure from the Byzantine emperor Michael III. He embraced the Eastern Orthodox Church over the Roman Catholic Church when the latter failed to appoint an archbishop for Bulgaria. Thus Bulgarians have remained predominantly Orthodox and have observed Christmas on January 7 according to the old Julian Calendar, despite a long history of totalitarian governments: five centuries by the Ottoman Empire, beginning in the fourteenth century, and some forty years of Soviet occupation following World War II. The preserved Christmas traditions are largely a blend of Orthodoxy and pagan, agrarian rituals, especially in rural regions.

The principal celebration is *Koleduvane* (Christmas Eve), the Christianization of a winter solstice festival that once heralded the birth of the sun. Often the head of the house cuts a large oak or peach log which burns through the night, a symbol of Christ who will be resurrected. Upon entering his home with the log, the man proclaims, "Do you glorify the young God?" whereupon the household responds with, "Yes, we do, welcome!" Christians keep a forty-day fast before Christmas (to commemorate Christ's ordeal of forty days in the wilderness following His baptism) by abstaining from all animal products. In memory of Christ's

Twelve Apostles, the Christmas Eve dinner consists of twelve meatless dishes, eaten on a table covered with straw which honors the manger. When someone sights the first star of the evening, believed to be the Star of Bethlehem, the dinner commences. Just prior to the dinner there are greetings from the host, who proclaims, "Christ is born," after which the family members respond with, "He is born indeed." The host offers grace, then purifies each room of the house with incense. The traditional menu consists of cabbage or vine leaves stuffed with rice, beans, lentils, boiled wheat, stewed fruit, and *saint*, a ritual bread loaf containing a coin. The eldest woman breaks this bread, then distributes the pieces, and whoever finds the coin in his piece will receive good luck.

Earlier in the day, groups of boys eight to twelve years of age tour neighborhoods with cornel sticks. To wish each home a good crop, they rap the thresholds with these sticks, whereupon the hostess anoints the boys with wheat seed. At midnight, groups of single men, or *Koledars*, also visit homes to sing *koledari* (Christmas carols) and to bestow wishes for health, good luck, and fertility. Attired in traditional *kalpaci* (fur hats) decorated with local flowers, *yamurluci* (hooded cloaks), ornate leggings, sandals, embroidered white shirts, and carved wooden staffs, the Koledars process through the streets. Each procession is led by an older man, the *stanenik*, who carries a cask of red wine and a cornel-tree branch decorated with popcorn and pretzels. At each home, the Koledars antiphonally serenade the members from a repertoire of scores of traditional songs and dances learned from childhood. Appropriate songs are especially sung to the male head of the household, his wife, senior citizens, unwed girls, soldiers, livestock, the fields, and so forth. Then the Koledars receive rewards such as *koledni gevreci* (round buns), *banisa* (cheese-filled pastry), fruit, nuts, popcorn, wine, and *rakia* (plum or grape brandy). A young girl typically presents a *kravai* (large bagel) to the *stanenik*, who raises it and blesses the house.

Christmas Day is celebrated with relatives and friends. The Koledars convene to distribute the kravais received the night before, and

each man seeks to receive the bagel baked by his special girl. Should more than one man desire a particular bagel, it is auctioned. Groups of children again visit homes, this time carrying *survaknitsa* (bunches of willow twigs woven together) with which to tap adults. Performing this act is termed *survakam*, which conveys wishes for good health and prosperity, and the children receive candy and money.

In more rural areas on Christmas Day, the head of the household sprinkles corn from a stocking on the doorstep with the same greeting and response uttered prior to the Christmas Eve meal. Next he strikes the Yule log, and with each blow pronounces a wish of good health to the land, the livestock, and a bountiful harvest. Then the ashes are placed in trees to assure a good harvest.

Other religious customs are similar to those of Ukraine.

"Merry Christmas" in Bulgaria is: *Tchestita Koleda*.

See also **Ukraine**.

The Burgundian Carol

Title applied to a carol from the Burgundy region of France, written by the poet Bernard de LaMonnoye around 1700 and published in his carol collection of 1701. Technically, all of LaMonnoye's carols could be generically titled "Burgundian Carols," but the specific carol here received its title from the Canadian-born folk singer and recording artist Oscar Brand (1920–), who provided an English translation and reworked the lyrics and traditional melody into a folk song. Brand introduced his version of the carol on the *Folk Song Festival*, a program which he had hosted for more than fifty years on New York City's WNYC radio. The carol was first recorded by a folk-singing group that had formed in 1948, The Weavers (Pete Seeger, Lee Hays, Fred Hellerman, and Ronnie Gilbert), who included it in their Christmas album *We Wish You a Merry Christmas* (Decca, 1952). Seeger had heard the carol when he appeared as a guest on Brand's program.

Consisting of three verses, "The Burgundian Carol" centers around the traditional ox and donkey who, according to legend, were the Christ Child's stable mates after His birth. In the first verse, the animals' presence keeps Him warm; in the second, their vigil is so intense that they fast; in the third, they kneel and kiss His feet. Following each verse is the refrain which asks a rhetorical question: How many oxen and donkeys today would pay such homage had they been present at Christ's birth? The carol seems to convey a moral, namely, that if animals feel compelled to worship at Christ's feet, how much more should mankind feel the same.

C

California Holly
See **Christmas Plants**

Calm on the Listening Ear of Night
See **It Came Upon the Midnight Clear**

Canada

The first Christmas in this land dates to 1535 in Ste. Croix, a series of forts which the French explorer Jacques Cartier and his crew built at the mouth of the St. Charles River. Although the fare was lean at that time, by 1606, the French observed the first "European" Christmas setting in Port Royal, Nova Scotia, founded by Sieur de Monts and Samuel de Champlain. Amid Christmas evergreens, the settlers feasted on roast moose and wild duck. Although the *crèche* (Nativity scene) dates to 1644 in Canada, the Christmas tree did not arrive until 1781 in Quebec, when Major General Friedrich von Riedesel, a German commander of British troops from Sorel to Montreal during the American Revolution, erected one in his home in Sorel.

Today all Canadians share the season's inauguration by witnessing the Christmas Lights Across Canada, held on the first Thursday of December. Citizens gather for the simultaneous lighting of government buildings and tree-lighting ceremonies over the whole nation as they enjoy hot cider, shortbread, fruitcake, and other light holiday cuisine.

Winter activities of cross-country skiing, sleigh-riding, and ice skating abound at sites such as Montreal's Mount Royal Park and Quebec City's Mont Ste.-Anne. Special Christmas services appeal to Canadians and tourists alike at such world-famous churches as St. Michael's Cathedral and The Church of the Transfiguration, both in Toronto; St. Joseph's Oratory (with its collection of Nativity scenes from around the world) and Notre-Dame Basilica, both in Montreal; and Quebec City's Ste.-Anne-de-Beaupre with its 240 stained-glass windows.

Canada utilizes some 100,000 acres across its land for the growing and marketing of six million Christmas trees annually, most notably the balsam fir. One-third of this land lies in Nova Scotia alone. Most of these trees are marketed nationally and to the United States, with some 10 percent exported to the Caribbean and Central and South America. Annually since 1973, Halifax has presented a 70-foot balsam fir to the city of Boston, Massachusetts, in gratitude for assistance received when, in 1917, an ammunition ship exploded in Halifax Harbor, destroying much of the city. Boston annually erects the tree in its Prudential Square.

• A DIVERSE CULTURE. The Canadian population is quite culturally diverse, with people of British, French, Acadian, German, Italian, Polish, Dutch, and Ukrainian heritages, in addition to the Indian tribes indigenous to Canada, who prefer the all-encompassing name First Nations. The Christmas traditions of European Canadians closely parallel those of their parent countries, and the following is a summary of those traditions which have arisen in addition to, or have been modified from, those found in Europe.

British traditions are preserved in museums and historical homes around the country. Christmas parades with Santa Claus date back to 1905 and the T. Eaton Department Store of Toronto, which hosted the first parade. On Prince Edward Island, the annual school concert, traditional for over 100 years, has become the social highlight of the season. Two favorite candies of the Maritime Provinces include "Chicken Bones," a hard cinnamon stick filled with chocolate, manufactured in St. Stephen, New Brunswick, since 1885; and "Barley Toys," colored candy molded into the shapes of animals or toys, manufactured in Yarmouth, Nova Scotia, for more than 175 years. Mumming is found almost exclusively in Newfoundland during the twelve days of Christmas. Boxing Day, December 26, while a national holiday, no longer carries the promise of gratuity to employees as in former times. During the week before Christmas since 1961, Vancouver, British Columbia, has sponsored a "Carol Ship" that is decorated with lights and a Christmas tree and carries bell ringers and children's choirs on board. As this ship sails through Vancouver Harbor during the evenings, a flotilla of private yachts and other ships follows, while crowds on shore build bonfires and sing along with the choirs. A "Santa Ship" distributes toys in mid–December to needy children living on U.S. and Canadian gulf islands.

To the French, *le réveillon*, the traditional meal following Midnight Mass, may consist of *tourtières* (meat pies), *ragout de boulettes* (meat ball and pork stew), pork spread, minced pork pie, partridge with cabbage, goose or turkey, oyster or pea soup, cheeses, condiments, cranberry sauce, numerous pastries such as maple syrup tarts, and *bûche de Noël* (Christmas cake shaped like a log). Children ask blessings from their father, older brother, or other patriarch on New Year's Day, a day that has traditionally been the day for gifts, though children often receive gifts at *réveillon* as well.

For French-and-English-speaking peoples (Acadians) of the Maritime Provinces, Christmas includes the major French and some British customs. *Réveillon* features rabbit pie and *pâté a la rapure* (meat pie with potatoes, onions, bacon, seasonings). For their parents, children make a *Bouquet Spirituel*, a decorative card

which contains all the prayers they have said in the weeks prior to Christmas. New Year's Day includes firstfooting, where a young boy arriving first at one's door brings a year's worth of luck, and older boys beat in the New Year by rapping the sides of homes with sticks. The Epiphany King's Cake includes a ring (predicts the next to marry) and silver coin (predicts the one who will become rich), along with the bean and pea (*see* **Epiphany** [TWELFTH NIGHT]).

Though the Mennonites do not subscribe to specific feast days as do their conventional German counterparts, their children set out plates on Christmas Eve, which their parents fill with treats for Christmas Day. For the Hutterites of Saskatchewan, although Christmas is a three-day holiday from labor, it is spent in strict meditation, prayer, and church services.

Ukrainian children usually receive gifts from St. Nicholas on his feast day, December 19 on the Julian calendar, instead of Christmas Day. The ceremonial Blessing of the Waters is observed on the Feast of Jordan (January 19) and is reenacted at the Ukrainian Cultural Heritage Village near Edmonton, Alberta.

• FIRST NATIONS. Winter solstice celebrations center around gift giving, feasting, dancing, and games of skill and strength. During a festival of eight days, the Iroquois burn tobacco and petition the Creator for blessings upon their crops. The children visit their mother's relatives on New Year's Day and carry bags which the relatives fill with treats. Cree children observe a similar custom on Christmas Eve, returning the next day for the filled bags. West Coast tribes observe *potlatch* ("giving"), which celebrates any special occasion during the year. Here, the more gifts a chief or tribe lavishes on the guests, the more prestigious the event. Other Christian tribes hold community-wide parties with carols sung in their native tongues and with appearances from Santa.

The Inuit also hold community feasts, which feature Santa and a menu of caribou, seal, and raw fish, along with the traditional Drum Dance, storytelling, harpoon throwing, wrestling, igloo building, rifle shooting, snowmobile racing, and other games of skill. In the unusual game of Throat Singing, Inuit women pair off and compete by imitating the sounds of the North without breaking the rhythm. For

Boxing Day or on New Year's Day, the Inuit observe *pallaq* ("charging"), in which family members with anything to celebrate stand on their roofs and throw gifts to their guests below. Snowmobile parades and rifle shooting again welcome the new year.

The Métis (of French-Canadian and First Nations heritage) of the Prairie Provinces also hold Christmas Eve family reunions with feasting on buffalo, moose, deer, potatoes, berries, and wild rice; gifts; music; dancing; and traditional gunfire. Their celebrations may extend for two weeks.

"Merry Christmas" among First Nations peoples might be *Mitho Makosi Mesikansi* (Cree); *Jutdlime pivdluarit ukiortame pivdluar-itlo* (Inuit); *Ojenyunyat sungwiyadeson honun-gradon nagwutut* (Iroquois). Christmas greetings in the various European languages are heard throughout Canada, depending on the heritage of the area.

See also **Epiphany; France; Germany; Great Britain; The Huron Christmas Carol; Italy; The Low Countries** (THE NETHERLANDS); **Poland; Ukraine.**

Candlemas

Observed by the Roman Catholic Church on February 2 and the Armenian Church on February 14, marks the purification of the Virgin Mary and presentation of Jesus in the Temple forty days after His birth. Until the Second Vatican Council (1962–1965), the date also terminated the Christmas season in the Catholic church.

According to ancient Jewish law, after a woman gave birth, she was considered to be unclean and was required to spend certain days in purification rites before she was accepted back into society. The time was forty days if the child was male, eighty if the child was female (Leviticus 12:1–4). A first-born child was redeemed through animal sacrifice (Numbers 18:15). Candlemas, a date forty days past Christmas Day, commemorates not only Mary's purification but the presentation of the infant Jesus in the Temple as well. At that time, according to Luke's Gospel, the prophet Simeon referred to Jesus as "a light to lighten the Gentiles, and the glory of thy people Israel" (Luke 2:22–33). To capitalize on this state-

ment, candle ceremonies play a significant role in Candlemas to symbolize Jesus as Light of the world. Blessed beeswax candles are distributed to worshippers. The candles are lighted, and the congregation participates in a procession.

The Church in Jerusalem first celebrated a feast of purification during the first half of the fourth century, prior to designating December 25 as Christmas Day. At that time, the feast was known only as "the fortieth day after Epiphany," which implied that, in the Eastern Rite, Epiphany was held as the date of Christ's birth. Originally, the feast was held on February 14, which had Christianized the ancient Roman purification feast of *Februa*. With the declaration of December 25 as Christmas Day during the latter half of the fourth century, the feast was moved to February 2. It is believed that the Byzantine emperor Justinian I instituted the Candlemas feast around 542 in the East and that Pope Sergius I (687–701) introduced it in the West, although the blessing of candles did not become widespread in the western Church until the eleventh century.

In the Middle Ages, Candlemas was not only the time for families to select next year's Yule log; it was the time to burn the Christmas plants (they were never thrown out) plus the remnants of the old Yule log as well, while saving a piece of the old log to light the one for the following year.

An old superstition holding that a sunny Candlemas predicts forty more days of winter weather forms the basis for "Groundhog Day" in the United States, February 2. According to this folklore, if the groundhog sees his shadow on that day, expect six more weeks of cold weather.

See also **Epiphany; Yule.**

Candy Canes

Hard, thin, sugar sticks with one end bent to form a crook, generally with red and white stripes or other colors. Originating in Europe during the seventeenth century, candy canes at first consisted only of straight, white sticks which mothers gave to their babies as pacifiers and which were hung on Christmas trees as decorations, along with other sweets. In 1670 the choirmaster at the cathedral in Cologne,

This illustration by M.E. Ohrumschalk, from an unidentified children's book ca. 1920s, shows a small elfin being, perhaps a Scandinavian jultomten, leading a child through the "Peppermint Stick Gate."

Germany, had a number of the sticks fashioned as small shepherds' crooks and passed them along to children who visited the cathedral's live Nativity scene that year. The treat, a memorial to the Christmas shepherds of long ago, was again designed to keep little ones quiet during those ceremonies. The innovation became quite popular, especially during the holidays, and spread throughout Europe. Later, candy canes were embellished with white sugar roses.

It is reported that candy canes first came to America with a German-Swedish immigrant, August Imgard, of Wooster, Ohio, who decorated his Christmas tree with the sweets in 1847.

Around the turn of the twentieth century, candy canes took on red and white stripes plus the flavors of peppermint and wintergreen, but the one responsible for these added accouter-

ments remains unknown. Evidence of the change can be observed in old Christmas cards: Those issued before 1900 show the plain, white canes, and those thereafter feature the striped versions.

Over centuries, assorted religious interpretations have surrounded the candy cane, all inspirational, but all without definitive source of origin. For example, turned upside down, the cane resembles a "J," indicative of Jesus; the red and white stripes are symbolic of the stripes of flogging that Jesus received prior to His crucifixion and the colors, His blood and purity, respectively; the hard texture symbolizes Christ as the Rock, the foundation of the Church; and the peppermint flavor is reminiscent of hyssop, an aromatic plant that ancient Hebrews used for purification rites. The story that persecuted early Christians used candy canes as secret means of identifying one another is most certainly a myth, given that this form of candy was a creation of the seventeenth century.

Lori Walburg's *The Legend of the Candy Cane* (1997), an inspirational children's book, incorporates many of the above interpretations surrounding this confection. In Ms. Walburg's story, John Sonneman, a candy merchant newly arrived in a small prairie town, teaches the candy cane's symbolism ("J," crook, red and white stripes) to a little girl, Lucy. Together the two, while delivering candy canes to each home in town, spread the story abroad until all have heard its message by Christmas Eve.

Cards
See **Christmas Cards**

Caribbean Islands
See **West Indies**

Carol for Another Christmas
See **A Christmas Carol** (FILM AND TELEVISION VERSIONS)

Carol of the Bagpipers
("Canzone d'i Zampognari"), Italian traditional carol, also known as "Bagpipers' Carol," "Song of the Bagpipers," "On That Most Blessed Night," and "When Christ, the Son of Mary." Reputed to be the best known of Italian carols, it originated in Sicily around the

seventeenth century, a period in which, some ten days before Christmas, it was customary for the *pifferari* (Calabrian shepherds) to journey to Rome, Naples, and other cities in southern Italy and Sicily to play their bagpipes before statues of the Virgin. Traditionally the music was believed to ease the Virgin's impending labor discomfort, and the shepherds also would stop by a carpenter's shop out of respect for Joseph. The custom has since fallen into neglect.

The baroque German composer George Frideric Handel, while touring Italy from 1706 to 1709, was much impressed by those enchanting bagpipe melodies and incorporated them into some of his works. The most notable of these is his oratorio *Messiah*, written in 1741, in which such melodies form the basis for the "Pifa" or "Pastoral Symphony." More specifically, the melody for the aria "He Shall Feed His Flock" is closely based on that of "Carol of the Bagpipers."

Carol of the Bells

Title of two twentieth-century songs, both Ukrainian-American hybrids. The far more popular version, also known as "The Ukraine Carol," was adapted from "Shchedryk," an ancient Ukrainian folk song, which is classified as a *shchedrivka* (New Year's carol). The adaptation was created by Ukrainian composer Mykola Leontovych (1877–1921) in his *Shchedryk*, a choral work that was first performed at Kiev University in 1916. The basis for his piece was an ancient Slavic legend which held that, at midnight when Christ was born, all the bells in the world pealed for joy. Indeed, the music simulates rapidly pealing bells. An American composer, lyricist, and conductor, Peter Wilhousky (1902–1978), added English lyrics, beginning with "Hark! How the bells," to Leontovych's music in 1936 and titled the match "Carol of the Bells." Today the appeal of this masterpiece still lies in its choral renditions.

A lesser-known variant, also titled "Carol of the Bells," appeared anonymously in 1972. Although it, too, kept Leontovych's melody, its lyrics began with "Hark to the bells." Two additional American songs, "Ring, Christmas Bells" by M. L. Holman (1947) and the anony-

Calabrian shepherds (pifferari) *playing in Rome at Christmas, reminiscent of the Italian "Carol of the Bagpipers." Wood engraving after an etching by D. Allan, from* Hone's Every-Day Book *(London: 1836).*

mous "Come, Dance and Sing" (1957), each borrowed Leontovych's haunting melody as the setting for original lyrics.

Of the 25 most frequently performed Christmas songs of the twentieth century listed by the American Society of Composers, Authors and Publishers (ASCAP), "Carol of the Bells" (Leontovych/Wilhousky) is ranked number 15.

Carol of the Brown King: Nativity Poems

Collection of six brief poems for young children about the Nativity. Five of the poems were written by the African American poet, novelist, playwright, and lyricist Langston Hughes (1902–1967), a key figure in the Harlem Renaissance of the 1920s and sometimes called the Poet Laureate of Harlem. The sixth Hughes translated from an anonymous Puerto Rican Christmas card. Ashley Bryan, noted illustrator of African American spirituals and poetry, compiled the poems and published them together with his illustrations in 1998.

"Carol of the Brown King," the title poem and best-known of the collection, asserts that one of the three Wise Men or Magi was black, or in Hughes's words, "a brown man" (some traditions hold that one Wise Man came from Ethiopia). "Shepherd's Song at Christmas" poses the rhetorical question of what fitting gifts a shepherd can bring to the manger. The answer is simple: a song from the heart, a gentle lamb, and one's own heart. "On a Christmas Night" and "The Christmas Story" are Nativity narratives. "On a Pallet of Straw" again recalls the Wise Men who found the Christ Child on a straw pallet. Hughes's translation of a Puerto Rican Christmas card consists of eight lines about replacing an orange that the "Child" has lost.

Carol of the Drum
See The Little Drummer Boy (carol)

Carol of the Mother
See Alfred Burt Carols

Caroling, Caroling
See Alfred Burt Carols

Carols
See Christmas Carols

Casper's First Christmas
(1979). Made-for-television animated cartoon, based on the character Casper the Friendly Ghost, featured in Harvey Cartoons.

Their old, abandoned haunt about to be torn down, mischievous ghost Hairy Scarey and his little friend Casper receive unexpected guests on Christmas Eve. Hanna-Barbera cartoon characters Quick Draw McGraw, Huckleberry Hound, Augie Doggie, Doggie Daddy, Snagglepuss, Yogi Bear, and Boo Boo, lost en route to a mountain lodge, stop at the house instead and make it festive.

Initially opposed to Christmas, Hairy attempts to drive them away until he discovers Casper's note to Santa, asking that Hairy's house be spared. Touched, Hairy forms a new opinion about Christmas, and the party resumes. As Casper had hoped, Santa arrives and presents Hairy with a deed to the house, which becomes Hairy's Haunting Lodge, and the gang agrees to celebrate Christmas each year thereafter with Hairy and Casper.

Voices: Daws Butler, Paul Dekorte, Don Messick, Hal Smith, Ida Sue McCune, Julie McWhirter, John Stephenson, Michael Redman. Written by Bob Ogle. Produced by Alex Lovy. Directed by Carl Urbana. Hanna-Barbera Productions. World Vision Home Video. Color. Half-hour.

Central America
Overwhelmingly Roman Catholic because the countries on this continent were former Spanish colonies dating to the sixteenth century, Central America celebrates Christmas traditions deriving from Spain. The principal customs common to Central American countries include *Nacimientos* or *Pesebres* (respectively, simple or more elaborate Nativity scenes); the Feast of the Immaculate Conception (December 8); the Midnight Mass, termed "Mass of the Rooster" (*Misa del Gallo*), celebrated on *Nochebuena* ("Good Night," Christmas Eve); a large Christmas Eve dinner for family and friends held either before or just after the Midnight Mass; Holy Innocents Day (December 28); New Year's Day (January 1); and *Día de los Reyes* (Kings Day, Epiphany, January 6).

Through foreign influences (predominantly from the United States), Santa Claus and Christmas trees are well known, but the Nativity scene remains the most important holiday symbol. It is customary for families to visit Nativity scenes of friends and relatives, as well as the scene erected in the local cathedral. Traditionally, the crib or manger within each Nativity scene remains empty until midnight on Christmas Eve, at which time each family or church adds a figure of the Christ Child to symbolize that Christ is born.

Pesebres are usually handmade and occupy a large space in the principal room of the home. Consisting of ornate landscapes with perhaps hills and waterfalls, they include figures of the Holy Family, animals, angels, shepherds, the Three Kings, and figures of local familiarity, such as the mayor, police officer, butcher, carpenter, and so forth, the latter figures bonding the past with the present.

Formerly, children received gifts only on Epiphany from the Three Kings, but it has become customary for children to receive gifts on Christmas Eve as well, brought either by Santa Claus or the Christ Child. More commonly, on Epiphany Eve, children place their shoes upon a window sill, and the Three Kings fill them with treats by morning.

Religious processions and festive parades with fireworks, music, singing, and dancing abound. Employers in some regions are compelled by law to provide employees with an *aguinaldo* ("gift," Christmas bonus).

The period from December 16 to 24 constitutes a Novena, on each day of which a special mass is held. The first mass is dedicated to the Annunciation; the second, to the visit between Mary and her cousin Elizabeth; the third, to the journey to Bethlehem; the fourth, to the Nativity; the fifth, to the shepherds; the sixth, to the Magi; the seventh, to the flight into Egypt; the eighth, to the boy Jesus in the Temple with the scholars; the ninth, to the boy Jesus' return to Nazareth. The Christmas season generally ends on Epiphany.

The following paragraphs summarize additional customs found in the individual countries. "Merry Christmas" is spoken in Spanish: *Feliz Navidad.*

• BELIZE (formerly British Honduras until 1973) has a population of mixed racial descent, consisting of Creoles, Native Americans (Caribs and Mayans), Mestizos, black Caribs (Garifuna), and Europeans (English and Spanish). Nearly 60 percent of the population is Roman Catholic. Despite the ethnic diversity, Christmas decorations and carols reflect American and European influences, and Santa Claus brings the children's gifts. Mestizos observe *Las Posadas* ("The Lodgings") as in Mexico, and the Garifuna follow the rituals of Jonkonnu, as principally found in the West Indies. The Christmas menu varies slightly between ethnic groups, but generally consists of beans, rice, potato salad, turkey with stuffing, *tortillas*, fish, ham, yams, black cake (dark fruitcake), and *rompope* (eggnog with rum). Favorites among those of Mexican descent are *bollos* (ground corn with chicken, rolled into palm leaves and steamed over an open fire). "Merry Christmas" is said in English, the official language. *See also* **Las Posadas; West Indies.**

• COSTA RICA. As mandated by law, around December 1, employers must provide annual *aguinaldos* (Christmas bonuses) to employees, equivalent to one year's salary plus that for one month (average annual salaries are quite low, perhaps $300). Beginning on Christmas Eve, churches observe the Prayer of the Rosary of the Holy Child, a celebration that extends until Candlemas (February 2). Families also observe the prayer before their private Nativity scenes, known in Costa Rica as *portals*. Collectively known as the *Paso* (from *Pasch*, "Passover"), the three most important figures in each *portal* consist of those of Mary, Joseph, and the Child.

Amid fireworks, Costa Rican celebrations include a menu of *tamales* (corn dough with meat filling and spicy sauce, wrapped in plantain leaves and steamed), *chica* (liquor with ginger spice), *escabeche* (vinegar relish of carrots, peppers, onions, cauliflower, and green beans), rum, eggnog, fruits, wine, and *queque Navideno* (Christmas cake). Children receive gifts from the Christ Child on Christmas Eve.

Although each local community sponsors fairs, plays, and other public events, those held in San Jose are of special interest. The Festival of Lights, resembling the American Mardi Gras, provides a carnival atmosphere with decorative lights, parades with tropical floats, fireworks, clowns, cartoon characters, and goblins, culminating in a grand street carnival held just before New Year's Eve. An equine parade, *El Tope*, fills December 26 (St. Stephen's Day) with displays of horses imported from Peru and Spain. Children ride with their parents, who are most elaborately dressed. Variations on Spain's "Running of the Bulls" are *Las Corridas* (The Bull Fights) of Zapote, a section of San Jose, in which the most daring of men approach bulls in the ring, touch them with the bullfighter's cape, then try to outrun the enraged animals to safety. Those who succeed are awarded small prizes. And from Christmas Day onward, Zapote also sponsors an open-air fair with rides, food booths, loud music, and all the ingredients similarly found in state or county fairs in the United States. *See also* **Candlemas.**

• EL SALVADOR. The Christmas season begins

with the Feast of the Immaculate Conception, followed closely by a similar celebration on December 12, the Feast of Our Lady of Guadalupe. This latter event commemorates the appearance of the Virgin to the Indian Juan Diego, believed to have occurred in 1531 in the city of Guadalupe Hidalgo (now known as Gustavo A. Madero), Mexico. These festivities include appearances from *Inditos* (children dressed as Diego), processions carrying statues of the Virgin, fireworks, dances, and soccer tournaments. Christmas trees, poinsettias, and *Pesebres* constitute the most common of decorations, the latter of those focusing upon the *Misterio* ("Mystery"), a collective term for the figures of Mary, Joseph, and the Child.

Unlike Mexico, which celebrates *Las Posadas* ("The Lodgings") for nine days prior to Christmas, El Salvador observes this custom only on Christmas Eve. The menu at this time usually features *tamales* (corn dough with meat filling and spicy sauce, wrapped in plantain leaves and steamed), turkey, chicken, pork, rice, green vegetables, assorted desserts, and liquors. Children receive gifts from Santa Claus, who places them either under the Christmas tree or under the children's beds. Christmas Day is marked with church services and beach activities. *See also* **Las Posadas**.

• GUATEMALA. The Christmas season commences simultaneously with the Feast of the Immaculate Conception and *La Quema del Mal* ("The Burning of the Evil"), the latter custom consisting of burning discarded items with fireworks. For the preceding week, people masked as demons chase children through the streets, a vestige of Mayan rituals now blended with those of Christmas, which culminates in the burning, a symbolic purging of evil prior to Christmas. Other Advent customs include painting and repairing the house, decorating with poinsettias, and, because Guatemalan law forbids the cutting of whole trees, the significant German population fashion Christmas trees from tree branches. The customary *Las Posadas* ("The Lodgings"), similar to that of Mexico, is also observed for nine days prior to Christmas.

Public festivities fill Christmas Eve with costumed parades and numerous fireworks throughout the day and especially at midnight, after which families congregate for the Christmas dinner. The menu often features *tamales* (corn dough with meat filling and spicy sauce, wrapped in plantain leaves and steamed) and *ponche* (liquor with brown sugar and fruits such as raisins, dates, plums). Although children receive gifts on Christmas Eve from the Christ Child, adults usually exchange gifts on New Year's Day. Fireworks resume on Christmas Day. *See also* **Las Posadas**.

• HONDURAS. Migrating from the West Indies, black Caribs (Garifuna) settled along the northern shore of Honduras, bringing their traditional dances and customs, such as Jonkonnu. During Advent, bands of Garifuna women perform dances at various homes, for which they receive monetary donations and sweet liquors, such as *guaro*. Spanish children perform *Pastorelas* (Nativity plays), employers grant *aguinaldos* (bonuses) to employees, and Christmas parties abound for employees and youths. On Christmas Eve, a masked dancer, the *Warini*, ushers in Christmas by dancing from house to house with an entourage of singers and drummers and a din of firecrackers. The Christmas dinner usually features turkey with stuffing, *lechonitos* (suckling pig), and *rompope* (eggnog with liquor). At midnight on New Year's Eve, families burn an effigy of an undesirable person or object, a custom termed *La Quema de los Años Viejos* ("Burning the Old Year"), which symbolizes cleansing for the new year. The *Warini* closes the season with dances on Epiphany.

• NICARAGUA. The Christmas season commences with the Feast of the Immaculate Conception, the night of which is termed *La Noche de Gritería* ("The Night of the Shouting"). Such a name arises from the highly intense, fervent singing of hymns and carols to the Virgin, which bands of singers present at homes so decorated for their reception. The processions bear *La Gigantona* ("The Giant Female" or "The Super Female"), a large figure of the Virgin. Amid fireworks, the hosts reward the singers with candy and treats such as *cañas de azúcar* (sugar canes), sweets, fruit, and cookies, among others. Christmas decorations include *Flores de Pastor* ("Shepherd's Flowers," poinsettias), *muérdagos* (aromatic decorations suspended overhead, imitative of mistletoe), colored streamers, and artificial Christmas trees (since pine trees are scarce). The Christmas Eve dinner usually features *gallina de patio* (stuffed chicken), Spanish rice, *nacatamal* (tamale), *tortillas*, and *ponche* (rum beverage). Gifts are hidden around the home, and children, believing that *El Niño Jesus* (Baby Jesus) brings them, search for them following Midnight Mass. New Year's Eve is filled with parties and fireworks. It is customary to withdraw a few pieces of straw from the *Pesebre* at church to place in children's shoes on the eve of Epiphany as symbolic fodder for the Three Kings' camels. The Kings remove the straw and fill the shoes with treats.

• PANAMA. During the novena, a *Misa del Aguinaldo* (Mass of the Gift) is held early each morning. Christmas dinner may feature a variety of seafood, rice with beans, *arroz con pollo* (chicken with rice, saffron, and vegetables), *arroz con piña* (rice with pineapple), and *rom ponche* (rum punch). Instead of writing letters to Santa Claus, children address them to Baby Jesus, care of St. Peter in heaven. Gifts are placed either under the Christmas tree or under children's beds.

See also **Epiphany; Feast of the Immaculate Conception; Holy Innocents Day; Mass of the Rooster; Nativity Scene; Spain.**

A Ceremony of Carols

Musical settings of medieval and fifteenth- and sixteenth-century English or Scottish poems, written in 1942 by English composer Benjamin Britten (1913–1976). Comprising Britten's Opus 28 and the first of his works to be scored for treble (boys') voices and harp, *A Ceremony of Carols* was written along with his *Hymn to St. Cecilia* during a perilous voyage from the United States to England. It was first published in 1943 and first recorded by the Morriston Boys' Choir and Maria Korchinska with Britten conducting. The following paragraphs summarize its twelve movements.

1 and 12. "Processional and Recessional" are identical, consisting of "Hodie Christus natus est" ("Today Christ Is Born"), the Latin antiphon plainsong from the Christmas Eve Vespers. 2. "Wolcom Yole" ("Welcome Yule"), anonymous from the fourteenth century, bids good cheer and welcome to personalities and events recognized during the Christmas season: feast days of St. Stephen, St. John, St. Thomas, the Holy Innocents, Twelfth Night, and Candlemas. 3. "There Is No Rose of Such Vertu [Virtue]," anonymous from the fourteenth or fifteenth century, likens the Virgin Mary to a rose, whose young flower is Christ. 4. "That Yonge [Young] Child," anonymous from the fourteenth century, asserts that the Virgin's lullaby song to the Babe is far sweeter than any music that a minstrel or nightingale may produce. 5. "Balulalow," by brothers James, John, and Robert Wedderburn, sixteenth-century Scottish balladists, sets forth the Virgin's lullaby, in which she pledges her heart and everlasting devotion to her Son. 6. "As Dew in Aprille," anonymous from ca. 1400, likens the birth of Christ to the still and gentle "falling" of April dew; that is, without ceremony. 7. "This Little Babe," by sixteenth-century English poet Robert Southwell, presents a series of metaphors in which the Babe, seemingly weak and helpless, nevertheless poses as a formidable Warrior, against whom the powers of Satan are no match. Thus, the Babe's breast serves as a shield; His cries, "battering shot"; His weeping eyes, arrows; cold and need, His ensigns; His flesh, a steed; the stable, a camp; the manger, a trench; the shepherds, the mustered army. 8. "Interlude," harp solo based on a plainchant. 9. "In Freezing Winter Night," also by Robert Southwell, metaphorically assigns royal significance to humble emblems of the Nativity: the stable, "a Prince's court"; the manger, a "chair of State"; a wooden dish, His plate; His poor attire and base surroundings, prized as royal pomp in Heaven. 10. "Spring Carol," by sixteenth-century poet William Cornish, looks forward past the harshness of winter to spring, a reminder to mankind that God is the source of all sustenance. 11. "Adam Lay I-Bounden [Bound]," anonymous from the fifteenth century, gives thanks to God for the Fall of Man through the sin of Adam, for without the Fall, Christ never would have been born.

Britten, a prolific composer of operas and other works, also wrote the Christmas Choral piece *A Boy Was Born* (1933).

See also **There Is No Rose of Such Virtue.**

Ceremony of Lessons and Carols
See A Festival of Nine Lessons and Carols

Chanukah
See Hanukkah

A Charlie Brown Christmas
(1965). Made-for-television animated cartoon based on the *Peanuts* comic strip characters created by Charles M. Schulz. Receiving both Emmy and Peabody Awards for program excellence, it was the first of the *Charlie Brown* television specials, the first prime-time cartoon without a laugh track, and the first in which children provided all the voices. Grammy Award–winning pianist Vince Guaraldi provided the jazz piano background score, not only for this special, but for sixteen subsequent Charlie Brown specials and one movie, *A Boy Named Charlie Brown*. *A Charlie Brown Christmas* featured his tunes "Christmas Time Is Here" (vocal) and "Linus and Lucy" (for group dance sequences).

According to Charlie Brown, commercialism is destroying the true meaning of Christmas. His little sister Sally wants money from Santa; Snoopy decorates his doghouse for the neighborhood display contest, which he wins; and the Christmas pageant is nothing more than a jazz festival. Derided for selecting a scrubby, real tree for the pageant, instead of a shiny, artificial one, Charlie Brown desperately asks if anyone knows what Christmas is all about. Linus steps to center stage and reverently recites the Nativity story from Luke's Gospel, which renews everybody's faith in the season.

Voices: Peter Robbins, Tracy Stratford, Christopher Shea, Chris Doran, Karen Mendelson, Cathy Steinberg, Ann Altieri, and Sally Dryer-Barker. Written by Charles M. Schulz. Produced and directed by Bill Melendez. A Lee Mendelson–Bill Melendez Production in Association with Charles M. Schulz Creative Associates and United Feature Syndicate. Paramount Pictures Home Video. Color. Half-hour.

See also Happy New Year, Charlie Brown; It's Christmastime Again, Charlie Brown.

The Cherry Tree
See The Cherry Tree Carol

The Cherry Tree Carol
Traditional English carol, thought to have arisen during the fifteenth century. Opinion varies regarding the original form of the carol. Some authorities feel that this title is merely a collective term for three separate, yet closely interrelated carols. Others believe that it names a single carol that comprises three distinct divisions or parts, with Part I having been dubbed "Joseph Was an Old Man," Part II "Joseph and the Angel" or "As Joseph Was A-Walking," and Part III "Mary and Jesus" or "Mary's Question."

Regardless of the form in which the carol initially appeared, its immense popularity over the centuries has generated countless folk versions, both in text and musical settings, such that no two versions are exactly alike. These alternate versions include titles such as "Joseph and Mary," "When Joseph Was an Old Man," "Oh, Joseph Took Mary Up on His Right Knee," and "The Cherry Tree," these latter four having appeared in the United States during the eighteenth or nineteenth century. The earliest and longest, printed version of the three-part text, assembled from a number of broadsides, appeared in William Hone's collection *Ancient Mysteries Described* (London, 1823). While that text is felt to be incomplete, it is considered to be the most satisfactory of those that are available.

"The Cherry Tree Carol" possibly evolved from one of the Coventry Plays, a cycle of mystery plays presented in Coventry, England, during the Middle Ages. Certain similarities exist between the play and Part I of the carol. The story line of both is apocryphal and derives in part from the Gospel of Pseudo-Matthew, which originally dealt with the Holy Family's flight into Egypt and a miracle whereby the infant Jesus commanded a palm tree to bend and yield its dates to Mary. For purposes of the play and carol, however, a cherry tree (more familiar to the British) and the prenatal journey to Bethlehem are substituted, in which Christ from the womb delivers a similar command to the cherry tree. Joseph, having previously expressed anger over his doubts about the Child's paternity ("Let him pluck thee a cherry that brought thee with child"), immediately repents upon witnessing the miracle. This version derives from the Protevangelium of James, another apocryphal book.

In Part II, also based on the Protevangelium, the angel heralds the impending birth of Jesus to Joseph: the Child shall be born in an ox stall, wrapped in "fair white linen," rocked in a wooden cradle, and christened with "fair spring water."

Part III, associated more with Easter, depicts the young Jesus sitting in Mary's lap and predicting the redemption of mankind through His own death, burial, and resurrection.

According to interpretations set forth in *The New Oxford Book of Carols*, the cherry tree represents the Tree of Life as presented in Genesis 2:9, and Mary represents the new Eve, whose immaculate conception Jesus prenatally confirms through the miracle involving the cherries. Thus Jesus predicts that, through His future death, the original sin of Eve in the Garden of Eden will be absolved.

See also **Christmas Drama; The Coventry Carol; Feast of the Immaculate Conception.**

Chestnuts Roasting on an Open Fire
See **The Christmas Song**

Childermas
See **Holy Innocents Day**

Children, Go Where I Send Thee
African-American spiritual, also known as "Little Bitty Baby" and "The Holy Baby." As with many spirituals, specific details regarding authorship and date of composition are lacking. Although the song was first discovered in a rural school for black children in Kentucky, where it was probably sung for many generations, an origin from Arkansas has also been suggested but not proven. It received more widespread attention through the Ritchie Family of Kentucky, particularly Jean Ritchie, who has collected, performed, and recorded American folk songs for more than fifty years.

A children's counting song sung in the same manner as the more familiar "The Twelve Days of Christmas," the lyrics for "Children, Go Where I Send Thee" describe one's going forth to preach the Gospel, based on Him who was "born in Bethlehem." Various sets of lyrics exist, the most frequently appearing counting scheme of which is as follows: "one for the little bitty Baby, two for Paul and Silas, three for the Hebrew children, four for the poor that came knockin' at the door" (alternatively, "four for the four that stood at the door"), "five for the Gospel preachers, six for the six that never got fixed, seven for the seven that went up to heaven" (alternatively, "seven for the seven that never got to heaven"), "eight for the eight that stood at the gate, nine for the nine that got left behind" (alternatively, "nine for the nine all dressed so fine"), "ten for the ten commandments." Other versions continue counting to twelve: "eleven for the eleven deriders, twelve for the twelve Apostles."

The Children's Carol
See **The Waltons**

The Children's Friend: Number III. A New Year's Present to the Little Ones from Five to Twelve
Believed to be the first Christmas book printed in the United States. Written and illustrated in 1821 by Arthur Stansbury, a New York Presbyterian minister, the eight-page picture book depicts St. Nicholas sitting in a sleigh pulled by a single reindeer. Whether Stansbury should receive full credit for contributing a reindeer sleigh to the St. Nicholas repertoire is not known. It is more likely that this concept was already an integral part of the St. Nicholas traditions which Dutch immigrants brought to New York. The book was published by William Gilley.

See also **Saint Nicholas; A Visit from St. Nicholas.**

Children's Mass
See **Holy Innocents Day**

A Child's Christmas in Wales
Nostalgic recollection of enjoying simple Christmases as a boy, written by Welsh poet, short-story writer, and playwright Dylan Thomas (1914–1953), published posthumously in 1954. Recalling few differences between Christmases from year to year, Thomas presents especially memorable anecdotes. He recalls hurling snowballs at cats with a friend, and the little fire in a neighbor's home, all on Christmas Eve. A Christmas without snow, church bells, or postal deliveries would be

unthinkable. Christmas is a time for dining with one's relatives, of partaking of the turkey, goose, pudding, mince pie, and brandy, of uncles falling asleep afterwards and at least one pleasantly inebriated aunt singing weirdly. Then ghost stories fill the afternoon, followed by singing and playing folk tunes in the evening. As a boy, Thomas categorizes his Christmas gifts into one of two categories. "Useful" gifts are dull and boring: mufflers, mittens, zebra scarfs, wool vests, nose bags, and books without pictures. "Useless" gifts are the most appealing: "jelly babies," folded flags, hatchets, celluloid ducks that make unnatural noises, painting books, toffee, fudge, marzipan and other sweets, tin soldiers, games, hobby sets, dog whistles, and cigarettes (not for smoking but for shocking old ladies into scolding about the evils of smoking).

Chile

See **South America**

The Chimes

See **Dickens, Charles, Christmas Stories of**

China

See **Asia and the South Pacific**

A Chipmunk Christmas

(1981). Made-for-television animated cartoon, featuring The Chipmunks, Alvin, Simon, and Theodore, with keeper David Seville. After Alvin makes a Christmas gift of his Golden Echo Harmonica to Tommy, a sick friend, the chipmunks learn that Dave has booked them for a concert at Carnegie Hall. Unable to afford another harmonica for the act, the chipmunks are unsuccessful at raising sufficient funds. A pleasant old woman whom Alvin meets, describing herself as lonely, far from home, and wishing to bestow gifts, surprises Alvin with a new Golden Echo Harmonica for the concert. On the mend, Tommy is Alvin's guest performer, and together they play a harmonica duet. The old woman's identity is withheld until the close, for she is Mrs. Santa Claus.

Featuring "The Chipmunk Song" ("Christmas Don't Be Late"). Voices: Ross Bagdasarian, Jr., and Janice Karman. Written and produced by Janice Karman, Ross Bagdasarian.

Directed by Phil Monroe. Bagdasarian Productions. Buena Vista Home Video. Color. Half-hour.

See also **The Chipmunk Song.**

The Chipmunk Song

Also known as "Christmas Don't Be Late," this popular American novelty song was composed by Ross Bagdasarian, Sr., in 1958. A Hollywood actor prior to that time, Bagdasarian created a truly novel Christmas song that featured three "singing" chipmunks, Alvin, Simon, and Theodore, named after three executives at Liberty Records. Recording under the pseudonym David Seville, Bagdasarian achieved the high-pitched, chipmunk-like harmony by speeding up recordings of his own voice. He had previously used the technique for another novelty song of 1958, "The Witch Doctor." The top Christmas song of 1958, "The Chipmunk Song" sold seven million copies and also received a Grammy Award for the Best Children's Recording of that same year. "The Chipmunk Song" launched the singing trio into two television cartoon series, *The Alvin Show* (1961–1962), followed by *Alvin and the Chipmunks* (1983–1990). In the latter series, Ross Bagdasarian, Jr., principally provided the chipmunk voices following his father's death in 1972.

Of the 25 most frequently performed Christmas songs listed by the American Society of Composers, Authors and Publishers (ASCAP), "The Chipmunk Song" is ranked number 23.

See also **A Chipmunk Christmas.**

Chrismon Tree

A display that converts the conventional Christmas tree into a more significantly religious emblem. A Chrismon tree utilizes only ornaments that specifically symbolize Christ, examples of which include monograms featuring the Greek letters "Chi" and "Rho," the first two letters in "Xristos," the Greek word for "Christ"; the Greek letters "Alpha" and "Omega," for Christ the beginning (Alpha) and end (Omega); doves (for the Holy Spirit that descended on Christ at his baptism); and various kinds of crosses. The ornaments feature the symbolic colors of white (for purity) and gold (for royalty).

See also **Jesse Tree.**

Christ in the Stranger's Guise
See **Alfred Burt Carols**

Christ Is Born a Child on Earth
See **He Is Born, the Holy Child**

Christians, Awake, Salute the Happy Morn

English carol with lyrics by Dr. John Byrom (1692–1763), music by John Wainwright (1723–1768). A native of Manchester, a non-practicing physician, an inventor of an early form of shorthand, and a Quaker late in life, Byrom wrote this carol in 1749 as a Christmas present for his daughter Dorothy ("Dolly"). In 1750, his friend Wainwright, assistant organist at the Manchester Collegiate Church, provided a musical setting. On Christmas Day, because Byrom had patterned the carol after those sung by the British street minstrels called "waits," Wainwright arrived with a group of men and boys and delivered a surprise rendition of "Christians, Awake" at the Byrom residence. The carol's first public performance was said to have occurred that same Christmas at St. Mary's Church in the neighboring village of Stockport, though that event is considered more tradition than fact.

Although "Christians, Awake" had been printed earlier on broadsides, it was included in a posthumous printing of Byrom's works, *Miscellaneous Poems* (1773), and Wainwright also published text and music in his *Collection of Psalm-Tunes, Anthems, Hymns, and Chants* (London, 1767) under the generic title "A Hymn for Christmas Day." The carol in other publications also received some ten alternate titles such as "Mottram," "Stockport," and "Yorkshire," among others.

Although Byrom's original text consisted of 52 lines without divisions into stanzas, he created a shorter, revised version of 46 lines, which a newspaper, the *Manchester Mercury and General Advertiser*, published in December 1752. Hymnals today present a text based on an adaptation of this revision, which includes division into stanzas of six lines. The bulk of the text first elaborates on the angelic "glad tidings of great joy" given to the shepherds, then emphasizes the hope of eternal life which Christ will provide through His death on the cross.

See also **Waits**.

Christkindl or Christkindlein
See **Germany**

C-H-R-I-S-T-M-A-S

American song written in 1949 by country music songwriter and performer Jenny Lou Carson (given name Lucille Overstake) from Decatur, Illinois, and "Tennessee Plowboy" country and pop music legend Eddy Arnold. In Carson's lyrics, a mother teaches her child the true meaning of Christmas by spelling "Christmas" and associating each letter with a specific symbol of the holiday: "C," Christ Child, "H," herald angels, "R," Redeemer, "I," Israel, "S," star, "T," three Wise Men, "M," manger, "A," all that Christ means, "S," shepherds. Arnold contributed the music and recorded the song on the RCA Victor label in 1949. That recording became a charted single. Independent recordings of the same song by Rosemary Clooney and Al Morgan the following year were not charted.

Arnold also recorded two other songs in 1949 with lyrics by Carson, "Don't Rob Another Man's Castle" and "The Echo of Your Footsteps." Known principally as a lyricist; her work includes, among many, "Never Trust a Woman" (1942), "Jealous Love" (1945), and "Let Me Go, Lover" (1955).

Christmas Auld Lang Syne
See **Auld Lang Syne**

Christmas Bell
See **Christmas Plants**

Christmas Berry
See **Christmas Plants**

The Christmas Box

Emotionally-packed, best-selling novel written in 1993 by Richard Paul Evans, who based the principal characters and their names on himself, his wife Keri, and three-year-old daughter Jenna.

Escaping the rat race inherent in a large city, the Evanses move from southern California to Salt Lake City a few weeks before Christmas.

In Salt Lake City, "workaholic" Richard opens a formal-wear store. The family becomes very close to a reclusive, elderly widow, Mary Parkin, in whose expansive home they live as caretakers.

In the course of storing their furniture in Mary's attic, Richard discovers an ornamented, walnut Christmas box with brass hinges shaped like holly leaves and with an etching of the Nativity on the lid. The box is worthless to Richard until he experiences a recurring dream, in which an angel descends with outspread wings. As he looks into its face, it turns to stone, and Richard next finds himself in an open field surrounded by indescribably beautiful music. Waking one night, he traces the music to the Christmas box in the attic. Oddly, nothing about it suggests a music box, yet the music ceases at his approach, and a cradle nearby, previously covered, is now bare. Within the box are passionate letters of sorrow addressed simply to "My Beloved," dated December 6 of 1914, 1916, and 1920.

As Richard ponders this mystery, Mary confides that she is terminally ill and expresses grave concern over Richard's obsession with achieving success to his family's neglect. Adding another mystery, she asks if Richard knows what the first gift of Christmas was. He discerns part of the answer after learning from a neighbor that Mary has grieved for years over the loss of her three-year-old daughter, Andrea, whose gravestone consists of a stone angel identical to the one in Richard's dream. The letters, then, are Mary's expression of unspeakable sorrow.

When Keri discovers Mary's Bible open to John's Gospel, its pages stained with fresh tears, the answer becomes quite clear. The first gift of Christmas was a Child, given and sacrificed for the world by a loving, Heavenly Father ("For God so loved the world, that he gave his only begotten son...," John 3:16). Richard realizes that, in his quest for success, he had been trading diamonds for stones, so to speak; he was unwittingly parting with his own child at a time in her life which should be most precious for them both.

Richard receives the Christmas box as a gift, the air ringing with its music one last time as Mary joins her little Andrea who waits for her on Christmas morning.

A 1995 television adaptation of Evans's story, starring Richard Thomas, Maureen O'Hara, Annette O'Toole, and Kelsey Mulrooney, won an Emmy Award for Outstanding Individual Achievement in Costuming for a Miniseries or a Special. Written by Greg Taylor. Based on the novel by Richard Paul Evans. Produced by Erica Fox. Directed by Marcus Cole. Bonneville Producers Group and The Polson Company. Hallmark Home Video. Color. 92 min.

A former advertising executive, Richard Paul Evans wrote *The Christmas Box* as an expression of a father's love for his two daughters, Jenna and Allyson. Initially keeping the story a private endeavor, he made some twenty copies and distributed them to family members as Christmas presents. Their enthusiasm and encouragement eventually led to its publication in 1995, following which the book sold a million copies. Evans subsequently wrote two prequels to this story, *Timepiece* (1996) and *The Letter* (1997), which revolve around the early lives of David and Mary (or MaryAnne) Parkin and which complete *The Christmas Box* trilogy. His other published works include *The First Gift of Christmas* (1996), *The Locket* (1998), and the children's book *The Christmas Candle* (1998).

Christmas Bush
See **Christmas Plants**

Christmas Cactus
See **Christmas Plants**

Christmas Cards
The custom of exchanging winter holiday greetings can be traced to ancient civilizations, such as the Egyptians and Romans, who not only bestowed verbal good wishes for the new year but with them presented gifts to friends, relatives, and persons of authority. Over time, these tokens assumed written form, first on ornamental, clay tablets; then on woodblock prints during the Middle Ages in Europe; and, with the invention of lithography in the late eighteenth century, on colored sheets of paper flanked with biblical scenes or other pleasing designs. The advent of Christianity subsequently saw greetings for the new year combined with those at what was considered to be

the more important season of Christmas, especially in England, where the modern Christmas card originated.

The advances in printing during the nineteenth century and the creation of the "penny post" by the British postal system in 1840 set the stage for the mass production of relatively inexpensive Christmas cards. Immediately preceding the advent of conventional, printed Christmas cards, English schoolboys presented their parents with "Christmas pieces," decorative paper on which the boys had written seasonal messages in their best penmanship. In 1844, a W. A. Dobson sent hand-painted cards to his friends, and a Rev. Edward Bradley issued lithographed cards to his acquaintances. As an alternative to cards produced by the rather expensive method of lithography, people sometimes chose to convert their printed calling cards into greeting cards by decorating them with strips of colored cloth or paper and writing an appropriate message.

The English artist John C. Horsley is generally credited with designing the first printed Christmas card, although sources are inconsistent regarding the exact year of this event; some state 1843, others 1846. Further, William Egley may have claim to the honor instead, should an obscure date on his card read "1842" rather than the other possibility of "1849"; the date has defied deciphering. Horsley's creation was commissioned by Sir Henry Cole, an English gentleman who, when etiquette dictated that he send seasonal notes to his numerous friends, elected instead to send cards. On the colored, 3-by-5-inch Horsley card, the prominent center panel displayed a large, happy family seated together consuming wine. Beneath, a caption read, "A Merry Christmas and a Happy New Year to You," and two side panels depicted biblical scenes, titled "Clothing the Naked" and "Feeding the Hungry." (Despite the religious panels, some of the more pious citizens strenuously objected to the center panel, claiming that the card encouraged drunkenness.) The card was issued as a limited edition of a thousand copies which sold for a shilling each. After Horsley, various card manufacturers added Christmas cards to their inventory as a sideline, Marcus Ward and Company achieving the forefront with their

Top: An English woodcut card of the shepherds by artist C.M. Gere, for 1893; bottom: An 1890 woodcut card designed by Frederich Mason, England, of the angel appearing before the shepherds in their field. From "The Story of the Christmas Carol," House & Garden, December 1921.

publication of seasonal greeting cards in 1867. By the 1870s, England was widely exporting Christmas cards to the United States.

R. H. Pease, a printer in Albany, New York, is credited with distributing the first American-made Christmas cards in the 1850s. These depicted a family exulting in the holiday with Santa Claus and his reindeer, presents, and a sumptuous feast. About the same time, German immigrant Louis Prang arrived in America and established himself as a printer in Roxbury, Massachusetts, where he took the Christmas card industry to new heights. Having developed an improved method of color printing, he initially designed a series of cards depicting famous paintings with holiday greetings and exported them to England in 1874. Their immense popularity prompted him to market his cards in America during the following year. Two factors contributed to Prang's success: Free mail delivery, newly established in 1863, which became a strong incentive for

Christmas post card from Great Britain, Valentine's S series. (Undivided back. Chromolithographed image.) Both the robin and the mistletoe have Christmas connections: The robin supposedly got its red breast by fanning the fire for the Holy Family. The mistletoe has a more varied story with a rich pagan connection. (See also **Mistletoe.***)*

sending holiday greeting cards; and Prang's sponsorship of annual design contests with considerable cash awards, whereby he acquired the work of the finest artists for his designs. Further, he exhibited the artists' works at the American Art Gallery in New York and captured the public's attention with 7-by-10-inch cards, which sold for one dollar each. By 1890, however, much cheaper cards produced by competitors in Germany succeeded in driving Prang out of the Christmas card market.

Christmas cards today are broadly segregated into the religious and the secular. The former usually focus on Nativity scenes, the Madonna and Child, the Magi, and so forth. The latter cards tend to feature neutral, winter scenes with generic expressions of "Season's Greetings," "Greetings," or "Happy Holidays."

Annually over two billion Christmas cards are sold in the United States.

A Christmas Carol

(Novella). Classic Christmas tale by the celebrated British author Charles John Huffam Dickens (1812–1870). It is also the title of a poem of five stanzas by the same author (see entry below). The novella is considered to be the most popular story ever written about Christmas, second only to the Nativity story in the Bible. This work, written in just six weeks and originally titled *A Christmas Carol in Prose: Being a Ghost Story of Christmas*, was first pub-

lished in 1843 by Chapman and Hall of London (Dickens financed the project himself) with illustrations by John Leech (four full-color etchings and four black-and-white woodcuts). The story was priced at five shillings (twenty-five cents) and quickly became so immensely popular that it sold some six thousand copies during the first five days of publication, figures which surpassed sales of the Bible at that time.

Despite this initial success, after the publishers recouped their costs, Dickens had earned some 230 pounds (one thousand dollars), a sum that was quickly consumed in litigation over an unauthorized version of the *Carol*, complete with musical score, that had appeared in a London newspaper. Although Dickens won his suit, he received nothing from the bankrupted defendants and was left with court costs instead. He eventually was able to turn this situation around by giving public readings of the *Carol*, at first for charity and later for profit. The first reading took place in December 1854, and subsequently such readings became annual holiday events. In 1865, Dickens brought the *Carol* and other works to the United States with a reading in Boston. Because the tale was a ghost story, for better effect, Dickens suggested that it be read aloud by candlelight in a cold room.

The plot is well known: Mean-spirited and miserly Ebenezer Scrooge is transformed on Christmas Eve into a kind philanthropist through the hauntings of four Ghosts, beginning with the Ghost of Scrooge's former partner, Jacob Marley, who is followed by the Ghosts of Christmas Past, Christmas Present, and Christmas Yet to Come. This story line, however, was not original in 1843, for Dickens based *A Christmas Carol* on one of his earlier short stories, titled "The Story of the Goblins Who Stole a Sexton," which had appeared as chapter 29 in his first novel, *The Pickwick Papers* (1836–37). Chapter 28 sets the stage for this story-within-a-story. Mr. Pickwick and his colleagues have arrived at Manor Farm, the estate of their friend, Mr. Wardle, who has invited them to spend the Christmas holidays with his other guests. The ladies and gentlemen present have whiled away Christmas Eve by drinking wassail and playing traditional games, and now midnight approaches. In keeping with

Famous illustrator John Leech drew this scene of Scrooge facing the second of the Christmas spirits: the Ghost of Christmas Present. From Charles Dickens, Christmas Books. *London: 1876.*

This is the happy scene of Mr. Fezziwig's Ball as illustrated by John Leech. Scrooge, who as a young man was apprenticed to the jolly Mr. Fezziwig, went to see him with the Ghost of Christmas Past. From Charles Dickens, Christmas Books. *London: 1876.*

the English tradition of telling ghost stories at Christmastime (which derived from the pre–Christian Teutonic and Norse belief that evil spirits prevailed during the winter solstice or Yule festival), Mr. Wardle spins the story about the goblins stealing a sexton.

Like Scrooge, sexton Gabriel Grub is a surly old man who despises Christmas and takes no pleasure in anyone's happiness. While digging a grave on Christmas Eve, he falls asleep and dreams that a troupe of goblins floods the cemetery while playing leap-frog over tombstones. The goblin king whisks Grub into an underground cavern, where he experiences various torments, one of which is the vision of a poverty-stricken, simple, loving family, whose youngest boy eventually dies (foreshadowing the Bob Cratchit family with Tiny Tim). Grub learns that those who snarl at the happiness of others are the "foulest weeds on earth," and he awakens on Christmas Day a changed man.

Dickens experienced an early life of poverty, including working long hours in a factory for a pittance prior to his teenage years. Outraged at the injustices which the rich upper class inflicted on the poor, he often incorporated memories of his unhappy childhood into his fictional works. The *Carol* is no exception, for it condemns greed and those who neglect the less fortunate. Dickens also felt a personal relationship with the characters in the *Carol*, for several of them were based on circumstances and personalities of some of his own relatives. Tiny Tim was a composite, drawn from Dickens's brother, Frederick, and his young nephew, Harry Burnett, the crippled son of Dickens's elder sister, Frances Burnett (nicknamed Fanny). She in turn became the basis for Scrooge's little sister, Fan, and Frederick served as the role model for Scrooge's nephew, Fred. At first, Dickens had considered using the name Tiny Fred for Bob Cratchit's ailing little boy, because Frederick had acquired that name at the age of two. But Dickens settled on the name Tiny Tim, because it sounded more diminutive and more suitable for a sickly child. Scrooge was partially the embodiment of Dickens himself. Strapped for cash at the time, Dickens wrote *A Christmas Carol* strictly for financial gain. Like Scrooge, he was obsessed with acquiring wealth (an attempt to escape his childhood poverty), but there the similarity between the two men ended. This compulsion to make money actually created feelings of guilt, which clashed with Dickens's strong sense of love for family, community, and simple virtues despite poverty, ideals which he believed should surpass all quest for material gain and which surfaced many times in his literary works.

The present-day tradition of regarding Christmas as a festive occasion owes much to the *Carol*. From the Middle Ages until the mid–17th century, Christmas in much of Europe was an all-too-festive occasion that often centered on recklessness and debauchery. The seizure of Parliament by the religiously fanatical Puritans in the 1640s, the execution of King Charles I in 1649, and the subsequent establishment of a Protectorate in 1653 under the direction of Oliver Cromwell essentially abolished all observances of Christmas in England until the ascent of King Charles II in 1660. Even with Christmas restored, the holiday period afterwards was quite subdued and generally consisted of one day of religious devotion and quiet rest at home, nothing more. That is, until *A Christmas Carol*. Despite the somber plot with Scrooge, the story was jam-packed with such wonderful cheer, feelings of goodwill and kindness toward all, feasting, and the joy of being with family and relatives on the happiest of holidays, that the public gradually became caught up in the sentiment. Thus people sought to recreate the jolly atmosphere of Christmas outlined in the *Carol*, not only for themselves, but for those less fortunate as well. In time the name of Charles Dickens essentially became synonymous with Christmas itself. To illustrate this point, upon Dickens's death, one saddened little girl was noted to ask if Father Christmas (the British equivalent of Santa Claus) was also going to die.

Probably no other secular story has been adapted for film, television, animation, and theater as often as *A Christmas Carol*. As a spe-

cial tourist attraction, the town of Rochester, County Kent, England, where Dickens lived in his Gad's Hill home, sports a production of the *Carol* each weekend in December. Dressed in period costumes, the citizens recreate the beloved story throughout the town.

Today the original manuscript of *A Christmas Carol* resides in the Pierpont Morgan Library in Manhattan.

• FILM AND TELEVISION VERSIONS. The immense popularity of the Dickens classic over the decades has produced numerous motion picture, television, and animated versions. The following alphabetical list summarizes the information that is currently known about film, television, and cartoon adaptations. The designation "Video N/A" indicates that a version is either not currently available on VHS videocassette or that specific video information is lacking. Unless otherwise indicated, all versions originate in the United States. Paul Sammon, in *The "Christmas Carol" Trivia Book*, also lists several dance adaptations and a compilation of spoken-word versions available on audiocassette and compact disc.

An All Dogs Christmas Carol (1998), Metro-Goldwyn-Mayer animated film. A mean-spirited bulldog planning to ruin Christmas experiences divine intervention. Voices: Steven Weber, Dom DeLuise, Sheena Easton, Ernest Borgnine, Charles Nelson Reilly, Bebe Neuwirth. Written by Jymn Magon. Produced by Jonathan Dern, Paul Sabella. Directed by Paul Sabella. MGM/UA Home Entertainment Video. Color. 73 min.

Alvin's Christmas Carol (1983), episode from the television animated series *Alvin and the Chipmunks*. Alvin's lack of concern for others and his obsession over Christmas presents spawns ghostly visits from his brothers, Simon and Theodore, as well as keeper David Seville. Also features "The Chipmunk Song (Christmas Don't Be Late)." Voices: Ross Bagdasarian, Jr., Janice Karman, Thom Watkins, Dody Goodman. Bagdasarian Productions. Buena Vista Home Video. Color. 23 min.

An American Christmas Carol (1979), U.S.A.–Canadian television movie set in depression-era New Hampshire. Benedict Slade (Henry Winkler), a miserly banker, is haunted by three ghosts resembling people who have defaulted on loans and from whom Slade has seized property as payment. Also starring David Wayne, Chris Wiggins, R. H. Thomson, Kenneth Pogue, Gerard Parks, Susan Hogan, Dorian Harewood. Credited writer Charles Dickens. Produced by Stanley Chase. Directed by Eric Till. Smith-Hemien Productions and Stanley Chase Productions. Vestron Video. Color. 98 min.

Bah, Humbug! The Story of Charles Dickens' "A Christmas Carol" (1994). Televised abridged dramatic reading of Dickens's story at the Pierpont Morgan Library in New York City where the original manuscript resides. Based on the adaptations which Dickens used for his own public readings. Featuring James Earl Jones, Robert MacNeil, and Martin Sheen. Video N/A.

Blackadder's Christmas Carol (1988). BBC television movie and comedic parody based on a 1980s BBC-TV comedy show, *Blackadder,* which satirized the Middle Ages. The parody features Ebenezer Blackadder (Rowan Atkinson), initially a kind-hearted soul, whom a drunken Christmas ghost converts into a scoundrel. Also starring Tony Robinson, Robbie Coltrane, Miranda Richardson, Hugh Laurie, Stephen Fry, Miriam Margolyes, Jim Broadbent, Nicola Bryant. Written by Richard Curtis, Ben Elton. Directed by Richard Boden. British Broadcasting Corporation. Fox Video. Color. 43 min.

Br'er Rabbit's Christmas Carol (1992). Animated cartoon featuring Uncle Remus characters such as Br'er Rabbit, Br'er Fox, and Br'er Bear. Video Treasures. Color. 60 min.

Bugs Bunny's Christmas Carol. See **Bugs Bunny's Looney Christmas Tales.**

Carol for Another Christmas (1964). Television movie. Written by *Twilight Zone* creator Rod Serling, this contemporary version features Sterling Hayden as a cynical Daniel Grudge who faces a world sliding toward nuclear destruction. Also starring Ben Gazzara, Peter Sellers, Eva Marie Saint, Steve Lawrence, Pat Hingle, Robert Shaw, Britt Ekland, James Shigeta, Percy Rodrigues. Directed by Joseph L. Mankiewicz. American Broadcasting Company. B & W. Video N/A.

A Christmas Carol (1901). British silent film directed by W. R. Booth. B & W. Video N/A.

A Christmas Carol (1908). Silent film starring Thomas Ricketts. B & W. Video N/A.

A Christmas Carol (1910). Silent film starring Charles Ogle, William Bechtel, Carey Lee. Produced by Thomas Edison. Directed by Ashley Miller. B & W. 17 min. Video N/A.

A Christmas Carol (1912). Silent film. Video N/A.

A Christmas Carol (1913). Also known as *Scrooge,* British silent film. Starring Seymour Hicks as Scrooge. with William Lugg, J. C. Buckstone, Dorothy Buckstone, Leedham Bantock, Leonard Calvert, Osborne Adair, Adela Measor. Written by Seymour Hicks. Directed by Leedham Bantock. B & W. 50 min. Video N/A.

A Christmas Carol (1914). British silent film starring Charles Rock as Scrooge, with George Bellamy, Mary Brough, Franklyn Bellamy, Edward O'Neill, Edna Flugrath, Arthur Cullin. Written and directed by Harold Shaw. B & W. 22 min. Video N/A.

A Christmas Carol (1938). Film starring British actor Reginald Owen as Scrooge, with Gene Lockhart, Terry Kilburn, Leo G. Carroll, Lionel Braham, Lynne Carver, Anne Rutherford, Barry Mackay, Kathleen Lockhart, June Lockhart (film debut). Although Lionel Barrymore was originally cast as Scrooge, illness led to the selection of Reginald Owen instead, at Barrymore's suggestion. Written by Hugo Butler. Produced by Joseph L. Mankiewicz. Directed by Edwin L. Marin. Metro-Goldwyn-Mayer. MGM/UA Home Video. B & W. 69 min.

A Christmas Carol (1940). Amateur film directed by Gregory Markopoulos. Video N/A.

A Christmas Carol (1945). Television movie from station WBKB, Chicago. B & W. Video N/A.

A Christmas Carol (1947). Television movie from station WABD, New York, on the Dumont Network, starring John Carradine, Barnard Hughes, Eva Marie Saint. Directed by James L. Caddigan. B & W. 60 min. Video N/A.

A Christmas Carol (1948). On *Philco Television Playhouse,* starring Dennis King, Frank M. Thomas, Valerie Cossart, John Baragray, Dennis King, Jr., Loring Smith, James MacColl. Directed by Gordon Duff. B & W. 60 min. Video N/A.

A Christmas Carol (1949). Television adaptation starring Taylor Holmes and Vincent Price. B & W. Video N/A.

A Christmas Carol (1951). Also known as *Scrooge.* British film starring Alastair Sim as Scrooge, with Mervyn Johns, Jack Warner, Kathleen Harrison, Michael Hordern, Miles Malleson, Francis De Wolff, Patrick Macnee. Considered to be the best filmed version. Written by Noel Langley. Produced and directed by Brian Desmond-Hurst. Renown Pictures Corporation Ltd. United Home Video. B & W. 83 min.

A Christmas Carol (1951). Television special on *Fireside Theatre,* starring Sir Ralph Richardson, Margaret Phillips, Arthur Treacher, Melville Cooper, Malcom Keene, Robert Hay Smith, Norman Barr. Directed by Gordon Duff. B & W. Half-hour. Video N/A.

A Christmas Carol (1952). On *Kraft Television Theatre,* starring Malcom Keene, Harry Townes, Valerie Cossart, Glenn Walker, Richard Purdy, Melville Cooper, Noel Leslie. Encore show in 1953 with virtually the same cast. Both shows directed by Fielder Cook. Both B & W and 60 min. Video N/A.

A Christmas Carol (1955). Television movie from New York City, on *Eye on New York.* Video N/A.

A Christmas Carol (1960). British film starring John Hayter, Stewart Brown, Gordon Mulholland. Directed by Robert Hartford-Davis. B & W. 28 min. Video N/A.

A Christmas Carol (1962). British film starring Basil Rathbone. Directed by Desmond Davis. Coronet Video/MTI Film and Video. B & W. 25 min.

A Christmas Carol (1962). BBC television movie. Video N/A.

A Christmas Carol (1969). Australian animated musical version. Voices: Ron Haddrick, Bruce Montague, John Llewellyn, Brenda Sanders, C. Duncan, T. Mangan. Vocals by T. Kaff, C. Bowden. Music by Richard Bowder. Directed by Zoran Janjica. Rhino Home Video. Color. 46 mins.

A Christmas Carol (1971). American-British animated television special. Voices: Alastair Sim, Sir Michael Redgrave, Sir Michael Hordern, Diana Quick, Joan Sims, Paul Whitsun-Jones, David Tate, Felix Felton, Annie West, Melvyn Hayes, Mary Ellen Ray. Considered to be the best animated version and the only *Carol* to win an Academy Award, for Best Short Subject, Animated Film (1972). Produced and directed by Richard Williams. The American Broadcasting Company and Richard Williams Productions. Goodtimes Video/Kids Classics Video. Color. 26 mins.

A Christmas Carol (1982). Australian animated film. Voices: Ron Haddrick, Robin Stewart, Barbara Frawley, Sean Hinton, Phillip Hinton, Liz Horne, Bill Conn, Derani Scarr, Anne Haddy. Directed by Jean Tych. A Burbank Films Production. Vestron Video. Color. 72 min.

A Christmas Carol (1982). Film adaptation starring Richard Hilger. Directed by Paul Miller. Video Treasures. Color. 90 min.

A Christmas Carol (1984). British television movie starring George C. Scott as Scrooge, with Frank Finlay, Nigel Davenport, David Warner, Susannah York, Anthony Walters, Edward Woodward, Angela Pleasence, Lucy Gutteridge, Roger Rees. Considered to be the best television version and the only version of its kind to introduce the character of Scrooge's father Silas (Nigel Davenport) into the story line. In 1985, the film won the Christopher Award for Distinguished Achievement in Television. Written by Roger O. Hirsom. Directed by Clive Donner. 20th Century–Fox Television. 20th Century–Fox Home Video. Color. 100 mins.

Christmas Carol (1984). French television adaptation starring Michel Bouquet as Scrooge. Video N/A.

A Christmas Carol (1990). Animated cartoon. Video Treasures. Color. 75 min.

A Christmas Carol (1997). Animated film. Voices: Tim Curry, Whoopi Goldberg, Michael York, Ed Asner. Directed by Stan Phillips. 20th Century–Fox Video. Color. 72 min.

A Christmas Carol (1999). Cable television movie starring Patrick Stewart as Scrooge, with Richard E. Grant, Joel Grey, Ian McNeice, Saskia Reeves, Desmond Barrit, Bernard Lloyd, Dominic West, Trevor Peacock, Liz Smith, Elizabeth Spriggs, Kenny Doughty, Laura Fraser, Celia Imrie. Only version to open with the burial of Jacob Marley. In 2000 this film received nominations for the following awards: Saturn Awards from the Academy of Science Fiction, Horror and Fantasy Films for Best Genre Television Actor (Patrick Stewart) and

Best Single Television Presentation; Emmy Award nomination for Outstanding Cinematography for a Miniseries Movie or a Television Special (Ian Wilson); and Screen Actors' Guild Award nomination for Outstanding Performance by a Male Actor in a Television Movie or Miniseries (Patrick Stewart). Written by Peter Barnes. Produced by Dyson Lovell. Directed by David Jones. Hallmark Entertainment. Turner Home Video. Color. 93 min.

A Christmas Carol II: The Sequel (1985). Television special on *George Burns Comedy Week*. One year after the reform of Scrooge (James Whitmore), Marley's Ghost returns to find that his former partner has become a wimpish philanthropist. Also starring Ed Begley, Jr., and Roddy McDowall. Color. Half-hour. Video N/A.

A Christmas Carol: Being a Ghost Story of Christmas (1991). British film directed by Moira Armstrong. Video N/A.

A Christmas Cruella. Episode from the Walt Disney Saturday morning television series *101 Dalmatians*, ongoing since 1996. Dalmatian pups assume the roles of Christmas Ghosts to reform Cruella de Vil, evil neighbor of the Dearly family. This episode appears with another *Dalmatians* tale, "Coup de Vil," in the video *101 Dalmatians Christmas* (1997). Voices: Jeff Bennett, Tara Charendorff, Rachael Crane, Jim Cummings, Marla Gibbs, David Lander, Tress MacNeille, Michael McKean, Rob Paulsen, Charlotte Rae, Kath Soucie, Frank Welker, Debi Mae West, April Winchell. Written by Ken Koonce and Michael Merton. Produced and directed by Victor Cook. Walt Disney Home Video. Color. 44 min.

Christmas Present (1985). BBC television special starring Peter Chelsom as Scrooge-surrogate Nigel Playfayre, with Bill Fraser. Directed by Tony Bicat. Color. Video N/A.

Czech Year (1947). Also known as *Spalicek*. Six-part, animated puppet Czech film, one episode of which features an adaptation of *A Christmas Carol*. Directed by puppet-master Jiri Trnka. Color. Video N/A.

Dickens Christmas Carol (1948). Television special from New York featuring the Rupert Rose Marionettes. B & W. Video N/A.

The Dream of Old Scrooge (1910). Italian silent film. B & W. 10 min. Video N/A.

Ebbie (1995). Canadian-American production made for cable television. In this change-of-gender adaptation, Susan Lucci stars as Ebbie Scrooge, a heartless CEO of a large department store, to whom Christmas is nothing but a season to boost store profits. Two Ghosts of Christmas Past appear as Valley Girls. Also starring Wendy Crewson, Ron Lea, Molly Parker, Lorena Gale, Jennifer Clement, Nicole Parker, Taran Noah Smith, Jeffrey DeMunn, Adrienne Carter, Bill Croft, Laura Harris. Written by Paul Redford, Ed Redlich. Produced by Harold Tichenor. Directed by George Kaczender. Crescent Entertainment Ltd. Color. About 2 hrs. Video N/A.

Ebenezer (1997). Canadian production made for cable television. Jack Palance stars as Ebenezer Scrooge, a ruthless saloon proprietor and card shark in this wild west adaptation. To Scrooge, Christmas is not "humbug," but "hogwash." Also starring Rick Schroder, Amy Locane, Daryl Shuttleworth, Richard Comar, Darcy Dunlop, Michelle Thrush, Linden Banks, Sam Coyne, Aaron Pearl, Albert Schultz. Written by Donald Martin. Produced by Douglas Berquist, Michael Frislev. Directed by Ken Jubenvill. A-Channel Drama Fund and Nomadic Pictures. Plaza Entertainment. Color. 84 min.

The Fat Albert Christmas Special (1977). Episode from Bill Cosby's Saturday morning animated television series, *Fat Albert and the Cosby Kids* (1972–1979). When Tightwad Tyrone, a junkyard owner and Scrooge surrogate, threatens to demolish Fat Albert's clubhouse erected in the junkyard, the Spirit of Christmas provides him with a change of heart. The Cosby Kids also come to the aid of Marshall Franklin, a boy whose father and pregnant mother are stranded in their car. This program received an Emmy Award nomination for Outstanding Children's Special (1977–1978 season). Voices: Bill Cosby, Jan Crawford, Gerald Edwards, Eric Suter, Erika Carroll, Eric Greene, Kim Hamilton, Julius Harris, Ty Henderson. A Filmation Production in Association with Bill Cosby Productions. Color. Half-hour. Video N/A.

A Flintstones Christmas Carol. See **The Flintstones.**

Humbug Not to Be Spoken Here. See **Bewitched.**

A Jetsons Christmas Carol. (1985). Episode from the Hanna-Barbera futuristic, animated television series *The Jetsons*, which aired in primetime from 1962 to 1963, on Saturday mornings periodically from 1963 to 1983, and again on Saturdays from 1985 to 1986 with new episodes. The principal characters included George Jetson, wife Jane, teenage daughter Judy, young son Elroy, pet dog Astro, robot maid Rosie, and George's boss, Mr. Spacely. In this episode, Scrooge surrogate Mr. Spacely demands that George work on Christmas Eve but allows him to leave at midnight. Falling asleep at his desk, Spacely dreams that his deceased partner announces the coming of three Christmas Spirits. They in turn not only reveal that Astro (a Tiny Tim surrogate) has eaten a Spacely product known as a Spacely Sprocket and will likely die, but that Jetson will bring a devastating lawsuit against the company. Spacely, a changed man upon awakening, rushes to Jetson's home with a veterinarian, saves Astro, distributes gifts to all, and avoids the predicted litigation. Voices: George O'Hanlon, Penny Singleton, Janet Waldo, Daws Butler, Don Messick, Jean Vander Pyl, Frank Welker, Mel Blanc. Produced and directed by William Hanna and Joseph Barbera. Hanna-Barbera Productions. Hanna-Barbera Home Video. Color. 23 min.

John Grin's Christmas. (1986). Television special with an all African American cast, starring Robert Guillaume as John Grin, a Scrooge surrogate toymaker. Also starring Roscoe Lee Brown, Ted Lange, Alfonso Ribiero, Geoffery Holder, Candy Ann Brown. Directed by Robert Guillaume. Color. 60 min. Video N/A.

Leyenda de Navidad (1947). Spanish film starring Jesus Tordesillas, Lina Yegros, Manuel Requena, Joaquin Soler Serrano, Angel Picazo. Directed by Manuel Tamayo. B & W. Video N/A.

Mickey's Christmas Carol (1983). Walt Disney animated film. This half-hour adaptation features classic Disney characters in the roles of Dickens characters: Scrooge McDuck as Ebenezer Scrooge, Mickey Mouse as Bob Cratchit, Pluto as Marley's Ghost, Jiminy Cricket as the Ghost of Christmas Past, Willie the Giant as the Ghost of Christmas Present, Black Pete the Dog as the Ghost of Christmas Yet to Come, and so forth. Only in this version does the latter character smoke a cigar. This cartoon received an Academy Award nomination for Best Short Film. Voices: Alan Young, Clarence Nash, Wayne Allwine, Hal Smith, Eddie Carroll, Will Ryan, Susan Sheridan, Pat Parris. Written by Burny Mattinson, Tony L. Marino, Ed Gombert, Don Griffith, Alan Young, Alan Dinehart. Produced and directed by Burny Mattinson. Walt Disney Home Video. Color. 26 mins. The first television release in 1984 included an additional half-hour, behind-the-scenes documentary titled *The Making of Mickey's Christmas Carol*, starring Alan Young, Clarence Nash, Burny Mattinson, Mark Henn, Wayne Allwine, Jimmy MacDonald, Hal Smith. Walt Disney Home Video. Color. Video versions come with or without the documentary.

Mr. Magoo's Christmas Carol (1962). The first made-for-television animated special. A myopic old curmudgeon, Magoo became the most popular creation of animators at United Productions of America (UPA) in 1949, particularly Stephen Bosustow, John Hubley, and Ernest Pintoff. This *Carol* features Magoo as Scrooge in a Broadway musical, the lyrics and music of which are provided by Bob Merrill and Jule Styne, respectively. It is considered to be the best musical version, with such songs as "Ringle, Ringle, Coins as They Jingle," "It's Cold, It's Cold, It's Cold!," and "All Alone in the World." Another UPA character, Gerald McBoing Boing (a little boy who usually communicates through odd sound effects, though he *speaks* here), portrays Tiny Tim. This also is the only version in which the Ghost of Christmas Present appears ahead of the other two Ghosts. In 1970, *Magoo's Carol* was released to theaters, double-billed with the feature-length *Mr. Magoo's Little Snow White*. *Carol* voices: Jim Backus, Jack Cassidy, Laura Olsher, Joan Gardner, Jane Keen, Royal Dano, Morey Amsterdam, Les Tremayne, Paul Frees, Marie Matthews, John Hart. Written by Barbara Chain. Produced by Lee Orgel. Directed by Abe Levitow. UPA Pictures. Paramount Home Video. Color. 52 min.

Ms. Scrooge (1997), cable television special. Cicely Tyson stars in this change-of gender, change-of-race version as Ebenita Scrooge, a miserly African American woman whom Christmas ghosts reform on Christmas Eve.

Also starring Katherine Helmond, Michael Beach, John Bourgeois, Rae'ven Kelly, Karen Glave, Ken James, Arsinee Khanjian, William Greenblatt, Michael J. Reynolds, Julian Richings. Written by John McGreevey. Produced by Julian Marks. Directed by John Korty. Power Pictures and Wilshire Court Productions. Paramount Home Video. Color. 87 min.

The Muppet Christmas Carol (1992). Film, musical comedy starring Michael Caine as Scrooge, with Muppet characters such as the Great Gonzo, Rizzo the Rat, Kermit the Frog, Miss Piggy, Fozzie Bear, and others portraying Dickens characters. Songs by Paul Williams. Written by Jerry Juhl. Produced by Martin G. Baker and Brian Henson, son of the late Muppets creator Jim Henson. Directed by Brian Henson. Jim Henson Productions and Walt Disney Productions. Walt Disney Home Video. Color. 85 min.

Old Scrooge (1910). Italian silent film believed to be a remake of *The Dream of Old Scrooge* (see above). B & W. 12 min. Video N/A.

Rich Little's Christmas Carol (1978). Canadian television special starring comedian Rich Little in a one-man adaptation of the *Carol*. Little impersonates a number of celebrities who in turn depict the major Dickens characters. Directed by Trevor Edwards. Canadian Broadcasting Corporation. SVS Inc. Color. 50 min.

The Right to Be Happy (1916). Silent film starring Rupert Julian, John Cook, Claire McDowell, Frankie Lee, Harry Carter, Emory Johnson. Directed by Rupert Julian. B & W. 60 min. Video N/A.

Scrooge (1923). British silent film starring Russell Thorndike, Jack Denton, Nina Vanna, Forbes Dawson. Directed by W. C. Rowden. B & W. Video N/A.

Scrooge (1935). Also known as *A Christmas Carol*. British film starring Sir Seymour Hicks as Scrooge, with Donald Calthrop, Barbara Everest, Philip Frost, Mary Glynne, Robert Cocha, Marie Nye, Oscar Ashe, Maurice Evans. Written by H. Fowler Mear (some also credit Seymour Hicks). Produced by Julius Hagen. Directed by Henry Edwards. Twickenham Company. United American Video. B & W. 61 min. In 1936, Henry Edwards received Special Recommendation at the Venice Film Festival for his work on this film.

Scrooge (1970). British film, elaborate musical, starring Albert Finney as Scrooge, with Alec Guinness, Dame Edith Evans, Kenneth More, Laurence Naismith, Michael Medwin, David Collings, Gordon Jackson, Roy Kinnear, Kay Walsh. Songs by Leslie Bricusse, Ian Fraser, Herbert W. Spencer. Although Rex Harrison was initially offered the role of Scrooge, Finney accepted the part. Written by Leslie Bricusse, Michael Medwin. Produced by Robert H. Solo. Directed by Ronald Neame. Cinema Center 100 Productions and Waterbury Films. 20th Century–Fox Video. Color. 115 min. In 1971, this film was nominated for Academy Awards for Best Art Direction — Set Decoration, Best Costume Design, Best Music — Original Song Score, and Best Music — Song ("Thank You, Very Much" by Bricusse). It was nominated for a British Academy Award for Best Art Direction. The film won a Golden Globe Award for Best Motion Picture Actor in a Musical/Comedy (Finney) and received Golden Globe nominations for Best Motion Picture — Musical/Comedy, Best Original Score, Best Screenplay, and Best Original Song ("Thank You, Very Much").

Scrooge: A Christmas Carol (1989). Television presentation of colorized version of the 1951 film which starred Alastair Sim (see above). Hosted by Patrick Macnee.

Scrooged (1988). This comedic parody set in contemporary New York City casts Bill Murray as Scrooge surrogate Frank Cross, a despicable television network president who sees Christmas only as a means to boost network ratings. He is reformed by a cab-driving Ghost of Christmas Past (David Johansen); a Ghost of Christmas Present fairy (Carol Kane), who administers corporal punishment; and a black-robed, silent Ghost of Christmas Yet to Come, whose face alternately appears as a skull or as a video monitor which in turn depicts Cross's face as a mutilated mass. Also starring Karen Allen; John Forsythe; John Glover; Bobcat Goldthwait; Robert Mitchum; Alfre Woodard; Buddy Hackett; John Houseman; Mary Lou Retton; Michael J. Pollard; and Bill Murray's three other brothers, John, Joel, and Brian Doyle Murray. Written by Mitch Glazer, Michael O'Donoghue. Produced by Richard Donner, Art Linson. Directed by

Richard Donner. Paramount Pictures. Paramount Home Video. Color. 101 min. In 1989, this film received an Academy Award nomination for Best Makeup.

Scrooge's Rock 'n' Roll Christmas (1984). Televised rock version with music from such groups as Three Dog Night and Rush. With Jack Elam as Scrooge. Sony Video. Color. 44 min.

Skinflint (1979). Television country music adaptation, starring Hoyt Axton, Mel Tillis, Lynn Anderson, Dottie West, Barbara Mandrell, Larry Gatlin, Martha Raye, Danny Davis and the Nashville Brass. Directed by Marc Daniels. Color. 120 min. Video N/A.

The Spirit of Christmas (1954). Television musical adaptation on *Shower of Stars*, hosted by William Lundigan. Starring Fredric March, Basil Rathbone, Bob Sweeney, Ray Middleton, Queenie Leonard, Christopher Cook. Directed by Ralph Levy. Lyrics by Maxwell Anderson. Music by Bernard Herrmann. A cappella performance by the Roger Wagner Chorale. The production depicts the Ghost of Christmas Yet to Come as a mynah bird. Viking Video Classics. B & W. 60 min.

The Stingiest Man in Town (1956). Television adaptation on *The Alcoa Hour*, starring Basil Rathbone as Scrooge, with Vic Damone, Patrice Munsel, Martyn Green, Dennis Kohler, Johnny Desmond, the Four Lads. Directed by Daniel Petrie. B & W. 90 min. Video N/A.

The Stingiest Man in Town (1978). Animated television special, featuring stop-motion puppets. An insect, B. A. H. Humbug (voice of Tom Bosley), narrates, as Walter Matthau voices for Scrooge. Additional voices: Robert Morse, Theodore Bikel, Dennis Day, Robert Rolofson, Darlene Conley, Paul Frees, Debra Clinger, Steffanie Calli, Eric Hines, Charles Matthau, Diana Lee. Produced and directed by Arthur Rankin, Jr., and Jules Bass. Rankin-Bass Productions. Warner Video. Color. 50 min.

The Trail to Christmas (1957). Western frontier adaptation on television's *The General Electric Theatre*, starring John McIntire, Richard Eyre, Jimmy Stewart, Sam Edwards, Will Wright, Kevin Hagen, Dennis Holmes. Directed by Jimmy Stewart and narrated by Ronald Reagan. B & W. 26 min. Video N/A.

See also **Dickens, Charles, Christmas stories of; Irving Washington, Christmas sketches of.**

A Christmas Carol

(Poem). Poem of five stanzas by British novelist Charles Dickens (1812–1870), author of the identically titled novella about the reform of Ebenezer Scrooge. The poem is found in chapter 28 of Dickens's first novel, *The Pickwick Papers* (1836–37). The time is Christmas Eve at Mr. Wardle's estate, Manor Farm, where Mr. Pickwick and his colleagues are spending the holidays with Wardle's other guests. As everyone awaits the midnight hour, Wardle entertains the crowd with this poem as a song, which holds that none of the other seasons can compare with Christmas, "the King of the Seasons all!" Later, the poem itself was set to a popular tune of the time.

Christmas Carols

Sacred or secular songs which celebrate all aspects of Christmas and which are considered popular or modern for the era of origin. By strict definition, because carols in general may celebrate religious as well as secular holidays and other special events, they appeal to the public with lyrics and music with which the majority can identify. The word "carol" ultimately derives from the Greek *choros* ("chorus"), a circling dance. The latter often appeared in ancient Greek plays, in which performers sang and danced in a circle. Greek also provides *choraules* ("flute player for chorus dancing"); thence evolves the Latin *choraula* and the Old French *caroler* to the English "carol."

Although songs celebrating the Nativity have existed since the early Christian era, true carols, Christmas or otherwise, did not arise until the fourteenth or fifteenth century. Prior to that time, most Christmas music consisted of somber, plainchant hymns originating in the Church, the Latin texts of which appealed little to the public, for only clerics and scholars at that time were proficient in the ecclesiastical language. Indeed, the earliest extant Christmas hymns are those composed by St. Ambrose (340?–397) of Milan, whose "Veni, redemptor gentium" ("Savior [or Redeemer] of the

English children carolling on Christmas morning as was the custom of the 1870s. According to the book in which the wood engraving appeared, they perhaps were singing "When Christ was born of Mary free,/In Bethlehem, in that fair citie,/Angels sang there with mirth and glee,/In Excelsis Gloria." From Robert Chambers, ed., The Book of Days *(London and Edinburgh: Chambers, 1879).*

This crude little woodcut of 3 Wise Men was one of several printed on penny sheets of Christmas carols, which were sold by their publisher, T. Batchelar of Moorfields, London, in the early nineteenth century. William Hone, who bought the original printing blocks in 1820, recollected that once a full sheet of carols with eight woodcut sold for a half-penny: "But alas! everything is changed; the present half sheets are raised in price to a whole penny." He also said that people would naturally buy Christmas Carols "as they long for mince pies and eat plum pudding." From William Hone, Ancient Mysteries Described *(London: 1823).*

Nations [or Gentiles] Come") is a more familiar example. His Incarnation themes set a precedent, for the Church subsequently incorporated abstract theology into its Christmas hymns and condemned all forms of jocularity, including dancing, at Christmastime and on other feast days until the appearance of St. Francis of Assisi, Italy.

Considered the parent of the carol, St. Francis (1182–1226) desired that his parishioners acquire a full understanding and appreciation for the Bible, particularly its messages regarding Bethlehem and Calvary. On Christmas Eve of 1223, he attained the first goal by assembling a live Nativity scene in a cave near the village of Greccio, Italy. Amid a reconstructed stable with ox, ass, shepherds, and Wise Men, St. Francis jovially sang the Christmas Mass as spellbound spectators saw the Nativity presented with tender emotion, realism, and humanity theretofore unknown. By interjecting a spirit of joy into religious song, St. Francis revolutionized hymnody and laid the groundwork for changes in the English miracle or mystery plays that would follow, all of which brought Christianity closer in tune with

the hearts of the laity and inspired the writing of new religious songs in the vernacular. (*See* **Christmas Drama.**)

Other medieval clerics following in the steps of St. Francis included the Italian Jacopone da Todi (1228–1306), a Franciscan mystic whose lyrical Christmas songs pervaded the thirteenth century, and John Audlay, a blind English priest of Haughmond Abbey, Shropshire, whose collection of Christmas carols

(1430) bore the following inscription in red: "I pray yow syrus boothe moore and las / syng these caroles in cristemas" ("I pray you sirs both more and less / sing these carols in Christmas"). It is clear that Audlay's goal was to provide spiritual mirth for Christmas.

The fourteenth and fifteenth centuries saw, with the coming of the Renaissance, an upswing in lay patronage of the arts and music, a decline in the plainsongs of the Church, and a rise in vernacular hymns and carols throughout Europe. By the fifteenth century, the word "carol" had become synonymous exclusively with sacred or secular Christmas songs. In England, traditional carols were patterned after ballads or contained refrains, while a "macaronic" variety (not unique to England and probably the contribution of clergymen) consisted of English verse peppered with familiar phrases from the Latin liturgy. The best-known example of the latter variety, the "Boar's Head Carol," survives in a printed collection of 1521 by Jan van Wynkyn de Worde and is the earliest English carol collection extant.

Christmas carols flourished throughout Europe during the sixteenth century but markedly declined with the advent of the Protestant Reformation. No country saw a greater suppression of carols at this time than did Great Britain, for in 1647 the Puritans, having gained control of Parliament earlier in the decade, completely outlawed all religious feast days and their trappings. Although the ascent of King Charles II in 1660 restored these holidays, Christmas observances never again attained the level of merriment known in former centuries, and the former traditional carols were all but forgotten. From that time into the early nineteenth century, the clergy generated several new hymns; (some were significant examples, Isaac Watts's "Joy to the World," 1692), and others are no longer remembered today. Generally, however, carols superficially survived as folk tunes sung by the wandering minstrels, or they sporadically appeared on broadsides.

Fearing a total demise of the English-language carol tradition, a number of prominent nineteenth-century scholars individually recovered their country's Christmas heritage in song through a series of carol compilations.

Collection of Christmas Carols (1822 and 1823) by Gilbert Davies, president of the Royal Society, was considered to be the first modern collection of traditional carols since the Reformation. Other notable collections included *Christmas Carols Ancient and Modern* (1833) and *Christmas Tide* (1852), both by the solicitor antiquary William Sandys; *Songs and Carols* (1836) by Thomas Wright, consisting of fifteenth-century carols; and William H. Husk's *Songs of the Nativity* (1868).

Two collections further boosted carols in the eyes of the nineteenth-century English clergy. One of these, *Carols for Christmas-Tide* (1853) by the Anglican priest John Mason Neale and musicologist Thomas Helmore, consisted of twelve carols which Neale had translated from *Piae Cantiones* (*Holy Songs*), a book of sixteenth-century Swedish carols. Among them were the now familiar "Good King Wenceslas" and "Good Christian Men, Rejoice." Rev. Henry Bramley, fellow of Magdalen College, Oxford, together with Dr. John Stainer, college organist, published the second collection, *Christmas Carols New and Old* (1871). This volume, consisting of a mixture of traditional and contemporary numbers, is reputed to have been the most influential in restoring the English carol tradition.

An interest in carols also blossomed in nineteenth-century America, owing in part to the popularity of such literary works as the poem "A Visit from St. Nicholas" (published 1823) and Charles Dickens's *A Christmas Carol* (1843), as well as to the clergy, who composed some of America's most popular religious carols. For example, "It Came upon the Midnight Clear" (1849), the work of Rev. Edmund Sears and Richard Willis, is considered to be America's first prominent carol. Other genres have included African American spirituals such as "Go Tell It on the Mountain" (1800s) and a host of secular carols that especially burgeoned into the twentieth century.

See also entries for individual carols.

Christmas Comes Anew
See **Sing We Now of Christmas**

Christmas Cometh Caroling
See **Alfred Burt Carols**

Christmas Crackers

See **Great Britain**

A Christmas Cruella

See **A Christmas Carol** (FILM AND TELEVISION VERSIONS)

Christmas Day

Feast commemorating the birth of Jesus Christ. It corresponds to December 25 on the Gregorian calendar in the Roman Catholic, Anglican, Episcopal, and Protestant churches; January 7 in divisions of the Eastern Orthodox Church; and January 6 in the Armenian Church (its branch in Jerusalem observes January 19). Whereas this entry will focus on December 25, detailed explanations for the other dates will be found under **Armenia**; **Christmas Old Style, Christmas New Style**; and **Epiphany**.

The word "Christmas" first appeared between the sixteenth and seventeenth centuries as a contraction of "Christ's Mass," based on the three Roman Catholic masses which comprised the liturgy of Christmas Day. "Christ's Mass" further derived from the late Old English *Christes Maesse* (or *Cristes Maesse*) of the early eleventh century, and through subsequent centuries, the phrase underwent a series of evolutions, such as *Cristes-messe*, *Kryst-masse*, *Crystmasse*, *Cristmasse*, *Chrysmas*, *Cristmas*, and so forth (*See* **Christmas Masses**).

The establishment of December 25 evolved, not from biblical precedent (indeed, the Bible provides no specific date for the birth of Christ), but from pagan Roman festivals held at year's end, such as the Saturnalia, Kalends, and the combined festivals of two sun gods, the Roman Sol and the Persian Mithras. Roman soldiers, enamored with the cult of Mithras during their campaigns of the first century A.D. in Persia, spread the new religion throughout the Roman Empire, such that Sol and Mithras were regarded as one god. The empire celebrated their birthdays on December 25, the winter solstice according to the Roman (Julian) calendar, with festivities which the emperor Aurelian established in 274 as *Natalis Solis Invicti* ("Birth of the Unconquered Sun").

Early Christian theologians deplored the parallel of celebrating Christ's birth as the pagans did with their gods. As examples, St.

Irenaeus (140?–202?) of Asia Minor and the Roman Tertullian (160?–220?) made no mention of a Nativity feast in their era. Clement of Alexandria (150?–215?) criticized his colleagues for attempting to assign a specific date to Christ's birth, and Origen of Alexandria (ca. 185–ca. 254) cited biblical implications that only sinners celebrated birthdays (Genesis 40:20; Ecclesiastes 7:1; Mark 6:21). Nevertheless, it is believed that early Christians did commemorate the Nativity at year's end, possibly to offset the revelry and unrestraint of those pagan festivals held simultaneously within the Roman Empire.

The earliest evidence that mentions December 25 lies in a church calendar that dates to 336, devised by Furius Dionisius Philocalus of Rome. In the civil portion of the calendar, December 25 is labeled *Natalis Invicti* ("Birth of the Unconquered," implying the solar birthday). In another portion of the calendar known as the *Depositio Martyrum*, a list of universally venerated martyrs, December 25 is labeled with a Latin phrase which translates as, "On the eighth before the Kalends of January [i. e., December 25], Christ is born in Bethlehem of Judea." Because several dates of other entries in this calendar clash with history and possibility, these and the reference to a December Nativity are felt to be "interpolations," that is, feasts added to the calendar based on popular trends of the time.

During his tenure, Pope Julius I (337–352) attempted to calculate the day of the Nativity based on the Scriptures and Jewish holy days. According to Luke 1:5–17, the priest Zacharias was serving in the Temple at the hour of burning incense when he received the angel's annunciation that his wife Elizabeth would bear John the Baptist. All the worshippers were praying outside the Temple and not within, which Julius inferred to mean that this was the Day of Atonement, or Yom Kippur, for only the priest could enter the Temple at this time to conduct the proper rituals. Further deductions, tenuous at best, placed this day in October; since Christ was six months younger than John, Christ was conceived in March and born in December. It is possible that Julius was additionally influenced by the traditional notion that Christ was conceived at the spring equinox, or March 25 on the Julian calendar, and died on that date exactly 33 years later (the so-called "astronomical" theory), but around 350, Julius declared December 25 as the official date to commemorate the birth of Christ. In so doing, he Christianized the former birthday of the sun (possibly also as an incentive for pagans to convert to Christianity), which drew support from Pope Liberius I around 353 and from St. John Chrysostom, a theologian from Asia Minor (ca. 349–407). The latter, drawing a comparison between Christ and *Natalis Invicti*, declared that Christ was the "Sun of Justice," a sentiment that essentially reiterated a Messianic prophecy from Malachi 4:2, which portrayed Christ as the "Sun of righteousness." Although the December feast had been well established by their time, some church leaders, such as St. Augustine (354–430) and Pope St. Leo I (reigned 440–461), remained critical, principally for fear that pagans converting to Christianity had retained the notion that Christ represented the sun.

From Rome, the December feast spread to the churches of the eastern Roman Empire, which had been observing the feast of Christ's Epiphany on January 6 since the second century. Constantinople received the feast of Christmas through St. Gregory of Nazianzus (ca. 329–389) in 379, but not until the Synod of Constantinople in 381 did Theodosius I, Roman Emperor of the East (379–395), sanc-

Engraving of a manuscript miniature of the 14th century, showing Charlemagne receiving homage from feudal barons. The picture originates in the Chroniqes de Saint-Denis.

tion the December feast in that part of the empire. Cappadocia had received the feast through St. Gregory of Nyssa (ca. 335–394) by 380; Antioch, through St. Chrysostom in 386; Alexandria, by 433; Jerusalem, in the latter sixth century. Armenia never accepted the December date.

• CHRISTMAS DAY IN HISTORY. Over the centuries, a number of historical events have transpired on or about Christmas Day. The following list recalls some of the most noteworthy:

496, Christmas Day: St. Rémi baptizes Clovis I, king of the Franks at Rheims in Gaul, which brings Christianity to France.

800, Christmas Day: Pope Leo III crowns Charlemagne emperor of the Holy Roman Empire.

1065, Christmas Day: Consecration of Great Britain's Westminster Abbey.

1066, Christmas Day: William the Conqueror ascends the British throne.

1492, Christmas Eve: Christopher Columbus's flagship *Santa Maria* runs aground off what is now the coast of Haiti in the West Indies. Columbus and his crew become the first Europeans to spend the first Christmas in the New World and construct a small settlement from the ship's remains, which they name *Villa de la Navidad* ("Village of the Nativity").

1776, Christmas Night: General George Washington and his Continental Army cross the Delaware River at Trenton, New Jersey, and rout Hessian troops who are otherwise engaged in celebrating Christmas. The victory is a major turning point for the colonists in the American Revolution.

1814, Christmas Eve: The United States and Great Britain sign a treaty at Ghent, Belgium, which terminates the War of 1812 between these two powers.

1931, Christmas Day: Engelbert Humperdinck's *Hansel and Gretel* becomes the first opera to be broadcast over the radio from New York City's Metropolitan Opera.

1941, Christmas Day: First radio broadcast of Irving Berlin's "White Christmas," sung by Bing Crosby on *The Kraft Music Hall*.

1943, Christmas Eve: General Dwight D. Eisenhower is appointed Supreme Commander of Allied Forces in Europe during World War II.

1951, Christmas Eve: Gian Carlo Menotti's *Amahl and the Night Visitors* is broadcast as the first opera written for television.

1968, Christmas Eve: Apollo 8 astronauts Frank Borman, James Lovell, and William Anders deliver the first televised Christmas message from space while orbiting the moon. Their text is taken from the first verses of Genesis 1.

Christmas Don't Be Late
See The Chipmunk Song

Christmas Drama

Four principal forms of historical drama were practiced in Europe during the holidays and particularly in Great Britain: masques, mumming, Nativity plays, and pantomime.

• MASQUES. Taken from the sixteenth-century French, "masque" (mask) denotes a formal, masked presentation prevalent at English courts during the seventeenth century, which consisted largely of spectacular pageantry and scenery, along with music and elaborate speeches based on allegorical, mythological, or historical themes. Designed to compliment and entertain the monarchy during holidays and at other special events, English masques derived from early mumming or disguising customs (see MUMMING, below) as well as from court spectacles practiced in the Renaissance Italy of Lorenzo de' Medici. Passing through France, which gave rise to the *ballet de cour* and the masquerades, masques then appeared in England at the time of the Tudors; King Henry VIII first introduced the formal masque to his court in 1512. Here, as in Italy and France, the masquers, whose disguises sometimes included blackened faces, paired with members of the audience as well as the monarch for a grand, central dance called the "revels."

Masques especially flourished during the reign of King James I (ruled 1603–1625). Whereas masques until that time had centered primarily around pageantry and scenic effects with minor emphasis upon text, the celebrated English dramatist Ben Jonson (1572–1637) perfected the masque into a work of lyrical literature, beginning with his appointment as court poet in 1603. Jonson also first applied the word "masque" to his work in this genre, which commenced with *Masque of Blackness* (Twelfth Night, 1605). With this work, he launched a collaboration with the genius of English architect and stage designer Inigo Jones that produced 28 masques until 1634, at which time the two parted because of professional differences. Notable examples of their work include *Oberon, the Fairy Prince* (1611) and *Pleasure Reconciled to Virtue* (1618). Although Jonson's masques frequently were performed at Christmastime, the themes were not necessarily related exclusively to the season. Like most other masques, they generally centered around the resolution of discord or the movement from disorder to order, thus incorporating a moral. In Jonsonian masques were skillfully interwoven elements of comedic satire as well. For example, *Christmas His Masque* (1616), Jonson's only masque written specifically for the holiday, features a host of allegorical characters which elegantly satirize those secular elements that were commonly associated with Christmas at the time: "Christmas" (the host), "Misrule" (The Lord of Misrule), "Carol," "Minced Pie," "Gambol" (one who frolics), "Post and Pair" (a card game), "New Year's Gift," "Mumming" (see below), "Wassail," "Offering," and "Baby Cake" (Twelfth Night cake with the bean and pea).

Masques virtually disappeared in England following the Puritan rise to Parliament in the 1640s but survived for another century in France and at other European courts. The improvements in changeable scenery and stage machinery later found in other art forms such as the ballet, opera, and pantomime owe much to those innovations developed for the court masque. *See also* **Christmas Pie; Epiphany; Feast of Fools.**

• MUMMING. The word derives from the German *Mumme* and the Greek *mommo* (both indicating "mask") and refers to masked street revels dating at least to the thirteenth century, the amateur participants of which were called "mummers." Their disguises, consisting of outlandish costumes, animal masks, and blackening of the face, led to other folk designations, all corruptions of the word "disguise," such as *guisers* and *guizards*, with further corruptions to "geese-dancing" in Scotland. Providing entertainment from house to house with song

Mummers — masqued revelers who performed folk plays and were often accused of mischief — existed in many countries, including Russia. Great Britain, Austria, and the United States, particularly in Pennsylvania. This engraving depicts a performance of the St. George and the Dragon play which also includes "Old Father Christmas." From Robert Chambers, ed., The Book of Days *(London and Edinburgh: Chambers, 1879).*

and dance, mummers sought money, food, and drink from their hosts. Their cavortings often included rowdy mischief, pranks, and sometimes crimes. Examples of the latter include the failed assassination attempt upon England's King Henry IV in 1400 under the guise of mummers and the rise in murders during the time of King Henry VIII using the same ruse.

It is believed that mumming derived from pre–Christian sources, such as the riotous masquerades of the Roman Saturnalia in December; agrarian ceremonies which symbolized the death of the old year and rebirth of the new, with perhaps the sacrifice of a mock king; and spring festivals, which celebrated the death of winter and the fertility of spring. As a parallel, the death and resurrection of a central character became prevalent in the so-called "mummers' plays" of England. These folk plays, performed primarily at Christmastime, arose probably during the seventeenth century, although written documentation about them did not appear until the close of the eighteenth century.

Mummers' plays generally incorporate subjects and characters from mythology or legends, and they can be classed as follows: hero-combat plays (by far the largest group), sword plays, and wooing plays. Of the hero-combat group, "The Play of St. George" remains the most popular, the legend of St. George (d. 303), patron saint of England, having acquired fame through Richard Johnson's *Famous History of the Seven Champions of Christendom* (1596). According to the allegorical legend, St. George thwarts the sacrifice of a Libyan king's daughter (the Church) by slaying her would-be devourer, a dragon (the Devil), then converts the kingdom to Christianity. In keeping with the oral tradition of all mummers' plays, however, there is no definitive St. George play; rather, there are a multitude of variations on dialogue and an odd assortment of characters that accrued over time, all built upon distortions of the St. George legend and interwoven around the pagan ceremonies mentioned above. Despite the variations, they revolve around the same basic plot: St. George, also known as Sir George, Prince George, or King George, introduces himself as a valiant knight and boasts of his former deeds, particularly having slain the dragon and rescued the "King of Egypt's daughter," whom he married. To this a Turkish knight (also known as "Slasher"), or perhaps even the dragon himself, issues a challenge. A mock battle leaves one combatant "dead" (it matters not which), whereupon a quack doctor arrives and, after boasting of his healing powers, restores the deceased to life. Should similar battles follow between St. George and the same or other heathen challengers, the victim is always resurrected with the doctor's assistance. At the conclusion, the players solicit money or food and drink.

Although the casts consisted overwhelmingly of men, mummers' plays sometimes included a feminine role. In the St. George play, she might be cast as the Presenter, a character who introduced the others; as Sabra, the King of Egypt's daughter; as St. Margaret, to whom Satan appeared in the form of a dragon; or simply as "Maiden." It is thought that the female role paralleled a mother goddess figure from pagan fertility rites. A female Presenter might preside at plays on other occasions such as All Souls' Day, Easter, and the Feast of St. George (April 23), but the character of Father Christmas became over time the most suitable Presenter for the Christmastime plays. Further analysis of mummers' plays and their variant characters may be found in Chambers' *The English Folk-Play* (1933).

Although mumming declined in England during the mid-nineteenth century, European immigrants had instituted mumming traditions earlier in North America; for example, the English brought mumming to Newfoundland during the seventeenth century, and the Swedes to the city of Philadelphia during the same period. The latter's celebrations centered around the new year, when masked revelers cavorted about, shouting with noise-makers and "shooting in the new year" with firearms. Observed through the American Revolution, this custom merged with the format of English mummers' plays and their trappings. English mumming also merged with the mythical Belsnickel or Pelsnickel, both derived from *Pelz Nicholas*, "Fur Nicholas," a demon who accompanied St. Nicholas and whom German immigrants ("Pennsylvania Dutch") introduced during the eighteenth century, to create the custom of "belsnickeling." Between Christmas and New Year's Day, belznickelers, clad in disguises or with blackened faces, tramped from house to house committing pranks and seeking treats in return for providing some comic entertainment. When Philadelphia banned Christmastime mumming in 1808 as a public nuisance, members of the working class continued to stage private masquerades on New Year's Day in lesser populated regions outside the city. In 1901, Bart H. McHugh, a Philadelphia theatrical producer and publicity agent, persuaded city officials to sponsor an annual New Year's Day Philadelphia Mummers' Parade. This event has continued to this day and is now a nationally known event consisting of competitions in four divisions: Comic, Fancy, String Band, and Fancy Brigade.

• NATIVITY PLAY. This presentation portrayed the birth of Jesus Christ and varied considerably in complexity. Precursors of these plays included the so-called liturgical dramas or tropes of the medieval Roman Catholic Church across Europe, the earliest of which arose during the tenth century in England as

A French scene from a mystery play, "Incarnation et Nativité de nostre saulveur et redempteur Jesuchrist," showing the arrival in Bethlehem. From Harper's New Monthly Magazine, *December 1888.*

tools for instructing the laity in biblical stories and principles. Brief and initially presented in Latin within the sanctuary, liturgical dramas elaborated upon particular sections of the mass with the clergy serving as sole actors. The earliest of these dramas focused at first upon the Easter story; later years saw the development of the *Pastores*, Christmas dramas regarding the annunciation to the shepherds. In the latter, a chorister posing as the herald angel sang the "Gloria in Excelcis" aloft as "shepherds" approached the altar. Following a brief dialogue with the attending "midwives," the latter drew back a curtain to reveal a statue of the Virgin and one of the Christ Child lying in a crib. Later dramas incorporated such subjects as the adoration of the Magi, the confrontation with King Herod the Great, Herod's rage, and the slaughter of the innocents. In the latter, bruised and "deceased" choirboys were deposited about the altar as "mothers" wailed their laments.

By the twelfth and thirteenth centuries, the Latin dialogue slowly waned in favor of English and Anglo-French vernacular, the latter a remnant of the Norman Conquest of 1066. With their growing complexity, the English liturgical plays gradually moved from the sanctuary to the church grounds, thence away altogether to the market places or other public arenas to be taken up by the trade guilds. In part this migration arose from the interjection of comedy and vulgarity into the dramas. As an example, Christmas dramas had developed prologues in which a series of Old Testament prophets proclaimed the coming Messiah. The sequence of Baalam, whose frightened, talking ass encounters an angel, provided such mirth that additional, boisterous and sacrilegious scenes later emerged to amuse the congregation. This, along with the Christmastime revelries surrounding the Boy-Bishop and the Feast of Fools of the era, contributed to the expulsion of liturgical dramas from the church.

With the establishment of the Feast of Corpus Christi (Body of Christ) by Pope Urban IV in 1264 (held on the Thursday after Trinity Sunday), it is generally believed that the liturgical dramas formerly performed in the church probably further evolved into elaborate "mystery plays," which comprehensively encompassed biblical stories from the creation to the final judgment. Along with the pomp and processions of Corpus Christi, trade guilds displayed their crafts through outdoor fairs and further cooperated to produce the cycles of religious plays regularly featured at this summer feast. According to one source, the mystery play acquired its designation from the guilds' "mastery" of crafts, and from the local pronunciation of "mastery" as "mystery." Because the guilds were responsible for furnishing appropriate sets and props, it was customary to assign certain segments or pageants from the plays to those guilds, the special crafts of which were most suited to the subjects at hand. Examples of such assignments regarding Nativity pageants can be seen from the York Cycle of England (see below): spicers, "Annunciation and Visitation"; pewterers and founders, "Joseph's Trouble About Mary"; tile thatchers, "Journey to Bethlehem"; chandlers, "Shepherds"; masons, "Coming of the Three Kings to Herod"; goldsmiths, "Adoration of the Magi"; grooms, "Flight into Egypt"; and girdlers and nailers, "Slaughter of the Innocents." The guilds were also responsible for stage construction, and in England particularly, these appeared as wagons for the individual pageants, which could be easily transported to the next station in the cycle. The actors were members of the laity or the guilds.

Probably the best known of the medieval mystery plays are four anonymous and essentially complete English manuscripts surviving from the fifteenth and sixteenth centuries. Named for the place of performance, they include the Wakefield (also known as Towneley, a family that once possessed the manuscript), consisting of 32 plays in the cycle; Chester with 24; York with 48; and "N. Town" or Coventry with 42. Though religious in theme, the plays interjected more comedy, farce, and other worldly sequences which, despite a certain dramatic license not in total compliance with Scripture, nevertheless served to illustrate the interaction of an imperfect human race with the divine. The Nativity pageants were no exception; among the notable examples of these are the two "Shepherds' Plays" of the Wakefield Cycle. Both cast shepherds as buffoons who rail against the aristocracy (the second play also weaves a stolen sheep into the plot), but the comedy abruptly ceases as the herald angel brings the tidings of good joy. Despite their elaborate complexity, some play cycles could be performed completely in one day, but most, not only in England but elsewhere in Europe, required several days. Between the fifteenth and sixteenth centuries in France, for example, mystery plays requiring up to forty days for a full performance were not uncommon.

Nativity plays elsewhere in Europe are believed to have evolved in much the same manner via early Latin liturgical dramas. The fourteenth century saw the development of two varieties of mystery plays in France: saints' plays, which revolved around the lives of saints, and passion plays. At first, the latter focused only upon the events of Passion Week (the final week of Christ's life); later they incorporated elements such as Christ's Nativity and childhood. Ranking as one of France's best-known passion plays, *Mystère de la Passion* (1450) by Arnoul Gréban incorporates Old Testament scenes as well as those from the life of Christ. In Germany, passion plays were identified from the thirteenth century onward, but vernacular Nativity plays were not as common and dated primarily from the fifteenth and sixteenth centuries. One exception is *St. Galler Kindheit Jesu* (*St. Gaul Childhood of Christ*) of 1330. Scholars believe that drama once thrived within the Eastern or Orthodox Church, yet the principal evidence is found in only three extant sources:

a group of Byzantine sermon plays from the ninth to eleventh centuries, focusing primarily upon the Annunciation to the Virgin, and two passion plays, both dating to the thirteenth century.

Nativity plays virtually disappeared simultaneously with the mystery plays following the Protestant Reformation and the Roman Catholic Church's opposition to the unsavory dialogue and sequences that occasionally appeared therein. In June of 1998, however, the University of Toronto sponsored a production of the complete York Cycle of mystery plays, the first production since the sixteenth century. Vestiges of mystery plays also survive in the *Herbergsuchen* ("Search for the Inn"), German and Austrian Advent plays which reenact the Holy Couple's search for shelter in Bethlehem with rebuffs from surly innkeepers; in *Las Posadas* ("The Lodgings") of Latin America and the American Southwest, a similar custom which Spanish missionaries instituted in the sixteenth century; and in children's Christmas pageants held annually in churches and schools throughout the world. *See also* **Boy-Bishop; Feast of Fools; Las Posadas.**

• PANTOMIMES. These art forms can be traced to the *pantomimus* (solo actor portraying characters via wordless gestures and masks, accompanied by music and a chorus) of ancient Greece and Rome, but the present term refers to traditional Christmastime entertainments developed in English theaters during the eighteenth century.

English pantomimes developed through the efforts of two men connected with London theaters: John Weaver, dancing master at Drury Lane Theatre, and John Rich, manager of Lincoln's Inn Fields Theatre, both of whom separately introduced the "harlequinade," a precursor of the modern pantomime. The harlequinade in turn derived from *commedia dell'arte* ("comedy of the profession"), an improvised comedy that arose in northern Italy during the sixteenth century. Utilizing masks, exaggerated gestures, music, and little dialogue, the *commedia* presented slapstick comedy situations through a series of stock character types, the most notable of which were "Pantalone" (English, "Pantaloon"), an aged, suspicious merchant; "Pulcinella," a cruel schemer; "Dottore" (English,

"Doctor"), a pedantic physician whose prescriptions could prove fatal; the "Captain," a cowardly braggart; "Columbine," a witty serving-wench; and two lowbrow clowns, the unscrupulous "Brighella" and the virtually amoral, greedy, and womanizing "Arlecchino" (English, "Harlequin").

The latter first appeared in French folk literature around 1100 as Herlekin, Hellequin, and later as Arlequin in the latter seventeenth century, when he appeared in the French fairground theaters. Because he had continued to maintain his diabolical reputation, he became the most popular and leading character in the *commedia* repertoire. Harlequin failed to gain popularity with his first appearance in an English play (John Day's *The Travailes of the Three English Brothers*, 1607), yet French *commedia dell'arte* performances in London prompted Rich and Weaver to construct a new entertainment around Harlequin and similar characters, hence the harlequinade.

Weaver first staged the harlequinades in short ballets at Drury Lane in 1716; then Rich (performing under the stage name of Lun) portrayed Harlequin at Lincoln's Inn Fields in his *Harlequin Executed* on December 26, 1717, a piece which Chambers' *The Book of Days* holds to be the first English pantomime. This type of Christmastime entertainment would become quite popular, and each production followed the pattern of opening with a serious story in mime taken from classic mythology, between the acts of which was interwoven a comedy segment (the harlequinade), which often consisted of the courtship between Harlequin and Columbine along with a number of special stage effects. This pattern continued until George Colman's *The Genius of Nonsense* (1780) replaced the mythological opening with a fairy tale as standard fare.

The nineteenth century also saw a number of changes: a decline of the harlequinade as the actor Joseph Grimaldi's creation of Joey the Clown shifted the comic emphasis away from Harlequin; the roles of the "dame" and the hero ("principal boy") were assumed, respectively, by cross-dressed men and women; and extravagant pantomimes featuring dialogue, music, and dance emerged as Christmastime theatrical attractions that focused upon fairy tales or other familiar stories such as *Cinderella* or *Aladdin*. Pantomimes continued into the twentieth century with acrobatics and slapstick humor interwoven around the fantasy story lines. Originally opening on Boxing Day, December 26, today the pantomime season runs a few weeks before Christmas until mid–January. *See also* **Boxing Day**.

Christmas Eve

(1986). Made-for-television drama which closely parallels an earlier television special, *The Gathering* (1977).

Suddenly faced with a terminal illness, wealthy New York widow Amanda Kingsley (Loretta Young) hires a private investigator, Morris Huffner (Ron Leibman), to locate her three adult grandchildren, who have been long estranged from their domineering, power-crazed, widower father, Andrew (Arthur Hill), chief executive of Kingsley International. With time uncertain, Amanda's one wish before she dies is that her grandchildren be reunited with their father by Christmas. While Huffner searches, Amanda and her faithful English butler, Maitland (Trevor Howard), trek into the slums, distributing coffee, sandwiches, cash, and good cheer to the city's poor and homeless, a nightly mission Amanda has performed for ages. She has come to know many of the destitute personally, and when the police try to haul away her friends, Amanda tries to stop them. She and Maitland are arrested, and she refuses to leave jail until Andrew arranges not only her bail but the others' as well. When "bag lady" Molly (Kate Reid) is terminally hospitalized in Bellevue, Amanda arranges her transfer to a private hospital, remains with her, then personally handles Molly's funeral arrangements.

A change in Amanda's will, bequeathing all 51 percent of her interest in Kingsley International to the homeless, finally prompts greedy Andrew to petition the courts to have him appointed as his mother's conservator. The court's decision is postponed until after the holidays.

Within a few days of Christmas, Huffner successfully locates the grandchildren: country music devotee Josh (Patrick Cassidy) in San Antonio, actress Melissa (Season Hubley) in Hollywood, and draft-dodger Harley (Wayne

Best) in Canada with his wife Nora (Amanda Hancox) and young son Adam (Richard Sole). Through Huffner, Amanda bids them all to return home for Christmas, withholding the principal reason. They make no commitments, but Amanda is not fazed; she has complete faith that her brood will return, and in anticipation of their arrival, she prepares a welcome-home party.

Late into the evening on Christmas Eve, just as she contemplates retiring, her grandchildren arrive *en masse*, which generates a profoundly emotional scene of tears, hugs, kisses, and profuse apologies on the part of the grandchildren for having neglected their grandmother. Even Andrew has softened. Withdrawing the petition against his mother, he first embraces little Adam, the grandson whom he has never seen, then his own children, and the family becomes one again.

With Charles Frank, Deborah Richter, Antony Parr. Written by Blanche Hanalis. Directed by Stuart Cooper. Color. Video N/A.

For her role in *Christmas Eve*, Loretta Young won a Golden Globe Award in 1987 for Best Performance by an Actress in a Mini-Series or Motion Picture for Television. The film was nominated that same year for a Golden Globe Award for Best Mini-Series or Motion Picture Made for Television. Rob Leibman and Trevor Howard also received Golden Globe Award nominations for Best Supporting Actor.

See also **The Gathering**.

Christmas Eve Lovefeast

See **Moravian Church**

Christmas Every Day

Classic short story by the American author William Dean Howells, first published in 1892.

As Christmas approaches, a little girl wonders what it would be like to experience the joys and fantasies of Christmas every day of the year. When she coaxes a story from her father, the wise gentleman delivers a moral in the form of a story-within-a-story, the subject of which is another little girl whose wish for a full year of Christmas is granted by the Christmas Fairy, and not just for her alone, but for everyone. People open presents each morning, but, because the next day will also be Christmas they must buy new presents daily. Because people sing carols and wish neighbors and passers-by "Merry Christmas" without end, they eventually become hoarse and lose their voices. Gifts, candy, and other holiday paraphernalia accumulate in homes and overflow into the streets from daily giving and receiving, and rampant poverty ensues as people exhaust their incomes and savings on gifts. In time all people come to despise Christmas, and the child, passionately regretting her wish, begs the Christmas Fairy to abolish the loathsome holiday altogether at the close of the term. Instead of that extreme, the fairy convinces her to accept the once-a-year Christmas that has always pleased humanity ever since Christmas began.

A 1986 made-for-television animated cartoon adaptation of the same title featured the voices of Stacy Q. Michaels, Brian Cummings, Miriam Flynn, Edie McClurg, Marla Frumkin, Dick Orkin. A CBS Television Production in Association with Orkin-Flaum Productions and Calabash Productions. Color. Half-hour. Video N/A.

A 1996 comedy adaptation of the same title for television starred Robert Hays, Bess Armstrong, Erik von Detten, Yvonne Zima, Robert Curtis-Brown, Robin Riker, Julia Whelan. Written by Stephen Alix, Nancey Silvers. Produced by Gary M. Goodman, Barry Rosen. Directed by Larry Peerce. MTM Enterprises, Inc., and The Family Channel. Color. Video N/A. For his role, Erik von Detten was nominated in 1997 for the Young Star Award for Best Performance by a Young Actor in a Television Movie.

William Dean Howells (1837–1920) served as editor for the *Atlantic Monthly* from 1871 to 1881. His works include literary criticisms and some thirty novels. *The Rise of Silas Lapham* (1885) is perhaps his most famous book.

Christmas Fern

See **Christmas Plants**

Christmas Flower

See **Christmas Plants**

Christmas for Cowboys

American country and western song writ-

ten in 1975 by Dallas native Steve Weisberg. At the time, Weisberg was a guitarist for singer John Denver, who was recording his Gold Record–winning *Rocky Mountain Christmas* album for RCA. This album comprised a mixture of established traditional and contemporary works as well as some of Denver's original pieces, such as "Aspenglow," "Please, Daddy (Don't Get Drunk on Christmas)," "A Baby Just Like You," "The Music Is You," "Perhaps Love," and "Dreamland Express."

Ordinarily Denver wrote his own material, but when the album was short one song, Weisberg offered "Christmas for Cowboys," which Denver included in the album. The album sold over 2 million copies, and the song became the top Christmas tune of 1975 (position 58 on the *Billboard Hot 100* chart).

While most people are enjoying traditional presents, football, eggnog, and Christmas parades in the city, according to the nostalgic lyrics, nature offers the cowboy gifts of the sky and open range, with the stars serving as Christmas lights.

Weisberg's other compositions include "Hitchhiker," "It's Up to You," "Love Is Everywhere," "Our Lady of Santa Fe," and "Pickin' the Sun Down."

The Christmas Gift

(1986). Made-for-television drama.

Having lost his wife a year ago at Christmas, New York City architect George Billings (John Denver) and his young daughter Alex (Gennie James) seek a holiday retreat in Georgetown, Colorado, a remote village in the Rockies, where everyone, regardless of age, truly believes in Santa Claus. George's employer, Thomas Renfield (Edward Winter), a land developer, has ordered him to size up the location for a new recreational development project while posing as a tourist.

George and Alex arrive a few days before Christmas on "Letter Day," a city-wide holiday in which everyone convenes at the post office with their letters addressed to Santa. Initially puzzled at such an eccentric community, George, through the hospitality of caring people such as Susan McMillan (Jane Kaczmarek), Georgetown's postmaster, cabby-innkeeper Bud Sawyer (Pat Corley), and his old-maid sister

Henrietta (Mary Wickes), soon learns why the town is so devoted to Santa. At the lighting of the community Christmas tree, citizens recall the legend of the Christmas miracle, now 100 years old, that led Georgetown into prosperity.

Caught in a blizzard (says the legend) while crossing the Rockies, their pioneer forefathers faced starvation. On Christmas Eve, when an old, white-bearded stranger begged food from they who had none to spare, a compassionate boy managed to find something for the man. The stranger promised to reward the boy one hundred fold, and on Christmas morning, each wagon was found filled with food, blankets, and new toys for the children. To them, the stranger had been Santa Claus himself. Now that a century has passed, the legend will soon repeat itself, for another miracle is about to save Georgetown again.

Charmed by the people's friendliness and warmth, and especially his and Alex's attraction to Susan, George, knowing that Renfield's project will forever disrupt the town, attempts to steer Renfield to alternate locations, but his employer is relentless. The bank having foreclosed on the ranch of Jake Richards (Kurtwood Smith), Renfield desires the property and reveals his plan to bring "progress" at a town meeting. Although George protests and is fired, Susan and Alex initially believe that he has betrayed the town. When Alex runs away, Jake is instrumental in finding her, which prompts George to make a final plea at the church's Christmas Eve pageant. To stop Renfield, at George's suggestion, the citizens pull together and pay off Jake's mortgage, then congregate at his ranch for a candlelight ceremony just as Jake and his children are about to leave. With no property, Renfield is defeated, and the miracle of Christmas again saves Georgetown.

With James Callahan, Anne Haney, Harvey Vernon. Written by Christopher Grabenstein, David Venable, Ronald Venable. Produced by David A. Rosemont. Directed by Michael Pressman. Color. Video N/A.

Christmas in Bedrock
See **The Flintstones**

Christmas in Connecticut
(1945). Motion picture comedy-romance. Elizabeth Lane (Barbara Stanwyck) is a highly successful writer whose magazine articles about country living, child rearing, and cuisine on her farm in Connecticut are in great demand. Unknown to her publisher, Alexander Yardley (Sydney Greenstreet), are the following facts: Elizabeth is single, lives in New York, receives her recipes from local restaurateur Felix Bassenack (S. Z. Sakall), and doesn't know a toaster from a coffee pot.

A sticky situation arises when Yardley wants Elizabeth to entertain war hero Jefferson Jones (Dennis Morgan) at her farm over the Christmas holidays. Even worse, Yardley plans to come along and see Elizabeth's Christmas decorations, husband, and child for himself. By coincidence, her suitor, John Sloan (Reginald Gardiner), owns a farm in Connecticut, and Elizabeth agrees to marry him at the farm to save her job. With Felix in tow for the cooking, all that's left in the ruse is to find a baby, so Elizabeth commandeers an infant that John's housekeeper Norah (Una O'Connor) keeps for a neighbor during the day.

They maintain the deception with difficulty — a difficulty increased by the attraction between Elizabeth and Jeff — until Christmas night, when everyone attends a dance in honor of Jeff, and Yardley becomes suspicious when Jeff dances too closely with Elizabeth.

Finally the ruse comes apart when Yardley sees the neighbor coming for her baby at the farm later that night and believes she is kidnapping Elizabeth's child. Yardley calls the state police and the press. Many explanations are in order, and Elizabeth and Jeff are thrilled to learn that each is neither married nor engaged to anyone else (there was never any time for that farm wedding), for they have fallen in love with each other during Christmas in Connecticut.

With Robert Shayne, Frank Jenks, Joyce Compton, Dick Elliott. Written by Lionel Houser, Adele Commandini. Produced by William Jacobs. Directed by Peter Godfrey. Warner Bros. Pictures. MGM/UA Home Video. B & W. 101 min.

This film was remade into a 1992 television movie of the same title, starring Dyan Cannon, Kris Kristofferson, Tony Curtis. Written by Aileen Hamilton, Lionel Houser, Adele Commandini. Produced by Cyrus Yavneh.

Directed by Arnold Schwarzenegger. Turner Pictures. Turner Home Video. Color. 93 min. In 1993 this version received a nomination for a Young Artist Award, Best Young Actor in a Cable Movie (Jimmy Workman).

Christmas in Killarney

Song written in 1950 by Irish-Americans John Redmond, James Cavanaugh, and Frank Weldon. With a melody in the style of an Irish jig, the lyrics claim that there is no happier Christmas on earth than that which is experienced in Killarney, a town in southwestern Ireland, "with all of the folks at home." Irish tenor Dennis Day, noted for his appearances on the radio-television hit program *The Jack Benny Show*, first introduced this song in 1951 with a successful recording on the RCA Victor label.

In addition to their separate contributions on other works, Redmond and Cavanaugh collaborated on such titles as "The Gaucho Serenade" (1940) and "Crosstown" (1940), together with Nat Simon. Cavanaugh and Weldon also paired for "I Like Mountain Music" (1933).

Christmas in Olden Times
See **Heap on More Wood**

Christmas Is

(Song). American song written in 1966 by Canadian-American Percy Faith (music) and Spence Maxwell (lyrics). This is also the title of a made-for-television animated cartoon (see entry below).

Recalling certain special items that are necessary for a meaningful Christmas, the song lyrics list sleigh bells, sharing, holly, caring, children with insomnia, fond memories, the warmth of carols, and the brightness of the very holiday when wishes really do come true. The song has been performed by numerous artists. Two of the first vocal recordings were by Johnny Mathis (1971) for Columbia and Tom T. Hall (1979) for RCA.

Faith, a composer, conductor, and arranger, assembled an orchestra that was respected for its renditions of popular favorites, the best-known of which was "Theme from *A Summer Place*" (1960). A prodigious lyricist, Maxwell collaborated with Faith on a few pieces, such as "Waitin' Round the Bend" and "Quiet Day."

Christmas Is

(Television cartoon, 1970). Underwritten by the International Lutheran Layman's League, this animated cartoon stressed the true meaning of Christmas by picturing young Benji and his dog Waldo transported back in time to witness the Nativity. Voices: Richard Susceno, Hans Conried, Don Messick, Colleen Collins, June Foray, Jerry Hausner, Vic Perrin. A Screen Images Production for Lutheran Television. Color. Half-hour. Video N/A.

Christmas Lilies of the Field

(1979). Made-for-television sequel to the motion picture *Lilies of the Field* (1963), in which Sidney Poitier starred as Homer Smith, a construction worker whom a group of East German nuns persuaded to build a church for them in the American Southwest. In the sequel, the nuns, led by Mother Maria (Maria Schell), run a makeshift orphanage and persuade Homer (Billy Dee Williams) to build a dormitory for the children by late December. Otherwise, a social worker will place the children in foster homes.

When the government rejects the nuns' request for financial aid and a local charity committee refuses its support because one orphan, Felicia (Julie Delgado), is a pregnant, unwed teenager, the orphans face immediate placement. Miraculously, a group of Pima Indians volunteer their labor, Homer acquires building materials from a dismantled charity bazaar, and the dormitory is finished by Christmastime.

On Christmas Eve, as the children prepare for a Nativity pageant, Felicia delivers her son, whom she names Jesus. Attired as shepherds, angels, and Wise Men, the children gather around Felicia and her child. Featured songs: "Amen" and the Christmas spiritual "Children, Go Where I Send Thee."

With Fay Hauser, Lisa Mann, Hanna Hertelendy, Judith Piquet, Donna Johnson, Bob Hastings, Fred Hart, Sam Di Bello. Written by John McGreevey, Ralph Nelson. Produced by Jack Reddish, Toby Martin. Directed by Ralph Nelson. Rainbow Productions. HPI Home Video. Color.

See also **Children, Go Where I Send Thee.**

Christmas Masses

Series of three masses held on Christmas

Day by the Roman Catholic Church, occurring at midnight on Christmas Eve (Midnight Mass), at dawn on Christmas Day (Dawn Mass), and later that same day (Christmas Day Mass). Respectively, they are also known as the "Angels' Mass," "Shepherds' Mass," and "Mass of the Divine Word," based on the Gospel text used for each service. They also symbolize the "triple birth" of Christ in eternity, in time, and in the soul. Although Christmas is currently the only time when the Catholic Church holds three masses, the Church had conducted a triple mass formerly on Easter, Whitsun, and the Transfiguration, as documented in the year 845 by Ildefonsus, a Spanish bishop.

The exact year of the inauguration of the triple Christmas mass is unknown, sources varying between the fifth and seventh centuries. Rome initially celebrated these masses in different churches around the city, with the pope conducting Midnight Mass in the chapel of the Church of Santa Maria Maggiore (St. Mary Major). This church on the Esquiline Hill was commissioned by the Virgin Mary, who supposedly appeared to Pope Liberius I in a dream in 352 and commanded that he build the church where he found snow. Liberius noted snow in August of that year, construction commenced, and the basilica, patterned after the Basilica and Grotto of the Nativity in Bethlehem, was completed around 440 under the auspices of Pope Sixtus III. Currently enshrined there are five relics, pieces of boards of sycamore wood believed to have supported Jesus' original stone manger or crib (popular theory holds that not only was Jesus born in a cave that doubled as a stable, but His crib was of stone). According to *The Catholic Encyclopedia*, Pope Theodore (reigned 640–649) probably acquired these relics, for which St. Mary Major was initially known as *Santa Maria ad Praesepe* (St. Mary to the Crib). These relics are exposed to the public annually on Christmas Eve.

The first of the three masses was held at midnight on the belief that Christ was born at that hour. Early evidence for this belief dates to a fourth-century Latin hymn, "Quando noctis medium" ("When in the Middle of the Night"), and the belief was perpetuated by Saint Elizabeth of Hungary (1207–1231), who allegedly performed a number of miracles.

The Dawn Mass was celebrated in St. Anastasia's Church on the Palatine Hill in Rome. According to legend, Anastasia, a fourth-century Sirmian martyr, was beheaded on Christmas Day during the reign of Diocletian, after which her remains were interred in Constantinople in the Anastasis Basilica ("Anastasis," Greek for "Resurrection"). Because the Palatine church, patterned after the Anastasis Basilica in Jerusalem, also originally bore the name of "Anastasis," Rome substituted the name of St. Anastasia for Anastasis and initially celebrated this second mass in honor of the legendary saint. Currently, the Dawn Mass replaces that for St. Anastasia.

The Christmas Day Mass was, and still is, celebrated in St. Peter's Basilica in Rome, as are the other two masses. Televised broadcasts of the Midnight Mass from St. Peter's have been an annual event since 1948.

Not only do Roman Catholic churches around the world hold the triple mass today, but many Protestant churches often hold comparable services on Christmas Eve (often terminating at midnight) and on Christmas Day.

See also **Nativity**; **Nativity Scene**.

A Christmas Memory

Classic autobiographical short story written in 1956 by American author Truman Capote. First appearing in *Mademoiselle* magazine, the story recalls a special Christmas during the years when Capote lived with a family of distant elderly cousins in rural Alabama until the age of ten. Capote developed a close relationship with one of those cousins, Miss Sook Faulk, who is known only as "my friend" in the story and whom he describes as being "still a child," simple and innocent. She, in turn, refers to seven-year-old Capote as "Buddy," the name of a childhood friend who died in 1880. This cousin is shy with everyone except strangers, who seem to be not only her truest friends, but Buddy's as well, for the other members of their household have little to do with either of them except to preach and scold.

The story opens late in November, when Buddy's cousin heralds the coming of Christmas by announcing, "It's fruitcake weather!" Having held rummage sales and done odd jobs through the year, she and Buddy scrape together enough cash to buy ingredients for baking thirty fruitcakes, the chief ingredient of which is bootleg whiskey purchased from a giant Indian named HaHa Jones. The cakes are presents for their friends and acquaintances, and one is even mailed to President Franklin D. Roosevelt. Returning from a hike in the woods with their Christmas tree (which is twice as tall as a boy), the two pass a traveler, who, remarking that they can always get another one, offers to buy the tree. The cousin's reply: "There's never two of anything."

Their simple decorations consist of homemade paper drawings of cats, fish, apples, watermelons, and tinfoil angels, hung on the tree with paper clips. Their gifts to each other are homemade kites which they fly together on Christmas Day in a pasture. Frustrated because she cannot afford a bicycle for Buddy, the cousin states that what's worse than not being able to have something you want is not being able to give somebody something you want them to have.

This is Buddy's happiest Christmas and the last with his friend. Shipped off to military school, he corresponds with her a few years and receives a fruitcake each November, until that morning when instinct alerts him that she will no longer arise and proclaim that it's fruitcake weather.

Miss Faulk died in 1938 while Capote was attending a military school in New York State. *Truman Capote's "A Christmas Memory"* (1966) was an adaptation for television starring Geraldine Page and Donnie Melvin with narration by Capote. The special won a Peabody Award. Video N/A.

A Christmas Memory (1997), another television adaptation, starred Patty Duke and Eric Lloyd. Written by Duane Poole. Produced by John Philip Dayton, Glenn Jordan. Directed by Glenn Jordan. Hallmark Entertainment and Holiday Productions. Color. Video N/A.

See also **One Christmas.**

Christmas New Style

See **Christmas Old Style, Christmas New Style**

Christmas Old Style, Christmas New Style

Terms respectively applied to Christmas observed on the old Julian calendar, authorized by Julius Caesar in 44 B.C., as opposed to the holiday observed on the present Gregorian calendar, developed by Pope Gregory XIII in 1582. Because of retrograde inaccuracies in the Julian calendar, which provided for a "leap" year every fourth year, the year was actually some 11 minutes and 14 seconds longer than the solar year, and important dates such as equinoxes and church feasts gradually fell out of season. By 1582, the vernal equinox occurred on March 11 instead of March 21. The Gregorian calendar corrected this error by dropping ten days from the calendar, retaining every fourth year as a leap year, and establishing every century divisible by 400 also as a leap year. Thus December 25 on the Gregorian or "New Style" calendar was January 4 on the Julian or "Old Style" calendar. Whereas most of central Europe's Roman Catholic nations had adopted the new calendar by the end of the sixteenth century, Protestant nations resisted for some one hundred years, the first changes occurring around 1600 as Scotland made the conversion. Eastern Europe converted in the early 1920s with Greece converting in 1923, the last European country to do so.

By 1752, when England adopted the Gregorian calendar, the difference between the two calendars had increased to eleven days, and an event from Glastonbury helped to establish the term "Christmas Old Style." For years, that community had traditionally gathered on Christmas Eve to witness the annual blooming of the Glastonbury Thorn, said plant allegedly having sprung from the staff of Joseph of Arimathea. When the thorn failed to bloom on Christmas Eve, 1752, by the new calendar, many citizens refused to observe Christmas until it bloomed eleven days later on January 4 by the old calendar, and this latter Christmas was dubbed "Christmas Old Style" or "Old Christmas," with the earlier date termed "Christmas New Style" or "New Christmas." For some 200 years, rural England observed "Christmas Old Style" on January 5 (January 6 after 1800). By the end of the twentieth century, the lapse had increased to thirteen days.

Most countries following the Eastern Orthodox faith adhere to the Julian calendar for ecclesiastical events but have adopted the

Gregorian calendar for civil purposes. With thirteen days' difference in the twentieth century between the two calendars, Eastern Orthodox Christmas is observed on January 7, "Christmas Old Style." Most Armenian Orthodox churches follow the Gregorian calendar but still observe Christmas on January 6. The exception is the Armenian Church in Jerusalem, which adheres to January 6 by the Julian calendar. Accordingly, their Christmas corresponds to January 19 on the Gregorian calendar.

See also **Armenia**; **Glastonbury Thorn**; **Epiphany**.

Christmas Orchid
See **Christmas Plants**

Christmas Pageant
See **Christmas Drama**

Christmas Pie

Also known as mince pie and mincemeat pie. This dish originated in medieval England following the Crusades, when returning knights introduced eastern spices to their land. Along with the spices, the ingredients

Illustrator Dan Beard drew "Ghosts from a Christmas Pie" for the December 18, 1888, issue of Harper's Young People. *It warns of the effects of eating too much Christmas pie on a little boy. Nursery rhyme characters, including Bo Peep and Jack and Jill, visit the boy's dream, along with Mother Goose and Santa.*

Printed label for a jar of minced pie meat. Monroe's Patent, dated October 12, 1869, was for the meat not the container.

included minced bits of meat from a host of game birds and other hunted animals, apples, raisins, sugar, suet, and molasses.

Mince pies were popular at elaborate court banquets of the Middle Ages, which often featured excessively bountiful tables. Probably the largest mince pie of that era was described as measuring nine feet in diameter, weighing 165 pounds, and containing two bushels of flour, twenty pounds of butter, four geese, two rabbits, four ducks, two woodcocks, six snipes, four partridges, two bovine tongues, two curlews, six pigeons, and seven blackbirds.

It was fashionable at Chrismastime to

bake a mince pie in the form of a manger topped with an image of the Christ Child fashioned from dough, for the spices and sweetmeats were held as symbols of the Magi's gifts. The Puritans, not only in England but also in the American colonies, strenuously objected to these pies and outlawed them under the Commonwealth of Oliver Cromwell, because they considered such images to be idolatrous abominations linked with Roman Catholicism. This sentiment eventually contributed to the modification of mince pies to circular forms divested of any religious ties.

It is said that when anti–Catholic King Henry VIII commenced phasing out England's monasteries in 1532 and seizing their properties, Richard Whiting, the abbot of Glastonbury Abbey, secretly attempted to curb the king's greed by sending him a Christmas pie wherein were hidden the deeds to several of the abbey's choicest estates. Whiting sent his "gift" via his servant, a Thomas Horner, who opened the pie and stole one or more of the deeds for himself. Horner's theft was immortalized in the well-known children's nursery rhyme "Little Jack Horner" which altered Horner's first name and in which the extracted "plum" represented the stolen deed. Despite Whiting's efforts, Henry VIII hanged him in 1539 for treason and added Glastonbury Abbey to his conquests.

Christmas Place Names

A number of cities or regions throughout the United States and its possessions are named for the Christmas season. The most frequently occurring name is "Bethlehem" or a variant thereof, which is found in twenty states: Connecticut, Florida, Georgia, Illinois, Indiana, Iowa, Kentucky, Maryland, Mississippi, Missouri, New Hampshire, New Jersey, New York, North Carolina, Ohio, Pennsylvania, Tennessee, Texas, West Virginia, and Virginia (Bethlehem Fork).

"Christmas" is the second most frequently occurring name, found in ten states: Alabama (Christmas Landing), Arizona, Florida, Maine (Christmas Cove), Michigan, Minnesota (Christmas Lake in Scott County), Mississippi, Oregon (Christmas Valley), Tennessee, and Utah (Christmas City). The citizens of Christ-

A collectible Christmas cover mailed from Santa Claus, Indiana, and postmarked December 25, 1948.

mas, Florida, keep a community Christmas tree decorated the year round.

"St. Nicholas" identifies cities in Florida, Michigan, Minnesota, and Pennsylvania; "Santa Claus" is found in Georgia and Indiana; "Santa" is located in Idaho. Santa Claus, Indiana, originally acquired its name of "Santaclause" on Christmas Eve, 1882, but changed it to its present form in 1928. The city sports a Santa Claus Theme Park with a 23-foot statue of the saint, and children may write to Santa at his "summer home" there and receive a personal reply.

Only one village in a U.S. possession bears a Christmas-related name: Bethlehem Old Work, Virgin Islands.

Christmas Plants

A listing of several plants that either incorporate "Christmas" into their common names, possess legendary holiday significance, or bloom at Christmastime. Major plants such as mistletoe and poinsettia are discussed as separate entries. Holly and ivy are discussed with the carol "The Holly and the Ivy."

• CHRISTMAS BELL. Two species native to Australia. *Blandifordia grandiflora* is a tufted plant with grass-like leaves and flower spikes having some ten bell-like flowers that vary from yellow to red with yellow tips. *Blandifordia nobilis* is similar but smaller; the flowers are cylindrical and always red with yellow tips.

• CHRISTMAS BERRY (*Heteromeles arbutifolia*). Toyon, an evergreen, rosaceous shrub or tree reaching 6 to 10 feet in height, forming a round crown with clusters of small, white flowers in terminal clusters, bright red berries,

An engraving of a Christmas Rose (Helleborus niger) *from a nineteenth century botanical.*

Another type of "Christmas Rose": This 1910 German craft how-to shows "Christrosen" blooms made of cut folded paper, then stuck on a rosemary sprig. From Berta Wegner-Bell, Herzblättchens Beitvertreib *(Berlin: Fleming, 1910).*

and elliptical leaves with finely dentate borders. Native to California and northern Mexico. Also known as California Holly.

• CHRISTMAS BUSH. Three species native to Australia. *Prostanthera lasianthos* exists as a shrub or small tree with green, fragrant foliage and small white, pink, or mauve flowers arranged in clusters. *Ceratopetalum gummiferum* is a shrub with light green, trifoliolate leaves and lance-like, tooth leaflets. Terminal sprays of white, stellate flowers yield red, swollen calyces. *Bursaria spinosa* is a thorny shrub with dark green, obovate, shiny leaves and masses of white flowers yielding brown fruits.

• CHRISTMAS CACTUS (*Schlumbergera brigesii*). Also known as crab cactus, a Central American and Brazilian true cactus blooming in December with flat, segmented stems rounded and scalloped at the margins. The flowers at the extremes of the stems are picturesque in shades of red, white, and orange.

• CHRISTMAS FERN (*Polystichum acrosti-*

choides). A clump-forming evergreen native to North America, growing 2 to 4 feet in height with variable spread and with fine leaves.

• CHRISTMAS FLOWER (*Helleborus viridis*). Green hellebore, a Eurasian perennial evergreen, the yellow flowers of which contain five large, petal-like sepals and eight to ten inconspicuous, tubular petals, blooming in late winter or early spring.

• CHRISTMAS ORCHID (*Calanthe triplicata*). An evergreen terrestrial orchid with soft, obovate leaves and white flowers on a spike. Native to Australia.

• CHRISTMAS ROSE (*Helleborus niger*). Black hellebore, also a Eurasian perennial evergreen. Bears large, white flowers in midwinter to early spring. According to legend, Madalon, a little shepherd girl, tended her flock as the three Wise Men passed by on their way to Bethlehem with gifts for the Christ Child. Desiring to present a gift but too poor to do so, Madalon wept, whereupon an angel appeared and brushed away the snow from the ground. Revealed was a beautiful white, pink-tipped flower, the Christmas rose, which Madalon carried to Bethlehem. In another version, the angel initially revealed only solid white flowers. Madalon gathered them for the Christ Child, and where He touched them, there remained small tips of pink.

• DESERT CHRISTMAS CACTUS (*Opuntia leptocaulis*). A bush growing 3 to 6 feet high with numerous tangled, reddish, spiny branches and quarter-inch stems. A long spine up to two inches grows from each cluster of bristles. Flowers of greenish-yellow bloom up to one inch wide on the stems in the late spring, while bright red, one-half-inch-long rounded fruits remain during the winter. Native to the desert American southwest and northern Mexico.

• LAUREL (Bay, *Laurus nobilis*, not to be confused with the unrelated mountain laurel). A large evergreen shrub growing to heights of 25 to 60 feet, with small, yellow flowers in clusters and broad, aromatic leaves and black berries, native to the Mediterranean region. Its leaves are primarily used for seasoning in cooking; its oil is an essence of perfumes and a topical medicinal. Its connection to Christmas derives from pre–Christian times, when, as the symbol of victory, crowns and wreaths of laurel were bestowed upon heroes and poets. During winter solstice festivals, such wreaths decorated statues of gods such as Apollo, to whom laurel was sacred. When Christmas Christianized pagan traditions, laurel symbolized the victory of Christ over death and evil.

• LAVENDER (*Lavandula angustifolia*). The common variant is a Mediterranean, evergreen shrub of the mint family with narrow leaves and small, pale purple flowers. Its aromatic oil is used in the manufacture of perfume, toilet water, aromatic vinegar, and clothes sachets. According to legend, the virgin Mary dried the Christ Child's garments by spreading them on a bed of common lavender, which supposedly thus acquired its sweet scent.

• PENNYROYAL (*Mentha pulegium*). A perennial herb of the mint family, which yields an aromatic oil used in potpourri, cosmetics, and insect repellents. Native to southern Europe and western Asia, it produces clusters of small, purple flowers. According to legend, the

The evergreen lavender plant is said to have been used by Mary to scent the Christ Child's clothes. From an unidentified late nineteenth century herbal.

manger was lined in part with pennyroyal, which bloomed at the very hour that Christ was born.

• ROSEMARY (*Rosmarinus officinalis*). An aromatic, evergreen shrub of the mint family, the linear leaves of which yield an oil used in seasoning, liniments, and perfumes. The common name derives from the Virgin Mary. Native to the Mediterranean region, rosemary produces small blue flowers in the spring. During the Middle Ages, because rosemary supposedly repelled evil spirits, it was spread on the floor at Christmastime, the aroma pervading the home as people walked on it. According to folklore, anyone breathing its fragrance on Christmas Eve would receive happiness during the coming year. The aroma and blue flowers are the subject of legend, that during the Holy Family's flight into Egypt, when Mary washed the Christ Child's garments and spread them on a rosemary branch to dry, the flowers, initially white, turned blue (the traditional color associated with the Virgin) and became aromatic. A variation states that Mary's blue cloak imparted the color to the flowers when she hung it on a rosemary branch. Another legend holds that on January 5, "Christmas Eve Old Style," rosemary blooms out of season for Christmas. *See* **Christmas Old Style, Christmas New Style.**

• WESTERN AUSTRALIAN CHRISTMAS TREE (*Nuytsia floribunda*). Considered to be a Christmas tree and a mistletoe, this evergreen tree grows over 30 feet in height with clusters of orange, golden flowers blooming in midsummer. The plant is parasitic, drawing its nourishment from other tree roots. It is native to western Australia.

• WILD THYME (*Thymus serpyllum*). A ubiquitous shrub of the mint family. Its creeping stem produces many tuft-forming branches with low, dense, oval leaves and purple flowers arranged in whorls, united in a head. Now used as a seasoning and to add aroma to potpourri, its pungent oil once was used as an antiseptic and was burned as incense. According to legend, wild thyme formed the Virgin Mary's bedding when she gave birth to Jesus.

Christmas Play
See **Christmas Drama**

Christmas Present
See **A Christmas Carol** (FILM AND TELEVISION VERSIONS)

Christmas Rose
See **Christmas Plants**

Christmas Seals
Decorative stamps issued each Christmas by various charitable organizations. These stamps encourage donations toward research in the fight against lung diseases.

Christmas Seals originated in Denmark in 1903 when postal worker Einar Holbøll, prompted by large numbers of children dying from tuberculosis (TB), initiated a fund-raising plan for building more TB sanitariums through the sale of special postage stamps, which received support from King Christian IX

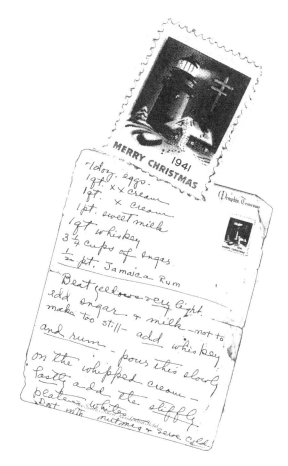

Affixed as decoration to a hastily scribbled recipe for eggnog is a 1941 Christmas Seal, showing a lighthouse in Maine and the double-barred Cross of Lorraine (not a telegraph pole, as some have supposed). Collection of Mary Mac & Robert D. Franklin.

at the time. Called "Christmas Seals," the first of these stamps, bearing the likeness of King Christian's wife, Queen Louise, was marketed in 1904 at Christmastime. They were designed as added decorations for Christmas cards. The stamps sold at one cent each that first year, and over four million were sold, which generated some $18,000 for the cause.

The American Red Cross became involved in the project by 1907 through the promotional efforts of Danish immigrant Jacob Riis, a New York City journalist. Emily Bissell, Delaware state secretary for the Red Cross, designed the first seals in the United States in December of that same year, and by 1908, Christmas Seals were a national entity. In 1910, the National Tuberculosis Association (now the American

Lung Association) assumed sponsorship. Originally the American seals bore the familiar Red Cross emblem, but in 1920, the double-barred cross, derived from the Lorraine Cross, became the new emblem.

In memory of Holbøll's contribution to mankind, his portrait appeared on the Danish seal in 1927, the year of his death. Currently, 45 countries have adopted the Christmas campaign.

The Christmas Song

Popular American song written in 1946 by well-known nightclub, radio, and television singer Mel Torme ("The Velvet Fog") from Chicago and Robert Wells Levinson (known only by his first two names) from Washington State, a producer of nightclub acts, motion picture scores, and television specials.

The song originated when Robert Wells, watching his mother stuff a holiday turkey with chestnuts, was inspired to compile a list of everything that made the season joyful, in addition to roasting chestnuts: Jack Frost's nip, carols sung by a choir, the aroma of holiday cuisine, mistletoe, and wide-eyed children waiting for Santa's visit. Torme created the melody, and his 1946 recording was successful, although it did not make the pop charts.

The song, also known by its first line, "Chestnuts Roasting on an Open Fire," did not achieve true fame until Nat "King" Cole's recording on the Capitol label was released in the same year. Cole's rendition, now a perennial classic, sold at least one million copies. A later recording of "The Christmas Song" by Herb Alpert on the A & M label became the top Christmas song for 1968 (position 1 on the *Billboard Christmas Singles* chart).

Of the 25 most frequently performed Christmas songs of the twentieth century listed by the American Society of Composers, Authors and Publishers (ASCAP), "The Christmas Song" is ranked number 3.

Christmas Stamps

On Christmas Day, 1898, to commemorate the inauguration of its penny postal system, Canada issued the world's first Christmas stamp, inscribed with "Xmas 1898." Since that time, a number of countries around the world have adopted the custom of printing special postage stamps for the holidays, many with elaborate designs or reproductions of classic works of Christmas art. Great Britain first produced Christmas "aerogrammes" in 1965, then followed with a Christmas theme on its postage stamps in 1966. The United States Postal Service (USPS) issued its first Christmas stamp in 1962, and from 1966 has issued a "traditional" (often religious) line depicting a classic work of Christmas art with the caption "Christmas." Its "contemporary" (secular) line, often with captions such as "Season's Greetings," "Greetings," "Merry Christmas," and sometimes "Christmas," dates from 1962.

The following list briefly describes the images found on those Christmas stamps issued by the USPS from 1962 to 2000 with their denominations.

1962 (4 cents). Wreath and two candles.

1963 (5 cents). National Christmas tree with White House in background.

1964 (5 cents). Four stamps, each depicting a different holiday plant: holly, mistletoe, poinsettia, sprig of conifer.

1965 (5 cents). Angel with trumpet.

1966 (5 cents). "Madonna and Child" by Hans Memling.

1967 (5 cents). "Madonna and Child" by Hans Memling.

1968 (6 cents). Detail of the angel Gabriel from "The Annunciation" by Jan van Eyck.

1969 (6 cents). Winter Sunday scene in Norway, Maine.

1970 (6 cents). Five stamps: "The Nativity" by Lorenzo Lotto; the other four each depict a different antique toy: tin and cast-iron locomotive, toy horse on wheels, mechanical tricycle, doll carriage.

1971 (8 cents). Two stamps: "Adoration of the Shepherds" by Giorgione; a partridge in a pear tree with the phrase "On the first day of Christmas my true love gave to me."

1972 (8 cents). Two stamps: detail of angels from "Mary, Queen of Heaven" by the Master of the St. Lucy Legend; Santa Claus with the phrase "'Twas the Night before Christmas."

1973 (8 cents). Two stamps: small Cowper "Madonna and Child" by Raphael; a Christmas tree in needlepoint.

1974 (10 cents). Three stamps: detail of angel from Perussis Altarpiece; "The Road — Winter" by Currier and Ives; dove weather

A triptych of Greek Christmas stamps from 1974 shows the Holy Family's flight into Egypt in color on a gold background.

vane atop George Washington's home, Mount Vernon, with phrase "Peace on Earth."

1975 (10 cents). Two stamps: "Madonna and Child" by Domenico Ghirlandaio; 1878 Christmas card designed by Louis Prang showing a cherub suspended from a holly-clad bell, captioned with "Merry Christmas."

1976 (13 cents). Two stamps: "Nativity" by John Singleton Copley; "Winter Pastime" by Nathaniel Currier.

1977 (13 cents). Two stamps: George Washington kneeling in prayer at Valley Forge; open, rural mailbox stuffed with holiday packages.

1978 (15 cents). Two stamps: "Madonna and Child with Cherubim" by Andrea della Robbia; child on hobby horse with Christmas tree background.

1979 (15 cents). Two stamps: "Virgin and Child with Cherubim" by Gerard David; Santa Claus Christmas tree ornament.

1980 (15 cents). Two stamps: "Madonna and Child" from the Epiphany window, Washington Cathedral; window sill with wreath and toys.

1981 (20 cents). Two stamps: "Madonna and Child" by Botticelli; felt bear on sleigh with "Season's Greetings."

1982 (20 cents). Five stamps: "Madonna and Child" by Tiepolo; children sledding; children building snowman; children ice skating; children trimming Christmas tree outdoors (the latter four captioned with "Season's Greetings"). *(13 cents).* Puppy and kitten in snow.

1983 (20 cents). Two stamps: Niccolini-Cowper "Madonna and Child" by Raphael; Santa Claus with "Season's Greetings."

1984 (20 cents). Two stamps: "Madonna

Three very colorful British Christmas stamps from 1969. All show a gold silhouette of Queen Elizabeth II. They have stylized depictions of three shepherds, a sheep, and the Star of Bethlehem; the three Magi in richly embroidered robes; and an angel bearing a star disk.

and Child" by Fra Filippo Lippi; child's drawing of Santa Claus with "Season's Greetings."

1985 (22 cents). Two stamps: Genoa "Madonna and Child" by Luca della Robbia; poinsettias with "Season's Greetings."

1986 (22 cents). Two stamps: "Madonna and Child" by Perugino; village scene with falling snow and "Greetings."

1987 (22 cents). Two stamps: "Madonna and Child" by Moroni; Christmas ornaments amid fir branches with "Greetings."

1988 (25 cents). Two stamps: "Madonna and Child" by Botticelli; one-horse open sleigh with village snow scene and "Greetings."

1989 (25 cents). Two stamps: "Madonna and Child" by Caracci; sleigh laden with presents and "Greetings."

1990 (25 cents). Two stamps: "Madonna and Child" by Antonello; elementary drawing of white Christmas tree decorated with green garland and colored ornaments, red background, and "Greetings."

1991 (29 cents). Six stamps: "Madonna and Child" by Antoniazzo Romano; Santa sliding down chimney; Santa checking list; Santa leaving a gift under the tree; Santa going up the chimney; Santa flying in sleigh.

1992 (29 cents). Five stamps: "Madonna and Child" by Giovanni Bellini; the remaining four stamps each depict an antique toy with "Greetings": race horse on wheels, steam locomotive, fire engine, steam boat.

1993 (29 cents). Five stamps: "Madonna and Child in a Landscape" by Giovanni Battista Cima da Conegliano; the remaining four stamps consist of cartoon drawings, each with "Greetings": jack-in-the-box, red-nosed reindeer, snowman, and toy soldier.

1994 (29 cents). Four stamps: "Madonna and Child" by Elisabetta Sirani; the remaining three stamps consist of cartoon drawings, each with "Greetings": Santa holding a present, stocking filled with gifts, cardinal in the snow.

1995 (32 cents). Seven stamps: "Madonna and Child" by Giotto di Bondone; two children on a sled; midnight angel; Santa Claus entering chimney; Santa Claus working on a sled; child holding a jumping jack; child holding a tiny Christmas tree.

1996 (32 cents). Seven stamps: Detail of Madonna and Child from "Adoration of the Shepherds" by Paolo de Mattels; "Hanukkah" stamp showing cartoon drawing of menorah with multicolored candles; four stamp cartoons depicting family scenes: sitting before fireplace, mother and daughter carrying wrapped gifts, father lifting child to place star atop Christmas tree; girl dreaming of Santa's descent into chimney; and cartoon drawing of ice skaters.

1997 (32 cents). Three stamps: "Madonna and Child with Saints and Angels" by Sano di Pietro; "Kwanzaa" stamp showing silhouette

drawing of two African Americans with the symbols of Kwanzaa; sprig of holly with caption "American holly."

1998 (32 cents). Five stamps: Florentine Madonna and Child terra cotta relief; the remaining four stamps depict holiday wreaths with representations from four different plant groupings, each with "Greetings": traditional, colonial, chili, and tropical.

1999 (33 cents). Two stamps: "Madonna and Child" by B. Vivarini; gold silhouette of prancing reindeer on red, blue, green or purple background with "Greetings."

2000 (33 cents). 1999 stamps were used; previously issued Hanukkah and Kwanzaa stamps were reprinted in 33-cent denominations.

See also **Christmas Seals.**

Christmas Star
See **Star of Bethlehem**.

Christmas Story
(Biblical account). *See* **Nativity**

A Christmas Story
(Animated cartoon, 1972). When little boy Timmy forgets to mail his letter to Santa, Gumdrop the mouse discovers it on Christmas Eve and sets out with Goober the family dog to intercept Santa and deliver the letter. Dodging alley cats and other obstacles, the two just manage to miss Santa at every turn. When a neighborhood animal relay also fails to locate Santa, the two dejected searchers return home, fearing that Santa will overlook Timmy. But as they sleep by the tree, Santa finds the letter nearby and fills Timmy's wish list. Voices: Daws Butler, Don Messick, Hal Smith, John Stephenson, Walter Tetley, Janet Waldo, Paul Winchell, Paul DeKorte, Randy Kemner, Stephen McAndrew, Susie McCune, Judi Richards. Written by Ken Spears, Joe Ruby. Produced and directed by William Hanna, Joseph Barbera. Hanna-Barbera Productions. Hanna-Barbera Home Video. Color. Half-hour.

Christmas Story
(Television episode). *See* **The Andy Griffith Show**

A Christmas Story
(1983). Motion picture comedy based on

In God We Trust, All Others Pay Cash (1966). A book by novelist and radio-television humorist Jean Shepherd.

Set in fictional Hohman, Indiana, in the mid–1940s, the film, narrated by Shepherd, takes most of its story from the chapter titled "Duel in the Snow, or Red Ryder Nails the Cleveland Street Kid." The story revolves around nine-year-old Ralph Parker (Peter Billingsley), who has but one wish for Christmas, a "Red Ryder Carbine Action 200-Shot Range Model Air Rifle" (a BB gun). So strong is his wish that Ralph lapses into daydreams. In the first, armed with the rifle, he rescues his family from Black Bart's gang.

Getting the gun may be a problem, however, because Mother (Melinda Dillon), his teacher Miss Shields (Tedde Moore), and even the demonic Santa (Jeff Gillen) at Higbee's Department Store are of one mind on that subject: "You'll shoot your eye out!" And the odds seem worse when Ralph, extolling the virtues of owning a Red Ryder in "What I Want for Christmas," a school theme, earns a miserable C+ (in his second daydream, Miss Shields had been so pleased with the theme that she wrote A+ *ad infinitum* as his class cheered hysterically).

In addition to Ralph's BB gun obsession, the film presents a number of digressional anecdotes which include his friends "Flick" (Scott Schwartz) and "Schwartz" (R. D. Robb), the latter of whom persuades Flick via a "triple-dog-dare" to stick his tongue to an icy schoolyard flagpole. Together, the three older boys and Ralph's younger brother Randy (Ian Petrella) endure harassment from the typical neighborhood bully, yellow-eyed Scot Farcus (Zack Ward) and his "little toadie" sidekick Grover Dill (Yano Anaya), noted for his green teeth. But following the seemingly undeserved C+ on his theme, Ralph is overcome with rage, pulverizes Farcus' face in the snow and sends Dill scurrying.

Home life is a circus of sorts. Ralph's father, the "Old Man" (Darren McGavin), frequently pits himself against either a belching furnace, raving and cursing all the while (viewers hear only wild gibberish), or against the foul-smelling hounds of his neighbors, the Bumpuses. His passion, newspaper sweep-stakes, nets a "major award" in the "Great Characters in American Literature" contest, a hideous lamp shaped like a stripper's leg. And Randy, never willing to eat, must have maternal encouragement. Other memorable pre–Christmas scenes include Ralph's bar-soap-in-the-mouth punishment for swearing (inducing the final "you'll-be-sorry" daydream of going blind from soap poisoning) and Ralph's pursuit of a Little Orphan Annie decoder.

When Christmas arrives, Ralph looks for a BB gun, but at first it seems he will be disappointed. But at last his wish comes true — and Ralph almost shoots his eye out with the Red Ryder as a pellet ricochets and breaks his glasses.

Bumpus's hounds raid the kitchen and grab the Christmas turkey, and an unsettling dinner at a Chinese restaurant, where waiters stumble over lyrics to "Deck the Halls" and serve roast duck with the head intact, rounds out the Christmas merriment.

Shepherd and his wife, Leigh Brown, made cameo appearances in the film as a couple waiting in line to see the department store Santa.

Written by Jean Shepherd, Leigh Brown, Bob Clark. Produced by Rene Dupont, Bob Clark. Directed by Bob Clark. Metro-Goldwyn-Mayer. MGM Home Entertainment Video. Color. 94 min.

In 1984 *A Christmas Story* won Genie Awards for Best Achievement in Direction and for Best Original Screenplay. It received a Genie nomination for Best Motion Picture. It also received nominations from the Writers' Guild of America for Best Comedy Adapted from Another Medium and from the Young Artist Awards for Best Family Motion Picture — Musical or Comedy, Best Young Actor in a Motion Picture (Peter Billingsley), and Best Young Supporting Actor in a Motion Picture (Ian Petrella).

Jean Shepherd, originally from Hammond, Indiana, appeared on radio for some thirty years as a humorous storyteller, using bits and pieces of his own life as subjects. His stories originally appeared in *Playboy*, where they often won awards for best humor stories of the year. Later he compiled these stories into several novels, including *Wanda Hickey's Night of Golden Memories and Other Disasters* (1971), *The Ferrari in the Bedroom* (1973), and *A Fistful of Fig Newtons* (1981).

The Christmas That Almost Wasn't

(1965). American-Italian children's fantasy motion picture. In this story possessing undertones of *A Christmas Carol* and *It's a Wonderful Life*, mean-spirited, wealthy Phineas T. Prune (Rossano Brazzi) has purchased the North Pole, and Santa (Alberto Rabagliati) is now his tenant. Strapped for cash, Santa must surrender all of the toys in his workshop to Prune if the rent is not paid by midnight on Christmas Eve. Santa turns to an old friend, attorney Sam Whipple (Paul Tripp), for help. Years before, a much younger Sam had written a letter to Santa, pledging to come to Santa's aid at any time.

Together, Sam and Santa appeal to Prune's memory of his own childhood Christmases, hoping that Prune will relent. Instead, he denies that he ever had a childhood and challenges Santa to prove otherwise. Prune does offer to cancel the rent, but only if Santa will never again deliver presents to children on Christmas Eve. Santa chooses to raise the money for the rent rather than deprive the children.

With only a few weeks left before Christmas, Santa takes a job as the "Santa" for Prim's Department Store with Sam serving as custodian. Despite Prune's inept attempts to disrupt Santa's visits with children in the store, all seems well, until closing time on Christmas Eve. Prune strikes again, buying the department store from Prim (Sonny Fox) and firing Santa and Sam.

Seeing the two dejected souls walking the streets, a little boy recognizes Santa and, upon learning of his plight, summons thousands of children to yield their penny banks. The two men arrive back at the North Pole just at the stroke of midnight to foil an awaiting Prune with the rent. As his adversary departs, Santa takes off on his rounds, together with Sam and Mrs. Claus (Lilia Brazzi alternating with Lydia Brazzi), while elf foreman Jonathan (Mischa Auer) tosses on board a last-minute gift. The latter, marked for Prune himself and the last

gift to be delivered, consists of a toy sailboat and a note from Jonathan, whom Santa had commissioned to find Prune's name in his record books. Unable to locate the name, Jonathan had found a lost postcard, which Prune as a boy had addressed to Santa, requesting a sailboat for Christmas. Santa's unintentional absence that year had embittered Prune toward children and Christmas ever since.

When Prune receives the sailboat, it melts his malignant feelings completely. To strengthen Prune's good will, Santa, his wife, and Sam turn Prune's gloomy home into a shining showplace of Christmas cheer.

With John Karlsen, Ruth Enders (wife of Paul Tripp), and David Tripp (son of Paul Tripp). Written by Paul Tripp. Produced by Barry B. Yellan. Directed by Rossano Brazzi. Bambi Productions. Color. 89 min. Video N/A.

Christmas Time's A-Coming

American song written by Tex Logan in 1949. Having grown up savoring the sounds of Bill Monroe and the Blue Grass Boys in the 1940s, Tex Logan became proficient on the fiddle and played with various country music groups while working on a Ph.D. degree in electrical engineering at the Massachusetts Institute of Technology. Although he had never met Monroe, Logan wrote "Christmas Time's A-Coming" specifically with Monroe in mind and received his chance to pitch the tune in 1951. Logan's band, together with a number of big-name country artists, including Bill Monroe, had completed a concert in Baltimore during the fall of that year. Backstage, Logan played his song for Monroe, who agreed on the spot to record it (Decca label) in time for the 1951 Christmas sales, although it was not charted. According to liner notes for the Bill Monroe record collection *Bluegrass: 1950–1958*, Logan probably based "Christmas Time's A-Coming" on an earlier tune, "Christmas Time Will Soon Be Over," which an artist known as Fiddlin' John Carson had recorded in 1927. Both songs possessed similar melodies and lyric patterns.

Christmas Tree

Any one of a variety of genuine or artificial trees erected in homes or public places

A rough adaptation of a late eighteenth century engraving by Joseph Kellner shows a German scene with a family admiring a Christbaum, *complete with fruit decorations, candles, and some sort of large, probably foil-paper stamped image of the Christ Child. From Clement A. Miles,* Christmas in Ritual and Tradition, Christian and Pagan *(London: T. Fisher Unwin, 1912).*

and decorated for the season. Although known throughout the world, the Christmas tree reigns as the chief physical symbol of Christmas primarily in northern Europe, America, Australia, and regions of Canada. (In southern Europe, Latin America, and in other Spanish-speaking regions, the Nativity scene predominates.)

• ORIGINS AND HISTORY. While the modern Christmas tree is a product of Germany, the origins for the custom are many and varied, taking root first with European pre–Christian conceptions that evergreen trees possessed magical powers because they remained green during the winter, when other trees shed their leaves. Across the Roman Empire at year-end festivals such as the Saturnalia and the Kalends, varieties of evergreen boughs adorned homes, temples, and public statuary. (Streamers, ribbons, and images of the god Saturn adorned trees during the Saturnalia.) At the winter solstice, pagan Germanic tribes erected fir trees in their homes and burned fir boughs to welcome the annual visit of a domestic goddess variously known as Hertha, Bertha, Berchta, or Perchta, who was believed to appear through the smoke bearing luck and blessings for the household. Regarded as symbols of longevity and eternal life for centuries prior to the Christian age, evergreens acquired a parallel sym-

bolism with the feast of Christmas despite a futile campaign by the early Church to suppress their use as decorations (Tertullian, third century; Second Council of Braga, Portugal, sixth century). During the Middle Ages, evergreen trees factored into certain mystery plays performed on December 24, a day that had originally commemorated Adam and Eve on the early church calendar. Such plays recalled the fall of man in the Garden of Eden; a "Paradise Tree," a fir tree decorated with apples, portrayed the Tree of Forbidden Fruit and served as the only prop for the plays.

Two legends further link the Christmas tree with Germany. The English missionary Winfrid, St. Boniface, while preaching to Germanic tribes in the eighth century, is said to have introduced the fir tree as a symbol of the Christ Child on Christmas Eve. Details and further elaboration of this legend are found in the entry "The First Christmas Tree: A Story of the Forest" (1897), a classic short story by the American author Henry Van Dyke. According to another legend, a German woodcutter and his wife offered food and shelter for the night to a freezing, starving child, who manifested himself at dawn as the radiantly beautiful Christ Child. To reward their generosity, the Child planted a small fir tree nearby which grew and bloomed annually at Christmastime. A third legend, originating as a story told by the tenth-century Arabian geographer George Jacob, stated that when Christ was born at midnight in the dead of winter, all the trees of the world bloomed to glorify Him. This legend, one of few traceable to a definitive source, is believed to have contributed significantly to the decorating of Christmas trees as imitations of those that allegedly bloomed two millennia ago.

The oldest evidence for decorated trees at Christmastime comes from Riga, Latvia (1510), and from Reval, Estonia (1514). Both instances occurred on Christmas Eve, with members of a local guild gathering at the market place, dancing around a fir tree adorned with paper roses, and then burning it. The first reports of German Christmas trees date to 1531 in Alsace, where trees (undecorated) were erected on tables because a local forest ordinance forbade cutting of firs more than four feet in height.

A typical German tabletop tree, with candles and an angel on top, is shown in this vignette from a nineteenth century engraving of a wood-paneled German parlor. Note the little boy's flag with the crossed swords. From the German magazine Fliegende Blätter, *1890.*

An account from Strasbourg in 1605 first mentioned home-decorated firs adorned with paper roses (symbols of the Virgin), flat wafers (symbols of the Communion Host), apples, gilded candies, sugar candy, and pretzels. In some circles, names such as "sugar tree" or *Christbaum* (Christ tree) respectively reflected the abundant sugar confections or religious symbols present. Children's gifts of small toys and trinkets were customarily placed among the branches, and the sweets remained on the tree until Epiphany, at which time the tree was dismantled and the children were afforded the pleasure of devouring the sweets.

German trees were first illuminated with candles. A popular myth attributes the custom to Martin Luther (1483–1546), who supposedly incorporated candles to symbolize the abundant stars that he had witnessed on a clear Christmas Eve. Before appearing on trees, however, candles adorned the related *Weihnachtspyramide* (Christmas pyramid), a contemporary structure that featured fir boughs wrapped around a triangular wooden frame containing several shelves decreasing in length from bottom to top and decorated with fruits, sweets, and small toys. Also known as a *Lichtstock* (light stick), the pyramid appeared in Germany about the same time as the use of evergreen trees; often the two co-existed in the same home, the pyramid sometimes hanging from the ceiling, the Christmas tree standing on a table. Documented use of candles on trees first appeared in southern Germany around 1660.

Christbaumhalters, or stands — one a revolving windup music box — are seen in two ads from the November 29, 1885, issue of Fliegende Blätter, *published in Munich. The tripod stand could have supported a much larger tree.*

Over the next two centuries, the German custom gained wide popularity and spread throughout northern Europe, the pyramid having migrated to Italy as the *ceppo* (log) long before it finally disappeared from Germany during the nineteenth century.

The Christmas Tree Book discusses another popular myth, that the Saxon-born Prince Albert, consort to England's Queen Victoria, erected a decorated tree at Windsor Castle in 1841 to celebrate the arrival of his first-born son, thereby introducing the custom to Great Britain. In reality, the English royal family had been decorating Christmas trees since the turn of the eighteenth century, but they achieved widespread appeal only with the publication in 1848 of a photograph of a tree at Windsor Castle decorated with expensive sweetmeats, candy, gilt gingerbread, and a winged angel for a tree topper. Charles Dickens provided an elaborate description of the British tree in "The Christmas Tree," a short story that appeared in 1850 in his weekly publication, *Household Words*. In addition to myriad candles, virtually every conceivable variety of sweets and toys hung on the branches.

Christmas trees first arrived in America in the form of pyramids brought over by members of the Moravian Church, German immigrants who established their first permanent settlement, Bethlehem, Pennsylvania, in 1747. It is sometimes said that Hessian troops decorated trees during the American Revolution, but initial evidence documenting the use of decorated fir trees in this country dates only from the 1820s. Examples include an entry from the diary of one Matthew Zahm (December 1821) of Lancaster County, Pennsylvania, and the so-called "Kris Kringle Tree" erected in one Pennsylvania-Dutch community in 1823. The latter was a table-size fir decorated with *matzebaum* (cakes of almond paste), *schnitz* (strings of dried apples), marzipan figures, assorted nuts, and other homemade ornaments fashioned from paper and cardboard. Although these trees very likely included candles, there were no reports of them until 1832, when Charles Follen, a German immigrant living in Boston, included candles on a tree decorated with toys and gilded half-eggshells filled with candy. The prohibitive cost of candles, however, prompted others to use simple wicks placed in nut half shells filled with oil. Decorated trees were so novel that they prompted public exhibitions to raise funds for charity and private exhibitions in homes which sold tickets for personal gain.

By the 1840s, the Christmas tree tradition had spread from a few principal cities in the Northeast to rural regions and farther west, thanks to German settlers, promotions from newspapers, and children's books such as *Kriss Kringle's Christmas Tree* (Philadelphia, 1845). The title page from the latter clearly depicts a table tree by the fireplace with an elfish, pipe-smoking Kriss Kringle arranging toys on its branches. In rural Pennsylvania, conservation-minded farmers stripped the needles from dried firs and wrapped cotton batting around the skeletons to simulate snow-covered trees that could be reused for several years. The bare branches of non-firs received similar treatment. Rural ornaments were typically simple: pastry, ribbons, candied fruit, nuts, colored paper chains, and strings of popcorn, cranberries, and raisins. In 1851 the Rev. Henry

E. FERRETT & CO.
PHILADELPHIA:
1845.

The title page of Kriss Kringle's Christmas Tree, *published 1845. Kriss Kringle is hanging a jointed toy on one branch, and he clutches his doll in his other hand.*

Schwan, a Lutheran pastor and German immigrant living in Cleveland, Ohio, created a furor by erecting the first Christmas tree in an American church; some of his congregation protested this "pagan throwback." By 1860, American Christmas trees had achieved ceiling height and stood on the floor rather than a table, as first depicted in a short story written by Lizzie McIntyre and published that year in *Godey's Lady's Book*, a women's magazine. (When trees were erected on floors, in time the gifts were transferred from the branches and placed beneath the tree.) At the turn of the twentieth century, only one in five United States families sported a Christmas tree; by 1930, the custom was almost universal.

• NEW PRODUCTS AND INNOVATIONS. The latter half of the nineteenth century saw an onslaught of commercially produced ornaments, accessories, and other innovations, both foreign and domestic, that extended far into the twentieth century. The following chronological list summarizes the most noteworthy of these:

1851. Mark Carr, a logger from the Catskill Mountains with two ox sleds of balsam firs, establishes the first Christmas tree lot in New York City's Washington Market.

1870. First glass-blown balls (*Kugel*) are imported from Lauscha, Germany's chief glass manufacturing city.

1870–1900. Height of popularity for flat, tin ornaments, produced in Germany since the eighteenth century.

1870–1910. Height of popularity for wire ornaments imported from Germany.

1875. German woodcarvers first produce a large variety of ornaments shaped like miniature toys; though a fire hazard, celluloid toys become popular.

1876. Philadelphians Hermann Albrecht and Abram Mott receive the first two U.S. patents for a three-legged tree stand.

1878. Nuremberg, Germany, first produces "icicles."

1880s. Germany produces "angel hair" composed of spun glass.

1880s–90s. Prime period when Eastern toy and variety stores import a wide assortment of glass-blown, decorative ornaments (fruit, animals, all imaginable shapes) from Germany. Other imports include silver, gilt paper, and

These glass tree ornaments were advertised in a 1939 catalog, but they are fashioned to resemble blown glass balls from the 1880s. Though mostly silver, red, green and blue, some were painted in multicolors with floral designs. Some were offered in the shape of fruit or Santa or pine cones. The most unusual shown here is the silver bead biplane with colored wings 4½″ × 4½″. From the Shure Winner Catalog *no. 132 (Chicago: N. Shure, 1939).*

cardboard ornaments; ornate cornucopias, doll-size baskets, and fine net bags for holding candy and nuts; and ornaments of cotton batting glued over a solid frame with chromolithographic images on paper.

1882. Edward Johnson, vice president of the newly formed Edison Electric Company, demonstrates the first electric lights on a Christmas tree in his New York City home. Eighty blue, red, and white lights were individually wired to the tree by a professional electrician.

1890s. Germany produces rope garlands of tinsel; metal hooks for ornaments (1892); Japan produces ornaments consisting of miniature lanterns, parasols, and fans.

1890s–1910. Prime period for the "Dresden ornaments," large variety of ornaments from Dresden, Germany, consisting of three-dimensional silver and gold embossed cardboard.

1900. Germany produces papier-mâché figures; tree toppers consisting either of foil angels or long, glass points; metal caps for glass ornaments with spring clips.

1901. W. V. McGalliard establishes the first Christmas tree farm in New Jersey with 25,000 Norwegian spruce and markets them six to seven years later at one dollar per tree. American poet Robert Frost also cites this price in his poem of 1916, "Christmas Trees."

1903. The Ever-Ready Company of New York City produces the first strings of Christmas light sockets in series (if one light goes out, they all go out), called "festoons." The General Electric Company, having bought out Edison's company in 1890, sold these strings with their own lights (clear, identical to the standard light bulbs of the time with pointed tips) but changed to parallel wiring in 1927.

1908. The Paper Novelty Products Company in New York produces honeycombed, red paper bells.

1909. Vienna, Austria, produces the first tree light bulbs in the shape of miniature figures, followed by General Electric with machine-blown figure light bulbs in 1917. With the onset of World War I, Austria ceased to export bulbs to American retailers, who then imported similar figure bulbs from the Japanese. Japan exported to the United States until World War II, then resumed exporting in the 1950s.

1910. General Electric changes to colored, ball-shaped lights.

1918. America manufactures its first ornaments, consisting only of round balls.

1920s. America manufactures "icicles" using lead foil to prevent tarnishing but changes to silver-mylar base in 1960s to lessen chances for lead poisoning.

1920s–30s. America imports Czech, Japanese, and Polish ornaments.

1930s. The Paper Novelty Products Company produces red and green crushed crepe paper ropes and garlands.

1936. NOMA Lights introduces series-wired lights with colored, plastic lampshades affixed with decals of standard Walt Disney cartoon characters.

1938. The Paper Novelty Products Company produces the first hand-blown glass figures in America, consisting of Snow White and the Seven Dwarfs.

1939. Corning Glass turns out the first mass-produced glass ornaments in America. Max Eckardt's "Shiney Brite" company, originally in New Jersey, decorates the glass "blanks," which are then distributed by the F. W. Woolworth Company. Following World War II, Shiney Brite became the largest ornament company in the world, and Corning became the largest supplier of glass ornaments beginning in 1960.

1945. Carl Otis, an accountant for Montgomery Ward, invents "BubbleLights," which incorporate a colored solution of methylene chloride that boils with minimum heat. By the 1960s, only the F. W. Woolworth Company continued to market them.

1950s. Aluminum trees illuminated with floodlamps using a rotating, colored wheel become popular in America. Midget light sets imported from Europe and Japan supplant BubbleLights.

1970s. Life-like artificial trees manufactured from polyvinyl chloride in Asia become popular, and twinkling "mini-lights" are developed, their negligible heat output providing a safer light source.

• PRESIDENTIAL CHRISTMAS TREES. Several traditions have centered around American presidents and Christmas trees.

In 1856, Franklin Pierce established an annual tradition by erecting the first tree in the White House.

Grover Cleveland first used electric lights on a tree in the White House in 1895.

After realizing that, by 1900, the demand for Christmas trees had decimated about 50 percent of all timber in the United States, conservationist president Theodore Roosevelt officially barred Christmas trees from the White House during his administration, beginning in 1901.

His children, however, secretly erected a tree of their own that year in a closet. Upon consultation with cabinet member and founder of the Yale School of Forestry Gifford Pinchot, who assured the president that proper cuttings would thin the timberland, Roosevelt permitted his children to have an "unofficial" tree each year.

Since 1966, the National Christmas Tree Association, the trade group for the Christmas tree growing industry, has presented a Christmas tree to the president and first family. The winner of the association's annual pageant in August has the honor of selecting the tree, which is displayed in the Blue Room of the White House.

Although President Woodrow Wilson instituted the national Christmas tree lighting ceremony on Christmas Eve, 1913, near the United States Capitol, he and several presidents to follow did not actually attend the event. When President Calvin Coolidge moved the ceremonies to the Ellipse near the White House in 1923, however, he became the first president to light the national Christmas tree. Subsequent locations included Sherman Plaza (1924–1933), Lafayette Park (1934–1938), the Ellipse (1939–1940), and the White House grounds (1941–1953).

On December 17, 1954, President Dwight Eisenhower officiated at ceremonies on the Ellipse which adopted an expanded program advocating worldwide peace through Christmas. This program was known as the Pageant of Peace. Pageants from this time through 1972 used cut trees as national Christmas trees, but in 1973 a live, 42-foot Colorado blue spruce was planted on the Ellipse. The national Christmas tree today is another Colorado blue spruce planted in 1978 on the Ellipse. Since 1954, the Ellipse has been the traditional site for the pageant. The national Christmas tree remained unlighted in 1942–1944 because of blackouts imposed during World War II. In 1979 and 1980, President Jimmy Carter ordered only the top ornament lighted in memory of the American hostages held in Iran. Although the tree was fully lighted in 1980 for only 417 seconds to commemorate the 417 days the hostages had been held, it was fully lighted again following the hostages' release on President Ronald Reagan's inauguration day, January 20, 1981.

• THE NATION'S CHRISTMAS TREE. Different from the national tree described above, this 267-foot giant Sequoia resides in California's Kings Canyon National Park near Sanger. About 4,000 years old with a circumference of 107 feet, this tree, known since 1867 as the "General Grant," has been the site of an annual Christmas ceremony at its base since 1925. Persuaded by Charles Lee and R. J. Senior, members of the Sanger Chamber of Commerce, President Calvin Coolidge designated the General Grant as the nation's Christmas tree in 1926. President Dwight Eisenhower subsequently proclaimed the tree a national shrine in 1956 as a living memorial to all United States veterans who gave their lives for their country. Because its lowest branch is some 130 feet from the ground, the General Grant is not decorated for Christmas. Instead, members of the National Park Service place a large wreath at its base during the Christmas ceremonies.

• OTHER NATIONALLY KNOWN CHRISTMAS TREES. Several notable trees receive annual trimming at Christmastime in the United States: "The Tree of Light," a 60-foot balsam fir in New York City's Madison Square Park, dedicated in 1912; "The Children's Christmas Tree," a 75-foot Norwegian spruce in Philadelphia's Independence Square, dedicated in 1913; numerous giant cedars bordering a mile-long avenue in Altadena, California, known since 1920 as "Christmas Tree Lane"; and the ninety-foot trees in New York City's Rockefeller Center.

• VARIETIES OF CHRISTMAS TREES. Virtually any tree may be decorated as a Christmas tree, but in North America, the types most commonly chosen are pines, firs, and spruces, all noted for their conical shape. Whereas some people with free access to open timberland may cut their own trees each year, most purchase a tree either from a tree lot or a tree farm. According to the National Christmas Tree Association, the top-selling Christmas trees in the United States include the Scotch pine (number 1), balsam fir, Douglas fir, Fraser fir, noble fir, Virginia pine, and eastern white pine. Other varieties include the Colorado blue spruce, Norwegian spruce, eastern red cedar, and red pine. Those with larger gaps between their branches, such as the balsam fir, Douglas fir, Fraser fir, and Virginia pine, are probably the easiest trees to decorate. Posing more difficulty is the Norwegian spruce with its drooping branches. Most of these varieties show good needle retention, except for the spruces, which shed their needles easily.

Over 37 million families in the United States annually erect real Christmas trees in their homes, followed by a roughly equal number of those who prefer artificial trees. Christmas tree farms in the United States currently number about 15,000 and require about one million acres for total production. A third of these farms allow individual buyers to select and cut their trees on site. Those states with the highest yields of Christmas trees include California, Michigan, North Carolina, Oregon, Pennsylvania, and Wisconsin.

See also **Chrismon Tree**; **Jesse Tree**.

Christmas Trees

Poem written in 1916 by American poet Robert Frost. Describing the poem as a "Christmas circular letter," Frost pits nature and the holiday against commercialism. A New England farmer owns a large expanse of land on which grow numerous fir trees. As he admires nature's handiwork, likening his trees to "fir churches" with prominent spires pointing toward heaven, a city buyer offers to purchase all the fir trees on his property for a Christmas enterprise. Estimating a thousand trees, the city dweller offers thirty dollars for the lot (three cents per tree). With Christmas trees selling for one dollar apiece in the city at that time, the farmer, figuring that his trees are worth three cents more to give away than to sell at the offered price, wishes that he could send all his friends a tree enclosed in a letter to wish them a Merry Christmas.

Christmas Vacation

See **National Lampoon's Christmas Vacation**

The Christmas Visitor

(1987). Australian drama made for television, also known as *Miracle Down Under*.

In 1891, the O'Day family faces Christmas on their sheep ranch in the outback amid poverty and summer drought. Only little Ned O'Day (Andrew Ferguson) possesses any Christmas spirit, for he is sure that a grizzled stranger with a white beard lurking about is Father Christmas, the British equivalent of Santa Claus. In reality this man is Max Bell (Charles Tingwell), former partner to now-wealthy landowner Trevor Watson (Bill Kerr). A fugitive from justice for twenty years for illegal horse trading, Bell has returned to claim his share of the profits from Watson. The latter, cynical and bitter following his wife's death years ago, welcomes the holidays by firing his three hired hands and denying water rights to his neighbor, Patrick O'Day (John Waters), Ned's father.

The O'Days' difficulties mount when Patrick, having hired Watson's former hands, strikes a well of salty water on Christmas Day, after which they successfully battle a grass fire, kindled from chimney sparks belched from Watson's Yule log. These disappointments, together with receiving no presents on Christmas morning, smother Ned's faith in Father Christmas. At this point his mother, Elizabeth (Dee Wallace Stone), reminds him that Christmas is truly a time for giving, not receiving.

In the spirit of the season, Ned presents a bouquet of wild flowers to Watson, and the little boy's simple gift so touches him that not only does Watson revoke the ban on water rights, but he and his son Angus (Grant Piro), formerly at odds, are reconciled, and he also gladly restores Bell's share of the profits. Bell in turn, after making restitution to a store he had robbed, arrives at the O'Day ranch with gifts for all, as would Father Christmas, and secretly plants a gold sovereign in each slice of plum pudding. On Christmas night, as the O'Days are making merry, Bell, having witnessed their happiness through the window, mockingly addresses the sky as he departs with, "Abracadabra!" To his great surprise, the heavens open with a welcome downpour, which ends the drought.

With Francis Bell, Nadine Garner, Callie Gary, Kym Gyngall, John Heywood, Christine Keogh, Bruce Kilpatrick, Neil Melville, Maggie Millar, Francine Ormond, David Ravenswood, Martin Redpath, Christopher Stevenson, and Rosie Sturgess. Written by Jeff Peck. Produced by Peter Beilby, Robert Le Tet. Directed by George Miller. Entertainment Media. Walt Disney Home Video. Color. 87 min.

The Christmas Waltz

American song written by Sammy Cahn

(lyrics) and Jule Styne (music) in 1954 after singer Frank Sinatra asked them to write a Christmas song for him. Styne's habit before writing any music was to run through one particular pair of songs at the piano, a Viennese waltz and a tango. This gave Cahn the idea for Sinatra's song. By slowing down the waltz tempo and tacking on some light lyrics regarding candles, painted candy canes, Santa, and Christmas wishes, the two created "The Christmas Waltz." Sinatra's 1954 recording on the Capitol label failed to make the pop charts, however, and the song never achieved quite the popularity as had an earlier Cahn-Styne seasonal collaboration, "Let It Snow! Let It Snow! Let It Snow!" (1945).

Of the 25 most frequently performed Christmas songs of the twentieth century listed by the American Society of Composers, Authors and Publishers (ASCAP), "The Christmas Waltz" is ranked number 22.

Together or separately, Cahn and Styne produced numerous works in the popular music field. Cahn supplied the lyrics for such pieces as "Love and Marriage" (1955), "All the Way" (1957), and "High Hopes" (1959). Styne provided the musical scores for such Broadway hits as *Gentlemen Prefer Blondes* (1949), *Gypsy* (1959), and *Funny Girl* (1964).

See also **Let It Snow! Let It Snow! Let It Snow!**

The Christmas Wife

(1988). Made-for-television drama based on a short story of the same title by Helen Norris.

Having lost his wife earlier in the year, retired architect John Tanner (Jason Robards) faces spending the holidays alone. In past years, he and his family traditionally had spent Christmas at their mountain cabin, but now his son Jim (James Eckhouse), daughter-in-law, and grandchildren live across the country in California. When Jim calls his father on Thanksgiving and offers to fly him to the West Coast for Christmas instead, John cannot break with tradition. Desiring to find a suitable female companion with whom to spend Christmas, he investigates a newspaper ad from "Alone Again, Inc.," an agency that arranges social engagements. Although the office is shabby and the "special agent" (Don Francks) is evasive, mysterious, and demands $500 for his services,

John allows the agent to draw up a list of "candidates" for a platonic relationship. But during their second meeting in a hotel lobby, the agent, claiming that suitable choices are virtually nil, has arranged for John to meet only one woman, Iris (Julie Harris), who is just as evasive and mysterious. She and John agree to spend the Christmas weekend together at John's cabin, but Iris insists that John not seek to know anything about her and requests that he meet her at a bus depot on Christmas Eve.

By Christmas Day in the cabin, the two have become well acquainted, considering the circumstances, and John presents Iris with a music box that plays Beethoven's "Für Elise." His gift to himself (he tells Iris that she gave it to him) is a new bow tie. A walk in the woods before Christmas dinner brings them even closer together, and soon he is entertaining her with songs on his ukulele, while she delivers a poem, Dorothy Parker's "One Perfect Rose."

On the day after Christmas, when John wishes for the relationship to grow, Iris, also most fond of John, breaks down and confesses that not only is she a married woman, but that her husband, the "special agent," put her up to the stunt because they needed the money. Without anger, John asks himself what was he trying to prove by running off with a strange woman. That he was not alone? Iris adds that perhaps he was trying to prove that, even though he had lost his wife, life wasn't over for him yet, and that he was really breaking a spell. Their parting is bittersweet, but they have given each other a beautiful Christmas.

With Patricia Hamilton, Deborah Grover, David Gardner, Tom Harvey, Christopher Andrade, Steven Andrade, Bill Lynn, Helen Frost. Written by Katherine Ann Jones. Produced by Patrick Whitley. Directed by David Jones. An Edie Landau Production. HBO Video (Canada). Color.

A Christmas Without Snow

(1980). Made-for-television drama. Ms. Michael Learned stars as Zoe Jensen, a recently divorced schoolteacher who moves from Omaha, Nebraska, to San Francisco in the fall to begin a new life. While she settles in, her young son Robbie (Matthew Hautau) remains with her parents in Omaha.

Zoe joins a church choir, the new director of which is a most condescending and exacting Ephraim Adams (John Houseman), whose goal is to whip the ragtag choir into shape to perform Handel's *Messiah* at Christmastime. The story principally revolves around this central theme, as Adams expertly handles trouble within the ranks, crushing the inflated ego of one new soprano while gently advising an older member that, because she sings off-key, she must leave the choir. Several digressions include Zoe's unsuccessful attempt at a relationship with choir member Henry Quist (Ramon Bieri); the choir's Thanksgiving dinner aboard a boat owned by Mr. Wood (William Swetland); Robbie's unexpected arrival in San Francisco, he having traveled across the country alone by bus to be with his mother; and the vandalizing of the church's pipe organ. The latter leads to a mistaken accusation by choir member Muriel Moore (Valerie Curtin) that Wendell Curtis (Calvin Levels), a black member, is the culprit, when the guilty party is in fact Terry (David Knell), the troubled teenage son of Rev. Lohman (James Cromwell). While the versatile choir pitches in to restore the organ, the church acquires a temporary electronic model, which frequently broadcasts police calls during services.

One week before the scheduled Christmas performance, Adams suffers a mild stoke. When Rev. Lohman suggests canceling the program, Zoe and the other members override him and persuade organist Seth Rubin (Ed Bogas) to take over for Adams. As Adams proudly watches from a wheelchair, the picture closes with the choir singing lengthy excerpts from *Messiah*, the last number of which is the "Hallelujah Chorus" as the credits roll.

With Ruth Nelson, Beah Richards, Daisietta Kim, Joy Carlin, Anne Lawder, Barbara Tarbuck. Written by John Korty, Richard Beban, Judith Nielsen. Produced by John Korty, Whitney Green. Directed by John Korty. A Korty Films/Frank Konigsberg Production. Warner Home Video. Color. 100 min.

See also **Messiah.**

Church of the Nativity

Shrine in Bethlehem, Israel, built over a cave traditionally held as the site of Christ's birth. The construction began in the year 326 at the order of the Roman emperor Constantine the Great (ca. 274–337), whose mother, St. Helena, had ascertained the particular site on a previous expedition to the Holy Land. The original church, which had replaced the Roman emperor Hadrian's (76–138) temple to the Greek god Adonis, was destroyed during a Samaritan revolt in 529 but was rebuilt on the same site by the Byzantine emperor Justinian I (483–565). Persians invaded the church in 614 and would have destroyed it, had they not seen a mural depicting the Magi in Persian dress. To deter radical and zealous groups from storming the church in the future, the entrance was subsequently reduced to a narrow opening four feet high which forced all to enter single file and stooping. To capitalize on the emotions of pilgrims visiting the shrine today, local tour guides hold that the entrance was designed to have everyone stoop as an act of reverence. Thus, the entrance has been dubbed "The Door of Humility." The nave and its four aisles are divided by four rows of red limestone Corinthian columns, eleven to a row, and the walls show traces of mosaics depicting Christ's ancestors and the first seven Ecumenical Councils.

Beneath the church is the Grotto of the Nativity, a ten-by-forty-foot marbled chamber lighted by 53 lamps, divided among the Eastern Orthodox, Roman Catholic, and Armenian churches which principally hold services there. At the eastern end, the traditional site of the Nativity is marked with an inlaid, fourteen-pointed silver star and a Latin inscription, "Hic de Virgine Maria Jesus Christus natus est" ("Here of the Virgin Mary Jesus Christ was born"). The star and inscription were originally installed in 1717; Franciscans subsequently replaced the star during the nineteenth century when the original vanished.

Although the shrine is now controlled by the Eastern Orthodox Church, a dispute over its possession and other holy places in what was once Palestine (dominated at the time by the Turkish Ottoman Empire) began in the sixteenth century between the Orthodox and Roman Catholic churches. In December 1852, the Turkish sultan, responding to pressure from Catholic France, decided in favor of the

Roman Catholics. This and other events such as the disappearance of the original star in the Grotto greatly contributed to the Crimean War (1853–1856), which brought Russia against Turkey, France, and Great Britain. In April 1873, armed Greek monks invaded the Grotto, ransacked the cave, and stole the marble slab which had covered the holy crib. Since then, the Grotto has remained under guard.

Today, the Orthodox, Roman Catholic, and Armenian churches share rights to the Grotto. While the Catholics control the Nativity scene there, the Orthodox and Armenians split the altar.

See also **Middle East**.

Claymation Christmas Celebration

(1987). Made-for-television animated presentation, featuring stop-motion, sculptured clay figures (Claymation) created by Will Vinton. Dinosaur figures Rex and Herb host a series of carol renditions performed by Claymation characters. "We Three Kings" features a jazz refrain by three camels. In Notre Dame Cathedral, the hunchbacked character Quasimodo conducts a group of bells which knock their own heads with hammers to play "Carol of the Bells." "O Christmas Tree" depicts variously decorated trees in Santa's workshop. To the strains of "Angels We Have Heard on High," walruses and penguins ice skate in the arctic. "Joy to the World!" is performed in African-American spiritual style, and the California Raisins swing to "Rudolph, the Red-Nosed Reindeer." Several characters have difficulty with the word "wassailing," pronouncing it "waffeling," "waddling," or "wallowing," but eventually everyone sings "Here We Come A-Wassailing" correctly.

This program received an Emmy Award for Outstanding Nighttime Animated Program (1987–88 season).

Voices: Tim Conner, Johnny Counterfit. Written by Ralph Liddle. Produced by David Altschul. Directed by Will Vinton. Will Vinton Productions. Family Home Entertainment Video. Color. Half-hour.

Colombia

See **South America**

Come All Ye Shepherds
See **Angels and Shepherds**

Come, Dear Children
See **Alfred Burt Carols**

Come, You Shepherds
See **Angels and Shepherds**

Costa Rica
See **Central America**

Cotton Bowl
See **New Year's Day**

The Coventry Carol

Name applied to a carol originating from the Pageant of the Shearmen and Tailors (two trade guilds sponsoring the pageant), one in a cycle of medieval mystery plays that was annually performed in Coventry, England, on the Feast of Corpus Christi (originally observed on the Thursday after Trinity Sunday, established in 1264 by Pope Urban IV). In this particular pageant, which depicted the birth of Christ from the angel's annunciation to Mary to the slaughter of the innocents by King Herod, three male voices, portraying women bereft of their children in Bethlehem (males commonly assumed female roles in productions at that time), sang what is now known as "The Coventry Carol," a chilling dirge in response to the massacre. It is sometimes known by its opening words in the medieval English vernacular, "Lully, lulla(y), thow littel tyne child" (Lullaby, lullaby, thou little tiny child).

Where in Coventry the pageant was held is a matter of minor controversy. According to some sources, carts with actors dramatizing various scenes rolled through the streets; other sources say that all the drama transpired on the steps of Coventry Cathedral itself.

The anonymous Coventry Plays are believed to date from 1392, although the oldest known manuscript of dialogue dates from 1534, copied by Robert Croo. Initially the pageant songs were handed down in folk fashion, but in 1591, Thomas Mawdycke added them to Croo's manuscript. In 1879, a fire consumed this manuscript, which had resided in a library in Birmingham, England, but two songs from the manuscript could be salvaged from other engravings: "The Coventry Carol" and "The Coventry Shepherds' Carol," both from the shearmen-tailors pageant.

There were two principal parts to the shearmen-tailors play: "The Coventry Shepherds' Carol" ended part one, which included the angel's annunciations to Mary and the shepherds plus the Nativity. "The Coventry Carol" was the climax of the second half, which included the Wise Men's visit, the Holy Family's flight into Egypt, and Herod's raid on Bethlehem. In the modern repertoire of best-known Christmas music, few carols address as dark an issue as does "The Coventry Carol."

In 1935, the folk music collector John Jacob Niles, best known for the carol "I Wonder As I Wander," published a carol with wording almost identical to that of "The Coventry Carol" but with a different tune. Titled "Lullay, Thou Tiny Little Child," this carol appeared in his *Ten Christmas Carols from the Southern Appalachian Mountains*. Although Niles claimed to have heard "Lullay" at an Old Timers' Day festival in Gatlinburg, Tennessee, in 1934, it has yet to be identified elsewhere, which leads one to speculate that Niles created the variant carol himself.

See also **Christmas Drama; I Wonder As I Wander.**

Coventry Shepherds' Carol
See **The Coventry Carol**

Crackers
See **Great Britain**

The Cricket on the Hearth
See **Dickens, Charles, Christmas Stories of**

Croatia
Soviet Communists dominated this former constituent republic of Yugoslavia and other nations in eastern Europe from the end of World War II until 1991, after which Soviet troops withdrew, and Croatia gained her independence from Yugoslavia in 1991. During the approximately fifty years of Communism's atheistic regime, Christmas was repudiated, the midwinter holiday was moved to New Year's Day with a secular agenda, and the St. Nicholas or Baby Jesus figure who had brought children's gifts was replaced by a Soviet "Santa" known as

"Grandfather Frost" (*see* **Russia**). Communism nearly extinguished the old holiday customs, yet a number of them still survive, primarily in rural areas; these customs revolve around agrarian rituals and repelling evil. The principal Christian faith in Croatia now is Roman Catholicism.

The Christmas season extends from Advent to Epiphany and officially commences with St. Barbara's Day (December 4). Wheat seeds are traditionally sown in plates either on this day or on St. Lucia Day (December 13) and should germinate by Christmas Eve, when the green wheat becomes a centerpiece for the Christmas Eve table; alternatively, it is placed beneath the Christmas tree, for the wheat is a symbol of the renewal of life. In the mid-nineteenth century, St. Nicholas Day (December 6) was observed along with St. Lucia Day in such northern cities as Osijek, where the saint brought apples and walnuts (denoting plenty and blessing) to deserving children. His accomplices varied among regions, from Luca the Hag (deriving from "Lucia"), to the fur-clad, chain-rattling Krampus, to a devil with an angel. Today, St. Nicholas brings gifts in northern and central Croatia, while it is St. Lucia in the southern and northeastern regions (*see* **Advent** [ST. LUCIA DAY]; **Saint Nicholas Day**).

Christmas decorations include holly; ivy; branches from an oak, maple, or evergreen tree; and the Christmas tree, the latter having arrived in Croatia around the mid–1800s from central Europe. The evergreen branches are often fashioned into wreaths, hung in a cluster above the Christmas table, and variously garnished with ornaments, which may include apples, walnuts, flowers, and chains and lanterns made from paper and straw. Depending on the locale, this decoration is known as a *kinč*, *ojić*, *vojić*, *božić*, or *cimer*. Sometimes a simple cluster of red apples (symbols of bounty and plenty, red offering protection against evil) is suspended above the table. Christmas trees, formerly decorated with homemade ornaments, may now include those commercially made. According to strict tradition, these decorations are put up only on Christmas Eve.

A Nativity scene, known as a *Betlehem* or *Jeruzalem*, often resides beneath the Christmas tree at home, certainly in every church, and a group of statues believed to be remnants of the oldest Croatian Nativity scene (sixteenth century) reside in a Franciscan monastery on the island of Krk (*see* **Nativity Scene**). Reliefs portraying such scenes as the Annunciation to the Virgin, the Nativity, and the Baptism in the River Jordan, are found in the Church of the Holy Sunday in Zadar; these date to the eleventh century and are among the earliest renderings of the Christmas story in Croatia. The Advent wreath appeared around the turn of the twentieth century.

Although *Badnjak* ("to be awake,"—the word refers to Christmas Vigil or Christmas Eve as well as the virtually extinct Yule log) is still a day devoted to the dead as ancient custom dictates, it is observed—as a meatless fasting day steeped in ritual—perhaps less today than before the Communist era. Nevertheless, traditionalists still prepare the table by placing straw (symbolic of the manger) beneath it and on it in the shape of a wreath or cross, covering the latter with a table cloth, sprinkling grains on top, then covering with a second, decorative table cloth. The centerpiece consists of several items: Christmas bread with a coin hidden inside, its top divided into quadrants by a cross of pastry, the four quadrants containing emblems of the four seasons of the year; a crucifix; a candle; a bowl containing all representative seeds sown on the farm; the green wheat sown earlier; and a personal object or small tool. Farmers may place their plowshares or other tools under the table to receive a blessing.

Badnje jelo (Christmas Eve menu) traditionally consists of foods ordinarily associated with funeral feasts for the dead: hazelnuts, walnuts, almonds, honey, poppy seeds, garlic, apples, legumes, turnips, corn, pasta, cured cod and other fish, potatoes, pumpkins. Thus, recalling ancient winter solstice customs, Christmas Eve commemorates not only the living but also the spirits of family ancestors and those living who otherwise cannot be present at this dinner, for it is customary for all able family members to attend. For the absent member(s), a vacant place is set, a candle or other light is kept burning all Christmas Eve night, and the leftover food remains on the table overnight for visiting spirits. The Christmas bread is displayed throughout the holidays, and it was once traditional for crumbs from the table to be saved and burned as incense for any family member who became ill in the new year.

At midnight, men still shoot firearms to herald Christmas, a throwback to ancient times when noise dispelled evil spirits at the winter solstice. After Midnight Mass, red apples exchanged beforehand between friends or sweethearts are thrown into wells as gifts to the water.

Christmas Day is spent with immediate family at home. The principal cuisine in northern regions usually consists of roasted goose or turkey, whereas the northeastern and southern regions feast upon pork or lamb; cakes and various liquors are universal.

Children no longer receive gifts from Grandfather Frost. Just before Christmas 1992, "Grandfather *Božićnjak*" appeared on the public scene, a weak invention of state television to replace the then-unpopular image of Communism's gift-giver. According to *Christmas in Croatia* by Dunja Rihtman-Auguštin, *Božićnjak* does not describe a specific being but instead refers to a decorated Christmas tree and formerly to a Christmas tax which bonded peasants once paid to landlords. In keeping with Roman Catholic tradition, therefore, the Croatian gift-giver is the Christ Child, Little Jesus, or more specifically His "messenger," depicted as a little girl with wings, crown, and bearing a small fir tree (*see* **Germany**, whence this concept arose). Gift-giving to children and exchanges among adults are more common today than previously.

Families visit relatives on St. Stephen's Day (December 26), and house-cleaning commences on St. John's Day (December 27), on which day the Christmas straw is tied to fruit trees as a talisman for fruitfulness. On Holy Innocents Day (December 28), bands of children parade about with willow branches and "flog" relatives and comrades, the act a symbolic wish for health and well being.

New Year's Eve is filled with parties and noisemaking as men again shoot firearms at midnight, and this night, as well as Christmas Eve, is devoted to rituals predicting the future.

An alternative name for New Year's Day in Croatia is "Little Christmas" or "Second Christmas," which derives from the combined celebrations of Christmas and New Year's Day observed in that part of the world from the fourth to the sixteenth centuries, after which the Gregorian calendar moved New Year's Day to January 1 (*see* **New Year's Day**).

On Epiphany Eve, parishioners carry home water and salt blessed in church to be used as talismans against sickness and evil, and on Epiphany, the fields, homes, and other properties receive anointings of blessed water. Groups of children may offer carols as they travel about with illuminated stars and mangers. Family members divide the aforementioned Christmas bread among themselves on this day, and the one finding the hidden coin will have good luck in the new year.

Christmastime well-wishers include the *polaznik* ("first guest"), who may appear on St. Barbara's Day, Christmas Day, or St. Stephen's Day. Tradition holds that a young man arriving as the first visitor at one's house on these days brings good luck, and he receives a gift from the household. *Kolede* (carol) processions, more often found in Croatia's Adriatic region, are usually held on Christmas Eve, Christmas Day, St. Stephen's Day, New Year's Eve, New Year's Day, and Epiphany. The *koledari* (carolers) consist of groups of young boys who go from house to house singing wishes for health and bounty with expectations for rewards. Failure to provide the latter invites curses through song upon the household. Related *zvjezdari* ("star processions") run from New Year's to Epiphany and consist of groups of three boys dressed as the Three Kings, one of whom carries an illuminated star on a pole.

Since the Communist era, a renewed air of nationalism has pervaded the Croatian Christmas. For example, Christmas candles now sport the red, white, and blue colors of the Croatian flag; Midnight Mass in Zagreb Cathedral has become a gathering of the political elite; and decorations in urban areas reflect not only the Christmas spirit but themes of power and the state.

Yet religious sentiment appears also to prevail. For example, many citizens now prefer to greet one another with more religious phrases such as *Čestit Božić* ("Holy Christmas") or *Blagoslovljen Božić* ("Blessed Christmas") over the former, more secular greeting of *Sretan Božić* ("Happy Christmas").

See also **Czech Republic**; **Epiphany**; **Poland**; **Slovak Republic**.

Cuba

See **West Indies**

Czech Republic

Czechs and Slovaks united in 1918 after World War I to form Czechoslovakia, which Soviet Communists dominated from the end of World War II until 1991, when Soviet troops withdrew. During the approximately fifty years of Communism's atheistic regime, Christmas was repudiated, the mid-winter holiday was moved to New Year's Day with a secular agenda, and St. Nicholas or Baby Jesus, who had brought children's gifts, was replaced by a Soviet "Santa" known as "Grandfather Frost" (*see* **Russia**). Following the cessation of Soviet occupation, Czechoslovakia split into two independent nations, the Czech Republic and the Slovak Republic, on January 1, 1993. Communism had nearly extinguished the old holiday customs, yet a number of them still survive, primarily in rural areas, which revolve around agrarian rituals, romantic matchmaking, repelling evil, and forecasting the future. The principal Christian faith in the Czech Republic now is Roman Catholicism.

During the Advent season, homes and villages display the *Betlem* (Nativity scene), and collections of these may be found in regional museums such as the Museum of Nativities in Karlstejn near Prague. Here, one may view twenty-five antique wooden Nativities. First introduced in Prague in 1560 by Jesuit priests, the *Betlem* was the chief Christmas symbol until 1812, when the first Czech Christmas tree appeared in Prague. *Betlems*, constructed of paper, wood, or other substances, now consist of elaborate scenes and figures not only of the stable, Holy Family, shepherds, and Wise Men, but also of characters from local surroundings.

Other Advent customs include thoroughly cleaning the house, displaying window decorations of wreaths and lighted stars, mailing out Christmas cards (popular cards feature the work of Czech artist Josef Lada), attending a myriad of Christmas markets and cultural events, and baking a host of Christmas sweets, popular servings of which include Linzer cookies (formed into shapes such as bells, stars and wheels, pasted together with jam) and vanilla rolls. Instead of writing letters to Santa Claus or St. Nicholas, children address their epistles to *Jezisek* (Baby Jesus), who brings the Christmas gifts. Television programs feature an assortment of Czech fairy tales and fantasies.

Although Advent observances may include St. Andrew's Day (November 30), St. Barbara's Day (December 4), and St. Lucia's Day (December 13), the only custom still practiced from these three days is the expectation that cherry sprigs cut and placed in vases on December 4 will bloom by Christmas Eve, a positive sign for luck or seeking a mate. The Advent holiday now widely observed is *Mikulas* (St. Nicholas Day), observed on December 6. Folklore holds that *Svaty Mikulas* (St. Nicholas) descends from heaven on a golden cord at this time and is accompanied by an angel, who distributes gifts to good children, along with the devil, formerly called "Cert," who rattles chains and brings switches or coal to naughty youngsters.

Festivities for *Mikulas* actually commence on St. Nicholas Eve with parades. Groups of three people dressed as Bishop Nicholas, the angel, or the devil travel from house to house to quiz the children about their behavior and pass out treats, all for the purpose of giving the children a frightening thrill. Before retiring to bed, children place their shoes on the window sill and awaken to find them filled with an assortment of fruits, nuts, and candy.

Principal customs center around *Stedry Vecer* (Christmas Eve), the first of three consecutive Christmas holidays. Because folklore holds that the spirits of one's ancestors are present with the living on Christmas Eve, on that date the oldest child places a lighted candle and a fir sprig on the graves of family members. The Christmas tree is decorated that afternoon. Formerly, the tree was suspended from a cen-

Two spicy Yule Dollies from the former Czechoslovakia. On the left is a Baby Cake, the image of the Christ Child in swaddling clothes, with a representation of what would have been a real sprig of rosemary, plain or gilded, stuck in after baking. Such Yule Dollies are common throughout the world for Christmas cakes or cookies; many were iced in brilliant colors. From the journal Český Lid *(published in Prague), 1898.*

tral, overhead beam, but most families now adhere to the western trend of a tree on a floor stand. Although tree decorations in the Communist era usually consisted of glass ornaments and chocolate figures supplied to workers as Christmas "bonuses" by the state, many families today prefer more natural decorations, such as wax candles, red apples, walnuts, gingerbread, pine cones, and homemade ornaments of paper, straw, or wood.

Prior to the Communist regime, a host of ancient traditions and superstitions dominated Christmas Eve, especially regarding the Christmas Eve supper. Family members and relatives convened after having fasted all day, and children were told that if they adhered to the fast,

Two children and an angel carry a small crèche, perhaps to be placed on the table for the Holy Supper on Christmas Eve. From the journal Český Lid (published in Prague), 1907.

This frightening masked creature is an image of the devil who accompanies Mikulas, or St. Nicholas, on his day, December 6, seeking out good and bad children. Here, the saint, far right with a bishop's crozier, directs the devil, who is carrying a bag of gifts for good children. In this eighteenth century print, no angel seems to be present. From the journal Český Lid (published in Prague), 1910.

they would see a golden pig on the wall that evening at the supper. Sources vary regarding the origin of such a fable. One source holds that it stems from Freya, Norse goddess of love, beauty, and fertility, who is depicted as riding a golden boar, and to whom Norsemen sacrificed a boar at their winter solstice festivals; another source states that the golden pig simply symbolizes wealth and abundance.

Because the events of Christmas Eve predicted the type of year to come, past grievances and quarrels were resolved, all objects previously borrowed were returned, and everyone behaved in their most genteel manner. The table was set with a white tablecloth, the legs adorned with garlands (a talisman against theft from the fields) and joined with iron chains (symbolic of family ties and a wish that the table bounty extend into the new year). The floor beneath the table was painted with white limestone, upon which straw was spread to symbolize the manger. At center table were found various emblems, such as a crucifix, bread (the staff of life), candles (symbol of Jesus as light of the world), and garlic (charm of strength that repelled evil). An additional place was set for any unexpected guests, such as the Holy Family, and a candle placed in a window beckoned the stranger to dine.

All preparations completed, the father dipped shocks of grain into holy water and sprinkled each room, thus sanctifying the house. Children watched for the first star of the evening, believed to be the Star of Bethlehem, for the supper commenced at its appearance. For good luck, an even number of diners had to be present. On the foreheads of everyone, the head of the household traced honey in the form of a cross to repel evil and bring a new year of health. Related customs consisted of eating a Christmas waffle laced with honey and garlic, or cutting a loaf of bread and dispensing a slice daubed with honey to each person at the table, beginning with the oldest. Slices remaining portended new birth(s) in the family, whereas insufficient slices signaled death during the coming year.

The menu consisted of twelve meatless courses in honor of the Twelve Apostles and featured assorted preparations of fish (symbolic of the Last Supper), *babalki* (small portions of baked dough topped with a mixture of hot water, crushed poppy seeds, and sugar), sauerkraut soup, peas garnished with sugar and gingerbread, dried fruit, *vanocka* (Christmas bread), nuts, candy, strudels, *kuba* (prepared from barley and mushrooms), and *kutia* (boiled wheat with honey, raisins, and nuts). Carp became a traditional dish only during the nineteenth century, and fish scales were placed under each plate to assure health and prosperity.

At some point during the meal, the head of the household threw a spoonful of *babalki* or *kutia* up to the ceiling. If most of it stuck, the harvest would be bountiful. Reading auguries from such items as cracked walnuts and sliced apples then followed the meal. A rotten walnut portended illness or death; a star pattern seen in one's apple slice forecasted long life; a cross pattern predicted the opposite. (Other superstitions are discussed below). During the meal, no one left the table, and at its conclusion, everyone rose in unison, for the first to rise was cursed to die during the coming year.

Today, families may elect to keep such strict traditions or follow a more contemporary menu of carp or breaded fish, potato salad, fish soup, sauerkraut soup, and *vanocka*. Afterwards, the children are escorted out and return only after Baby Jesus has rung a small bell, the signal that He has arranged their presents under the Christmas tree and has now departed the scene. The livestock receive the table leftovers, and the family sing *kolady* (Christmas carols) around the Christmas tree or watch television Christmas programs. Christmas Eve concludes with Midnight Mass, at which churches often feature the *Czech Midnight Mass*, written in 1796 by Czech organist and composer Jakub Jan Ryba (1765–1815). This work has become popular because it replaces the original Latin lyrics of the Roman Catholic Christmas Mass with Ryba's own version of

Christ's birth and is patterned after folk Christmas plays.

Hod Bozi Vanocni (Christmas Day) and *Svateho Stepana* (St. Stephen's Day, December 26), the two remaining Christmas holidays, are spent in feasting, visiting, and receiving guests. On the latter day, caroling groups of children parade from house to house and receive treats as rewards.

New Year's Eve, also known as *Silvester* (so named for Sylvester I, the first pope to hold office after the Roman emperor Constantine accepted Christianity in the fourth century), is a rowdy period of family gatherings and parties. To bring luck, one consumes lentils and avoids poultry on New Year's Day. *Tri kralu* (Three Kings Day, Epiphany) closes the season as groups of boys dressed as the Three Kings again carol in the villages and receive treats.

• OTHER EXAMPLES OF CHRISTMAS EVE SUPERSTITIONS. After a candle is blown out, uprising smoke forecasts health and fortune; falling smoke predicts death.

A small, burning candle is placed in half of a walnut shell and floated in a bowl of water. If the shell remains afloat, long life is in store; if it sinks, the opposite. In another interpretation, the farther the "boat" travels from the side of the bowl, the farther one will travel from home.

Three walnuts are split and the meat removed. One of the shells is refilled with dirt, a second with a bit of bread, the third with money. The shells are glued back together and placed in a batch of walnuts. At midnight, each person selects a nut. He who receives the dirt can expect poverty; the bread, a life of comfort; the money, wealth.

An unmarried girl throws her shoes over her head. Toes pointing toward the door forecast marriage within the coming year; toes pointing back inside indicate another year's wait. If she who must wait ties a strand of her hair to a ring and holds it near a glass, the number of times the ring hits the glass before settling predicts the number of years to wait.

The shape of a piece of wood blindly drawn from a woodpile predicts the physical makeup of a girl's future husband.

A girl receives a clue about her future or her future husband's appearance by the shape that melted lead attains when poured into cold water. Another variation requires that the lead be poured through a key ring.

If, when a girl taps a henhouse door, a rooster crows, she will wed in the coming year; if a hen clucks, she must wait another year.

By cutting a hole in the ice of a frozen lake or pond and looking therein at midnight, one may see his future.

A girl learns the direction from which her future spouse will come by listening for the first dog bark heard after supper. Another variation requires her to shake a lilac tree beforehand and then listen for the bark.

"Merry Christmas" is *Prejeme Vam Vesele Vanoce.*

See also **Advent**; **Croatia**; **Epiphany**; **Poland**; **Slovak Republic.**

Czech Year

See **A Christmas Carol** (Film and Television Versions)

D

The Day Before Christmas, *or* Rudolph, the Red-Nosed Reindeer

See **Rudolph, the Red-Nosed Reindeer**

Day of the Innocents

See **Holy Innocents Day**

December 25

See **Christmas Day**

Deck the Halls with Boughs of Holly

Welsh traditional dance-carol, believed to date from the sixteenth century or earlier. The tune was originally the setting for a number of different merry-making or romantic texts which had nothing to do with Christmas. It belongs to a tradition in which people, dancing in a ring around a harpist, in turn contributed new verses to a song or were eliminated if they could not. What is now known as the "Fa la la la la," or "answering" section, the harpist originally played alone. Use of these nonsense syllables arose when no harp was present and eventually became a refrain for folk songs throughout the Middle Ages, not only in Wales but elsewhere. In some instances, the "Fa la la" allowed the ring dancer enough time to com-

pose a new verse on the spot. Over time in Wales the tune became permanently associated with anonymous texts for *Nos Galan* (New Year's Eve) celebrations, with titles such as "Oer yw'r gwr sy'n methu caru" ("Soon the Hoar Old Year Will Leave Us").

The anonymous lyrics to the familiar carol sung in America, "Deck the Halls with Boughs of Holly," first appeared with the traditional Welsh tune in *The Franklin Square Song Collection,* compiled by J. P. McCaskey (New York, 1881). This led to the assumption that these lyrics also arose in nineteenth-century America, but documentation to this effect is lacking. The lyrics recall pre–Christian traditions of decorating manor halls with holly and intense merrymaking at Yuletide and at the New Year. Variations of these lyrics exist, some of which take considerable interest in holiday imbibing. Line 3 of the first verse has read "Don we now our gay apparel." Line 1 of verse 2 has read "See the blazing Yule before us," and "See the flowing bowl before us!" Line 3 of verse 3 has read "Sing we joyous all together" and "Laughing, quaffing, all together."

Denmark

The Danes have enjoyed Christmas since the tenth century, when Viking king Harald

Bluetooth introduced Christianity to his kingdom, and Christmas traditions derive in part from those of the Norse pre–Christian *Jul* (Yule) celebrations. Denmark experiences only six hours of daylight at Christmastime, and cities and villages through the country light thousands of candles during the holidays as a reminder of bygone days when, during the winter solstice, their Viking ancestors set great fires to encourage the return of the sun and to dispel the hordes of spirits which were believed to haunt the long hours of darkness.

Another vestige is the *Julnisse*, shortened to *nisse* (plural *nisser*), a small, mischievous, aged male elf attired in gray homespun, red hood, long red stockings, white clogs, and sporting a long, gray beard. Whereas *nisser* do resemble the American Santa Claus except for size, some have suggested that they also bear a relationship to Satan, an opinion which most Danes dismiss. As the Vikings believed that the spirits of their dead returned home annually during the winter solstice (a belief commonly found in the folklore of many cultures), so the modern Danish folklore holds that the *nisser*, the spirits of each family's forefathers, return at the time of Advent as guardians of the home and remain until the end of the Christmas season. Allegedly, they can be seen only by cats, and their favorite haunts are attics or barns. Prone to committing endless pranks, they require a bowl of rice porridge on Christmas Eve to keep them pacified. The *nisser* are Denmark's favorite Christmas characters, and figures of them abound in homes and store displays.

Early in December, families ritually clean their homes and stables in anticipation of the guests that will arrive. Decorations include evergreens in various arrays and, because the state church is Lutheran, Advent wreaths, Advent candles, and Advent calendars, all attributed to Martin Luther himself.

The Swedish custom of observing December 13 as St. Lucia Day or Lucia Bride became popular in Denmark following World War II. The Danish ritual is similar to that for Sweden. *See also* **Sweden.**

Tradition dictates that all holiday guests must receive refreshment, for should they leave otherwise, with them the Christmas spirit departs from the house. Therefore, Danes keep a ready supply of sweets available, which may include *brune kager* (round, brown cookies topped with half an almond), *klejner* (fried cookies twisted into knots), *pebernødder* (peppernuts or spice cookies), marzipan (almond fondant molded into shapes of fruits, vegetables, or animals), *vanillekranse* (vanilla wreaths), *julekage* (Christmas coffee cake), and *kringle* (a pastry with raisins and almonds).

At least once, but usually several times during Advent, people attend evening parties ironically known as "Christmas lunches." Employers most often sponsor these events at the workplace for their employees, and because spouses are generally not invited (although some sources state that family members do attend), these "lunches" have gained a reputation for unrestrained behavior. Along with various Christmas beers and schnapps, the menu may feature herring, curry salad with eggs, ham, sausage, cheese, biscuits, fruits, and sweets.

Two holiday traditions originating in Denmark have gained world renown: collectible Christmas plates and Christmas seals. In previous centuries, aristocrats annually provided their servants with Christmas gifts of sweets and delicacies served on highly decorative, valuable plates, which the servants collected over the years. Finding that a lucrative market existed in such plates, two porcelain manufacturers introduced limited edition Christmas plates with a different design each year, Bing and Grondahl in 1895 and Royal Copenhagen in 1908. Four years earlier in 1904, Danish postal worker Einar Holbøll had introduced Christmas seals to his country as a means of raising money to build tuberculosis hospitals (*see* **Christmas Seals**).

Christmas trees have existed in Denmark since 1808, when they were imported from Germany to Holsteinborg on the island of Fyn. For those adhering to tradition, the preferred tree is a fir which is decorated on *Juleaften* (Christmas Eve) behind closed doors, for children are not allowed to view the tree until it is fully decorated. Danish families generally make their own ornaments, keeping them as heirlooms from year to year. Ornaments may consist of hearts interwoven from red and white paper, the most favored of decorations; garlands of miniature Danish flags; woven heart baskets and colored paper cones, both of which are filled with candy; *nisser*; stars; "crackers" (noisemakers that pop when both ends are pulled); and sparklers (similar to those used on the American Independence Day) which are placed in the tree and lit on Christmas Eve. A large star usually serves as a tree topper. Whereas Christmas trees in homes are traditionally illuminated by real candles despite the significant fire hazard, Christmas trees in public places are decorated with electric lights, which are illuminated on the first day of December.

On *lille Juleaften* ("little Christmas Eve," December 23), as families prepare the Christmas Eve dinner, they traditionally may invite friends to their homes for *glögg* (spiced red wine with cloves, cinnamon, raisins, and almonds) along with "apple-pieces," small hot cakes which, ironically, contain no apples.

Although most businesses close at noon on Juleaften, the ringing of church bells at 4 P.M. heralds the official commencement of Christmas, and all commerce ceases until December 27 (for many, until January 2). Tradition also dictates that each household hang a *juleneg* (sheaf of grain) for the birds as the Birds' Christmas Tree, and that their livestock receive extra rations of food, for no creature must be neglected at Christmastime. To that end, each house displays a burning candle in a window to welcome the stranger that may pass by.

The traditional Juleaften dinner, served after the early evening Lutheran church services (or following Roman Catholic Midnight Mass), usually includes *risengrød* (rice porridge) containing a single almond, and the person finding the almond in his or her serving receives an extra little treat. Alternatively, the almond may be hidden in a cold rice pudding dessert. Other courses include roast goose, turkey, duck, pork, variously prepared potatoes, cucumber salad, *rødkål* (red cabbage), *rombudding* (rum pudding), *æblekage* (apple crumb cake), red wine, and Christmas beers.

A Christmas tree celebration follows the dinner. The tree is finally revealed to the little ones, and, joining hands, everyone in the household walks around the tree while singing traditional carols. Children then open their gifts, which come from the Julemand ("Christmas Man"), the Danish equivalent of the American Santa Claus and the British Father Christmas, who commands a reindeer sleigh with *nisser* for assistants. Often the father or another male will retire and return dressed as the Julemand, distributing gifts from a pack and quizzing the youngsters about their behavior over the past year. In Danish folklore, the *Klapparbock* ("Goat with Yule Gifts," derived from two mythical goats, Gnasher and Cracker, which pulled the chariot of the Scandinavian god Thor) also accompanies the Julemand and administers punishment to naughty children (in some locales, a man dressed in goatskins may personify this creature, chasing and frightening children). Amid coffee, *glögg*, and other confections, the family then opens and reviews all Christmas cards that have been received heretofore.

Christmas Day and the day after, termed Second Christmas Day, are reserved for visiting relatives. Again, a sumptuous table is spread, this time a *kolde bord* (cold table), consisting of cold foods for noonday meals. Following each course, the host offers a *skål* (toast), after which guests reciprocate. In addition to dining, there are outdoor activities such as ice skating and cross-country skiing. On December 26, theaters offer plays and pantomimes, some presenting the same production year after year. For example, Copenhagen's *Folketeatret* has presented *Christmas in Nøddebo Rectory* annually since 1888.

New Year's Eve is filled with parties, fireworks, the committing of numerous pranks, and the monarch's televised address to the nation. The Christmas season ends on Epiphany Eve, Twelfth Night, when Christmas trees are dismantled and their sweets eaten, and families light three candles in memory of the traditional three Wise Men.

"Merry Christmas" in Danish is *Glædelig Jul*.

See also **Advent; Epiphany; Greenland; Yule.**

Desert Christmas Cactus
See **Christmas Plants**

Devil's Knell

See **Great Britain**

The Dick Van Dyke Show

Popular television situation comedy series that aired on the CBS network from 1961 to 1966. Dick Van Dyke played the lead, Rob Petrie, a television writer for a fictional variety show, *The Alan Brady Show*. The rest of the regular cast included Carl Reiner as Alan Brady; Rose Marie and Morey Amsterdam as Petrie's assistant writers, Sally and Buddy; and Mary Tyler Moore as Rob's wife, Laura.

Of the 158 episodes in the series, only one featured a Christmas theme. That episode, titled "The Alan Brady Show Presents," aired on December 18, 1963. In this show-within-a-show, the staff of *The Alan Brady Show* joins Alan for some holiday merriment on the air. In the most memorable scene, characters Rob, Laura, Sally, and Buddy dress up as a marching band quartet and sing "We All Are Fine Musicians." Pretending to play different musical instruments and imitating their sounds, Rob mimics a trombone, Laura a piccolo, Sally a trumpet, and Buddy a tuba. As this routine closes, each person "plays" and retreats one by one until Laura is left alone. Unable to face the sudden loneliness, the little piccolo squeaks a final measure and runs off in "tears." Also in this episode, Sally, whom the series portrayed as a man-hungry single woman, appropriately delivers her rendition of an original tune, "Santa, Send a Fella." Interestingly, the Christmas episode is the only one that ever depicted an actual performance of *The Alan Brady Show*; the other 157 episodes only revolved *around* that show.

The script and most of the musical numbers for this episode originated with Sam Denoff and Bill Persky, both former writers for *The Andy Williams Show*. "We All Are Fine Musicians" had appeared in an earlier *Dick Van Dyke Show* episode titled "The Sam Pomerantz Scandals" which aired in March of 1963. Vacationing in the Catskill Mountains, *The Alan Brady Show* staff performs an identical routine at a local resort as they do for the Christmas show. Dick Van Dyke first became acquainted with "We All Are Fine Musicians" (originally known simply as "The Musicians") from an obscure record in 1953 while hosting a children's television show in Atlanta. He and the children had initially performed the same act that later was incorporated into two episodes of *The Dick Van Dyke Show*.

Carl Reiner at first rejected Denoff's and Persky's idea of making any Christmas episode at all, because he felt that a holiday show would not fit well into the summer rerun schedule. He finally agreed when he realized that he could rerun the same episode every year at Christmastime instead.

Dickens, Charles, Christmas Stories of

In keeping with the British tradition of telling ghost stories at Christmastime, Dickens created five novellas, now collectively termed *Christmas Books*, wherein, with one exception, the supernatural pervades the holiday. The first and best-known example of these is *A Christmas Carol* (1843). But whereas ghosts in that tale transform a basically mean-spirited person into one of compassion and generosity, the spirits in *The Chimes* (1844), *The Cricket on the Hearth* (1845), and *The Haunted Man and the Ghost's Bargain* (1848) serve to reform the flawed attitudes of basically good people. The fifth book, *The Battle of Life* (1846), not only contains no supernatural elements but also is not a Christmas story in the strictest sense of the term and is therefore not discussed in detail here. Although Dickens surely considered its theme of love between two close sisters and the romantic sacrifice that one makes for the other as a tale in keeping with the Christian spirit of the holiday, *The Battle of Life* remains the least known of the collection.

A Christmas Carol is discussed as a separate entry; the following paragraphs summarize the best-known of the remaining novellas.

The Chimes: A Goblin Story of Some Bells That Rang an Old Year Out and a New One In (1844). Toby Veck, a poor ticket porter, initially manifests an optimistic outlook on life, despite his station, and imagines that the hourly pealing of the church bells signifies good omens. When harsh words from the upper classes suggest that the poor have no rightful place in the upcoming new year, however, Toby's self-esteem falls, and he imagines that even the chimes mock him. Wallowing in self-pity, Toby meets the Goblin of the Great Bell, who upbraids him for actually believing that the working class and the poor are "born bad." The Goblin paints a futuristic scene of a world without Toby's positive influence, showing him the devastating consequences if others, like his dear daughter, Meg, abandon all hope of rising above their stations. At the moment when Meg is about to commit suicide rather than remain destitute, Toby awakens from his nightmare at midnight on New Year's Eve. He no longer doubts his capabilities, having learned this "from the creature dearest to his heart." *The Chimes* was twice adapted in 1914 for the silent screen, once in the United States and once in Great Britain.

The Cricket on the Hearth: A Fairy Tale of Home (1845). A series of interconnected doubts and deceptions plagues the characters in this complex New Year's Eve tale. John Peerybingle, a carrier, reasons that his much younger wife, Dot, has deprived herself of a young and active life by marrying him and now only feigns affection for him. Caleb Plummer, a poor toy-maker, has deceived his blind daughter, Bertha, from her birth regarding their lifestyle. Believing that she lives in luxury, Bertha falls in love with Mr. Tackleton, her father's sarcastic employer, and Caleb shields her from Tackleton's verbal abuse by explaining that Tackleton is only "joking" with her because his feelings are mutual. Tackleton actually plans to wed Dot's friend, May Fielding, but May still yearns for an old flame, Edward Plummer, Caleb's son, who is presumed dead. Years earlier, John had provided Edward with the means of going abroad; hearing that May will marry, however, Edward returns, disguised as an old man to learn the truth. Dot recognizes him and, meeting him secretly, promises not to reveal his identity. When John, discovering their meetings and mistaking their intentions, would end his marriage, a fairy emerges from a cricket on the hearth and bids John to reconsider, for Dot has never ceased to love him; her love is genuine. They are reconciled, and Caleb eventually confesses his deception to Bertha, who forgives her father's misplaced intentions. And for a sunny ending, Edward and May wed on New Year's Day.

United States adaptations of *The Cricket on the Hearth* for the silent screen were released in 1909, 1915, and 1923; a United States/Russian version also appeared in 1915.

A musical, animated cartoon adaptation for television aired on *The Danny Thomas Hour* in 1967 and featured the voices of Danny and Marlo Thomas, Roddy McDowall, Ed Ames, Hans Conried, Abbe Lane, and Paul Frees. Produced and directed by Arthur Rankin, Jr., and Jules Bass. A Rankin-Bass Production in association with Videocraft International. Sony Wonder. Color. 50 min.

The Haunted Man and the Ghost's Bargain: A Fancy for Christmas Time (1848). Memories of past sorrows haunt Mr. Redlaw, a kind yet most unhappy chemist. Christmastime is at hand, and whereas a servant remarks that the happiest of his own memories are greatest at this time of year, Redlaw plunges himself into melancholy at this season. When his miserable ego appears as a phantom, Redlaw, seeking relief, petitions the specter to abolish all memories of past injustices. The specter complies but stipulates that those who have any contact with Redlaw henceforth will also lose similar memories. While this request seems merciful, Redlaw rapidly discovers that the inability to recall sorrow or injustice produces a cold, callous behavior devoid of compassion. He revokes his wish, and the phantom reverses the spell. The experience teaches Redlaw that, at Christmastime, the memory of every remediable sorrow and wrong should be especially active, for we remember Christ, who suffered wrong for us and redeemed us. And as Christ forgave those who wronged Him, it is proper to remember those who wrong us, that we may forgive them.

In 1850, Dickens founded *Household Words*, a weekly journal in which he expressed his views on current affairs and which, at year's end, included the special feature of a Dickens Christmas short story. This tradition continued when this journal was incorporated in 1859 into *All the Year Round*, which Dickens edited for the remainder of his life. His initial contributions to the 21 tales now collectively known as the *Christmas Stories* consisted of a traditional approach to Yuletide, with recollections of childhood and family festivities. As time passed, however, Dickens, ever concerned for the neglected poor and alert to social injustice in England, generally dropped Christmas themes as such and used this medium instead as a sounding block for social reform. In four of these stories, Dickens collaborated with Wilkie Collins, who wrote portions of the text.

Dickens's *Christmas Stories* consists of the following titles: "A Christmas Tree" (1850, the only one of his works to mention this decoration); "What Christmas Is as We Grow Older" (1851); "The Poor Relation's Story" (1852); "The Child's Story" (1852); "The Schoolboy's Story" (1853); "Nobody's Story"; "The Seven Poor Travelers" (1854); "The Holly-Tree" (1855); "The Wreck of the Golden Mary," with Wilkie Collins (1856); "The Perils of Certain English Prisoners" (1857); "Going into Society" (1858); "The Haunted House" (1859); "A Message from the Sea," with Wilkie Collins (1860); "Tom Tiddler's Ground" (1861); "Somebody's Luggage" (1862); "Mrs. Lirriper's Lodgings" (1863); "Mrs. Lirriper's Legacy" (1864); "Doctor Marigold" (1865); "Mugby Junction" (1866); "No Thoroughfare," with Wilkie Collins (1867); "The Lazy Tour of Two Idle Apprentices," with Wilkie Collins.

See also **A Christmas Carol.**

Dickens Christmas Carol

See **A Christmas Carol** (FILM AND TELEVISION VERSIONS)

Ding Dong! Merrily on High

French-English carol. The music is a French folk dance tune, "Branle de l'official" ("Dance of the Official"), which Thoinot Arbeau (1519–1595) included in *Orchesographie* (1588), a collection of sixteenth-century music and dance. Anglican priest George R. Woodward (1838–1934) supplied the text, written in a style commensurate with the music. In fact Woodward, seeking artistic worth in church music over the Victorian styles at the turn of the twentieth century, preferred to compose hymn lyrics in the style of the sixteenth- or seventeenth-century, then select appropriate melodies from that era to fit his lyrics. Woodward was responsible for many of the reforms in *The English Hymnal* (1906) and compiled three collections, *Songs of Syon* (1904), *An Ital-*

ian Carol Book (1920), and *The Cowley Carol Book* (1901, 1919, for the Fathers at Cowley, Oxford), the latter three in collaboration with Cambridge musician Charles Wood (1866–1926).

The subject of "Ding Dong! Merrily on High," as the title suggests, is the merry ringing of bells both in heaven and on earth at the birth of Christ. Macaronic (vernacular words mixed with Latin), the carol features a Latin refrain, "Gloria! Hosanna in excelsis!" ("Glory! Hosanna in the highest!"), which is similar in wording and musical phrasing to the refrain of another macaronic carol, "Angels We Have Heard on High": "Gloria in excelsis Deo!" ("Glory to God in the highest!").

See also **Angels We Have Heard on High.**

A Disney Christmas Gift

(1982). Television presentation of excerpts from classic Disney animated cartoons. Included are scenes from four feature films: *Bambi* (1942), *Cinderella* (1950), *Peter Pan* (1953), and *The Sword in the Stone* (1963). Also included are scenes from four holiday cartoon "shorts": *The Night Before Christmas* (1933); *Once upon a Wintertime* (1952), sung by Frances Langford; *Pluto's Christmas Tree* (1952), with Mickey Mouse and chipmunks Chip and Dale; and *The Clock Watcher* (1945), with Donald Duck wrapping Christmas gifts by the clock.

This program received an Emmy Award nomination for Outstanding Animated Program (1983-84 season). Prepared by Ed Ropolo, Frank Brandt, Darryl Sutton, Joan Spollino. Executive producer William Yates. Walt Disney Company. Walt Disney Home Video. Color. One hour.

See also **Walt Disney Christmas.**

Do You Hear What I Hear?

Popular American carol written in 1962 by Noel Regney and Gloria Shayne, the sole work of any significant note from either songwriter. An indirect yet quite unique telling of the Christmas story, this carol personifies nature who first learns the good news of Christ's birth, and from there the tidings cascade around the world. More specifically, the night wind, the first informant, asks a lamb if it has seen the bright star overhead. The lamb in turn asks a shepherd boy if he has heard the glorious song that fills the air. The boy then inquires of a king if he knows that a Child shivers from cold and suggests that gifts be brought in homage. Turning to all nations of the world, the king calls for everyone to pray for peace, for the Child is destined to bring goodness and light to an ailing world.

The Harry Simeone Chorale first recorded the carol in 1962 for Mercury Records, but it was not charted. Bing Crosby's recording a year later on the Capitol label was ranked number 2 on the *Billboard Christmas Singles* chart, and Andy Williams's 1965 recording for Columbia placed 18th on the same chart.

Dr. Seuss's How the Grinch Stole Christmas
See **How the Grinch Stole Christmas**

Dominican Republic
See **West Indies**

The Dream of Old Scrooge
See **A Christmas Carol** (FILM AND TELEVISION VERSIONS)

E

Ebbie
See **A Christmas Carol** (FILM AND TELEVISION VERSIONS)

Ebenezer
See **A Christmas Carol** (FILM AND TELEVISION VERSIONS)

Echo Carol
See **While by My Sheep**

Ecuador
See **South America**

Eggnog
Thick, rich, holiday drink consisting of beaten eggs, spices, cream, sugar, and some form of alcohol. The name derives from "noggin" or "nog," a strong ale known in Great Britain since the seventeenth century. The British thus are generally credited with creating the drink, which originated from posset, a hot drink consisting of eggs and milk with nog or wine added. The basic recipe passed to other countries, where variations in the drink were known by names such as *advocaat* (Netherlands), *eggedosis* (Norway), *lait de poule* (non-alcoholic drink of France), and *Biersuppe* (an egg-and-beer soup of Germany). Subsequent to eggnog's arrival in the early American colonies, the alcoholic portion consisted of rum, brandy, bourbon, sherry, and so forth. Despite the variety of liquor added, however, eggnog retains an association with the British "nog."

The eggnog that is sold in grocery stores in the United States is most commonly spiced with nutmeg. Grocery store eggnog has been cooked to prevent possible salmonella contamination.

Egypt
See **Africa**

El Salvador
See **Central America**

Elmo Saves Christmas
(1996). Children's video, a musical parody of William Dean Howells's classic short story "Christmas Every Day," featuring the Jim Henson Muppets of Sesame Street.

Stuck in Elmo's fireplace because of an oversized bag of toys, Santa (Charles Durning) receives some much-needed assistance from Elmo, who pulls him out. The reason the bag is so large is that Lightning, a curious little reindeer in training, has hidden there. A grateful Santa offers Elmo a special gift, the choice between a pink bear doll or a magical snow globe which grants three wishes. Choosing the globe, Elmo wastes his first wish on a glass of water. His second wish is worse, for he wishes that every day of the year could be Christmas. At Santa's command, Lightning escorts Elmo forward into time to glimpse the future impact of his folly: work piles up because people are on Christmas break, daily carol singing produces hoarse voices, and endless shopping for gifts breeds contempt for the season. Repenting, Elmo accidentally breaks his globe while casting his final wish for all to be restored as it was. The only hope is for Lightning and Elmo to reverse their path and return to that part of time before Elmo received the globe. This time he chooses the bear doll.

With Maya Angelou, Harvey Fierstein, and singing group "14 Karat Soul." Written by Christine Ferraro, Tony Geiss. Produced by Karin Young Shiel. Directed by Emily Squires. Children's Television Workshop and Jim Henson Productions. Sesame Street Home Video. Color. 55 min.

See also **Christmas Every Day.**

Elves

See **Denmark; Finland; Iceland; Norway; Saint Nicholas; Sweden**

England

See **Great Britain**

Epiphany

(Greek, *Epiphaneia,* "appearance, manifestation"). Feast observed on January 6 by the Roman Catholic, Anglican, and Eastern Rite (Orthodox) churches. It commemorates the three-part manifestation of Jesus as the Son of God: (1) physically manifested to the Gentiles through the Magi at Bethlehem (Matthew 2:1–12); (2) spiritually manifested at His baptism in the River Jordan when the Holy Ghost descended as a dove (Luke 3:21–22); (3) miraculously manifested at the marriage in Cana when Jesus performed His first miracle by turning water into wine (John 2:1–11). Sometimes

called "Little Christmas," in many parts of Europe Epiphany is considered the end of the Christmas season, the last day in the period known as the Twelve Days of Christmas. Thus Epiphany Eve is often called "Twelfth Night" and Epiphany itself "Twelfth Day," if one considers Christmas Night as the first night and December 26 as the first day in this period. Custom dictates that all Christmas decorations be stored away at this time and that holiday greenery be burned; according to superstition, anyone failing to adhere to this tradition invites bad luck. Other designations include "Feast of Light," for the early Christians celebrated with lighted torches; "Feast of Jordan"; and "Three Kings Day" in honor of the Magi.

The fixing of January 6 remains largely traditional in Roman Catholic circles. One theory, however, proposes reckoning backward from April 6, Easter as kept by the Phrygian Montanists, who followed the second-century heretical prophet Montanus. Assuming that Jesus lived exactly 33 years, Epiphany would have fallen on January 6. On the other hand, an Internet article on "The Feast of Lights" by the Rev. George Mastrantonis of the Greek Orthodox Archdiocese of America implies that Epiphany Christianized the birthday of Aeon, patron god of Alexandria, Egypt.

Epiphany was first celebrated in the East by the second century, with emphasis placed primarily on Christ's baptism and secondarily on His Nativity. This rationale stemmed from two concepts: one, that Christ's baptism constituted His true, or spiritual, Nativity; two, by tradition, His baptism occurred exactly thirty years from His Nativity; thus the two events were celebrated together. Clement of Alexandria (150?–215?), a Greek theologian and church father, wrote that, although the followers of Basilides (second-century Alexandrian teacher who founded a gnostic sect) commemorated the baptism and Nativity on January 6, the Church at that time had not embraced Epiphany as an ecclesiastical feast. While Epiphanius (315?–403), a father of the Greek Church and a theologian of Jewish birth, also referred to January 6 as the Epiphany, the Roman historian Ammianus Marcellinus provided the first definite evidence of church involvement by mentioning that in 361, the

Roman emperor Julian the Apostate (331?–363) attended an Epiphany feast in Vienne of Gaul.

Because Epiphany also Christianized certain pagan spring festivals, which honored the gods of running water, rivers, and streams through water purification rituals, it became commonplace to hold baptisms on this date with a special "Blessing of the Waters" ceremony. Whereas Epiphany baptisms survived in the African Christian Church, the sanctification of water has remained in the Eastern Orthodox churches, for example, the Greek Orthodox and Russian Orthodox faiths. The blessing often consists of a priest tossing a cross into a nearby body of water, after which men compete to retrieve it. Believing that the holy water will cure sickness and yield bountiful crops, worshippers return home with some of the water.

The Western (Roman) Church did not observe Epiphany until the fourth century, when it is believed that the theologian St. Athanasius (c. 293–373) of Alexandria introduced it to Gaul. This new feast came to Western knowledge about the same time that the Western Church established December 25 as the Feast of the Nativity, thus Christianizing the birthday of Mithras, the Persian sun god. With two established dates for the Nativity, the East adopted December 25 and retained January 6 as the anniversary of Christ's baptism; the West, while also embracing Epiphany, placed far more emphasis on the Magi's visit to Bethlehem on that date. Regarding the miracle at Cana, Epiphanius asserted that water, even rivers and probably the Nile itself, had turned to wine on January 6, a miracle that has never been noted in the literature of the Western Church.

• TWELFTH NIGHT. Beginning in the Middle Ages, Twelfth Night in Europe was spent in revelry with music, singing, dancing, masques and masquerades, bonfires, pageants portraying the Magi, and feasting, with a mood much akin to that of the Roman Saturnalia. Throughout European courts, it was initially customary to elect a mock king, the Lord of Misrule, to supervise a series of festivities held all during the Christmas season, in which those in attendance were subject to this mock king's ludicrous fancies. By the time of Edward II of England (1284–1327), the mock king had become known as "King of the Bean" from the manner in which he was elected. A large plum cake was served with a bean hidden inside. Each participant took a slice of cake, and whoever found the bean was dubbed King of the Bean. If a woman found the bean, she became queen and chose a king. Following the festivities, a portion of the cake was donated to the poor. The cake itself, called a "Kings' Cake" in honor of the Three Kings or Magi, originated in France during the twelfth century as a means of choosing the mock king for Christmas court festivities. The hidden object might be a bean or perhaps a pea, nut, or a coin, and the one finding the object was either dubbed king for a day or would receive good luck in the coming year. During the Renaissance, the custom of choosing a King of the Bean had become more associated with Twelfth Night rather than the entire Christmas season as before, and the Kings' Cakes appeared as works of art, often of enormous sizes.

The seventeenth century saw increasing popularity for an innovative custom: drawing slips of paper which contained the names of fictitious, ridiculous characters for revelers to impersonate. This practice gained preference over the King of the Bean game, and by the eighteenth century, the Twelfth Night mock king had become virtually obsolete. The paper slips evolved into sets of professionally printed cards with names and illustrations.

A somewhat related custom, the so-called Urn of Fate, was found in Italy and Spain. On Twelfth Night, Italians filled a large urn with wrapped boxes containing either gifts or nothing at all, and each guest had one chance of drawing either a prize or a dud. Instead of gifts, the Spanish urn contained paper slips, each with the name of a guest, and the slips were drawn out by twos on Christmas Day. The pairs were encouraged to become good friends during the new year, which prompted matrimony for some pairs of unmarried men and women.

By the nineteenth century, the boisterous mood of Twelfth Night had considerably waned, yet a number of countries retain vestiges of this festival. For example, the Kings' Cakes found in the United States today are rounded to symbolize the circuitous route which the Magi supposedly took to evade King Herod and are decorated in purple, green, and gold, colors not only symbolic of justice, faith, and power, respectively, but also resembling a jeweled crown. The hidden object often consists of a tiny plastic doll, symbolic of the Christ Child. Twelfth Night initiates the Carnival season in Louisiana which terminates with Mardi Gras, and the objects once hidden in the Kings' Cakes of England have found a new home in plum puddings.

See also **Christmas Day; Great Britain; Nativity; Saturnalia.**

Ernest Saves Christmas

(1988). Motion picture comedy, one in a series of *Ernest* pictures starring Jim Varney as the wacky, drawling, accident-prone know-it-all, Ernest P. Worrell.

For centuries, the role of Santa Claus has been passed from one deserving man to the next, each endowed with that special spirit, a love for children, that makes him worthy of receiving the role. The time has arrived when the present Santa (Douglas Seale), now 150 years of age, must name his successor by 7:00 P.M. on Christmas Eve, lest the magic of Christmas die forever. Santa's choice is Joe Carruthers (Oliver Clark) in Orlando, Florida, a gentle, highly moral man whose children's television show has been canceled and who now has the opportunity to star in a Christmas movie. With two days remaining, Santa, using no alias and dressed as a businessman, arrives by commercial aircraft with his reindeer and sleigh crated on board. To find Joe, he receives help from Ernest, a cabby filled with the Christmas spirit, and reluctantly from Harmony Starr (Noelle Parker), a cynical, runaway teenager in much need of Santa's Christmas spirit.

Adept at trickery, disguise, and deception, Ernest serves Santa well by bailing him out of jail after he is arrested for vagrancy, discovering Joe's whereabouts from a talent agency, and sneaking Santa onto the movie lot where Joe will star. There, Joe declines Santa's proposal, yet he is dissatisfied with the movie and his role, for this "Christmas" film incorporates violence and profanity. As Joe ponders his future, Santa discerns that Harmony has run off with his magic bag but knows that her conscience, longing for a reconciliation at home, will bring her back.

Christmas Eve wanes as Ernest and two of Santa's elves claim the sleigh and eight reindeer at the airport baggage hangar after shocked workmen discover the reindeer attached upside down to the ceiling (they possess a natural affinity for roofs). When Ernest hitches them to the sleigh, they rocket into space. Zipping wildly through the skies, Ernest fights for control and manages to evade two military jets bent on shooting them all down as UFOs.

With minutes to spare, Harmony returns, as does Joe, whom Santa, through a simple handshake, transforms into his successor, complete with all the trappings. As Ernest lands the sleigh in one piece, the new Santa bids him guide his sleigh this one night, and the former Santa resumes his original identity as Seth Applegate.

With Gailard Sartain, Bill Byrge, and Robert Lesser. Written by Bosco Kline, Ed Turner. Produced by Stacy Williams, Doug Claybourne. Directed by John Cherry. Touchstone Pictures in association with Silver Screen Partners III. Touchstone Pictures Home Video. Color. 95 min.

Estonia
See **Baltic States**

Ethiopia
See **Africa**

Evergreens
See **Christmas Plants; Christmas Tree; The Holly and the Ivy; Mistletoe**

Everywhere, Everywhere Christmas Tonight
See **O Little Town of Bethlehem**

The Exeter Boar's Head Carol
See **The Boar's Head Carol**

F

A Family Circus Christmas

(1979). Made-for-television animated cartoon, based on the comic strip *The Family Circus*, created by Bill Keane.

As Mommy, Daddy, Billy, Dolly, Jeffy, and PJ decorate the Christmas tree, a sentimental crisis arises when the family cannot find the handmade star fashioned by the children's late grandfather years ago. After dreaming about riding with Santa to the North Pole to see wondrous holiday inventions, Jeffy asks a department store Santa to bring his grandfather back from heaven for Christmas. With faith in such an impossible request, Jeffy does receive a miraculous alternative. On Christmas Eve, the spirits of Santa and his grandfather guide Jeffy to the star, which had been misplaced. Atop the tree and lit, the star symbolizes that Grandfather is still among them.

Voices: Anne Costello, Bob Kaliban, Mark McDermott, Missy Hope, Nathan Berg, Allen Swift. Vocalist: Sarah Vaughan. Written by Joseph C. Cavella. Produced by Edward F. Cullen. Directed by Al Kouzel. A Cullen-Kasdan Production in association with the Register and Tribune Syndicate. Family Home Entertainment Video. Color. Half-hour.

Fantasia on Christmas Carols

See **The First Nowell**

Farolitos and Luminarias

Respective Spanish-language designations for "little fires" and "illuminations," two simple holiday lighting decorations found outdoors in the American Southwest. Farolitos, which line walkways, roofs, buildings, and plazas, consist of brown paper bags filled with several inches of sand and lit by a votive candle wedged into the sand. The tops are cuffed to keep the bags open. Forerunners of farolitos were Chinese paper lanterns which first appeared in Mexico during the sixteenth century as a result of Spanish trade with the Orient. By the nineteenth century, these lanterns had spread into Spanish territory north of Mexico, where brown wrapping paper subsequently proved to be a more durable medium for construction.

Luminarias, on the other hand, are bonfires of piñon pine logs stacked in squares three feet tall. Most commonly found in rural regions and the pueblos on Christmas Eve, they adorn homes and churches especially in New Mexico. Although luminarias are less prevalent now in metropolitan areas, larger cities such as Albuquerque sponsor tours of luminaria displays in selected neighborhoods. Where luminarias originated is a matter of conjecture. They supposedly derived either from bonfires tended by the Bethlehem shepherds of 2,000 years ago, or from ancient Native American customs which sixteenth-century Spanish missionaries Christianized into Christmas celebrations, or from customs which these missionaries originally brought to Mexico.

Use of the two terms depends on one's locale. In northern New Mexico, "farolitos" implies only the paper bags, but in locales where the bonfire custom is not routinely practiced, farolitos are also known as luminarias.

The Fat Albert Christmas Special

See **A Christmas Carol** (Film and Televisions Versions)

Father Christmas

(Book). Classic children's picture book written and illustrated in 1973 by British author Raymond Briggs. It received Great Britain's Kate Greenaway Medal, equivalent to the Caldecott Medal in the United States.

On the morning of Christmas Eve, Father Christmas, the British equivalent of Santa Claus, awakens from dreams of vacations on warm, tropical isles and reluctantly prepares for his annual rounds. With no elves about to help him and knowing that soon he must drive his two-reindeer sleigh through snow, sleet, rain, and fog to deliver presents, he makes preparations while muttering favorite expressions such as "Blooming snow!" and "Blooming chimneys!" Yet he performs his duties faithfully, arriving at Buckingham Palace, his last stop, at sunrise. He is happiest back home at the North Pole, where he concludes with a turkey dinner and tea. Retiring to bed for another year, he wishes everyone a "Blooming Christmas!"

In 1991, the story was adapted as a motion picture animated cartoon "short," in which Father Christmas fulfilled his dreams by taking a vacation around the world. William Dennis Hunt provided the voice of Father Christmas, the only character with dialogue. Written by Raymond Briggs. Produced by John Coates. Directed by Dave Unwin. Blooming Productions in association with Palace Video, Ltd., and Gaga Communications. Columbia Tristar Home Video. Color. 25 min.

See also **The Snowman.**

Father Christmas
(gift-giver) *See* **Great Britain**

Feast of Asses
See **Feast of Fools**

Feast of Dedication
See **Hanukkah**

Feast of Fools
Collective term for a series of mock-religious festivals in force by the twelfth century, which divisions of the lower clergy, particularly in France, England, and central Europe, observed between Christmas and Epiphany (January 6). As a release from the solemnity of Christmas itself, deacons observed a feast on St. Stephen's Day (December 26), the priests on St. John the Evangelist's Day (December 27), the choirboys on Holy Innocents Day (December 28), and the sub-deacons generally on the Feast of the Circumcision (January 1) or sometimes on Epiphany. The mood of each of these feasts, held within the church, was riotous and often blasphemous, with clowning, buffoonery, obscene songs, the wearing of hideous masks (often depicting wild animals), transvestism,

"When Friars, Monks, and Priests of former days,
Apocrypha and Scripture turn'd to Plays,
The Festival of Fools and Asses kept,
Obey'd Boy-Bishops, and to crosses crept,
They made the mumming church the People's rod,
And held the grinning Bauble for a God."

An engraving end verse from William Hone's Ancient Mysteries Described *(1823).*

and the reversed roles of superiors and subordinates. Each feast was supervised by an elected Archbishop of Fools, Lord of Misrule, or Abbot of Unreason, the entire affair closely resembling the extravagant license of the ancient Roman Saturnalia, which had included the crowning of a mock king.

Coupled with the Feast of the Circumcision and the revels was the Feast of the Asses, a mock Christianization of the pagan feast of Epona, Roman goddess of horses, mules, and asses, which had been observed near the new year. On January 1, the local church would stage a parody on the biblical flight into Egypt

(Gospel of Matthew 2:13–15). In this parody a young woman holding a baby would ride into the sanctuary on an ass (traditionally the Virgin Mary had ridden an ass into Egypt as well as to Bethlehem). Rituals would praise the ass; then, to conclude the service, the priest would imitate an ass by braying three times, and the congregation would respond in like manner.

The Feast of Asses emerged from a church drama dating to the eleventh century or earlier, which portrayed a series of Old Testament prophets attesting to the birth of Christ. One of these, Baalam, rode upon a wooden ass and reenacted the biblical story about his talking ass and an angel (Numbers 22:22–38). This segment gained wide popularity and, by the thirteenth century, had become an independent play that eventually merged with the year-end revels.

Although the Feast of Fools as a whole had existed for centuries, the Church never officially sanctioned the abuses that occurred and largely succeeded in driving the celebrations from its cathedrals by the fifteenth century, although some persisted until the early eighteenth century. The peasantry then took up the merriment by electing a Prince or Pope of Fools, often bestowing upon him a hood with the ears of an ass.

French author Victor Hugo (1802–1885) provides another picture of the Feast of Fools in his historical novel *The Hunchback of Notre Dame* (1831), set in late fifteenth-century Paris. Amid bonfires, a maypole, and a mystery play, the hunchbacked bellringer Quasimodo, crowned with a tiara and vested with a cloak, is elected Pope of Fools on Epiphany.

See also **Christmas Drama; Epiphany; Holy Innocents Day; Saturnalia.**

Feast of Jordan
See **Epiphany**

Feast of Light
See **Epiphany**

Feast of the Circumcision
See **New Year's Day**

Feast of the Holy Innocents
See **Holy Innocents Day**

Feast of the Immaculate Conception

Observed on December 8 in the Roman Catholic Church, proclaimed by Pope Pius IX in the bull *Ineffabilis Deus* of 1854. The feast commemorates the dogma that the Virgin Mary, chosen from the foundation of the world to be the mother of God, was preserved free from all stain of original sin, as recognized in the Roman Catholic Church. According to that belief, Mary was immaculately conceived. Coming early in December, the feast often launches Christmas celebrations in Roman Catholic countries, particularly Spain and Latin America.

An early proponent of the Immaculate Conception was St. Ephrem, a fourth-century theologian and poet from Syria, dubbed the Patriarch of Antioch. A feast honoring the Immaculate Conception had been observed in the Eastern Church on December 9 as early as the fifth century. The Roman Church began observances some two centuries later. Opposition arose in the twelfth and thirteenth centuries from the French monastic St. Bernard of Clairvaux and the Italian philosopher St. Thomas Aquinas, respectively, and defenders included the thirteenth-century Scottish theologian John Duns Scotus.

In 1846, Catholic bishops in the United States consecrated the immaculate Virgin Mary as patron to the United States and assigned December 8 as her feast day. Pope Pius IX followed suit in 1854 with a decree that also assigned the Immaculate Conception to December 8.

Feliz Navidad

(Spanish, "Merry Christmas"). Popular song written in 1970 by the blind Puerto Rican–American singer-guitarist José Feliciano. His simple lyrics first wish the listener a Merry Christmas and a prosperous New Year in Spanish, followed by a similar sentiment in English. Feliciano first recorded his song on the RCA label that same year, and despite the fact that this recording was not charted, the song has become a Christmas standard. Of the 25 most frequently performed Christmas songs of the twentieth century listed by the American Society of Composers, Authors and Publishers

(ASCAP), "Feliz Navidad" is ranked number 24.

Feliciano remains popular primarily in Spanish-speaking countries. He has produced forty gold and platinum albums, principally outside of the United States.

Festival of Lights
See Hanukkah

A Festival of Nine Lessons and Carols

Also known as "Ceremony of Lessons and Carols." Annual musical event held on Christmas Eve in the chapel of King's College, Cambridge, England, since 1918. The format consists of nine readings of Messianic-related biblical texts (the lessons) by members of King's; following each lesson, the King's choir sings at least two carols. Whereas the lesson texts remain constant, the carols may vary from year to year with one exception. Since 1919, the festival has traditionally opened with the carol "Once, in Royal David's City," performed by a single choirboy singing the first verse of the carol *a cappella*. Also by tradition, the choirboy attaining this honor is not selected until a few moments before the festival begins.

The festival evolved from a small Christmas Eve service in 1880 that was built around nine biblical texts and nine carols drawn up by the Rev. Edward W. Benson, a pastor in Truro, Cornwall, who later achieved the office of Archbishop of Canterbury. The concept became quite popular, and other churches quickly incorporated the festival for their own Christmas services, the best known of which became that at King's College. The first festival at King's in 1918 was planned by the dean, Eric Milner-White, with organist Arthur Henry Mann directing the music. With the exception of 1930, the festival has enjoyed annual BBC radio broadcasts since 1928 and television broadcasts since 1963. Broadcasts continued through World War II, during which time the chapel glass was removed and the location withheld from broadcasts for security reasons.

Although the order and specificity of the nine lessons may show slight variation from church to church, here listed are the biblical references for, and summaries of, the lessons as observed at King's:

Lesson One: Genesis 3:8–15, 17–19. The Fall of Man and the promise that the seed of woman shall ultimately conquer the seed of the serpent.

Lesson Two: Genesis 22:15–18. God's promise to Abraham that, because of his faith, through his line all nations of the earth will be blessed.

Lesson Three: Isaiah 9:2, 6–7. Prophecy that those who walked in the darkness of sin will see the light of redemption in the Child to be born, who will also be known as "Wonderful, Counselor, the mighty God, the everlasting Father, the Prince of Peace."

Lesson Four: Isaiah 11:1–4, 6–9. Prophecy that the Messiah will be a descendant of King David (a branch of Jesse, David's father); also metaphorical prophecy of the coming peace through Christ.

Lesson Five: Luke 1:26–35, 38. The Annunciation to the Virgin Mary.

Lesson Six: Luke 2:1, 3–7. Mary and Joseph's journey to Bethlehem and the birth of Jesus.

Lesson Seven: Luke 2:8–16. The angelic host appears to the shepherds.

Lesson Eight: Matthew 2:1–12. The account of the Magi.

Lesson Nine: John 1:1–14. Expounds upon Jesus as the Word, the Light, and the Incarnation.

See also **Once, in Royal David's City.**

Fiesta Bowl
See **New Year's Day**

Fiji Islands
See **Asia and the South Pacific**

Finland

From the influences of the Eastern Orthodox Church and the conquest by Roman Catholic Sweden, Finland accepted Christianity over a period of years from 1050 to 1300. When the country broke from Rome in the sixteenth century, the Evangelical Lutheran Church replaced Catholicism and remained as the principal faith.

• *Joulua* (Christmas) commences with the Advent season and citywide bazaars. Since the 1920s, most organizations, businesses, and families have organized social gatherings,

A reindeer pulls a Laplander in his sledge across the icy snow. From the Sunday School Visitor, *1897.*

called *pikkujoulu* ("Little Christmas"), as typical Christmas parties. Additional lights to combat the long periods of darkness fill the windows of shops and businesses, and decorations include Advent candles, Advent wreaths, Advent calendars, and winter greenery. It is also customary to erect a sheaf of grain on a pole outdoors for the birds ("Birds' Christmas Tree").

Since 1950, Finland has observed December 13 as St. Lucia Day, a tradition acquired from Sweden in the 1920s and introduced by the Swedish-language newspaper *Hufvudstadsbladet* as well as the Finnish national health organization *Folkhalsan*. Although families select a Lucia among their own kindred, a national, fund-raising competition selects one teenage girl annually as Finland's Lucia, who graces various functions, schools, and hospitals. Proceeds fund *Folkhalsan*.

Christmas trees are usually erected a few days before Christmas Eve and decorated with candles, miniatures of the national flag, *himmeli* (straw mobiles) of various sizes and shapes, and paper and wood ornaments.

Christmas Eve officially commences with the "Peace of Christmas," a Scandinavian custom dating to medieval times. An annual ceremony dedicated to this custom is televised throughout Finland and Sweden at noon from Finland's former capital, Turku, which now refers to itself as Finland's "Christmas City." From the balcony of Brinkkala Mansion in the Old Great Square, a public official reads the text of a medieval document, which orders that all citizens must maintain peace during the Christmas season or suffer criminal penalties. Included in the telecast is a service from Turku Cathedral, in which bishops from the Lutheran, Orthodox, Roman Catholic, and Methodist faiths plead for world peace.

At sundown on Christmas Eve, families adorn graves of their ancestors with lighted candles and wreaths and visit the sauna prior to the evening's festivities. Whereas manufactured gifts were popular in the early twentieth century, homemade gifts have once again become popular, as they were in the nineteenth century. Children personally receive gifts on Christmas Eve from *Joulupukki* (literally "Yule Buck," Father Christmas), who arrives in the form of a friend or relative dressed similarly to Santa Claus and who traditionally inquires, "Are there any good children here?" Children often dress as *Joulutonttuja* (elves or gnomes) in red suits and caps, while adults entertain the special visitor with carols. According to a tradition established by the Finnish Broadcasting Company in 1927, Father Christmas, who resembles the American Santa Claus with his reindeer and elves, resides with his wife, Mother Christmas, atop Mount Korvatunturi in the eastern region of Lapland belonging to Finland. Children address their Christmas letters to this location, where special postal workers answer each letter in the guise of Father Christmas.

The association of a goat figure with gift bringer derives from pre–Christian Yule festivals, which paid homage to the gods. At the winter solstice, it was believed that Thor, as he rode through the skies in a chariot pulled by two billy goats named Gnasher and Cracker, distributed gifts to the Vikings while his father and chief of the gods, Odin, riding his white, eight-legged steed Sleipner, escorted the souls of slain heroes into Valhalla. Men costumed as goats portrayed this belief by making surprise entrances at Yule parties, and after dancing about, "died" and then returned to life. During the Middle Ages, the goat figure evolved into the devil in Scandinavian Christmas folk revels, and men costumed in goat skins and masks frolicked about, much to the dismay of the Church, which banned such behavior in the sixteenth century. In more remote regions today, the gift bearer may be known as Wainamoinen, who arrives on his goat steed, Ukko. The former, depicted as an old man clad in a red coat and sporting a long, white mustache, derives from the principal worker of mighty deeds and hero of the *Kalevala*, a series of anonymous, centuries-old poems that collectively comprise the national, epic poem of Finland. In that work, Ukko is the supreme god.

The Christmas Eve meal follows the distribution of gifts and often includes salmon, ham, herring, *lutefisk* (codfish), assorted casseroles, liver pâté, mixed fruit soup with cinnamon, *joululeipä* (Christmas bread), *joulutortut* (Christmas fruit pastry), *piparkakut* (ginger cookies), *korvapuustit* (cinnamon buns), and *glögg* (warmed, spiced drink composed of red wine, sugar, raisins, cinnamon, cloves, orange peeling, and almonds). A traditional, holiday dish served throughout Scandinavia includes rice porridge with one almond in the batch; the person receiving the almond in his serving will have good luck in the coming year. After dinner, there may be readings from the Bible or the singing of carols as family members join hands and walk around the Christmas tree.

Christmas Day is spent with family attending early morning church services and enjoying quiet devotion at home. St. Stephen's Day or "Second Day of Christmas" is also a holiday, while traditions for New Year's Eve include fortune-telling games such as interpreting shadows cast from the shapes created after molten lead or tin is cooled in water. The Christmas season ends on Epiphany, January 6.

"Merry Christmas" is *Hyvaa Joulua*.
See also **Advent; Epiphany; Sweden.**

The Fir Tree

The only fairy tale by the celebrated Danish author Hans Christian Andersen with a Christmas setting. Clearly presenting a strong moral, the story features a young Fir Tree that cannot appreciate its youth or its lovely environment in the forest because it yearns to be taller, older, or somewhere else. When the Tree

desires to be a ship's mast, the Sunbeams caution it to rejoice in its youth. When the Sparrow brings news of gorgeous Christmas trees decorated in town, the Fir Tree impatiently wishes to be one. But the elements again caution the Tree to rejoice in the Air, the Wind, and its youth.

At last, the mature Tree is cut down, erected in a grand home, and trimmed exquisitely for Christmas Eve. Now, the Tree believes, it will live in splendor forever. But one of its burning candles scorches a branch, and then children plunder gifts from its branches, leaving its appearance disheveled.

Expecting to be redecorated the next day, the Tree instead is thrown into an isolated garret, where it remains alone for days. Inquisitive mice prompt the Tree to tell them its history, and in doing so, the Tree realizes too late that it really had a good life in the forest. Withered, yellow, and now considered ugly by the children, the Tree is soon burned for firewood.

It is uncertain whether Andersen deliberately incorporated a particular piece of European folklore about Christmas evergreens into the ending, but it is in keeping with the old superstition that, at holidays' end, Christmas evergreens should be burned rather than thrown out. The story also implies that gifts were hung on the tree and not placed beneath, which further implies that the tree was set on a table (*see* **Christmas Tree**).

Hans Christian Andersen (1805–1875) wrote some 150 fairy tales. His life's work as a writer of children's fairy tales and stories commenced with a small volume, *Fairy Tales Told for Children* (1835). Although a number of his tales have winter settings, such as "The Snow Queen," only two, "The Fir Tree" and "The Little Match Girl," are set amid the holidays. The latter story is a tale of New Year's Eve.
See also **The Little Match Girl.**

The First Christmas: The Story of the First Christmas Snow

(1975). Made-for-television animated story using stop-motion puppets (Animagic).

Three nuns in a French abbey provide care for a little shepherd boy, Lucas, an orphan who is struck and blinded by lightning a few weeks before Christmas. The nuns become fond of Lucas and wish for him to remain, but Father Thomas is set on sending him to an orphanage after the holidays. Lucas's only wish is to have snow for Christmas, though he's never seen it and never will. Having nothing with which to buy Christmas presents, Lucas gives Sister Theresa his dog Waggles and his little flock of sheep, his only possessions.

During the Christmas Eve Nativity pageant, as Lucas sings in the angel choir, snow miraculously falls from a cloudless, starlit sky, the first Christmas snow. When flakes touch Lucas's eyes, his sight is restored. In addition to this wonder, Father Thomas grants that Lucas may remain with them always.

Featuring the Irving Berlin classic "White Christmas." Narrated by Angela Lansbury. Voices: Cyril Ritchard, David Kelley, Dina Lynn, Greg Thomas, Iris Rainer, Joan Gardner, Don Messick, Sean Manning, Hilary Momberger, Dru Stevens, The Wee Winter Singers. Written by Julian P. Gardner. Produced and directed by Arthur Rankin, Jr., and Jules Bass. Rankin/Bass Productions. ABC Video/Golden Book Video. Color. Half-hour.

The First Christmas Tree: A Story of the Forest

Classic short story written by the American clergyman and author Henry Van Dyke (1852–1933), who first delivered the story as a sermon to his congregation in New York City in 1897. It is based on the legend of Winfried (or Winfrid), the English missionary known as St. Boniface, the Apostle of Germany, who brought Christianity to Germanic tribes in the eighth century and who supposedly was responsible for the dramatic introduction of the first Christmas tree.

On Christmas Eve in the year 722, Winfried, during a visit to the cloister of Pfalzel in Germany, convinces young Prince Gregor, grandson of King Dagobert, to take up the life of a pilgrim and join him in converting the pagans. On Christmas Eve two years later, Winfried leads his party of twenty to the sacred, giant thunder-oak at Geismar, sacred to the Scandinavian god Thor, where a multitude has gathered to celebrate Yule, to worship Thor, and to appease his wrath with a human

sacrifice. The old priest Hunrad chooses Chief Gundhar's young son, Bernhard, who is prepared to enter Valhalla (the hall of the chief god, Odin, into which the souls of slain heroes are received). Staying Hunrad's hand, Winfried announces his intent to deliver them from evil and reads a parchment from the bishop of Rome which summarizes his mission. To prove that Thor is a false god, Winfried and Gregor begin chopping down the great oak, when a sudden mighty wind, the hand of God, rips the oak from its roots and splits it into four pieces. As Winfried commands the pagans to build a church on that spot with the wood, he notices a little fir tree among the pieces and declares this to be the tree of the Christ Child, the substitute symbol of their new worship. He also commands that they no longer meet secretly in forests but keep their feasts at home with laughter and love. After the fir tree is erected in Gundhar's hall and decorated, the pilgrims chant a Christmas hymn while Winfried shares the Nativity story with everyone.

See also **Christmas Tree; The Other Wise Man.**

The First Nowell

English traditional carol, a narrative of the Nativity, believed to have arisen during the fifteenth century from the Cornwall region. Often the French word "Noel" (Christmas) is substituted, resulting in the misconception that the carol is French. Because the English word "Nowell," itself dating at least from the fourteenth century, derives from either "Noel" or "Nouvelle" (New), the source for the mistitle becomes apparent.

The earliest known publication of the lyrics alone, which had previously surfaced as nine verses on broadsides printed near Cornwall, appeared in the second edition of Davies Gilbert's collection *Some Ancient Christmas Carols* (London, 1823). Ten years later, the tune was first published along with the lyrics in William Sandys' collection *Christmas Carols, Ancient and Modern* (London, 1833). According to *The Christmas Carol Reader*, the notes to "Born Is the King" in the original refrain were subsequently altered to those in common usage today; *The New Oxford Book of Carols* names John Stainer as having modernized the Sandys tune and published it in *Christmas Carols New and Old*, co-edited with Henry Bramley (London, 1871).

Music scholars now believe that Sandys's version derives from several alternate (and earlier) renderings of the carol, the first of which was discovered in 1913 in Camborne by English carol collector Cecil Sharp. Whereas verse 1 of Sharp's discovery opens with "Nowell and nowell," the same words also appearing in the refrain instead of "Nowell, nowell," other versions include either "O well and O well" or "Nowell and nowell," which open verse 1 as well as the refrain.

The English composer Ralph Vaughan Williams (1872–1958) incorporated "The First Nowell" into several of his works: as excerpts in *Fantasia on Christmas Carols* (1912, for baritone, choir, orchestra); as opening and closing themes in the masque *On Christmas Night* (1925–26); and as the title theme in *The First Nowell* (1958, for soloists, choir, orchestra), a Nativity play.

Firstfooting
See **Great Britain**

A Flintstone Christmas
See **The Flintstones**

A Flintstone Family Christmas
See **The Flintstones**

The Flintstones

The first primetime, made-for-television animated cartoon series created by the animation giant Hanna-Barbera Studios. Featuring the Stone Age characters of Fred and Wilma Flintstone, daughter Pebbles, pet dinosaur Dino, neighbors Barney and Betty Rubble with son Bamm-Bamm, and Fred's boss at the rock quarry, Mr. Slate, *The Flintstones* revolved around Fred's and Barney's shenanigans in the town of Bedrock, where every name was derived from some form of stone or prehistoric creature.

The Flintstones and Rubbles enjoyed Christmas in four productions:

How the Flintstones Saved Christmas (1964), an episode from the original series. Needing some extra Christmas cash, Fred acquires a part-time job in the Bedrock Depart-

ment Store. Inept as a gift wrapper and stock boy, he avoids termination by playing the part of the store's Santa Claus, for which he is most qualified. On Christmas Eve, two elves sent by the real Santa, Winkie and Blinkie, offer Fred the opportunity of taking Santa's place that year, because the jolly old elf is sick with a cold. Glad to help, Fred speeds around the world in a sleigh drawn by three little dinosaurs with antlers.

He drops presents from the sleigh, and the presents parachute into the chimneys of homes. After the elves depart, Fred realizes that he has nothing for his own family, for their gifts were aboard the sleigh. Dejected, he returns home and rejoices to find that Santa had rallied and had made a special delivery to everyone there, sneezing all the way. Voices: Alan Reed, Mel Blanc, Jean Vander Pyl, Gerry Johnson, Don Messick, Harvey Korman. Written by Herbert Finn, Alan Dinehart. Produced and directed by William Hanna and Joseph Barbera. Hanna-Barbera Productions. Hanna-Barbera Home Video. Color. Half-hour.

A Flintstone Christmas (1977), special telecast, virtually a remake of the 1964 episode with an additional story line. To keep his job at the rock quarry, Fred agrees to play Santa at a benefit for the Bedrock Orphanage, as requested by his boss, Mr. Slate. But when the real Santa slips on Fred's roof and sprains his ankle in addition to catching a cold, Fred and Barney must take over Santa's Christmas Eve rounds. With Fred in Santa's own suit and with Barney dressed as an elf, the two bumble their way around the world, losing half of the presents in a snow storm. Forced to return to the North Pole for another load with time drawing nigh for the benefit, Fred kicks the sleigh into high gear, dropping presents like bombs into chimneys. The two arrive back at the orphanage just in the (St.) Nick of time as Mr. Slate is about to fire Fred. Arriving with an empty sack, Fred quickly takes advantage of Santa's magical suit and conjures up abundant gifts for the children. Voices: Mel Blanc, Lucille Bliss, Henry Corden, Virginia Gregg, Gay Hartwig, Don Messick, Hal Smith, John Stephenson, Jean Vander Pyl. Written by Duane Poole, Dick Robbins. Creative Producer, Iwao Takamoto. Directed by Charles A. Nichols. Hanna-Barbera

Productions. Hanna-Barbera Home Video. Color. 60 min.

A Flintstone Family Christmas (1993), special telecast. On Christmas Eve, Stoney, a "caveless" boy dressed as Santa who cares nothing for Christmas, robs Fred and Barney while they are out shopping. Rather than see him spend the holidays in Juvenile Hall, Wilma persuades a reluctant Fred to bring the boy home to share the season with the Flintstones. In time, Fred and Stoney warm to each other, and the gang heads to a Christmas tree lot, where Stoney sets up a quick game of chance to help raise money for a special tree that Fred cannot afford. The scene further deteriorates when Fred, defending Stoney against a thug who accuses the boy of cheating, is slugged, hospitalized, and unable to play Santa in the Bedrock Christmas Parade as previously planned. Mr. Slate, in charge of Fred's float, must find a replacement, and when he retrieves the Santa suit at Fred's house, Stoney, wishing to do Fred a good turn, locks Slate in the bathroom and rushes the suit to the hospital. Fred's attempt to free Slate lands him and Stoney in jail temporarily on kidnapping charges, but Slate bails Fred out, and a social worker takes Stoney away. Just making the parade, Fred takes to the skies in his sleigh drawn by six flying pterodactyls, plucks Stoney from the car headed to Juvenile Hall, and takes him home to stay. That evening, after Pebbles, husband Bamm-Bamm, and the grandchildren arrive for merriment, Stoney, the newest member of the family, places the star (lit by a firefly) atop the Christmas tree. This program received an Emmy Award nomination for Outstanding Nighttime Animated Program — One Hour or Less (1993-94 season). Voices: Charlie Adler, Hamilton Camp, Christine Cavanaugh, Didi Cohn, Henry Corden, Nick Jameson, Megan Mullally, Robert Ridgely, Kath Soucie, John Stephenson, Jean Vander Pyl, B. J. Ward, Frank Welker, Alan Young. Written by Sean Roche, David Ehrman. Produced by Larry Huber. Directed by Ray Patterson. Hanna-Barbera Productions. Color. This program is included in the video collection *Christmas in Bedrock* (see below).

A Flintstones Christmas Carol (1994), television movie in which the Flintstones and Rubbles star in the Bedrock Community Theater's production of *A Christmas Carol* with the usual cast of "Charles Brickens'" characters modified to the Stone Age: Scrooge (Fred); Bob and Mrs. "Cragit," daughter Martha, and Tiny Tim (Barney, Betty, Pebbles, and Bamm-Bamm, respectively); and "Marbley's" Ghost (Mr. Slate). Because the city has been hit with the Bedrock Bug, a nasty 24-hour virus, and many cast members are out ill, Wilma, originally the stage manager and costume designer, also doubles as the Ghost of Christmas Past and as Belle, Scrooge's fiancee. Betty takes over the makeup department, while Dino steps in as a white-hooded Ghost of Christmas Yet-to-Come. As the play closes and Bamm-Bamm forgets Tiny Tim's famous last line, Pebbles finishes with, "God bless us, every one!" This movie was the recipient of an award from the Film Advisory Board. Voices: Henry Corden, Jean Vander Pyl, Frank Welker, B. J. Ward, Russi Taylor, Don Messick, John Stephenson, Marsha Clark, Will Ryan, Brian Cummings, Rene Levant, John Rhys Davies, Joanie Gerber, Maurice LeMarche, Howard Morris, Jan Rabson. Written by Glenn Leopold. Produced and directed by Joanna Romersa. Hanna-Barbera Productions. Hanna-Barbera Home Video. Color. 70 min.

Christmas in Bedrock (1996), video collection of previously aired Flintstones productions: *A Flintstone Family Christmas* (1993) and *How the Flintstones Saved Christmas* (1964), plus two Hanna-Barbera cartoon "shorts," *Breezly and Sneezly in Noodrick of the North* (1965) and *Dino in The Great Egg-Scape* (1995). Hanna-Barbera Productions. Hanna-Barbera Home Video. Color. 60 min.

A Flintstones Christmas Carol
See **The Flintstones**

Football Bowl Games
See **New Year's Day**

The Fourth King
(1977). Made-for-television animated cartoon.

Upon learning that a bright star in the sky heralds Jesus' birth and that three human kings are going to visit Him in Bethlehem, the animal kingdom decides to send a representative of its own. Uno, the lion, feels that he should go, because he's the strongest and wisest. Feathers, the sparrow, insists on accompanying him, and a beaver, rabbit, and turtle join them along the way. Uno, haughty and self-reliant, reluctantly requires his companions' help twice to escape danger, once after he plunges into a river while fleeing Roman soldiers set on capturing him, and again when he is caged after falling into a lion pit. Following the star to Bethlehem, a more humble lion and his friends realize that they have no gift for the Christ Child, as do the Three Kings. An inspired Feathers offers a gift on behalf of all of the animals: a song of love.

Voices: Ted Ross, Laurie Beechman, Arnold Stang, Bob McFadden, and Ed Klein. Written by Alvin Cooperman, Seymour Reit. Produced by Alvin Cooperman, Bruno Caliandro. Directed by Romano Scarpa. A Production of RAI Corporation in association with Fourth King Productions. J2 Communications Video. Color. 23 min.

The Fourth Wise Man
See **The Other Wise Man**

France

Predominantly Roman Catholic, this nation has celebrated Christmas since 496, when St. Rémi, bishop of the region formerly known as Gaul, baptized Clovis I (ca. 466–511), King of the Franks, along with 3,000 of his army at Rheims on Christmas Day. Clovis's Christian wife, Clotilda of Burgundy, is believed to have had the greatest influence upon his conversion, after which Clovis championed Christianity throughout Gaul.

The Christmas season extends from St. Nicholas Day (December 6) to Epiphany (January 6). To honor the Archbishop of Myra, most cities host pageants in which men attired as St. Nicholas parade through the streets, followed by Nicholas's antithesis, *Père Fouettard* ("Father Whipper"). The latter, a forbidding figure with a long, unkempt beard and a dark robe, carries a basket of switches with which to discipline naughty youngsters. Children customarily receive candy and other treats on this day.

While the Miracle Play was going on in a medieval French town, armed guards roamed the streets to watch people's houses, and householders hung many lights from their houses and above the streets to discourage burglaries. From Harper's New Monthly Magazine, *December 1888.*

Families prepare their homes with a thorough cleaning and decorate them with fir branches, holly, mistletoe, assorted flowers, poinsettias, and Christmas roses. Candles arranged by the hearth symbolize hope. *Sapins* (Christmas trees) are decorated a few days before Christmas with colored balls, figures of animals and angels, paper fruit and flowers, tinsel, pine cones, walnuts, bags of candy and lollipops, electric lights, and perhaps candles. The Christmas tree was first known in France by 1605, for an account from Strasbourg in eastern France stated that Christmas trees at that time were decorated with apples, paper roses, candy, and other treats. This custom arrived in Paris in 1837 through Princess Helene of Mecklenburg, wife of the Duke of Orléans.

Churches and theaters throughout the country sponsor *pastorales*, miracle plays about the Nativity and French legends surrounding it, many of which date to the Middle Ages. In Provence especially, such plays feature living *crèches* ("cribs") or Nativity scenes (see below), the characters of which form candlelight processions en route to the church on Christmas Eve. Other theatrical events include noted puppet shows in Paris and Lyon, one popular, contemporary example of which is de Marynbourg's "Bethlehem 1933."

By far the most treasured of Christmas symbols is the *crèche*, which decorates every Roman Catholic home and church. Although the family of St. Francis of Assisi first introduced the *crèche* to Avignon during the first half of the fourteenth century, the custom did not become popular until the sixteenth century. Antique *crèches* may be found in the cathedrals at Chartres, Chaource, Nogent-le-Rotrou, Sainte-Marie d'Oloron, and in several museums, such as those in Marseille and Orleans. *Crèches* are usually erected a week to several days before Christmas Eve, and it is customary to advance the Wise Men closer to the manger with each succeeding day until Epiphany. The figure of the Christ Child is not placed in the manger until Christmas Eve. *Crèches* may be fashioned from wood, paper, porcelain, or from unusual items such as lumps of sugar and bread crumbs. Some may also feature animated figures.

The most famous *crèches* are those from the region of Provence, which traditionally consist of rather expansive scenes depicting not the setting of Bethlehem but the French countryside in elaborate detail, because folklore contends that Jesus was born in France. Amid the miniature figures of the Holy Family, shepherds, ox and donkey, angels, and Wise Men are those portraying people from all modern walks of life, such as the butcher, baker, miller, police officer, and so forth. The Provençal Nativity figures, or *santons* ("little saints"), are just as famous, having been brought to France by Italian artisans who arrived in Marseille in the early 1800s. The figures became popular, and fashioning them became an art that has remained within several French families for succeeding generations. Provence offers two basic varieties of *santons*, those of clay (*santons d'argile*) and those clothed in period costume (*santons habillés*), all of which are displayed at the annual *santon* fair in Marseille, held since December 1803.

Children receive gifts either from *le petit Jésus* ("the little Jesus") or from *père Noël* ("Father Christmas"), whom Baby Jesus sends in His place and who, in addition to riding a donkey, closely resembles the white-bearded St. Nicholas clothed in a red cleric's robe, hood, and wooden shoes. Having written their letters to *père Noël* at the North Pole earlier in the season, children place their shoes near the hearth or *crèche*, or under the Christmas tree on Christmas Eve to be filled with presents and treats overnight, and they usually prepare a small snack for *père Noël* and his donkey. In the spirit of the season, families may welcome children's shoes from homes of lesser means. Traditional receptacles of former days, *sabots* (wooden shoes) now survive as confections molded from chocolate. Before the children retire, parents may treat them to a Christmas story, a favorite of which is "The Three Masses" by Provençal author Alphonse Daudet (1840–1897). In this story, a priest, greedily anticipating the sumptuous meal to follow, receives divine punishment for irreverently rushing through the three Christmas Eve Masses.

With the exception of young children, everyone attends Midnight Mass on Christmas Eve, after which people congregate either in their homes with friends and relatives or in restaurants for *le réveillon* ("the awakening"). This traditional Christmas meal considerably varies from region to region, may feature as many as fifteen courses, and often extends until dawn. A broad range of cuisine includes beef, lamb, fowls, venison, assorted seafood and fruits, pastries, pâtés, cheeses, breads, candies, *sotelties* (confections created in the shapes of miniature castles, biblical scenes, or animals), and wines. *Bûche de Noël* ("Christmas log"), a traditional dessert shaped like a Yule log, consists of an elongated sponge cake rolled with chocolate butter cream filling and covered with brown icing. Scoring the latter creates the appearance of tree bark, and the cake is garnished with powdered sugar, nuts, and

Christmas images. This dessert symbolizes the Yule log, which was popular in France in previous centuries but largely has been abandoned with the advent of modern heating technology. In the Alpine regions, where torchlight ski processions down mountainsides are common, *le réveillon* may feature beef or an omelet with *escargot* (snails); in Brittany, where it is believed that the angel of the seas guides lost ships on Christmas Eve, there are buckwheat cakes and cream; in Burgundy, turkey with chestnuts. Provence, in addition to lobster, pheasant, and lamb, traditionally serves thirteen desserts, symbolic of Christ and His Twelve Apostles. In Paris and the *Ile de France*, oysters on the half shell and *pâté de fois gras* (goose liver pâté) are quite popular.

New Year's Day is devoted to family visitations and a repetition of *le réveillon*, where the principal course is roast chicken. Domestic help customarily receive a Christmas bonus, and adults, not children, exchange *étrennes* (gifts) at this time. This term derives from the Latin *strennae*, which were gifts given to honor the Roman goddess Strenia during the Saturnalia.

On *jour de rois* (Three Kings Day, Epiphany, January 6), the principal custom is to cut a *galette des rois* ("Kings' Cake") in which is hidden a bean or a small porcelain figure. A small child customarily distributes the slices, and whoever finds the object in his slice becomes "king for a day"; all guests at such parties are subject to his whims. Instead of receiving gifts on Christmas Day, children in the South of France near Spain receive gifts on Epiphany from the Three Kings.

"Merry Christmas" in France is *Joyeux Noël*.

See also **Epiphany; Nativity Scene; Saturnalia; Yule.**

The Friendly Beasts

Carol of uncertain origin but thought to have arisen in England during the twelfth century. Its anonymous tune is said to have been the setting for a hymn used during the medieval Feast of the Asses or Donkey Festival, which formed a part of the larger Feast of Fools. More doubt surrounds the origin of its lyrics. While some sources simply identify the carol as "English traditional," *The Christmas Carol Reader* suggests that Robert Davis, an otherwise totally obscure American, may have written the lyrics to "The Friendly Beasts," and that they were first printed in 1934 (publisher not listed) but not registered for copyright until 1949. However, until this or any other alleged lyricist for this carol is identified beyond question, "The Friendly Beasts" must remain "traditional."

The subject of the carol is based on legends holding that when Christ was born, the stable animals either presented Him with gifts or performed various services and good deeds for Him. He rewarded their kindness with the gift of speech at midnight, not only at the first Christmas, but annually thereafter. In this instance, several animals tell of their gifts to the Babe. A shaggy brown donkey carried Mary to Bethlehem; a red-and-white cow donates her manger for a cradle and her hay for a pillow; a curly-horned sheep yields its wool for a warm blanket; two doves in the rafters coo the Babe to sleep; and a yellow-and-black camel brings one of the Magi with a gift in his pack. A similar gift theme is found in "The Burgundian Carol."

According to other gift legends, the rooster was the first animal to herald the birth of Christ by crowing at midnight (*see* **Mass of the Rooster**); the robin acquired its red breast by having stood too near the Holy Family's fire while fanning the flames with its wings; the stork donated its feathers to line the manger; the nightingale, by caroling the "Gloria in excelsis" along with the heavenly host, acquired the sweetest of avian voices. A legend paralleling that of Italy's *La Befana* and Russia's *Baboushka* involves the owl, who decided not to follow the other animals to Bethlehem. Like these two spirits, the owl repented and now forever seeks the Christ Child under the cover of darkness by crying "Whooo," a plea to be led to the Babe.

See also **The Burgundian Carol; Feast of Fools; Italy; Russia.**

From Bethl'em's City
See **Angels and Shepherds**

From Heaven Above to Earth I Come
("Vom Himmel hoch, da komm ich her").

German carol, the only original Christmas carol written by Martin Luther (1483–1546), initiator of the Protestant Reformation. Designed as part of a family Christmas Eve ceremony for 1534, the carol consisted of fifteen verses, the first five of which were sung by a man dressed as an angel standing beside a crib to announce that Christ is born. Luther's children took the remaining verses, a running commentary on the Nativity and the divinity of the Babe, with the angel joining them on the last verse, the final praise to God.

Luther initially set the lyrics to a folk tune of the time and published his carol in the *Geistliche Lieder*, printed by a Herr Klug (revised edition, Wittenberg, 1535), then republished the carol with his own, original music in another *Geistliche Lieder* (Leipzig, 1539), edited by Valentin Schumann. It is this latter setting that established "Vom Himmel Hoch" as one of Germany's most popular carols. Great Britain's Catherine Winkworth (1827–1878), a translation specialist, published the best-known English version in 1855.

Not only has Luther's melody been the setting for other hymn texts (Luther's "Vom Himmel kam der Engel Schar," 1543 ["From Heaven Came the Angel Host"] for example), but the German composer J. S. Bach (1685–1750) also used it for the closing chorale of Part I of his *Christmas Oratorio* (1734, BWV 248). In addition, there are a number of organ chorale preludes based on "Vom Himmel Hoch," notably those by Bach: *Orgelbüchlein* (BWV 606), BWV 700, 701 fughetta, 738, and 769 canonic variations.

Frosty Returns

(1993). Made-for-television animated cartoon sequel to *Frosty the Snowman*.

Beansboro's annual winter carnival is approaching, but there may be no snow for the occasion because of Summer Wheeze, a snow repellent invented by factory tycoon Mr. Twitchel. Frosty, reincarnated by the magic hat of young Holly DeCarlo, also faces extinction. To save him, Holly presents Frosty at the carnival, where the two expose the evils of Summer Wheeze and the benefits of snow. Twitchel is foiled, and the citizens crown Frosty king of the carnival.

Featuring the song "Frosty the Snowman." Narrated by Jonathan Winters. Voices: Jan Hooks, Andrea Martin, Brian Doyle-Murray, Elizabeth Moss, Michael Carter, John Goodman, Steve Stoliar, Philip Glasser, Gail Lynch, and Mindy Martin. Written by Oliver Goldstick. Produced by Eryk Casemiro, Bill Melendez. Directed by Bill Melendez, Evert Brown. CBS Entertainment Productions. Sony Wonder Video. Color. 25 min.

See also **Frosty the Snowman (animated cartoon); Frosty the Snowman (song); Frosty's Winter Wonderland; Rudolph and Frosty: Christmas in July.**

Frosty the Snowman

(Animated cartoon, 1969). Made-for-television cartoon based on the children's song of the same title by Walter E. "Jack" Rollins and Steve Nelson.

Frosty, a snowman with a corn cob pipe, two lumps of coal for eyes, and a button for a nose, comes to life only when children place Professor Hinkle's magic hat on the head of their Christmas Eve creation. Announcing "Happy Birthday" with each resurrection, Frosty frolics with his young friends until he boards a refrigerated train bound for the North Pole to stay alive. Desiring his hat, Hinkle dogs Frosty and traps him in a greenhouse, where Frosty melts. Santa arrives to restore Frosty and threatens to ignore Hinkle's Christmas list if he harasses Frosty any further. Although Frosty accompanies Santa back to the North Pole, he promises to return to the children with each new Christmas snow.

Narrated by Jimmy Durante. Voices: Jackie Vernon, Billy DeWolfe, June Foray, Paul Frees. Written by Romeo Muller. Produced and directed by Arthur Rankin, Jr., and Jules Bass. A Rankin/Bass Production. Sony Wonder Video. Color. 30 min.

See also **Frosty the Snowman (song); Frosty Returns; Frosty's Winter Wonderland; Rudolph and Frosty: Christmas in July.**

Frosty the Snowman

(Song). Popular American children's song written by New York natives Walter E. "Jack" Rollins and Steve Nelson in 1950. Having almost rejected an earlier children's piece, "Rudolph, the Red-Nosed Reindeer," which he ultimately recorded in 1949, cowboy singing star Gene Autry wisely took his wife Ina's advice about "Frosty" as well. First recorded by Autry in 1950 on the Columbia label, "Frosty the Snowman," a tune about a talking snowman who frolics with children, made the pop charts for the next two years, and the Frosty character was subsequently featured in several animated productions for television. Of the 25 most frequently performed Christmas songs of the twentieth century listed by the American Society of Composers, Authors and Publishers (ASCAP), "Frosty the Snowman" is ranked number 13.

See also **Frosty the Snowman (animated cartoon); Frosty Returns; Frosty's Winter Wonderland; Rudolph and Frosty: Christmas in July.**

Frosty's Winter Wonderland

(1976). Made-for-television animated cartoon sequel to *Frosty the Snowman.*

Wedding bells ring for Frosty, who takes Crystal as his snow wife. With beads for eyes, a thimble for a nose, pink yarn for a mouth, and a dust mop for hair, Crystal comes to life when Frosty bestows a gift of frost flowers made of snow.

Jealous of Frosty's popularity with children, Jack Frost blows a strong blizzard which almost cancels the snow nuptials, until Frosty invites Jack to be his best man.

Featuring the songs "Frosty the Snowman"

and "Winter Wonderland." Narrated and sung by Andy Griffith. Voices: Shelley Winters, Dennis Day, Paul Frees, Jackie Vernon, Shelly Hines, Eric Stern, Manfred Olea, Barbara Jo Ewing, The Wee Winter Singers. Written by Romeo Muller. Produced and directed by Arthur Rankin, Jr., and Jules Bass. A Rankin/Bass Production. Warner Home Video. Color. 23 min.

See also **Frosty Returns; Frosty the Snowman (animated cartoon); Frosty the Snowman (song); Rudolph and Frosty: Christmas in July; Winter Wonderland.**

Fum, Fum, Fum

Spanish traditional carol from the region of Catalonia, thought to have arisen during the sixteenth or seventeenth century. Held as the most popular of carols from Spain, it has received several English translations, the best-known of which begins, "On this joyful Christmas Day sing fum, fum, fum." Another opens with, "On December five-and-twenty, fum, fum, fum." In each of the two or three verses, depending on the translation, the first line is repeated, including the "fum, fum, fum," which also concludes each verse. It is thought that the words "fum, fum, fum" imitate either the beating of a drum or the strumming of a guitar. Whatever the translation, the carol calls for all to be joyful on Christmas Day and to seek the Infant Son of Heaven, who brings peace and good will to earth.

A Garfield Christmas Special

(1987). Made-for-television animated cartoon, based on the comic strip *Garfield*, a lasagna-eating cat created by Jim Davis.

Jon, Garfield's master, packs up Garfield and Odie, the dog, and heads to his parents' farm for Christmas cheer. On Christmas morning, Garfield surprises Jon's lonely grandma with a stack of old love letters written by her late husband which he discovered in the barn, and Odie gives Garfield a back scratcher which

he built with his own paws. According to Garfield, the giving and receiving are not nearly as important as the loving.

This program received an Emmy Award nomination for Outstanding Nighttime Animated Program (1987-88 season).

Voices: Lorenzo Music, Thom Huge, Greg Berger, Pat Carroll, Pat Harrington, David Lander, Julie Payne. Written by Jim Davis. Produced and directed by Phil Roman. A Phil Roman Production in association with United

Media-Mendelson Productions and Paws. CBS Video/Fox Video. Color. 24 min.

Gather Around the Christmas Tree
See We Three Kings of Orient Are

The Gathering

(1977). Made-for-television drama with one sequel.

Having sacrificed a fulfilling family life for the pursuit of success, Adam Thornton (Edward Asner), president of Thornton Industries, suddenly faces Christmas with the news that he is terminally ill. Though estranged from his four grown children and separated from his wife Kate (Maureen Stapleton) for years, Adam solicits Kate's help to reunite the family one last time at Christmas before he dies. His children, Julie (Rebecca Balding), Tom (Lawrence Pressman), Peggy (Gail Strickland), and Adam "Bud" Jr. (Gregory Harrison), are scattered across the continent. A regretful Adam especially wishes a reconciliation with Bud, his youngest, whose sentiments against the Vietnam War had offended Adam to the point that he had expelled his son from home. Bud then left the country, fleeing to Canada under a false identity to escape the draft.

After Kate issues the invitations, taking care only to plead that Adam wishes to see his children again (he would not have them return simply because of his illness), she and Adam make preparations by decorating the family homeplace and the Christmas tree together, as though they had never separated. The holiday spirit overtakes Adam, who, rummaging through the attic for toys to give to his grandchildren, finds and repairs a doll house and an electric train.

On Christmas Eve, the three older children arrive with their families to fellowship, love, carols, and a rendering of "A Visit from St. Nicholas," all of which Adam considers quite a miraculous event, given his neglect of former days. Only Tom suspects his father's motives for calling everyone together when Adam, opening a gift box of fireworks from Dr. John Hodges (John Randolph), refers to him as "my doctor," an unusual phrase for the self-reliant Adam. Yet Tom keeps the secret and the

two are drawn closer as they light up the Christmas Eve darkness with fireworks.

Bud's arrival on Christmas Day brings the long-expected meeting and forgiveness, along with two new family members whom Adam has never seen, Bud's wife Toni (Stephanie Zimbalist) and infant son, christened Adam Thornton III that same day in a home ceremony. Before everyone departs, Adam's last acts of generosity include offering Bud and Julie's unemployed husband, George (Bruce Davison), positions in his company.

With Sarah Cunningham, Veronica Hamel, James Karen, Edward Winter. Written by James Poe. Produced by Harry R. Sherman. Directed by Randal Kleiser. Hanna-Barbera Productions. Color. Video N/A.

The Gathering received an Emmy Award for Outstanding Special and received Emmy nominations for Outstanding Actress in a Special (Stapleton), Outstanding Director, Outstanding Writing, and Outstanding Art Direction.

A sequel, *The Gathering, Part II*, followed in 1979. Kate assumes control of Thornton Industries and receives amorous advances from a wealthy industrialist (Efrem Zimbalist, Jr.), who wishes to buy the business. Written by Harry Longstreet. Directed by Charles S. Dubin. Color. Video N/A.

See also **Christmas Eve**, a later television drama which closely parallels *The Gathering*.

Gentle Mary Laid Her Child
See Good King Wenceslas

George Balanchine's "The Nutcracker"
See The Nutcracker

Germany

This nation has enjoyed Christmas since the eighth century, when the English Benedictine missionary Winfrid, St. Boniface (ca. 675–754), brought Christianity to the Germanic tribes of Europe. It is the country from which a number of worldwide holiday customs originated (for example, Advent wreaths, candles, and calendars, and Christmas trees), richly interwoven with pagan rites of pre–Christian times.

Christmas is preceded by Advent and its associated customs and symbols. Also commencing at this time is the *Christkindlmarkt* (Christ Child market), a large, open-air market hosted in virtually every German city, sporting all manner of Christmas merchandise. The largest and most famous of these markets is that in Nuremberg, an annual tradition of more than 400 years. Roman Catholics erect a *Krippe* (crib), a Nativity scene, in churches and homes. Often these displays are heirlooms featuring wooden figures hundreds of years old, hand-carved by family ancestors.

On December 5, the eve of St. Nicholas Day, men dressed as the Bishop St. Nicholas in full clerical attire ride about cities on white horses, while children set out their shoes for the saint to fill with toys and treats overnight. A St. Nicholas personage usually visits homes in neighborhoods for the traditional quizzing of children in church doctrine and the assessing of their behavior over the past year. Accompanying Nicholas is a personification of Satan, known, depending on the region, by a host of names such as Knecht Ruprecht, Krampus, Grampus, Hans Muff, Hans Trapp, Butz, Klaubauf, Bartel, Budelfrau, Pelznickel, Belsnickel, Habersack, Klaasbuur, Burklaas, Rauklas, Ru-klas, Bullerklaas, Aschenklas, Shaggy Goat, or simply Rider. A hideous, fur-clad figure with blackened face, dark beard, long tail, and red, serpentine tongue, this antithesis of St. Nicholas growls, rattles chains, and sports a whip with which to beat naughty children and those ignorant of their catechism. Some characters tote bags or baskets in which they threaten to stuff and whisk away the little offenders. Traditionally, as the Satan figure is about to spring, St. Nicholas intervenes and saves the children from a fate worse than death. In their shoes on St. Nicholas day, naughty children find switches, coal, or dirt, gifts from the evil one.

St. Nicholas Day continues with vestiges of pagan rituals. In south Germany, St. Nicholas personages lead processions to bonfire ceremonies, recalling the bonfires of ancient Yule festivals, which were believed to drive away the spirits of darkness. Donning straw sheafs and wearing grotesque masks, the *Buttenmandelhaut* (Riddle-Raddle Men) of the

Knech Ruprecht *or* Krampus, *the devilish companion of St. Nicholas who carries the toy bag and helps St. Nick decide who is to get a gift, and who is to be punished. Old engraving reprinted in Phillip Snyder,* The Joys of Christmas Past: A Social History *(New York: Dodd, Mead, 1985).*

Bavarian Alps run through valleys creating a din with cow bells and other noisemakers as they symbolically drive away evil, recalling the pagan belief that not only fire, but loud noises, would drive away the evil spirits of winter. Following this commotion and a ceremony honoring St. Nicholas, the Riddle-Raddle Men accompany the saint as he journeys from house to house delivering gifts to children. Finally, in a scene derived from pagan fertility rites, the Riddle-Raddle Men enter homes and simply carry the single women outdoors.

On the three Thursdays before Christmas, Bavarian children observe *Klopfelnachten* (Knocking Nights), a ritual similar to Halloween in the United States. Wearing masks, they go about creating as much noise as possible to banish evil spirits. They recite rhymes beginning with the word "knock" at each home visited. The children then receive treats.

By Christmas Eve, the seasonal baking is completed, featuring such confections as gingerbread men and gingerbread houses, *Springerle* (cookies with raised designs), *Lebkuchen* (spiced cookies with candied fruit), *Stollen* (candied fruit loaf or fruit cake), *Pfeffernüsse* (pepper nuts), *Aachener Printen* (Aachen almond biscuits), and marzipan (almond confection molded into shapes of animals or other characters). Families decorate their Christmas trees behind closed doors, and children are not allowed to view the tree until it has been decorated with the traditional gingerbread or marzipan figures, candles, and *Wunderkerzen* (sparklers). A tinkling bell then signals that the children may enter the room and partake of the tree's culinary delights.

In Bavaria on Christmas Eve, the Berchten Runners (named for Berchta, a variant of Hertha, Norse goddess of the home) don grotesque masks and parade about, rhetorically asking what people have done for them during the year. Makers of mischief, they must be placated with gifts. In the city of Berchtesgaden, the minutes before midnight ring with gunfire as shooters attempt to drive away the last remaining evil spirits before Christmas arrives. Around most of the country, it is customary to visit the graves of loved ones on Christmas Eve and place lighted candles or small Christmas trees with candles by their tombstones. Another Christmas Eve custom is *Herbergsuchen* ("Searching for Shelter"), a custom similar to the Latin American *Las Posadas*, in which groups reenact the Holy Couple's search for shelter in Bethlehem and which terminates with *Mitternachtsmette* (Midnight Mass) (*see* **Las Posadas**).

Children also receive gifts on Christmas Eve, the traditional gift bearer being either the Roman Catholic *Christkindl* (Christ Child) or the Protestant *Weihnachtsmann* (Christmas Man). These spirits sprang from the influence of Martin Luther (1483–1546), the German Roman Catholic priest who initiated the Protestant Reformation. Observing that the Church made much ado about honoring St. Nicholas at Christmastime, Luther strongly advocated a Christ-centered season with far less emphasis on the saint. After the Reformation, Catholics adopted the concept of the *Christkindlein* (little Christ Child, later shortened to *Christkindl*) as the Christmas gift bearer, yet it was inconceivable to imagine the Son of God in such a role. Therefore, tradition has held that an angelic messenger brings the gifts instead. Also confusingly termed the "Christ Child," this spirit is depicted as a little girl with golden wings who wears a white robe, and jeweled crown and carries a tiny fir tree, a symbol of eternal life. The Christ Child supposedly helps decorate the Christmas tree, and it is she who rings the bell when all the gifts are spread beneath it.

The Protestants, on the other hand, rejecting all saints and Church-sanctioned entities as gift bearers, created the Weihnachtsmann, an altered conception of St. Nicholas. His appearance is remarkably similar to that of the American Santa Claus. In past centuries, parents in North German villages sent their children's gifts to one man who, attired as Knecht Ruprecht, visited all the village homes on Christmas Night in the name of his master Jesus. After hearing an account of the children's behavior, he either distributed the gifts or presented the parents with a rod, urging them to discipline the naughty ones.

Christmas Eve dinner may consist of roast goose with stuffing, turkey, carp, *Spätzle* (dumplings), *Königinpasteten* (meat-filled "kings' pastries"), vegetables, *Bayerisches Kraut* (Bavarian red cabbage), potato salad, spiced cakes, *Stollen*, marzipan, assorted cookies, and wines. Church services are held in the afternoon or evening. Catholics attend *Mitternachtsmesse* (Midnight Mass), and *Turmblasen* (brass ensembles) herald the coming of Christmas as they play chorales from church towers. This latter tradition, called "Blowing in the Yule (or Christmas)," is often repeated on New Year's Eve.

Christmas Day is spent in resting and visiting family members. December 26, Second Christmas Day (St. Stephen's Day), is a legal holiday. Because St. Stephen is the patron saint of horses, many cities host mounted processions in honor of this saint.

The twelve days of Christmas, from

Christmas Day to Epiphany (January 6), are known as *Die Zwölf Rauhnächte* (The Twelve Smoking Nights), a vestige of *Jul* (Yule), so named because it is customary during this period to burn incense and build bonfires, the smoke of which was once believed to dispel evil spirits at Yuletide. Additionally, people wear demon masks and make loud noises.

New Year's Eve, St. Sylvester's Day, honors the early fourth-century pope Saint Sylvester I. Typically featured are gunfire, fireworks, other forms of noisemaking, and parties. Citizens of Bavaria turn off their lights just prior to midnight, then turn them on to welcome the new year.

Community parties on Epiphany often feature two pastries, each with a single bean baked inside, which derive from medieval Twelfth Night customs. The man and woman finding the beans become the Bean King and Bean Queen of the event and are vested with authority to issue ridiculous commands, which all guests must obey. Should the king and queen both be single, superstition holds that they will eventually marry. Other superstitions include the consecrating of salt and chalk. The salt is fed to livestock, and with the chalk people write the traditional names of the three Wise Men, Melchior, Gaspar, and Balthasar, on their homes, thus providing protection for their property. In Bavarian Processions of Light, people carry torches and lanterns through the streets and light bonfires on mountains. *Sternsinger* (star singers), groups dressed as the Magi, make rounds singing carols, and one person carries a lighted star on a pole. Pastors bless homes with holy water, by burning incense, and by writing "G+M+B," the Magi's initials, on door posts.

"Merry Christmas" in Germany is *Fröhliche Weihnachten*.

See also **Advent; Christmas Tree; Epiphany; Saint Nicholas; Saint Nicholas Day; Yule.**

Gesu Bambino

("The Infant Jesus"). Best-known composition of the Italian-American organist and composer Pietro A. Yon (1886–1943). Originally written in Italian, with an English version provided by Frederick Martens, "Gesu Bam-

A German youth, perhaps a baker's boy, carries perhaps a Weihnachtstollen, Stollen, *or fruit loaf under each arm. From the German magazine* Deutscher Kinderfreund, *1910.*

bino" centers around the Nativity, recalling the legend of flowers blooming at Christ's birth ("When blossoms flowered 'mid the snows") and applying other metaphorical attributes such as the "Christmas Rose" and "King of Love and Light" to the Child. Following each verse is the familiar refrain to the carol "Adeste Fideles": "O come, let us adore Him, Christ the Lord." The carol's popularity is attested by the various vocal and instrumental arrangements that have appeared.

Pietro A. Yon served as organist for St. Peter's, Rome (1905–1907), after which he immigrated to the United States. Securing posts as an organist in New York City, first at St. Francis-Xavier's (1907–1919, 1921–1926), then at St. Patrick's Cathedral (a post held for some seventeen years until his death), Yon was renowned as an organist, composer, and teacher. In addition to numerous organ compositions, masses, and religious services, Yon's works include an oratorio, *The Triumph of St. Patrick* (1934).

The Yule of 1889 is "blown in" by a troupe of musicians with horns, while the householders, their cats, and the postman are surrounded by a sky full of symbolic figures for a happy New Year. From the German magazine Fliegende Blätter, *December 30, 1888.*

Ghana
See Africa

The Gift of the Magi

Classic short story by the American writer O. Henry (pseudonym for William Sydney Porter), published in 1905. Contrary to its title, this is not a story of the literal Magi, but of a young, truly loving couple. With a weekly income of only twenty dollars, eight dollars of which rents a furnished flat in the city, Della Young has been able to save up a mere $1.87 with which to buy her husband, Jim, a gift on Christmas Eve. In desperation, she sells her one prized possession, her own long, gorgeous hair, for twenty dollars to buy a platinum fob for Jim's gold watch. But Jim's gift for Della is a set of jeweled, tortoise shell hair combs, which he purchased after having sold his most prized possession, his watch. Here the story ends, and the author unveils the hidden moral of the story. Superficially, these two "foolish children" unwisely sacrifice their most precious treasures. But compared to the Magi, who gave wisely to the Babe, those giving gifts in the manner of Jim and Della are truly wisest of all.

One of O. Henry's most popular stories, "The Gift of the Magi," has also appeared in other forms, including a ballet by The American Ballet Theatre, an off–Broadway musical, a segment of a motion picture, and more than one television special.

Five of O. Henry's stories form the setting for the 20th Century–Fox motion picture *O. Henry's Full House* (1952), which stars Farley Granger and Jeanne Crain in "The Gift of the Magi" segment (written by Walter Bullock, produced by André Hakim, directed by Henry King). The other stories depicted are "The Cop and the Anthem," "The Clarion Call," "The Last Leaf," and "The Ransom of Red Chief." Narrated by John Steinbeck. B & W. 117 min. Video N/A.

Television adaptations include *The Gift of the Magi* (1958), starring Gordon MacRae, Sally Ann Howes, and Tammy Grimes; and *The Gift of Love* (1978), hosted by Henry Fonda, starring Timothy Bottoms and Marie Osmond (written by Carol Lendner, directed by Don Chaffey). In the latter, a wealthy orphan is about to enter into an arranged marriage until a Swiss immigrant captures her heart. Videos for both N/A.

Glastonbury Thorn

Hawthorne tree (*Crataegus mongyna biflora*) found in the town of Glastonbury, Somerset, southwestern England, that blooms at Christmastime. Its association with Christmas further stems from legends surrounding the biblical character Joseph of Arimathea, a Jewish leader who donated his own tomb in which to bury the body of Christ following the Crucifixion (Luke 23:50–53). According to one of the numerous legends that also fill the significant hiatus in the Gospel accounts of Jesus' life between the ages of twelve and thirty (the so-called "lost" years of Jesus), the boy Jesus accompanied Joseph on one or more of the latter's voyages to the region of what is now Glastonbury. From a composite of other legends, Joseph, having obtained the Holy Grail following the Crucifixion, returned with it to Glastonbury around Christmastime of A. D. 63 to establish the first English Christian church. After ascending Wearyall Hill, Joseph thrust his staff of hawthorne wood into the ground and slept, then awoke to find not only that the staff had become a hawthorne tree with blooms, but also that it bloomed annually thereafter at Christmastime.

Although the thorn's yearly "miracle" attracted thousands over the centuries, the Puritan regime in the latter sixteenth century scorned its association with the supernatural. Some tales hold that one Puritan man, on attempting to destroy the tree, was either blinded or perished for his act of desecration, struck by the hand of divine providence.

Although the Glastonbury Thorn itself had perished by the seventeenth century (specific dates are lacking), cuttings believed to have been taken from the original tree continued to survive in Glastonbury and other locations. By this time, people had anticipated its annual Christmas Eve blooms as a natural sign that Christmas had arrived. When England dropped the old Julian calendar and adopted the present Gregorian calendar in September of 1752, which placed Christmas Eve eleven days earlier, the Glastonbury Thorn failed to bloom on the new date. Instead, it bloomed on January 5, Christmas Eve by the old calendar, for which many refused to celebrate Christmas until they witnessed the blooms. The calendar change prompted the terms "Old Christmas Day" or "Christmas Old Style" for Christmas observed on January 6 and "New Christmas Day" or "New Style Christmas" for the holiday observed on December 25.

Descendants of the Glastonbury Thorn survive in England and abroad. Annually on Old Christmas Eve, the mayor and vicar of Glastonbury send a clipping to the reigning English monarch, a custom dating to the Middle Ages. In 1901, the bishop of Washington, D.C., received a clipping from the Glastonbury Thorn to commemorate the building of the National Cathedral there. Planted on cathedral grounds, the thorn often blooms on Christmas Day.

Glastonbury was the site of a prominent Celtic abbey, first erected during the fourth century, and was also believed to be the "Island of Avalon" mentioned in the tales of King Arthur. Indeed, during the Middle Ages, monks from Glastonbury Abbey claimed that King Arthur himself was buried in their cemetery. Although the abbey declined around 1539 and ultimately fell into ruins following King Henry VIII's dissolution of British monasteries, the Church of England now controls the estate.

See also **Christmas Old Style, Christmas New Style.**

Gloucestershire Wassail

Eighteenth-century folk carol from the Gloucestershire region of England, also known as "Wassail, Wassail All Over the Town" and "Gloucestershire Wassailers' Song." Wassailers from this region reportedly made their rounds carrying a large, decorative wassail bowl while singing this carol, whose merry lyrics call to mind the revelry and the drinking (wassailing) to the health of not only friends during the holidays but of the hired help and livestock as well. The number of verses varies, usually between five and eight, but in most versions, the carol toasts horses named Cherry and Dobbin; cattle named Broad May, Fillpail, and Colly; the butler and maid; and the wassail leader as well. Other versions permit the carolers to supply the names of those being toasted. Similar Eng-

lish folk carols with like sentiment bear the names of their locales of origin, for example, "The Yorkshire Wassail Song" ("We've Been a While A-Wandering") and "The Somerset Wassail" ("Wassail, O Wassail All Over the Town").

See also **Here We Come A-Caroling; Wassail.**

Gloucestershire Wassailers' Song
See **Gloucestershire Wassail**

Go Tell It on the Mountain

African American spiritual. Sources vary regarding its origin. Whereas some believe that it arose as an anonymous slave song during the early 1800s, others attribute it to John Wesley Work, Jr. (1871–1925), a black instructor of Greek and Latin at Fisk University in Nashville, Tennessee (founded in 1865 with the purpose of educating freed slaves). Together with his composer brother, Frederick Jerome Work (1880–1942), John Work collected, harmonized, and published several collections of slave songs and spirituals, the first of which was *New Jubilee Songs as Sung by the Fisk Jubilee Singers* (1901). John Work, Jr., allegedly wrote the lyrics to "Go Tell" and then paired them with the musical setting for an older spiritual titled "When I Was a Seeker" (also the first words to one of the verses to "Go Tell"), for which his son, John W. Work, III (1901–1967), also provided a harmonization. It remains uncertain, however, whether John Work, Jr., wrote the original lyrics to "Go Tell."

According to sources from the Reader's Digest Association, the Jubilee Singers of Fisk University introduced "Go Tell" around 1879 during their fund-raising concert tours in America and in Europe. With the exception of the refrain, which remains constant and from which the title derives, the lyrics vary from source to source. Therefore, it is conceivable that John Work, Jr., his brother, or his son could have contributed additional lyrics after the song became established.

God Rest Ye Merry, Gentlemen

English traditional carol, a narrative of

the Nativity, thought to have arisen during the sixteenth century. The "Rest" is an archaic term for "keep." One of the earliest tangible settings is found in *The Roxburghe Ballads*, a manuscript collection of verses and tunes which resides in the British Museum in London. Although the manuscript itself dates to 1770, the pieces contained therein are believed to be much older. Whereas the well-known tune is said to have been initially published in 1827 with a variant text, the lyrics commonly sung today appeared in William Sandys' *Christmas Carols, Ancient and Modern* (London, 1833) with a variant tune, while *Christmas Carols New and Old*, edited by Henry Bramley and John Stainer (London, 1871), provided a more reliable source for the present melody.

Needless to say, variant tunes and lyrics exist, developed from the eighteenth century onward. For example, in the first verse, the original lines, "For Jesus Christ, our Savior, / Was born upon this day" have read, "Remember Christ, our Savior, / Was born on Christmas Day." Some versions omit verse two entirely, which begins as, "In Bethlehem in Jewry," or if it is retained, change the first line to the less archaic, "In Bethlehem in Israel." From the original refrain, "O tidings of comfort and joy, comfort and joy, O tidings of comfort and joy," has evolved "O tidings, O tidings of comfort and joy. / For Jesus Christ, our Savior, / Was born on Christmas Day," or simply, "And it's tidings of comfort and joy." Even the original "Ye" in the title is often replaced with a more modern "You." The eighteenth century also saw at least one additional folk tune setting from Cornwall in western England, and in the nineteenth century, Lewis Redner (of "O Little Town of Bethlehem") contributed another melody. The latter two settings are rarely used, however.

A typical wassailing song, "God Rest Ye Merry, Gentlemen" probably was included in the repertoire of songs commonly sung by the Waits of London, licensed bands of holiday singers and town criers. Charles Dickens alluded to this old tradition in *A Christmas Carol*, in which Scrooge threatens to throttle a young boy for singing this carol on the street outside his office.

See also **Waits**; **Wassail**.

Going on the Wren
See **Hunting the Wren**

Good Christian Men, Rejoice

English title for the German macaronic (mixture of vernacular German and Latin) Carol "In dulci jubilo" ("In Sweet Jubilation"), attributed to the German mystic and Dominican monk Heinrich Suso (1295–1366). In his autobiography of 1328, *Das Büchlein der ewigen Weisheit* (*The Little Book of the Eternal Wisdom*), Suso claimed to have been visited by a company of angels who, to relieve his monastic sufferings, engaged him in ecstatic, heavenly dancing to a tune, the lyrics of which began as "In dulci jubilo." Although this questionable story allegedly inspired Suso to create the carol, it is believed that an anonymous version of this, the oldest of the German macaronic carols, existed before the year 1328.

The oldest known manuscript of the carol, currently residing in Leipzig University, dates to ca. 1400 and consists of a one-verse dance-carol. By the fifteenth century, "In dulci jubilo" had acquired an additional three anonymous verses. Whereas its first printing consisted of only three verses in a Lutheran hymnal in 1533, with one verse expressing Roman Catholic views omitted, Protestant hymnals later adapted and rearranged some of the verses to improve the lyrical sense of the carol.

The best-known English language version was provided by the English clergyman and hymn translator John Mason Neale (1818–1866), who based his very free translation on a Swedish-Latin version of the carol as found in *Piae Cantiones*, a carol collection published in 1582. Beginning as "Good Christian men, rejoice," the English version retained none of the Latin phrases. Neal's musical associate, Thomas Helmore, upon transcribing the tune from that same source, mistook two short notes in the middle section for notes of longer duration, which resulted in a score that did not quite fit the lyrics. Rather than alter the tune, Neal simply added a two-word phrase to each verse as a form of exclamation and published his version in *Carols for Christmas-Tide* (London, 1853–54). Thus, in the midst of verse one, there is "News! News!"; in verse two, "Joy! Joy!"; and in verse three, "Peace! Peace!" Some hymnals now omit the extra words. The lyrics simply express joy at the coming of Christ, that He has opened the door to heaven, and that there is no longer any need to fear death.

"In dulci jubilo" has enjoyed numerous musical settings, notably by the German composer J. S. Bach (1685–1750): BWV 368, which his son C. P. E. Bach (1714–1788) published in a collection of his father's vocal chorales (1769); *Orgelbüchlein* (BWV 608) and BWV 729, both of which are organ chorale preludes. Other organ chorale preludes include those by Johann Michael Bach (1648–1694), Dietrich Buxtehude (1637–1707), Johann G. Walther (1684–1748), and Friedrich Wilhelm Zachau (1663–1712). Michael Praetorius (1571–1621) published several settings in his *Musae Sioniae* (1607, 1609), and the English composer Robert Pearsall (1795–1856) created a popular setting with a solo vocal octet and five-part chorus, published in 1836.

Good King Wenceslas

(Song). English carol, the lyrics of which were written in 1853 by clergyman and greatest of English hymn translators John Mason Neale (1818–1866) as a moral poem to illustrate the virtues of charity to children. Historically Wenceslas (Czech: Vaclav the Good), known for his piety and zeal for spreading Christianity in his country, reigned as duke, not king, of Bohemia from 922 to 929, was murdered by his power-crazed brother Boleslav, and eventually became the patron saint of the former Czechoslovakia. As with St. Nicholas, legends regarding Wenceslas's generosity multiplied, and Neale included one particular legend in his lyrics: As Wenceslas and his page carry food and logs through deep snow to a peasant, the heat radiating from his master's footprints prevents the page from freezing. Another reference to charity (indirectly linking the carol to Christmas) is the "feast of (St.) Stephen," which honors the first Christian martyr on December 26. Also known as Boxing Day in Great Britain, that date was a special time for remembering the poor (*see* **Boxing Day**).

Neale had discovered a thirteenth- or fourteenth-century Scandinavian spring song, "Tempus adest floridum," within *Piae Cantiones*, a carol collection published in 1582, and wrote the lyrics to "Good King Wenceslas" around this melody. He first published the two together in his own collection, *Carols for Christmas-Tide* (London, 1853–54), co-edited by Thomas Helmore. The spring song has also been matched with "Gentle Mary Laid Her Child," a Canadian carol written in 1919 by Joseph S. Cook.

Good King Wenceslas

(Television productions). In 1994 came a television dramatization of Wenceslas's life of benevolence and political struggle with brother Boleslav, starring Jonathan Brandis, Stephanie Powers, Joan Fontaine, and Charlotte Chatton. Written by James Andrew Hall. Produced by Adam Clapham, Michael Deakin. Directed by Michael Tuchner. The Griffin Company. Color. Video N/A.

A 1994 animated cartoon version of the same title features the voices of Bing Crosby and Bob Burrows. Directed by Keith Scoble. BFS Entertainment and Multimedia Video. Color. 25 min.

Grandfather Frost

See **Russia**

Grandma Got Run Over by a Reindeer

Novelty song written by Randy Brooks and popularized by the former husband-and-wife singing group "Elmo & Patsy" (Dr. Elmo Shropshire, a former veterinarian, and Patsy Trigg). The pair were performing at Lake Tahoe, Nevada, in 1979 when Brooks, whose band had rejected "Grandma," persuaded them to record his piece. Although it was first released that same year on Elmo & Patsy's label, Oink Records, no major radio stations or recording studios were interested in promoting "Grandma" until 1983, when a station in San Francisco played it, generating the sale of ten thousand copies in one week. It was the first time in thirty years that a Christmas song had received more time on the air and more sales in one year than Bing Crosby's recording of "White Christmas." Among other examples of its success: A disc jockey in Davenport, Iowa, once played "Grandma" 27 consecutive times on the air (after which he was fired), while another in Godfrey, Illinois, played it 310 consecutive times and made the *Guinness Book of World Records.*

Epic Records released "Grandma" in 1984. The tune, which shot to No. 1 on the Christmas hits charts from 1983 to 1987, has consistently remained a Top 10 Christmas hit since 1987 and has sold over four million copies.

According to the lyrics, Grandma, tipsy from eggnog, is returning home after visiting relatives on Christmas Eve when she is accidentally run down and killed by Santa's reindeer sleigh racing through town. The lyrics, intending humor, nevertheless created a storm of protest from some, including the Gray Panthers, who once picketed an Elmo & Patsy performance with signs reading "What's so funny about a dead grandma?" The press coverage generated by such controversy only boosted "Grandma" sales even further. To appease those troubled over the tune, however, Elmo & Patsy produced a music video in 1983 in which Grandma survived the accident.

Originally known as "The Homestead Act," Elmo & Patsy adopted their professional title on the advice of the late pianist Liberace. Although they recorded some fifty songs together on five albums during the 1970s and 1980s, "Grandma" was their only hit. One such album recorded in 1984 included "Grandma" as the title track, along with humorous songs such as "Percy, the Puny Poinsettia" and "Señor Santa Claus," as well as traditional favorites. After Elmo & Patsy divorced in 1986, Kentucky-native Dr. Elmo, as he is now known, founded Laughing Stock Records in 1995. His latest compact disc album, *Dr. Elmo's Twisted Christmas,* not only features "Grandma," but also a series of sequel novelties such as "Grandpa's Gonna Sue the Pants Off of Santa," "Grandma's Spending Christmas with the Superstars," "Grandma's Killer Fruitcake," and "Please Don't Make Me Play That 'Grandma' Song Again."

Great Britain

Three countries, England, Scotland, and Wales, comprise the island of Great Britain; with Northern Ireland, they form the United Kingdom of Great Britain and Northern Ireland. For purposes of discussion, however, this entry focuses on the countries of Great Britain alone; Irish customs are detailed in a separate entry.

Although there is evidence that Christianity was first introduced with the Roman invasions into Britain for several hundred years after Christ, Saint Columba, an Irish missionary to what is now Scotland, was most influential in spreading Celtic Christianity to the island, beginning in 563. In 596, Pope Gregory I ordered a troupe of missionaries led by St. Augustine (who later became the first archbishop of Canterbury) to Kent, where the baptism of King Ethelbert succeeded in Christianizing the island's southern kingdoms. Although Saint Aidan had established a Celtic branch of the Church by 635 in Northumbria, a northern kingdom of what is now England, its King Oswy embraced the Roman Church in 664 at the Synod of Whitby. Thus the Celtic Church yielded to Rome, and Wales became an English principality following some 200 years of invasions, beginning in the eleventh century. As a result of the Protestant Reformation, the Church of England (Anglican) and Church of Scotland (Presbyterian) survive as respective state churches. The principal faiths in Wales include the Welsh branch of the Church of England and the Presbyterian Church of Wales (actually a Calvinistic Methodist church).

During the Middle Ages, Christmastime in Great Britain was filled with considerable merriment, revelry, and excesses not unlike those of the Roman Saturnalia. Such feasting and imbibing, gaming and gambling, mumming and masquerading were abominations to the Puritans, a radical, religious group born from the Protestant Reformation. While an exhaustive account of Puritan history is beyond the scope of this text, their actions from the mid-sixteenth century into the seventeenth century had a significant impact upon the future of the British Christmas. After Queen Elizabeth I (reigned 1558–1603) established a compromise in 1559 between Roman Catholicism and Protestant reforms within the Church of England, the Puritans, deploring all Christian feast days for which no biblical precedent existed, further sought a shift to a considerably more fundamental church doctrine. Calling for reforms that included completely abolishing Christmas, in 1642 the Puritans waged a

A Puritan (left) forbids Father Christmas to enter his town, while a commoner welcomes him in this early woodcut from a cartoon-like broadsheet printed in the late seventeenth or early eighteenth century. Reprinted in J.M. Golby and A.W. Purdue, The Making of the Modern Christmas *(Athens: University of Georgia Press, 1986).*

civil war against the reigning monarch, King Charles I. They gained control of Parliament in 1644, executed the king in 1649 for treason, and established a Protectorate in 1653 under the direction of Oliver Cromwell, who had played a significant military role in the revolution.

During their regime, the Puritans enacted severe punishments against those who acknowledged Christmas through merry-making, who attended special church services at this time, or who closed their businesses for a holiday. As town criers paraded through the streets with strict admonitions of "No Christmas!" many families covertly celebrated the holiday within their homes, while the citizenry occasionally countered forced compliance with riots and brawls.

Following Cromwell's death in 1658, the Protectorate collapsed, and Parliament restored the monarchy when King Charles II ascended the throne in 1660. Although Charles restored Christmas and other religious observances, the Puritan influence had taken its toll, for these celebrations never fully achieved their height of fervent merriment seen in the days of yore. Nowhere in Britain was the impact of

Puritanism greater than in Scotland, which had outlawed Christmas in 1561. The holiday remained virtually suppressed despite the British Restoration, and the Scots reserved their winter celebrations for New Year's Day. Indeed, Scotland did not legalize Christmas as a holiday until 1958.

Today the Christmas season extends from Advent until Epiphany. Because of common heritage, the Christmas customs of Great Britain share much with those of the United States, such as Christmas trees, cards, and carols; Nativity scenes, pageants, and plays; decorating with lights and evergreens; church services on Christmas Eve or Christmas Day and a large family meal on either day; wassail; and New Year's celebrations with parties and fireworks.

"Father Christmas," an entity peculiar to Great Britain, not only brings the Christmas gifts today but has also assumed the likeness of the American Santa Claus. Yet Father Christmas once personified only the raucous merry-making and secular pleasures of the holiday. According to Phyllis Siefker's *Santa Claus, Last of the Wild Men*, Father Christmas derived from the "Fool" who choreographed the revelry at year-end festivals. At the Roman Saturnalia, this was the *magister ludi* (master of the games); at the medieval Feast of Fools, this was the Archbishop of Fools, Abbot of Unreason, or Lord of Misrule. Also used to describe the master reveler were terms such as "syre Cristemas" of medieval English carols, "Kyng Crestemasse" in the revels at Norwich in 1443, and "Yule" in those at York in 1572. At some point, a Father Christmas figure also presided over the mummers' plays, which E. K. Chambers (*The English Folk-Play*) believes occurred around the seventeenth century. A personification of Christmas gained wider popularity through the dramatist Ben Jonson's (1572–1637) court masque, *Christmas His Masque* (1616), the principal character of which is "Christmas," who refers to himself as "old Christmas," "Captain Christmas," and "Christmas of London." Although the term "Father Christmas" was probably in use much earlier, it first appeared in two pamphlets related to the Puritan decimation of the feast, *The Arraignment, Conviction, and Imprisonment of Christmas*

(1645) and *The Examination and Tryal of old Father Christmas* (1678). His appearance also evolved over time. Jonson portrayed him as an elder man attired in round hose, stockings, doublet, high hat with brooch, long thin beard, and white shoes; following his "imprisonment" during the Puritan regime, the once-corpulent, gray-bearded elder shrank to emaciation. On the other hand, Charles Dickens, in his desire to revive the failing customs of the holiday during his era, portrayed a bare-chested, younger, virile, and jolly Father Christmas through the Ghost of Christmas Present in *A Christmas Carol.* Undoubtedly patterned after popular images, Dickens's Ghost, amid the cornucopia symbolic of the "Golden Age" of the Roman god Saturn, sported a cornucopia-like torch, a green robe lined with white fur, and a holly wreath which crowned his head (*see* **Saturnalia**).

"Firstfooting," a custom once widespread throughout Europe, has been peculiar to Scotland and northern England since at least the eighteenth century. On New Year's Eve, according to superstition, the physical characteristics of the first person ("firstfooter") to cross one's threshold after midnight predicts what luck is in store for the year. A strong, dark-haired man is the most desirable firstfooter, who enters bearing the traditional gifts of coal and bread, along with money or salt (respective symbols of warmth, food, and wealth) or a sprig of holly. Women, fair-haired or red-headed men, and people with flat feet, crossed eyes, or other physical deformities are generally considered to bring bad luck, although some regions make exceptions. Hired firstfooters are not uncommon, and some homes may attach a sprig of prickly holly (the so-called "man's plant") to the door to dissuade women from entering after midnight. The household customarily serves the firstfooter with food, drink, and perhaps money. Those taking the custom most seriously are also quite familiar with spells to counter any infractions of the taboos. For example, should a woman become the firstfooter, several little boys must march through each room of the house to restore the luck. Firstfooting similarly applies to the first person that one encounters on the road; children and oxcarts supposedly bring the best luck.

A favorite English Christmas Eve party game in the nineteenth century and long before that was "Snapdragon." All the lights in a room were extinguished, and a quantity of raisins in a large bowl were covered with brandy and ignited. The party-goers "now endeavor, by turns, to grasp a raisin, by plunging their hands through the flames; ...a considerable amount of laughter and merriment is evoked." Part of the rhyme about Snapdragon reads: "But old Christmas makes him come,/Though he looks so fee! fa! fum!/Snip! Snap! Dragon!" From Robert Chambers, ed., The Book of Days *(London and Edinburgh: Chambers, 1879).*

The following paragraphs summarize additional customs found in the individual countries.

• ENGLAND. During the German occupation of World War II, Norway's King Håkon found political asylum in England. As an annual token of its appreciation, since 1947 the city of Oslo has shipped one of its best Christmas trees to London, where it decorates Trafalgar Square. Some weeks before Christmas, children write letters to Father Christmas, who appears much like the American Santa Claus. Instead of mailing them to the North Pole, the children throw them into the fire, for it is

A MERRY CHRISTMAS AND A HAPPY NEW YEAR!

Everyone gets in on the Christmas Feast parade in this wood engraving for Punch, *December 1858. A turkey, with the body of a plum pudding, is pulled along on a sleigh, while children and the irascible Punch and some nursery rhyme characters skate alongside.*

believed that Father Christmas will favor those letters that burn quickly; otherwise, they must be rewritten.

Noteworthy Christmas Eve celebrations include "A Festival of Nine Lessons and Carols," held annually at King's College in Cambridge, and the "Devil's Knell" ("Old Lad's Passing Bell"), the latter a formerly widespread custom throughout Europe that originated in the Middle Ages. For at least one hour before midnight on Christmas Eve, churches tolled the death of Satan who, according to folklore, had perished at the midnight birth of Christ. One bell tolled once for each year that had passed since that time; then bells pealed joyfully upon the stroke of midnight to herald the arrival of Christmas. Although the Protestant Reformation virtually eliminated the custom, it survives in the village of Dewsbury in Yorkshire.

The Christmas dinner menu often features roast turkey, goose, or beef, along with potatoes, vegetables, and plum pudding, the latter a traditional dessert also known as Christmas pudding or figgy pudding. "Plum" pudding is a misnomer today because the dessert contains no plums. Instead it consists of dried fruit (particularly raisins), spices, sugar, butter, flour, eggs, and suet, and is usually topped with a brandy syrup. Plum pudding evolved from medieval porridge or pottage dishes, which were concoctions of meat, currants, and spices that, by the sixteenth century, also included plums and dried fruits; hence the early name of "plum porridge." During the seventeenth and eighteenth centuries, the evolving recipes omitted the meat and replaced plums or prunes with raisins. Because the seventeenth-century use of the word "plum" broadly implied any form of dried fruit, these recipes were dubbed "plum puddings" (the same reasoning applied to raisins and the term "figgy"). They became popular Christmas dishes by the nineteenth century.

Most puddings were prepared several weeks in advance of Christmas, principally on the Sunday preceding the first Sunday of Advent. Called "Stir-Up Sunday," this day acquired its designation not only from the Anglican prayer offered in church to "stir up" the faithful for Advent, but also because it was customary on this day for family members to stir the pudding batter for luck while making a wish. In 1819 the village of Paignton in Devon cooked a 900-pound pudding, the largest recorded in history.

Today's plum puddings feature a hidden coin, and the person finding the coin in his slice will receive good luck. Alternatively, some puddings include not only a coin, but other objects such as a ring, a small wishbone, an anchor, or a thimble; the coin signifies wealth; the ring, marriage; the wishbone, luck; the anchor, safety; the thimble, thrift, or spinsterhood to an unmarried woman. Inserting objects in plum pudding is a vestige of the Kings' Cakes of Twelfth Night, virtually extinct in England since the nineteenth century.

At each person's plate is found a Christmas "cracker," a traditional party favor which consists of a small, cardboard tube covered with a twist of colored paper. When both ends are pulled simultaneously, a small pyrotechnic device explodes, producing a loud pop (hence the name "cracker"), and the favor bursts open to reveal a written joke or riddle, a colorful paper hat, a balloon, and a variety of small toys. Crackers, the innovation of Tom Smith, a London confectioner, evolved over a period of seven years, commencing in 1840 with the Christmastime marketing of wrapped bonbons, which Smith had discovered earlier that year in Paris. Later he added bits of love verses or

A beautiful plum pudding, stuck with almonds and holly, decorates this Christmas postcard, printed in Germany for the English-speaking market. The postmark is 1909. The artist was Ellen H. Clapsaddle, whose cards are avidly collected today.

mottos. When a crackling fire inspired him to develop a chemical strip that popped with the application of friction, he abandoned bonbons for this new device, which retained the mottos and included surprise gifts. First marketed in 1847, these "cosaques," as Smith initially called them, were Great Britain's first crackers. Following the Victorian age, jokes and riddles supplanted the love poems, and by the turn of the twentieth century, the demand had considerably grown for crackers not only at Christmastime but also for a host of other special occasions, the mottos bearing suitable verses as well. Today the Tom Smith Group Limited, the largest manufacturer of crackers in the world, produces an estimated 38 million crackers annually and ships about 15 percent of these to some 34 countries abroad.

Another postcard printed in Germany about 1910 shows a British Punch-like figure and a Germanic pinecone pulling a Christmas cracker — a party favor that exploded with a "pop," when pulled, revealing tiny toys, printed jokes, and so forth.

On Christmas Day, families often occupy themselves with parlor games, a custom dating to the Middle Ages, and listen to the monarch's annual Christmas message. King George V first broadcast the latter in 1932, and it has been televised since 1956. The traditional fare at Queen's College, Oxford, is to serve the "boar's head" with pomp and ceremony, and some regions observe the ancient custom of "hodening" (from "hobby horse"). The latter, which entails a horse skull or a wooden effigy thereof, is much akin to the Welsh *Mari Lwyd* (see below).

Boxing Day, December 26, also known as St. Stephen's Day, is a legal holiday given to various sporting and theatrical events, such as fox hunting, soccer matches, and pantomimes. On Epiphany Eve or "Christmas Old Style" (January 5), the mayor and vicar of Glastonbury send a clipping from the Glastonbury Thorn to the reigning monarch, having done so for some 400 years. The thorn, said to be a descendant of a tree that sprouted from the staff of Joseph of Arimathea, is also said to have bloomed annually on "Old Christmas Eve" prior to England's adoption of the Gregorian calendar in 1752.

See also **Advent; The Boar's Head Carol; Boxing Day; Boy-Bishop; Christmas Cards; Christmas Drama; Christmas Old Style,** Christmas New Style; Christmas Tree; Epiphany; Feast of Fools; A Festival of Nine Lessons and Carols; Glastonbury Thorn; The Holly and the Ivy; Mistletoe; Nativity Scene; Wassail.

• SCOTLAND. The principal winter festival is *Hogmanay*, observed on New Year's Day. The term is of obscure origin, thought by some to derive from an old French phrase for Christmas, "*Homme est né*" ("Man is born"), or *aguillaneuf* (French, "New Year's gift"). Other likely sources include *haleg monath* (Anglo-Saxon, "holy month") and *oge maidne* (Gaelic, "new morning").

The festival commences with the firing of guns at midnight on New Year's Eve, a custom dating to ancient winter solstice festivals, in which loud noises supposedly drove away the spirits of darkness. Men meeting the requirements of "firstfooters" then make their rounds, (see subentry ENGLAND, above), bearing *handsels*, the customary offerings. The host accepts the food and drink by sharing it with all present, especially the firstfooter, who adds fuel to the fire (or a token lump of coal for the home without a fireplace) and pronounces wishes for a good new year with many more to come. The stranger then receives the customary rewards of a bottle of whiskey and an oatcake. A gift to the host may include the "black bun" (fruitcake with almonds, spices, and whiskey), a traditional holiday cake deriving from the Kings' Cake of Twelfth Night.

Some countries of eastern Europe (for example, Bulgaria and Romania) feature the New Year's custom of children tapping adults with decorated poles to convey good wishes for health and prosperity. A related custom is found on the islands of Lewis and South Uist in the Hebrides of western Scotland. Groups of boys bearing sticks enter homes and chant Gaelic rhymes. The leader, clad in sheepskin, walks clockwise around a chair while his comrades tap the sheepskin with the sticks.

Following the ritual, the boys receive oat cakes. The custom recalls ancient fertility rites, in which beating with sticks on certain holidays supposedly aided health and growth.

Hogmanay was once associated with a host of customs and superstitions, most of which have long been abandoned or are no longer widely practiced. For example, Hogmanay was the chief day for giving gifts, and children went from door to door requesting a "hogmanay," a gift of cheese or oat cakes. Today, whether children receive gifts varies from region to region. People were on their best behavior, for whatever happened on New Year's Day would influence the entire year; the old year's bad luck was burned with the *cailleach*, a small wooden effigy of an old woman that represented the Spirit of Winter; and a girl would surely marry that year if she was the first to draw water from the well that day and her beau drank thereof, a custom once known as "creaming the well."

Scotland's Shetland Islands terminate the winter holidays with "Up-Helly-Aa" (the name possibly derives from the old Scotch "Uphaliday" or "Epiphany"), a fire festival held most notably in the town of Lerwick on the last Tuesday of January. Believed to postdate the Napoleonic Wars (1799–1815), initial celebrations occurred on Epiphany Eve with all manner of noisemaking, drinking, gunfire, brawling, and music. By 1840 the festival included "guizers" (slang, men in disguises) who pulled sledges with burning tar barrels through town and then visited the homes of friends. Torchlight processions replaced the tar barrels when Lerwick banned the latter in the early 1870s. Guizers dressed as Vikings who burned a replica of a Viking galley (the ritual commemorated 600 years of Viking domination ending in 1472) topped the festivities in the late 1880s. The festival gradually shifted to January 29 (twenty-four nights after "Christmas Old Style"), then again to its present day in the twentieth century. Today a "Guizer Jarl" or chief guizer initiates Up-Helly-Aa by posting "The Bill," a farcical proclamation containing a year's worth of gossip and local humor, in the town square. A torchlight procession of some 900 guizers then marches through the streets to the harbor in the evening to burn the thirty-foot galley, after which, amid a night of revelry and imbibing, they perform skits in entertainment halls instead of homes.

"Merry Christmas" in Scots Gaelic is *Nollaig Chridheil*.

• WALES. The most traditional of Welsh customs include *Eisteddfod*, *Plygain*, *Calenigg*, and *Mari Lwyd*, all of which involve some form of carol singing.

Lord Rhys is reputed to have first instituted the *Eisteddfod* ("A Sitting of Learned Men") in 1176 at Castle Cardigan, an event which sought the best works of musicians and poets around the country. Numerous Eisteddfodau have been held throughout Wales since that time, and in 1880 the National Eisteddfod Association was formed to sponsor an annual festival, the location of which alternated between North and South Wales. With the exception of the years 1914 and 1940, the festivals have been held in July or August thereafter. Although they broadly encompass arts and crafts with special emphasis on music and poetry, they are a neverending source for original Welsh Christmas carols, one of which is hailed as the most outstanding for the year. An International Eisteddfod, established in 1947, is held annually in the city of Llangollen.

Following the Protestant Reformation, *Plygain* ("daybreak" or "cockcrow") replaced the Roman Catholic early dawn mass held on Christmas morning. Originally, it commenced between 3 and 6 A.M. and consisted of candlelight processions and Christmas services with unaccompanied carol singing which only men attended. Women remained at home with their children and attended to the baking and preparation of treacle coffee. Following the quite lengthy service, the Christmas feasting began with toasted bread and cheese ("Welsh rabbit"), ale, and perhaps a fowl. Although women and children joined the services during the nineteenth century, Plygain had begun to decline by that time because of increasing drunkenness among those in attendance. With its revival in the twentieth century, Plygain now retains the custom of carol singing but at more reasonable hours and only in a few locales. No longer confined to Christmas morning, it may be held anytime during December or early January, usually without religious services.

The *Calenigg* ("small gift") evolved from the Roman Kalends, in which it was customary to exchange olive branches as peace offerings for the new year. On January 1, Welsh children armed with water and evergreen branches toured their neighborhoods singing carols and anointing their friends' faces with the water. In exchange for these good luck wishes, they received a few coins or Caleniggs. In some areas, the children also dispensed good-luck charms, also known as Caleniggs, which consisted of apples set on three sticks and decorated with almonds, raisins, greenery, colored ribbons, and one candle wedged on top. It was said that only those charms given between dawn and noon would bring luck, and that this luck would remain for the life of the Calenigg. The custom survives in a few locales.

In pre–Christian times, the Teutonic and some Asian pagans sacrificed horses to their gods, then placed the heads or skulls upon poles (spite-stakes or nithing-posts) and propped open the jaws as talismans against their enemies. During the Middle Ages, such devices were believed to ward off werewolves, witches, illnesses, robbers and other bogies, and it was commonplace to note carved, wooden images of horses' heads on house gables or horseshoes over thresholds as good-luck charms. Because it was believed that the powers of darkness were especially prevalent at Christmastime, horse skulls played a significant role in the British holidays. Known as the *Mari Lwyd* ("Grey Mare"), this Welsh equivalent consisted of a horse's skull, the jaws of which opened and shut by means of a wooden pulley. Bedecked with false eyes, ears, and ribbons, the Mare was operated by a man hidden under a white sheet. Together, the Mare and its entourage of black-faced men went from house to house, at each of which arose a series of competitive verses in song (*pwnco*) between the occupants and the Mare, who sought entrance. At some point the occupants usually failed to counter with an appropriate verse (by reputation, the Mare's repertoire was prodigious), whereupon the revelers invaded the house and committed all forms of mischief, then received food and drink as "rewards." Although the Mare had declined into the twentieth century because of its frequent association with drunkenness and acts of vandalism, it has been revived in some regions such as Llantrisant, where it is a feature of New Year as well as Christmas festivities.

"Merry Christmas" in Wales is *Nadolig Lawen.*

The Greatest Gift
See **It's a Wonderful Life**

The Greatest Story Ever Told
See **The Nativity on Film**

Greece

A number of Christ's apostles first introduced Christianity into Greece during the first century. By the sixth century, Greece was incorporated into the Byzantine Empire, from which evolved the Orthodox Church, and it is to this church that the vast majority of Greek Christians adhere. Although a number of countries following this faith cling to the old Julian calendar for ecclesiastical events, Greece now observes Christmas on the present Gregorian calendar. To the Greeks, however, Easter is a holiday of far greater importance than Christmas (*see* **Christmas Old Style, Christmas New Style**).

To commemorate the forty days of temptations that Christ suffered in the wilderness following His baptism, the Greek Orthodox Church observes a forty-day fast or Lenten season prior to Christmas Eve, commencing on November 14. Such a fast prohibits the consumption of any animal products, olive oil, or liquor. During this period, St. Nicholas, the patron saint of sailors, among others, is commemorated on December 6, but with much less ado than is found in central Europe (*see* **Saint Nicholas Day**).

The Christmas season extends from Christmas Eve until Epiphany (January 6). It was once believed that specters roamed the earth during this twelve-day period, a throwback to pre–Christian times, when winter solstice celebrations throughout Europe devised rituals to dispel the supernatural forces believed to lurk in the winter darkness. To the Greeks at this time, the *kallikantzari*, mythical gremlins from the underworld, temporarily ceased their year-long attempts to destroy the roots of the Tree of Life, which held up the physical world, and came to the surface to wreak havoc and mischief. While they were topside, the roots recovered. Initially appearing at the first Christmas, they have returned annually ever since and remain popular in Greek Christmas folklore. Because kallikantzari gain access to the home through the chimney, a fire must burn throughout the twelve days of Christmas to keep them at bay, and all visitors to the home must stir the fire. Additional charms to thwart them include hanging the lower jaw of a pig behind the door, burning old shoes in the fireplace, throwing salt into the flames, and throwing a cake up the chimney for the gremlins to eat. Children born during these twelve days (or only on Christmas Day, according to some sources) may also become kallikantzari, and mothers may counter the spell by binding their newborns in garlic or straw, or by singeing their toenails. The "Blessing of the Waters" on Epiphany (see below) drives the gremlins back to their abode for another year.

The principal Christmas observances occur on December 24. Groups of children travel from house to house singing *kalanda* (Christmas carols), the lyrics of which traditionally not only relate the Nativity story, but also offer good wishes and effusive praise to the household regarding the social and financial status of the occupants therein (regardless of their actual station in life). Along with drums, triangles, and other simple instruments, the carolers often bear small, intricately carved ships that are illuminated from within and decorated with colored ribbons. These ships are vestiges of the Panathenaea, the oldest and most famous festival of ancient Athens, which honored the goddess Athena. As part of this festival, processions of young girls carried small, wooden ships, symbols of mythical vessels which supposedly brought wondrous gifts from the ends of the world. Today, carolers receive rewards of money, fruits, nuts, and sweets, which are tossed into the ships.

Christmas trees decorated with candles and sweets, first introduced to Greece by King Otto I of Bavaria (who ascended the throne in 1832), did not become fashionable until the 1930s. In recent years the Society of the Friends of the Trees, an organization in Athens devoted to conserving fir trees, has begun a campaign to substitute the "lighted ship," described above, for the foreign Christmas tree as Greece's chief Christmas symbol. The society organizes displays which feature miniature replicas of not only historic Greek ships but also those which depict pure fantasy.

The long fast is broken on Christmas Eve with the family dinner, which always features *Christopsomo* ("Christ bread"). This is a sweet loaf with nuts and dried fruit, the surface of which is usually carved with images of the family's trade. This bread often forms the table centerpiece, along with representations of the "bounty of the earth," such as nuts, figs, dates, and fruits. Such a centerpiece is said to derive from pre–Christian thanksgiving oblations to Demeter, goddess of agriculture. As the meal begins, the host makes the sign of the cross over the bread, then slices it and distributes the pieces according to family rank, with the first piece reserved for the first beggar who passes by. Hidden within the bread is a coin, and the person finding it in his slice will receive luck in the coming year. The meal may also include pork, turkey, chicken, lamb, *kourabiedes* (small cakes covered with powered sugar), *melomacarona* (similar, but soaked in diluted honey), and *loukoumades* (fried dough puffs with honey). Other Christmas Eve customs include pouring drops of oil or wine over the hearth, which derives from libations once offered to Hestia, goddess of the home, and feeding small cakes to the livestock at this time and at the New Year.

Christmas Day begins with Orthodox mass, which extends from 4 A.M. until dawn, at which time worshippers take communion. Some families wait until after this mass to break their long fast with the Christmas meal.

Until recent years, children received holiday gifts only on St. Basil's Day (January 1), which commemorates the death of St. Basil (329–379), one of the Patriarchs of the Orthodox Church. Because of western influences, *Agios Vassilis* (St. Basil) now brings the gifts at Christmastime, and his appearance closely resembles that of Santa Claus in the United States. At midnight on St. Basil's Eve, families often ritually slice and distribute a *Vasilopita* ("St. Basil cake"), which also contains a hidden coin. The recipient of the first slice varies among sources, some noting St. Basil, others Christ and the Virgin Mary. Family members receive slices as with the Christ bread, and slices are reserved for the poor and any absent family members. Children again make their rounds to present kalanda, and card games traditionally determine one's fate for the new year. On New Year's (St. Basil's) Day, the first person to enter the home is also a portent for the new year. A strong person entering predicts health; a person carrying a religious icon predicts blessing; a wealthy person, riches; and so forth. The more bountiful the table, the more plentiful will be the year.

Epiphany closes the Christmas season, the principal ritual of which includes the Blessing of the Waters. After a priest dips a cross with a sprig of basil into basins of water, the worshippers take samples of the blessed water home to be used as medicinals. In cities near rivers and the sea, the priest throws the cross into the water, after which young men compete to retrieve the cross by diving into the water. (In the United States, the best known sites for this ritual include Tarpon Springs, Florida, and Asbury Park, New Jersey.) The priest also personally blesses the homes of his parish. Both rituals supposedly drive the kallikantzari back underground.

"Merry Christmas" in Greece is *Kala Christougenna*.

Greenland

A Danish province since 1721, Greenland is the largest island in the world. Because it is the nearest land mass to the North Pole, children from the United States often write letters addressed to Santa Claus in Greenland, and

these are forwarded to Copenhagen, Denmark. There, members of the Department of Tourism provide an appropriate response in the guise of the jolly gentleman.

Christmas traditions in Greenland center around the cultures of the two principal societies inhabiting the island, the Inuit (Eskimo) and the Europeans of Danish-Norwegian descent. Danish and Norwegian customs are discussed under entries for those individual countries, and Inuit customs are found primarily in the entry for Canada.

In addition to decorating imported Christmas trees, caroling, dancing, and giving gifts, the Greenland Inuit enjoy such holiday cuisine as *mattak* (whale skin with blubber) and *kiviak* (young auks buried in seal skins for several months, "aged" to an advanced level of decomposition). Christmas night is the only time of year when Inuit men will attend to their women, such as serving them coffee and stirring it for them. A popular game consists of passing a revolting object (usually round, clammy, and rough) from hand to hand under the table.

"Merry Christmas" may be said in Inuit, *Jutdlime pivdluarit ukiortame pivdluaritlo*; in Danish, *Glædelig Jul*; or in Norwegian, *Gledelig Jul*.

See also **Canada**; **Denmark**; **Norway**.

Grenada
See **West Indies**

Guatemala
See **Central America**

Guyana
See **South America**

H

Hail the Blest Morn
See **Brightest and Best of the Sons of the Morning**

Hamlet
(ca. 1601). Play in five acts by English play-

wright William Shakespeare (1564–1616). *Hamlet* is the only one of Shakespeare's plays that makes any significant reference to Christmas, and that quite briefly. Near the end of Act I, scene I, the officers Marcellus and Bernardo, together with Hamlet's friend Horatio, behold the ghost of Hamlet's father, which vanishes as the cock crows at daybreak. Then Marcellus remarks,

Some say that ever 'gainst that season comes
Wherein our Saviour's birth is celebrated,
The bird of dawning singeth all night long:
And then, they say, no spirit can walk abroad;
The nights are wholesome; then no planets strike,
No fairy takes, nor witch hath power to charm;
So hallow'd and so gracious is the time.
                                        [I.i. 158–164]

Marcellus implies that, according to tradition, the cock, ordinarily crowing with the dawn, also proclaimed the birth of Christ by crowing at midnight. British legends also held that evil spirits were powerless during the twelve holy days of Christmas. This was in marked contrast to folklore in some parts of Europe, particularly Germany and Poland, where it was believed children born during the twelve nights of Christmas could become werewolves. According to a similar, Greek superstition, newborn babies during this period could become *kallikantzari*, evil, half-human monsters. These beliefs undoubtedly carried over from pre–Christian times, when, in the minds of many, spirits populated the darkness of long winter months.

See also **Greece; The Twelve Days of Christmas; Winter Solstice; Yule.**

Hanukkah

(Hebrew, "Dedication"). A Jewish celebration of eight days commencing on the 25th day of Kislev, the third month on the Jewish calendar, which corresponds approximately to the month of December on the Gregorian calendar. It commemorates the victory of Judah Maccabee and his Jewish army over the Hellenist Syrians in 165 B.C., the miraculous burning of a cruse of oil for eight days, and the purification and rededication of the Temple in Jerusalem which the Greeks had desecrated.

Hanukkah, also known as Chanukah, Festival of Lights, and Feast of Dedication, bears no historical relationship to Christmas, yet because its observance frequently falls at Christmastime, Hanukkah forms a trio of principal year-end festivals in the United States, along with Christmas and the seven-day African American holiday, Kwanzaa.

• HISTORY OF HANUKKAH. Upon the death of Alexander the Great (356–323 B.C.), who had conquered the Near East including Palestine, his empire split into smaller kingdoms termed the Seleucid Dynasty, which perpetuated the dominion until the first century B.C. In 167 B.C., Antiochus IV Epiphanes (ca. 215–164 B.C.), king of Syria and overlord of Palestine, captured Jerusalem. Determined to hellenize the Jews, Antiochus introduced Greek gods, desecrated the Temple with an altar erected to Zeus (upon which pigs were sacrificed), and abolished all Jewish rituals. Individuals who resisted died as martyrs.

The Jewish priest Mattathias with his five sons initiated a guerrilla war against the Greek invaders. At Mattathias's death, son Judah Maccabee assumed command and lead his army to defeat Antiochus, thus reclaiming Jerusalem and the Temple for the Jews in 165 B.C. (by 160 B.C., Jewish forces had completely expelled Antiochus from Palestine). In purging the Temple, the Maccabees recovered only one cruse of sealed, undefiled olive oil, which ordinarily would have supplied fuel to light the Temple menorah for one day. Instead, this cruse miraculously fueled the menorah for eight days, during which time the Jews rededicated the Temple with festivities.

The accounts of Hanukkah, as recorded in several historical sources, reflect the holiday's changing role with the Jews over time. For example, the earliest versions, found in the First and Second Books of Maccabees (included in the Apocrypha) and the writings of Josephus, a first-century A.D. Jewish historian (who referred to the holiday as "Light"), stress the martyrs and military victory of the Maccabees but omit the miracle of the oil. The later rabbinic material (Gemara) of the Talmud, while briefly mentioning the victory, focuses primarily on the miracle, and a medieval work, *Megillat Antiochus* (*Scroll of Antiochus*), also speaks of victory and miracle.

At one time, the importance of the Maccabees' victory diminished in favor of the miracle, possibly because the independence gained by the Maccabees lasted for less than 100 years. Yet with the establishment of the State of Israel in the twentieth century, nationalist and military aspects of the festival have returned to play key roles.

• CUSTOMS AND TRADITIONS. Whatever the emphasis placed on Hanukkah, the menorah remains the chief symbol of the festival, representing the light of religious, national, and cultural freedom, and lighting the menorah remains the chief activity. The *Hanukkiah* (Hanukkah menorah) is a candelabrum consisting of nine candles or oil lamps, one of which is more prominent and is located either centrally or to one side. Called the *Shamash* ("servant light"), this special lamp is used to light the others successively from right to left, one for each night of Hanukkah. Following this ritual, which includes the recitations of blessings and traditional songs, the Hanukkiah is usually displayed in a window. Custom also dictates the eating of certain foods made with oil, such as *latkes* (potato pancakes) and *sufganiyot* (doughnuts without holes).

As a result of the influence of Christmas, many American Jewish children now receive gifts, especially *gelt* (money) or chocolate candy wrapped to simulate shekels. Festivities also include games, the most common of which is *dreidel* (or *dreidl*: "rotate, turn"). In this game of chance, children spin a four-sided top, the *dreidel*, the sides of which each contain one of the following Hebrew letters: *Nun, Gimel, Heh,* and *Shin*. These are the first letters to the words in the Hebrew phrase, "*Nes Gadol Haya Sham*" ("A great miracle happened there").

Hanukkah is the only major Jewish festival not recorded in the Hebrew Bible.

Happy Holiday
See **Holiday Inn**

Happy New Year, Charlie Brown
(1986). Made-for-television animated cartoon, based on the characters in the *Peanuts* comic strip created by Charles M. Schulz.

Compelled to read Tolstoy's *War and Peace* as a school assignment over the holidays, Charlie Brown lugs the tome wherever he goes, including the New Year's Eve party thrown by Marcie and Peppermint Patty. He had invited Heather, the "little red-haired girl," but she never responded. Isolating himself, Charlie

Brown falls asleep while reading at the party. While he is asleep, Heather arrives and dances with Linus instead. By the time Charlie Brown awakens, the midnight revel is past, and Heather has departed. He finishes his book-report assignment a few hours before school resumes, receiving a D-minus for his efforts. Upon receiving the next assignment, to read Dostoyevski's *Crime and Punishment*, Charlie Brown falls into a swoon.

Voices: Chad Allan, Kristi Baker, Melissa Guzzi, Aron Mandelbaum, Jeremy Miller, Jason Mendelson, Elizabeth Lyn Fraser. Vocalists: Sean Collins, Tiffany Billings, Desiree Goyette. Written by Charles M. Schulz. Produced by Bill Melendez. Directed by Bill Melendez, Sam Jaimes. A Lee Mendelson-Bill Melendez Production in Association with Charles M. Schulz Creative Enterprises and United Feature Syndicate. Paramount Video. Color. 24 min.

See also **A Charlie Brown Christmas**; **It's Christmastime Again, Charlie Brown**.

Hark! The Herald Angels Sing
Highly popular English carol, the lyrics of which were written by Charles Wesley (1707–1788), a founder of Methodism and author of some 9,000 hymn poems including "Christ the Lord Is Risen Today" and "O for a Thousand Tongues to Sing." Inspired by the pealing of London church bells on Christmas morning, Wesley first published the poem as "Hymn for Christmas Day" in his *Hymns and Sacred Poems* (1739). The poem has undergone various revisions over the years. Originally consisting of ten four-line verses, it began as "Hark, how all the welkin [heaven] rings / 'Glory to the King of Kings.'" The wording of this first couplet was too archaic for George Whitefield, a Calvinist and Wesley's associate, who revised the couplet to "Hark! The herald angels sing: / 'Glory to the new-born King!'" Likewise, verse five, beginning as "Hail the heav'nly Prince of Peace" was altered to "Hail the heaven-born Prince of Peace." These changes, together with omitting verses eight and ten entirely, Whitefield published in his *Hymns for Social Worship* (1753). In 1760 the Reverend Martin Maldan revised the second couplet of verse two, from "Universal nature say / 'Christ the Lord is

born today'" to "With the angelic hosts proclaim, / 'Christ is born in Bethlehem!'" Repeating the opening couplet as a refrain first appeared when the poem was included in an Anglican publication, the Supplement to *New Version of the Psalms* (1782). And the final alteration appeared in *Hymns Ancient and Modern* (1861), in which "Pleased as man with men to appear / Jesus, our Immanuel here" in verse 4 was replaced with "Pleased as man with men to dwell, / Jesus, our Immanuel." By this time the established printing had paired the four-line verses together, creating three eight-line verses with refrain.

For more than one hundred years Wesley's poem was sung to a number of tunes, including that for "Christ the Lord Is Risen Today" and "Take My Life, and Let It Be." None of these musical settings seemed suitable, however. Finally, William Cummings, organist for Waltham Abbey, Essex, discovered an obscure work, *Festgesang*, a cantata in four movements by German composer Felix Mendelssohn. Commissioned in 1840 for the 400th anniversary of the Johann Gutenberg printing press in Leipzig, *Festgesang* featured a spirited second chorus, "God Is Light." Cummings adapted this melody to Wesley's poem and published the two together in 1856. Cummings's arrangement has become the carol version most often sung today.

Of *Festgesang*, Mendelssohn had ironically remarked from the outset that only lyrics expressing something gay and popular, and not sacred words, best suited the music.

The Haunted Man and the Ghost's Bargain
See **Dickens, Charles, Christmas Stories of**

Have Yourself a Merry Little Christmas
Popular American song written for the 1944 MGM motion picture *Meet Me in St. Louis* by Oklahoma native Ralph Blane Hunsecker (lyrics), better known as Ralph Blane, and Alabama native Hugh Martin (music), both of whom also wrote the picture's musical score. The movie, which can hardly be classified as a "Christmas film" in the strictest sense of the

term, featured such other numbers as "The Trolley Song" (nominated for an Academy Award), "The Boy Next Door," and "Skip to My Lou." Judy Garland played a much older sister to young Margaret O'Brien (recipient of the Juvenile Award for Most Outstanding Child Actress of 1944) and was supposed to make their imminent move from St. Louis to New York City seem less distressing by singing "Have Yourself a Merry Little Christmas." When Garland found the original lyrics too depressing to sing to a child and requested something more optimistic, actor Tom Drake convinced producer Arthur Freed to have the composers alter the lyrics accordingly rather than abandon the number altogether. Though the lyrics anticipate celebrating Christmas in new surroundings, the music is quite nostalgic and sentimental. Garland recorded the song on the Decca label in 1944 and 1954, but neither recording made the pop charts. Of the 25 most frequently performed Christmas songs of the twentieth century listed by the American Society of Composers, Authors and Publishers (ASCAP), "Have Yourself a Merry Little Christmas" is ranked number 7.

The Hawaiian Christmas Song
See **Mele Kalikimaka**

He Is Born, the Divine Christ Child
See **He Is Born, the Holy Child**

He Is Born, the Holy Child
("Il est né, le divin Enfant"). French traditional carol thought to date from the eighteenth century. It is also known as "Christ Is Born a Child on Earth" and "He Is Born, the Divine Christ Child." As with many traditional carols, text and music were first published separately, and how or by whom they were paired is not known. The text was first published in a collection by Dom Georges Legeay, *Noêls anciens* (Paris, 1875–1876), the music in *Airs des noêls lorrain* (1862) by an R. Grosjean. In the latter, the tune appears as a hunting song. Although the lyrics appear in various English translations, basically the mood of the three verses is joyful praise and adoration of the Child who has come to earth.

He Is Sleeping in a Manger
See **Infant Holy, Infant Lowly**

He Smiles Within His Cradle

("Ein Kindlein in der Wiegen"). Austrian traditional carol, the text of which is thought to date from the fourteenth century. Although it appeared with an altogether different tune in a publication of 1590, the more familiar tune with text appeared in a Viennese hymn collection published in 1649 by the theologian David Gregor Corner (1585–1648). Whereas a number of hymn texts in that collection bear Corner's initials, supporting his authorship, "He Smiles" does not, yet Corner has on occasion received credit for its tune. It is generally felt, however, that the tune is of folk origin. The best-known English translation was made by English poet and novelist Robert Graves (1895–1985), better known for his novel *I, Claudius*. The carol is also known as "A Baby Lies in the Cradle" and "A Baby in the Cradle."

Consisting of four stanzas, the text pictures the joy and peace of viewing the Babe being gently rocked in a cradle, a brilliant halo surrounding him. It is believed that the repertoire of Christmas songs used in German medieval cradle-rocking services included this carol.

See also **Rocking**.

Heap on More Wood

One of several popular titles assigned to Christmas verse written by the Scottish novelist and poet Sir Walter Scott (1771–1832). Other titles include "Christmas in Olden Times" and "Old Christmas." Scott's poem beginning with the lines, "Heap on more wood!—the wind is chill; / But let it whistle as it will, / We'll keep our Christmas merry still," lies within his work *Marmion* (1808), a romantic, narrative poem built around the fictitious character Lord Marmion, amid a setting of knighthood and chivalry. This expansive poem consists of six Cantos, each preceded by its own introduction, and the 85-line "Heap on More Wood" comprises approximately the first half of the "Introduction to Canto Sixth."

"Heap on More Wood" first recalls the pre–Christian, winter solstice festivals (*Iol* or Yule) of Scotland's ancestors from Scandinavia, who celebrated with unrestrained revelry by feasting, drinking, pelting each other with bones, fighting, and dancing around pine-tree fires (according to Scott's notes, a reveler accidentally falling into the fire, if rescued, was required to drink a measure of ale for spoiling the king's fire). The poem next reviews the merrymaking of medieval Christmases, in which the nobility opened their manor halls, bedecked with holly and mistletoe, for purposes of sharing the spirit of the holiday with peers and commoners alike. Christmas dinner featured a boar's head served with pomp, along with wassail, plum porridge, goose, sirloin, and Christmas pie. Entertainment included dancing, caroling, mumming, stories, and card games, all sufficient to brighten "The poor man's heart through half the year."

Marmion is also the source of the familiar proverb, "Oh what a tangled web we weave / When first we practice to deceive," as found in Canto Sixth.

One of the foremost authors in English romanticism and considered to be the first significant, historical novelist, Sir Walter Scott portrayed Great Britain and particularly his native Scotland from the Middle Ages to the eighteenth century. Among his best-known works are the poem *The Lady of the Lake* (1810) and the novel *Ivanhoe* (1820).

See also **The Boar's Head Carol; Christmas Drama; Christmas Pie; The Holly and the Ivy; Mistletoe; Wassail; Winter Solstice; Yule**.

Hear What Great News We Bring
See **Angels and Shepherds**

Heidi

(1937). Motion picture drama, based on the classic children's book of the same title by Johanna Spyri. A key scene takes place on Christmas Eve.

In the nineteenth-century Swiss Alpine setting in the little village of Dorfli, seven-year-old Heidi (Shirley Temple), orphaned since infancy and reluctantly raised by her Aunt Dete (Mady Christians), is now cast upon her grandfather, Adolph Kramer (Jean Hersholt). A recluse of the mountains, Adolph holds only bitterness for his kin and humanity because of a family dispute years ago. But Heidi's winsome ways eventually touch Adolph's heart, and the old man is soon humming the same little tune favored by his granddaughter. At first rebuffing a personal invitation from Pastor Schultz (Thomas Beck) to return to church and society, if only for Heidi's sake, Adolph, after reflecting on having given Heidi her first Sunday school lesson, "The Prodigal Son," repents and becomes a respected member of the community.

While Adolph is away, Aunt Dete, having made financial arrangements to provide a companion for Klara Sesemann (Marcia Mae Jones), the crippled daughter of a wealthy widower in Frankfurt, returns to steal Heidi. Though circumstances are unfavorable, Heidi still brings joy to this new household, including Andrews (Arthur Treacher) the butler, but not to Fraulein Rottenmeier (Mary Nash), Klara's no-nonsense governess. To Rottenmeier, as long as Klara remains an invalid, her position as governess remains secure. Heidi's presence jeopardizes that position, for Klara grows stronger each day through Heidi's influence.

On Christmas Eve, Herr Sesemann (Sidney Blackmer), previously away on business, arrives home to a formal holiday reception with his family and staff, where the song of the evening is "Silent Night." Klara receives a lovely porcelain doll, and her gift to Heidi is a snow globe, precious because its figures of a cabin and an old man remind Heidi of her grandfather. The climax of the evening is Klara's gift to her father, the best he has ever received: Klara steps from her wheelchair and haltingly walks unaided, falling into his arms with, "Merry Christmas, Father!" Weeks prior to Christmas, Klara had learned to walk again with Heidi's faithful assistance, and the two have kept the secret until now.

Rottenmeier, enraged, causes a scene and is discharged. That night, she seeks revenge by attempting to sell Heidi to gypsies. Heidi escapes into the street, where she is reunited with Adolph, who has walked 100 miles from Dorfli to find her. The two flee in a sleigh but are apprehended, Adolph is jailed on Rottenmeier's charges of child abduction, and a hysterical Heidi begs the law to interview Herr Sesemann to clarify all points.

The final scene cuts to springtime, where a fully recovered Klara and her father visit Heidi and Adolph back on the mountain.

With Helen Westley, Pauline Moore, Delmar Watson, Egon Brecher, Christian Rub, George Hambert. Written by Walter Ferris, Julien Josephson. Produced by Darryl F. Zanuck. Directed by Allan Dwan. 20th Century–Fox Film Corporation. Fox Video. B & W. 88 min.

Here Comes Santa Claus

(Film). French motion picture (1984) with English dialogue. This film bears no relationship to the popular Christmas song of the same title (see below).

Touring an airport at Christmastime, a little boy and his friend mistakenly board a plane bound for Rovaniemi in Lapland, where they seek out Santa to help locate the boy's parents, who are political prisoners in Africa. With the help of a good fairy, Santa journeys to the Dark Continent, while the two children suffer hardships at the hands of a forest ogre living near Santa's workshop.

With Karen Cheryl, Armand Meffre, Emeric Chapius, Little Alexia, Jeanne Herviale, Dominique Hulin, Helene Ruby, Jean-Louis Foulquier, Raye Fall. Written by Didier Kaminka. Produced and directed by Christian Gion. Lanaca Productions. Star Maker Video. Color. 78 min.

Here Comes Santa Claus

(Song). Popular American children's song written in 1946 by cowboy singing star and Texas native Gene Autry and California native Oakley Haldeman.

Serving as the grand marshal for the Hollywood Christmas Parade of 1946, Autry was riding his horse Champion when the procession came to that section of Hollywood Boulevard locally known to merchants as "Santa Claus Lane." Some distance ahead of Santa's float, Autry heard throngs of children screaming, "Here comes Santa Claus!" The scene inspired Autry to write "Here Comes Santa Claus," which he outlined to Oakley Haldeman, manager of his music publishing firms at the time. Haldeman and another colleague, Art Satherly, created a lead sheet and prepared a demonstration tape for Autry, with lyrics sung by guitarist Johnny Bonds. It is said that, during this informal recording, the clinking of ice cubes in a drink which Satherly held prompted the use of sleigh bells in Autry's recording of 1947 on the Columbia label. That recording sold over 2.5 million copies and made the pop charts for the remainder of the 1940s and into the 1950s. Autry re-recorded the song in 1957 on the Challenge label and in 1969 on the Republic label, but neither recording made the charts.

"Here Comes Santa Claus" was Autry's first Christmas release. He was also the first to record two other holiday standards, "Rudolph, the Red-Nosed Reindeer" (1949) and "Frosty the Snowman" (1950). Of the 25 most frequently performed Christmas songs of the twentieth century listed by the American Society of Composers, Authors and Publishers (ASCAP), "Here Comes Santa Claus" is ranked number 17.

See also **Frosty the Snowman** (song); **Rudolph, the Red-Nosed Reindeer** (song).

Here We Come A-Caroling

English traditional carol thought by some to date from the sixteenth century in the Yorkshire region. Also known as "Wassail Song," "Here We Come A-Wassailing," and "Here We Go A-Caroling," the carol was one of many sung by the Waits who went from door to door wishing everyone "wassail" (good health), their reward often being a cup of hot wassail.

Although a medieval origin has been suggested, the earliest known written sources include a Manchester pamphlet and a Bradford, Yorkshire, broadside dating from about 1850. This prompted William H. Husk, in his *Songs of the Nativity* (London, 1864), to surmise that the carol was a more recent composition by northern carolers. In Husk's collection, the tune is the familiar one for "God Rest Ye Merry, Gentlemen," with the refrain patterned after a tune known as "Brigg Fair." Although variant tunes and refrains have appeared over the years (the verses remaining fairly constant), the tune and refrain most frequently sung today are derived from Henry Bramley and John Stainer's collection, *Christmas Carols, New and Old* (London, 1871), the tune again originating in Yorkshire.

Some Yorkshire children singing carols on Christmas morning. In the nineteenth century, carolers went out on Christmas Eve as well as Christmas day, but popular opinion was beginning to think that the Eve was a more appropriate time to go around and sing. This may have been because the adult carolers were often given money, which they saved and spent on the merry-making on Twelfth Day. From Robert Chambers, ed., The Book of Days *(London and Edinburgh: Chambers, 1879).*

Another carol, possibly a variant of "Here We Come A-Caroling," is "We've Been a While A-Wandering" ("The Yorkshire Wassail Song"), which contains very similar lyrics but is also sung to a variant tune for "God Rest Ye Merry, Gentlemen."

See also **God Rest Ye Merry, Gentlemen**; **Gloucestershire Wassail**; **Waits**; **Wassail**.

Here We Come A-Wassailing
See **Here We Come A-Caroling**

Here We Go A-Caroling
See **Here We Come A-Caroling**

Holiday Affair

(1949). Motion picture romance.

Christmastime in New York presents two marriage proposals for Connie Ennis (Janet Leigh), a comparison shopper (commonly known as a commercial spy) and young widow with a six-year-old son, Timmy (Gordon Gebert). Her faithful boyfriend, attorney Carl Davis (Wendell Corey), practically lives at her apartment and has popped the question too many times to count, yet Connie, seemingly satisfied with the status quo, refuses to take the leap. Carl's competition arrives in the form of Steve Mason (Robert Mitchum), a toy salesman with a keen eye for sizing people up, whom Connie meets at Crowley's Department Store. Pegging Connie as a spy for the competition when she pretends to return the same electric train set that she had "purchased" from him, soft-hearted Steve is fired for failing to blow the whistle on her.

Steve pursues Connie, despite the fact that she has suddenly decided to marry Carl on New Year's Day, and rapidly becomes friends with Timmy, something Carl has not achieved. Learning that Timmy wants an electric train for Christmas but that Connie cannot afford it, Steve, now broke, somehow provides the surprise gift, after which Connie attempts to refund his money. Instead, he proposes after knowing her only four days, frankly arguing that she would be marrying Carl strictly for security and not love. Torn by this thought, Connie receives another shock when Timmy, realizing Steve's financial need, walks alone to Crowley's and sacrifices his train for a refund, and from Mr. Crowley (Henry O'Neill) at that. When Connie asks Carl to deliver Steve's refund in her place, Carl realizes that she is truly in love with Steve and, citing the evidence, bows out.

On New Year's Eve Steve, believing that Connie still desires Carl, boards a train bound for the West Coast, where he plans to establish himself in building boats. Amid the evening's festivities, however, he receives a message, at which he suddenly rushes through the cars and sweeps Connie and Timmy into his arms. Letting go of the past, Connie has made her choice, and with the new year, a new way of life commences.

With Griff Barnett, Esther Dale, Henry Morgan, Larry Blake, and Helen Brown. Written by Isobel Lennart. Based on a story by John D. Weaver. Produced and directed by Don Hartman. RKO Radio Pictures. Turner Home Video. B & W. 87 min.

In 1996 the picture was remade for television under the same title, starring David James Elliott, Cynthia Gibb, Tom Irwin. Produced by Vicky Herman. Directed by Alan Myerson. Video N/A.

Holiday Inn

(1942). Motion picture musical, the idea for which originated with American songwriter Irving Berlin. The songs were not composed to suit the film; instead, the picture was written to revolve around a series of original Berlin songs that depict the most important American holidays: "Happy Holiday" and "Let's Start the New Year Right" (New Year's Day); "Abraham" (Lincoln's Birthday); "Be Careful, It's My Heart" (St. Valentine's Day); "I Can't Tell a Lie" (Washington's Birthday); "Easter Parade," composed in 1933 (Easter); "Say It with Firecrackers" and "Song of Freedom" (Independence Day); "I've Got Plenty to Be Thankful For" (Thanksgiving Day); "White Christmas" (Christmas). No songs commemorate Armistice Day (now Veterans Day) or Memorial Day. Other songs include "I'll Capture Her Heart," "Lazy," and "You're Easy to Dance With."

A loosely constructed plot ties these songs together. New York's Pierre Club features the song-and-dance act of crooner Jim Hardy (Bing Crosby) and dancer Ted Hanover (Fred Astaire), with Lila Dixon (Virginia Dale) as Ted's dancing partner. Jim, leaving the show for the "easy life" on a farm in Connecticut, returns after a year and decides to convert the farm into an inn that is open only on holidays, "Holiday Inn," which features an appropriate floor show for each occasion. While recruiting Ted and Lila for the inn, Jim meets Linda Mason (Marjorie Reynolds), who aspires to enter show business, and convinces her to become his vocal partner for the show.

In New York, when Lila throws her fiancé Ted over for a Texas millionaire, a drunken Ted retreats to Holiday Inn on New Year's Eve and dances with Linda by accident. They are a perfect match choreographically, and the next few holidays at the inn find Ted resolved to have Linda romantically and professionally, though she and Jim are already engaged. But when Hollywood plans a film based on the Holiday Inn concept, Ted and Linda accept, while Jim remains in Connecticut to write the musical numbers.

By Thanksgiving, when a dejected Jim closes the inn, a pep talk from Mamie the housekeeper (Louise Beavers) puts him out in Hollywood on Christmas Eve, as the movie studio is about to shoot the Christmas finale. Also sick at heart, Linda falters while singing "White Christmas" on the set, at which Jim steps on stage, carries the tune, and rekindles their love. Reopening the inn on New Year's Eve, the foursome (Lila returns because her "millionaire" actually *owed* millions) sings a happy ending.

Despite the many holidays honored, *Holiday Inn* is now regarded as a Christmas classic. Nominated for three Academy Awards, including Best Song, Best Score of a Musical Picture, and Best Original Story, it received only one, which went to Irving Berlin for "White Christmas." This film also promoted one of the most popular Christmas songs ever written, "White Christmas," which Bing Crosby had first introduced on his Kraft Music Hall radio show on Christmas Day, 1941. He sang the song twice in this film, accompanied both times by Marjorie Reynolds. *Holiday Inn* was remade as *White Christmas* (1954).

Written by Claude Binyon. Story by Irving Berlin. Produced and directed by Mark Sandrich. Paramount Pictures. MCA Home Video. B & W. 101 min.

See also **White Christmas** (song); **White Christmas** (film).

Holland

See **The Low Countries** (THE NETHERLANDS)

Holly

See **The Holly and the Ivy**

The Holly and the Ivy

Traditional, allegorical English carol, probably the best known of the so-called medieval "holly and ivy" carols, which draw analogies between Christmas and the pagan symbols of holly and ivy. Although the exact date for this carol is unknown, Joshua Sylvester (believed to be the pseudonym of English carol collectors William Sandys and William H. Husk) first published the lyrics in *A Garland of Christmas Carols* (London, 1861), based on a broadside from Birmingham dating to 1710. But it is believed that the carol was written at a much earlier date. English folk song collector Cecil Sharp first published the lyrics with the tune in his *English Folk-Carols* (London, 1911), which has become the standard version.

Holly and ivy were pre–Christian symbols of rival entities, predominantly male versus female, respectively, but also good versus evil, and they were popular decorations for homes and public places during winter solstice festivals and other holidays. It has been established that in the British Isles, holly was the "man's plant" and clinging ivy the "woman's plant," these two evergreen plants symbolizing the sexes vying for dominance over each other; yet the precise connections of these plants to such contention remain obscure.

Ivy was used primarily as a fertility charm (girls believed that wearing three ivy leaves would enable them to dream of their future husbands, and ewes fed a few leaves supposedly bore twin lambs more often) and as a protective for dairy products and flocks. In Greek mythology, Dionysus, god of wine and vegetation, placed the spirit of the dancing girl Ivy into the plant that bears her name after she had expired at his feet. Thereafter, Ivy clung to and embraced all with whom she came in contact.

According to English folk custom, holly was symbolically superior to ivy, a concept tauntingly suggested in a number of fifteenth-century "holly and ivy" carols. One of these depicts the fair "Holly and his merry men" reveling in a gala winter event, while "Ivy and her maidens" must stand and weep outside in the cold, and a recurrent refrain calls for Holly to have the mastery over Ivy. Holly was also the subject of superstition in that it repelled

A botanical engraving of the 1850s shows the holly leaves and its berries. Holly and other evergreens were used to decorate English churches, and remained until the end of January. The ecclesiastical canons decreed that they must be gone by Candlemas Day, February 2, probably in part because of local superstitions that if the holly were left up, goblins would proliferate.

witches, its presence encouraged pleasant dreams, and arguments could be settled more quickly under a holly tree.

When Christianized as Christmas symbols, holly initially came to represent the masculine features of Christ's birth and ivy the feminine, that is, the Virgin Mary, and the latter theme was emphasized in various medieval carols. In time, holly further symbolized not only the attributes of Christ but those of the Virgin as well, to the neglect of ivy, the latter's loss of popularity in song and as a Christmas decoration stemming primarily from its association with mistletoe as a pagan fertility symbol.

As suggested in the lyrics to "The Holly and the Ivy," the white blossoms of holly represent the purity of Virgin and Babe; the red berries, Christ's blood; the sharp thorns, Mary's travail in childbirth and Christ's crown of thorns; the bitter bark, Christ's agony at the Crucifixion.

With ivy now ostracized from Christmas, so-called "prickly" and "smooth" varieties of holly, respectively, acquired the competitive male and female symbolism, particularly regarding superstitions about which sex would rule the household in the coming year. If prickly holly was brought into the home first on Christmas Day, the man would rule; if smooth holly, the woman. The folk belief of masculine dominance at Christmas also carried over into the British custom of "firstfooting," a quaint tradition which still holds that a woman as the first person to enter a home on Christmas Day brings bad luck. In years past, on Christmas and New Years' Day, a holly sprig would be placed outside the door to ensure that only a man would be the first to enter.

See also **Great Britain; Mistletoe; Winter Solstice.**

A Holly Jolly Christmas

Popular American song written in 1962 by composer John D. (Johnny) Marks, best known for his classic hit of 1949, "Rudolph, the Red-Nosed Reindeer." Encouraging all to have the merriest Christmas ever, the bubbly "A Holly Jolly Christmas" achieved public attention when it became one of several of Marks's creations featured in the 1964 television ani-

Punch hands Queen Victoria a bouquet of holly. Punch, *December 1847.*

mated special *Rudolph, the Red-Nosed Reindeer,* with vocals rendered by Burl Ives. Ives's Decca recording of "Holly Jolly Christmas" ranked 13th on the *Billboard Christmas Singles* chart in 1964 and 29th in 1968.

Of the 25 most frequently performed Christmas songs of the twentieth century listed by the American Society of Composers, Authors and Publishers (ASCAP), "Holly Jolly Christmas" is ranked number 25.

See also **Rudolph, the Red-Nosed Reindeer** (television special).

The Holy Baby
See **Children, Go Where I Send Thee**

Holy Innocents Day

Also known as Day of the Innocents or Feast of the Holy Innocents in the Roman Catholic and affiliated churches, and as Childermas (Children's Mass) in England. Traditionally observed on December 28, it is a memorial to those children two years old and under whom King Herod the Great massacred in Bethlehem following the Wise Men's visit to the manger, as described in the Gospel of Matthew 2:1–18. In the Armenian tradition, because the Innocents died fifteen weeks after Christ was born, that church observes the Monday following the second Sunday following Pentecost. The official color for the Catholic Mass is purple, symbolic of mourning; if the date falls on Sunday, the Church prescribes red, symbolic of the young martyrs' blood.

Exactly when the Roman Church instituted this feast is not known. The earliest records of its observance date from the end of the fifth century, but its first celebrations could have occurred by the end of the fourth century. During those early feasts, abstinence from meat and from foods cooked in fat was mandatory. During the Middle Ages, Holy Innocents Day was considered unlucky, because the Bethlehem children theoretically had not been baptized prior to their deaths. On the other hand, because these children were regarded as martyrs for Christ, children were venerated and given places of honor in homes and religious orders; in some locales, the youngest member of a community, regardless of his or her age, was fed baby food. Holy Innocents Day was also the final day of reign for the "Boy-Bishop," a young boy who had been elected on Saint Nicholas Day (December 6) to act as bishop from then until December 28.

Parents symbolically whipped their children as a reenactment of Herod's slaughter and to drive out evil spirits, a carry-over from year-end fertility rites of ancient pagans. Children in turn would seek out women and girls, brush them with twigs, and chant fertility verses. Related customs whereby children tap elders and contemporaries with sticks occur today in many areas of Europe. In France, children who overslept on this day were punished with whippings.

By the eleventh century, Holy Innocents Day had also become a riotous feast for students and choirboys, which recalled those revels of the pre–Christian Roman Saturnalia, and was one of four degenerate post–Christmas holidays collectively termed the Feast of Fools.

A number of churches now claim to enshrine the remains of several of the Holy Innocents, including the Church of St. Justina at Padua and the cathedrals of Lisbon and Milan, among others.

See also **Boy-Bishop**; **Feast of Fools**; **Nativity**; **Saturnalia**.

Home Alone

(1990). Motion picture comedy that spawned two sequels. The family of eight-year-old Kevin McAllister (Macaulay Culkin) accidentally leaves him behind in Chicago while they travel to France for Christmas vacation. Initially, the situation is a dream come true for Kevin, who is often at odds with his family and had even wished that they would disappear. Now with the house at his command, he learns self-reliance amid self-indulgence (such as reading his older brother's *Playboy* magazines, eating junk food, and watching videos with titles like *Angels with Filthy Souls*).

As Kevin prepares for Christmas alone, robbers Harry (Joe Pesci) and Marv (Daniel Stern) have targeted Kevin's seemingly empty, well-to-do home as the next one to hit. When Kevin spots them outside and overhears that they plan to strike at 9 P.M. on Christmas Eve, he booby traps the entire house from top to bottom.

By now, Kevin misses his family. Feeling pensive while out on a walk early on Christmas Eve, he stops by a church, where a children's choir is singing "O Holy Night." Inside, he is joined by Mr. Marley (Roberts Blossom), the next-door neighbor wildly rumored to have murdered his own family years ago, and the two become friends after sharing some personal problems. Marley, a crusty but kindly old man, has actually been estranged from his son for years and is reluctant to call him, for fear that the son still bears ill will. Kevin encourages the call anyway, and Marley lifts Kevin's spirits about his family (who, unbeknownst to Kevin, are desperately searching for a way to get home to him).

On schedule, inept crooks Marv and Harry find that evading Kevin's twelve challenges is virtually impossible, for they are seared, stuck, gouged, struck, and bashed by a hot coil, sticky tar, sharp ornaments, an iron, a spike, a trip wire, and paint cans turned wrecking balls. Calling 911, Kevin steers the police to a house across the street, then lures the crooks there. Although the crooks initially nab Kevin, Marley appears and bashes the two with a shovel, and the police arrive shortly for the arrest.

On Christmas morning, Kevin's family returns, having at last found a flight home. Gazing outside, Kevin observes Marley embracing his son and family, a sight that gladdens his heart as much as having his own family back again.

With John Heard, Catherine O'Hara, Angela Goethals, Gerry Bamman, Hillary Wolf, Larry Hankin, John Candy, Kieran Culkin. Written and produced by John Hughes. Directed by Chris Columbus. A John Hughes Production with 20th Century–Fox Pictures. Fox Video. Color. 105 min.

Home Alone received Academy Award nominations in 1991 for Best Original Score and Best Song, "Somewhere in My Dreams," by Leslie Bricusse and John Williams. It also received Golden Globe nominations in 1991 for Best Motion Picture Comedy/Musical and Best Performance by an Actor in a Motion Picture Comedy/Musical (Macaulay Culkin).

Home Alone 2: Lost in New York (1992) reunites the principal cast in another holiday comedy that should be classified as a remake of the 1990 film rather than a sequel, for although the location has changed, the characters, plot, and sometime-seasonal sentiment are virtually identical. Boarding the wrong aircraft, Kevin finds himself in the Big Apple at Christmas, while his family jets to Florida, and robbers Marv and Harry, now escaped prisoners seeking revenge, fall victims to Kevin's ingenious booby traps once more. With Rob Schneider, Dana Ivey, Tim Curry, Brenda Fricker, and a cameo appearance by multi-millionaire Donald Trump in the Plaza Hotel, owned by Trump. In 1993 the film won the People's Choice Award for Favorite Comedy Motion Picture. Production credits identical to *Home Alone.* Fox Video. Color. 120 min.

Home Alone 3 (1997), again written by John Hughes, presents a similar plot but with a new cast of characters featuring eight-year-old Alex D. Linz. In 1998 the film was nominated for a Razzie Award for Worst Remake or Sequel. Produced by Hilton A. Green, John Hughes. Directed by Raja Gosnell. 20th Century–Fox Film Corporation. Fox Video. Color. 102 min.

Home for the Holidays

Popular American song written by the New York–born songwriting team of Al Stillman (lyrics) and Robert Allen (music) in 1954. It recalls the all–American sentiments and pleasures of being at home for the holidays, including homemade pumpkin pie. Because Christ-

mas is never actually mentioned in the lyrics, the song might also be appropriate for Thanksgiving. Yet it remains inexorably linked with Christmas, popularized by Perry Como's 1954 recording on the RCA Victor label, which became the top Christmas song that year.

Of the 25 most frequently performed Christmas songs of the twentieth century listed by the American Society of Composers, Authors and Publishers (ASCAP), "Home for the Holidays" is ranked number 18.

Stillman and Allen also contributed such titles as "It's Not for Me to Say" (1956), "No, Not Much" (1956), and "Chances Are" (1957).

The Homecoming: A Christmas Story
See **The Waltons**

Honduras
See **Central America**

The Honeymooners

Highly popular television situation comedy series that initially aired on the DuMont network in 1950 and went on to become a popular show on CBS. Starring Jackie Gleason as New York City bus driver Ralph Kramden and Art Carney as sewer-working friend Ed Norton, the series, Gleason's creation, featured the domestic, argumentative lives of loud-mouthed Kramden and his nerves-of-steel wife Alice, along with Ed Norton's wife, Trixie. In various incarnations the show lasted until 1970.

The episodes from *The Honeymooners'* DuMont Network years are lost, but the existing *Honeymooners* Christmas episodes consist of the following:

"Santa and the Bookies" (December 12, 1953): Needing fast cash because he believes that Alice is pregnant, Ralph answers a newspaper ad for a sidewalk Santa Claus who will supposedly solicit funds for charity. Unknown to Ralph and Ed (dressed as an elf), the operation is a front for bookies. The two initially land in jail but eventually assist the police in capturing the real culprits.

"Honeymooners Christmas Party" (December 19, 1953): This episode is a remake of a now-lost DuMont sketch. Alice is decorating the apartment on Christmas Eve and sends Ralph on a grocery errand. After Trixie arrives and describes to Alice what Ed gave her for Christmas (a juice squeezer in the image of Napoleon that squirts juice out of its ear), a series of "guests" drop by that are characters played by Gleason, including "Fenwick Babbit," the beer-and-ice man; "Joe the Bartender"; "The Poor Soul"; "Rudy the Repairman"; and "Reginald Van Gleason III." Other stars visiting the Kramdens are Frances Langford, who sings "Great Day" and "I Love Paris"; child star Eddie Hodges, who sings "Walking My Baby Back Home"; and the June Taylor Dancers, regulars on the Gleason variety shows. With the exit of the final guest, Ralph returns, and he and Alice exchange gifts, a pair of gloves for him and a Napoleon juice squeezer for her.

"New Year's Eve Party" (December 26, 1953): Not wishing to go out on New Year's Eve but anticipating that Alice will, Ralph attempts to dissuade her by being overly obnoxious. His attitude changes when bandleaders Jimmy and Tommy Dorsey, arriving to retrieve a stack of their sheet music that Alice had found in a telephone booth, invite the Kramdens and Nortons to be their New Year's Eve guests at the Statler Hotel. To avoid having to work on New Year's Eve, Ralph feigns illness to his boss, who in turn has lied to his mother-in-law about spending the evening with her, and heads for the Statler instead. On seeing Ralph there, the boss fires Ralph for lying but reconsiders when his wife reminds him about his own lie. With all forgiven, everyone enjoys dancing to the Dorsey band.

"'Twas the Night before Christmas" (December 24, 1955): This is a remake of an earlier episode, "The Anniversary Gift" (February 21, 1953), with a Christmas theme substituted. It's Christmas Eve, and Ralph has bought Alice a supposedly one-of-a-kind hairpin box made of 2,000 matches, which, according to the salesman, once belonged to the emperor of Japan. Before Ralph can present his gift, a neighbor drops by with a gift for Alice: another hairpin box exactly like the one Ralph bought. Chagrined, tricked, and without additional funds for another gift, Ralph almost finds a way out when Uncle Leo arrives with his present for the Kramdens, a gift certificate for

$25 to a local department store. Alice, however, is aware of this present, which precludes Ralph from using it to buy her a more practical gift, so he hocks his prized bowling ball instead. On Christmas morning, Alice gives Ralph a bag for his bowling ball, and when she insists on seeing if it fits, Ralph confesses all. Instead of the hairpin box, Ralph's gift to Alice is a Napoleon orange juice squeezer, just like the one Ed gave to Trixie (an idea borrowed from the 1953 "Honeymooners Christmas Party"). The sentiment is not unlike that presented in O. Henry's short story "The Gift of the Magi."

After 1970, the Kramdens and Nortons returned for several *Honeymooners* specials, none of which are currently aired on television. In *The Honeymooners Christmas Special* (November 26, 1977), Ralph stages a presentation of Dickens's *A Christmas Carol* for the Gotham Bus Company, with Ralph and Ed playing multiple characters. In *Jackie Gleason Honeymooners Christmas* (December 10, 1978), Ralph persuades people to buy hundreds of lottery tickets.

Series written by Marvin Marx, Walter Stone, Syd Zelinka, Leonard Stern, Andy Russell, Herb Finn. Executive producer, Jack Philbin. Produced by Jack Hurdle. Directed by Frank Satenstein.

The Honeymooners appears in the following video collections: *The Honeymooners Classic 39 Collection* (8 cassettes, 20th Century–Fox Video, B & W) and *The Honeymooners—The Lost Episodes* (12 cassettes, MPI Home Video, B & W, 600 min.).

Honeymooners Christmas Party
See The Honeymooners

The House Without a Christmas Tree

(1972). Made-for-television drama based on a story by Gail Rock, later published as a book (1974).

The setting is Nebraska, 1946. Each year Addie Mills (Lisa Lucas) begs her father James (Jason Robards) for a Christmas tree; each year he refuses. Embittered over losing his beloved wife after Addie's birth ten years ago, James has put Christmas aside, for its symbols remind him too much of his Helen, who had cherished the season. Undaunted, Addie persists in dropping hints about her wish, even singing the carol "O Christmas Tree" with her friends before her father.

A severe altercation erupts after Addie brings home the tree from her class that she "won" at school. Spewing brimstone, James orders the tree out of his house, as expected, after which Addie attaches a note "From Santa" and anonymously gives it to a school chum who has no tree. Shortly thereafter, James recognizes Addie's former tree in a neighbor's home. Hearing how it arrived through Addie's unselfishness more than melts James's stony heart. He brings home a Christmas tree and shares memories with Addie about the mother she never knew. And from the attic, he retrieves the precious, hand-made star that Helen had intended for Addie's first Christmas tree. Their house had Christmas trees from then on.

With Mildred Natwick, Alexa Kenin, Kathryn Walker, Gail Dunsome, Maya Ryan, Brady MacNamara. Written by Eleanor Perry. Produced by Alan Shayne. Directed by Paul Bogart. CBS Productions. Fox Video. Color. 90 min.

How Brightly Beams the Morning Star
See **How Brightly Shines the Morning Star**

How Brightly Shines the Morning Star
("Wie schön leuchtet der Morgenstern"). German chorale written in 1598 by Philipp Nicolai (1556–1608), Lutheran pastor of Unna in Westphalia. Nicolai wrote only four chorales, of which this and "Sleepers, Awake! A Voice Is Calling" are the best known, the two having achieved the distinctions as the queen and king of chorales, respectively. All four were written following a six-month outbreak of bubonic plague in Unna between July 1597 and January 1598 and were published in Frankfurt in 1599.

The text is founded on Psalm 45, which consists of songs from a royal wedding party. From this, Nicolai developed the variant theme of a spiritually royal bridal song between the Christian soul (bride) and Christ (Bridegroom). References to Christmas appear in the first two of seven verses, in which Christ, symbolized as the "Morning Star" (not the Star of Bethlehem), is the light born to save a lost world from the darkness of sin (Malachi 4:2 and Luke 1:78). Verse one also refers to Christ as the branch from Jesse, King David's father, as found in the Messianic prophecy of Isaiah 11:1. And verse two refers to Christ as Mary's son who has come down to earth as the pearl and crown. In the remainder of the chorale, the soul expresses undying love for Christ.

The Unna plague claimed the life of one of Nicolai's former students, fifteen-year-old Wilhelm Ernst, Count of Waldech. According to *The New Oxford Book of Carols*, Nicolai memorialized him in "Morning Star" by using the first letter of each of the seven verses as an acrostic, creating the initials "W. E. G. U. H. Z. W.," which stand for "*Wilhelm Ernst, Graf und Herr zu Waldech*" (Count and Lord of Waldech).

"Morning Star" has appeared in other settings, such as the accompaniment for "Die Könige" ("The Kings"), an Epiphany carol written in 1859 by the German composer Peter Cornelius (1824–1874) and published in 1871. J. S. Bach's Cantata No. 1 (1725) is also based on the Nicolai chorale.

The best-known English translations have been provided by Great Britain's Catherine Winkworth (1827–1878), a translation specialist who has rendered the title as "O Morning Star, How Fair and Bright" and "How Brightly Beams the Morning Star."

See also **Sleepers, Awake! A Voice Is Calling**.

How Great My Joy
See **While By My Sheep**

How the Flintstones Saved Christmas
See **The Flintstones**

How the Grinch Stole Christmas
Classic children's book by Dr. Seuss (Theodor Seuss Geisel) with animated cartoon and motion picture adaptations. The book, published in 1957, features the Grinch, a nasty creature who hates Christmas because his heart

is two sizes too small. Hearing the little Whos preparing gaily for Christmas in the nearby town of Whoville only irritates him that much more. Determined to keep Christmas from coming, the Grinch, disguised as Santa, steals into Whoville on Christmas Eve with his dog, Max (disguised as a reindeer), and strips the town of every Christmas item, including the Who-pudding, the roast beast, and the last can of Who-hash. When tiny Cindy-Lou Who discovers him stealing her Christmas tree, the lying Grinch claims that he's merely taking the tree away to replace a broken light bulb and will return it shortly.

On Christmas morning, instead of witnessing a scene of despair, the Grinch hears joyful singing as the Whos welcome Christmas despite the absence of gifts and decorations. Learning that the true meaning of Christmas doesn't come from a store, he restores the Whos' possessions and joins in the festivities.

Geisel also co-produced the animated cartoon *Dr. Seuss's How the Grinch Stole Christmas* for television (1966). Narrated by actor Boris Karloff and featuring a green Grinch, it became a favorite annual telecast. Original songs "Welcome Christmas" and "You're a Mean One, Mr. Grinch" by Dr. Seuss and Albert Hague. Voices: Thurl Ravenscroft (singing), June Foray. Written by Dr. Seuss. Co-produced by Chuck Jones. Directed by Chuck Jones. A Chuck Jones Enterprises production in association with The Cat in the Hat Productions and Metro-Goldwyn-Mayer Television. MGM/UA Home Video. Color. 26 min.

A motion picture comedy adaptation released in 2000 stars Jim Carrey, Christine Baranski, Molly Shannon, Josh Ryan Evans, Jeffrey Tambor, Frankie Ray. Written by Peter S. Seaman, Jeffrey Price. Produced by Brian Grazer. Directed by Ron Howard. Imagine Entertainment. Color. Video N/A.

Humbug Not to Be Spoken Here
See Bewitched

Hunting the Wren

Also known as "Going on the Wren." Archaic custom once prevalent in the British Isles and France, a modified version of which survives in Ireland. Dating at least from the eighteenth century and possibly earlier, the custom originally took place on Christmas Eve or Christmas Day but, for unclear reasons, shifted to December 26 ("Boxing Day" or St. Stephen's Day). Groups of "Wren Boys," attired in outlandish costumes which included masks and women's clothing, would hunt and kill a wren, and, after fastening it to a decorative pole, placing it in a cage, or attaching it to a cluster of holly ("wren bush"), they would carry this token while serenading homes in the village with a repertoire of wren songs for the purposes of soliciting food, drink, and money. To those who complied, the Wren Boys bestowed a wren feather for good luck; otherwise, they offered songs of derision and sometimes buried the wren in the yard of an offender as a sign of bad luck. The collected cash then supported a Wren Dance in the village either that night or the night after, to which the public was invited. Rarely, as in one region in Wales, the wren was captured for the ritual but not slain. The ritual was virtually nonexistent in Scotland, except for that on New Year's Day, when a wren occasionally would be captured, decorated, then released with no further ceremony.

Although these wren hunts essentially vanished by the turn of the twentieth century, the Irish custom incorporates either a wren effigy or a caged live wren. The songs and costumes remain, the singers now include women who often appear as transvestites as do men, and the money collected now benefits charities or sponsors traditional Wren Dances.

Precise origins for hunting wrens at Christmastime are lacking, and proposed theories are paradoxical, especially when coupled with wren legends and folklore. According to legends, as Jesus and St. Stephen fled from persecution, the wren betrayed them by directing their captors to them (one possible explanation for hunting wrens on St. Stephen's Day). Another holds that as the Irish army secretly approached the camp of invading Vikings, the wren's pecking on a drum alerted the sleeping enemy, who successfully routed the Irish. The Celts particularly regarded the wren as the "Druid's bird," that is, a bird of omen. Elsewhere, it was a bird favored of God along with the robin, and the harming of either would bring bad luck. It was the "king of birds" in wren verses and folklore. The latter stems from a tale in which the bird that flew the highest would be crowned king. To deceive its competitors, the wren, hiding on the back of an eagle, suddenly appeared above all other birds in flight and won the title.

While some theories have proposed that hunting wrens was an act of vengeance for the birds' alleged betrayals and deceptions, the most plausible theory holds that the custom derived from those pagan New Year's festivals which offered a mock king as a sacrifice following a period of revelry. Examples are found in the ancient Mesopotamian festivals of Akitu and Zagmuk (discussed in the entry for **Saturnalia**). Because some Victorian Christmas cards, for reasons unknown, cast the wren as a symbol of the old year, it is possible that killing wrens also symbolized the death of the old year.

See also **Boxing Day; Ireland; Saturnalia.**

The Huron Christmas Carol

(Huron, "Jesous ahatonhia," "Jesus Is Born"). First Canadian carol, written in 1641 by French Jesuit missionary Father Jean de Brébeuf (1593–1649). Residing at a mission set among the Huron Indians of Georgia Bay, Ontario, since 1626, Father Brébeuf created "Jesous ahatonhia," a poem in the Huron language, which adapted the biblical Nativity story to an equivalent concept in the Huron culture. For a musical setting, Father Brébeuf chose a sixteenth-century folk tune, "Une jeune pucelle" ("A Young Virgin").

Thus, angel choirs sent from Gitchi Manitou (God) appear to a throng of hunters (shepherds) with the news that Jesus is born. As the hunters approach a lodge of "broken bark" (stable), they find the Babe within wrapped in ragged rabbit skins (swaddling clothes), and three chiefs (Wise Men) present gifts of fur skins (gold, frankincense, myrrh).

The Hurons kept the carol in their oral tradition until 1649, when a band of Iroquois Indians destroyed the mission, killed Father Brébeuf, and drove the Hurons out, with many escaping into Quebec. There, a century after its composition, another Jesuit priest, a Father Villenueve, committed the carol to paper after hearing it sung by Huron descendants. Attorney and Huron member Paul Picard subsequently produced a French translation of the carol. The popular English version known today, beginning with the words "'Twas in the moon of wintertime," was translated by J. E. Middleton and was first published in 1942 by the *Canadian Messenger of the Sacred Heart.*

I

I Heard the Bells on Christmas Day

American carol, the lyrics of which were written by the celebrated poet Henry Wadsworth Longfellow (1807–1882) during Christmas 1863 and published in 1867 under the title "Christmas Bells." A pacifist, Longfellow, whose son Charles was wounded in 1862, wrote the poem as a lament over the American Civil War which raged at that time and as an expression of grief over the loss of his wife in 1861 during a fire. At first the joyous pealing of church bells on Christmas Day, according to the lyrics, seem to mock the concept of "peace on earth, good will to men" in a time of war. But, listening more closely, the bells assure that God is neither dead nor asleep, and eventually that "the wrong shall fail, the right prevail."

The lyrics have been sung to two principal melodies, one by the English organist John Baptiste Calkin (1827–1905), the other composer Johnny Marks (1909–1985) of "Rudolph, the Red-Nosed Reindeer" fame. Calkin's tune of 1872, "Waltham," was originally paired with an older missionary hymn written in 1848, "Fling Out the Banner! Let It Float." Further details regarding the match between "Waltham" and "I Heard the Bells" remain obscure. Whereas Johnny Marks composed both lyrics and music for his multitude of Christmas songs, he simply supplied a popular tune for "I Heard the Bells" in 1956, a version that has received wide exposure by numerous recording artists.

See also **The Three Kings.**

I Know a Rose Tree Springing
See **Lo, How a Rose E'er Blooming**

I Love Lucy

Probably the best-known situation comedy series in the history of television, running on the CBS network from 1951 to 1960 and first sponsored by Philip Morris cigarettes. Its weekly episodes featured the domestic antics of zany Lucy Ricardo (Lucille Ball), often to the dismay of her Cuban bandleader-husband, Ricky (real-life husband and bandleader Desi Arnaz), and their older neighbors, Fred and Ethel Mertz (William Frawley and Vivian Vance).

Although none of the 179 regular episodes of the Emmy Award–winning *I Love Lucy* centered around Christmas, the series did feature one Christmas special that was not numbered with the other episodes. Titled "'I Love Lucy' Christmas Show," it aired on Christmas Eve, 1956. In this episode, Lucy and Ricky have a five-year-old son, Little Ricky (Keith Thibodeaux, who first came to the series in May 1956), whose Christmas-Eve curiosity about Santa's arrival is satisfied with appropriate, quickly improvised tales; for example, Santa slides down the chimney like a fireman and brings the North Pole with him. With the child in bed, Fred and Ethel arrive with a five-dollar Christmas tree, which, at Lucy's suggestion, Fred begins to shape by cutting off branches. As Ricky reminisces, the scene flashes back to an earlier episode, "Lucy Is *Enceinte*" (December 1952). There, during his act at the Tropicana Club, Ricky received an anonymous note requesting that he sing "We're Having a Baby," because a couple in the audience were expecting a baby. Of course, when he saw Lucy sitting nearby, Ricky quickly deduced that his wife was pregnant. Listening so intently to the tale, Fred hacks the tree to shreds and departs for a replacement.

As the other three strike up "Jingle Bells," Lucy's off-key singing prompts a second flashback to another episode, "Lucy's Show Biz Swan Song" (also December 1952), in which Lucy, the fourth member of a barbershop quartet, sang "Sweet Adeline" as miserably as ever.

Decorating Fred's second tree (purchased for fifty cents) yields the final flashback to "Lucy Goes to the Hospital" (January 1953), in which Ricky and the Mertzes "rehearsed" their plan to get pregnant Lucy to the hospital as quickly as possible. When the real moment arrived, as expected, pandemonium reigned.

Christmas morning now finds the Ricardos and Mertzes all dressed as Santas, who hide in the kitchen as Little Ricky races to his gifts. The presence of a fifth Santa (Cameron Grant) among them prompts a systematic pulling of beards as the true Santa suddenly vanishes before their eyes. Shaken, the others manage to close with a "Merry Christmas" for the audience. This five-Santa routine originated as a four-minute seasonal "tag" to the episode "Drafted" (aired Christmas Eve, 1951), in which a fifth Santa (Vernon Dent) magically joined the four Santa-clad stars as they frolicked around the Ricardos' Christmas tree. Stunned, the principals again provided a similar closing.

Written by Bob Carroll, Jr., Madelyn Pugh, Bob Schiller, Bob Weiskopf. Produced by Desi Arnaz. Directed by James V. Kern. Desilu Productions. CBS Video. B & W. 26 min.

I Saw Mommy Kissing Santa Claus

American novelty song written in 1952 by British songwriter Tommie Connor, the only song of note from that composer. Recorded by twelve-year-old Jimmy Boyd on the Columbia label, it sold over 2.5 million copies and was the top Christmas song for 1952. As the title suggests, the lyrics feature a young child's account of witnessing his mother kissing "Santa" beneath the mistletoe and tickling the old gent under his white beard. As part of its naive flavor, the song does not specify whether Mommy's interest lies in the real Santa, Daddy dressed up as Santa, or a third party bent on Yuletide hanky-panky, about which the child would probably not have been aware, at least not in 1952. In the closing segment, though, the youngster believes that it would have been amusing if Daddy could have seen Mommy's actions.

Of the 25 most frequently performed Christmas songs of the twentieth century listed by the American Society of Composers, Authors and Publishers (ASCAP), "I Saw Mommy Kissing Santa Claus" is ranked number 20.

I Saw Three Ships

English traditional carol believed to have arisen during the fifteenth century. The carol is based on a legend which claims that relics of the three Wise Men eventually came to rest in Germany's Cologne Cathedral in 1162, having been transported up the Rhine River in three ships. Many variant lyrics and tunes exist, the earliest of which was published in John Forbes's second edition of *Cantus, Songs and Fancies* (Aberdeen, 1666).

The earlier versions presented more graphic accounts of the ships' contents, that is, three skulls being transported to Cologne. Later versions softened the lyrics, describing that the ships carried "Our Savior Christ and His lady [the Virgin Mary]," as found in William Sandys's *Christmas Carols, Ancient and Modern* (London, 1833), with no mention of Cologne. However, in virtually all versions, three ships sail either into or from landlocked Bethlehem. Explanations for this physical impossibility have included suppositions that early Britons, knowing virtually nothing about the geography of Bethlehem, pictured it as a coastal town. Alternatively, the ships have been conceived as allegorical media for Father, Son, and Holy Spirit; Jesus, Mary, and Joseph; or Faith, Hope, and Charity.

A remarkably similar English traditional carol, "As I Sat on a Sunny Bank," again mentions three ships sailing by on Christmas Day and that "Joseph and his fair lady [Virgin Mary]" are with them, but specifies neither the ships' destination nor whence they have come. Therefore, although the titles are different, "I Saw Three Ships" and "As I Sat on a Sunny Bank" must be considered as variants of each other.

See also **Nativity**.

I Wonder As I Wander

American carol attributed to John Jacob Niles (1892–1980). A native of Kentucky, a folk singer, and composer, Niles began collecting American folk tunes at an early age. Although he had studied classical music in Paris and Cincinnati following World War I, he journeyed to New York during the Depression to pursue a folk music career. There he met and became a guide for famed photographer Doris Ullman, who was undertaking a project in the southern Appalachian Mountains. Niles claimed that while he and Ullman were touring North Carolina in 1933, he heard a young girl singing a most haunting tune in the town of Murphy, and this tune became the basis for "I Wonder As I Wander," which Niles published in his collection *Songs of the Hill-Folk: Twelve Ballads from Kentucky, Virginia, and North Carolina, Collected and Simply Arranged with Accompaniment for Piano* (New York, 1934). If this latter title is an accurate reflection of its contents, then "I Wonder" is simply a Niles arrangement of a true folk song rather than an original composition. However, because Niles once remarked that his involvement with folk material ranged anywhere from simple arrangement to original composition, it is equally likely that this carol is original. A definitive conclusion on this point is lacking.

The provocatively plaintive tune suggests a spiritual, while the lyrics ponder the mystery that Christ would be born, only to die for "poor on'ry (ornery) people like you and like I."

Iceland

Although Irish monks are believed to have first arrived in Iceland in the ninth century, the island was settled principally by Nordic tribes, who accepted Christianity and Christmas around the year 1000. Christmas customs blended with those of pagan *Jol* (Yule), a midwinter festival honoring the return of the sun at the winter solstice.

In the holidays of yesteryear, villagers helping to process the autumn wool before Christmas received as reward an article of new clothing. Exchanging Christmas presents as such did not become common until the nineteenth century. Because of the scarcity of grain, the poor stretched their supply of bread by creating *laufabraud* (leaf bread), fried, flat cakes of flour and water rolled into extremely thin sheets and cut into shapes of leaves or other objects. Christmas was also the time for taking annual baths and washing clothes. The principal course for the wealthy consisted of *hangikjot* (smoked lamb), whereas the less fortunate feasted on wild grouse.

Since evergreen trees were not native to Iceland, Christmas trees originally consisted of twigs nailed onto a pole and decorated with native foliage, sweets, and candles. The first Christmas tree imported to Iceland is said to have arrived in 1862 from Germany, and decorating homes was not common until the arrival of U.S. servicemen during World War II.

Today the majority of Icelanders belong to the Evangelical Lutheran Church and follow typical Advent traditions. Children enjoy two to three weeks of vacation from school, which commences after "Little Christmas," a day devoted to lighting candles at school, singing carols, and reading holiday stories. Families prepare by cleaning their homes and baking spiced cookies for guests, and many traditionally make their own leaf bread. Because of the limited supply of evergreen Christmas trees grown locally, most families purchase imported trees and decorate them on December 23rd, a day which commemorates the death of a native saint, Thorlakur Thorhallson, bishop of Skalholt (d. 1193). Tree decorations vary, but almost always include miniature Icelandic flags and a star or crown for a tree topper. Families do not light their trees until 6 P.M. on *Adfangadagur* (Christmas Eve), for at that time the national broadcast of the ringing of the bells at the Lutheran Cathedral in Reykjavik officially heralds Christmas.

Family members strive to return to their native homeplace for the holidays and the Christmas Eve supper, the table of which usually features smoked lamb, along with perhaps pork, beef, chicken, grouse, and porridge. Another traditional dish is rice pudding containing one almond in the batch. The person who receives this almond in his serving will have a successful year. Fish is conspicuously absent, as is any form of liquor. (Although social standards permit full alcoholic consumption on New Year's Eve, drinking in moderation is acceptable on December 26, the Sec-

ond Day of Christmas). Afterwards, children may open their gifts, brought by the thirteen *Jolasveinarnir* ("Christmas Lads," see below). A new article of clothing remains a traditional gift, as are books or other useful items. Earlier on Christmas Eve, families honor their dead by decorating graves with pine or fir branches and by leaving lighted candles which burn through the night.

• JOLADAGUR AND ANNAR JOLADAGUR. Translated as "Christmas Day" and "Second Day of Christmas," respectively, these two days are spent in feasting and fellowship with family, the menu remaining virtually the same as on Christmas Eve. The new year is greeted with fireworks and parties. According to native folklore, animals acquire speech at this time, seals assume human forms, the dead rise, elves move their homes, and one may receive gold from elves on New Year's Eve by waiting at crossroads as they pass by.

• JOLASVEINARNIR ("Christmas Lads"). These creatures plus the *Jolakkotur* ("Christmas Cat"), discussed below, constitute the most significant of Icelandic Christmas folklore. The Lads first appeared in the seventeenth century as the sons of two thirteenth-century trolls, Gryla and her husband Leppaludi, both of whom stole and ate naughty children at Christmastime. Over the centuries, the sons, having assumed the Yuletide role of their parents, now deliver the Christmas gifts. Yet they are still notorious as pranksters and thieves and appear in red suits similar to the western Santa Claus. Although some seventy names exist for the Lads, thirteen are most commonly accepted, each name reflecting a particular preference for mischief, often the pilfering of food: "Gimpy," "Gully Imp," "Most Tiny," "Pot Scraper Licker," "Pot Licker," "Bowl Licker," "Door Slammer," "Yogurt Eater," "Sausage Grabber," "Window Peeper," "Doorway Sniffer," "Meat Hooker," and "Candle Beggar." Residing in the mountains, the Lads appear thirteen days before Christmas, one new Lad arriving each day with a Christmas gift. Children prepare for their arrival by hanging up a sock or by placing their shoes on the windowsill only on Christmas Eve. If they have been good, the Lads fill their shoes with treats, whereas naughty children receive either some undesirable object or nothing at all. The Lads begin their sequential departure on Christmas Day and have returned to their mountain abode by Epiphany (January 6), at which time the Christmas season ends.

• JOLAKKOTUR ("Christmas Cat"). A pet monster of the parent trolls mentioned above, the gigantic Christmas Cat devours those who have received no new Christmas clothes. In former days when the only Christmas gift consisted of a bonus of new clothing for processing the autumn wool, the cat was used to threaten those less-productive villagers who would not have received such a bonus. Although the oldest written sources about the cat date to the nineteenth century, a twentieth-century Icelandic poet, Johannes Ur Kotlum, immortalized the beast in a poem, which Vignir Jonsson translated into English as "The Christmas Cat." According to the poem, the cat stalks about on Christmas Eve and peers into windows in search of poor children, the least likely recipients of new garments. At its conclusion, the poem makes an appeal for all to help children in dire need at Christmastime, not because of a mythical beast, but for the sake of their happiness and well-being.

"Merry Christmas" in Iceland is *Gledileg Jól*.

See also **Advent; Epiphany; Yule.**

I'll Be Home for Christmas

(Film, 1998). Motion Picture Comedy.

Initially refusing to return home to New York for Christmas because he disapproves of his father's remarriage, California college student Jake Wilkinson (Jonathan Taylor Thomas) receives an offer he cannot refuse. If he returns home by 6 P.M. on Christmas Eve, Jake's father David (Gary Cole) promises the gift of a Porsche. Jake and his girlfriend Allie (Jessica Biel) prepare for the cross-country road trek, but Eddie (Adam LaVorgna), Jake's archrival, alters their plans by foiling Jake's scheme to sell answers for an examination to the school's football team. Now seeking revenge, the team waylays Jake and deposits him in the California desert with nothing but a Santa Claus suit and a white beard glued to his face.

Stranded and alone, Jake, drawing upon his prowess as a con artist, hitchhikes and freeloads his way East, befriending a number of eccentric characters along the way, including petty thief Nolan Briggs (Andrew Lauer), and all the while tracking down Allie who is traveling with Eddie instead. Predictably, Jake accomplishes his goal, gains the Porsche, wins back Allie, and enjoys a Christmas reunion with his family in the Big Apple. With Sean O'Bryan, Lesley Boone, Eve Gordon. Written by Michael Allin, Harris Goldberg, Tom Nursall. Produced by David Hoberman, Tracey Trench. Directed by Arlene Sanford. Leo Productions, Mandeville Films, and Walt Disney Productions. Walt Disney Home Video. Color. 86 min.

I'll Be Home for Christmas

(Song). Popular American song written by James Kimball (Kim) Gannon, Walter Kent, and Buck Ram in 1943.

Created during the height of America's involvement in World War II, "I'll Be Home for Christmas" was especially endearing because it brought visions of home to the thousands of men and women serving in the Armed Forces who were unable to be with their loved ones for the holidays. The song is a wish for snow, mistletoe, presents, and all the secular ideals that make Christmas what it is. But, even if the one wishing cannot be present in body, he will still revel in a family Christmas "if only in my dreams."

Bing Crosby, who had enjoyed overwhelming success with his recording of "White Christmas" a year earlier, also recorded "I'll Be Home for Christmas" on the Decca label in 1943, backed by the John Scott Trotter Orchestra. In position 3 on the pop charts, it became the top Christmas song that year, sold over a million copies (producing Crosby's fifth gold record), and was back on the charts in 1944. To illustrate the lasting popularity of this song, Gemini 7 astronauts James Lovell and Frank Borman, having completed 206 orbits, requested to hear the Crosby recording as they returned to earth on December 17, 1965.

Of the 25 most frequently performed Christmas songs of the twentieth century listed by the American Society of Composers,

Authors and Publishers (ASCAP), "I'll Be Home for Christmas" is ranked number 12.

I'll Be Home for Christmas

(Television drama, 1988). The Bundy family of New England experiences a bittersweet wartime Christmas of 1944. Returning home for the holidays are son Terrell (Jason Oliver), who has completed military basic training, and daughter Leah (Nancy Travis), who works away at a steel plant. While Terrell and his father Joseph (Hal Holbrook) must mend a years-long rift in their relationship, Leah, coping with the loss of her boyfriend abroad, invites a lonely G.I., Aaron Kaplan (Peter Gallagher), to spend Christmas with her family. On Christmas Eve, after attending a USO party, expectant mother and daughter-in-law Nora (Courteney Cox) receives news that her decorated pilot-husband Michael has perished in a plane crash en route home from overseas. Amid the tragedies, Nora gives birth to a son on Christmas Day.

As the servicemen depart, youngest son Davey remarks about the irony of Christmas songs that impart messages of "peace on earth" when there is no peace. To that, Joseph replies that those songs still give us hope.

With Eva Marie Saint, David Moscow, Whip Hubley, Kieran Mulroney, Charles R. Nelson, Drew Pillsbury, Tarrish Potter, John Shepherd, Charles Tyner, Harvey Vernon. Written by Blanche Hanalis. Produced and directed by Marvin J. Chomsky. In 1989 this picture was nominated for a Young Artist Award, Best Young Actor in a Special, Pilot, Movie of the Week or a Miniseries (Jason Oliver). Video N/A.

I'll Be Home for Christmas

(Television drama, 1997). Filled with guilt because he could not save his wife's life four years ago, Minneapolis surgeon Dr. Mike Greiser (Robert Hays) suffers a breakdown before the holidays and retreats to his small hometown of St. Nicholas, Iowa, for a vacation. The citizens welcome their favorite son by electing him as the "Grand Electrician" who will light the community Christmas tree on Christmas Eve, and Mike also rekindles a romance with his high school sweetheart, Dr.

Sarah Gladestone (Ann Jillian), now St. Nicholas's mayor and veterinarian. The town, lacking a doctor, offers Mike a position, but Mike quickly returns to Minneapolis. There he abandons his practice and assumes an administrative role instead. He attains the courage to continue in medicine, however, when his father Bob (Jack Palance), having returned with him rather than spend Christmas in St. Nicholas alone, suffers a heart attack and requires immediate coronary bypass surgery. Further inspired when his young daughter Jilly (Ashley Gorrell) begs him to save her grandfather, Mike throws off his fears and performs the surgery successfully.

The news that St. Nicholas's hospital will close without a doctor prompts Mike to make his final career move, for he and Jilly relocate to St. Nicholas on Christmas Eve to start a new life together with Sarah.

With Linda Sorensen, Eric Peterson, Bernard Behrens, and Tom Harvey. Written by Darrah Cloud. Produced by Susan Murdoch. Directed by Jerry London. Jaffe Braunstein Productions. Video N/A.

In the Bleak Mid-Winter

English carol, the text for which was written in 1872 by poet Christina Rossetti (1830–1894). Consisting of five verses, each with eight lines, its first verse, filled with stark imagery of a bitter winter at Christmastime, contrasts much with the remaining four verses, which describe the Nativity on a more positive note. The final verse crowns the poem with an admonition for us to give Christ our best gift, our heart.

Two musical settings for this carol remain foremost. That by the English composer of Swedish descent Gustav Holst (1874–1934) was written for the first edition of *The English Hymnal* (1906), which retained Ms. Rossetti's then-shocking phrase "breastful of milk" in verse three (censored in other hymnals of the period). The other setting (1911) by Harold Darke (1888–1976), organist at London's Church of St. Michael for fifty years, also included the controversial phrase.

Christina Rossetti is one of England's best-known female poets. Two of her most noted works are *Sing-Song: A Nursery Rhyme*

Book and a collection of children's stories, *Speaking Likeness* (both 1872). She also penned the poem "Christmastide," destined to become the famous carol known as "Love Came Down at Christmas."

See also **Love Came Down at Christmas.**

India

See **Asia and the South Pacific**

Indonesia

See **Asia and the South Pacific**

Infant Holy, Infant Lowly

("W zlobie lezy"). Polish traditional carol, considered to be the best-known and earliest significant carol from that country. Thought to date from the thirteenth or fourteenth century, its title has also been translated as "Jesus Holy, Born So Lowly," "Baby Jesus, in a Manger," and "He Is Sleeping in a Manger." The most often sung English version today, beginning with "Infant Holy," is an adaptation of the translated text that was first published in *Music and Youth* (1921), an English journal founded and edited by Edith M. G. Reed (1885–1933). Consisting of two verses, the lyrics recall the manger, the oxen lowing nearby, the shepherds keeping watch over their flocks, and the angelic message that the Babe has been born.

Iran

See **Middle East**

Iraq

See **Middle East**

Ireland

Although St. Patrick (?389–?461) is credited with introducing Christianity to Ireland in the fifth century, the Irish became acquainted with the British Christmas through King Henry II of England, who initiated the Norman conquest of Ireland (1171–1172). Today Roman Catholicism predominates in the southern five-sixths of the island, known as the Republic of Ireland, while the smaller Northern Ireland remains a constituent of Protestant Great Britain. For the sake of simplicity, this entry discusses Irish Christmas customs as a whole.

The holiday season extends from Advent until Epiphany, and preparations include baking Christmas cakes a month or two in advance. Fortified with brandy and enveloped in a marzipan coating, these fruitcakes, which also double as Irish wedding cakes, improve with age and are frosted only a few days before Christmas. Roman Catholics may voluntarily fast for periods during Advent, and their homes and churches feature Nativity scenes, often with Celtic figures. While it is customary to pray the rosary each night before the manger, a figure of Baby Jesus is not placed therein until Christmas Eve, and those of the Wise Men are not added until Epiphany. Families thoroughly clean their homes, often whitewashing the exteriors in rural regions, and send Christmas cards only to those friends and relatives which they will most likely not see during the holidays because of distance or illness. Charitable organizations, schools, and churches stage Nativity plays and mummers' plays during Advent, and Christmas markets peak on the Saturday before Christmas, with their patrons said to "bring home the Christmas." Christmas trees, fairly recent innovations, are usually firs decorated with strings of electric lights and homemade garlands of paper and tinsel. These together with evergreens are usually put in place on Christmas Eve or a few days beforehand. At noon on Christmas Eve, most commerce ceases and will remain in abeyance until January 2; the usual exceptions are pubs and taverns, which offer free drinks on Christmas Eve.

Christmas in Ireland centers around family, and all unmarried members are expected to return to their parents' home by Christmas Eve if at all possible, regardless of whether they reside locally or abroad. Married children celebrate Christmas in their own homes, not those of their parents. Families place candles in their windows on Christmas Eve, beginning with a large "principal candle" two feet tall that is set in the central window. Depending on the region, this candle is either red, green, blue, yellow, or pink and may be the only candle that is displayed; should smaller candles adorn other windows, they are lighted only from the principal candle, and custom dictates that either the youngest daughter or one named Mary light all candles. Then families often walk about, admiring the candle glow from neighbors' windows. Origins for the custom are surrounded in legend. According to one, it was believed that, on Christmas Eve, Mary and Joseph annually retraced their steps to Bethlehem, and that lighted candles in windows offered them shelter. Another dates to the Protestant Reformation, holding that the custom secretly alerted passing priests that the occupants therein were Catholics who desired to receive mass on Christmas Eve. A fable about the Holy Family's wanderings then supposedly evolved to quell the suspicions of Protestant authorities.

The Church no longer requires fasting all day on Christmas Eve, yet some still prefer this tradition, breaking the fast with a simple, meatless meal of fish and potato soup. Going to confession on Christmas Eve is no longer universal, as was once the custom. Whereas Catholics in other countries attend Midnight Mass, this is a relatively new innovation for the Irish, whose Christmas masses were formerly held at dawn on Christmas morning, the so-called "First Light Masses."

Before retiring for the evening, children hang up their stockings in anticipation of a visit from Santa Claus, who may also leave gifts in a pillow case at the foot of the bed. Some families cater to old superstitions by setting out food on the table, unlocking the doors, and keeping at least one candle lit in a window all night. These latter acts not only serve to bid the Holy Family welcome, but they also welcome the spirits of deceased ancestors, who are believed to return home at Christmastime. Other favorite Christmas Eve superstitions once held that Satan had perished at midnight when Jesus was born, for which church bells annually tolled the "Devil's Knell" (the tradition survives locally in Great Britain); further, those who died on this night would never suffer Purgatory, for the Gates of Heaven mercifully remained open to receive all souls.

Families spend Christmas Day quietly together at home. Noted traditions among them include simple gift exchanges that are limited to members living under the same roof, and the distribution of meals and other necessities to those in need, prior to assembling for Christmas dinner. The latter usually features turkey or goose with stuffing, vegetables, plum pudding, bread pudding, mincemeat pie, Christmas cake, and Irish whiskey. Afterwards, families amuse themselves with assorted games and the telling of yarns and stories.

The remainder of the holidays center around St. Stephen's Day (December 26), New Year's Day, and Epiphany. On St. Stephen's Day, the Irish engage in "hunting the wren," attend mummers' plays (notably in Wexford, Dublin, and Ulster) and sporting events such as horse racing and fox hunting, and visit friends and relatives. Parties, fireworks, bonfires, and parades greet the new year, along with a few superstitions which may still be observed in rural regions. For instance, to thwart hunger and assure plenty in the coming year, consume a heavy meal on New Year's Eve, dash a New Year's cake against the principal door of the house, or strike the door thrice while holding the cake. To protect livestock against hunger, throw the cake against the barn door. Although girls are less likely today to induce dreams of future husbands by placing holly or ivy leaves beneath their pillows, the custom of "firstfooting" on New Year's Day survives as in Great Britain. Three candles often decorate windows to honor the Wise Men on Epiphany, also known as "Women's Christmas," so named because it was once commonplace to serve a meal more delicate than the goose and potent whiskey of Christmas. Some families may still practice an old superstition on this last day of Christmas: Each member is assigned a candle which is placed atop a cake and lit. The order in which the flames extinguish predicts the eventual order of each person's death.

"Merry Christmas" in Irish Gaelic is *Nollaig Shona Dhuit.*

See also **Advent**; **Boxing Day**; **Epiphany**; **Great Britain**; **Hunting the Wren**.

Irving, Washington, Christmas Sketches of

Series of five consecutive, interrelated tales by this American author of wit (1783–1859), published in his collection *The Sketch Book of Geoffrey Crayon, Gent* (1819–1820), the title also reflecting Irving's pseudonym. This collection is probably best known for two classics, "The Legend of Sleepy Hollow" and "Rip Van Winkle."

A romantic historian fond of antiquated customs, Irving developed a keen interest in English Christmases as celebrated in days of yore and the customs that had been largely neglected since the decline of the Puritan regime in the latter 1600s. Although England once again observed Christmas with the ascent of Charles II in 1660, it was with much less fervor than in times past, the Puritan influence having stamped out Christmas observances altogether.

Living in England for some years since 1815 and fearing that England's rich holiday traditions were in jeopardy of falling into oblivion, Irving created a series of nostalgic tales which served to remind the British of their Yuletide heritage. His *Sketch Book* won wide acclaim on both sides of the Atlantic, and the Christmas stories especially moved British author Charles Dickens to express like sentiments by letter in 1841. Influenced by Irving, Dickens greatly contributed to the resurrection of his country's centuries-old holiday customs through his own Christmas stories, most notably in *A Christmas Carol.*

The following paragraphs briefly summarize Irving's five Christmas sketches:

Christmas. In this sketch, which is more of an essay than a tale, Irving recalls the specifics of the bygone Christmas era and yearns to return to those days. At that time, friends and families, in addition to observing the religious rites of Christmas, joined together in merry fellowship around blazing fires in evergreen-bedecked homes and halls with one purpose: to celebrate "Peace on earth" with traditional carols, feasts, and games.

The Stage Coach. A stranger in England, Irving initially plans to spend Christmas at a Yorkshire inn, where he will be more likely to witness the surviving holiday customs, and whiles away a portion of Christmas Eve with a coach tour of the county. His excursion paints a scene of holiday bustle and happiness that has seized the countryside, including the butchers' and merchants' displays of trappings for the traditional feast, the much-anticipated deliveries of packages from the coachman, and the exuberance of schoolboys just released for their vacation. Arriving at the inn, he meets an old traveling companion, Frank Bracebridge, who persuades Irving to spend Christmas at his father's manor hall.

Christmas Eve. Well into the evening, the two friends arrive at Bracebridge Hall, where Squire Bracebridge is hosting a gala affair amid a large company of family and relatives. The Squire is a strict proponent of the old customs, and his holiday agenda consists of music and dancing; caroling; and games such as "hoodman blind," "shoe the wild mare," "hot cockles," "steal the white loaf," "bob apple," and "snap dragon." The Yule log, Christmas candles, mistletoe, mince pie, spiced beverages, and romance add much flavor to the festivities. The younger set particularly enjoy the wit and mischief of the elderly bachelor, Simon Bracebridge, and Robert Herrick's (1591–1674) poems are the favored texts for songs of the evening. As Irving retires, a band of Waits (carolers of the time) serenade the Hall outdoors.

Christmas Day. Christmas commences with early morning religious services, first in the chapel at Bracebridge Hall, then in the village church. There, the parson, also clinging to the past, exhorts all to make merry at this time and supports this seemingly novel opinion with innumerable quotes from ancient church authorities. Following a brief, historical account of the Puritan banishment of Christmas, restored with Charles II, the Squire, keeping ancient custom, throws open the Hall to the poor and peasantry, who partake of beef, bread, and ale, the products of the Squire's Christmas charity, as the rustics make merry among the gentry.

The Christmas Dinner. In this most popular of Irving's Christmas sketches, Squire Bracebridge's family and guests assemble at the table to participate in a series of ancient customs which include the ceremony of the boar's head, brought in on a silver platter to the tune of "The Boar's Head Carol" (a ceremony annually observed at Queen's College, Oxford, since the Middle Ages); a pheasant pie decorated with peacock feathers (patterned after the peacock pie served at court during the Middle Ages, in which the peacock's head protruded from one end, the tail feathers from the other); and drinking from the wassail bowl. Afterwards, the children play at games such as blind man's buff, the parson spins tales of superstitions and ghost stories, and the children round out the day by performing a Christmas masque or mummery for their elders.

In neither this nor any of the previous four sketches is special mention made of Father Christmas's visit to children or the giving of gifts; instead, the bestowing of charity and the pure happiness of being together with family and other loved ones is considered the essence of Christmas.

Since 1927, the Ahwahnee Hotel in Yosemite National Park in the United States has hosted an annual, modern-day Bracebridge Dinner, patterned after that in this latter sketch. The dinner features minstrels, Druids, Bach chorales, a medieval pageant, the boar's head, wassail, and Yorkshire pudding.

Washington Irving's contributions to the concept of Santa Claus are discussed under the entry **Saint Nicholas.**

See also **A Christmas Carol; Waits; Wassail; Yule.**

Israel
See **Middle East**

It Came Upon the Midnight Clear

(Song). America's first prominent carol, the lyrics of which were written in 1849 by Edmund Hamilton Sears (1810–1876), pastor of First Church Unitarian in rural Wayland, Massachusetts, from 1848 to 1865. His poem of five verses was first published in Boston in the *Christian Register* on December 29, 1849. The editor for Boston's *Monthly Religious Magazine* (1859–1871), Sears was a strong opponent of slavery.

The principal musical setting is that by Richard Storrs Willis (1819–1900), who studied music in Germany with Felix Mendelssohn and later became a music critic for the New York *Tribune*. In 1850 Willis published his *Church Chorals and Choir Studies*, of which "Organ Study No. 23" was adapted as the setting for "It Came Upon the Midnight Clear" in America. Sources vary regarding who actually produced the adaptation, either Willis himself or Uzziah Christopher Burnap. It is known that by 1860, Willis also adapted the same tune as one setting for the carol "While Shepherds Watched Their Flocks," and it has sometimes been matched

with a lesser-known carol by Rev. Sears, "Calm on the Listening Ear of Night" (1834).

"It Came Upon the Midnight Clear" reached Great Britain in 1870, when the Sears-Willis version was published in London in Edward Bickerseth's *Hymnal Companion to the Book of Common Prayer*. The setting most commonly applied in Great Britain, however, is a traditional English melody adapted by Arthur Sullivan, which was first published in *Church Hymns with Tunes* (London, 1874), edited by Sullivan.

See also **While Shepherds Watched Their Flocks by Night.**

It Came Upon the Midnight Clear

(Television movie, 1984). Mickey Rooney stars as an old man who promises to take his grandson, played by Scott Grimes, to New York City for Christmas. Although he dies beforehand, Rooney as an angel returns to Earth to fulfill his promise and brings the spirit of Christmas to the Big Apple. In 1986 the program was nominated for a Young Artist Award, Exceptional Performance by a Young Actor in a Television Special or Miniseries (Scott Grimes).

Written by Frank Cardea, George Schenk. Produced by George Schenk. Directed by Peter H. Hunt. An HGV Production. Color. Video N/A.

It Happened One Christmas
See **It's a Wonderful Life**

Italy

This nation has officially celebrated Christmas since the middle of the fourth century, when the Church in Rome selected December 25 as the date to celebrate the birth of Christ. Since the first century A.D., Roman legions had embraced the cult of the Persian sun god Mithras and had observed his birthday on December 25 with ceremonies titled *Natalis Solis Invicti* ("Birth of the Unconquered Sun"). The Church, seeking an alternative to this and other pagan practices held in mid- to late December (Saturnalia and the Kalends), replaced December 25 with celebrations honoring the birth of Christ. From the example of the Roman Catholic Church, much of the world now celebrates Christmas on this date.

Although Advent commences four weeks before Christmas, the official Christmas season begins with a Novena, a period of nine consecutive days before Christmas Eve, during which time worshippers attend a series of masses which climax with the Midnight Mass on Christmas Eve. The season terminates on Epiphany, January 6.

During Advent on December 6, cities commemorate the death of St. Nicholas, the fourth-century archbishop of Asia Minor. Men dressed as the saint deliver gifts to children, and festivals, processions, and parades abound, especially in cities along the coast of the Adriatic Sea. According to legend, mariners enshrined the remains of St. Nicholas in the city of Bari in the eleventh century.

St. Lucia, a young girl martyred in Sicily for her Christian faith in the fourth century, is honored on December 13. Riding a donkey, a woman attired in a blue cloak portrays the saint in processions. On the night before, Sicilian children place their shoes outside their doors in expectation of gifts from St. Lucia.

Early in December, virtually every city sponsors a Christmas market, wherein may be found all manner of foods, decorations, sweets, gifts, toys, and other paraphernalia pertinent to the season. Around mid–December, the *zampognari*, rustic shepherds from the mountains, arrive in Rome and other villages, as they have for centuries, to play their bagpipes at churches, markets, and before shrines of the Madonna. Legend states that their droning music eased the Virgin Mary's travail of labor. To honor Joseph the carpenter as well, they customarily serenade carpenters' shops. Less often than in the past, the *zampognari* present their repertoire from door to door, as would carolers, and receive rewards of food or cash.

Since 1968, the Vatican has held a special ceremony for children on the last Sunday of Advent. On this day, children bring their manger figures of Jesus to be blessed by the Pope.

The *presepio* ("manger") or Nativity scene ranks as the most popular of Christmas symbols. St. Francis of Assisi, Italy, is credited with having created not only the first Nativity scene, but also the first "live" Nativity scene in 1223 in a cave near Greccio, Italy. Desiring to make the Nativity story of the Bible more meaningful to his parishioners (most people of the time could not understand the Latin of the Church liturgy and relied upon the priests to interpret the scriptures for them), Francis incorporated live people to portray Mary, Joseph, the shepherds, angels, and Wise Men, along with a traditional ox and ass. After saying the mass, Francis placed a wax figure of Baby Jesus in the manger. Over the centuries artisans produced likenesses of these characters, and today *presepi* appear in a large variety of sizes, from miniatures with a few figures to those which occupy several rooms. Residing in places of honor in homes, churches, and other public places, *presepi* often depict elaborate Italian landscapes rather than those of Bethlehem, and include such items as trees, waterfalls, rivers, mountains, mills, and characters from all walks of Italian life. By custom, the Christ Child figure is placed in the manger only on Christmas Eve, and the figures of the Wise Men are advanced a few paces until their "arrival" on Epiphany.

Historic *presepi* may be found throughout the country. One of the oldest resides in the Church of Santa Maria Maggiore in Rome and dates to the end of the thirteenth century. A *presepio* constructed by Charles IV, king of the Two Sicilies (ruled 1754–1759), boasts 1,200 carved pieces and resides in the Royal Palace of Caserta, and Rome's Basilica of Saints Cosmos and Damian houses a gigantic, 200-year-old Neapolitan *presepio* that measures: 45 × 21 × 27 ft. Living *presepi* remain popular and may attain elaborate proportions, such as that of Rivisondoli, held in its mountain setting on Epiphany Eve with a cast of some 600 characters.

During World War II, American soldiers in Italy popularized Santa Claus and Christmas trees, the latter especially in the North; Christmas trees still rank second to *presepi* in the southern regions. An alternative decoration and vestige of the Yule log is the *ceppo* ("log"), a pyramidal-shaped, wooden or cardboard structure with several shelves on which can be placed gifts, ornaments, and a *presepio*.

Vestiges of the "Boy Bishop," a custom that honored St. Nicholas during the Middle Ages, lie in traditions surrounding the *Santo*

Bambino ("Holy Child"), a jewel-studded Nativity figure of Christ in Rome's Church of Santa Maria Ara Coeli. After the figure is placed in the manger on Christmas Eve, children stand before it and deliver sermons or some other form of holiday address. The figure is believed to possess healing powers.

At sundown in Rome on Christmas Eve, cannonfire from the Castle of St. Angelo announces the arrival of Christmas. Whereas the season generally is spent among friends and relatives, Christmas Eve and Christmas Day are reserved for the immediate family. Catholics observe a strict 24-hour fast which terminates with the Christmas Eve dinner, a meatless affair extending for several hours before Midnight Mass. Typical cuisine includes *capitone* (eel), *calamari* (squid), *vongoli* (clams), *baccalà* (codfish), pickled or fried vegetables, beans, salads, breads, pasta, various sweets including *pizzele* (lacy cookies), *caffé espresso*, wines, and champagne. In Rome, the Pope celebrates Midnight Mass at 11 P.M., and this mass is televised worldwide from St. Peter's Basilica.

On Christmas Day, children customarily write letters to their parents requesting forgiveness for having committed any misdeeds during the year with promises to improve, and they hide these letters under the parents' plates or somewhere else on the dinner table. The menu for Christmas Day features meat, such as turkey or ham, *tortellini* (meat pasta), lentils with sausage (for prosperity), and *panettone* (glazed yeast cake with currants and candied fruit). Many other desserts contain nuts and honey, which stem from ancient superstitions regarding the former's role in fertility and the latter's magical properties. Visitations resume on St. Stephen's Day (December 26).

Noise, clamor, and parties fill New Year's Eve. People may throw objects from windows or fire guns, activities that stem from ancient winter solstice festivals which held that loud noises dispelled evil spirits lurking in the winter darkness. Some still believe that whatever happens at this time determines the fate of the year, and girls may observe quaint rituals to determine whether they will marry soon. In one of these, a girl tosses her shoe overhead toward the door. If the toe points to the door, she will wed, but not if it points away. The first person one meets on New Year's Day is predictive: a strong man, a healthy year; a priest, a funeral; a woman, bad luck.

Children traditionally receive gifts on Epiphany from *La Befana* (or simply *Befana*, derived from *Epiphania*, Epiphany), a mythical witch whose legend otherwise is virtually identical with Russia's "Baboushka." According to the legend, an old woman was sweeping her house when the three Magi passed by en route to Bethlehem. When they invited her to accompany them, she refused, claiming that her housework precluded a long journey. Later, she repented and, after collecting a few toys for the Christ Child, set out to overtake the Magi. Because she found neither them nor the Christ Child, she returns annually via her broomstick and descends into chimneys on Epiphany Eve to examine each sleeping child, hoping to find Jesus. She then fills the stockings or pockets of deserving youngsters with gifts. For the naughty, she leaves a piece of coal. Children write letters to her, describing what gifts they desire, and they hang effigies of the witch as decorations. While Epiphany is the principal giftgiving day, children commonly receive gifts at Christmas as well, and in some regions, *Babbo Natale* ("Father Christmas," Santa Claus), has replaced Befana.

It is believed that Befana derives from a winter goddess and fertility figure of Germanic-speaking tribes who protected the home, hearth, motherhood, children, and fields. Dispensing rewards and punishments to deserving adults and children at the winter solstice, this goddess was variously known as Berchta, Bertha, Hertha, Holda (Holde, Holle), and Perchta. In the Christian age, she appeared during the twelve days of Christmas, especially on Epiphany or Twelfth Night, considered to be magical times by the superstitious. How Befana became a witch is open to speculation. Germanic folklore depicts Berchta as an old, disheveled woman; and the name of Holde, and perhaps others, became synonymous with witchcraft upon the advent of Christianity. Thus, Befana is also known as *La Strega* ("witch") and *La Vecchia* ("old woman").

"Merry Christmas" in Italy is *Buon Natale*. *See also* **Advent**; **Boy Bishop**; **Christmas Day**; **Epiphany**; **Nativity Scene**; **Russia**; **Yule**.

It's a Wonderful Life

(1946). Highly popular motion picture drama based on "The Greatest Gift," a short story by New York writer Philip Van Storen Stern. Unsuccessful at selling his story to a magazine, Van Storen Stern ordered 200 copies printed at his own expense and sent them out to his friends as twenty-four-page Christmas "cards." His Hollywood agent was one of those recipients and pitched the story to various movie studios. At actor Cary Grant's suggestion, it initially became the property of RKO Radio Pictures, but when this company failed to produce a workable script, RKO sold the story for $10,000 to a new studio, Liberty Pictures, formed in 1945 by director Frank Capra (*Mr. Smith Goes to Washington*, *Meet John Doe*). From "The Greatest Gift" evolved *It's a Wonderful Life*, Liberty's first motion picture and the favorite film of Frank Capra, who watched it every Christmas Eve thereafter.

THE SHORT STORY. George Pratt, a small-town bank clerk who has grown weary of his dead-end job and a life seemingly without meaning, wishes that he had never been born. As he contemplates suicide on Christmas Eve, he encounters an angel posing as a brush salesman who grants his wish. Seeing the tragedies in the world that would have come to pass had he not been present to prevent them, George realizes that his life has truly been a blessing to all around him, and that people really need him. He renounces his wish, life resumes as before, and George has learned that the greatest gift to humanity is always one's self.

THE MOTION PICTURE. The film adaptation changes the principal character to George Bailey (Jimmy Stewart), a man filled with creative ideas and a thirst for adventures that is never fulfilled. Jimmy Stewart was Frank Capra's sole choice for George from the beginning. When Stewart, having recently completed his military service, did not feel prepared to make pictures so soon after World War II, actor Lionel Barrymore convinced him to take the role.

As the film opens, it's Christmas Eve in the little town of Bedford Falls, New York, where numerous prayers rise from house to house on behalf of George, who is in trouble. Heaven decides to investigate George further by sending to earth the former clockmaker Clarence Odbody (Henry Travers), a simple-witted angel possessing childlike faith and in need of earning his wings (presently Clarence is "angel second class, AS2"). Before sending him, heaven briefs Clarence on George's life of unwitting self-denial and good will as the picture turns to an earlier point in time.

As a boy, George saves his younger brother, Harry, from drowning and prevents the druggist Mr. Gower (H. B. Warner) from unwittingly filling a prescription with poison. When his father dies, instead of going to college, George assumes control of the Bailey Building and Loan Company, which otherwise would have fallen into the hands of the unscrupulous banker Henry Potter (Lionel Barrymore), and provides for Harry's (Todd Karns) college education. After George's wedding to childhood friend Mary Hatch (Donna Reed), a run on the bank threatens to close the Building and Loan, which George saves with $2,000 of his own cash that was intended for the honeymoon. Ordinary people like cabbie Ernie Bishop (Frank Faylen) receive loans through the Building and Loan to build homes, which Potter's bank would have never financed, and George spares pocket cash for financially strapped "fast girl" Violet Bick (Gloria Grahame) to begin a new life out of town.

This brings the story line back to the Christmas Eve that began the film. On that day, George's Uncle Billy (Thomas Mitchell) misplaces $8,000 that belongs to the Building and Loan. Suddenly facing Potter's charges of embezzlement and misappropriation of funds, George transforms from a gregarious family man into a hunted animal. Returning home, he suddenly despises his surroundings, including the old house that he, Mary, and their four children occupy, a house that now seems to be falling apart with George's life. He argues severely with Mary, upbraids daughter Janie (Carol Coomes) for practicing "Hark! The Herald Angels Sing" interminably on the piano, and delivers telephone insults to the school teacher of little daughter Zuzu (Karolyn Grimes). An altercation with the teacher's husband at Martini's bar leaves George with a bleeding lip, and after running his car into a tree, George is about to jump into an icy river when Clarence dives in, forcing George to save him instead.

Bewailing his life, George wishes he had never been born. Clarence grants him his wish, allowing him to see what Bedford Falls would have been like had he never entered the picture. Several signs herald the transformation: the Christmas Eve snowfall suddenly ceases; George's deaf ear (present since childhood) and bleeding lip are healed; and Zuzu's wilted flower petals, which George had placed in his pocket moments earlier, have vanished, as has his demolished car. As George walks through what should be Bedford Falls, he finds it has become "Pottersville," corrupted with saloons and burlesque halls. He learns that Uncle Billy lost his business and suffered insanity. Gower served a prison term for poisoning a child and became a drunken bum. "Bailey Park," a neighborhood of homes financed by the Building and Loan is a cemetery; in that cemetery is the grave of George's younger brother Harry, who drowned (and because he did not live to adulthood, he did not perform his act of war heroism that saved the lives of many men; instead, all these men are also dead). George's mother (Beulah Bondi), now cynical and heartless, runs a second-rate boarding house. Violet is arrested for prostitution. George's home is an abandoned building, and Mary wastes away as an old-maid librarian. A dime-a-dance dive had replaced the Building and Loan; Nick the bartender (Sheldon Leonard), now cold and callous, has replaced the jovial Mr. Martini (Bill Edmunds) as proprietor of the Italian restaurant and bar. Ernie, his wife and child having deserted him, now lives in a shack in "Potter's Field."

Facing such ghastly alternatives, George repents of his wish and begs to return to his former life, at which the signs are reversed (the snow falls, his lip bleeds, and so on). Gladly willing to face prison as long as no one else suffers, he races through town screaming, "Merry Christmas!" and arrives home just as Mary returns from alerting the town about his predicament. It seems a miracle: Scores of citizens come forth with ready cash to pay the debt, many saying that they never would have had homes had it not been for George. In the collection basket George notes a copy of Mark Twain's *The Adventures of Tom Sawyer*, which Clarence had carried around with him. Inside, an inscription reminds George that no man is a failure who has friends, with thanks for the wings. At that moment, a little bell on the family's Christmas tree rings, at which Zuzu remarks that, according to her teacher, every time a bell rings, an angel gets his wings. Serviceman Harry, having won the Congressional Medal of Honor for saving a transport plane, arrives to toast his big brother as "the richest man in town," and the film concludes with everyone singing "Auld Lang Syne." (Originally the closing song was to have been "Ode to Joy" from Beethoven's ninth symphony, but "Auld Lang Syne" seemed more appropriate).

With Ward Bond, Samuel S. Hinds, Larry Simms, Harry Holman, Jimmy Hawkins. Written by Frances Goodrich, Albert Hackett, Frank Capra. Produced and directed by Frank Capra. Liberty Films. Republic Pictures Home Video. B & W. 132 min.

Over the years, attention has focused on several incidental scenes which have especially contributed to the picture's lasting popularity. A high school graduation dance scene with the swimming pool beneath the floor took place on location at Beverly Hills High School, the gymnasium of which sported such a pool. At that time, such a device was considered a high-tech innovation. Mary's date in these scenes, Freddie, is played by Carl Switzer, better known as "Alfalfa" in the *Little Rascals* and *Our Gang* comedies. In another scene, George saves the Building and Loan patrons with his $2,000 by pleading that they withdraw only what is essential for the moment. When a young woman (Ellen Corby, who later portrayed Grandma Walton in the television series *The Waltons*) requests the odd and incredibly low sum of $17.50 (unscripted, Capra having secretly prompted Corby with the line), George leans over and gives Corby a big, unscripted kiss, which blends perfectly. A third popular scene has the inebriated Uncle Billy leaving Harry's wedding reception. When he steps off camera, a loud crash leaves the impression that Uncle Billy has fallen into some trash cans, and he calls out that he's not injured. Actually, a technician backstage had dropped some equipment at that moment, and Capra worked the "blooper" into the final print. Finally, during the scene in which a devastated George prays for deliverance in Martini's bar before meeting Clarence, Stewart was so moved that he began weeping. Capra had originally filmed Stewart from a distance and wanted to get a closer retake. When Stewart could not reproduce the authentic emotion, Capra enlarged that segment frame by frame.

This film received five Academy Award nominations in 1947: Best Actor (Stewart), Best Director (Capra), Best Film Editing, Best Picture, and Best Sound Recording. It won the Golden Globe Award that year for Best Motion Picture Director. In 1990 it received the National Film Registry Award from the National Film Preservation Board.

• ANOTHER VERSION. Frank Capra cowrote a version for television with Lionel Chatwynd, titled *It Happened One Christmas* (1977). There, Marlo Thomas starred as the principal character, Mary Bailey Hatch, along with Richard Dysart, Christopher Guest, C. Thomas Howell, Cloris Leachman, Wayne Rodgers, and Orson Welles. In 1978 the program received an Emmy Award nomination for Outstanding Performance by an Actress in a Drama or Comedy Special (Cloris Leachman). Produced by Carole Hart, Marlo Thomas. Directed by Donald Wrye. A Universal Television production. Color. Video N/A.

It's Beginning to Look a Lot Like Christmas

Popular American song written in 1951 by Meredith Willson. With its descriptive theme of Christmas symbols (Christmas trees, candy canes, holly) appearing all over town as the season approaches, the song concludes with the philosophy that the best holiday music is the carol that is sung within your own heart.

The public became aware of this piece principally through two means. First, Perry Como with the Fontane Sisters first recorded it that same year on the RCA Victor label, hitting the pop charts at position 19. Then, Willson incorporated it as the theme song for his 1963 Broadway musical *Here's Love*, which was based

on the 1947 motion picture *Miracle on 34th Street*.

Of the 25 most frequently performed Christmas songs of the twentieth century listed by the American Society of Composers, Authors and Publishers (ASCAP), "It's Beginning to Look a Lot Like Christmas" is ranked number 16.

It's Christmastime Again, Charlie Brown

(1992). Made-for-television animated cartoon sequel to *A Charlie Brown Christmas*, based on characters from Charles M. Schulz's comic strip, *Peanuts*.

The gang returns in a loosely connected spoof about Christmas commercialism. Charlie Brown unsuccessfully attempts to sell Christmas wreaths before Thanksgiving; Linus waxes philosophic over the Nativity story as Sally complains about the cost of giving gifts; and Charlie Brown sells his entire comic book collection to buy his girlfriend a pair of expensive gloves, only to find that her mother has already bought them for her. Peppermint Patty must play a sheep in the school Christmas pageant and is appalled that Marcie, who wears *glasses*, would be selected to play Mary. And Sally, after having interminably rehearsed her single-word line of "Hark!" as the angel, breaks up the pageant with "Hockey sticks!" instead.

Voices: Mindy Ann Martin, John Christian Graas, Philip Lucier, Lindsay Bennish, Brittany M. Thornton, Jamie E. Smith, Marne Patterson, Matthew Slowik, Deanna Tello, Sean Mendelson, Bill Melendez. Written by Charles M. Schulz. Produced and directed by Bill Melendez. A Lee Mendelson-Bill Melendez production in association with Charles M. Schulz Creative Associates and United Media Productions. Paramount Home Video. Color. 22 min.

In 1993 this program was nominated for a Young Artist Award, Outstanding Young Voice-Over in an Animated Series or Special (John Christian Graas).

See also **A Charlie Brown Christmas**; **Happy New Year, Charlie Brown**.

Ivy

See **The Holly and the Ivy**

J

Jack Frost

(1979). Made-for-television animated fantasy.

Invisible, Jack Frost lives in Father Winter's Kingdom of the Winter Clouds. Because Jack is in love with Elisa, a lovely peasant girl of January Junction, Father Winter conditionally grants his request to be human until spring. Posing as Jack Snip, a tailor, Jack finds that Kubla Kraus the Cossack has taxed January Junction so heavily that Christmas gifts must be imaginary "dream" presents. Attempting to rescue Elisa from Kraus's clutches, Jack resumes his icy form and blows a blizzard which buries Kraus. But it is Elisa's other suitor, Sir Ravinoe Rightflow the knight, who saves her and marries her. Although Jack acquires Kraus's castle, horse, and gold by spring, he fails to obtain a wife, the last of Father Winter's four conditions necessary to achieve permanent human status.

Narrated by Buddy Hackett. Voices: Robert Morse, Debra Clinger, Larry Storch, Dee Stratton, Paul Frees, Don Messick, Dina Lynn, Dave Garroway, Sonny Melendez. Written by Romeo Muller. Produced and directed by Arthur Rankin, Jr., Jules Bass. Rankin/Bass Productions. Warner Home Video. Color. 50 min.

Japan

See **Asia and the South Pacific**

Jesse Tree

Through medieval art, a Jesse tree originally depicted Christ's progenitors as the branches of a tree rooted from Jesse, King David's father, the topmost branches of which were crowned with Christ. This concept derived from the Messianic prophecy in Isaiah 11:1, which stated that a Branch (Christ) would spring from the roots of Jesse. Today the Jesse Tree offers a way of connecting a Christmas tree with religious symbols. A contemporary Jesse tree utilizes ornaments which symbolize Christ's ancestors (such as Abraham, Isaac, Jacob, David) or other noted biblical characters.

Jest 'Fore Christmas

("Just Before Christmas"). Humorous poem written by the American poet and journalist Eugene Field (1850–1895). With deliberate misspellings of words to convey a rural dialect, the poem's five verses feature "Bill," a mischievous little boy, who in the first four verses details his typical variety of pranks and antics committed throughout the year. But knowing that Santa would disapprove, for example, of anyone getting a ride by hitching a sled to a horse-drawn grocery cart, Bill suddenly curbs his foolishness "jest 'fore Christmas" when he's as good as he can be. In the fifth verse, Bill's sage advice improves any wayward child's chance of having a happy Christmas: wash your face, brush your hair, keep your shoes in good condition, say "Yessum" and "Yessur," and never ask for a second serving of dessert.

Missouri native Eugene Field is best known for his children's poems, such as "Little Boy Blue," "Wynken, Blynken, and Nod," and "The Gingham Dog and the Calico Cat."

Jesu, Jesu, Baby Dear

See **Rocking**

Jesu Parvule

See **Alfred Burt Carols**

Jesus (motion picture)

See **The Nativity on Film** (FILM AND TELEVISION DEPICTIONS)

Jesus Christ

See **The Nativity**

Jesus Holy, Born So Lowly

See **Infant Holy, Infant Lowly**

Jesus of Nazareth

See **The Nativity on Film** (FILM AND TELEVISION DEPICTIONS)

A Jetsons Christmas Carol

See **A Christmas Carol** (Film and Television Versions)

Jingle All the Way

(1996). Motion picture adventure-comedy.

Neglecting his wife Liz (Rita Wilson) and young son Jamie (Jake Lloyd), workaholic Howard Langston (Arnold Schwarzenegger) has also forgotten that Jamie wants a Turbo-Man action figure, the hottest-selling toy that Christmas. It's now Christmas Eve, and Howard vainly dashes through a myriad of toy stores and packed crowds, creating havoc while racing against Myron Larabee (Sinbad), a mail carrier who needs the same toy. Their numerous escapades include a fight for TurboMan lottery numbers in the mall; Howard's failed deal with a black market Santa (James Belushi) and his escape from a police raid; their assault on a radio station that offers a TurboMan to the first caller who can name Santa's reindeer; Myron's attempt to stall police with two "fake" bomb threats, the second of which actually explodes after they both escape; and Howard's failed attempt to steal the TurboMan from his neighbor Ted Maltin (Phil Hartman), whose angry pet reindeer prevents the robbery. Ted, divorced and nosy, in the meantime has taken every opportunity to flirt with and be "helpful" to gorgeous Liz while Howard has been away.

Totally disgraced, Howard can only watch as Liz, Jamie, and Ted leave together for the Christmas parade, which features TurboMan as the main attraction instead of Santa Claus. Drafted at the last minute to replace the parade's TurboMan, Howard must select a child from the crowd to accompany him on the float and receive a coveted TurboMan toy. Howard, certain that this role will atone for his misdeeds, summons Jamie, when suddenly a crazed Myron, dressed as TurboMan's arch enemy Dementor, arrives to resume the battle for the toy that Jamie now possesses, and ultimately Myron chases Jamie to a high pinnacle. Forced to use the jet pack and other weapons built into his costume, Howard rockets into the air and saves Jamie as he tumbles from a building. His boy safe, Howard reveals his identity to an ecstatic Jamie and Liz and vows

to be a more attentive husband and father. Content to have his dad as the real TurboMan, Jamie unselfishly gives his action figure to Myron.

With Robert Conrad, Martin Mull. Written by Randy Kornfield. Produced by Chris Columbus, Mark Radcliffe, Michael Barnathan. Directed by Brian Levant. 20th Century–Fox Film Corporation. Fox Video. Color. 85 min.

Jingle Bell Rock

Popular American song, the only significant collaboration of Joseph Beal from Massachusetts and James Boothe from Texas, who otherwise were engaged in public relations and advertising, respectively. Written in 1957 on the centennial anniversary of the perennial favorite "Jingle Bells," it was the first song of the rock and roll era to blend that musical style with Christmas. Despite the fact that the lyrics follow no particular train of thought, consisting merely of meaningless, rhyming phrases about such items as "Jingle Bell Square" and "jingle bell time," this song of easy rhythm became a real hit after rocker Bobby Helms recorded it that same year on the Decca label. The top Christmas song for 1957 (position 6 on the pop charts), it sold some ten million copies and continued to make the pop charts into the 1980s.

Of the 25 most frequently performed Christmas songs of the twentieth century listed by the American Society of Composers, Authors and Publishers (ASCAP), "Jingle Bell Rock" is ranked number 11.

See also **Jingle Bells**; **Rockin' Around the Christmas Tree.**

Jingle Bells

Highly popular American song written in the mid–1800s by James S. Pierpont (1822–1893). Sources differ regarding the exact year; some say 1850, others 1857. A composer and native of Medford, Massachusetts (a community outside of Boston), Pierpont was inspired to write a lively winter piece based on the annual sleigh races held in Medford. The song would have been known by its original title, "The One-Horse Open Sleigh," had Pierpont not sought an opinion from a Mrs. Otis Waterman, reportedly the only person in Medford at the time with a piano in her boarding house. Hearing the tune, she commented that it certainly was "a merry little jingle," whereupon Pierpont, considering these magic words, altered the title to "Jingle Bells." It is known that, in 1857, "Jingle Bells" made its public debut as the highlight of a Thanksgiving pageant held at Pierpont's church where, under his direction, a choir of forty Sunday school children performed the song. An immediate success, it was repeated at Christmastime that same year and was published in 1859.

James Pierpont, who served in the Georgia Cavalry, now rests in Savannah, Georgia, where he was originally married. This city has also laid claim to "Jingle Bells," claiming that Pierpont penned the song there in memory of those Medford sleigh races. The Medford Historical Society, however, refutes that claim and cites an entry from Mrs. Waterman's diary which corroborates Pierpont's composition in Medford. Although Pierpont wrote a number of other songs, among them "The Coquette" (1853), "Geraldine" (1854), "Know Nothing Polka" (1854) and "Ring the Bell, Fanny" (1854), his memory survives only through "Jingle Bells."

The lyrics to "Jingle Bells" mention absolutely nothing about Christmas. They simply reflect the joy of racing over the snow in a one-horse open sleigh. Yet the song has become a Christmas classic through popular association.

Some people have difficulty with one phrase in the first verse: "Bells on bobtail ring." Although this obviously refers to the bells on the horse that pulls the sleigh, some have wondered if "Bobtail" is really the horse's name. An examination of the lyrics shows that "bobtail" is not capitalized; hence, the lyrics imply only a bobtailed horse.

"Jingle Bells" is arguably the most popular of all American secular Christmas songs.

John Grin's Christmas

See **A Christmas Carol** (FILM AND TELEVISION VERSIONS)

Jolly Old St. Nicholas

American children's song, possibly composed in the latter nineteenth century. Aside from African American spirituals, "Jolly Old ["Ole" in some printings] St. Nicholas" is the only American Christmas standard that is completely anonymous. It has been suggested that Benjamin R. Hanby, composer of another American holiday standard, "Up on the Housetop" (published in 1866), also wrote "Jolly Old St. Nicholas," but the evidence is only superficial: both songs mention a child named Nell or Nellie, and some music scholars believe that the two songs are written in a virtually identical style. If Hanby was the composer, the "Nellie" mentioned in "Jolly Old St. Nicholas" could have referred to a runaway slave named Nellie, whom Hanby's father had sheltered in pre–Civil War days and about whom Hanby wrote in his song "Darling Nellie Gray."

See also **Up on the Housetop**.

Joseph and Mary

See **The Cherry Tree Carol**

Joseph and the Angel

See **The Cherry Tree Carol**

Joseph, Dearest Joseph Mine

("Joseph, lieber Joseph mein"). Anonymous, late-medieval German carol. Leipzig University holds the earliest-known manuscript of the text, which dates from ca. 1400. Incorporated into various church dramas or mystery plays, "Joseph" centers around the tradition of cradle rocking, which prevailed in Germany at Christmastime during the Middle Ages. Its eight verses include parts for Mary, Joseph, and four Attendants. Mary opens the carol by bidding Joseph to help her rock Jesus in His cradle and promises that God will reward him for this service. Joseph, gladly responding in the affirmative, voices his faith that he and Mary shall see paradise, after which each Attendant pronounces a blessing or summarizes a prophecy fulfilled concerning Jesus' birth. In the remaining two verses, the Attendants join together in praise. Then follows a lengthy refrain which proclaims that Emmanuel is born in Israel. The last two lines of this refrain consist of Latin text derived from a fourteenth-century Latin hymn, "Magnum Nomen Domini Emanuel" ("Great Is the Name of the Lord Emmanuel").

Predating "Joseph" is another cradle-rocking carol with Latin lyrics, "Resonet in

Laudibus" ("Let Our Praises Resound"), the tune of which is identical with that for "Joseph." The text is a series of praises for the birth of Jesus. The earliest source is the Moosburg Gradual, a manuscript dating to the mid-fourteenth century, which resides in the University Library of Munich. Similar to "Joseph," "Resonet" likewise includes a refrain drawn from "Magnum Nomen Domini Emanuel." "Resonet" was especially associated with the erection of a model of the *Krippe* ("Crib") in medieval churches, around which boys would leap and dance in time to the music as an expression of the carol's praise.

"Joseph" and "Resonet" are two prime examples of the *Wechselgesang* (antiphonal singing) tradition, which originated in pre–Reformation Bohemia and from there migrated to Lutheran Germany, where it supplanted the Roman Catholic Christmas masses. According to the tradition, different groups of singers or instrumentalists, placed at different stations around the church, performed certain sections of carols for more dramatic effect. Because "Joseph" and "Resonet" contained extensive passages of vernacular German along with separate sections of Latin lyrics, they often were sung together, with one group performing the vernacular and another the Latin.

The tune was given a number of later vocal settings, notably among them "Geistliches Wiegenlied" ("Spiritual Cradle Song") by Johannes Brahms (1833–1897). W. A. Mozart (1756–1791) also incorporated the tune in the original second movement of his Symphony No. 19 in E flat (K132, 1772).

See also **Rocking.**

Joseph Was an Old Man
See **The Cherry Tree Carol**

Joy to the World!

Highly popular English carol, the words for which were contributed by Isaac Watts (1674–1748). A clergyman who penned some 700 hymns, among them "When I Survey the Wondrous Cross" and "O God, Our Help in Ages Past," Watts reworked the biblical Psalms, paraphrasing and even discarding some, and published his *Psalms of David Imitated in the Language of the New Testament* (London, 1719). "Joy to the World!" is derived from the latter half of Watts's paraphrase of Psalm 98, which he titled "To Our Almighty Maker, God." The lyrics initially began with "Joy to the earth," but "world" in time replaced "earth."

While the origins for the lyrics are clear, the composer of the melody (now known as "Antioch") remains unidentified, although G. F. Handel and Lowell Mason have been named without definitive proof. John Wilson (*Bulletin of the Hymn Society of Great Britain and Ireland*, June 1986) traced the origin of "Antioch" initially (and presumably) to a tune titled "Comfort," which anonymously appeared in two volumes, *Collection of Tunes* (1833) by the Methodist Thomas Hawkes and the non-denominational *Congregational Harmonist* (1835) by Thomas Clark. A revised tune also appeared in William Holford's *Voce di Melodia* (1834). Holford attributed the melody to Handel because it resembled the opening measures of "Glory to God" and "Lift Up Your Heads," two choruses from Handel's oratorio *Messiah*. Musicologists have since considered the brief similarity, among other complex reasons, as merely coincidental.

Lowell Mason (1792–1872), the noted American Presbyterian composer who supplied the music for such hymns as "My Faith Looks Up to Thee" and "Nearer My God to Thee," perpetuated the Handel myth. Mason made further arrangements of the "Comfort" tune, changed its name to "Antioch," and published it together with Watts's lyrics for the first time in his collection *Occasional Psalm and Hymn Tunes, Selected and Original* (Boston, 1836). Deeply devoted to Handel's works and undoubtedly influenced by Holford's premise, Mason included the phrase "from Handel," which appeared in Mason's subsequent collections of 1839, 1841, and 1848. Mason's arrangement has enjoyed widespread popularity in the United States, but it has never attained quite the same appeal in Great Britain, which seems to prefer the original "Comfort" version.

Joys Seven
See **The Seven Joys of Mary**

K

Kenya
See Africa

King of Kings
See The Nativity on Film

Kissing Bough
See Mistletoe

Kwanzaa

A secular, seven-day African American celebration which commences on December 26 and bears no historical relationship to Christmas. The name is derived from the Swahili phrase "matunda ya kwanza"—"first fruits." Its roots lie in ancient African first-fruit harvest celebrations, and the present concept of Kwanzaa strives to assist African Americans in relating to their cultural past. In so doing, they will be better equipped to understand the present and cope with the future. Kwanzaa, together with Hanukkah and Christmas, is one of the trio of principal year-end festivals in the United States.

Conceived by Dr. Maulana Karenga, currently professor and chairman of the Department of Black Studies at California State University at Long Beach, Kwanzaa originated in 1966 following the Watts riots in Los Angeles. Believing that social revolutionary change for African Americans could be achieved by exposing them to their heritage of African culture (Kawaida Theory), Dr. Karenga created Kwanzaa as an alternative to Christmas, a holiday which many blacks have otherwise viewed as "white" and Eurocentric.

Kwanzaa is organized around five fundamental activities and seven cardinal principles, the latter of which Dr. Karenga emphasized by duplicating the final "a" in "Kwanza" to form the seven-letter "Kwanzaa." The five fundamental activities are the gathering together of family, friends, and community; reverence for the creator and creation; remembering the past by honoring ancestors and learning from African achievements; adherence to the highest cultural ideals; and celebrating the "Good of Life." The seven principles, termed *Nguzo Saba*, focus on family and community and include *umoja* (unity), *kujichagulia* (self-determination), *ujima* (collective work and responsibility), *ujamaa* (cooperative economics), *nia* (purpose), *kuumba* (creativity), and *imani* (faith).

Kwanzaa celebrations include rituals, dialogue, narratives, poetry, dancing, singing, music, and feasting. A major ritual, somewhat similar to that of Hanukkah, is the lighting of a *kinura*, a candelabrum with seven candles (*mishumaa*) in colors of the Black Liberation Flag: three red, three green, and one black. One candle is lit on each of the seven days of Kwanzaa to commemorate the seven principles, after which celebrants, drinking from a *kikombe cha umoja* (unity cup), toast their ancestors by exclaiming, "Harambee" ("Let us pull together"). January 1 features a final feast (*karumu*), the table of which must include symbols of the seven principles, beginning with a straw placemat (*mkeka*), on which lie the remaining symbols: candelabrum; candles; assorted fruits (*mazao*); one ear of corn for each child present (*vibunzi*); the unity cup; and gifts (*zawadi*) for the children. These gifts traditionally include a book highlighting black achievement, a heritage symbol, and a toy.

Over 20 million blacks now celebrate Kwanzaa in North America, the Caribbean, and Africa.

L

Lamb's Wool
See **Wassail**

Latvia
See **Baltic States**

Laurel
See **Christmas Plants**

Laurel and Hardy in Toyland
See **Babes in Toyland**

Lavender
See **Christmas Plants**

Lebanon
See **Middle East**

The Legend of the Candy Cane
See **Candy Canes**

Let It Snow! Let It Snow! Let It Snow!
Popular American song written in 1945 by New York–born lyricist Sammy Cahn and London-born composer Jule Styne. While suffering through a California heat wave, the two "cooled" themselves by writing this generic, winter song. The picturesque lyrics suggest a romantic fireside interlude as cares are left to the wind, or better, to the blizzard outside. No holiday is mentioned, yet the song has become firmly linked with Christmas, a trend noted with a number of other popular, nonspecific winter songs, such as "Jingle Bells," "Frosty the Snowman," "Winter Wonderland," and others. "Let It Snow!" became an instant hit with Vaughn Monroe's 1945 recording on the Victor label, which was also the top Christmas song for that year.

Of the 25 most frequently performed Christmas songs of the twentieth century listed by the American Society of Composers, Authors and Publishers (ASCAP), "Let It Snow!" is ranked number 9.

Another Cahn-Styne holiday collaboration resulted in "The Christmas Waltz" (1954). *See also* **The Christmas Waltz.**

The Life and Adventures of Santa Claus
Classic children's novel, published in 1902 by L. Frank Baum, author of *The Wizard of Oz.* It is a biographical fantasy which outlines the life of Santa Claus.

Discovering an abandoned baby boy near the enchanted Forest of Burzee, the wood nymph Necile raises him as her son among the other Immortals of Burzee. Named "Claus" (meaning "little one"), the boy grows to manhood among his friends, the Fairies, Knooks, Ryls, and Nymphs. The great Ak, Master Woodsman of the World, guides Claus on a journey around the world, where he studies mankind and their sufferings. It is the poor little children who capture Claus's heart the most, and he vows to spend his life making them happy.

Leaving Burzee, Claus settles in the Laughing Valley of Hohaho as the beloved friend of children. Fashioning a wooden cat in the image of his pet Blinkie, Claus launches his career as a toymaker and gradually provides toys to neighboring children at their will, regardless of their status. When his enemies, the fiendish Awgwas, repeatedly thwart his efforts by kidnapping Claus (whom the Fairies and Knooks rescue) or by stealing and hiding his toys, an army of Immortals, lead by Ak, annihilate them.

To speed his deliveries, Claus eventually acquires ten reindeer, Flossie, Glossie, Racer, Pacer, Reckless, Speckless, Fearless, Peerless, Ready, and Steady, to pull his gigantic sledge of toys. The Knooks, the reindeer's masters, allow them to work for Claus only one night a year, Christmas Eve, with the stipulation that they be back in Burzee by daybreak.

Finding doors locked, Claus gains entrance to homes through chimneys and leaves toys sometimes in stockings hung by the chimney or sometimes on fir trees which he brings along for the children (origin of the Christmas tree). Parents, believing that only a saint could bestow such gifts, lay upon Claus the title of Santa Claus (contrary to the traditional Santa Claus, who leaves coal or sticks for naughty children, Baum's Santa Claus delivers gifts to the naughty as well as the nice).

As Santa Claus ages and the Spirit of Death seeks him, Ak convinces the Immortals that Claus, having done so much good for the world, deserves to wear the Mantle of Immortality, which they gladly confer. According to Baum, that is why Santa still lives today.

A 1985 made-for-television animated version of the same title features stop-motion puppets (Animagic). Principal voices: Alfred Drake, Earl Hammond, J. D. Roth, Lesley Miller, Earle Hyman. Vocalists: Al Dana, Margaret Dorn, Arlene Mitchell, Marty Nelson, David Ragaini, Robert Ragaini, Annette Sanders. Written by Julian P. Gardner. Based on the book by L. Frank Baum. Produced and directed by Arthur Rankin, Jr., and Jules Bass. Rankin/Bass Productions. Warner Home Video. Color. 50 min.

Lithuania
See **Baltic States**

Little Bitty Baby
See **Children, Go Where I Send Thee**

Little Christmas
See **Epiphany**

The Little Drummer Boy

American carol composed by Katherine Davis, Henry Onorati, and Harry Simeone in 1958. Originally published in 1941 as "Carol of the Drum" solely by Davis, it remained obscure until Onorati and Simeone became collaborators. Changing the title to "The Little Drummer Boy" added that tender touch for personal appeal. Simeone, a former choral conductor for Fred Waring (of Fred Waring and the Pennsylvanians), directed the Harry Simeone Chorale for its definitive 1958 recording on the 20th Century–Fox label, which attained position 13 on the *Billboard Hot 100* chart that year. It sold over six million copies, continued to make the pop charts into the early 1980s, and was also the top Christmas song for 1959, 1964, 1965, and 1966. The drummer boy character was the subject of two television animated specials, *The Little Drummer Boy* (1968) and *The Little Drummer Boy, Book II* (1976).

Similar to the much older carol "Pat-a-Pan," "The Little Drummer Boy" focuses on the age-old desire to give gifts to the Christ Child. With musical imagery of a drum softly beating in the background ("rum-pum-pum-pum"), a little boy speaks of his approaching the manger with nothing to offer but the simple gift of music on his drum. As Mary nods and the animals keep time, the Babe smiles in acceptance.

Of the 25 most frequently performed Christmas songs of the twentieth century listed by the American Society of Composers, Authors and Publishers (ASCAP), "The Little Drummer Boy" is ranked number 10.

See also **The Little Drummer Boy** (television special); **The Little Drummer Boy, Book II**; **Pat-a-Pan**.

The Little Drummer Boy

(Television special, 1968). Made-for-television animated story using stop-motion puppets (Animagic), based on the carol of the same title by Katherine Davis, Henry Onorati, and Harry Simeone.

Hating all people because bandits killed his parents, six-year-old Aaron, a shepherd boy, is captured and taken to Jerusalem. There, together with his three dancing pets, a donkey, a camel, and a lamb, Aaron must entertain the populace by playing his drum. Aaron is released when his captors sell his camel to the Wise Men en route to Bethlehem, and Aaron pursues their caravan. Although he finds his camel at the stable with the Holy Family, a chariot runs the lamb down at their reunion. Only the Babe in the manger can save it, say the Wise Men, whereupon Aaron produces his only gift, a song on his drum. Because Aaron gives out of the simple desperation of pure love, the lamb is healed, and Aaron learns the meaning of joy again.

Narrated by Greer Garson. Title song sung by the Vienna Boys Choir. Voices: Teddy Eccles, Jose Ferrer, Paul Frees. Written by Romeo

Muller. Produced and directed by Arthur Rankin, Jr., and Jules Bass. A Videocraft International, Limited Production in Association with NBC. Sony Wonder Video. Color. 30 min.

See also **The Little Drummer Boy** (song); **The Little Drummer Boy, Book II**.

The Little Drummer Boy, Book II

(1976). Made-for-television animated story using stop-motion puppets (Animagic). A sequel to *The Little Drummer Boy* (1968). The story continues with drummer boy Aaron having finished his performance for the Christ Child at the stable. He and his dancing pets then accompany Wise Man Melchior to tell Simeon the bell maker that Christ is born, for Simeon has cast a series of silver bells to be rung at the blessed event. Before they arrive, however, a troop of tax-collecting Roman soldiers raid Simeon's home and carry away his bells, because he cannot pay the tax. Melchior, Simeon, and Aaron pursue the soldiers to their camp, where Aaron offers to entertain them as a ruse. But the soldiers, bent on melting the bells into silver bricks, sacrifice Aaron's drum and sticks to start a fire instead. While the Romans harass Aaron, his pets slip away with the bells, and the three humans hide them in the desert until the soldiers tire of searching for them. Safe in Bethlehem, the bells peal forth the joy of the Nativity, after which Simeon presents Aaron with a new drum and bids him to return to the stable for an encore performance.

The Little Drummer Boy, Book II was nominated for an Emmy Award for Outstanding Children's Special (1976-77 season).

Narrated by Greer Garson. Instead of delivering a vocal rendition of "I Heard the Bells on Christmas Day," Garson simply reads the lyrics. Other principal songs are "The Little Drummer Boy" and "Do You Hear What I Hear?"

Voices: Zero Mostel, David Jay, Robert McFadden, Ray Owens, Allen Swift. Written by Julian P. Gardner. Produced and directed by Arthur Rankin, Jr., Jules Bass. Rankin/Bass Productions. Warner Home Video. Color. 24 min.

See also **Do You Hear What I Hear?**; **The Little Drummer Boy** (song); **The Little Drummer Boy** (television special).

Little Jesus, Sweetly Sleep
See **Rocking**

The Little Match Girl

A tragic yet unspeakably tender fairy tale by the celebrated Danish author Hans Christian Andersen (1805–1875). On New Year's Eve, a poorly clad little girl is forced to roam bitterly cold streets and sell matches in the snow. She cannot return home empty-handed, otherwise her wretched father will beat her. Starving at the end of the fruitless day, she crouches in a corner and begins to strike one match after another, desperately trying to keep warm. With each match, glorious visions appear before her: first a large, polished stove with a roaring fire; next a splendid dinner of roast goose stuffed with apples and plums; then a gorgeous Christmas tree trimmed with candles and colored pictures. Gazing into the night sky, she notes a falling star and recalls what her late grandmother once said about such a sign, that a soul was going to God. Striking another match brings the grandmother smiling before her, whereupon the girl, clinging to the image, strikes all the remaining matches and begs to be taken away. As the light swells brilliantly, the grandmother folds the little girl into her arms and, rising high and joyfully into New Year's Day, carries her granddaughter forever into the presence of God.

Several motion picture and animated versions introduce a more positive or romantic element into the otherwise somber tale:

La petite marchande d'allumettes (1928). Silent French film starring Catherine Hessling, Manuel Raaby, Jean Storm, Amy Wells, Ann Wells. Written by Jean Renoir. Directed by Jean Renoir, Jean Tédesco. B & W. 40 min. Video N/A.

Little Match Girl (1937). Animated cartoon "short" from the Color Rhapsodies series of Screen Gems/Columbia Pictures. In 1938 it received an Academy Award nomination for Best Short Subjects, Cartoons. Produced by Charles Mintz. Video N/A.

The Little Match Girl (1983). Motion picture version starring Sandy Duncan, Dan Hays, Matt McKim, Monica McSwain. Directed by Wally Broodbent, Mark Hoeger. Video N/A.

The Little Match Girl (1987). British musical, in which a young girl learns that true beauty lies in friendship and love. Starring Twiggy Lawson, Roger Daltrey, Natalie Morse, Paul Daneman, Nicola Dawn, Jennie Linden, Jemma Price. Written by Jeremy Paul, Leslie Stewart. Produced by Peter Jefferies. Directed by Michael Custance. Harlech Television and Picture Base International Productions. Color. 90 min. Video N/A.

The Little Match Girl (1987). Television special in which a woman attempts to reconcile her husband and estranged son at Christmastime, while a match girl's matches create positive outcomes. Starring Keshia Knight Pulliam, Rue McClanahan, John Rhys-Davies, William Daniels. Written by Maryedith Burrell. Produced by Robert Hargrove. Directed by Michael Lindsay-Hogg. Color. 96 min. Video N/A.

The Little Match Girl (1990). Animated cartoon in which homeless match girl Angela experiences an adventure that promises new beginnings on New Year's Eve, 1999. Narrated by F. Murray Abraham. Other voice: Theresa Smythe. Written by Maxine Fisher. Produced and directed by Michael Sporn. Family Home Entertainment Video. Color. 30 min.

Such Is Life (1924). Silent film comedy starring Baby Peggy, Joe Bonner, Thomas Wonder, Jack Henderson, Arnold MacDonald, Paul Stanhope. Directed by Alfred J. Goulding. Century Film Corporation. B & W. Video N/A.

Andersen wrote a number of tales with winter settings, such as "The Snow Queen," yet only two, "The Little Match Girl" and "The Fir Tree," are set amid the holidays.

See also **The Fir Tree**.

Little Women

Autobiographical novel by American writer Louisa May Alcott (1832–1888), published in 1868–69. Based on her childhood experiences in New England, it features the closely knit March family with daughters Meg, Jo, Beth, Amy, and "Marmee," their mother. Initially set during the American Civil War, the first two chapters depict a holiday scene amid the anxiety over their father, who has volunteered as a chaplain in the Union army, and who will not be home for Christmas. Because money is scarce, the girls, renouncing gifts for themselves, prepare a few treasures for Marmee instead. For her girls, Mrs. March places a New

Testament under each of their pillows early Christmas morning, then departs on an errand of mercy to the Hummel home before daybreak. There lies a sick mother with a newborn and six other children freezing and starving. With love, the girls sacrifice their meager meal and provide for the wretched family. Then follows an original melodramatic play, *The Witch's Curse, an Operatic Tragedy*, written by Jo and performed by the girls for their childhood friends. Afterwards, the children are delighted to find special treats of ice cream, fruit, and candy awaiting them. Rich old Mr. Laurence, their reclusive next door neighbor, upon hearing of their good deed earlier that morning, had sent over the repast. Indeed, despite the times, it is "A Merry Christmas."

The remainder of the novel follows the girls' lives as they grow.

The Littlest Angel

Classic children's book written in 1939 by American author Charles Tazewell, with television and animated versions.

A little boy, between four and five years old and known simply as "The Littlest Angel," finds that living in heaven requires much painful adjustment. His innocent mischievousness, his off-key singing in the celestial choir, his chasing his halo, and his swinging on the heavenly gates prompts a conference with the Understanding Angel. Homesick for Earth, the Littlest Angel is allowed to keep his most prized possession, a rough little wooden box that contains a butterfly, a bird's egg, two stones from a river, and his mongrel dog's collar.

When Jesus is born, all the angels lay gifts before the throne of God to honor the birth. With no other gift to offer, the Littlest Angel presents his little box, a seemingly blasphemous gift to the heavenly host. Yet to God this simplest of gifts is the most pleasing of all, because it represents unselfishness and sacrifice. At this blessing, the little box soars into the heavens, where it transforms into the shining Star of Bethlehem.

The Children's Press of Chicago first published the story as a book in 1946, and actor Helen Hayes narrated it on the Christmas radio show *Manhattan at Midnight. Coronet* magazine also published the story three years later.

In 1969 the *Hallmark Hall of Fame* sponsored an adaptation for television, which starred Johnny Whitaker ("Jodie Davis" of the 1970s television series *Family Affair*) as Michael, the Littlest Angel. With James Coco, Fred Gwynne, E. G. Marshall, Tony Randall, George Rose, Connie Stevens, Cab Calloway. Directed by Joe Layton. Bridgestone Multimedia Video. Color.

A 1997 animated cartoon version for television featured the voices of Maxine Miller, Blu Mankuma, L. Harvey Gold, William Samples, Walter Marsh, Peter DeLuise, Paulina Gillis. Written by Kayte Kuch, Sheryl Scarborough. Based on the book by Charles Tazewell. Produced by Chris Delaney, Arnie Zipursky. Directed by John Delaney, Don Boone. Delaney and Friends Productions and Littlest Productions. Family Home Entertainment Video. Color. 24 min.

Sound recordings include those narrated by Loretta Young (Decca, 1940s) and Dame Judith Anderson (Caedmon, 1973).

Charles Tazewell (1900–1972), a scriptwriter and author of children's books, performed on Broadway during the 1930s. His books include *The Small One*, *The Littlest Tree*, and *The Littlest Snowman*, the latter of which won the Thomas A. Edison Prize for the best children's story of 1956. He wrote *The Littlest Angel* in just three days, and at the time of his death, it was in its 38th printing. It has sold some five million copies.

See also **The Littlest Snowman**; **The Littlest Tree**; **The Small One**.

The Littlest Snowman

Children's book written by American author Charles Tazewell (1900–1972). The story initially appeared in the December 1955 issue of *Coronet* magazine and won the Thomas A. Edison Prize for the best children's story of 1956.

Each December a little boy on Winter Avenue creates the Littlest Snowman, who comes to life when clad with a candy heart inscribed with "I Love You Truly." When rising temperatures threaten to obliterate any chance for snow on Christmas Eve, the Littlest Snowman, thin from partial melting, devises a counter-plan. Consuming great quantities of colored ice cream on Christmas Eve, the now-obese Snowman climbs to the top of the community Christmas tree, where a fierce north wind blows him into multicolored snowflakes all over town. On Christmas Day, the villagers collect all the white flakes and return them to the boy on Winter Avenue, who restores the Littlest Snowman. Thereafter, his heart beats "I Love You Truly" throughout the Christmas season as another way of saying "Merry Christmas."

Tazewell is also the author of the bestselling children's story *The Littlest Angel*, as well as *The Littlest Tree* and *The Small One*.

See also **The Littlest Angel**; **The Littlest Tree**; **The Small One**.

The Littlest Tree

Children's book written by American author Charles Tazewell (1900–1972), published posthumously in 1997.

Whenever people on Earth select and decorate their Christmas trees, exact replicas of the trees grow in the Forest of the Nativity in Heaven. Saint Isadore, the forest gatekeeper, maintains a meticulous record of each tree's history, for on Christmas Eve the Son of God annually selects the best loved of those trees in the forest to be His birthday tree.

All Heaven looks to Solomon, a celestial sage and former king on Earth, to predict the Son's choice, and his accuracy has been flawless each year, with one exception: the year of the Littlest Tree. A mere scrub of a branch, decorated with lipstick, green ink, blueing, yellow twine, a military general's silver insignia, shards of glass, gearshift knobs, and tin foil, the Littlest Tree was a loving Christmas gift from a pack of war-ravaged, homeless orphan boys to a little girl, Laus, their newest member, who had never experienced a Christmas tree of her own, much less seen one. Though this Christmas symbol reflected the waste of war, to Laus, the Littlest Tree radiated breathless beauty, which brought tears of joy to her eyes. And to the Son, it was the perfect birthday tree.

Tazewell is also the author of the bestselling children's story *The Littlest Angel*, as well as *The Littlest Snowman* and *The Small One*.

See also **The Littlest Angel**; **The Littlest Snowman**; **The Small One**.

Lo, How a Rose E'er Blooming

("Es ist ein Ros' entsprungen"). German traditional carol which originated around the fifteenth century. The basis for the carol lies in the Messianic prophecy of Isaiah 11:1, "And there shall come forth a rod out of the stem of Jesse, and a Branch shall grow out of his roots." The modern interpretation of this scripture is that Jesus (the "rod" or "branch") was descended from King David, whose father was Jesse. According to medieval interpretation at the time, however, the rod-branch of Jesse was pictured allegorically as the Virgin Mary, further symbolized as a rose in bloom, with the Christ Child as her young flower.

The text, which centers on this flowering rose concept, exists in numerous versions, with variable numbers of verses ranging from two to twenty-three. The more lengthy versions elaborate on the entire Nativity and include all events from the Annunciation to the Magi. Such variability is thought to have originated from a simple Annunciation carol, to which shorter verses centering on the remaining details of the story were added at different times.

Because the carol contained Roman Catholic themes, it was not printed until 1599 in Cologne, for the Protestant Reformation had succeeded in preventing such material from reaching the presses until that time. The carol gained further recognition when, in 1609, the German composer Michael Praetorius (1571–1621) published a well-received musical arrangement in his *Musiae Sioniae*, which is the setting in use today. In 1896, another German composer, Johannes Brahms (1833–1897), based an organ chorale prelude around the carol (Opus 122, Book II).

The best-known English translation, "Lo, How a Rose E'er Blooming," is by the American music scholar Theodore Baker (1851–1934), who in 1900 published his *Biographical Dictionary of Musicians*. Alternate translations have included such titles as "I Know a Rose Tree Springing," "Behold a Branch Is Growing," "The Noble Stem of Jesse," and "Of Jesse's Line Descended," among others.

Love Came Down at Christmas

English carol, the text for which was written by Christina Rossetti (1830–1894), considered to be England's foremost female poet. A simple poem consisting of three verses of four lines each, "Love Came Down" proclaims that God's gift of love to the world was Jesus; that God, being Love, was born at Christmas. The poem originally appeared with the title "Christmastide" in Rossetti's collection *Time Flies: A Reading Diary* (1855), a book of daily devotions and meditations for the year, in which "Christmastide" was intended for December 29. This collection, together with two other volumes, *Called to be Saints* (1881) and *The Face of the Deep* (1892), were all combined to form a larger volume, *Verses* (1893). There, the final line of "Christmastide," which originally read "Love the universal sign," was altered to "Love for plea and gift and sign."

The poem was first published as a carol in *Church Praise* (1907), an English Presbyterian hymnal (Rossetti was Anglican), and in *Songs of Praise* (1925). These and several other musical settings never gained widespread popularity. Two additional tunes, one known as "Hermitage" by the Englishman Reginald O. Morris (1886–1948) and another, a traditional Irish melody known as "Gartan," are the two leading settings, though neither shows particular dominance. Despite lacking a suitable tune, "Love Came Down at Christmas" remains a favorite carol. Another of Ms. Rossetti's poems, "In the Bleak Mid-Winter," has also become a carol of note.

See also **In the Bleak Mid-Winter.**

Lovefeast, Christmas Eve

See **Moravian Church**

The Low Countries

Comprised of Belgium, Luxembourg, and the Netherlands (Holland). Christmas customs of Belgium are varied and are patterned after its three principal cultures, French, German, and Dutch. The predominantly Roman Catholic Luxembourg observes the feast days of the Church, as does Belgium, and customs in the Netherlands are roughly an equal mix of Catholic and Protestant observances.

Common to these countries are the Christmas markets, which are set up early in

December in cities throughout and consist of Christmas arts and crafts, toys, floral arrangements, decorations, cuisine, music, exhibits, and spirits (for example, mulled wines and schnapps known as *Drepp*). The Christmas tree and crèche or Nativity scene are the principal Christmas symbols, and it is traditional to leave a gift for the poor when passing an outdoor crèche. St. Nicholas brings gifts on the eve of his feast day, December 6, the principal gift-giving holiday of the season, and church services are held on Christmas Eve and Christmas Day. December 25 and 26 (Second Christmas Day) are minor holidays compared to St. Nicholas Day. The following paragraphs summarize other customs peculiar to these countries.

• BELGIUM. Children set out their shoes for St. Nicholas. Churches in Flanders traditionally present Nativity plays in sixteenth-century fashion with period costumes, and characters must resemble those found in the works of Flemish painter Jan Brueghel (1568–1625). Villages usually appoint three men to portray the three Magi. Dressed in regal attire, they parade from door to door collecting for charities and singing carols, especially the Flemish version of "O Tannenbaum" ("O Christmas Tree"). Because the three are offered food and beverage, which are consumed immediately at each house, the Wise Men are chosen for their gastronomic prowess. In Belgium one may hear "Merry Christmas" as *Joyeux Noël* (French) or *Fröhliche Weihnachten* (German).

• LUXEMBOURG. The St. Nicholas ("Kleeschen") and Black Peter ("Houseker") customs are similar to those of the Netherlands. In addition, children set out plates as well as their shoes to receive gifts. At Christmas, it is the Christ Child who brings the gifts. Traditional foods include *Stollen* (candied fruit loaf), *bûche de Noël* (Christmas cake in the shape of a Yule log), black pudding, hare, venison, and turkey. Fireworks and *Bals* (dance parties organized by university students) usher in the New Year. "Merry Christmas" is *Schei Chreschtdeeg* (Letzebuergesch).

• NETHERLANDS. A custom deriving from pagan Yule practices of creating loud noise to drive away evil spirits is Midwinter Horn Blowing. From the first Advent Sunday through Christmas Eve, farmers primarily in the rural eastern sections of the country daily blow horns over wells, producing sounds like foghorns. These horns are made from hollowed limbs of elder trees and range three to four feet in length.

Since tradition holds that St. Nicholas, *Sinterklaas*, was born in Spain, on the last Saturday in November he arrives in Amsterdam and other harbor cities by boat from Spain along with his antithesis, *Zwarte Piet* (Black Peter), a sixteenth-century Moorish personification of the devil. Dressed in full bishop's attire, the person portraying the saint rides a white horse and, with Peter walking behind, is the center of a parade to the city square; the queen welcomes him in Amsterdam. On the eve of St. Nicholas Day, St. Nicholas and Peter visit a number of public establishments as well as private homes to determine whether children are deserving of gifts. It is Peter, black-faced from jumping down chimneys, who actually distributes the gifts, and he also carries a sack in which to stuff naughty children and a rod for beating them. Often Peter knocks at doors and tosses in *peppernøtter* (hard spice cookies). Other seasonal sweets are *letterbanket* (cakes made into shapes of letters) and *speculaas* (gingerbread-like pastry). During the evening, elaborately wrapped gifts are hidden around the house. Recipients find them through a series of clues, and each gift contains a poem which satirizes the recipient. Then children set out their shoes filled with hay and carrots for St. Nicholas's horse, and overnight the fodder is replaced with treats; naughty children receive switches.

Although schools may be closed for two to three weeks, the adult holidays consist of First Christmas Day (December 25), Second Christmas Day (December 26), and New Year's Day. The Christmas tree, generally sporting real candles, is lit on Christmas Eve, and the Christmas dinner often consists of rabbit, venison, goose, and turkey with flaming or cold pudding. Families remain at home at this time and engage in carol singing or reading aloud by the Christmas tree. Second Christmas Day is reserved for activities away from home, such as attending concerts and plays. The Dutch again remain at home on New Year's Eve and play parlor games, then toast the new year as fireworks, pealing of church bells, and the blowing of boat whistles herald the midnight hour. "Merry Christmas" is *Zalig Kerstfeest.*

See also **France**; **Germany**; **Saint Nicholas**; **Saint Nicholas Day.**

Lullaby
See **Rocking**

Lullay, Thou Tiny Little Child
See **The Coventry Carol**

Luminarias
See **Farolitos and Luminarias**

Luxembourg
See **The Low Countries**

M

Madeline's Christmas

Classic children's picture book, the last in a series of six *Madeline* books written by the Austrian-American author Ludwig Bemelmans. Told in simple verse with illustrations by the author, the books feature the adventures of Madeline, one of twelve little girls attending a boarding school in Paris. *Madeline's Christmas* was originally published as a book insert in the 1956 Christmas edition of *McCall's* magazine.

It's Christmas Eve, and everyone at the boarding school is sick in bed with a cold, except Madeline, who ministers to her schoolmates and Miss Clavel, the head mistress. A mysterious rug merchant seeking shelter from the winter storm appears and magically dispatches Madeline's household chores in short order, then whisks away the girls on twelve flying carpets to their parents' homes for Christmas.

In 1990 the story was adapted for television as an animated cartoon, in which a magic-wielding Madam Marie replaced the rug merchant. Voices: Marsha Moreau, Judith Orban, Sonja Ball, Liz Macrae, Anik Matern, Mark Hellman. Written by Stephan Martiniere and Peter Landecker. Based on the book by Ludwig Bemelmans. Produced by Ronald A. Weinberg. Directed by Stephan Martiniere. A Cinar Films and France Animation production. Sony Wonder Video. Color. 25 min.

Ludwig Bemelmans (1898–1962), a world traveler, painter, and illustrator as well as a writer, sustained injuries in a car accident off the coast of France. As he lay in an island hospital, a little girl recovering there provided inspiration for the *Madeline* books.

Magi
See **Nativity**

The Man in the Santa Claus Suit

(1979). Made-for-television comedy.

Besides delivering toys to children on Christmas Eve, Santa finds time to help three troubled men out of sticky situations in New York City: a milksop math teacher fearful of proposing to his fashion model neighbor, a street bum dodging the mob, and a senator's aide estranged from his wife and little boy. Posing out of "uniform" as the owner of a costume shop that ordinarily does not exist, Santa (Fred Astaire) rents Santa suits to each man. Wearing the suits enables them to work through their problems just in time for Christmas. Besides a shop owner, Santa poses as a chauffeur, a policeman, a taxi cab driver, a floor walker at Macy's, a street food vendor, and a song leader, all in connection with his three "charges."

With Gary Burghoff, John Byner, Bert Convy, Tara Buckman, Brooke Bundy, Eddie Barth, Ron Feinberg, Nanette Fabray, Harold Gould. Written by George Kirgo. Story by Leonard Gershe. Produced by Lee Miller. Directed by Corey Allen. Dick Clark Cinematic Productions. Media Home Entertainment Video. Color. 104 min.

March of the Wooden Soldiers
See **Babes in Toyland**

Marks, John D. (Johnny)

See **Rudolph, the Red-Nosed Reindeer** (song)

A Marshmallow World

Popular American song written in 1949, the only collaboration of New York natives Carl Sigman (lyrics) and Peter De Rose (music). A generic song about winter which does not mention Christmas, its gimmick, besides a catchy tune, lies in likening snow to white confections, primarily marshmallows and whipped cream. According to the lyrics, winter is a "yummy" time for sweethearts. The song was not completed in time to be recorded for the 1949 season, but 1950 saw recordings by Bing Crosby on the Decca label, Vic Damone on Mercury Records, Arthur Godfrey on Columbia Records, and Vaughn Monroe on RCA Victor. Of these, only Crosby's recording was charted.

Separately, Sigman is known for his contributions to other popular pieces, such as "Pennsylvania 6-5000" (1939), "Enjoy Yourself, It's Later Than You Think" (1948), and "Ebb Tide" (1953). De Rose is perhaps better known for "Deep Purple" (1934), originally a piano instrumental.

Mary and Jesus

See **The Cherry Tree Carol**

Mary Had a Baby

African American spiritual of anonymous authorship, thought to have originated in South Carolina during the nineteenth century. Its twelve verses each consist of one line that is repeated three times, with the seemingly spontaneous phrases of "Oh, Lord!" or "Oh, my Lord!" interrupting the repetitions. The verses are as follows: 1. "Mary had a baby." 2. "Where did she lay Him?" 3. "Laid Him in a manger." 4. "What did she name Him?" 5. "Name Him Jesus." 6. "Who heard the singing?" 7. "Shepherds heard the singing." 8. "Star keep a-shining." 9. "Moving in the elements." 10. "Jesus went to Egypt." 11. "Traveled on a donkey." 12. "Angels went around Him." Each verse then concludes with the same, seemingly incongruous statement, "Oh, Lord! The people keep a-coming and the train done gone."

Mary's Little Boy Child

Popular American song written in 1956 by the African-American composer Jester Hairston. Friend and singer Harry Belafonte popularized this lively, West Indies calypso-style narrative of the Nativity with his 1956 recording on the RCA label. It became the top Christmas song that year, ranking number 12 on the *Billboard Hot 100* chart. As the lyrics summarize, the human race may now achieve immortality because of what transpired on Christmas Day 2,000 years ago.

A Pennsylvania native, classically trained musician, and actor, Jester Hairston (1901–2000) was a musician for the Eva Jessye Choir, a conductor for the Hall Johnson Choir, and a collector of spirituals. He has arranged choral music for more than forty motion pictures and has appeared in such films as *In the Heat of the Night* (1967) and *I'm Gonna Git You Sucka* (1988). He is best known for his choral work "Amen," a spiritual based on the life of Christ.

Mary's Question

See **The Cherry Tree Carol**

Masque

See **Christmas Drama**

Mass of the Rooster

(*Misa del Gallo*). The Spanish term applied to the Roman Catholic Midnight Mass held on Christmas Eve in Spain and Latin American countries. The term derives from a legend which holds that the only time in history when a rooster crowed at midnight was to herald the birth of Jesus at that alleged hour. The legend is certainly of European origin, Shakespeare also having made reference to it in Act I of his play *Hamlet*.

According to one medieval legend, the rooster crowed in Latin, "*Christus natus est*" ("Christ is born"), to which other stable animals witnessing the Nativity took up a litany of responses: The raven asked, "*Quando?*" ("When?"); the crow, "*haec nocte*" ("This night"); the ox, "*Ubi?*" ("Where?"); the lamb, "*Bethlehem*"; the ass, "*Eamus*" ("Let us go").

See also **Christmas Masses; The Friendly Beasts; Hamlet.**

Mass of the Divine Word

See **Christmas Masses**

Mele Kalikimaka (The Hawaiian Christmas Song)

Novelty song written in 1949 by Hawaiian businessman R. Alex Anderson, an amateur songwriter who created such other island pieces as "The Cockeyed Mayor of Kaunakakai," "Lovely Hula Hands," "White Ginger Blossoms," and "Lei of Stars." Translated into English, the words "Mele Kalikimaka" mean "Merry Christmas." As opposed to most secular Christmas songs that focus on snow and sleighing, Anderson's simple lyrics state the obvious: that Christmas in Hawaii will be green and bright, and that palm trees will sway on Christmas Day. Bing Crosby and the Andrews Sisters first recorded the song on the Decca label in 1950.

Merry Christmas, Darling

Popular American song written in 1970 by Richard Carpenter and Frank Pooler. Richard Carpenter and his sister, Karen, originally from New Haven, Connecticut, at that time were students at the Long Beach campus of California State University, where Pooler was director of choral studies. With Karen's melancholy solo in the lead, The Carpenters first recorded the song as a single in 1970 on the A & M label, which charted #1 in 1970, 1971, and 1973, then charted #4 in 1972 and #5 in 1983, all on the *Billboard Christmas Singles* chart. Karen reportedly was never truly satisfied with her track for this recording and rerecorded "Merry Christmas, Darling" in 1978. The new recording appeared in The Carpenters' gold record–winning album, *Christmas Portrait*, charted as the #1 Christmas album for 1978.

Like another popular standard, "I'll Be Home for Christmas" (1943), "Merry Christmas, Darling" centers around a young couple who cannot be together for the holidays. Sitting alone by the fire and the glittering tree on Christmas Eve, the singer sends a mental wish of "Merry Christmas" to the absent lover. Yet while they are physically apart, they will still be together for Christmas in their dreams.

The Carpenters enjoyed a number of hit tunes, including "Close to You" (1970), "We've Only Just Begun" (1970), "For All We Know" (1971), and many others.

See also I'll Be Home for Christmas (song).

Messiah

Oratorio in three parts, the best-known work of George Frideric Handel (1685–1759), composed in 1741 to a libretto by Charles Jennens. German by birth, Handel had relocated by 1711 to London, where his opera *Rinaldo* significantly helped to further the Italian style of opera. Other notable operas from that point included *Radamisto* (1720), *Giulio Cesare* (1724), *Tamarlano* (1724), and *Rodelinda* (1725). Except in the most elite circles, however, public taste eventually wearied of operas written in Italian (the only accepted language for opera at that time) and demanded something more English. With the premiere of John Gay's *Beggar's Opera* (1728), a highly popular English satire on the Italian opera, together with the folding of two of Handel's opera companies by 1737 and the failure of two other operas by 1741, Handel chose to pursue the oratorio as a principal alternative. Similar to an opera with parts for soloists, chorus, and orchestra but without elaborate scenery or costumes, the oratorio, always based on a religious subject, could employ English. Ironically, because oratorios were often performed in theaters, the form was not considered to be church music in the strictest sense.

Handel had written some fifteen oratorios prior to 1741, among them *Israel in Egypt* (1739), *Saul* (1739), and *L'Allegro–Il Penseroso–Il Moderato* (1740), the latter two librettos having been supplied by an eccentric friend, Charles Jennens. Aspiring to raise Handel's spirits, in 1741 Jennens presented the libretto for *Messiah*, a compilation of scriptures from the King James Bible and the Anglican Burial Service about the life of Christ. Jennens expected that Handel would complete the oratorio within a year. Instead, Handel set to work on August 21, 1741, and completed *Messiah* on September 14, 24 days later. During this time, the power and majesty of the subject consumed Handel such that he rarely ate or slept. Upon completing the "Hallelujah Chorus," he was found weeping over his work. Handel told the servant who so found him that he thought he had seen all Heaven before him and God Himself.

Having received an invitation from William Cavendish, Lord Lieutenant of Ireland, to give a series of benefit concerts in Dublin, Handel first presented *Messiah* at Dublin's New Music Hall, Fishamble Street, on April 13, 1742. The hall, ordinarily seating 600, on that date accommodated 700, for men left their bulky swords behind, as did women their hoop skirts. Although the world premiere of *Messiah* was much applauded, the use of a theater and theatrical singers to perform scriptural texts created mixed emotions after the first London performance at Covent Garden Theatre in March, 1743.

At a later performance that same season in London, King George II rose to his feet during the "Hallelujah Chorus." While popular trend holds that the king, overcome with emotion, rose in reverence to this monumental chorus, critics believe that he merely rose to stretch his legs during the oratorio's hours-long performance. Regardless of the reason, when a monarch rose, custom dictated that all present follow suit. Thus King George's act not only established the custom of rising during any performance of the "Hallelujah Chorus" today, it served to boost London's acceptance of *Messiah* overall.

Handel began closing his annual Lent season at Covent Garden with *Messiah* in 1750, which coincided with annual benefit performances at London's Foundling Hospital. The first performance on the Continent was in Hamburg, 1772, and, although excerpts had been played in New York City in 1770, the first full American performance was in Boston on Christmas Day, 1818, the same Christmas when "Silent Night" was introduced in Austria.

Yielding to Jennens's criticisms and influenced by the availability of vocalists, instruments, and players' musical abilities, Handel often revised *Messiah*. As a result, no definitive version exists today. Shortly after Handel's death, a movement arose to enlarge the chorus and orchestra from their initial numbers of forty members each. Originally no part had been written for organ or harpsichord, yet Handel, while improvising, had often conducted performances from the latter instrument. In 1789, Baron van Swieten commissioned W. A. Mozart to update the sparse orchestration, which had consisted primarily of strings, with selected numbers employing trumpets and tympani. Even though the chorus grew into the thousands by the late nineteenth and early twentieth centuries, an increased appreciation of Baroque instrumentation in recent times has prompted a return to a more "original" setting.

Messiah was originally intended as an Easter oratorio, as the dates of its early performances suggested, but popular usage has since brought it into the realm of Christmas music. The three principal parts comprise 53 numbers, but most Christmas performances utilize only Part I, which emphasizes the Old Testament prophecies of the coming of Christ and a few passages from New Testament accounts of the Nativity. Favorite choruses include "For Unto Us a Child Is Born" and "Glory to God." Often the "Hallelujah Chorus," which concludes Part II, is used as a finale to the Christmas section. Part II portrays Christ's passion, resurrection, and the spreading of the Gospel; and Part III, an epilogue, depicts the promise of redemption through Christ at the final Judgment.

Whereas in most of Handel's other oratorios the soloists represent specific characters, no characters exist in *Messiah*. Instead, soloists and chorus alike describe the life of Christ indirectly and almost completely through Old Testament prophets, the New Testament being used primarily in Part III for the thanksgiving when Christ conquers death. Music scholars cite two possible reasons for this. First, in the eighteenth century, the general was more often favored over the particular, the abstract preferred over the concrete. Second, avoiding direct biblical quotations often (though not always) circumvented the puritanical objection that sinful entertainers defiled holy writ in theaters.

Mexico

Local customs may vary from region to region, but a number of traditions prevail throughout the country. As in most Latin American countries, the Mexican Christmas season begins with the nine days' fiesta of *Las Posadas* ("The Lodgings"), celebrated from December 16 to 24. (*See* **Las Posadas.**) A Novena also commences at this time with special *Misas del Aguinaldo* ("Masses of the Gift") during the nine days before Christmas. (The subjects of the Novena are discussed in the introductions to **Central America** and **South America**.) Following the *Misa del Gallo* ("Mass of the Rooster," Midnight Mass) on *Noche Buena* (literally "Good Night," Christmas Eve), families return to their homes for a traditional Christmas dinner of roast turkey, ham, suckling pig, steak, fish, regional dishes, doughnuts, *rompope* (eggnog with cinnamon and rum or grain alcohol), *ponche* (hot fruit punch), and *sidra* (cider); for the thrifty reveler, *tamales* with *atole* (corn gruel) and *tortillas*. Festivities, which extend into the early hours of Christmas morning, include gifts for the children from *El Niño Dios* ("The Christ Child"), a *piñata* (discussed under *Las Posadas*), and *luces de Belen* ("sparklers"). *Navidad* (Christmas Day) itself is a day of rest.

Los Santos Inocentes (Holy Innocents Day), observed on December 28, is a memorial to those children whom King Herod the Great slaughtered in Bethlehem in his attempt to exterminate the infant Jesus. A day for foolishness and pranks similar to the American April Fool's Day, its activities are vestiges of the European medieval Feast of Fools. Victims of practical jokes receive mock gifts and are branded "Fool Saints" or *inocentes*.

Día de los Reyes (Day of the Kings), Epiphany, January 6, commemorates the Three Kings' visit to the manger and is the principal gift-giving day of the season. On the night before, children fill their shoes with hay for the Magi's camels and set these out on window sills for the *Reyes Magos* (Magi) to fill with gifts. A special event is the cutting of a *Rosca de Reyes* (Kings' Cake), a round, sweet bread with a small, ceramic *muñeco* (doll) symbolizing the Christ Child baked inside. Whoever receives the doll in his slice must host a party for the others present on *Día de Candelaria* (Candlemas), February 2, a day which once ended the Christmas season in the Roman Catholic Church.

Santa Claus and Christmas trees play minor roles if any, and only through American influence. The principal holiday display in each home consists of the *Nacimiento* (Nativity scene) or the *Pesebre*, a more elaborate version

with miniature reconstructions of pastoral scenes along with the traditional stable, *misterios* (figures of the Holy Family), animals, angels, shepherds, and Wise Men. Custom dictates that the manger receives the Christ Child figure only on Christmas Eve, and the Magi are moved forward each day, "arriving" only on Epiphany. A tiny, decorated Christmas tree, often a local shrub, may accompany the scene. Other typical decorations include poinsettias.

"Merry Christmas" is in Spanish, *Feliz Navidad*.

See also **Candlemas; Epiphany; Feast of Fools; Holy Innocents Day; Las Posadas; Mass of the Rooster; Nativity Scene; Poinsettia**.

Mickey's Christmas Carol

See **A Christmas Carol** (Film and Television Versions)

Middle East

Christmas is observed in only a few countries because Islam and Judaism are the prevailing religions in this part of the world. Because Armenia is predominantly Christian, Christmas in that country is discussed as a separate entry.

A favorite bit of folklore among the Christians in this part of the world holds that, at midnight on Epiphany Eve (January 5), all the trees of the world pay homage to the Christ Child by bowing their trunks and branches. According to another legend, traced to the tenth-century Arabian geographer Georg Jacob, when Christ was born, all the trees of the world bloomed in midwinter to His glory.

• Iran. As opposed to Easter, known as the "Big Feast," Christmas is known as the "Little Feast." The first 25 days of December are spent in fasting with abstinence from animal or dairy products. The fast is broken after the early morning mass on Christmas Day, when the traditional *harasa* (chicken stew) is served. Although Santa Claus is unknown and gift exchanges are not traditional, children usually receive a new outfit of clothes. "Merry Christmas" is spoken in Farsi: *Cristmas-e-shoma mobarak bashad*.

• Iraq. The Christian minority generally belongs to the Coptic Church, which follows the Julian calendar for ecclesiastical observances. Thus Christmas is observed on January 7. On Christmas Eve, the family, carrying lighted candles, gathers outdoors around a bonfire of thorns for a reading of the Gospel. The complete burning of the thorns to ash predicts good luck. Afterwards, each family member makes a wish and jumps over the ashes three times. A similar fire burns in the churchyard on Christmas Day as the priest, holding an effigy of the Christ Child, leads a procession. At the conclusion of the service, the priest initiates the Touch of Peace by touching the person next to him, who in turn touches his neighbor, and so forth, until the touch has fallen on all the congregation. "Merry Christmas" is said in Arabic *Idah Saidan Wa Sanah Jadidah. See also* **Christmas Old Style, Christmas New Style.**

• ISRAEL. Christmas celebrations are observed principally in Bethlehem by the Eastern Orthodox, Roman Catholic, and Armenian faiths, the chief Christian denominations. On the eastern fringes of the city are a series of open plains, where tradition holds that the shepherds keeping watch over their flocks by night received the "good tidings of great joy" from the angelic host. Thus, these plains are known as the Shepherds' Fields; one is controlled by the Orthodox, one by the Catholics, and a third by the YMCA, the latter featuring a Christmas Eve carol singing service in the early evening.

Also on Christmas Eve, the Latin (Catholic) Patriarch of Jerusalem and his procession travel the five miles to Bethlehem, and, passing through Manger Square, arrive at the Church of St. Catherine, where Midnight Mass is held. During the ceremony, the procession crosses a courtyard to the Church of the Nativity, a medieval structure built over the cave that tradition reveres as the place of Christ's birth. There, the Patriarch descends to the Grotto of the Manger and places a life-size statue of the Infant Jesus in a crib. The service is telecast on large screens to thousands congregating in Manger Square. The only Protestant service is Anglican, which is held in a Greek monastery near the Church of the Nativity.

Because the Armenians of Jerusalem and the Orthodox Church subscribe to the Julian calendar for ecclesiastical services, their Christmas observances are held on January 19 and January 7, respectively.

"Merry Christmas" might be heard in Hebrew, *Mo'adim Lesimkha,* or in Arabic, *Idah Saidan Wa Sanah Jadidah. See also* **Armenia; Christmas Old Style, Christmas New Style; Church of the Nativity.**

• LEBANON. Some 25 percent of the population is Christian, belonging to the Maronite (branch of the Roman Catholic Church), Orthodox, Armenian, and Protestant churches. The Orthodox and Armenian faiths particularly adhere to the Julian calendar for ecclesiastical observances.

The Christmas season opens on St. Barbara's Day, December 4, with feasting, charitable acts, and masked children soliciting goodies from homes. At the family feast, someone portrays St. Barbara dressed in white with a crown. Muslims in Lebanon often participate in secular Christmas Eve celebrations including a dinner and presents, particularly when the Muslim holy month of Ramadan coincides with the Christmas season.

During the weeks prior to Christmas, shops are decorated with western paraphernalia, and Christmas trees, consisting of plastic varieties or of cypress branches, are decorated with shooting stars, colored balls, tinsel, or homemade ornaments. Tradition once held that children received holiday gifts only on New Year's Day, but now Christmas brings *Papa Noel* (Santa Claus) and gifts as well, and the Social Affairs Ministry in Beirut may sponsor gift parties for those children and orphans who have suffered from the ravages of war.

Christmas Eve is spent strictly as a religious holiday, and total fasting commences at sundown in preparation for the Midnight Mass and communion. Immediately prior to the mass, young men demonstrate their skill in ringing an array of church bells, heralding the service. During the service, which extends nearly until dawn, it is customary to have a young infant brought forward to the altar. There, as the priest rests the Holy Book on its head, he reads the Gospel account of the Nativity. As the service closes, the priest initiates the *Salaam* (Touch of Peace) by touching the person to his right, who touches the one next to him, and so forth, until the touch has fallen on all the congregation. Afterwards, families retire to social gatherings and visitations, where the traditional offering is sugar-coated almonds, and the Christmas menu features roast turkey.

Christians and Muslims celebrate New Year's Day alike with social gatherings and games of chance which predict the future. Children traditionally receive a monetary token from their father at this time. "Merry Christmas" is said in Arabic, *Idah Saidan Wa Sanah Jadidah.*

• SAUDI ARABIA. The country is entirely Muslim, and public celebrations of Christmas are not tolerated in any form. However, European and other foreign Christian settlements, such as those housing personnel working with various oil companies, are permitted to hold private holiday observances according to the customs of their parent countries.

• SYRIA. The Christian minority primarily belongs to the Orthodox and Armenian churches. Families gather outdoors on Christmas Eve with lighted candles and ignite a bonfire. While singing carols, the family observes the fire, for its pattern of burning predicts the type of luck in store for the new year. After the fire dies out, each person makes a

A view of Bethlehem (also called Beit Lahm in some older sources) in the 1850s. From William M. Thomson, The Land and the Book *(New York: Harper & Bros., 1859[?]).*

wish and jumps over the embers. Christmas Eve services also include a bonfire of vines to honor the Magi. Christmas Day is spent quietly with a pre-dawn church service, and the dinner may consist of chicken, oranges, nuts, and pastries.

On Epiphany Eve, the Gentle Camel of Jesus or Youngest Camel brings gifts to children. According to legend, the youngest camel in the Magi's caravan en route to Bethlehem nearly expired from exhaustion. Determined to see the Christ Child, the camel's faith and resolve brought great reward, for the Babe granted the little camel immortality. He now returns each year as the bearer of Syrian Christmas gifts. Before retiring for bed, children often prepare bowls of water and wheat for the Camel, who rewards the good with gifts and the naughty with a black mark on the wrist. "Merry Christmas" is *Idah Saidan Wa Sanah Jadidah* (Arabic).

• TURKEY. Islam predominates, Turkey's Christians numbering less than 1 percent of the population. Following the Orthodox faith, they observe Christmas by the Julian calendar, January 7. Christmas is a three-day festival with feasting and entertaining. Typical cuisine includes coffee, sweetmeats, fruit, *lebban* (sour milk), *baklava* (honey cake), *etli fasulye* (broth with beans and lamb), *ic pilar* (rice with pinenuts), *labmacun dolmasi* (stuffed cabbage leaves), *borek* (fried pastry stuffed with meat or cheese), tomato-and-cucumber salad with olive oil and vinegar, and *kadayif* (fruit pastry). "Merry Christmas" in Turkish is *Noeliniz Ve Yeni Yiliniz Kutlu Olsun. See also* **Christmas Old Style, Christmas New Style; Epiphany.**

Midnight Mass
See **Christmas Masses**

Miracle Down Under
See **The Christmas Visitor**

Miracle in the Wilderness

(1992). Made-for-television adventure, based on a novella of the same title by Paul Gallico.

Having settled on a ranch in the northwestern American frontier, Jericho Adams (Kris Kristofferson), his wife Dora (Kim Cattrall), and his infant son are captured by a raiding party of the Blackfoot Nation, led by Chief Many Horses (Sheldon Peters Wolfchild). Four years ago, the chief's son had died after attempting to attack Adams. Now Many Horses would avenge the death by giving Adams's baby to a barren wife, Little Deer (Joannelle Nadine Romero), by giving Dora to one of his braves, and then by having Adams die as a warrior.

After burning Adams's home and escorting the prisoners into their camp, the Blackfoot witness an unusual scene: a doe giving birth in winter out of season. They infer that something magical is at hand. Because the occasion happens to be Christmas Eve, Dora, a "church-going woman," seizes the opportunity to share the miracle of Christmas with her captors. As Many Horses translates to his people, Adams, well versed in Indian lore, converts Dora's narration into characters more familiar to the Blackfoot.

In Adams's version, Mary, a fourteen-year-old Indian maiden, is to be wed to the brave Joseph, a mighty hunter. An eagle ("winged messenger") brings the Annunciation to Mary, while the Great Spirit, appearing as a white stallion, encourages Joseph in a dream to take Mary as his wife, regardless of her pregnancy. The two journey across the plains to the annual Sun Dance, where many different tribes convene, such as the Sioux, Cheyenne, Cherokee, and Cree. At Jesus' birth, the ox kneels and, empowered with speech, asks that the animals be protected from hunger and thirst, and that everyone live together in peace. Three Wise Men come bearing gifts: a Sioux with a peace pipe, a Mandan with a medicine bag and beaver skin, and a Plains Cree with a bow and quiver of arrows. Dora concludes the story with Jesus' death and resurrection and hopes that someday, all mankind will live together as brothers.

Apparently discarding the story as a fable for children, Many Horses is more impressed when Dora prevents Adams from killing one of the braves. Such an action is most remarkable for a woman in his eyes, and believes that she possesses great power. Adams prevails in a final duel with the chief but spares him as well, for Dora's sake. This and the strange story of a baby have worked their magic on Many Horses, however, for he elects to push onward into

Canada with his people and leave Adams, Dora, and son in peace. On Christmas Day, a cavalry unit rescues them.

The picture concludes by showing a portion of a statement made in 1896 by Mountain Chief, last war chief of the Blackfoot Nation. He asked, regarding the time of winter feasting, was it because of the cold that everyone sat around honoring each other, or was it because that was the time when the white man's God was born a baby boy?

With John Dennis Johnston, David Oliver, Rino Thunder, Steve Reevis, Peter Alan Morris, Otakuye Conroy, Matthew E. Montoya. Written by Michael Michaelian, Jim Byrnes. Based on a novella by Paul Gallico. Produced by Wayne Morris. Directed by Kevin James Dobson. A Ruddy and Morgan production. Warner Home Video. Color. 88 min.

Miracle on 34th Street

Highly popular motion picture drama of 1947 with two principal remakes, among others, based on a story by screenwriter Valentine Davies about a man convinced that he is Santa Claus. Having annually enjoyed Macy's Thanksgiving Day parade from his New York City apartment, Davies, concerned over Christmas commercialism, is said to have conceived the idea for *Miracle* while waiting in line at a department store.

Motion pictures are often based on a previously published book or story, but with *Miracle on 34th Street*, the film came first. Davies pitched the idea to his friend, George Seaton, who not only wrote the screenplay for the 1947 picture and the 1994 remake, but directed the original picture as well. Only after the 1947 film's release did Davies receive any invitation to publish his story as a little novel. Compared to the film versions, though, the novel pales in popularity.

• 1947 MOTION PICTURE VERSION. When a jolly old gentleman named Kris Kringle (Edmund Gwenn) replaces a drunken Santa in Macy's Thanksgiving Day parade, store representative Doris Walker (Maureen O'Hara) hires him to play Santa in their toy department. Kris forms a close friendship with Doris and her six-year-old daughter, Susan (nine-year-old Natalie Wood), but finds that personal problems have made them skeptics toward fantasy, Santa Claus, and love.

Realizing that Susan has lead a much too serious life devoid of simple childhood pleasures, Kris introduces her to the world of imagination by teaching her how to pretend to be a monkey. Kris's kind manner, real beard, and ability to converse with a little Dutch girl in her native language at Macy's almost convince Susan that Kris is truly Santa. To test him, she requests a real house in which to live, instead of her mother's New York apartment.

Because Kris insists that he is Santa Claus, an altercation with Macy's psychologist lands Kris in a mental hospital, and a mental competency hearing follows on Christmas Eve. Defended by Doris's friend, attorney Fred Gailey (John Payne), Kris is declared to be Santa Claus when the U.S. Postal Service delivers thousands of letters to Kris at the courthouse.

On Christmas morning Fred, Doris, and Susan attend a social at the Brooks Memorial Home for the Aged, where Kris is resident and host, but Susan's failure to find some evidence of her dream house under the Christmas tree there practically shatters her newly acquired faith in Kris. On the way home, however, a beaming Susan discovers a particular house for sale and insists that it's *her* house, that Kris meant for her to have it. Doris and Fred only humor her whim, until they spy Kris's cane standing by the fireplace and become total believers.

With Gene Lockhart, Porter Hall, William Frawley, Jerome Cowan, Philip Tonge. Written and directed by George Seaton. Produced by William Perlberg. 20th Century–Fox Film Corporation. 20th Century–Fox Home Entertainment Video. B & W. 96 min.

In 1948 this original version received four Academy Award nominations, including Best Picture, and won three Awards for Best Original Story (Davies), Best Screenplay (Seaton), and Best Supporting Actor (Edmund Gwenn). On receiving his Award, Gwenn, who played Kris Kringle, remarked, "Now I know there's a Santa Claus!" That same year the original film also won Golden Globe Awards for Best Screenplay and Best Supporting Actor.

• 1973 Made-for-Television Version. This remake closely follows the original picture, with the following minor differences. Doris Walker becomes Karen Walker (Jane Alexander), and attorney Fred Gailey becomes Bill Schaffner (David Hartman). The characters of Susan Walker (Suzanne Davidson) and Kris Kringle (Sebastian Cabot) remain as before. Kris converses with a little girl in Spanish instead of Dutch; Dr. Pierce at the Brooks Memorial Home for the Aged receives an emphysema machine instead of an x-ray machine; in Kris's game of pretending, Susan is a clam instead of a monkey.

With Roddy McDowall, Jim Backus, Tom Bosley, David Doyle. Written by Jeb Rosebrook. Produced by Norman Rosemont. Directed by Fielder Cook. Color. 120 min. Video N/A.

• 1994 Motion Picture Version. Because neither Macy's nor Gimble's department store would allow the use of its name for this film (though both allowed it for the previous two versions), Macy's becomes C. F. Cole's, and the competition is Shopper's Express. This time Kriss (spelled with a double "s"— Richard Attenborough) resides at the Mt. Carmel Senior Center, wears glasses, sports a shorter beard, communicates with a deaf child by sign language, and falls victim to a plot by Shopper's Express to remove him legally as their competition. Dorey Walker (Elizabeth Perkins) and her daughter Susan (Mara Wilson) remain skeptical as before, and Dorey's friend, attorney Bryan Bedford (Dylan McDermott), defends Kris without the help of the U.S. Postal Service. Dorey and Bryan wed (in the previous two versions, the couple only contemplate marriage), and Susan wishes for a dream house as well as a baby brother.

Two particular scenes reflect a 1990s sensibility: Bryan does not invoke the name of any specific deity while saying grace over a meal with Dorey and Susan, and the name on the newlyweds' mailbox reads "Walker-Bedford."

With J. T. Walsh, James Remar, Jane Leeves, Simon Jones, William Windom, Robert Prosky. Written by George Seaton, John Hughes. Produced by John Hughes. Directed by Les Mayfield. 20th Century–Fox Film Corporation. Fox Video. Color. 114 min.

• Other Versions. Obscure television adaptations include those for 1955, 1956 (*Meet*

Mr. Kringle), and 1959. The 1947 *Miracle* was also the basis for Meredith Willson's 1963 Broadway musical, *Here's Love*.

Mr. Magoo's Christmas Carol
See **A Christmas Carol** (FILM AND TELEVISION VERSIONS)

Mistletoe
Common name for a variety of small, parasitic, evergreen shrubs with small, green flowers and white, sticky berries, native to the United States (*Phoradendron flavescens*) and Europe (*Viscum album*). They infest trees such as apple, pine, fir, juniper, and (rarely) oak; the leafless, flowering, dwarf variety (*Arceuthobium pusillum*) is an especially lethal parasite.

The holiday custom of kissing under sprigs of mistletoe derives in part from the pre–Christian Celtic Druids of Gaul and the British Isles, who held oak trees and mistletoe as highly sacred, probably because they rarely found the latter growing on oaks. In ceremonies to gather the mistletoe from oak trees during the sixth day of the moon, Druid priests wearing long, white robes cut the shrub with golden sickles, after which worshippers below caught the mistletoe in white sheets, taking care that the holy plant never touched the ground. Two white bulls were then sacrificed to consecrate the event.

With a name that means "all-heal" in the Celtic language, mistletoe was sought as a medicinal, an antidote for poisons (mistletoe itself is quite toxic), an aphrodisiac, a fertility agent for humans and animals (symbolized by a kiss), and a talisman against evil. Homes usually sported sprigs fastened over doorways for good luck and as an emblem of good will, and guests who passed beneath received kisses of friendship. Along the same line, two enemies meeting under trees bearing mistletoe traditionally observed a truce for a day.

A tale from Scandinavian mythology lends further support for kissing under mistletoe. The tale concerns Balder, god of light and son of Odin (Woden) and Frigga, king and queen of the Norse gods, respectively. When Balder foresaw his own death in a dream, Frigga exacted a promise from all creatures, elements, and everything that existed on the earth and under it that no harm would befall her son. But in her haste, Frigga overlooked the mistletoe, an error used to the advantage of Balder's enemy, the evil god Loki. As the other gods hurled spears and arrows at the now seemingly invincible Balder, Loki armed an arrow with mistletoe and gave it to Balder's brother, the blind god Hoder, who delivered the fatal shot. Weeping bitter tears that were transformed into the white berries of mistletoe, Frigga ultimately succeeded in reviving her son with acts of love and kindness. In her joy, she vowed that nevermore would mistletoe cause harm to anyone, but would symbolize love and good will. As a token of those symbols, Frigga kissed all who passed beneath any tree which bore mistletoe and decreed that her subjects would forever do likewise.

Whereas kissing is well associated with

A branch of mistletoe, hung by a cord from a rafter. Illustration by Randolph Caldecott from The Sketch Book of Washington Irving.

Punch with a woodland sprite in the mistletoe. Punch, *December 1849.*

mistletoe, the precise origins of its association with Christmas remain unknown. Unlike most pagan winter holiday symbols which have received Christian analogies, no Christian substitute definitively exists for mistletoe. Some have preferred to interpret the biblical admonition to salute one another with a holy kiss (the kiss of peace, Romans 16:16) as a free license for kissing under the mistletoe.

Until Christmas trees became fashionable in England in the mid–1800s, mistletoe in that country had gained considerable popularity in decorative devices variously termed "kissing boughs," "kissing rings," "kissing balls," and "kissing bunches." These consisted of hoops overlaid with evergreen garlands and with streamers extending upward to a central point. Added features may have included apples, nuts, oranges, lighted candles, three small dolls representing the Holy Family, and a sprig of mistletoe hung from the center. Mounted from conspicuous points overhead, kissing boughs encouraged holiday romance, especially during the Victorian era. Traditionally, ladies caught under the bough were to allow them-

selves to be kissed by a gentleman, and for each kiss bestowed, the gentleman plucked one berry and gave it to the lady; when no berries remained, the kissing bough lost its romantic spell. Another superstition held that a maiden not kissed under the mistletoe at Christmastime would not marry during the coming year.

Banning mistletoe from churches was common during the nineteenth century, the reasons cited ranging from its association with the fertility rites of Druids to an abuse of the kiss of peace as mentioned above. Mistletoe was not altogether banned from medieval churches, however, for at York Minster the clergy often placed a bough of it on the altar at Christmas as a prelude to the traditional pardoning of criminals and other malefactors for the season. The ban was unknown in eighteenth-century England, as attested by the dramatist and poet John Gay (1685–1732), who wrote of contemporary "temples" (churches) bedecked with holly, laurel, and mistletoe.

In England and the United States, kissing under the mistletoe has survived as a popular Christmas custom. In Austria, a related custom on New Year's Eve (St. Sylvester's Day) involves the grotesque creature "Sylvester." An old, ugly, pagan entity who wears a wreath of mistletoe and was renamed for the fourth-century Pope St. Sylvester I, Sylvester lies in wait for maidens to pass beneath evergreen boughs hanging from the ceiling, when he seizes and kisses them. But at midnight, as a representative of the old year, he is symbolically driven out with the dawning new year.

See also **Christmas plants.**

Moore, Clement Clarke

See **A Visit from St. Nicholas**

Moravian Church

An evangelical Protestant denomination founded in Saxony in the eighteenth century, the Moravian Church is the originator of the Christmas Eve lovefeast, a service that has become popular in other denominations. Other Moravian Christmas traditions are also worthy of note.

Moravians (officially the *Unitas Fratrum* or Unity of the Brethren) arrived in America in 1735, establishing a temporary settlement in Savannah, Georgia, and then permanent settlements in Pennsylvania (e. g., Bethlehem and Lititz) in 1740 and in Salem (now Winston-Salem), North Carolina, in 1753. Today the Moravians number about 750,000 worldwide, the Moravian Church in America comprising over 54,000 members.

Moravian Christmas customs commence with Advent, its four Sundays offering alternative concepts to those embraced by the Roman Catholic, Episcopal, Lutheran, and Anglican churches regarding the coming of Christ. Specifically through Gospel passages, the first Advent Sunday is devoted to Jesus' triumphal entry into Jerusalem as the Messiah; the second, Christ's second coming at the Final Judgment; the third, His work of missions and healing in the world; the fourth, John's proclamation that Jesus is Christ. The services include hosannas and other hymns of praise.

Christmas decorations include those commonly present in respective countries or locales, yet two remain traditionally Moravian. One is the Christmas Star, large, three-dimensional, multi-pointed, and illuminated, which originated in the mid–1800s at a Moravian school in Niesky, Germany. Subsequently such stars were produced by a former student, Pieter Verbeek, with son Harry at their Herrnhut Star Factory. When war closed this establishment, other Moravian groups produced the decoration. Hanging in the home, the star was fashioned as a reminder of the stars of Heaven, the star that guided the Wise Men, and Christ as the star that arose from Jacob (Numbers 24:17). The second decoration, the *Putz* (German, "finery"; sometimes translated "decoration"), consists of an elaborate Nativity scene with traditional figures of the Holy Family, shepherds, Wise Men, and angels, along with realistic landscapes that feature period buildings, streams, animals, moss, other flora, and whatever else the imagination may invent. The figures may be centuries-old heirlooms or purchased elsewhere. A *Putz* may be arranged on a table in the home, adorn the floor beneath the Christmas tree, or consume an entire room, and communities may sponsor a large *Putz*, such as that created annually in Bethlehem, Pennsylvania. Perhaps it was not the first *Putz* to arrive in America, but one of the earliest on record was that erected in Bethabara, North Carolina, in 1760.

A feature of Christmas Eve services is the "lovefeast," a custom observed not only at this time of year but also during other church festivals. First introduced into the Moravian Church in 1727, the lovefeast is patterned after the agape fellowships of the early Apostolic Church. The lovefeast is primarily a song service, and usually there is no formal sermon. During the service the congregation also partakes of a simple, symbolic meal, which usually consists of slightly sweetened buns and a beverage (usually sweet coffee) served by women sacristans or *dieners* (servers) in white dress with *haube* (lace cap) assisted by men of the congregations. The congregation consumes these two emblems in unison, yet they have no sacramental significance.

During the Christmas Eve lovefeast each member of the congregation also receives a lighted, beeswax candle, the Moravian Christmas candle, trimmed with red or white paper. The church is darkened, and after all have received their tapers, a child sings two lines of "Morning Star," a Moravian hymn composed by

Dr. John Scheffler (1624–1677). The congregation antiphonally repeats these lines, and all sing the final line in unison. This custom originated in 1747 at a children's Christmas Eve service in Marienborn, Wetteravia, during which Bishop John Watteville provided instruction by singing lines of hymns in the form of questions, and the children would respond with the next lines in song as well. Then, to impress the Nativity message upon the children more fully, the bishop distributed lighted tapers trimmed with red ribbons as respective symbols of Christ's burning love and His sacrificial blood. Herrnhut adopted the practice a year later, and the custom spread to Bethlehem, Pennsylvania, in 1756, then to the communities of Bethabara and Bethania, North Carolina, in 1762.

For those congregations that still adhere to the waning custom of a New Year's Eve "Watch Night," church musicians at Watch Night services abruptly terminate the sermon, which often remains unfinished, at the stroke of midnight. The congregation then sings the German chorale "Now Thank We All Our God."

For Epiphany, missions receive emphasis on or near January 6, traditionally the date commemorating the Wise Men's arrival in Bethlehem.

See also **Advent**; **Epiphany**.

Mrs. Santa Claus

(1996). Made-for-television musical starring Angela Lansbury in the title role.

The year is 1910. Feeling neglected by her husband Santa (Charles Durning) each year during the Christmas rush, Mrs. Anna Claus yields to a whim and takes the reindeer sleigh out for a spin around the world six days before Christmas. She becomes trapped in the Big Apple when she attempts an emergency landing in Manhattan's Lower East Side because of inclement weather and Cupid suffers an injury.

While Cupid recuperates, Anna, posing as a revolutionary Mrs. North, participates in a women's suffrage march and fights for better child labor laws after observing intolerable working conditions at the Tavish Toy Company, which employs children. Outraged by Tavish's cheap toys and its motto, "It only has to last till Christmas," she succeeds in staging a citywide boycott of Tavish Toys.

Augustus Tavish (Terrence Mann), seeking revenge, discovers Anna's true identity and captures her reindeer on Christmas Eve. But Tavish's desire to ruin Christmas stems from his having lost a prized Christmas teddy bear as a child. Discerning this, Anna replaces the bear, Tavish reforms, and Anna returns to a more appreciative Santa just in time for Christmas Eve rounds.

In 1998, *Mrs. Santa Claus* won an Emmy Award for Outstanding Individual Achievement in Hairstyling for a Miniseries or a Special. It received Emmy nominations for Outstanding Achievements in Art Direction, Choreography, and Costume Design.

With Michael Jeter, Lynsey Bartilson, Bryan Murray, David Norona, and Debra Wiseman. Music and lyrics by Jerry Herman. Choreography by Rob Marshall. Written by Mark Saltzman. Produced by J. Boyce Harman, Jr. Directed by Terry Hughes. Hallmark Entertainment. Hallmark Home Entertainment Video. Color. 91 min.

Ms. Scrooge

See **A Christmas Carol** (Film and Television Versions)

Mumming

See **Christmas Drama**

The Muppet Christmas Carol

See **A Christmas Carol** (Film and Television Versions)

N

National Lampoon's Christmas Vacation

(1989). Motion picture comedy, also known as *Christmas Vacation*. It is the third in a series of four *Vacation* films, the other three being *National Lampoon's Vacation* (1983), *National Lampoon's European Vacation* (1985), and *National Lampoon's Vegas Vacation* (1997). In each of these, Chevy Chase stars as the well-meaning but wacky Clark Griswold, Jr., to whom life seems bent on dealing a consistently bad hand. Despite his slapstick antics, misadventures, and nearly-completed-but-never-finished projects, his lovely wife Ellen (Beverly D'Angelo) remains patiently supportive. The actors for their two children, teenager Audrey and younger Rusty, vary from film to film. These and seventeen other films comprising the *National Lampoon* collection are based on the satire and humor rampant in the *National Lampoon Magazine*.

Sporting a loose plot, *National Lampoon's Christmas Vacation* satirizes all of the traditional family values of the holiday. At Clark's invitation, obnoxious, argumentative parents and in-laws crowd into the Griswold home, the most disgusting of whom is Eddy (Randy Quaid), a lazy, hillbilly cousin. Chaos commences as Clark wrestles to decorate his house with 25,000 twinkling lights and battles poorly wired circuits. Aunt Bethany (Mae Questel), a senile lady bearing boxed, wrapped gifts of a live cat and lime Jell-O, arrives on Christmas Eve along with Uncle Lewis (William Hickey), whose cigar promptly flash-incinerates the Griswolds' dried-out Christmas tree. Although the tree is replaced, the cat, having escaped from its prison, settles down to gnawing on a string of Christmas lights and succeeds in vaporizing herself through electrocution. Aunt Bethany deems the "Pledge of Allegiance to the Flag" as an appropriate grace before dinner and the family sits down to eat. Later, pandemonium erupts when a squirrel residing in the Christmas tree springs out at Clark and attracts

Cousin Eddy's dog. The two varmints run amok, making a shambles of the house.

Topping off the evening, Clark's much-anticipated Christmas "bonus" arrives: a one-year membership in the "Jelly-of-the-Month Club." An irate Clark delivers a litany of unseasonal adjectives against his employer. Suddenly Eddy the vigilante appears with Clark's boss in tow. Soon thereafter, a police squad arrives and prepares to arrest the hillbilly on kidnapping charges. After realizing, however, that cutting Christmas cash bonuses has seriously damaged not just Clark's morale but that of his other employees, the boss reconsiders, reinstates the gift, and drops all charges.

As the family gathers outdoors for a final scene, Clark waxes sentimental over what appears to be the Christmas Star in the heavens. Uncle Lewis, tossing his lit cigar into the storm drain, shatters the illusion with a terse reminder that it's just the beacon atop the sewage treatment plant. Just then, exploding sewer gas shatters the heavens and sends the Griswold reindeer display rocketing into space. Inspired, Aunt Bethany renders a chorus of "The Star-Spangled Banner."

With Diane Ladd, John Randolph, E. G. Marshall, Doris Roberts, Juliette Lewis, Johnny Galecki. Written by John Hughes. Produced by John Hughes, Tom Jacobson. Directed by Jeremiah Chechik. Hughes Entertainment in association with Warner Brothers Pictures. Warner Home Video. Color. 97 min.

Nativity

Derived from the Latin *nativus* (birth). The capitalized form implies not only the birth of Jesus Christ, but also the account of His birth as described in New Testament narratives. Of the four Gospels (Matthew, Mark, Luke, and John), which detail the life of Christ, only Matthew and Luke present the familiar Nativity or Christmas story, and the two versions differ in some respects.

Luke's version begins with the angel Gabriel's appearance to the Virgin Mary in

Bethlehem, where indeed they find "Mary, and Joseph, and the Babe lying in a manger" (2:15–16). When they depart, they spread the news of the Child's birth (2:17–18).

Although Matthew's account first centers on Joseph's doubts about Mary's pregnancy (which he supposes to be illegitimate) and the reassurance bestowed through God in a dream (1:18–25), Matthew primarily focuses upon the "wise men from the east" (2:1–18). Guided by a star, they first visit King Herod the Great in Jerusalem, looking for the child who is "born King of the Jews." Fearing that his throne is in jeopardy, Herod feigns a desire to worship the child and orders the Wise Men to find Him and report his whereabouts. The Wise Men find the child and present gifts of gold, frankincense, and myrrh. But instead of reporting back to Herod, they depart, after which an irate Herod, hoping to destroy the child, orders the massacre of (presumably) all male children in Bethlehem who are two years old and under, "according to the time which he had diligently enquired of the wise men" (2:16 states that *all* children in this age range were slaughtered, which would imply females as well). Warned by God in a dream, however, the Holy Family flees beforehand into Egypt to escape Herod's wrath.

Speculations vary widely concerning the number of children that were killed in the massacre (which has come to be known as "the Slaughter of the Innocents"). According to Greek, Syrian, and medieval sources, the victims totaled 14,000, 64,000, and 144,000, respectively. Because the Bethlehem of 2,000 years ago was quite small, modern writers are more realistic, estimating six to twenty casualties. Oddly, the Jewish historian Flavius Josephus (ca. 37–101) makes no mention of the event, yet he describes other atrocities which Herod the Great committed in his final years. It is thought that the number dying in Bethlehem paled in comparison with the numbers of others whom the king had executed.

See also **Star of Bethlehem; Wise Men.**

• POPULAR ASSUMPTIONS. From the Nativity story, several other popular notions have arisen, for which no biblical evidence exists:

1. *Mary rode a donkey to Bethlehem and during the flight to Egypt.* Because Mary was either pregnant or holding the infant Jesus, it is

Mary, Joseph, and the Baby Jesus are depicted in an embossed, chromolithograph scrap. The scrap was made in Germany in the 1870s or 1880s.

Nazareth of Galilee with the news that she, being blessed among women, will bear Jesus, that He will be called the "Son of the Highest," and that His kingdom will be everlasting (1:26–38). (This announcement is known as the Annunciation.) As the story continues (2:1–7), the Roman emperor, Augustus Caesar, has levied a tax or census on all Roman provinces. Because each man must report to his city of birth, Joseph, also presently of Nazareth, journeys with Mary, his "espoused" wife, down to Bethlehem of Judea. Pregnant and at term, Mary delivers a son in Bethlehem, wraps Him in swaddling clothes, and places Him in a manger, "because there was no room for them in the inn." The only other group of people who receive news of this special birth are shepherds, to whom an angelic host pays a nocturnal visit, declaring that a Savior is born in Bethlehem (2:8–11).

The angels give the shepherds a sign for recognizing the Child: "Ye shall find the babe wrapped in swaddling clothes, lying in a manger" (2:12). The shepherds decide to go to assumed that she rode on some beast of burden, such as a donkey; however, this is only an assumption.

2. *Jesus was born at midnight.* That shepherds were "keeping watch over their flocks by night" when herald angels appeared is fuel for the assumption of a midnight birth.

3. *Jesus was born in a stable.* That Jesus' cradle was a manger evokes the image of a conventional stable. At that time and in that part of the world, however, inns and other establishments often housed their livestock close by in sections of the same building, for stables as we know them did not exist. Instead, Jesus could have been born in one of several caves around Bethlehem. We find this evidence from the early Christian writer Justin Martyr (ca. 100–ca. 165), who spoke of Jesus' birth in one such cave. Lending further support, Origen reported that even the pagans had known of the cave where Jesus was born.

4. *Jesus was born in the spring.* The uncertainty surrounding the specific year of Jesus' birth also applies to the time of year when Jesus was born. Many believe, however, that shepherds tending flocks in fields implies the spring of the year, especially the lambing season. Some have suggested that Caesar would have demanded a census only during the convenience of spring but this suggestion is unreliable, for Rome took little note of its subjects' lifestyles. With no reliable evidence either for or against a springtime birth, by the fourth century the Church had established Dec. 25 as the date for marking Christ's birth. By the eighth century, the Church was observing the Feast of the Annunciation in the spring on March 25, a logical date nine months prior to Christmas. (*See* "Christmas Day.")

5. *Shepherds and Wise Men visited the manger on the same night.* Although Nativity scenes traditionally show shepherds and Wise Men or Kings together around the manger, Matthew's Gospel suggests otherwise. Luke clearly states that the shepherds "came with haste" to the manger after learning of Jesus' birth. But there may have been a two-year hiatus until the Wise Men came on the scene, and this is implied in Matthew's story. King Herod ordered the slaughter of Bethlehem children two years old and under after learning

A fifteenth century woodcut shows Mary and the Baby Jesus on a donkey, followed by Joseph on their flight to Egypt. The popular imagination often pictures Mary riding a donkey on the journey to Bethlehem and the flight into Egypt, but there is no mention of a donkey in the scriptural story. From Henry Poulaille, La Grande et belle Bible des noëls anciens *(Paris: Michel, 1941).*

specifically when the Wise Men first saw the star. It has also been suggested that, if the Magi visited Jesus at some time after His birth, the visit would have taken place in His parents' home, and not in a cave or stable. Indeed, Matthew's account states that the Wise Men found the Child in a "house" in Bethlehem.

6. *An ox and an ass stood by the manger and watched over the Babe.* Since the Middle Ages, Nativity scenes and other depictions of the Nativity have included at least these two animals. They first appeared as beasts adoring the Christ Child in the Gospel of Pseudo-Matthew from the New Testament Apocrypha, which derived from Isaiah 1:3, "The ox knoweth his owner, and the ass his master's crib...."

• WORKS OF ART. Artistic portrayals of the Nativity originated in the early Church principally after the Roman emperor Constantine the Great (ca. 274–337) embraced Christianity. In the West, the Church initially utilized paintings and mosaics to teach biblical scenes and stories to a largely illiterate laity, for only the clergy and a handful of scholars understood the Latin liturgy and Latin translations of the Scriptures at the time. One of the earliest subjects was the Madonna or Virgin Mary herself; legend, but only legend, claims that St. Luke the Evangelist created some of the oldest extant pencil sketches of her. Some of the earliest mosaics of Madonna and Child appear on the walls of Roman Catacombs. Those of St. Priscilla depict the prophet Isaiah pointing to a star above their heads. Another shows shepherds and the Three Kings visiting the Child in His crib, while in a similar scene from a fourth-century sarcophagus, the Magi are kneeling. The Virgin rarely appeared on Christian sarcophagi, however. Early depictions of Madonna and Child within a church also include those found on fifth-century medallions of the triumphal arch in Rome's Church of Santa Maria Maggiore. Because the Church especially favored the subject of Madonna and Child, artists rendered them not only in portraits but

in scenes from the early life of Christ. Religious Christmas art in the West, therefore, can be divided into the following principal themes: "The Annunciation," "The Nativity," "Adoration of the Shepherds," "Adoration of the Magi," and "The Flight into Egypt."

"The Annunciation," one of the most frequent scenes of Renaissance art, is usually rendered in a home setting with Mary and the angel Gabriel elegantly dressed. An open text nearby implies her piety in reading the Scriptures. Positions of the angel and Mary vary, the angel kneeling with Mary standing or *vice versa*, while Giotto (Italian, 1267?–1337) has both kneeling (Padua). Gabriel, usually winged, generally bears a spray of lilies, symbolic of purity, or these flowers may appear in a vase nearby. There may be a banner somewhere on the work with the words "Ecce Ancilla Domini" ("Behold the handmaid of the Lord"), for Mary's reaction is most often that of quiet submission. The work of Fra Angelico (Italian, 1400?–1455) in the Prado Museum, Madrid, conveys the medieval notion regarding Mary's

An eighteenth-century woodcut of the Angel Gabriel announcing to Mary the news that she is to give birth to the Son of God. This woodcut shows Mary interrupted while reading the Scriptures, a common theme. From Henry Poulaille, La Grande et belle Bible des noëls anciens *(Paris: Michel, 1941).*

The Annunciation in a late nineteenth century, highly romanticized version, showing all the common elements: the stem of lillies that Gabriel holds, the dove, and a pious Mary reading Scriptures (here in a very modern-looking book). From John Fleetwood, The Light in the East *(National Publishing Co. and Jones Brothers, 1874).*

divine conception: Rays of light from heaven beam toward her through which a dove emerges, symbolic of the Holy Spirit. Robert Campin (Flemish, 1378?–1444) replaces the dove with a minute figure of the infant Christ bearing a cross as a futuristic emblem (Metropolitan Museum of Art). Other works may depict the dove hovering nearby. Whereas most renderings feature one angel, Andrea del Sarto (Florentine, 1486–1530), Tintoretto (Venetian, ca. 1518–1594), and Fra Bartolommeo (Florentine, 1472?–1517) present an angelic choir. Later renderings such as those of the nineteenth century incorporate a greater sense of realism. For instance, in a painting by Dante Gabriel Rossetti (English, 1828–1882) titled "Ecce Ancilla Domini" (a portrait of his younger sister Christina, Tate Gallery, London) Mary is frankly terrified at the presence of a wingless Gabriel, and in a rendering by James Tissot (French, 1836–1902) the ghostly specter of Gabriel hovers above Mary slumped on the floor (Brooklyn Museum). Other noted artists include Leonardo da Vinci (Florentine, 1452–1519), Simone Martini (Sienese, ca. 1280–1344), Domenico Veneziano (Florentine, 1405?–1461), Fra Filippo Lippi (Florentine, ca. 1406–1469), Sandro Botticelli (Florentine, 1445–1510), and Jan van Eyck (Flemish, 1390?–1441), the latter of whom presents the Annunciation outdoors, a most unusual setting (Metropolitan Museum of Art).

Set at the mouth of a cave (Fra Angelico's school) or in a traditional stable (Giotto's school), in daylight or at night, "The Nativity" may feature Jesus in a manger and Mary with or without Joseph kneeling or sitting in adoration beside Him. Joseph, seemingly of secondary importance, often occupies a place behind Mary and Jesus, as in works by a follower of Jan Joest (Flemish, active ca. 1515, Metropolitan Museum of Art) and Hugo Van der Goes (Flemish, 1440?–1482, Uffizi Gallery, Florence). Many Nativities feature angels hovering above or beside the manger (in contrast to Luke's Gospel, where they return to heaven after appearing to shepherds); others include shepherds near the manger ("Adoration of the Shepherds"), and still others set the shepherds in the background to receive the message from the heavenly host. Examples include works by

Hugo van der Goes (Uffizi, Florence), in which Jesus lies on the ground with adoring angels and shepherds nearby; a work by Piero Della Francesca (Italian, 1420?–1492) again shows Jesus lying on the ground, with Mary kneeling, and with angels playing lutes and singing (National Gallery, London). Botticelli (National Gallery) combines stable roof with entrance to a cave in which angels not only hover above, but also freely embrace those in attendance around the manger, which symbolizes the union of heaven with mankind through Christ's birth. Virtually all Nativities include the traditional ox and ass (see above), and frequently Jesus, to symbolize the Light of the World, is the principal source of light. Other noted artists who painted Nativity scenes include William Blake (English, 1757–1827), Philippe de Champaigne (French, 1602–1674), Jacopo Bassano (Venetian, ca. 1510–1592), Francisco de Zurbarán (Spanish, 1598–1664), Luca Signorelli (Italian, ca. 1445–1523), Carlo Crivelli (Italian, 1430?–1494?), and Andrea Mantegna (Italian, 1431–1506).

A favorite subject among Catacomb dwellers was the Magi, featured in some twenty mosaics. Numbering from three to six, the Magi appear before Mary, who is enthroned with Jesus lying in her arms. The great masters portrayed the traditional three Magi from two perspectives. In works titled "Journey of the Magi," the Magi, riding on horses (more familiar to the artists than camels), either lead, or are surrounded by, long processions that wind through the countryside. This treatment stems from the *Compagnia de'Magi*, Epiphany processions that were popular in Florence during the Middle Ages, whose members dressed as the Magi and paraded on horses. In one such fresco by Benozzo Gozzoli (Florentine, 1420–1497), the three Magi are likenesses of Lorenzo de' Medici, his grandfather Cosimo, and his father Piero, all of whom were influential Florentine bankers and patrons of the arts during the Renaissance (Medici Chapel, Florence). In "Journey" by Sassetta (Sienese, ca. 1400–1450) the Magi appear as scholars (Metropolitan Museum of Art). On the other hand, works titled "Adoration of the Magi" again incorporate either a cave setting (Fra Angelico, National Gallery) or a stable (Giotto, Padua) with traditional ox

The three Wise Men "saw the young child with Mary his mother, and fell down, and worshiped him; and when they had opened their treasures, they presented unto him gifts, gold, and frankincense, and myrrh" (Matthew 2:11). From John Fleetwood, The Light in the East *(National Publishing Co. and Jones Brothers, 1874).*

and ass present. The Infant Jesus is now somewhat older, for He often is shown sitting naked in Mary's lap with one hand raised in benediction. His nakedness symbolizes His identity with the poor. Usually a large company again has accompanied the three Magi, who appear as lavishly dressed kings. Most often the eldest is shown kneeling before the Babe and kissing His feet in humility while the other two stand or kneel. Whereas their southern colleagues usually featured white-skinned Magi, painters of Northern Europe followed the tradition of portraying one Magus as black. Examples of such "Adorations" include those by Albrecht Dürer (German, 1471–1528, in the Uffizi, Florence) and Quentin Massys (Flemish, 1466?–1530, in the Metropolitan Museum). Yet in these, the eldest white Magus still remains in closest proximity to the Babe. Besides ox and ass, animals such as monkeys and peacocks also have appeared and respectively symbolize sin in the world and the resurrection. Other noted artists include Peter Paul Reubens (Flemish, 1577–1640), Giorgione (Venetian, 1478?–1510), Gentile da Fabriano (Italian, 1370?–1427), Fra Filippo Lippi, Rogier van der Weyden (Flemish, 1399?–1464), and Giovanni di Paolo (Sienese, 1403?–1482?).

The escape from Bethlehem, the "Flight into Egypt," sometimes features Mary riding a donkey and holding the Babe as Joseph or an angel leads the beast. Examples include those by Giotto (Padua), Fra Angelico (Uffizi), and Hans Memling (Flemish, 1435?–1494, in the *Alte Pinakothek*, Munich). Many of the masters preferred a scene in which the Holy Family, now exhausted from a flight through the desert, rests in some fertile locale, hence the title "Rest on the Flight." To this repose, artists sometimes depicted miracles which the Infant Jesus allegedly performed on this flight as detailed in the eighth- or ninth-century apocryphal book the Gospel of Pseudo-Matthew. The "Rest" painting in the Prado Museum, Madrid, by Dutch artist Joachim Patenier (active 1515–1524) depicts a group of King Herod's soldiers in the background questioning laborers cutting grain. This scene is based upon the legend that as the Holy Family journeyed, Jesus obtained some seed from a farmer sowing grain and threw it onto the ground, which instantly yielded fully mature sheaves. Later, in reply to the soldiers' interrogations, the farmer stated that he had seen a woman and child pass by while he was sowing. Seeing the tall sheaves and inferring that months had passed since the sighting, the soldiers abandoned their pursuit. The repose setting was especially favored by German and Flemish masters.

In virtually all western frescoes and paintings, the Virgin wears a blue robe, the traditional color associated with her, and Joseph is depicted as considerably older than Mary, a tradition that coincides with the theme set forth in carols such as "The Cherry Tree Carol."

• FILM AND TELEVISION DEPICTIONS. While several motion pictures dramatize the entire life of Christ, few are centered entirely around the Nativity story alone. The following is a brief summary of notable productions which devote some footage to the Nativity.

The Greatest Story Ever Told (1965), based on a novel of the same title by Fulton Oursler, opens with a brief, anonymous narration from the first chapter of John's Gospel, "In the beginning was the Word...." The scene pauses in a darkened stable, in which the only evidence of humanity lies in the close-up of an infant's hand. Because John does not present an account of the Nativity, the story takes up Matthew's version as the Wise Men seek Jesus through King Herod (Claude Rains). Their individual identities are revealed neither to Herod nor to Joseph (Robert Loggia) nor to Mary (Dorothy McGuire). Each states the significance of the gift he has brought: gold, for the sovereignty of a King; frankincense, to worship God; myrrh, for preservation until time everlasting. The shepherds (from Luke's Gospel) are only incidental characters observing the preceding scenario from a distance, and there are no herald angels. As the Wise Men depart, Joseph hears a voice (not in a dream) telling him to flee. An irate Herod quotes the prophet Jeremiah (35:15): "In Rama was there a voice heard, lamentation, and weeping, and great mourning." He decides to fulfill this prophecy by killing all "newborn" babies in Bethlehem (Matthew 2 indicates all children two years old and under). As the raid commences, the camera pans to an empty manger draped with swaddling clothes. This film was nominated for five Academy Awards, including Best Color Cinematography, Best Art Direction, Best Costume Design, Best Special Effects, and Best Original Music Score. With Max von Sydow, Cyril Delevanti, Frank Silvera, Mark Lenard. Written by James Lee Barrett, Henry Denker, George Stevens. Produced by George Stevens. Directed by George Stevens, David Lean, Jean Negulesco. United Artists. MGM/UA Home Video. Color. 199 min.

Jesus (1979), a motion picture filmed on location in the Holy Land, is reputed to be the most accurate chronicle of the life of Christ, based entirely on Luke's Gospel. With Eli Cohen, Brian Deacon, Peter Frye, Niko Nitai, and Rivka Noiman. Written by Barnet Fishbein. Produced by Richard F. Dalton, John Heyman. Directed by John Krish, Peter Sykes. Inspiration Films and The Genesis Project. Color. 117 min. Video N/A.

Jesus of Nazareth (1977), British-Italian television miniseries based on all four Gospels, is the most complete portrayal of the life of Christ, although it does not always follow the Scriptures to the letter. Opening with the betrothal of Joseph (Yorgo Voyagis) and Mary (Olivia Hussey) in Nazareth, the movie depicts key pre–Nativity events as outlined in Luke 1: the angel's Annunciation to Mary (she converses with a brilliant light flooding through her window; the viewer neither sees nor hears the angel); Mary's meeting with her cousin Elizabeth (Marina Berti), the expectant mother of John the Baptist (the film makes Elizabeth a widow, although Luke states that her husband Zacharias is alive and serves as a priest); Joseph's anguish over Mary's unexpected pregnancy; and Joseph's dream from God about the coming of Jesus. After their wedding comes the journey to Bethlehem, where Joseph settles Mary into a cave that doubles as a stable. As the Star shines over the cave, shepherds arrive following the birth, saying that a "man" told them to come because a Savior had been born (again, no herald angels). Eight days pass, after which Jesus is circumcised in the local synagogue, and the devout Simeon (Ralph Richardson) delivers his prophecy of Jesus as a light unto the Gentiles, outlined in Luke 2:25–35 (according to Luke, Simeon delivers his soliloquy when Jesus is presented in the Temple in Jerusalem forty days after His birth). Returning to the cave, Mary and Joseph find the three Wise Men waiting. Balthasar (James Earl Jones) presents frankincense to perfume the halls of the Mighty; Gaspar (Fernando Rey) presents gold for Kingly rule; and Melchior (Donald Pleasence) presents myrrh, the most precious herb of the Orient as well as the most bitter. It is they who give the warning to flee into Egypt until Herod is dead (Luke writes that Joseph receives the warning from God). The viewer never sees the Wise Men's meeting with Herod (Peter Ustinov), only Herod's rage on their departure from Bethlehem. In the aftermath of the massacre in Bethlehem, Simeon laments over the children by quoting Jeremiah 35:15. This miniseries devotes over one hour to the Nativity. In 1978 the production won a Silver Ribbon Award from the Italian National Syndicate of Film Journalists for Best Cinematography, Best Costume Design, and Best Production Design. With Robert Powell. Written by Anthony Burgess, Suso Cecchi D'Amico, Franco Zeffirelli. Produced by Vincenzo Labella. Directed by Franco Zeffirelli. RAI-ITC Entertainment Productions with Sir Lew Grade. Family Home Entertainment Video. Color. 382 min.

King of Kings (1961) bases its Nativity

scenes on the Gospel of Matthew. The film opens in 63 B.C. during the Roman conquest of Jerusalem, and after some fifty years, according to narrator Orson Welles, Emperor Caesar Augustus appoints an Arab, Herod the Great (Gregoire Aslan), as king of Judea. Following a brief scene in which Joseph (Gerard Tichy) leads Mary (Siobhan McKenna) riding a donkey into Bethlehem, the three Wise Men present their treasures. Instead of the Wise Men revealing their names through character dialogue during their visit, the narrator identifies the Wise Men as Melchior, Caspar, and Balthasar, of Mesopotamia, Persia, and Ethiopia, respectively. They are not shown meeting with Herod beforehand; neither are there shepherds nor an angelic host. Joseph, warned in a dream about Herod's imminent raid on Bethlehem, awakens and flees into Egypt with his family as the soldiers arrive. The film devotes about as much time to the death of Herod alone as it does to the preceding Nativity events. With Jeff Hunter, Edric Connor, Jose Nieto, Adriano Rimoldi, Hurd Hatfield, Ron Randell. Written by Philip Yordon, Ray Bradbury. Produced by Samuel Bronston. Directed by Nicholas Ray. A Metro-Goldwyn-Mayer and Samuel Bronston production. MGM/UA Home Video. Color. 171 min.

Mary, Mother of Jesus (1999) is a television movie that focuses on the relationship between Mary and Jesus and is based on the Gospels of Matthew and Luke. The film opens in Nazareth as the Romans declare that a tax will be due in nine months. Mary (Melinda Kinnaman) receives the Annunciation from the white-robed angel Gabriel (John Light) beside a road where she is working, after which she visits her elder cousin Elizabeth (Geraldine Chaplin), who has been pregnant six months with John the Baptist (Luke 1:5–25). Her husband-priest Zacharias (Edward Hardwicke), previously struck dumb when he doubted Gabriel, recovers his speech at John's birth. After Joseph's (David Threlfall) turmoil over Mary's pregnancy and his dream, the scene turns to Bethlehem, where Jesus has been born in a conventional stable. The shepherds are the first to arrive and relate their experience with the heavenly host (not shown). At the court of King Herod (Hywell Bennett), the Star of Bethlehem is quite visible (contrary to Matthew's account), and Herod receives the three Magi, whose identities otherwise are not revealed. On the following day the Magi visit the manger, after which Herod orders the slaughter of all male children born in Bethlehem within the last six months (also contrary to Matthew). Instead of receiving a warning from God, the Holy Family escapes during the raid. Written by Albert Ross. Produced by Howard Ellis. Directed by Kevin Connor. Hallmark Entertainment and the Shriver Family Film Company. Hallmark Home Video. Color. 94 min.

The Nativity (1978), a television movie, is primarily a romantic, fictional account of the meeting between Joseph and Mary prior to the Nativity, starring John Shea and Madeleine Stowe. Written by Millard Kaufman. Directed by Bernard L. Kowalski. 20th Century–Fox Television. 20th Century–Fox Video. Color. 97 min.

See also **Epiphany; Holy Innocents Day; The Nativity on Film.**

The Nativity (television special)

See **The Nativity** (FILM AND TELEVISION DEPICTIONS)

Nativity Play

See **Christmas Drama**

Nativity Scene

Also known as "manger scene" and "crib." A three-dimensional replica of those characters and events surrounding the birth of Christ as outlined in the Gospels of Matthew and Luke. Traditional Nativity scenes include figures of the infant Jesus, manger or crib, Mary, Joseph, three Wise Men or Kings, shepherds, sheep, and perhaps one or more angels, all of which are usually arranged before or within a rustic, conventional stable or the entrance to a cave. Also traditionally included are the ox and ass, two animals not specifically mentioned in the Gospels (*see* **Nativity** [POPULAR ASSUMPTIONS]). Although they are known worldwide, Nativity scenes reign as the principal, physical symbols of Christmas primarily in southern Europe and Latin America, and in other Spanish-speaking locales. Nativity scenes range from the miniature to life-size.

The earliest Nativity scenes featured a simple replica of the manger. At the Grotto of the Nativity in Bethlehem, St. Helena, mother of Emperor Constantine the Great, is said to have replaced Christ's original manger of clay with one of silver in the fourth century and thus established a shrine at the traditional site of Christ's birth. Rome's Church of St. Mary Major, completed around 440, housed a shrine patterned after that in Bethlehem, to which were added in the seventh century six pieces of wooden boards believed to have served as supports for the original manger (*see* **Church of the Nativity**). During the late Middle Ages, Christmas vespers often included so-called "crib-rocking" ceremonies that recalled the earliest Nativity scenes. In this custom, especially popular in Germany, the priest would place a figure of the Christ Child in a crib and rock it before the altar during the Mass and sing appropriate *Wiegenlieder* (cradle songs). Children in the congregation often rocked a second crib.

Commencing in the tenth century, medieval liturgical dramas first incorporated simple statues of the Virgin with Child lying in a crib (*see* **Christmas Drama** [NATIVITY PLAY]), yet the popularity of the Nativity scene as we know it today is attributed to St. Francis of Assisi, Italy (ca. 1181–1226), a Catholic priest who spent most of his clerical life as missionary and evangelist among the poor. Always believing

that people should understand the Gospel in their own language, St. Francis preached in the vernacular rather than in Latin, which only clerics and scholars understood at the time. In 1223, he laid before Pope Honorius III a novel project designed to bring the Nativity story closer to the minds and hearts of the populace. With Church approval, on Christmas Eve of that same year St. Francis recreated the stable setting in a cave near Greccio, Italy, using live people and animals. One account states that as he sang the Gospel story of the Nativity, the Christ Child radiating brilliant light suddenly appeared in his arms; another version holds that he simply placed a wax figure of the Christ Child in the crib. Many also believe that his musical Nativity served as a foundation for the first Christmas carols (*see* **Christmas Carols**).

The realism that St. Francis brought to the Nativity so profoundly impressed the masses that multiple variations on this theme appeared throughout Christendom. Figures of traditional Nativity characters crafted by professional artisans became popular additions to the crib scene in churches during the sixteenth century, and by the seventeenth century, families were erecting simple Nativity scenes in their homes and either making or collecting figurines as heirlooms. Throughout Europe the

A variety of buildings from what the cataloger called "Christmas Villages," to be spread out under the tree, or with an electric train set-up. They were cardboard with colored cellophane windows like stained glass. The colored sides and roofs were sprinkled with colored glitter, and each building could be electrified by inserting one Christmas tree light bulb in the back. From the Shure Winner Catalog, no. 132 (Chicago: N. Shure, 1939).

A 1939 catalog offered this Nativity scene; also available for half the price was a smaller 14-piece crib set that didn't include the Star of Bethlehem. From the Shure Winner Catalog, *no. 132 (Chicago: N. Shure, 1939).*

eighteenth century brought considerable expansion to the Nativity scene as depictions of local countrysides and characters joined those of Bethlehem. Probably designed to create an even greater sense of familiarity with the subject, such Nativity scenes featured vast landscapes in miniature with trees and forests constructed from twigs or branches, along with moss, grass, flowers, mountains, working waterfalls, rivers with water, and perhaps volcanoes. Contemporary villages included buildings such as the baker's, blacksmith's and butcher's shops; a mill; police force; town hall; fashionable residences; and appropriately costumed figures. In the midst of these remarkable yet historically inaccurate settings stood the simple stable or cave with the Holy Family, shepherds, Three Kings, ox, ass, and angels.

Elaborate Nativity scenes are still constructed today, especially in primarily Roman Catholic countries or areas such as France, Italy, Mexico, Spain, and the southwestern United States, and their dimensions range from those fitting under the Christmas tree to table models to those that fill one or more rooms of the house. In addition to static Nativity scenes which adorn churches and homes, living tableaux involving stately processions through city streets are popular in France and Italy, and the *Putz* (from the German, "to decorate") that is annually built in Bethlehem, Pennsylvania, a city founded by German Moravian immigrants, is a prime example of the community Nativity scene.

Although static Nativity scenes may be erected a few days to several weeks prior to Christmas, a custom prevailing throughout all Roman Catholic regions of the world keeps the crib or manger symbolically empty until Christmas Eve, at which time churches and homes usually participate in ceremonies which add the Christ Child figure. Figures for the Three Kings are either added only on Epiphany (January 6), or, to symbolize their journey, they may be placed some distance away and moved forward each day to arrive at the manger on Epiphany. In Protestant Nativity scenes, all figures usually remain in place from initial setup. Information on specific Nativity scenes and further discussion may be found in the entries for individual countries.

Up to the mid-twentieth century, Nativity scenes sponsored by city officials or private enterprises often graced public property in the United States. Following controversies over the separation of church and state which erupted in the 1960s, many cities across the nation abolished public religious displays, including Nativity scenes, and the trend continues to the present.

Nestor, the Long-Eared Christmas Donkey

(1977). Made-for-television animated story using stop-motion puppets (Animagic), based on a song of the same title written in 1975 by Gene Autry, Don Pfrimmer, and Dave Burgess. They had hoped that their donkey character would gain as much popularity through recordings as had Rudolph with his red nose, but that popularity never materialized. Instead, the animated version has become a holiday favorite.

Raised on Olaf's donkey farm in northern Europe during the Roman Empire, young Nestor receives nothing but taunts and abuse from all the other animals because of his long, floppy ears. Olaf wrongly accuses him of ruining a potentially lucrative deal with a Roman soldier and banishes him from the farm during a hard blizzard. Determined to protect her little colt, Nestor's mother follows, covers him with her body, and sacrifices herself to the elements. Moving southward on his own, Nestor meets Tilly, a little cherub sent to guide him toward Bethlehem, his destiny. Tilly instead leaves him in the care of a desert merchant. In time Joseph, seeking a donkey to carry Mary to Bethlehem, tries to buy Nestor, but the merchant, seeing a halo around Mary, releases him as a gift. When a sudden sandstorm hinders their journey, the spirit of Nestor's mother appears, urging him to listen to the angels and follow them. Guided by their sweet song that only his long ears can appreciate, Nestor safely arrives in Bethlehem and takes Mary to a stable of his own choosing. After the Nativity, Nestor returns to Olaf's farm, where he receives a hero's welcome.

Narrated and sung by Roger Miller. Voices: Eric Stern, Linda Gary, Brenda Vaccaro, Paul Frees, Iris Rainer, Shirley Hines, Don

Messick. Written by Romeo Muller. Produced and directed by Arthur Rankin, Jr., Jules Bass. Rankin/Bass Productions. Warner Home Video. Color. 25 min.

The Netherlands
See **The Low Countries**

New Christmas
See **Christmas Old Style, Christmas New Style**

New Style Christmas
See **Christmas Old Style, Christmas New Style**

New Year's Day
First day of the new year, January 1 on the present Gregorian calendar. In the Roman Catholic Church, the day marks the "Solemnity of Mary," known prior to 1969 as the "Feast of the Circumcision"; in the Orthodox Church, it is the "Feast of the Circumcision of Our Lord"; Episcopal Church, "Feast of the Holy Name of Our Lord Jesus Christ"; Lutheran Church, "Feast of the Circumcision and the Name of Jesus." The new year is customarily viewed as a period of ending and of new beginning, respectively symbolized by Father Time, a wizened, white-bearded old gentleman carrying a scythe and Baby New Year, a toddler in diapers.

• CALENDAR DATES. The date for New Year's Day has varied over the centuries between different civilizations. For example, to the ancient Greeks, the year commenced with the new moon after the summer solstice of June 21; the Chinese new year begins on the second new moon after the sunset of the winter solstice (now celebrated sometime between January 10 and February 19 on the Gregorian calendar); and the Jews celebrate *Rosh Hashanah* on the first and second days of the month of Tishri (principally in September on the Gregorian calendar). Although the new year in the Roman Empire originally began on March 1, Julius Caesar (100–44 B.C.) changed it to January 1 in 46 B.C. with a revision of the calendar now known as the Julian calendar. Prior to the Norman Conquest (1066), the English new year coincided with Christmas Day, but it changed to January 1 after that point. Incorporating the

Father Time holding a baby Punch. Punch, *December 1847.*

Julian calendar during the Middle Ages, however, most of Europe observed the new year on March 25, a day exactly nine months prior to Christmas Day and traditionally held as the day that the Virgin Mary received the angel's Annunciation that she was to be the mother of Christ. The institution of the Gregorian calendar in 1582 again set New Year's Day on January 1, which Roman Catholic countries readily adopted. Although Scotland converted to the new calendar in 1600, the Puritans in England, objecting to the association of January with its namesake Janus, the pagan two-faced god, succeeded in delaying England's adoption of the Gregorian calendar until 1752, a delay that also extended to the British colonies in America (*see* **Christmas Old Style, Christmas New Style**).

• ASSOCIATED TRADITIONS. One principal tradition, regardless of the date, included the giving of gifts, a custom that preceded Christmastime exchanges in Europe and which derived principally from similar customs which the Romans observed during the Saturnalia and the Kalends (*see* **Saturnalia**). During the Middle Ages, courtiers and royalty also exchanged gifts, and Queen Elizabeth I was especially noted for taking advantage of the custom by requesting specific gifts. King Henry VIII's gifts of expensive gold lapel pins to ladies became so

This wood engraving from about 1890 shows not a Christmas party, but a typical nineteenth century New Year's Day reception. A New York woman festoons her gas chandelier with holly and greens while another brings in a fancy layered cake.

popular that they were commercially reproduced; the expression "pin money" supposedly arose as gentlemen set aside cash over periods of time to purchase the cherished items. New year gift-giving at court faded during the eighteenth century, but the citizenry, who had taken up the custom in the seventeenth century, carried it into the nineteenth. It was during that century that holiday gift-giving became more associated with Christmas than with the new year. The reasons for the shift are not clear but probably centered around the "Christmas renaissance" that followed the Puritan ban on Christmas. Christmas gift-giving had been recorded in Germany since the early seventeenth century, which date also corresponds to the first records of home-decorated Christmas trees (1605) (*see* **Christmas Tree**).

Whereas the Christmas Day of history was spent quietly at home with the immediate family, for centuries people have greeted the new year with revelry in the form of parties, imbibing, fireworks, and all manner of noise-making, the latter two stemming from pagan winter solstice festivals which attempted to frighten away the spirits of darkness. Custom dictated calling upon and receiving one's

friends and acquaintances on New Year's Day, and in mid-nineteenth-century America, it was fashionable for bachelors to call upon unmarried ladies, the latter of whom reserved visitations among themselves for January 2.

According to Old World customs, New Year's Day was the time to consult auguries regarding the weather for the new year, the likelihood of a good crop, the prospects for marriage, and the chance of death during the year. Many countries recall old superstitions which held that whatever transpired on New Year's Day predicted what was in store for the new year. Therefore, families made every effort to be pleasant, clean, well, debt-free, and to have a bountiful feast at this time. The present custom of making New Year's resolutions undoubtedly stems from this superstition.

• CHURCH FEASTS. After the Roman Catholic Church had established December 25 as Christmas Day in the fourth century, January 1 took on significance as "Octave of the Birth of Our Lord" ("octave" signifying any holy day and the seven days which follow) as well as the day to commemorate Christ's circumcision, which occurred eight days after His birth in compliance with the covenant with Abraham and the Mosaic Law (Genesis 17:9–14; Leviticus 12:3; Luke 2:21). With circumcision He also received the name Jesus. The early Church did not universally observe January 1, however, because pagan revelry and abandon associated with the Kalends significantly overshadowed the date. Nevertheless the Council of Tours, France (567), first instituted the Feast of the Circumcision on that date as an effort to offset pagan practices. Spain adopted the feast sometime during the life of St. Isidore of Seville (ca. 560–636), and Rome, having first established the Octave of the Birth of Our Lord in the seventh century, combined this feast with the Feast of the Circumcision in the ninth century. Since the eighth century, the Orthodox Church has observed January 1 as the Circumcision as well as the anniversary of the death of St. Basil (ca. 329–379), one of the Orthodox Patriarchs. Many regard the January feast as the earliest in the Catholic Church dedicated to the Virgin Mary, for in the mass are prayers that specifically make reference to her virtues; hence, the new title "Solemnity of Mary."

• New Year's Day in the United States. Broadcast nationwide is the New Year's Eve celebration from New York City's Times Square, where at least one million people annually crowd together to revel and to watch a large, illuminated ball atop the Times Square Building descend from its pinnacle at 11:59 P.M. Eastern Standard Time. At the stroke of midnight, a large "Happy New Year" sign beneath the ball flashes, as cheers and "Auld Lang Syne," the theme song for the new year, fill the air (*see* **Auld Lang Syne**).

New Year's Day is devoted to parades and nationally televised college football games or "bowl" games. One of the foremost parades, the annual Tournament of Roses Parade in Pasadena, California, dates to January 1, 1890, as the highlight of a festival that originated with Charles F. Hunt of the Pasadena Valley Hunt Club. Designed to display California's roses and other native flora, the first parade included horse-drawn carriages covered with flowers. In 1895, the Tournament of Roses Association relieved the Valley Hunt Club and took charge of the festival. Today, complex floats built by professional companies are appropriately decorated with thousands of flowers according to the annual theme selected for the event. In addition to these floral floats which pass down Colorado Boulevard, the two-hour parade also includes marching bands, equestrians, and the float for the reigning Rose Queen and her Royal Court of six Rose Princesses. The latter, selected in September during a month-long competition of poise, personality, public speaking, and scholastic achievement, also reign over the Rose Bowl Game.

Added to the festival in 1902, a college football game served to revive the seemingly waning interest in the Tournament of Roses festival at the time. After this first game, however (in which the University of Michigan defeated Stanford University 49–0), football games did not return to the festival until 1916, chariot races having temporarily filled the interim. Football resumed in Tournament Park, then moved to the "Rose Bowl," a new 57,000-seat stadium (subsequently enlarged to more than 93,000) which hosted the first Rose Bowl Game and the first formal college bowl game on New Year's Day, 1923. The Rose Bowl Game has

This December 1949 magazine ad for Capehart televisions capitalized on the draw of New Year's Day football to attract buyers.

been played from this stadium since that time, except for 1942 following the Japanese attack on Pearl Harbor on December 7, 1941, which moved the bowl to Duke University Stadium, Durham, North Carolina. Dubbed "The Granddaddy of Them All" in 1947, the Rose Bowl Game has featured the championship teams of the Big 10 and the Pacific 10 conferences. Since the 1998 season, the Rose Bowl has participated in the Bowl Championship Series, which schedules a championship game between the two highest ranked teams in the country. Once the pair is determined, this and other bowls are free to invite the teams of their choice.

Other principal college bowl games that are played on or about New Year's Day include the following:

Orange Bowl, first played in 1933 as a feature of the Palm Festival in Miami, Florida. From 1935 to 1995, it was played in the Orange Bowl Stadium, but from 1996 has been played in Ft. Lauderdale's Pro Player Stadium (seating 75,192). Since 1998, it has participated in the Bowl Championship Series, usually a Big East or Atlantic Coast Conference champion vs. an at-large opponent.

Sugar Bowl, played from 1935 to 1974 at Tulane Stadium in New Orleans, Louisiana. Since 1975, it has played at the Superdome (seating 77,446) in New Orleans and is the first and only bowl to be played indoors. The Sugar Bowl has participated in the Bowl Championship Series since 1998.

Cotton Bowl, played in Dallas, Texas. The first Cotton Bowl matched two high school teams on New Year's Day, 1936, with college teams following in the years thereafter. This bowl was played in Fair Park Stadium in 1937 and has been played in the Cotton Bowl Stadium (seating 68,252) since 1938. Currently, the Cotton Bowl features teams from the Big 12 and the Southeastern Conference.

Fiesta Bowl, played in Arizona State University's Sun Devil Stadium (seating 73,656) in Tempe since December 27, 1971. The Fiesta Bowl first matched Arizona State against an at-large opponent. The game moved to January 1 after the 1981 season and has been played on that day or thereabouts since then. The Fiesta Bowl has participated in the Bowl Championship Series since 1998.

Another annual New Year's Day parade is the Philadelphia Mummer's Parade (*see* **Christmas Drama** [MUMMING]).

New Year's Eve Party
See **The Honeymooners**

Nicaragua
See **Central America**

Nigh Bethlehem
See **Alfred Burt Carols**

The Night Before Christmas
See **A Visit from St. Nicholas**

The Night They Saved Christmas
(1984). Made-for-television adventure.

Santa (Art Carney) and his workshop at North Pole City face annihilation when an oil company drilling in the Arctic Circle plans a blasting project on Christmas Eve, not knowing the project is near Santa's hidden abode. After geologist Michael Baldwin (Paul Le Mat) dismisses Santa's emissary and chief elf Ed (Paul Williams) as a practical joke, Ed convinces Michael's wife, Claudia (Jaclyn Smith), to meet with Santa about the problem. Skeptical, Claudia accompanies Ed in a "reindeer zephyr," a self-propelled sleigh, to North Pole City, along with her children, David (Scott Grimes), Maryanne (Laura Jacoby), and C. B. (R. J. Williams). Not only do they become instant believers in awe of Santa's high-tech domain, which boasts a time deceleration device that allows Santa to get around the world in one night and a world-wide language communicator/translator, but Santa also reveals the location of an abundant oil site farther away. Then it's a race against time to inform the oil company before it carries out the scheduled detonation, and Christmas is saved after all.

The picture won a Young Artist Award in 1986 for Best Young Actress starring in a Television Special or Miniseries (Laura Jacoby).

With June Lockhart as Mrs. Martha Claus, Mason Adams. Written by Jim Moloney, David Niven, Jr. Produced by David Kappes, Robert Halmi, Jr. Directed by Jackie Cooper. RHI Entertainment. Hallmark Home Entertainment Video. Color. 95 min.

The Nightmare Before Christmas
(1993). Animated motion picture musical using three-dimensional, stop-motion action, based on a poem by director, producer, writer, and actor Tim Burton. Burton conceived *The Nightmare Before Christmas* while working as an animator for Disney studios in 1983. A dual celebration of Halloween and Christmas — Burton's two favorite holidays, this is the story of Jack Skellington, the skeleton king of Halloween Town, whose inhabitants, ghouls, vampires, and other typically frightful creatures plan each Halloween celebration a year in advance.

Weary of creating the same screams and nightmares each year, Jack longs for something more meaningful. Wandering through a forest, he chances upon several trees with doors fashioned in various holiday symbols that are alien to him: an Easter egg, a turkey, and a Christmas tree. He opens the latter door and plummets into a magical world of snow, toys, and Santa Claus — in short, Christmas Town. Anxious to share Christmas with Halloween Town, he returns with sample toys and commissions everyone in his domain to duplicate them as well as create a Santa suit, reindeer, and sleigh. Their efforts are anything but Christmasy, for their limited imaginations are capable of producing only fiendish toys with fangs and a coffin sleigh with skeleton reindeer.

Overcome with the desire to participate in Christmas, Jack decides to assume Santa's role on Christmas Eve. To get Santa temporarily out of the way, Jack orders three mischievous creatures, Luck, Chuck, and Beryl, to kidnap the jolly old elf. The creatures deliver Santa to the Bogey Man, Oogie Boogie. Sally, a Frankenstein-like creation of Dr. Finkelstein, senses that Jack is completely out of his element and conjures up a fog that almost puts a halt to Jack's midnight ride, until Zero, his red-nosed ghost dog, leads the skeleton team skyward in the spirit of Rudolph, the Red-Nosed Reindeer. As Jack disperses his toys, they wreak havoc by chasing and attacking children while Jack, spotted as an impostor, is shot from the sky by artillery. With Christmas nearly a disaster, Jack realizes that attempting to venture beyond his realm was a serious error. Just as Oogie Boogie is about to dispatch Santa, Jack returns to his role as skeleton king and saves Christmas.

This film was nominated in 1993 for an Academy Award, Best Visual Effects; nominated for a Golden Globe Award, Best Original Score for a Motion Picture; nominated for a Hugo Award, Best Dramatic Presentation; and nominated for a Grammy Award, Best Album for Children.

Principal voices: Danny Elfman (also provided the musical score, songs, lyrics, and lead vocals), Chris Sarandon, Catherine O'Hara, William Hickey, Glenn Shadix, Paul Reubens, Ken Page. Written by Caroline Thompson. Adapted by Michael McDowell. Produced by Tim Burton, Denise DiNovi. Directed by Henry Selick. Touchstone Pictures. Touchstone Video. Color. 76 min.

The Noble Stem of Jesse
See **Lo, How a Rose E'er Blooming**

Noel
See **The First Nowell**

Noel! A New Noel
See **Sing We Now of Christmas**

North Pole
See **Saint Nicholas**

Norway

A succession of Norwegian kings gradu-ally introduced Christianity into Norway from the mid-tenth century and thereafter. The first was King Haakon I (914?–961, a son of the Norwegian King Harold I), who had been raised in the Christian faith by King Athelstan of England. Haakon first decreed that the long-established winter solstice festival of *Jul* (Yule) would coincide with that for the birth of Christ on December 25, a change that initially alienated many of his subjects and hindered their conversion. Norway completely converted during the subsequent, iron-fisted rules of Harold's descendants, Kings Olaf I (968–1000) and St. Olaf II (995–1030), the latter of whom was canonized as the patron saint of Norway. Following the Protestant Reformation in the sixteenth century, the Evangelical Lutheran Church emerged in Norway as the principal Christian faith. Norway continues to celebrate Christmas with customs that blend the spiritual with remnants of pagan Yule.

The Advent season includes Advent candles, calendars, and wreaths. For the latter decoration it is still customary for many families to make their own candles (a related superstition in some regions holds that if someone's candle is extinguished on Christmas night, death lingers nearby). Employers customarily host Christmas buffets for their employees and customers during the weeks of Advent, and a favorite dish served at these occasions is half-fermented trout.

The Christmas season, formerly beginning on St. Thomas's Day (December 21) in Norway's Roman Catholic past, now begins on St. Lucia Day (December 13) with customs akin to those of Sweden, which has become the prototypical country for observing St. Lucia Day. This night was termed *Lussinatten* (Lussi Night) in Norway after Lussi, a vengeful spirit who punished those who did any work at this time. It was also believed that gnomes and trolls were given free rein from this day until Christmas.

Other Advent customs include thoroughly cleaning the house and decorating with fir boughs, erecting a sheaf of grain on a pole outdoors for the birds ("Birds' Christmas Tree"), providing the livestock with extra fodder, withdrawing of hunting traps and snares, sending Christmas cards, and baking traditional

Christmas cookies. Consisting of at least seven varieties, Christmas cookies include, among others, *peppernøtter* (pepper nuts), *sirupssnipper* (syrup snaps), *berlinerkranser* (Berlin wreaths), *sandkaker* (sand tarts), *krumkaker* (curled cookies), *strull* (sour cream cookies), and *fløtekaker* (cream cakes). For special events, it is customary to serve a *kransekake* (almond wreath cake) stacked in the shape of a pyramid, and gingerbread "houses" frequently take intricate shapes of castles, perhaps even entire village scenes.

Christmas trees, a custom adopted from Germany in the early nineteenth century, decorate many public places. The public trees are lighted on the first Advent Sunday, whereas families light those trees in their homes only on Christmas Eve. Families usually include a combination of homemade and commercially manufactured ornaments. The homemade ornaments often consist of small candles, strands of small Norwegian flags, hearts of red felt, and heart-shaped baskets filled with candies. As a gesture of her appreciation to England for granting political asylum to King Håkon during the German occupation of World War II (1940–1945), Norway has, since 1947, shipped one of her best Christmas trees annually to England, where the tree decorates London's Trafalgar Square.

Although Norwegians are quite familiar with Santa Claus through western influences, it is not he who brings the Christmas gifts but the *Julenissen*, a composite of St. Nicholas and the *nisse*, a small, mischievous elf or gnome of Norwegian folklore. Attired in a red stocking cap, knee breeches, stockings, and fur, and sporting a long, white beard, the *nisse* ordinarily protects the homestead and its inhabitants during the year, and any mishaps occurring thereabouts are said to result from his pranks. Assuming the name *Julenissen* at Christmastime, he requires an annual bowl of rice porridge on Christmas Eve to control his antics. Children not only in Norway but throughout the world may mail their Christmas wish lists to *Julenissen* at his special post office in Drøbak, a small village south of Oslo, and for each letter received, *Julenissen* sends a reply. Decorative versions of the *Julenissen* are known as *smånisser* ("small Santas").

Christmas Eve officially commences at 5 P.M., when church bells throughout all cities ring in Christmas, for most churches hold services at this hour. Families usually place lighted candles and wreaths on the graves of loved ones and then retire to their homes for the traditional Christmas Eve feast, the menu of which will vary from region to region. In general, coastal and northern regions feature *lutefisk* (codfish); eastern regions, pork ribs, sausages, and cabbage; western regions, mutton and pork. Dishes widely found include *lefse* (flat bread), cloudberry cream, caramel pudding, rice, and fruit. A most traditional Scandinavian dish is rice porridge, which contains one almond in the batch. Whoever finds the almond in his serving will receive luck in the new year. In those households that follow old customs, the food remains on the table overnight for the spirits of deceased family members, who are believed to return at this time of year to partake of the Christmas feast.

Following the meal, families may engage in reading from the Bible and joining hands to walk around the Christmas tree while singing carols. Sometime after the meal, someone dressed as the *Julenissen* and toting a sack of gifts knocks on the door, then asks the traditional question before distributing gifts to children: "Are there any good children here?" Some regions may still perform the archaic custom of "Shooting in Christmas," in which marksmen fire a number of rounds on Christmas Eve to greet Christmas. The custom derives from Yule festivals, which held that much commotion and loud noise at the winter solstice would ward off evil spirits.

After church on Christmas Day, families enjoy a large buffet of hot and cold dishes similar to those of Christmas Eve, including fish and pork, cheese and fruit, *lefse*, beer, and a liquor, Norwegian *aquavit*. Activities include various competitive games along with a popular tradition, *Julebukk* ("Christmas Goat"). Resembling the American custom of trick-or-treating at Halloween, *Julebukk* involves bands of costumed children traveling through neighborhoods, leading a billy goat, and singing carols in return for treats. Instead of a goat, a man dressed in goat skins and wearing a goat mask may accompany the children for the purpose of imitating a goat's unruly behavior and frightening the children into maintaining proper deportment. The *Julebukk* derives from pre–Christian Yule festivals, which paid homage to the gods. At the winter solstice, it was believed that, as he rode through the skies in a chariot pulled by two billy goats named Gnasher and Cracker, Thor distributed gifts to the Vikings while his father Odin, riding his white, eight-legged steed Sleipner, escorted the souls of slain heroes into Valhalla. Men costumed as goats portrayed this belief by making surprise entrances at Yule parties, and after dancing about, "died," then returned to life. During the Middle Ages, the goat figure symbolized the Devil in Scandinavian Christmas folk revels, and men costumed in goat skins and masks frolicked about, much to the dismay of the Church. Although the Church banned such behavior in the sixteenth century, today's *Julebukk* is a relatively tame vestige.

Celebrations after Christmas include St. Stephen's Day (December 26), on which people visit friends and relatives, and costumed men in villages render folk songs about the saint; New Year's Eve, which allows for another round of merrymaking, noise, and parties; and Epiphany (January 6), marked by parades of "Star Boys" (dressed in white with tall, pointed hats bedecked with stars) who provide carols.

The Christmas season terminates twenty days after Christmas Day on St. Knut's Day (January 13), a day named in honor of the Danish king Knut IV (Canute, Cnut, Knud), who was assassinated in 1086. A strong supporter of the Church through acts of piety and charity, he was canonized in 1100. Sources vary regarding the exact origin of the twenty-day feast. One source holds that Knut himself decreed it; another claims that because the Vikings feasted and offered human sacrifices on this day, the Church sought to stamp out such practices by extending Christmas through that day. In festivals today, home parties on St. Knut's Day light the Christmas tree one last time, then remove all decorations and dismantle the tree. Children retrieve the decorative sweets, and trees are often burned in communal bonfires.

"Merry Christmas" in Norwegian is *God Jul*.

See also **Advent**; **Epiphany**; **Sweden**.

Nowell, Sing Nowell
See **Sing We Now of Christmas**

The Nutcracker

Ballet in two acts, the last of three ballets for which the celebrated Russian composer Peter I. Tchaikovsky (1840–1893) provided the music, the other two being *Swan Lake* (1876) and *The Sleeping Beauty* (1889). The only major Christmas ballet currently performed, *The Nutcracker* is loosely based on a fantastic fairy tale, *The Nutcracker and the Mouse King*, written in 1816 by the German author E. T. A. Hoffmann. A synopsis of this story is essential to appreciate the significant alteration of the story that subsequently emerged in the ballet.

• THE ORIGINAL STORY. Christmas Eve provides unusual festivities for Dr. Stahlbaum's children, seven-year-old Marie and her older brother, Fritz. Their mysterious and eccentric clockmaker-godfather, Judge Drosselmeier, has fashioned a series of ingenious toys, one of which is an ugly yet fascinating nutcracker doll dressed as a prince. Fritz damages the nutcracker in a childish scuffle, and Marie, most attached to the doll, remains with it long after everyone has retired. At midnight, she witnesses a strange battle between an army of Fritz's toy soldiers, led by the nutcracker, and an army of mice, led by a seven-headed mouse king. When the tide turns against nutcracker, Marie saves him by throwing her slipper at the mouse king, but her arm is lacerated by broken glass in the process. Fainting, she is found in the morning lying in her own blood, having almost perished from exsanguination. During her recovery, her family scoffs at her wild story about the Christmas Eve battle, and Drosselmeier, who has repaired the nutcracker, entertains Marie with the intriguing tale about how that doll became so ugly.

Here begins a complex subplot, "The Story of the Hard Nut." Madam Mouserinks, a mouse witch, vows revenge on a king's baby daughter, Princess Pirlipat, because the king ordered the execution of the witch's seven-headed son and other relatives when the witch ruined the king's feast. She transforms baby Pirlipat into a monstrosity, after which Drosselmeier, the court wizard, determines that eating the rare and exceedingly hard

Krakatuk nut will reverse the spell. The king promises his daughter to the man who can crack such a nut, and Drosselmeier sets off to find both man and nut. Finding the nut in Nuremberg after a fifteen-year search, Drosselmeier also discovers that his young nephew from the same locale, who cracks the hardest nuts with his teeth, is most suited to perform the vital nut-cracking ritual. Restored as a beautiful young lady, Pirlipat scorns the nephew, who, having taken the spell upon himself, is transformed into an ugly nutcracker and is banished from the kingdom. In the commotion, the nutcracker accidentally crushes the mouse witch to death. To break this new spell, nutcracker must kill the mouse witch's second, seven-headed son who now reigns as the new mouse king.

Marie now realizes that the battle of Christmas Eve was her beloved nutcracker's initial attempt to break the spell and that he is actually the bewitched nephew of Godfather Drosselmeier. At a magical moment, the nutcracker begs a sword from Marie and ultimately slays the mouse king. In gratitude, he escorts Marie into an incredible fairyland of sweets, beauty, and pleasure, where he is the prince of Marzipan Castle. Awakening as from a dream, Marie vows that, if nutcracker had been human, she would never have spurned him for his ugliness. Her confession of love erases the spell, for Godfather Drosselmeier immediately appears with his handsome, quite-human nephew in tow, who, as the new king of Marzipan Castle, secures Marie's hand in marriage.

• ORIGINS OF THE BALLET. The two-act ballet is a considerably reduced adaptation of a French translation of Hoffman's tale titled *The Nutcracker of Nuremberg*, made in 1845 by Alexandre Dumas (the elder, author of *The Three Musketeers*). The adaptation originated with Ivan Vsevolozhsky, director of Imperial Theaters in St. Petersburg, the imperial choreographer Marius Petipa, and Petipa's assistant, Lev Ivanov (who completed the choreography when Petipa fell ill). The former two had collaborated with Tchaikovsky on *The Sleeping Beauty*, and they persuaded the composer to provide the musical score for *The Nutcracker*. This was a hard sell, for their adaptation (which

changed the character of Marie Stahlbaum to Clara Silberhaus) reduced Hoffmann's complex, often violent, and erotically weird plot to a bland children's Christmas party (first half of Act I) and a little girl's fanciful dream (latter half of Act I and all of Act II) that retained only the initial Christmas Eve scene and a series of dances in the contrived "Kingdom of Sweets." Tchaikovsky, feeling that this abbreviated version suffered from a complete lack of drama and emotional appeal, reluctantly commenced work on it in early 1891.

• "THE NUTCRACKER SUITE" AND THE BALLET. By March of 1892, Tchaikovsky, dividing his time between conducting tours in Europe and America and working on *The Nutcracker*, faced a series of concerts previously booked for St. Petersburg, about which he had forgotten and for which he was unprepared. In desperation, he threw together eight selections from his unfinished *Nutcracker* ballet and presented them at the Maryinsky Theatre in St. Petersburg on March 19, 1892, as *The Nutcracker Suite*. This best-known collection from the ballet consists of the "Miniature Overture," "March" (accompanies the children's entrance in Act I), "Dance of the Sugar-Plum Fairy" (whom Tchaikovsky characterizes with a celesta, an instrument he had discovered in Paris in June 1891), "Russian Trepak," "Arabian Dance" (personifies coffee), "Chinese Dance" (personifies tea), "Dance of the Reed-Pipes" (also known as "Dance of the Flutes" and "Dance of the Shepherds"), and "Waltz of the Flowers" (concludes the entertainment divertissement in the Kingdom of Sweets). The latter six numbers appear in Act II, and the latter five represent a portion of the entertainment that Clara enjoys during her magical visit to the Kingdom of Sweets. The "Spanish Dance," which personifies chocolate in Act II, is not included in the *Suite*.

The *Suite* was an instant success, not only in St. Petersburg, but abroad as well. It debuted in the United States in Chicago on October 22, 1892, and in London on October 17, 1896.

Tchaikovsky completed the ballet *The Nutcracker* in April 1892, but in keeping with its theme, deliberately delayed its premiere until Christmastime. Performed by the eminent Kirov Ballet on December 18, 1892, in St.

A shelf of nutcrackers of carved, painted wood flank a tiny Christmas tree in this illustration from a German children's periodical, Deutscher Kinderfreund, *1909.*

Petersburg, the ballet generated surprisingly mixed emotions. The chief complaint voiced was that romping children dominated the entire first act, leaving the heart of the ballet for the second act. Today, of course, it is the children, the fantasy, and the opportunity to create spectacular visual effects such as flying sleds and dancing snowflakes that make *The Nutcracker* a popular, holiday attraction.

The Nutcracker was performed only within Russia for over forty years. Nicholas Sergeyev staged the first complete performance of the ballet abroad in London in 1934. A shortened version followed in the United States in 1940, performed by Ballet Russe de Monte Carlo, and a complete performance debuted in the United States in 1954, staged by Kirov-trained George Balanchine. It is this latter staging on which many modern American productions are based.

• FILM VERSIONS OF "THE NUTCRACKER." Numerous motion picture or animated versions exist, most of them titled *Nutcracker* or *The Nutcracker*. The following list summarizes a few of the noteworthy releases:

George Balanchine's "The Nutcracker" (1993), performance featuring Macaulay Culkin. Narrated by Kevin Kline. Choreography by George Balanchine. With Bart Robinson Cook, Jessica Lynn Cohen, Darci Kistler, Peter Reznick, Robert LaFosse, Heather Watts, Robert W. Lyon. Written by Susan Cooper. Produced by Robert Hurwitz, Robert A. Krasnow. Directed by Emile Ardolino. Elektra Entertainment and Regency Enterprises. Warner Home Video. Color. 92 min.

The Nutcracker (1977), television performance featuring Mikhail Baryshnikov, Gelsey Kirkland, Alexander Minz. Choreographed by Baryshnikov. Directed by Tony Charmoli. MGM/UA Home Video. Color. 79 min.

The Nutcracker (1978), Russian production featuring Yekatarina Maksimova, Vladimir Vasilyev, and Nadiya Pavlova of the Bolshoi Ballet. Directed by Yelena Macheret. Kultur Video. Color. 100 min.

The Nutcracker: A Fantasy on Ice (1983), performance featuring champion figure skater Dorothy Hamill. Narrated by Lorne Greene. Vidmark/Trimark Video. Color. 85 min.

Nutcracker Ballet (1968), performance featuring Rudolph Nureyev. Kultur Video. 100 min.

Nutcracker Fantasy (1979), Japanese production featuring animated puppets, dubbed in English. In 1980 the film won a Young Artist Award for Best Musical Entertainment Featuring Youth and was nominated for Best Motion Picture Featuring Youth. Narrated by Michele Lee. Voices: Melissa Gilbert, Lurene Tuttle, Christopher Lee, Jo Anne Worley, Dick Van Patten, Roddy McDowall, Eva Gabor. Music adapted and arranged by Akihito Wakatsuki, Kentaro Haneda. Written by Eugene A. Fournier, Thomas Joachim. Produced by Mark L. Rosen, Walt deFaria. Directed by Takeo Nakamura. Sanrio Films. Color. 82 min. Video N/A.

Nutcracker on Ice (1994), television performance featuring champion figure skaters Oksana Baiul, Viktor Petrenko, Vladimir Petrenko. Choreographed and directed by Minnie

Madden. 20th Century–Fox Video. Color. 110 min. A 1995 television production by the same title featured champion figure skater Peggy Fleming.

The Nutcracker Prince (1990), Canadian animated cartoon feature, in which the nutcracker is named Hans. In 1991 the film received a Young Artist Award nomination for Most Entertaining Family Youth Motion Picture — Animation. Music arranged by Victor Davies and performed by the London Symphony Orchestra. Principal voices: Kiefer Sutherland, Megan Follows, Mike MacDonald, Peter Boretski, Phyllis Diller, Peter O'Toole. Written by Patricia Watson. Produced by Kevin Gillis. Directed by Paul Schibli. Lacewood Productions. Warner Home Video. Color. 74 min.

The Nutcracker: Tchaikovsky (1994), performance by the Kirov Ballet at the Maryinsky Theatre in St. Petersburg, Russia. Starring Larissa Lezhnina. UNI/Philips Video. 95 min.

Nutcracker: The Motion Picture (1986), performance by the Pacific Northwest Ballet Company with sets and costumes by Maurice Sendak. In 1988 the film received a Young Artist Award nomination for Best Family Motion Picture — Drama. With Hugh Bigney, Vanessa Sharp, Patricia Barker, Wade Walthall, Russell Burnett. Produced by Willard Carroll, Donald Kushner, Peter Locke, Thomas L. Wilhite. Directed by Carroll Ballard. Hyperion Films. Color. Video N/A.

The Nuttiest Nutcracker (1999), made-for-video animated cartoon comedy. Voices: Jim Belushi, Phyllis Diller, Cheech Marin, Cam Clarke, Debi Derryberry, Desiree Goyette, Tress MacNeille, Jeff Bennett, Jim Cummings, Kevin Schon. Directed by Harold Harris. Dan Kretch Productions. Columbia/Tristar Home Video. Color. 48 min.

The Nutcracker: A Fantasy on Ice
See **The Nutcracker**

Nutcracker Fantasy
See **The Nutcracker**

Nutcracker on Ice
See **The Nutcracker**

The Nutcracker Prince
See **The Nutcracker**

Nutcracker: The Motion Picture
See **The Nutcracker**

The Nuttiest Nutcracker
See **The Nutcracker**

Nuttin' for Christmas
American novelty song written in 1955 by the New York-born songwriting team of Sid Tepper and Roy Bennett. Inspired by an occasion when Bennett's daughter Claire spilled some ink, the lyrics are an actual compilation of childish pranks pulled by Tepper's and Bennett's own children at various times and presented as though a mischievous little boy is the sole culprit. The misdeeds include head-bashing with a bat, hiding a frog, eating bugs, using metal slugs in gum machines, placing tacks in chairs, tying knots in hair, trampling plants, tearing clothes, and adding ants to the sugar bowl. Having been a bad boy all year, the child anticipates getting "nuttin' for Christmas." Five-year-old Barry Gordon introduced the song on television's *The Milton Berle Show*, and his recording with Art Mooney and His Orchestra on the MGM label was the top Christmas song for 1955 (position 6 on the *Billboard Hot 100* chart), selling over one million copies.

Tepper and Bennett collaborated on a number of other hits, such as "Red Roses for a Blue Lady" (1948), the holiday favorite "Suzy Snowflake" (1951), and "The Naughty Lady of Shady Lane" (1954).

See also **Suzy Snowflake.**

O

O Christmas Tree

("O Tannenbaum," literally translated as "O Fir Tree"). Traditional carol of Germany, one of the most popular holiday songs in that country. The tune is believed to have arisen in the sixteenth or seventeenth century, although it did not appear in print until 1799, paired with lyrics unrelated to Christmas. Prior to that time, it had also been the setting for Latin lyrics often sung by students, "Lauriger Horatius." Verse 1 of the carol known today is of folk origin as well and first appeared with the same tune in a book of folk songs for elementary schools published by August Zarnack (1820). The German poet Ernst Anschütz (1800–1861) contributed verses 2 and 3 around 1824. A number of English translations exist, no one superior to the others. Because translators report difficulty in producing a faithful yet sensible set of lyrics from the original words, rather free interpretations of the German are made.

The American James R. Randall, a native of Maryland, adapted the tune in 1861 to his poem about that state's involvement in the Civil War, "Maryland, My Maryland." The melody has been matched with other songs about states, such as "Delaware, My Delaware" and "Kentucky, O Kentucky."

O Come, All Ye Faithful

("Adeste Fideles"). Highly popular Latin carol generally attributed to John F. Wade between the years 1740 and 1743. During this time Wade, having fled his native England because of his Roman Catholic faith, was working at an English college in Douai, France, as a music teacher and music copyist. In his work he dealt frequently with Latin lyrics. When Wade produced a Christmas hymn of four Latin stanzas titled "Adeste Fideles," the general assumption was that he had merely stumbled upon another song and copied it.

For some 200 years, "Adeste Fideles" was attributed to various sources, including an adaptation of an aria in Handel's *Ottone* (1723); a parody of a tune from a Parisian vaudeville play, *Le Comte d'Acajou* (1744); and the seventeenth-century English organist John Reading. The carol did not actually appear in England until the eighteenth century, however, and the modern version (Wade had originally used several different tempo settings) was first published anonymously in *An Essay on the Church Plain Chant* (London, 1782). It is believed that Wade and a colleague, Samuel Webbe, organist for the Portuguese embassy chapel in London, were responsible for this essay. In 1795 Webbe played "Adeste Fideles" at the Portuguese embassy, and the Duke of Leeds was so impressed with the carol that it was introduced at a series of concerts in 1797 which he patronized. Through these concerts, it was assumed that the carol had arisen in Portugal, which led to its sobriquet, the "Portuguese Hymn."

In 1947, research published by Dom Jean Stéphan of Buckfast Abbey, Devon, England, revealed a newly discovered manuscript in Wade's handwriting that dated between 1740 and 1743 (the earliest known copy of the carol) and that further supported Wade as the composer, an opinion with which carol authority William Studwell concurs in *The Christmas Carol Reader*. *The New Oxford Book of Carols*, however, does not completely concur with Stéphan's conclusion; among other points *Oxford* suggests that Wade's setting and the remarkably similar tune in the Paris vaudeville (see above) both probably originated from another source as yet unidentified. Therefore *Oxford* lists the composer as anonymous.

The complete "Adeste Fideles" as we know it today consists of a hybrid of seven stanzas, although most modern publications include only Wade's original four. According to *The New Oxford Book of Carols*, the French clergyman Abbé Étienne Jean F. Borderies contributed two additional Latin stanzas, along with an anonymous third of Gallic origin, and published the seven-stanza carol in 1822. Altogether, the seven verses were arranged as follows: 1, 2, 6, 7 were Wade's original four; 3 and 5 were Borderies's; and verse 4 was truly anonymous. The Latin text was first published in the United States in 1795; a copy of that publication resides in the Newberry Library, Chicago.

Although there have been some fifty English translations of the Latin lyrics, the second of two translations by English clergyman Frederick Oakeley (1802–1880) remains the most-accepted version. As canon of London's Westminster Abbey, Oakeley's initial translation in 1841 of Wade's original text (verses 1, 2, 6, 7) opened with "Ye faithful, approach ye." When he later converted to Catholicism, he published a second translation of only three verses in 1852, the opening line of which read, "O come, all ye faithful," by which the carol is better known. William Brooke translated the remaining four verses and combined them with Oakeley's in the *Altar Hymnal* (London, 1884).

O Come, Little Children

("Ihr Kinderlein, kommet") German carol, the lyrics of which were written around 1850 by Christoph von Schmidt (1768–1854) and the music by Johann Abraham Peter Schulz (1747–1800). A Roman Catholic priest, Schmidt was known for publishing religious literature for children, and Schulz, an organist and conductor, had studied in Berlin with Johann Philipp Kernberger, a former student of J. S. Bach. Although it is not known exactly when Schulz composed the melody for this carol, it is thought to have originated during his tenure (1787–1795) as court musician to the king of Denmark. The lyrics to its four verses bid first the little children, then "one and all" to hasten to see the Child Jesus, whose bed is a manger, whose pillow is hay, now wrapped in swaddling clothes, and more lovely than all the angels together.

O Come, O Come, Emmanuel

("Veni, Veni, Emanuel"). Advent carol, about which music scholars are not in agreement regarding its origins. According to *The New Oxford Book of Carols*, the original Latin lyrics to this carol derive from a series of seven

"O Antiphons" dating to at least the eighth century, which were sung in monasteries at vespers for seven nights from December 17 to December 23. Disregarding the letter "O," the initial letter of each antiphon, when read from last to first, spelled the Latin acrostic "ERO CRAS" (freely translated "I shall be with you tomorrow"), which implied the imminent coming of Christ and Christmas. The lyrics sung today, originally beginning as "Veni, Veni, Emanuel" and comprising five verses, are thought to date from the thirteenth century, yet the country of origin remains unknown. In 1851 the Anglican priest John Mason Neale (1818–1866) translated these lyrics into English, revised them in 1853, and produced "O Come, O Come, Emmanuel." Other English translations of the lyrics have been made, particularly by Henry Sloane Coffin (1877–1954), and some hymnals and carol collections have replaced one or more of Neale's verses with those of Coffin. The lyrics are filled with metaphors and allusions to biblical prophesies about the coming Messiah.

Neale's associate, Thomas Helmore, adapted the translation to a plainsong tune, and the two were first published together with harmony in part 2 of *The Hymnal Noted* (London, 1854), edited by Neale and Helmore. Although it is not known exactly where Helmore found the tune, it is now believed to be of French origin, for in 1966 in the French National Library in Paris, the melody was discovered in a fifteenth-century French funeral processional, which had been used by Franciscan nuns. It also has been argued that the refrain, "Rejoice! Rejoice! Emmanuel…," was not a part of the original verses, but was added later to balance them. If that is true, it was not added anytime within the past 500 years, for the plainsong manuscript in the French National Library includes the refrain.

Another school of thought contends, however, that the Latin words upon which Neale based his English translation cannot be traced earlier than 1710, that the musical setting is consistent with a period 300 years later than other scholars surmise, and that in reality, "O Come, O Come, Emmanuel" is more of an original composition by Neale and Helmore with a medieval flair.

O Hearken Ye
See **Alfred Burt Carols**

O Holy Night
("Cantique de Noël"). French carol, the lyrics of which were written in 1847 by Placide Cappeau (1808–1877), a wine merchant, amateur poet, and mayor of the village of Roquemaure in the Rhone Valley. Having received a commission from the local priest to write a Christmas poem, Cappeau produced some verses beginning with "Minuit, Chrétiens, c'est l'heure solennele" ("Midnight, Christians, it is the solemn hour"). The priest desired the poem for a vocalist from his congregation, Madame Laurey, who subsequently sought the popular Parisian composer Adolphe Adam (1803–1856) for a musical setting. A prolific composer primarily of light opera and ballet, Adam is best known for his ballet *Giselle* (1841).

Titled "Cantique de Noël" ("Song of Christmas"), Cappeau's and Adam's new carol debuted at the Christmas Eve Midnight Mass of 1847 in Roquemaure, with Madame Laurey performing the solo. The song was first published as an organ arrangement in 1855 and later was translated into many languages, the best-known English version being that by the American John Sullivan Dwight (1818–1893), a music critic and journalist. Compared with the original French, Dwight's translation incorporated a rather free interpretation, beginning as "O holy night, the stars are brightly shining."

Although "O Holy Night" is now one of the world's most beloved Christmas carols, church officials at the time, especially the bishop of Paris, initially condemned it as lacking in musical taste with total absence of religious spirit. It is believed that such undue criticism stemmed from prejudices formed against Cappeau's and Adam's personal backgrounds: Neither man embraced Christianity in the strictest sense of the word. Adam composed for theaters, arenas of sin and abomination in the eyes of the Church, and Cappeau was viewed as a radical socialist.

"O Holy Night" would have an impact on the Franco-Prussian War (1870–1871) to some extent. It is said that on Christmas Eve, 1870, as French and German troops fought in trenches outside of Paris, a French soldier suddenly sprang from his position and began singing "Cantique de Noël" amid the din of gunfire, which soon ceased, at least for a time. Instead of raining bullets on the French soldier, at least one German, perhaps more, responded with "Vom Himmel hoch, da komm ich her" ("From Heaven Above to Earth I Come"), one of Germany's favorite carols by Martin Luther.

See also **From Heaven Above to Earth I Come.**

O How Joyfully
See **O Sanctissima**

O Little Town of Bethlehem
Arguably the best-known of America's sacred carols, written in 1868 by Phillips Brooks (1835–1893) and Lewis Redner (1831–1908). Brooks, who was pastor of the Holy Trinity Episcopal Church in Philadelphia and would later become the Episcopal Bishop of Massachusetts, took inspiration from his sojourn in the Holy Land three years earlier, when on horseback he had ridden from Jerusalem to Bethlehem on Christmas Eve. Having paused by the Shepherds' Field, a plain outside the city traditionally held as the site where herald angels brought the "good tidings of great joy," he had attended services at the Church of the Nativity, built over the traditional site of Christ's birth. Later producing a poem of five stanzas, which the Sunday school children of his church were to sing at the annual Christmas program, Brooks sought a musical setting from the church organist, Lewis Redner. A successful real estate broker and director of Holy Trinity's Sunday school, Redner composed nothing suitable until the night before the program when, it is said, he awoke to an "angel strain," "a gift from heaven," which he quickly transcribed. Holy Trinity's Sunday school children first presented "O Little Town of Bethlehem" on December 27, 1868. It was first published as early as 1874 and also appeared in *The Church Hymnal* (1892) of the American Episcopal Church.

In place of Redner's tune, the English composer Ralph Vaughan Williams substituted his arrangement of a folk ballad, "The Ploughboy's Dream," a setting which he titled "Forest Green." This alternate tune for "O Little Town

The small town of Bethlehem, on a hilly rise, as depicted in Reverend John Fleetwood's The Light in the East *(National Publishing Co. and Jones Brothers, 1874). Fleetwood was a missionary for 40 years in the Middle East.*

of Bethlehem," now the best-known in Great Britain, was first published in *The English Hymnal* (1906). A melody by Henry Walford Davies (1869–1941), organist of London's Temple Church for twenty years, is sometimes used.

Brooks and Redner collaborated on another carol, "Everywhere, Everywhere Christmas Tonight," composed sometime between 1862 and 1868, which never gained the immense popularity as did "O Little Town of Bethlehem."

See also **Church of the Nativity.**

O Morning Star, How Fair and Bright

See **How Brightly Shines the Morning Star**

O Most Wonderful

See O Sanctissima

O Sanctissima

("O Thou Most Holy"). Anonymous sixteenth-century Latin hymn to the Virgin Mary which originally bore no relationship to Christmas. Since that time its text has been the source for a series of Christmas adaptations variously known as "O Thou Joyful Day," "O How Joyfully," and "O Most Wonderful." Although the earliest known Christmas versions were published anonymously in London in 1792 and 1794, probably the best-known version is that composed in 1819 by Johannes Falk (1768–1826). Superintendent of an orphanage in

Weimar, Germany, Falk adapted the first verse of "O Sanctissima" for a children's Christmas play, while a colleague, Heinrich Holzschuher, added two additional verses for the event. There, Falk's text appeared under the title "O du fröhliche" ("O Most Wonderful").

Other lesser known text variations, titled "O Thou Joyful Day," have appeared in the United States in the twentieth century. While most are anonymous, one bears the name of William Glass. The German composer Ludwig van Beethoven also published an arrangement of "O Sanctissima" for three voices, piano, violin, and cello (1814–15).

A factor common to all of these variations is the musical setting itself, known as "The Sicilian Mariners' Hymn," a traditional tune believed to have arisen during the eighteenth century. Despite the title of this tune, however, no direct relationship between the hymn text, Sicily, or mariners has ever been documented.

O Thou Joyful Day

See **O Sanctissima**

O Thou Most Holy

See **O Sanctissima**

Of Jesse's Line Descended

See **Lo, How a Rose E'er Blooming**

Of the Father's Heart Begotten

See **Of the Father's Love Begotten**

Of the Father's Love Begotten

("Corde natus ex Parentis"). Latin carol, also translated as "Of the Father's Heart Begotten." The text derives from "Hymnus omnis horae" ("Hymn for Every Hour"), a poem of 37 stanzas by Aurelius Clemens Prudentius (348–ca. 410), a Spanish attorney who, in his latter years, retired to a monastery to write religious poetry. Prudentius included "Hymnus" in his *Cathemerinon*, a collection of daily hymns. The best-known English translation was provided by the Anglican clergyman John Mason Neale (1818–1866), who, together with colleague Thomas Helmore, matched the translation with an anonymous, thirteenth-century tune found in *Piae Cantiones*, a Swedish carol collection published in 1582. Neale and Helmore published text and music together in their *Carols for Christmas-Tide* (London, 1853–54), and Sir Henry Williams Baker (1821–1877) revised the piece for *Hymns Ancient and Modern* (London, 1861, edited by William Clowes).

Instead of a conventional narrative of the Nativity, Neale's translation of ten stanzas first outlines the creation of the Earth by the Trinity, that the Father is Alpha and Omega, then recalls that Christ was made incarnate to redeem mankind from the sentence of death by the Law (Mosaic Law). The latter half of the carol is an elaborate exhortation for all creation to praise God.

Oh, Joseph Took Mary Up on His Right Knee
See **The Cherry Tree Carol**

Old Christmas
See **Christmas Old Style, Christmas New Style**

Old Christmas, poem
See **Heap on More Wood**

Old Lad's Passing Bell
See **Great Britain**

Old Scrooge
See **A Christmas Carol** (FILM AND TELEVISION VERSIONS)

Old Style Christmas
See **Christmas Old Style, Christmas New Style**

On Christmas Night
See **The First Nowell**

On That Most Blessed Night
See **Carol of the Bagpipers**

On the Morning of Christ's Nativity
Ode written during the Christmas of 1629 by the English poet John Milton (1608–1674), who placed this work first in his *Poems* (1645). Milton's first great English poem, written shortly after his 21st birthday, "Christ's Nativity" begins with a short prelude of six stanzas, which ponders the paradox between the Babe's divine power and His mortality. Then follows *The Hymn*, the principal work consisting of 27 stanzas. Rather than elaborate directly upon the Gospel texts of Matthew and Luke, Milton views the Nativity as an event which creates a closer harmony between heaven and earth (Nature), which the music of the angels and the planets herald. But compared with the Advent of the creator, Nature regards herself as most inconsequential. Peering into the future, the poem's latter stanzas emphasize the Incarnate's redemption of mankind through the recovery of righteousness and the overthrow of idolatry, followed by the Day of Judgment. The final stanza returns quietly to the manger and the sleeping Babe, with angels and the Star in attendance nearby.

Regarded as the greatest English poet since Shakespeare, Milton is especially known for his epic poem *Paradise Lost* (completed in 1667), along with its companion *Paradise Regained* (1671).

Once, in Royal David's City
Irish carol, the lyrics of which first appeared in *Hymns for Little Children* (London, 1848), a collection of poems by Mrs. Cecil Frances Alexander (1823–1895). The wife of the bishop of Ireland, Mrs. Alexander created the collection for her godsons to facilitate their appreciation and understanding of the catechism. Thus, "Once, in Royal David's City" serves not only as a simple narrative of the Nativity but also as an elementary treatise on the divinity of Christ as both man and the Son of God. The designation "Royal David's City" implies Bethlehem, as mentioned in the second chapter of Luke's Gospel. Mrs. Alexander's collection also featured another well-known hymn, "All Things Bright and Beautiful."

The music for "Once, in Royal David's City" was written by Henry J. Gauntlett (1805–1876), an Englishman who published the tune as "Irby" in his *Christmas Carols: Four Numbers* (London, 1849). When Mrs. Alexander issued a second edition of her hymns in 1858, all of them included musical settings for piano by Gauntlett, including his 1849 setting of the present carol.

Traditionally, "Once, in Royal David's City" opens the Festival of Nine Lessons and Carols, a world-broadcast, annual musical presentation held on Christmas Eve in the chapel of King's College, Cambridge, England.

See also **Festival of Nine Lessons and Carols.**

One Christmas

Autobiographical short story written by American author Truman Capote (1924–1984).

When his parents divorce after a year of marriage, young Capote is placed with his mother's family in rural Alabama, where he will live until the age of ten. His mother essentially abandons him for a career in New York, while his father returns to his native New Orleans. Capote develops a lasting friendship with one elderly cousin, Miss Sook Faulk, who instills spiritual values, teaches him about Santa Claus, and nicknames him "Buddy." When Buddy is seven years old, his father arranges a Christmas visit with him in his luxurious home in New Orleans. Life in a large city is overwhelming with cumbersome new clothes, disagreeable Creole food, and a man who is more a stranger than a father. Two additional rude awakenings are in store for the boy. One: his thirty-five-year-old father chases rich, elderly widows, marries one for her cash, then finds another when she passes away. Two: Santa Claus is not real, or so it seems, when Buddy discovers his father piling presents under the tree on Christmas Eve.

In the morning, when his father asks if he is pleased with Santa's gifts, Buddy turns the question around and asks what his father will give him. Stunned, the father grants Buddy's wish for a rather expensive model airplane he had seen earlier in town.

Inebriated, raving, and agonizing over Buddy's imminent departure for Alabama, his father, denying God and Santa Claus, wishes that he and Buddy's mother had committed suicide. He begs to hear Buddy say, "I love you, Daddy," but the boy is not prepared to commit.

Back home, Sook supplies the "straight" story of Santa: He exists in all of us, as the Lord would have it, for no single person could do all that Santa must do. And knowing that he must complete a task, also as the Lord would have it, Buddy sends a simple message via postcard to his father that concludes with "…yes I love you Buddy" [sic].

In 1994, a television dramatization of this story starred Katharine Hepburn, T. J. Lowther, Henry Winkler, Swoozie Kurtz, Tonea Stewart, Pat Hingle, Julie Harris. For her performance, Hepburn was nominated in 1995 for the Screen Actors Guild Award for Outstanding Performance by a Female Actor in a Television Movie or Miniseries. Written and produced by Duane Poole. Directed by Tony Bill. Davis Entertainment. Hallmark Home Entertainment Video. Color. 96 min.

See also **A Christmas Memory.**

The One-Horse Open Sleigh
See **Jingle Bells**

One-Hundred-One Dalmatians Christmas
See **A Christmas Carol** (Film and Television Versions)

One Magic Christmas

(1985). Motion picture drama-fantasy.

Each year Santa Claus (Jan Rubes) sends the Christmas angel Gideon (Harry Dean Stanton), a gentle and rather shabby figure dressed in black with a broad-brimmed hat, on a mission to restore the Christmas spirit to one dispirited individual. This year his assignment is Ginnie Grainger (Mary Steenburgen), a grocery store cashier, wife, and mother, whose husband Jack (Gary Basaraba) has lost his job. Despite this and the fact that, as tenants in a company home, his family must vacate the premises by January 1, optimistic Jack retains the Christmas spirit and dreams of opening his own bicycle shop someday. When Jack suggests taking $200 of their $5,000 savings to buy presents for their two young children, six-year-old Abbie (Elisabeth Harnois) and Cal (Robbie Magwood), Ginnie strongly objects, fearing for their savings and scoffing at the notions of Christmas, Santa, and fantasy at a time when they all should be packing.

Appearing to Abbie one night, Gideon reveals his mission and the fact that she will be involved in its fulfillment. As Ginnie reluctantly mails Abbie's letter to Santa on the night of December 23, Gideon exhorts her to find the Christmas spirit, at which all the neighborhood Christmas lights suddenly go out.

Tragedy strikes Ginnie's life from that point, for on Christmas Eve, Ginnie, pulling a double shift, is fired from the store. Worse, Harry Dickens (Wayne Robson), also down on his luck, robs the bank, kills Jack in the attempt, and escapes in Ginnie's car, kidnapping her children. As Harry crashes through a roadblock, losing control and plunging into a river, Gideon rescues the children while Harry perishes.

Learning of her dad's death, Abbie searches for Gideon at the city's community Christmas tree, as he had instructed her, and pleads for him to bring her dad back. Instead, Gideon magically transports Abbie to the North Pole, where Santa retrieves a letter that a young Ginnie had written to him on December 21, 1959. Since only Ginnie's faith can return Jack, according to Santa, she must see this old letter, for then she will remember, and her faith in Christmas will be restored.

The scene now returns to the night of December 23, before Ginnie mailed Abbie's letter to Santa. Ginnie refuses to believe Abbie's tale of an angel having taken her to the North Pole until she examines the old letter that Abbie had brought back. Now convinced, she gladly mails Abbie's own letter and, as the neighborhood Christmas lights suddenly flash back on, Jack returns from a stroll up the street. With a chance of seeing how sad her life would be had she continued without the Christmas spirit, Ginnie spends Christmas Eve with her family, her Scrooge-like manager Herbie (Timothy Webber) demanding that she be at work all the earlier on the day after Christmas. She buys a camp stove from Harry Dickens for $50, which prevents the bank robbery and its consequences, and writes Jack a check for $5,000, the capital he needs to open a bicycle shop. She has learned the spirit of Christmas, the spirit of giving.

This film won Genie Awards in 1986 for Best Overall Sound and Best Sound Editing. It was nominated for a Genie for Best Motion Picture.

With Arthur Hill, Elias Koteas, Michelle Meyrick, Sarah Polley. Written by Thomas Meehan. Produced by Peter O'Brian. Directed by Phillip Borsos. Walt Disney Pictures in Association with Peter O'Brian Productions, Fred Roos, Silver Screen Partners II, and Telefilm Canada. Anchor Bay Entertainment Video. Color. 88 min.

Orange Bowl
See New Year's Day

The Other Wise Man
Classic short story written in 1896 by the American clergyman and author Henry Van Dyke.

Artaban, of the Persian priesthood of the Magi, summons eight of his order together and reveals that, by his astrological calculations, the time is at hand when the Anointed One, the Prince, is to be born as King in Israel. He has sold all of his possessions to purchase a sapphire, a ruby, and a pearl as tribute for the new King. Believing that Artaban is chasing a dream, the others refuse to accompany him to Jerusalem when the astronomical sign appears, the convergence of the planets Jupiter and Saturn.

Setting off to rendezvous with three other Magi bound for Jerusalem — Melchior, Caspar, and Balthazar — Artaban delays his arrival to minister as physician to a critically ill Hebrew exile found near Babylon. Rescued from death, the Hebrew, learning of Artaban's mission, directs him to Bethlehem to find the Messiah, for so say the prophets. But when Artaban's companions leave without him, he returns to Babylon and acquires a caravan with the sapphire.

He arrives in Bethlehem three days after the other Magi have departed and learns from a young mother that they had visited Joseph of Nazareth, whose wife had borne a son. Strangely, she says, Joseph fled with his family to Egypt. As Herod's soldiers raid Bethlehem and begin the "Slaughter of the Innocents," Artaban saves the mother's child by bribing the captain with the ruby, declaring that he is alone.

With only the pearl remaining, Artaban spends years searching for the Messiah in Egypt, to no avail. A Jewish rabbi in Alexandria advises him that the Messiah will be found among the poor and suffering, for so say the prophets. Walking thus among the wretched, Artaban delays his search further in order to feed the hungry, clothe the naked, heal the sick, and comfort the captive.

His search of 33 years finally brings him much aged to Jerusalem, where he ransoms a young girl from slavery with the pearl. Receiving a mortal wound during a sudden earthquake, he hears a voice gently and faintly addressing him. Artaban replies by denying that he has ever fed, clothed, or visited his Lord and King. The voice: "Verily I say unto thee, inasmuch as thou hast done it unto one of the least of these my brethren, thou hast done it unto me" (the story directly quotes the Gospel of Matthew 25:40). Artaban, his gifts accepted, has found the King, for it is the day that Christ is crucified.

Dramatized for television, *The Fourth Wise Man* (1985) starred Martin Sheen as Artaban, with Alan Arkin, Eileen Brennan, Ralph Bellamy, Richard Libertini, Lance Kerwin, Harold Gould. Written by Tom Fontana. Produced by Michael Ray Rhodes, Lewis Abel. Directed by Michael Ray Rhodes. A Paulist Production. Vestron Video. Color. 72 min.

Henry Van Dyke (1852–1933), a Presbyterian minister, first delivered "The Other Wise Man" as a sermon to his congregation, the Brick Presbyterian Church in New York City, in 1896. In the foreword to a later edition of the story, Van Dyke replied to the many queries that he had received regarding why the noble Artaban had lied to save the child in Bethlehem. He stated that lying, hardly justifiable, is sometimes inevitable, and that Artaban could more easily be forgiven a lie than for the betrayal of innocent blood. Van Dyke is also the author of "The First Christmas Tree: A Story of the Forest."

See also **The First Christmas Tree: A Story of the Forest.**

Over the River and Through the Woods

American song, the lyrics for which originated as a poem written in 1844 by Lydia Maria Child (1802–1880) of Medford, Massachusetts. Originally titled "A Boy's Thanksgiving Day," the poem was based on Child's pleasant experiences of traveling to her grandfather's house for Thanksgiving. Her original opening lines read, "Over the river and through the woods/ To Grandfather's house we go," but the name "Grandmother" subsequently replaced "Grandfather," and the lyrics, otherwise lauding the sights and delights of winter holidays, have become associated with Christmas as often as with Thanksgiving. Indeed, "Christmas Day" may substitute for "Thanksgiving Day" in the lyrics. Ms. Child first published her poem in *Flowers for Children*, Volume 2 (New York, 1845). The composer of the musical setting remains anonymous.

The Oxen

Short poem by English novelist and poet Thomas Hardy (1840–1928), penned in 1915.

While sitting by the fireside on Christmas Eve, the poet muses over the ancient legend which holds that, since the first Christmas, oxen have always knelt in reverence at the stroke of midnight on Christmas Eve. Certain that they are kneeling at that very moment, he admits that such a "fancy" would not be accepted today if it was a newly created idea. Yet if someone challenged him to see it all for himself, he would still go, truly hoping that he would witness the miracle.

Not mentioned in the poem is the related legend that animals are also empowered with speech at this magical hour. Neither does Hardy speak of the caveat which applies, that those daring souls intent on witnessing such miracles endanger their lives.

Hardy's best known novels include, among others, *The Mayor of Casterbridge* (1886) and *Tess of the D'Urbervilles* (1891).

See also **The Friendly Beasts; Mass of the Rooster; Superstitions.**

Pakistan

See **Asia and the South Pacific**

Panama

See **Central America**

Pantomime

See **Christmas Drama**

Paraguay

See **South America**

Los Pastorelas

See **Las Posadas**

Pat-a-Pan

Carol from the Burgundian region of France, written by poet Bernard de la Monnoye (1641–1728), who published a carol collection of his poems set to folk tunes of the region in 1701. The lyrics encourage the drum-and-flute team of boys Willie and Robin to celebrate Christmas with joy and praise through their music. The title "Pat-a-Pan" is derived from a portion of the lyrics which imitates the beating of a drum, "pat-a-pat-a-pan," as well as the basic, underlying droning rhythm, the latter also identified in a contemporary drum carol of the twentieth century, "The Little Drummer Boy." Above this, a light melody brings to mind the trilling of a flute, written as "tu-re-lu-re-lu." The carol was first published in English in 1907.

See also **The Little Drummer Boy** (song).

The Peace Carol

American song written in 1965 by Bob Beers of the Beers Family, a folk-singing troupe from upstate New York. Beers wrote the carol in honor of the Reverend Edith Craig Reynolds, a Baptist minister, whose gentle demeanor and wisdom were a source of inspiration to the composer. The Beers Family recorded this piece on two albums, *Christmas with the Beers Family* (Columbia) and *Seasons of Peace: A Great Family Sings* (Biograph), both released in the 1970s. Consisting of three verses, "The Peace Carol" assures that the peace inherent in Christmas Day will abolish all worldly cares and woes. Following each verse, a refrain simply lists some key symbols of that peace: a holly branch, a dove, and the light that is Christmas.

Pennyroyal

See **Christmas Plants**

Peru

See **South America**

Philippines

The only Asian nation where Christianity predominates, the Philippines has enjoyed Christmas since the sixteenth century, when it initially became a Spanish colony. Although the culture and, hence, Christmas customs largely reflect those of Spain and the Roman Catholic Church, traditions are quite diverse from region to region and include those of British, Indian, Chinese, Japanese, and American origins. This discussion will center on the Spanish influence.

The holiday season begins with the Feast of the Immaculate Conception on December 8, followed by the nine-day Novena of *Misas del Gallo* (Masses of the Rooster), a series of predawn masses beginning on December 16. In the Tagalog language, the masses are known as *Simbang Gabi* (Night Mass). Originally a post-harvest mass of thanksgiving, *Simbang Gabi* eventually blended with Christmas. Firecrackers, bands, and carols sung over the church public address system summon villagers to these morning masses; alternatively, the parish priest makes rounds awakening his parishioners by knocking on their doors. Afterwards, food booths set up in the church courtyard offer rice cakes with coconut, ginger tea, and hot chocolate. Other traditions during *Simbang Gabi* include groups of carolers parading through the neighborhoods from 6 P.M. until midnight, and the performance of *Pastores* ("Shepherds"), Nativity plays.

Although Santa Claus, Christmas trees, wreaths, candles, colored lights, and Christmas cards are quite familiar through Western influence, the principal Christmas decoration is the *parol*, a five-pointed star symbolic of the Star of Bethlehem. Bedecked with tassels at each point and affixed to bamboo poles, typical *parols* are covered with colored rice paper and may be lit with candles or electric light bulbs within the structures. They actually are variants of the Latin American *piñata*, replacing the piñata's candies and trinkets with a source of light. Families traditionally fashion their own *parols* and may interlace them together to form Christmas trees. Alternatively, because pine trees are quite expensive, people may construct Christmas trees from cardboard or decorate palm branches with tiny *parols*, fruit, small wooden or bamboo carvings, tiny baskets, rice paper ornaments, tinsel, and icicles.

Another favorite decoration is the Nativity scene, known as the *belén* (Bethlehem).

During the days before Christmas, villages sponsor lantern festivals, the most famous and elaborate of which is that in San Fernando, capital of Pampanga province. These festivals originated from the *parol* parades of the nineteenth century, which preceded the pre-dawn masses of *Simbang Gabi*. With incentives for cash prizes, entrants vie to construct the largest and most spectacular lanterns of the most complex shapes, illuminated by thousands of colored electric lights and paraded through the streets as floats. The winning float from San Fernando is then taken to Rizal Park in the capital city of Manila and displayed as a feature attraction.

Other holiday activities in Manila include various cultural events at public parks and museums; children's events during the week before Christmas at the Malacanang Palace, once the presidential palace and now a museum; the collection and distribution of gifts for needy children by government-sponsored organizations; and the *Fiesta Intramuros*, a month-long festival within the old walled original city.

Prior to the Christmas Eve Midnight Mass, known here as the *Misa del Aguinaldo* (Mass of the Gift), villages often sponsor a *panunuluyan*, a pastoral street play reenacting the search by Mary and Joseph for shelter in Bethlehem. The performance, which ends at the local church around midnight, features either live players or statues with citizens supplying the dialogue. As crowds and brass bands follow along, the scene closely resembles *las posadas* (the lodgings) processions of Latin America.

Following the Christmas Eve Midnight Mass, families return home for a sumptuous meal, known as the *Noche Buena* (Good Night). This may consist of stuffed chicken or fish, stuffed rolls, noodles, rice pudding with ground coconut, ginger tea, rice cakes, and fruit. Although children may traditionally hang up their stockings for Santa Claus, the principal gift giver is the family's *lola* (grandmother), who distributes presents either during *Noche Buena* or on Christmas Day.

Children visit their godparents on Christmas Day and receive gifts after performing a ritual of respect by kissing the godparents'

hands, then touching the hands to their own foreheads. For Christmas dinner, there may be roast suckling pig with caramel custard.

Holy Innocents Day, December 28, is filled with pranks. Those who are successful in their endeavors are absolved of all wrongdoing, and debts need not be repaid. People in costumes may roam the streets portraying King Herod's soldiers in search of the Christ Child.

Noise, fireworks, and superstitions usher in the new year, and the noisier the merriment, the more prosperous will be the outlook. At midnight repasts on New Year's Eve, because round objects are symbols of good luck at this time, revelers customarily follow Spanish tradition by eating twelve grapes at the stroke of twelve. House lights are turned on to ensure a bright year, and the first animal heard at midnight predicts the quality of the coming year. For example, a cow portends abundance; a chicken, poverty. Similarly, a sunny New Year's Day forecasts a good year; rain, a miserable year. Families also must remain at home on New Year's Day to guard against being called away from home during the year.

Epiphany, Three Kings Day, originally observed on January 6, is now celebrated on the first Sunday in January with a mass and pageants about the Magi. On Epiphany Eve, villagers adorned as the Magi hold street processions, and children place their shoes on window sills to receive gifts overnight from the royal trio.

"Merry Christmas" is *Maligayang Pasko* (Tagalog).

See also **Epiphany; Feast of the Immaculate Conception; Holy Innocents Day; Las Posadas; Mass of the Rooster; Spain.**

Pinocchio's Christmas

(1980). Made-for-television animated story using stop-motion puppets (Animagic), loosely based on the classic children's book, *The Adventures of Pinocchio* (1883), by Italian author Carlo Collodi (pseudonym for Carlo Lorenzini).

Pinocchio, a talking marionette fashioned by the old wood carver Geppetto, joins Maestro Fire Eater's side show to earn money to buy Geppetto a Christmas gift. He falls in love with Julietta, a plain marionette, and carries her away when Fire Eater plans to change her into a Wise Man. Pinocchio escapes into the Forest of Enchantment, pursued by Fox and Cat, who pose as friends but secretly plan to sell him to a duke who wants an unusual Christmas gift for his son. The forest spirit Lady Azura rescues the two marionettes and teaches Pinocchio that the best Christmas gifts that he can bestow upon Papa Geppetto are simply his love and obedience, neither of which can be purchased with money.

Eventually kidnapped and taken to the duke's castle on Christmas Eve, Pinocchio imparts the lesson he learned, that Christmas means much more than presents. Upon his release, Pinocchio hitches a ride with Santa and returns to a joyful Geppetto just in time for Christmas. Pinocchio receives the best gift of all, a living Julietta, thanks to Lady Azura.

Voices: Todd Porter, Alan King, George Irving, Robert McFadden, Pat Bright, Allen Swift, Diane Leslie, Gerry Matthews, Ray Owens, Tiffany Blake, Carl Tramon, Alice Gayle. Written by Romeo Muller. Produced and directed by Arthur Rankin, Jr., and Jules Bass. Rankin/Bass Productions. Vestron Video. Color. 60 min.

Plum Pudding
See **Great Britain**

Poinsettia

(*Euphorbia pulcherrima*). Popular decorative plant native to Central America and tropical Mexico. Regarded as symbols of purity, poinsettias originally grew to heights of 10 feet. Below inconspicuous floral whorls are large, colored leaves, or bracts, which serve the function of petals. The poinsettia's white sap is known as latex.

Prior to the Spanish conquest of the Americas in the sixteenth century, the Aztecs had used this plant, which they called *cuetlaxochitl* ("false flower"), as a textile and cosmetic dye and its sap as an antipyretic.

As Christmas decorations, poinsettias date from the seventeenth century, when Franciscan priests of Taxco del Alarcon in southern Mexico first incorporated them to add color and festivity to holiday processions. They became the subject of a legend, several variations of which explained their significance to Christ-

mas. According to a composite legend, Pepita, a poor Mexican girl, despaired because she had no gift to lay before the altar at Christmas Eve Midnight Mass. Comforted by her cousin Pedro, who believed that any gift, no matter how small or unsightly, would be accepted if given in love, Pepita plucked a few weeds and placed them before the *Pesebre* (Nativity scene). Miraculously, the weeds were transformed into large, brilliantly red leaves, which led to their Spanish designation, *Flores de la Noche Buena* (Flowers of the Holy Night).

Poinsettias were named for Dr. Joel R. Poinsett (1779–1851), a botanist from Greenville, South Carolina, who took a keen interest in the plant while serving as the first U.S. ambassador to Mexico from 1824 to 1829. In 1828, Poinsett first dispatched a number of the Mexican specimens to his home, where they were cultivated and circulated to other botanical gardens, and by 1836, the plants had acquired their common name, poinsettias. From 1923 on, selective breeding by horticulturists in southern California, such as the Paul Ecke family, produced a shorter variety of poinsettia with more branches and with bracts of green, yellow, white, or pink. In 1963 came the cultivars that grew best as potted plants. Contrary to popular belief, poinsettias are nontoxic.

National Poinsettia Day, December 12, commemorates the death of Dr. Poinsett.
See also **Christmas Plants**.

Poland

This nation has enjoyed *Gwiazdka* ("little star"), Christmas, since the late tenth century, when Mieszko, son of the legendary king Piast, introduced Christianity to his land. The holiday traditions are firmly rooted in ancient folklore and superstitions which center primarily around seeking a mate, repelling evil, and forecasting the future. Roman Catholicism is the predominant Christian faith which observes typical Advent customs, including the *Roraty*, a mass held early each morning during the four weeks of Advent. Homes and churches display the traditional *szopka* (Nativity scene or crèche), and the city of Kraków annually hosts a national crèche competition at its Historical Museum, where the entries are displayed from early December until February.

Also during Advent are observed *Andrze-jki* (St. Andrew's Day, November 30), *Baborka* (St. Barbara's Day, December 4), and *Mikolaj* (St. Nicholas' Day, December 6). Amid the social gatherings of *Andrzejki*, unwed girls place their left shoes in a row from a wall to a door. The first girl whose shoe crosses the threshold is soon to wed. The direction in which a needle points when thrown into water indicates the direction in which a boy should seek his mate, and melted wax poured through the eye of a door key into cool water forms shapes, the shadows of which are believed to predict forthcoming events. Festive gatherings also celebrate St. Barbara, patron saint of lightning, artillery, and miners. *Swiety Mikolaj* (Saint Nicholas) arrives on his feast day to examine children in their catechism and to leave them treats such as apples, nuts, and cookies, which are placed under their pillows on the evening prior. A small rod of chastisement accompanies these gifts as a reminder that youngsters should maintain proper deportment.

With the preliminary cooking, baking, and traditional house cleaning accomplished, festivities climax on *Wigilia*, Christmas Eve (from the Latin *vigilare*, "watch on the eve of a feast"), commencing with the *Polaznik*, a custom similar to "first footing" of Great Britain. (*See* **Great Britain** [ENGLAND]). Because it is believed that a man first visiting a home on this day portends good luck (the opposite if the visitor is a woman), families customarily arrange for the appropriate visitor. Upon his arrival at dawn, the man tosses wheat over the family for luck. After feasting with them and receiving a gift, he departs at evening. It is also believed that events transpiring on this day will impact the coming year. Thus, family members and friends strive to resolve quarrels and disputes, lest these precipitate a troublesome year. The *choinka* (Christmas tree) is decorated at this time with an assortment of items, often handmade, including stars, painted egg shells, nuts, candy, apples, oranges, glass ornaments, candles, "angel hair" (strips of clear paper), and paper chains. Mistletoe hung above the front door serves as a talisman against evil.

Sighting the first star of *Wigilia* (thought to be the Star of Bethlehem) heralds Christmas and the Christmas Eve supper, which breaks a fast observed throughout the day. The table is set with a white tablecloth, under which is placed straw to commemorate Christ's manger. An extra place is also set for any unexpected guest, commemorative of Mary and Joseph who sought shelter, for no one is turned away on this night.

The meal begins with the solemn ceremony of breaking the *Oplatek* (communion wafer, now commercially available but formerly baked by church organists, who distributed them about the parish during Advent). The father or eldest member breaks the wafer in half and gives half to the mother with wishes for love, prosperity and happiness for the coming year. After he breaks and eats a portion of her half, the mother reciprocates, after which the ceremony is repeated between the father, children, and other relatives present. Then follows the meatless meal which traditionally must consist of an odd number of courses (at least twelve in memory of the Twelve Apostles) and an even number of diners for luck. The menu often includes cooked or dried carp; herring; assortment of soups such as red beet, fermented rye, fish, and *barszcz* (mushroom soup); sauerkraut with beans; dried fruit compote; *pierogi* (dumplings stuffed with mushrooms, cabbage, or fruit); *makowiec* (baked poppy seed bread); strudel; and *kutia* (poppy seed and wheat pasta with honey, raisins, almonds, and spices). To assure fertility, livestock are fed the *Oplatek*, and fruit trees are beaten with branches. In some rural areas, a fertility ritual involves a man throwing dried fruit upon fruit trees with threats to cut them down. His wife intercedes and ties a straw rope around them, which assures a bountiful harvest.

After the meal, children receive gifts from the Star Man, who symbolizes the Star of Bethlehem. Similar to St. Nicholas, he arrives to quiz youngsters in their catechism and is accompanied by a host of Star Boys dressed as Wise Men, shepherds, or other personae from the Nativity. The latter sing *kolady* (Christmas carols) and receive some remuneration for their efforts. *Wigilia* concludes with the *Pasterka* (Mass of the Shepherds), the term for Midnight Mass.

Christmas Day is spent at home, while visitations are reserved for St. Stephen's Day (December 26). *Herody* (carolers), consisting of troupes of twelve boys, wander from house to house with a repertoire of carols and, upon admission, reenact scenes from the life of King Herod. On Epiphany, January 6, the final day of the season, the Star Boys once again travel door to door, marking a cross over doorways with the letters "C. M. B.," the initials of the traditional names of the three Wise Men, Caspar, Melchior, and Balthasar.

• OTHER WIGILIA FORECASTS:

Girls grinding poppy seed will wed soon.

The direction of the first barking dog heard after dinner points the direction from which a girl's future husband will come.

En route to the *Pasterka*, if a blindfolded girl touches a smooth picket fence, her future husband will be resourceful; a rough fence portends a clumsy spouse.

The first object pulled from a river reveals the profession of a girls' future spouse: wood, a carpenter; iron, a blacksmith, and so forth.

If Christmas sees no snow, Easter will.

A sunny Christmas Eve brings fair weather all year round.

A green straw drawn from beneath the tablecloth foretells of marriage; a withered straw, a period of waiting; a yellow straw, spinsterhood; a short straw, an early grave.

If smoke from extinguished candles moves toward a window, the harvest will be bountiful; toward a door, a family member will die soon; toward the stove, a marriage.

"Merry Christmas" in Polish is *Wesolych Swiat*.

See also **Advent; Czech Republic; Epiphany; Slovak Republic.**

The Polar Express

Children's book written and illustrated in 1985 by American children's author Chris Van Allsburg (1949–), who won a Caldecott Medal for its illustrations.

Late one Christmas Eve, a little boy boards a mysterious train waiting at his house. The Polar Express, says the conductor, is bound for the North Pole, where Santa will give the first gift of Christmas to one of the many children on board. After a meal of candies and hot cocoa, the children arrive at Santa's toy factories and see hundreds of elves cheering Santa.

When asked what he wants for Christmas, the same little boy requests only one silver bell from Santa's sleigh, which becomes the first gift of Christmas. But when the boy loses the bell through a hole in his pocket, he finds it wrapped in a little box under his Christmas tree back home. Although he and his little sister Sara enjoy the bell's sweet ring, their parents are unable to hear the bell and think that it is broken. Over time the bell falls silent for Sara, but never for the boy, now grown, because the bell is audible only to those who truly believe in Santa Claus.

Chris Van Allsburg (1949–) also won the Caldecott Medal for *Jumanji* (1981). Other works include *Ben's Dream* (1982), *The Wreck of the Zephyr* (1983), and *The Sweetest Fig* (1993). He also illustrated Mark Helprin's adaptation of *Swan Lake* (1989), based on the Tchaikovsky ballet.

Portugal

Contiguous with Spain, Portugal shares much of its neighbor's holiday traditions. After the Christmas Eve *Missa do Galo* (Mass of the Rooster), families return for the traditional *Consoada* (Christmas Supper), which may consist of cod fish with boiled potatoes, cabbage, and *bolo rei* (a fruit cake), the latter stuffed with small trinkets plus one bean. Whoever receives the bean in his slice must furnish the cake next Christmas. Remembering their deceased relatives, families set empty places at the table for the *alminhas a penar* (souls of the dead) and leave crumbs for them on the hearth. Formerly, the offering consisted of seeds in the belief that the souls would ensure a bountiful harvest next year. If a household burns a *fogueira da consonda* (Yule log), the ashes are kept and burned with pine cones in the stormy season, for, according to legend, where the smoke drifts, no thunderbolt will strike.

"Merry Christmas" in Portuguese is *Boas Festas*.

See also **Mass of the Rooster; Spain.**

Posadas

See **Las Posadas**

Las Posadas

(Spanish, "The Lodgings"). An important fiesta commemorating the difficulties that Mary and Joseph encountered in finding lodging in Bethlehem. Because, by tradition, their journey from Nazareth to Bethlehem required nine days, this fiesta is observed from December 16 through 24 in a number of Latin American countries, most prominently in Mexico, and in Spanish-speaking communities of the United States. Las Posadas dates from the colonial period, from the Spanish conquest of the Americas in the early sixteenth century. In Mexico, to induce the native Aztec people to accept Christianity more readily, Franciscan friars introduced Las Posadas in order to Christianize a portion of the Aztec winter solstice festival, observed from December 7 to December 26, which commemorated the annual rebirth of the Aztec sun god Huitzilopochtli.

Within neighborhoods, those homes determined beforehand to represent the *posadas* are colorfully decorated with such items as Spanish moss, evergreens, and colored paper lanterns. Regardless of whether they are chosen as *posadas*, most homes typically display *Pesebres*, Nativity scenes erected on a special altar in one or more rooms, often completely landscaped with little trees, ponds, a stable or cave with figures of Mary and Joseph, livestock, shepherds, and an empty cradle (Wise Men figures traditionally do not "arrive" until Epiphany). The presence of evil in the world is also represented with a serpent or devil statue.

On each of the nine nights, families form a procession, led by a child dressed as an angel. Two other children dress as Mary (who may ride a burro) and Joseph, while the others, singing *villancicos* (Christmas carols), follow with lighted candles and *faroles* (paper lanterns). Some may be dressed as the three Wise Men or as shepherds carrying decorated *baculos* (walking staffs). In one version, as the procession arrives at the *posada* for the evening, it splits into two groups, the Holy Pilgrims and the Cruel Innkeepers. Marching through the house, the Pilgrims sing a ritualistic dialogue, asking for shelter, while the Innkeepers respond in the negative. The Pilgrims then identify Mary and Joseph as the expectant parents of Jesus, whereupon the Innkeepers grant lodging. In another version, as the procession travels from house to house requesting lodging in like manner, the occu-

pants (Innkeepers) turn them away, until they reach one designated house, at which the procession enters. Lodging having been granted, the participants gather around the candle-lit *Pesebre* for prayers and special blessings.

On Christmas Eve, a statue of Baby Jesus is laid in the crib, followed by the traditional singing of the lullaby "El Rorro" (translated as "The Babe" but also known as "Rocking the Child" and "O, Ru-Ru-Ru, My Little Jesus"), a folk carol thought to date from the eighteenth or nineteenth century.

Following the ceremonies of each evening come festivities with fireworks, singing and dancing, *buñuelos* (thin, fried pastries), *colacion* (assorted candies), fruit, *ponche* (hot fruit punch, laced with rum or tequila for the adults or sweetened with brown sugar, cinnamon and vanilla for the children), *tamales*, *atole* (corn gruel), and a *piñata* (particularly in Mexico). The latter consists of a decorative earthenware jar in the shape of an animal, doll, or other attractive figure, suspended overhead and filled with all manner of treats, nuts, and sweets. Blindfolded children try, one by one, to break the *piñata* with a long stick, and when broken, there is a happy scramble for the prizes.

Morality plays, *Los Pastorelas* (Shepherds Plays), also depict the journey to Bethlehem during these nine days, but from the shepherds' point of view. Like Las Posadas, these plays date from the Spanish conquest of Mexico and Central and South America. Roman Catholic missionaries, seeking converts, took Native American dramatizations, which the nations had built around historic events in their own culture, and adapted them to key biblical events. Although such plays originally mirrored the strictly religious plots from the mystery plays of medieval Europe, they, like their European counterparts, eventually fell into the hands of folk performers, where they evolved into comedies in which the principal characters, the shepherds, were depicted as lazy oafs and buffoons, along with less-than-spiritual dialogue. But whereas the Shepherds Plays and other mystery plays of Europe declined with the Protestant Reformation, these plays have thrived in the Americas, despite their less formal evolutions, and frequently appear as popular public performances during the holidays. As this traditional story of good versus evil now stands, shepherds, having received the annunciation of Christ's birth from an angel, reluctantly set out for Bethlehem. En route, Satan and his legions attempt to thwart their progress through a series of mishaps; yet the shepherds, whom angels and an old hermit shield from harm, persevere and arrive to worship the Christ Child.

See also **Mexico**.

Prancer

(1989). Motion picture drama.

Rebecca Harrell plays nine-year-old Jessica Riggs, who claims that one of Santa's reindeer, Prancer, is wounded and loose in the woods around Three Oaks, Michigan. She developed this notion from two sources: First, a reindeer figure that she identified as Prancer fell from the city's overhead Christmas display and crashed to the street. Second, she saw a reindeer in the woods and noticed that it had markings identical to a magazine's rendering of the mythical reindeer. Jessica's father, an impoverished, no-nonsense apple farmer and widower (Sam Elliott), who pays little attention to her except to scold, dismisses her story as mere childishness.

Discovering Prancer lying in their barn, Jessica hides him in a remote shed, feeds him Christmas cookies, engages a veterinarian (Abe Vigoda) to treat his wound, and, to buy fodder, works on the sly for a cantankerous old recluse (Cloris Leachman), whose life Jessica also brightens by adorning her roof with Christmas lights discovered in her attic.

Jessica entrusts a photograph and a letter outlining Prancer's condition to a Santa (Michael Constantine) at the local shopping mall with faith that he will forward these on to the *real* Santa. Instead, he delivers them to the editor at the city newspaper with an idea for a heart-warming, human-interest story. By next morning, an editorial titled "Yes, Santa, There Are Still Virginias" (a slant on the famed Francis Church editorial "Yes, Virginia, There Is a Santa Claus") extols the virtues of Jessica's belief in Santa, and curiosity seekers storm Riggs's farm to see Prancer.

When Riggs, irate over Jessica's actions,

sells Prancer to a local merchant as an advertising gimmick, Jessica runs away. Feeling that, without Prancer, there is nothing left for her in Three Oaks, Jessica attempts to free him in time for Christmas but falls from a tree and sustains minor injuries. The accident softens Riggs's heart, and on Christmas Eve, the two release Prancer in the woods and follow him to the edge of Antler Ridge, where his tracks end. They never see Prancer again, but the viewer sees a white streak mounting to the sky which meets Santa's team flying in the distance.

In 1990 the picture received Young Artist Award nominations for Best Young Actress Starring in a Motion Picture (Rebecca Harrell) and Best Young Actress Supporting Role (Ariana Richards).

With Rutanya Alda, John Joseph Duda, Mark Rolston, Walter Charles, Michael Luciano. Greg Taylor, who wrote the script, created the story for his own seven-year-old daughter. Produced by Raffaella De Laurentiis. Directed by John Hancock. Nelson Entertainment in Association with Cineplex Odeon Films. MGM/UA Video. Color. 103 min.

See also **Yes, Virginia, There Is a Santa Claus**.

The Preacher's Wife

See **The Bishop's Wife**

Pretty Paper

American song written in 1963 by country singer-songwriter Willie Nelson. The lyrics are a reminder that, amid the sparkle, bustle, and dazzle of the holiday, others such as the lonely, despondent, and homeless must not be forgotten, for it is at Christmastime that they suffer want more than ever. Nelson's friend, singer Roy Orbison, brought "Pretty Paper" to the forefront, for Orbison's recording on the Monument label placed number 15 on the *Billboard Hot 100* chart in 1963.

Willie Nelson is one of country music's biggest stars. Among many other songs, he wrote the Grammy Award winner "Always on My Mind" (1982) as well as "Crazy" (1961).

Puerto Rico

See **West Indies**

R

Reindeer
See **Saint Nicholas**

Remember the Night
(1940). Motion picture comedy-romance. Assistant New York district attorney John Sargent (Fred MacMurray) takes compassion on Lee Leander (Barbara Stanwyck), a beautiful larcenist arrested just before Christmas. With the trial postponed until after the holidays, John bails her out of jail and, because she has nowhere to turn, invites her to spend the holidays at his mother's farm in Indiana. John's family, simple, wholesome, down-home folks, quickly accept Lee as one of the family, despite her past, and shower her with warmth and love.

The holidays, the most memorably touching moments that Lee has ever experienced, pass all too quickly, and as the hour approaches when they must return to New York, Lee and John realize that they are desperately in love with each other. John, wishing to have Lee acquitted, attempts to throw the case, but Lee, unwilling to compromise John's position, breaks down with a full confession of her guilt in court. Although a few years must separate them, John and Lee vow to be married upon her release.

With Beulah Bondi, Elizabeth Patterson, Sterling Holloway. Written by Preston Sturges. Produced and directed by Mitchell Leisen. Paramount Pictures. MCA Universal Home Video. B & W. 94 min.

Republic of South Africa
See **Africa**

Resonet in Laudibus
See **Joseph, Dearest Joseph Mine**

Revenge Is Sweet
See **Babes in Toyland**

Rich Little's Christmas Carol
See **A Christmas Carol** (Film and Television Versions)

The Right to Be Happy
See **A Christmas Carol** (Film and Television Versions)

Ring Out, Wild Bells
Carol for the New Year, the lyrics to which were written by English poet Alfred, Lord Tennyson (1809–1892). The lyrics are taken from the 106th canto of the elegy *In Memoriam*, Tennyson's tribute to a close friend and his sister's fiancé, Arthur Henry Hallam, who died in 1833 at the age of 22. Plunged into deep, spiritual depression, Tennyson composed the elegy over sixteen years (1833–1849) and published it in 1850, the same year that he was appointed Poet Laureate of England. *In Memoriam* consists of 131 cantos, each a separate poem with independent thought. Together, they celebrate Hallam's life, lament Tennyson's loss, express his search to find a way to cope with his feelings of abandonment and depression, and find justification for human immortality by working through the loss of faith which plagued English society at that time (the scientific revolution and secularization had begun to challenge Christian principles, thus creating a spiritual crisis).

With the old year waning quickly, "Ring Out, Wild Bells" is an appeal to ring out false pride, slanderings, and spite, and ring in that which is new, the common love of good, truth and right, and the Christ that is to be. Although the musical setting remains anonymous (as does the one who joined words and music together), it was once attributed to Mozart. It has also been attributed to Carl Zulehner and to Wenzel Muller; both of these names are obscure.

Alfred, Lord Tennyson was one of the foremost English poets of the Victorian era. His best-known works include the poems "Morte d'Arthur" and "The Charge of the Light Brigade."

Rise Up, Shepherd, and Follow
Anonymous, African American spiritual collected during the American Civil War and

first published in *Slave Songs of the United States*, edited by William Allen, Charles Ware, and Lucy Garrison (New York, 1867). The song received its title from the repetitive phrase traditionally sung by a choir in response to a soloist's rendering of the verses. Urging the shepherds to forsake their flocks, the text bids them to "take good heed to the angel's words" and follow the star in the East to Bethlehem (which takes liberties with the biblical account of the Wise Men and the star as recorded in the second chapter of Matthew's Gospel). The African American soprano Dorothy Maynor (1910–1996), who recorded with Serge Koussevitsky and the Boston Symphony and who founded New York City's Harlem School of the Arts in 1963, popularized this spiritual in the United States.

Rockin' Around the Christmas Tree

Popular American song written by Johnny Marks in 1958. A writer of numerous Christmas songs and known especially for his hit of 1949, "Rudolph, the Red-Nosed Reindeer," Marks entered the rock and roll era by contributing "Rockin'," which was the second major rock Christmas song, the first being "Jingle Bell Rock" (1957) by Joseph Beal and James Boothe. The lyrics center around the Christmas "hop" (1950s teenage term for a dance gathering), where the boys and girls are dancing the "new old-fashioned way."

Thirteen-year-old Brenda Lee (nicknamed "Little Miss Dynamite"), a most promising recording artist since age eleven, recorded "Rockin'" on the Decca label in 1958. It did not attract radio disc jockeys for two years, until Lee had accumulated a number of other big-time hits, after which radio stations across the country were more than willing to play "Rockin'." When the song finally became a hit in 1960 as the top Christmas song that year (position 14 on the *Billboard Hot 100* chart), it sold some 6.5 million copies. Subsequently it was charted each year during the 1960s.

Of the 25 most frequently performed Christmas songs of the twentieth century listed by the American Society of Composers, Authors and Publishers (ASCAP), "Rockin' Around the Christmas Tree" is ranked number 19.

See also **Jingle Bell Rock**; **Rudolph, the Red-Nosed Reindeer** (song).

Rocking

("Hajej, nynej"). Czech traditional lullaby with variant titles of "Rocking Carol," "Lullaby," "Little Jesus, Sweetly Sleep," "Shepherd's Rocking Carol," and "Jesu, Jesu, Baby Dear." Thought perhaps to be the oldest of carol lullabies, it originated sometime between the fourteenth and sixteenth centuries. The carol's two verses, each with six lines, mimic gentle cradle rocking, particularly through the repetitious phrase of "We will rock you, rock you, rock you" found in line three of both verses. A number of English translations exist, some of which repeat the entire "We will rock you" phrase for line four as well. In others, line four reads "Gently slumber as we rock you." The melody is somewhat reminiscent of that for the children's tune "Twinkle, Twinkle, Little Star."

Because "Rocking" arose during the Middle Ages, it is believed to have been included in a repertoire of cradle songs used for Christmas cradle-rocking ceremonies of the time. Originating in Germany and thence to all of Europe, cradle rocking was once a feature of Christmas vespers, wherein the priest rocked a cradle containing an image of the Christ Child to an appropriate cradle song. Groups of children rocking cradles would also parade through the streets while singing a lullaby.

Rocking Carol

See **Rocking**

Romania

Having received Christianity from Bulgaria of the Byzantine Empire (of which it was once a subject), Romania has enjoyed Christmas since the ninth century. The principal Christian faiths include the Eastern Orthodox Church and Roman Catholicism. Because the Orthodox Church follows the older Julian calendar for ecclesiastical purposes, Christmas Day falls on January 7 by the current Gregorian calendar.

The Christmas season extends from Christmas Eve until Epiphany, thirteen days later. A preliminary event, St. Nicholas Day, is observed on December 6, when children place their boots near an entrance on the eve before, so that *Mos Nicolae* (Old Nicholas) can fill them with candy and treats; naughty children receive sticks.

Colindatul (caroling) on Christmas Eve constitutes the most important tradition of the season and involves community-wide participation. Large groups of *colindatori* (carolers) organize and travel from door to door singing a mixture of sacred and secular *colinde* (carols). The texts of secular folk carols widely vary and include fairy tales and themes of romance and marriage. Other folk carols center around legends of God and the saints, placing them in fictitious situations. Those carols most inspired by the Scriptures are known as *cantece de stea* (star songs) and are usually sung by children, who carry icons of Jesus and painted or illuminated paper stars, *steaua*, on poles. For their participation, the children receive fruit, nuts, pastries, bread, or money. Accompanied by flute and drum in many areas, the carolers call upon the names of each person in the house, beginning with the head and including members deceased during that year, and offer a specific carol of blessing with good wishes for each of them, based upon their marital state, profession, and so forth; hence, the repertoire of carols is quite extensive. Traditional dances always accompany the carols, after which the host offers the troupe food, drink, and gifts.

Christmas Eve customs also include decorating the home with fir branches and the Christmas tree with multicolored ornaments and candles. In Hunedoara of Transylvania, *pizarai*, groups of children bearing a *pizara* (lance) on which is tied a headkerchief, travel from house to house with recitations for health, happiness, and good fortune during the holiday. As they recite, they touch members of the household with the lance as a means of transferring the wishes. This tradition closely resembles the *sorcova* of New Year's Day (see below). The region of Moldavia features the unique *umblatul cu ursul* (bear custom), in which a man portrays a bear by wearing a bear mask and animal skins adorned with red tassels. The man growls and imitates the grotesque steps of a dancing bear, while throngs of people, especially children and mu-

sicians, accompany him. Christmas Eve concludes with Midnight Mass, and Christmas Day traditions mirror those in the United States.

Throughout the season, Nativity plays and masked dances are popular. Best known among the latter is the *Capra* (Goat), which is performed from Christmas until New Year's Day. In Wallachia and Oltenia, this dance is termed *Brezaia* because the masks feature a host of colors; in other regions, the custom is known as "Stag." The masks are fashioned after goats, oxen, or deer with movable jaws which champ together as the performers, clad in animal skins, dance and contort in a comic routine, accompanied by clamoring children and men shouting *strigaturi* (humorous remarks). While the goat once symbolized fertility at the winter solstice, it is said that this goat custom most likely derives from ancient Jewish rituals once performed on the Day of Atonement (Yom Kippur). As detailed in Leviticus 16, one of two goats became a sacrificial sin offering, and the other became a scapegoat that was released into the wilderness, bearing away the sins of the congregation (the scapegoat concept of transferring disease or bad luck onto an animal or human to be sacrificed also was known to the Assyrians, Babylonians, and Greeks). This ritual foreshadowed Christ, who would become the ultimate scapegoat for the sins of all humanity through His crucifixion, and the Romanian goat custom recalls this theme during celebrations of His birth. Some performances include an Old Man mask, representative of the man who led the scapegoat into the wilderness.

Parties, fireworks, and clamor greet the new year as in the West, and the fertility tradition of *Plugusorul* (Little Plow) brings wishes for a bountiful crop and success in the new year. Bearing a plow adorned with colored paper or embroidered cloth, teenagers travel from house to house and deliver an elaborate, poetic recitation which petitions the spirit of the plowman to bless the crops. The text, delivered amid the din of bells, cracking whips, and a bellowing *buhai* (bagpipe), makes special mention of the foundation of Romania in the days of the Roman emperor Trajan, who conquered the land formerly known as Dacia about the year A.D. 106. In another fertility tradition known as *Sorcova* (from the Slavic *soroku*, "forty"), groups of children wish their parents, friends, and neighbors a long and prosperous life through the *sorcova*, a fruit-tree branch decorated with colored paper and artificial flowers. While reciting a traditional poem of forty lines, the children, all of whom bear a *sorcova*, touch their elders forty times with the branch as a symbolic means of transferring the wishes. For their participation, the children receive rewards of sweets and coins.

Forecasting the future remains a favorite New Year's pastime. *Obiceiul Mesei* (Table Custom) involves hiding either a coin, corn, mirror, or lump of coal at each of the four corners of a table under a tablecloth. Then four children arrange themselves at the corners and uncover the objects before them. The coin forecasts wealth; the corn, abundant food; the mirror, beauty and nobility of soul; the coal, bad luck. For *Obiceiul Puntilor* (Bridge Custom), children take a forked branch and place a stick between the two forks, which symbolizes a bridge between the old and new years. With such a bridge, a child may dream of his destiny on New Year's night.

On Epiphany, the priest, using a branch of basil to sprinkle holy water about, blesses the homes of his parishioners.

"Merry Christmas" is *Sarbatori Vesele*.

See also **Epiphany**; **Saint Nicholas Day**.

Rose Bowl

See **New Year's Day**

Rosemary

See **Christmas Plants**

Rudolph and Frosty: Christmas in July

(1979). Made-for-television animated sequel to *Rudolph, the Red-Nosed Reindeer* and *Frosty the Snowman*, using stop-motion puppets (Animagic).

In order to help the foundering "Circus by the Sea," Rudolph, Frosty the Snowman, and Frosty's wife and two children head south to become the circus's star attractions in its "Christmas in July" show over the Fourth of July weekend. The evil Winterbolt, King of the

Two children set off with their sorcova, *a branch decorated with fruit and ribbons on New Year's Day. From the journal* Cesky Lid *(published in Prague), 1910.*

North, forms an elaborate plot to eliminate Rudolph and Santa, so that he will be sole ruler of the North. This involves framing Rudolph for a circus robbery (said crime extinguishing the magic behind his bright, red nose), and Rudolph's promise of silence about the truth of the robbery in exchange for the lives of Frosty's family, who wear Winterbolt amulets which prevent their melting. To silence Frosty, Winterbolt tricks him into relinquishing his hat, his source of life. Rudolph pursues Winterbolt and recovers the hat, the wearing of which also restores Rudolph's bright nose. He returns to the circus, recovers the stolen money, and names the perpetrator, a crooked showman named Sam Spangle.

The shattering of his ice scepter defeats Winterbolt, but his amulets also fail, and the

Frosty family melts. Only the icy winds of Jack Frost, wintering in South America in July, can restore the Frostys. Brought in by Clockwork Big Ben (a whale introduced in an earlier sequel, *Rudolph's Shiny New Year*), Jack accomplishes a happy ending as Santa, delayed by Winterbolt's storm, arrives to return everyone to the North Pole.

Featuring the songs "Rudolph, the Red-Nosed Reindeer," "Frosty the Snowman," "Rockin' Around the Christmas Tree," "I Heard the Bells on Christmas Day." Principal voices: Red Buttons, Ethel Merman, Mickey Rooney, Alan Sues, Jackie Vernon, Shelley Winters, Paul Frees, Billie Richards, Hal Peary, Shelby Flint, Don Messick. Written by Romeo Muller. Produced and directed by Arthur Rankin, Jr., and Jules Bass. Rankin/Bass Productions. Warner Home Video. Color. Half-hour.

See also the animated cartoons **Frosty the Snowman; Frosty Returns; Frosty's Winter Wonderland; Rudolph, the Red-Nosed Reindeer; Rudolph's Shiny New Year.**

Rudolph, the Red-Nosed Reindeer

Highly popular character created in 1939 by Robert L. May (1905–1976), an advertising writer born in New Rochelle, New York, and immortalized in a song written by his brother-in-law, New York City songwriter John D. (Johnny) Marks (1909–1985). The song was released in 1949.

• BACKGROUND WITH ROBERT MAY. May created Rudolph as a Christmas promotional gimmick for the Montgomery Ward Company, a department store chain based in Chicago. Instead of buying coloring books to give away to holiday shoppers as it had done in years past, Ward assigned May, one of its writers at the Chicago office, the task of producing a give-away booklet of its own, to save money. Small, frail, and ostracized from school teams as a youngster, May used his own childhood experiences to create a story about a little reindeer whom other reindeer taunted for his physical abnormality, a big, shiny red nose. But the reindeer's "deformity" became an asset in guiding Santa's sleigh through heavy fog on Christmas Eve.

Tossing around names such as "Rollo" and "Reginald," May hit on an alliterative name, "Rudolph, the Red-Nosed Reindeer," in keeping with the style of cartoon names in the 1930s, then wrote the story as a poem consisting of rhyming couplets. Although May's original title read "The Day Before Christmas, or Rudolph, the Red-Nosed Reindeer," Montgomery Ward shortened the title to its now-famous version. Denver Gillen, an artist for Ward, provided the illustrations, based on sketches he had made of reindeer at Chicago's Lincoln Park Zoo.

Montgomery Ward distributed some 2.4 million copies of May's 32-page creation in 1939 alone, and by 1946, the number had reached 3.5 million. Although Ward initially owned the copyright, in 1947 the company generously assigned the rights to May, who formed Rudolph the Red-Nosed Enterprises, Inc. A large host of Rudolph products followed, including a two-disc record album in 1947, narrated by Paul Wing with music by George Kleinsinger, and an animated cartoon "short" feature for theaters in 1948, directed by Max Fleischer, from the Detroit-based Jim Handy Company, with narration and music by Wing and Kleinsinger. The revenues thus generated offset debts which May had incurred while caring for his terminally ill wife, who had died during Rudolph's inception.

For more than 25 years, May displayed on the front lawn of his Chicago-area home a life-size, papier-mâché figure of Rudolph with a red light bulb nose. In 1958, he donated the original manuscript and other Rudolph memorabilia to his alma mater, Dartmouth College. Rudolph is considered to be the only original addition to the Santa Claus folklore in the twentieth century.

• MAY'S ORIGINAL STORY. In the reindeer community, far removed from the North Pole, the reindeer are at play on Christmas Eve, except red-nosed Rudolph. Although he is a good little buck, he is jeered by his peers and barred from their games because of his nose. That night, thick fog hinders Santa's trip, and his blind, low flying results in several mishaps, until he drops by Rudolph's house. Impressed by the red nose, Santa, worried that he will not finish his rounds before morning, persuades Rudolph to bail him out by leading the team. After a successful night, the other reindeer treat Rudolph as a celebrity, and Santa promises to call on him again, should foul weather threaten future Christmas Eves.

• "RUDOLPH" BOOK SEQUELS. Robert May created other stories about Rudolph. In *Rudolph Shines Again* (Follett Publishing, 1954, illustrations by Marion Guild), Rudolph's self-pity as a taunted reindeer snuffs out his beacon nose with Christmas at hand. The light is restored only when he performs the selfless deed of rescuing two lost bunnies. Follett reissued this book in 1981 with new illustrations by Diana Magnuson. *Rudolph's Second Christmas* (Applewood Press, 1992, illustrated by Michael Emberley) consists of three recently discovered Rudolph pieces which May had written in 1947.

• THE SONG. Although Johnny Marks claimed to have conceived his song about Rudolph in 1939, ten years lapsed before it was released. Numerous music publishers had rejected it on the notion that a song about a misfit reindeer couldn't possibly sell. Eventually a determined Marks established his own publishing house in New York City, appropriately named St. Nicholas Music, Inc., to issue the sheet music, and then he sought a recording artist. When Perry Como allegedly wanted to change some of the lyrics, Marks approached cowboy singing star Gene Autry. Having recorded a most successful "Here Comes Santa Claus" in 1947, Autry also would have declined, had not his wife, Ina, moved by the ugly duckling sentiment in "Rudolph," convinced her husband otherwise.

Autry introduced "Rudolph" during his rodeo show at Madison Square Garden in the fall of 1949, and his recording on the Columbia label became the top Christmas song on the pop charts for three consecutive years, selling two million copies in 1949 alone and over 25 million copies through the years. These figures rank Autry's "Rudolph, the Red-Nosed Reindeer" as the second largest-selling Christmas single in the world, behind Bing Crosby's version of "White Christmas." Autry also achieved a hit with his remake of "Rudolph" in 1957 on the Challenge label.

Marks's song inspired *Rudolph, the Red-Nosed Reindeer*, a 1964 animated television special with Burl Ives that also launched two sequels.

Of the 25 most frequently performed Christmas songs of the twentieth century listed by the American Society of Composers, Authors and Publishers (ASCAP), "Rudolph" is ranked number 5.

Johnny Marks studied music in Paris and produced shows for the army overseas during World War II. Working primarily as a radio producer, he published some 175 songs, most of which contained Christmas themes, and he is probably the most prolific writer of popular Christmas music in the twentieth century. Although he is known best for "Rudolph," some of Marks's other holiday treasures include "When Santa Claus Gets Your Letter" (1950), "'Twas the Night Before Christmas Song" (1952), "Everyone's a Child at Christmas" (1956), "I Heard the Bells on Christmas Day" (1956), "A Merry, Merry Christmas to You" (1958), "Rockin' Around the Christmas Tree" (1958), "Run Rudolph Run" (1958), "A Holly Jolly Christmas" (1962), "Jingle, Jingle, Jingle" (1964), "Silver and Gold" (1964), "The Most Wonderful Day of the Year" (1964), "We Are Santa's Elves" (1964), and "A Caroling We Go" (1966).

See also **I Heard the Bells on Christmas Day**"; "**Rockin' Around the Christmas Tree**"; and television specials **Rudolph, the Red-Nosed Reindeer; Rudolph's Shiny New Year; Rudolph and Frosty: Christmas in July.**

Rudolph, the Red-Nosed Reindeer

(Television special, 1964). Made-for-television animated story using stop-motion puppets (Animagic), loosely based on the 1949 hit tune of the same title by Johnny Marks; also remade for video in 1998 as *Rudolph, the Red-Nosed Reindeer: The Movie*. The television special premiered on the *General Electric Fantasy Hour* in December 1964 and has since become the longest-running television animated special.

Unpopular because of his glowing red nose, young Rudolph runs away from Christmas Town with a misfit elf, Hermy, who aspires to be a dentist. Yukon Cornelius, a prospector, joins them in adventures that lead to the Island of Misfit Toys, populated by toys whose owners have rejected them. Such toys include, among others, a white elephant with red spots, a train whose caboose has square wheels, and a water pistol that squirts jelly instead of water.

Convinced that Santa could find homes for these toys, Rudolph returns to Christmas Town, where he learns that the Abominable Snow Monster has captured Clarise, his doe friend, and his parents, who had been out looking for him. Rudolph tracks down the Monster, Cornelius incapacitates him, and Hermy pulls his teeth, which renders him docile.

Only when foggy weather sets in and Santa is about to cancel Christmas does Rudolph realize the true value of his red nose. Leading Santa's team, Rudolph proves that even misfits can lead useful lives.

A copyright "blooper" seen during the opening credits reads "MCLXIV" (1164) instead of "MCMLXIV" (1964).

Narrated and sung by Burl Ives. Featuring songs by Johnny Marks: "Rudolph, the Red-Nosed Reindeer" (1949), "A Holly Jolly Christmas" (1962), "Silver and Gold" (1964), "Jingle, Jingle, Jingle" (1964), "We Are Santa's Elves" (1964), "We're a Couple of Misfits" (1964), "There's Always Tomorrow" (1964), and "The Most Wonderful Day of the Year" (1964). Voices: Billie Richards, Paul Soles, Larry Mann, Stan Francis, Janet Orenstein, Corinne Connely, Peg Dixon, Paul Kligman, Alfie Scopp. Written by Romeo Muller. Produced by Arthur Rankin, Jr., and Jules Bass. Directed by Larry Roemer. A Videocraft International Ltd. Production. Sony Wonder Video. Color. Half-hour.

The 1998 animated cartoon remake follows essentially the same plot as its predecessor, with Stormella, the evil Ice Queen, brewing a blizzard that threatens to bury the North Pole. In 1999, this video was nominated for the Golden Reel Award by the Motion Pictures Sound Editors, United States, for Best Sound Editing, Animated Feature. It was also nominated for the Young Artist Award for Best Family Features, Animated. Principal voices: John Goodman, Eric Idle, Bob Newhart, Debbie Reynolds, Richard Simmons, Whoopi Goldberg, Eric Pospisil, Kathleen Barr, Alec Willows, Garry Chalk, Vanessa Morley, Myriam Sirios. Written by Michael Aschner. Produced and directed by Bill Kowalchuk. Tundra Pro-

ductions and Cayre Brothers Productions. Good Times Home Video. Color. 90 min.

See also **Rudolph, the Red-Nosed Reindeer** (song); **Rudolph's Shiny New Year**; **Rudolph and Frosty: Christmas in July.**

Rudolph's Shiny New Year

(1975). Made-for-television animated sequel to *Rudolph, the Red-Nosed Reindeer*, using stop-motion puppets (Animagic).

Ashamed of his large ears, Happy, the Baby New Year, has run away from Father Time's castle on Christmas Night. Unless Happy is found, time will stop on December 31. Embarking with companions Clockwork Big Ben, a whale; One Million B.C., a caveman; Quarter-Past-Five, a camel; and Sir Ten-To-Three, a knight, Rudolph traces Happy to the Island of No Name, home of Aeon, the evil buzzard, who is Happy's captor. With half an hour remaining before midnight on December 31, Rudolph and friends foil Aeon and, with Santa's help in the (St.) Nick of time, return Happy to Father Time with a fraction of a second to spare. Narrated and sung by Red Skelton. Featuring an original musical score by Johnny Marks. Voices: Frank Gorshin, Morey Amsterdam, Hal Peary, Paul Frees, Billie Richards. Written by Romeo Muller. Produced and directed by Arthur Rankin, Jr., and Jules Bass. Rankin/Bass Productions. Warner Home Video. Color. 50 min.

See also **Rudolph, the Red-Nosed Reindeer** (song); **Rudolph, the Red-Nosed Reindeer** (television special); **Rudolph and Frosty: Christmas in July.**

Russia

In 988, Vladimir I (956–1015), grand prince of Kiev, also known as Saint Vladimir and Vladimir the Great, accepted Orthodox Christianity from the Byzantine Empire and hence introduced Byzantine culture to Russia. For nearly one thousand years, the Russian Orthodox Church, adhering to the Julian calendar, celebrated Christmas on January 7 and Epiphany on January 19 with customs that blended Orthodoxy with Slavic agrarian customs and superstitions. In 1917, however, the Bolshevik Revolution in St. Petersburg ended czarist rule and set the stage for the rise of the

Communist Party and the creation of the Soviet Union. Upon implementing its atheistic political platform, the new regime forbade most religious practices, closed many (but not all) churches, and replaced the Christmas season with a secular "Winter Festival." Despite the government's adopting the present Gregorian calendar during this period, the Orthodox Church rejected such change and retained its ecclesiastical days on the Julian calendar as before. With the collapse of the Soviet empire in 1991, Russia now struggles to regain its Christmas heritage and other religious traditions, large portions of which were lost, possibly forever, during the Communist era.

Prior to the Revolution, the twelve-day Christmas season extended from January 6, Christmas Eve, until Epiphany on Jan 19. A 39-day fast preceded this period, which prohibited the consumption of any animal products. This conditional fast continued into Christmas Eve with the traditional holiday meal for the immediate family, which commenced upon sighting the first star of the evening, believed to be the Star of Bethlehem. Then followed twelve meatless courses honoring the twelve months of the year and Christ's Twelve Apostles. Typical cuisine included, among other dishes, *borscht* (cabbage soup), assorted fish, *kissel* (berry dessert), and *kutya* (wheat porridge with honey and poppy seeds). Some of the kutya would be thrown up to the ceiling, and the amount that stuck predicted the fate of the next harvest. This and a host of other superstitions, now abandoned, embellished the holidays (they derived from ancient winter solstice folklore which held that danger and evil lurked in the winter darkness). Rituals foretold the weather for each of the following year's months, predicted whether a girl would marry in the new year, dispelled evil spirits, assured good health and fortune for the coming year, and so forth. Following Christmas Eve Midnight Mass, which frequently extended until dawn, it was permissible to serve meat as families with friends gathered for Christmas dinner.

Other customs included groups of people traveling about their villages singing *kolyadki* (Christmas carols). Originally commemorating the renewal of the year and other folk themes, these carols later incorporated the message of the Nativity. The carolers customarily expected rewards of confections, but if these were not forthcoming, the subsequent carols bestowed curses upon the household. Other groups, "mummers," donned outlandish costumes as clowns, spirits, and especially as wild animals and entertained at homes and public places. (The Russian author Leo Tolstoy provides a vivid description of Christmas mumming practices among Russian aristocrats in a passage from his novel *War and Peace* [1865–1869]). Christmas trees became popular in the 1800s, and their decorations included fruits, candy dolls and animals, walnuts, wooden figures, paper lanterns and chains, and a star tree topper.

Russian folklore holds that two spirits have brought holiday gifts. One possibly derived from the "Frost," an entity of rural society encompassing all that was bitterly cold. To prevent this unseen menace from harming the crops, it was customary to "invite the Frost to supper" by setting out food for it. In the nineteenth century, the Frost took on human qualities as urban regions concocted the legend of *D'yed Moroz* ("Grandfather Frost"). Residing in the Russian forests, Grandfather Frost arrived at Christmastime with gifts for children in a *troika* (sleigh pulled by three horses abreast). His long red, fur-trimmed suit with hat and long, white beard somewhat resembled the St. Nicholas of Europe. In Europe, however, naughty children were threatened with punishment by St. Nicholas's demon antithesis; Grandfather Frost merely ignored them.

The second spirit, *Baboushka* ("Grandmother"), brought gifts on Epiphany Eve. According to legend, Baboushka was sweeping her house when the three Magi passed by en route to Bethlehem. When they invited her to accompany them, she refused, claiming that her housework precluded a long journey. Later, she repented and, upon collecting a few toys for the Christ Child, set out to overtake the Magi. Because she found neither them nor the Christ Child, she returned annually on Epiphany Eve to examine each sleeping child, hoping to find Jesus, then left a small gift behind. In variations of the story, all with the same conclusion, Baboushka either deceived the Magi or refused them lodging, or she denied asylum to the Holy Family in their flight from King Herod's soldiers.

In 1699, Czar Peter the Great established January 1 as New Year's Day in Russia. At the czar's command, celebrations included the lighting of bonfires on New Year's Eve. Homes were decked with evergreen garlands, and feasting abounded. All of this activity took place just prior to Christmas and thus extended the holiday season.

Seeking to eradicate Christmas (formerly observed on January 7), the Communists established a secular Winter Festival during the last half of December, a period devoted to feasting, fantasy, fireworks, and parades. During his rule (1929–1953), dictator Joseph Stalin declared New Year's Day as a national family holiday instead of Christmas and replaced the Christmas tree with the New Year's tree in 1935. Grandfather Frost, now appearing in either blue or red, was retained to bring gifts on New Year's Eve instead of Christmas Eve, and two more figures were added to complement him. One of these, *Snegurochka* ("Snow Maiden"), was based on a secular legend about a childless elderly couple who, desiring a child of their own, fashioned a little girl out of snow. Although she achieved mortality and became their daughter during the winter, she melted as spring approached but returned annually with the winter snows. Snow Maiden, portrayed by a beautiful young girl with blond braids, white fur hat, blue robe or short fur coat, and knee boots, became Grandfather Frost's granddaughter who assisted him on his rounds. A youth portrayed the other figure, New Year's Boy, who depicted the freshness of the new year, and his costume bore the numerals of that year. Secular equivalents to Mary, Joseph, and the Christ Child, groups comprising Grandfather Frost, Snow Maiden, and New Year's Boy made public appearances throughout the country, the most notable of which was at the annual New Year's children's festival held at the Palace of Congresses in the Kremlin. Adults imbibed vodka on New Year's Eve, champagne on New Year's Day, and feasted on suckling pig, *karavay* (round bread), and *baba* (round coffeecake). Few could afford such luxuries as caviar, smoked fish, and other roast meats. For many older Russians, the holidays extended until January 13, New Year's Day on the Julian calendar.

Since the collapse of the Soviet Union, New Year's celebrations have continued to dominate the holidays. Still popular are the children's festival in the Kremlin and other parties, Grandfather Frost, Snow Maiden, and gift exchanges. Typical cuisine is returning to that of former centuries, such as *borscht*, *blini* (small pancakes served with sour cream, caviar and smoked salmon), fish, *baba*, *kissel*, and *piroshki* (turnovers stuffed with meat, fish, chicken, eggs, vegetables). Yet *Sviatki* (Christmas season, January 7–19) is slowly resurfacing and changing, as manifested by the appearance of Christmas trees, Nativity scenes (novelties to Russia), the adoption of western traditions such as Santa Claus decorations and American and English carols (*kolyadki* only occasionally appear in stage performances), and the increasing attendance at Christmas Eve Midnight Mass. The latter remains a service of many hours which compels the worshippers to stand during its entirety, with peripheral benches reserved only for the aged and infirm. Then follows *Krestny Khod* ("Walking with the Cross"), a candlelight procession that forms outside around the church as the congregation bears religious symbols. Although it is not customary to exchange gifts on Christmas Day at present, the Museum of Folk and National Arts in Moscow sponsors "The Christmas Gift," an exhibit of traditional toys and gifts that were commonly found prior to the Revolution.

"Merry Christmas" is *S Rozhdestvom Khristovym*.

See also **Epiphany; Ukraine.**

S

Saint Andrew's Day
See Advent

Saint Barbara's Day
See Advent

Saint John's Day
See The Twelve Days of Christmas

Saint Kitts and Nevis
See West Indies

Saint Lucy's Day
See Advent

Saint Nicholas

(?304–?345). Archbishop of Myra in Asia Minor (now Demre, Turkey) and popularly accepted as the personage on whom the mythical Santa Claus is based.

With the exception of a few fairly certain facts, virtually everything written about St. Nicholas is based on legends. He is known to have lived during the fourth century and was present at the Council of Nicea in the year 325. Tradition states that St. Nicholas was a native of Patara, a city in the district of Lycia. After serving as a monk in the monastery of Sion near Myra, he rapidly advanced to the office of bishop at a rather early age (for which he was dubbed the "Boy Bishop") and finally achieved the rank of archbishop of Myra. He is said to have been quite wealthy, and his acts of secret charity and munificence became legendary to the point that, following his death, any gift received under mysterious circumstances was automatically attributed to the spirit of St. Nicholas.

Tradition also held that his death occurred on December 6, which subsequently became St. Nicholas Day, and that his remains initially rested at the Church of St. Nicholas in Myra, with the exception that in the year 1000, that church transferred some of the relics to Kiev in Russia. In 1087, however, when Muslim occupation of Turkey allegedly threatened to desecrate Nicholas's tomb, sailors from Bari in southern Italy relocated the remains to the Church of St. Stephen in Bari. Today St. Nicholas's relics lie not only in Bari but at the Greek Orthodox Church in New York City, where some were transferred in 1972. This latter church subsequently transferred most of the relics to the Shrine of St. Nicholas in Flushing, New York.

St. Nicholas's various legendary miracles and acts of charity led a number of people and places to adopt him as their patron saint. After he supposedly compelled a group of thieves to return their stolen goods, thieves in general earned the title of "clerks of St. Nicholas" during the Middle Ages. In another story, St. Nicholas miraculously restored life back to three young boys whom an innkeeper in Myra had murdered, dismembered, and stuffed in a salting tub. (Later portraits of St. Nicholas depicted him as a stern, ascetic archbishop standing beside three boys who were sitting in a tub.) Another legend holds that on making a voyage to the Holy Land, St. Nicholas allegedly quieted a violent storm and later saved some sailors when they had invoked his name. Finally, when his remains came to rest in Bari, it is said that thirty people were cured of distemper after calling upon his name. Thus, St. Nicholas has not only become the patron saint of thieves, children, and sailors, but also of Russia, Greece, Sicily, Liege, Lucerne, Freiburg, Laplanders, scholars, lawyers, and travelers.

The legend that firmly linked St. Nicholas with hanging up stockings and the spirit of giving at Christmastime centered around three dowerless maidens. A father in Myra was unable to give his three daughters in marriage because they lacked sufficient dowries. The desperate father was about to give his daughters up to lives of slavery or prostitution when Nicholas heard about their plight. On each of three successive nights, Nicholas secretly tossed a purse of gold through the father's window and supplied the dowries (in another version, St. Nicholas climbed onto the roof and tossed the purses down the chimney). Instead of landing

St. Nicholas, according to the book from which this picture is taken, was "a saint of great virtue, and disposed so early in life to conform to ecclesiastical rule, that when an infant at the breast he fasted on Wednesday and Friday, and sucked but once on each of those days, and that towards night." This illustration depicts the legend of St. Nicholas miraculously restoring three dismembered boys to life. From William Hone, Ancient Mysteries Described *(London: 1823).*

on the hearth, where he had aimed them, the purses landed in stockings hanging by the chimney to dry. Because of this legend, some portraits depict St. Nicholas holding three gold balls, which symbolized the purses of gold. When the Medici family of Florentine bankers adopted the three gold balls on their coat of arms in honor of St. Nicholas, the symbol eventually became that of lenders, especially pawnbrokers. From this, pawnbrokers also adopted Nicholas as their patron saint — as did virgins, in recognition of his act of compassion for the three young women.

• SAINT NICHOLAS AND SANTA CLAUS. The European conception of St. Nicholas had always centered around a sternly pious, ascetic elder dressed in crimson robes. He was often pictured with a long white beard and tall mitre,

carrying a crozier (the staff that symbolizes the bishop's office) and riding a white horse. Saint Nicholas often traveled with a demon antithesis known by a host of aliases such as Black Pete, Grampus, Knecht Ruprecht, and others, and the two annually brought joy and terror to villages as they entered homes on St. Nicholas Day (December 6) for purposes of quizzing young children in their catechism. Those successful in their recitations received gifts from the saint, but should the recitations prove wanting, the hideous demon, fur-clad with blackened face, would growl, rattle chains, brandish a rod with which to "beat" the youngsters, and then (so ran the threat) stuff them into a large sack to be "whisked away" to oblivion. Thus the saint and demon personified good and evil, heaven and hell. Although St. Nicholas always interceded for naughty children at this point, he customarily left them with a lump of coal or a switch instead of goodies.

Popular notion holds that Protestant Dutch settlers founding New Amsterdam (now New York City and the Hudson Valley) were responsible for bringing the St. Nicholas customs to the North American continent and ultimately to Christmas itself. There, the saint's demeanor and physiognomy radically transformed from that of austere archbishop into that of a stereotypical "Dutchman," that is, a short, plump, jolly fellow with a broad hat and short breeches, smoking a long-stemmed pipe. Over time, the story goes, American children slurred the saint's formal Dutch name of *Sint Nikolaas* into the vernacular *Sinterklaas*, thence into the immortal "Santa Claus," and a new Christmas personage was born.

On the other hand, Phyllis Siefker's book *Santa Claus, Last of the Wild Men* contends that the phenomenal popularity of American author Washington Irving's novel *Knickerbocker History* (1809) was ultimately responsible for creating a mythical association between the Catholic St. Nicholas and Protestant Dutch immigrants. Author of such memorable tales as *The Legend of Sleepy Hollow* and *Rip Van Winkle*, Irving published his *History* as a satire on Dutch life in New Amsterdam; there, St. Nicholas flew across the skies in a wagon as he brought children their gifts and gained access to homes by descending into chimneys.

Irving supposedly modeled his St. Nicholas after the ideas of the Saint Nicholas Society of New York, a political society founded by John Pintard after the Revolutionary War which adopted St. Nicholas as an anti–British symbol. Other accounts note that Irving's saint bore a remote similarity to Thor, the wild Scandinavian god of war and thunder, who was pictured as clothed in red fur and who commanded a golden, airborne chariot pulled by two white goats, Gnasher and Cracker. According to popular belief, Irving's story further inspired the writing of the poem "A Visit from St. Nicholas" ("'Twas the Night Before Christmas"), first published anonymously in 1823, which featured a flying sleigh pulled by reindeer instead of goats and which clad a small, elfish, but portly St. Nicholas in sooty fur, not an archbishop's robes. The poem, in turn, inspired political cartoonist Thomas Nast (1840–1902) to portray "Santa Claus" and all of his now-familiar trappings (red suit trimmed with white fur, buckled shoes, wide belt, pointed stocking cap, reindeer sleigh) in a series of cartoons which appeared annually in *Harper's Illustrated Weekly* from 1863 to 1900.

Interestingly, it was also Nast who first depicted Santa as living at the North Pole, for an 1885 sketch depicted two children gazing at a map and tracing Santa's route from the North Pole to the United States. Although Nast never stated why he specifically chose the North Pole, no doubt Santa's furry costume and reindeer sleigh influenced Nast to pick the polar region. In 1886, American writer George P. Webster went further, stating that Santa's polar abode was ordinarily hidden in the ice during summer months.

Siefker asserts that not only the fur-clad, American Santa Claus, but also the host of antithetical demons which have accompanied the European St. Nicholas, can be traced to a formidable, dark, hairy beast-god of primordial civilizations. Virtually omnipotent, this god commanded all elements of nature including the cycles of reproduction and death, planting and harvesting; thus, to renew the earth, at year's end he "recycled" himself by dying and was resurrected in the following spring. Ancient civilizations reenacted this death which included sacrifices of people or animals in the

A sheet of embossed, diecut, chromolithographed Santas, some with blue and red hats, ready to be trimmed and pasted into scrapbooks or homemade Christmas cards. These Santas still bespeak their St. Nicholas heritage, with their rather thin faces and long beards. Printed in Germany, about 1900.

god's name. A seer, healer, and god of fertility as well as storm and destruction, he became known as the so-called "Wild Man" of the Middle Ages. Because his pagan popularity vied with conversions to Christianity, the Church branded him as evil and, in the seventh century, declared him to be the personification of Satan. Traces of the Wild Man figure are still seen in year-end celebrations throughout Europe and elsewhere, which almost always feature people dressed variously as masked animals or devils.

Siefker concludes that Santa Claus is actually a more recent derivative of the Teutonic being "Pelz Nicholas" (Furry Nicholas) and not St. Nicholas. Another alias for the Wild Man, Pelz Nicholas (also with numerous spellings such as Pelznickel, Pelznichol, Belznickel, Belsnichol, Bellsniggle) migrated to America with German immigrants, the so-called "Pennsylvania Dutch," as he who brought not only Christmas gifts but punishment to naughty children. In the perennial favorite poem "A Visit from St. Nicholas," Siefker sees a number of characteristics which link Santa to the Wild Man–turned–Pelz Nicholas: dressing completely in sooty fur, shouting to reindeer whose names reflect those of the elements or mythical beings ("Dasher" resembling Thor's "Gnasher," "Vixen" the fox, the astronomical "Comet," the god "Cupid," the respective German "Donder" and "Blitzen" for "thunder" and "lightning"), erratic behavior such as disturbing the peace with a clatter on the lawn, and toting a sack of toys (the sack originally symbolized the article with which to kidnap children). And Santa's trademark phrase of "Ho Ho Ho" is identical to that of the "devil's bluster" of medieval mystery plays, the literary and folk prankster Robin Goodfellow (a god of vegetation), and those spirits who participated in the "Wild Hunt" during the twelve days of Christmas (*see* **Austria**; **Christmas Drama**; **Winter Solstice**).

Santa now lived at the North Pole, and new traditions would add elves as his assistants in making Christmas toys for children. Although mythical elves originated in the rich Viking folklore of Scandinavia and northern Europe which long predated St. Nicholas and Santa Claus, they seemed to be ideal polar assistants. Denmark's *julnisse* and Sweden's *jultomten*, prototypical elves, are mischievous little beings who live in the attic, under floorboards, or out in the barn. Guardians of the home and livestock, these elves must receive a bowl of rice pudding on Christmas Eve; otherwise, the homeowner falls victim to their pranks, and harvests will be poor.

Another Scandinavian myth contributed to the concept of Santa's personal descent into chimneys on Christmas Eve to deliver gifts. During pre–Christian Germanic feasts at the winter solstice (December 21), families prepared altars of flat stones in their homes and laid fires of fir boughs. It was believed that these fires would invite Hertha, Norse goddess of the home, to descend through the fire and smoke to bring health and good fortune to all. Not only was Hertha another forerunner of Santa, but the flat stone altars became the modern hearths of today.

Santa's appearance changed somewhat again in the early twentieth century. Beginning in 1931, the Coca-Cola Company ran a series of commercial ads that featured a full-sized Santa as pitchman for the beverage. We find Santa's second evolution from small elf back to robust human size in the art of Haddon Sundblom, who enlarged the "standardized" Santa image for Coca-Cola.

Popular all through America, Santa Claus has not only crossed the Atlantic to a warm re-ception in Europe, but has influenced the celebration of Christmas the world over.

See also **Boy Bishop**; **Saint Nicholas Day**; **United States**; **A Visit from St. Nicholas**.

Saint Nicholas Day

December 6 on the Roman Catholic Church calendar, this day honors the legendary and charitable fourth-century archbishop of Myra in Asia Minor, now Demre, Turkey. Posthumously canonizing Nicholas to sainthood, the Church declared December 6 (traditionally held as the day of his death) as St. Nicholas Day by the twelfth century. During pre–Christian times, December 6 was a feast day to the Greek god Poseidon and the Roman god Neptune, both of whom were regarded as the "givers of good things." When the Church began Christianizing pagan feast days, St. Nicholas, also a giver of good things, proved an ideal replacement for the pagan gods for a December 6 celebration.

Celebrations of St. Nicholas Day prevailed in the Low Countries and Rhine provinces of Europe as early as the tenth century with Church-sponsored dramas, which further fostered legends about the saint. Imitating Nicholas's charity, parents secretly placed small gifts in their little ones' shoes or stockings on St. Nicholas Eve; French nuns anonymously left small gifts of fruit or nuts on the doorsteps of the poor. Awakening on St. Nicholas morning, the children learned that their delightful surprises had come from the good St. Nicholas. Because of the proximity of December 6 to Christmas Day (established in the fourth century), the customs of the St. Nicholas holiday gradually merged with those of the increasingly important Christmas, with St. Nicholas as the principal gift-giver.

Today, a number of European countries still observe St. Nicholas Day with gifts and festivities. In the Netherlands, for example, Amsterdam holds an annual pageant in which the white-bearded St. Nicholas, dressed in red clerical robes with a tall mitre, carrying a gold crozier, and riding a white horse, makes his first appearance of the season on the last Saturday in November. His horse derives from Sleipnir, the mythical eight-legged steed of the wild Scandinavian god Odin. St. Nicholas arrives by boat from Spain for, according to Dutch tradition, he was born in Spain, not Asia Minor. Accompanying St. Nicholas to the Netherlands is *Swarte Piet* (Black Peter), the Moorish personification of Satan, whose task is to walk behind St. Nicholas while toting a black bag of gifts. On St. Nicholas Eve, tradition holds, the austere saint and Peter visit every home to determine if the children deserve gifts or punishment. It is not Nicholas but Peter who enters homes by jumping down chimneys to deliver the gifts or chastisement; hence, Peter's appearance is black and sooty. Peter carries another bag into which he is said to stuff particularly naughty children and carry them off to Spain to be imprisoned for a year. Commonly on St. Nicholas Eve, someone playing the part of Peter thrusts a black-gloved hand just inside the door and tosses spice cookies known as *peppernøtter* for the children. Just as commonly, someone dressed like St. Nicholas rides about town on a white horse while dispensing presents.

Children throughout Europe prepare for St. Nicholas's visit by setting out gift receptacles, usually shoes or stockings, into which they stuff carrots or hay for the saint's horse. On St. Nicholas morning, those children judged to have been good are delighted to see that the animal fodder has been replaced with little gifts and sweets. For naughty Dutch children, though, Peter leaves a bundle of sticks and ignores the fodder. Other countries observing St. Nicholas Day hold related customs suited to their culture.

The Netherlands is not the only country having folklore in which a demon antithesis accompanies St. Nicholas on his feast day. In the Czech and Slovak Republics, *Svaty Mikulas* (St. Nicholas) descends from heaven on a golden cord along with an angel who bestows the gifts and a representation of the Devil, sometimes called "Cert." Dressed in black, the Devil carries a whip and rattles chains, at which good children must say their prayers or receive a lashing. The demon is known by many names throughout Germany and Austria: "Knecht Ruprecht" (Servant Rupert), "Ru-Klas" (Rough Nicholas), "Krampus" (Grampus), "Klaubauf," "Hans Muff," "Hans Trapp," "Pelz Nicholas" (Furry Nicholas), "Bartel," "Butz,"

"Bullerklas," "Pulterklas," "Aschenklas" (Ash Nicholas), and others. By whatever name it is known, this demon, often portrayed as a dark, hideous, furry creature with horns, is thought to derive from the wild king of the Norse gods, Odin. Similar to Black Peter, it carries a sack of gifts and a rod of chastisement.

See also **The Low Countries** (THE NETHERLANDS); **Saint Nicholas.**

Saint Stephen's Day
See **Boxing Day**

Saint Thomas Day
See **Advent**

Salvation Army

International Christian and charitable organization, initially founded as the Christian Mission in London in 1865 by Methodist minister William Booth. Dedicated to spreading the Gospel and rendering material aid to such destitutes as thieves, gamblers, prostitutes, and alcoholics, Booth worked among the slums and gained a number of converts, who, calling themselves the "Hallelujah Army," preached, marched, and sang hymns in the streets of not only London but other cities as well. In 1878, the organization acquired its present name after Booth corrected a printed statement, which had described his organization as a "volunteer army"; Booth substituted "Salvation Army" instead. He adopted a military structure and served as General Superintendent (his followers called him "General"), while his uniformed officers held appropriate ranks commensurate with their duties. From the outset, Booth placed iron cooking kettles around London as a novel means of attracting donations for the poor. The response to this appeal was most significant during the Christmas season. The Salvation Army thus maximized its efforts to relieve the poor during the weeks prior to Christmas, and the kettle became its symbol.

Lieutenant Eliza Shirley, an English immigrant, introduced the Salvation Army into the United States by holding the first meeting in Philadelphia in 1879. A year later, George Scott Railton and seven other Salvationists arrived from England to begin work in New York City and beyond. The concept in the United States of the Christmas kettle with its accompanying bell ringer originated in San Francisco in December 1891, with Salvation Army captain Joseph McFee, a former sailor who recalled such kettles at the docks in Liverpool, England. By 1895, the kettles had spread along the West Coast, and Army officers William A. McIntyre and N. J. Lewis brought the idea to the East Coast. McIntyre's kettle efforts in Boston in 1897 alone provided for 150,000 Christmas dinners to those in need. Through kettle contributions in New York City, the first large-scale dinner for the poor was held at Madison Square Garden in 1901 and became an annual tradition that persisted for years.

Following the first presidential endorsement by Grover Cleveland in 1891, the Army rapidly expanded throughout the world and now serves in 103 countries. In the United States, The Salvation Army aids more than seven million people annually at Thanksgiving and at Christmastime.

Santa and the Bookies
See **The Honeymooners**

Santa and the Three Bears

(1970). Motion picture animated cartoon.

The picture opens in live-action with a grandfather (Hal Smith) telling a story to his two grandchildren, Beth (Beth Goldfarb) and Brian (Brian Hobbs). Merging into animation, the story continues in Yellowstone National Park, where elderly and portly Mr. Ranger settles Momma Bear Nana and her two cubs, Nikomi and Chinook, into their cave for hibernation. Curious about seeing the ranger bringing a Christmas tree back to park headquarters, the cubs follow and are beside themselves with delight over the brilliantly decorated tree. They press the ranger to tell them all about Christmas. He presents an abbreviated version of the Christmas story, then expounds on the legend of Santa Claus and all his trappings.

The excited cubs hurry back and, waking their mother, persuade her to get them a Christmas tree. But when their frolicking and singing keep her awake, Nana seeks out the ranger for a chat. The ranger, learning that the cubs expect a visit from Santa on Christmas Eve, decides to humor them by playing the part

himself, which will satisfy all parties concerned, and the bears can finally return to hibernation. A howling blizzard, however, hinders the costumed ranger from reaching Nana's cave and forces him to take shelter in a park bus depot.

As Christmas Eve wanes, Nana must tell her disappointed cubs the truth about Santa and the ranger's plan to surprise them. But just as the little ones settle down to sleep, Santa, whom the cubs now believe is the ranger, arrives with two gift-filled stockings and hurries away. Shortly before daybreak the storm abates, and the cubs, seeing the ranger–Santa, are now convinced that the real Santa had visited earlier. A booming "Ho Ho Ho" from the sky signals Santa's departure as the cubs revel in their first Christmas.

Although the original picture is 63 minutes in length, often the live-action scenes are cut when it is rerun on television in one-hour time slots with commercials.

Voices: Hal Smith, Jean Vander Pyl, Annette Ferra, Bobby Riha. Vocalist, Joyce Taylor. Written, produced, and directed by Tony Benedict. Live action direction by Barry Mahon. An Ellman Enterprises and Key Industries Ltd. Production. United American Video. Color.

Santa Claus (character)
See **Saint Nicholas**

Santa Claus

(Motion picture, 1985). British-American motion picture fantasy, also known as *Santa Claus: The Movie*.

Perishing in a blizzard while delivering Christmas toys to children in their village, woodcarver Claus (David Huddleston) and his wife Anya (Judy Cornwell) find themselves the expected immortals in a magical, polar world of toymaking elves. According to the Ancient Elf (Burgess Meredith), Claus, thereafter dubbed "Santa Claus," has fulfilled the prophecy of a childless "Chosen One," an artisan sent to deliver the elves' gifts of toys to children throughout the world on Christmas Eve.

As time passes and Santa enters the twentieth century, he chooses an assistant, Patch (Dudley Moore), an elf bent on modernizing the workshop with automated technology. But when Patch loses his position because his assembly lines produce inferior toys, he journeys out into the world and unwittingly falls into the hands of a greedy New York City toy magnate, "B.Z." (John Lithgow), whom a Senate subcommittee has investigated for marketing cheap, dangerous toys. Desiring to create something special that will restore Santa's faith in him, Patch produces the "Puce Pop," a lollipop that, when eaten, allows the consumer to walk on air. That Christmas, the Puce Pop takes the world by storm, Patch having distributed the candy via his jet sleigh, and Santa, seemingly outdone, questions whether children will ever need him anymore.

Richer beyond measure, B.Z. demands that Patch alter his invention to enable people to fly, then confides to his assistant, Dr. Towzer (Jeffrey Kramer), his plan to take financial control of Christmas. His young step-niece Cornelia (Carrie Kei Heim) and a homeless street urchin named Joe (Christian Fitzpatrick), whom Cornelia and Santa have befriended, overhear the plan, but B.Z. discovers Joe and kidnaps him.

When Cornelia learns that the new candy will explode if overheated, she writes to Santa for help, the letter magically disappearing up the chimney in British fashion and reappearing on Santa's hearth, as do all letters addressed to Santa. Meanwhile Patch finds Joe bound in his basement, and the two, unaware of the danger, head up to the North Pole with a jet sleigh full of explosive candy. En route, the sleigh overheats and the candy explodes, but Santa and Cornelia, executing the "super-dooper-looper" maneuver with the reindeer, overtake and rescue the other two.

Joe finds a new home with Santa, and Cornelia remains until the following Christmas. B.Z., attempting to escape from the law by eating a mouthful of new candy, floats away into outer space and oblivion.

With John Barrard, Anthony O'Donnell. Written by David Newman, Leslie Newman. Produced by Ilya Salkind and Pierre Spengler. Directed by Jeannot Szwarc. A Calabash Corporation and TriStar Pictures Production. Anchor Bay Entertainment Video. Color. 104 min.

Santa Claus (song)
See **Up on the Housetop**

Santa Claus Conquers the Martians

(1964). Motion picture science fiction fantasy, also known as *Santa Claus Defeats the Aliens.*

When Martian children Bomar (Chris Month) and Girmar (Pia Zadora) become mesmerized with video shows from Earth about Santa Claus, their father, Martian chief Kimar (Leonard Hicks), is convinced that Santa will have a positive influence on all Martian children. He abducts the jolly old elf (John Call) along with two Earth children, Billy and Betty Foster (Victor Stiles and Donna Conforti), after which Santa establishes a toy factory on Mars as if nothing had ever happened. Officer Voldar (Vincent Beck) attempts to foil Santa's mechanized setup, but Santa remains ever jovial, despite the circumstances, and succeeds in spreading Christmas cheer to the Red Planet. Its inhabitants, however, manifest a deep shade of green.

According to the noted film reviewer Leonard Maltin, this film is "absurd."

With Bill McCutcheon, Leila Martin, Charles Renn, James Cahill. Written by Glenville Mareth. Produced by Paul L. Jacobson. Directed by Nicholas Webster. An AVCO Embassy Pictures and Jalor Production. Jef Films Int. Video. Color. 81 min.

Santa Claus Defeats the Aliens
See **Santa Claus Conquers the Martians**

Santa Claus Express

Generic name applied to a number of holiday railroad excursions throughout the United States. Often sponsored by railroad museums and incorporating appropriately decorated vintage locomotives and cars, the Santa Claus Express may offer scenic tours beginning in late November and continuing through December. By other schedules, the Express stops at towns and villages along the line, at which time professional or amateur performers aboard provide a Yuletide concert or show for citizens awaiting outside.

The Santa Claus Express also is a vehicle

for delivering toys and gifts to underprivileged children, an example of which can be found in Appalachia. Since the mid–1940s on the Saturday after Thanksgiving, officials of CSX Transportation have furnished a locomotive and cars so that the Santa Claus Express could wind its way from Pikeville, Kentucky, across Virginia, and into Kingsport, Tennessee. All along the tracks, children and their families gather, many having camped overnight to secure strategic positions. When the train slows at each whistlestop, children run behind as Santa, who addresses everyone as "darlin'," and his assistants (local businessmen) toss candy, small toys, and other gifts from a platform on the last car into eager hands. Local merchants, some of whom were once among those children chasing the train, donate the gifts, which become the only Christmas presents that many children in this region will receive each year.

Santa Claus Is Coming to Town

(Song). Popular American children's song written in 1932 by Haven Gillespie of Kentucky and J. Fred Coots of Brooklyn.

The song did not debut until 1934, when the wife of singer-comedian Eddie Cantor persuaded Cantor to perform it on his radio show just before Thanksgiving. The song, whose lyrics cautioned children to be on their best behavior for Santa, had been a hard sell, for numerous publishers initially had rejected it as another unimportant kiddie tune — as had Cantor himself until his wife intervened.

The 1943 Decca recording by Bing Crosby with The Andrews Sisters sold over six million copies and has probably become the most popular rendition of this classic tune. It is the best-known work by either Gillespie or Coots, although in the 1950s singer Pat Boone popularized Coots's 1931 tune, "Love Letters in the Sand."

Of the 25 most frequently performed Christmas songs of the twentieth century listed by the American Society of Composers, Authors and Publishers (ASCAP), "Santa Claus Is Coming to Town" is ranked number 2.

Santa Claus Is Coming to Town

(Television special, 1970). Animated story incorporating stop-motion puppets (Animagic) and loosely based on the Gillespie-Coots hit song (*see* above). A biographical fantasy, it traces the life of Santa from his adoption as an orphan by the Kringle elf brothers, toymakers who name him Kris; his victory over the Winter Warlock; his determination to bring toys to children in defiance of Sombertown's burgermeister, who outlaws all toys; his marriage to Jessica, Sombertown's school teacher; and his eventual establishment at the North Pole to escape persecution from the burgermeister.

Narrated by Fred Astaire. Voices: Mickey Rooney, Robie Lester, Keenan Wynn, Joan Gardner, Paul Frees, Dina Lynn, Greg Thomas. Written by Romeo Muller. Produced and directed by Arthur Rankin, Jr., and Jules Bass. Rankin/Bass Productions. Sony Wonder Video. Color. Half-hour.

The Santa Clause

(1994). Motion picture comedy.

Divorced father Scott Calvin (Tim Allen) discovers that Santa has taken a fatal tumble off his roof on Christmas Eve. As he watches, the body of Santa vanishes, leaving only the red-and-white suit behind. A card inside requests that the finder don the suit and mount the reindeer sleigh on the roof. Complying, Scott and his son, Charlie (Eric Lloyd), resume Christmas Eve rounds. (Scott finds that the suit enables him to change his shape to enter any home magically through any sort of entrance.)

Following their rounds, Scott and Charlie ride the reindeer sleigh back to Santa's headquarters at the North Pole. There, Scott learns from chief elf Bernard (David Krumholtz) that, by wearing the former Santa's suit, he has now become Santa Claus, according to a microscopic clause written on the card, known as the "Santa Clause."

Through the following year, Scott assumes Santa's physical qualities, rapidly gaining weight and developing a full, white beard which instantly reappears despite repeated shavings. Scott's evolving appearance and Charlie's frequent bizarre tales about the North Pole cause Charlie's mother and his psychiatrist stepfather, Laura and Dr. Neal Miller (Wendy Crewson and Judge Reinhold), to revoke Scott's visitation privileges with Charlie.

Despite this restriction, the boy again

accompanies Scott on Christmas Eve rounds, which forces Laura, who mistakenly believes that Scott has kidnapped her son, to summon the law. Although Scott is arrested while performing Santa duties, Charlie and a squad of elves with "attitude" liberate him from jail.

Returning Charlie to his mother, Scott-Santa, true to his character, also returns good for evil, so to speak, by providing gifts which Laura and Neal had always wanted as children but never received: a Mystery Date game for Laura and an Oscar Meyer Wiener whistle for Neal. In return, Laura arranges unlimited visitation privileges between Santa and Charlie.

For his work on this film, in 1995 Tim Allen received MTV Award nominations for Best Breakthrough Performance and Best Comedic Performance. The film also won a People's Choice Award for Favorite Comedy Motion Picture.

With Larry Brandenburg, Mary Gross, Paige Tamada, Peter Boyle. Written by Leo Benvenuti, Steve Rudnick. Produced by Brian Reilly, Jeffrey Silver, Robert Newmyer. Directed by John Pasquin. Hollywood Pictures, Outlaw Productions, and Walt Disney Productions. Walt Disney Home Video. Color. 97 min.

Santa Comes to Visit and Stays and Stays
See Bewitched

Santabear

Series of collectible bear dolls and related products manufactured since 1985 by the Dayton-Hudson Corporation, America's fourth largest general merchandise retailer, based in Minneapolis, Minnesota. Santabear prompted the production of two stories, both of which have appeared on video.

Santabear's First Christmas (1986) consists of static cartoon drawings, illustrated by H. B. Lewis and narrated by Kelly McGillis. Separated from his family when the arctic ice cracks, a little polar bear is swept out to sea on an ice pack and lands in a region of forests previously unknown to him. Marie, a young girl who lives in a cottage with her grandfather, adopts him as her pet, and over time, the three become quite close. As Christmas approaches, Marie introduces the bear to stories of Santa Claus, reindeer, and gifts.

On Christmas Eve, the grandfather falls into an icy pond and lies at home nearly frozen. Desperately needing firewood, the bear hurries into the forest but cannot acquire a sufficient supply. He happens to meet Santa on his rounds. When Santa offers to grant him any wish for Christmas, the bear, instead of wishing to return to his family in the Arctic, requests firewood for the grandfather instead.

With Santa felling a few trees and the bear sawing logs, Marie builds a large fire which soon revives her grandfather. Santa, touched by the bear's unselfishness but now behind on his rounds, commissions the bear to help him by delivering gifts to the forest creatures in his stead, and it is done so efficiently that Santa offers the bear an annual job as his assistant. Dubbing him thereafter as "Santabear," Santa presents the bear with a festive cap and scarf and personally returns him back up North to his family.

Written by Barbara Read. Produced by Mark Sottnick, Joel Tuber. Directed by Mark Sottnick. A Rabbit Ears/Children's Video Library Production. Vestron Video. Color. Half-hour.

In the sequel, *Santabear's High Flying Adventure* (1987), Santa asks Santabear to deliver Christmas toys to children at the South Pole, for they have never experienced a Christmas. Bullybear jeopardizes the mission by stealing the toys and impersonating Santabear. Narrated by Kelly McGillis, Bobby McFerrin, John Malkovich. Written by Lenore Kletter. Produced by Mark Sottnick, Michael Sporn, Joel Tuber. Directed by Michael Sporn. A Rabbit Ears Production. Vestron Video. Color. 23 min.

Santabear's First Christmas
See Santabear

Santabear's High Flying Adventure
See Santabear

Saturnalia

A pre–Christian harvest and winter solstice celebration held throughout the Roman Empire in honor of Saturn or Saturnus (from the Latin *satus*, "to sow"), god of agriculture, who reigned during the so-called Golden Age

An imagined scene of a winter solstice Saturnalia celebration in pre–Christian Rome. Harper's New Monthly Magazine, *December 1889.*

of Rome, a time of peace and prosperity. Under the Caesars, the festival was lengthened from one day (December 17) to seven (through December 24), in which the spirit of gaiety and frolic prevailed, recalling that Golden Age. All work, businesses, schools, and matters of court were suspended, criminals received reprieves from punishment, war was not waged, and no humans were sacrificed to Saturn; the lighting of numerous candles in his temple symbolized such mercies.

Instead, festivities began with the sacrifice of a young pig in the temple. Each community selected a *Magister Ludi* (Master of the Games) or a *Saturnalicus Princeps* (Chief of the Saturnalia), a mock king, who supervised the feasting, revelry, singing, and dancing. He was chosen by lots, sometimes as the one who found the coin hidden in servings of pudding. Masters and slaves traded places, with masters serving their slaves, who could bid the former to perform any task and could exact ludicrous punishments should they fail to execute them. Class distinctions were suspended as well, as a spirit of humanity seized everyone to do good unto his neighbor, including dispensing money to the poor. Transvestism was common, and, in keeping with the tradition of masquerades, in northern provinces, Germanic tribes often donned masks in the likenesses of horned beasts and hideous creatures, symbolic of spirits which were believed to inhabit the winter darkness.

Statues of Saturn, as well as homes, were decorated with holly, sacred to this god; with evergreen wreaths, symbolic of the sun; and with evergreen garlands, symbolic of the renewal of life at the approaching winter solstice, December 25 on the Roman or Julian calendar. (In the Christian era, these evergreens would come to symbolize eternal life through Christ.)

At the conclusion of the week came the exchanging of gifts: *signillaria* (clay dolls) for the children and *streniae* (olive branches honoring the woodland goddess Strenia) or *cerei* (wax tapers or candles) for the adults.

The festivities were essentially repeated for three days at the Kalends, beginning on the first day of the new year (January 1). This was especially the time when the populace presented the emperor with *votae*, gifts.

Although the Saturnalia was not the sole winter solstice festival of the Roman Empire (among other festivals, a feast on December 15 honored Consus, god of the storeroom; one on the 17th honored his consort, Ops, a mother goddess), it was by far the most important in terms of its traditions and symbols, many of which the early Christian Church adopted into the Christmas season. The lighting of candles, decorating with holly and evergreens, giving of gifts (the Wise Men that visited the manger had no monopoly on gift-giving), holiday charity, and the unrestrained merrymaking all were most recently derived from the Saturnalia.

The basis for these traditions actually originated some 4,000 years before the birth of Christ in the land of Mesopotamia, which included Sumer, later corresponding to Babylonia; through northern and western routes, the customs reached Greece, Rome, and other parts of Europe. The equivalent Sumerian and Babylonian celebrations, respectively, were the *Zagmuk* ("Beginning of the Year") and *Akitu* ("New Year's Festival"). The Sumerian festival was semiannual, held in the fall (month of Tishri) and in the spring (month of Nisan), commemorating the two principal solar points of the year (winter and summer). Akitu, however, occurred only at the first new moon after the spring equinox.

The mythology surrounding these festivals held that as the year drew to a close, the world, created by the supreme god, Marduk, lay dying. During the festivals it was traditional for the king to perform rituals to atone for any sins of man against Marduk and to assist him in battling the monsters of chaos in the underworld to restore the world of the living for another year. To begin the rituals, the king entered the temple of Marduk. There, he suffered humiliation by being stripped of his regal vestments; then he swore annual allegiance to Marduk, after which he was reinstated as king. It is likely that the king then symbolically "sacrificed" himself by allowing the appointment of a mock king in his stead from the ranks of criminals (his mock counterpart is seen in the Master of the Games of the Saturnalia and Archbishop of Fools of the Feast of Fools), arrayed in regal raiment, and sacrificed sometime during a twelve-day celebration, which consisted of feasting, socializing, and gift-giving (a parallel is seen in the twelve days of Christmas). Wooden images depicting the monsters of chaos were burned to assist Marduk in his battle for life, and such images are believed to be the earliest form of Yule log.

These, then, were some of the world's earliest known plans for year-end festivals, which most modern civilizations have since adapted to their own cultures.

See also **Christmas Day; Feast of Fools; Winter Solstice; Yule.**

Saudi Arabia
See **Middle East**

Scotland
See **Great Britain**

Scrooge
See **A Christmas Carol** (FILM AND TELEVISION VERSIONS)

Scrooge: A Christmas Carol
See **A Christmas Carol** (FILM AND TELEVISION VERSIONS

Scrooged
See **A Christmas Carol** (FILM AND TELEVISION VERSIONS)

Scrooge's Rock 'n' Roll Christmas
See **A Christmas Carol** (FILM AND TELEVISION VERSIONS

Seals
See **Christmas Seals**

Second Christmas Day
See **Boxing Day**

The Seven Good Joys
See **The Seven Joys of Mary**

The Seven Joys of Mary
Best-known generic title given to a number of English folk songs based on the "Joys of Mary," a series of devotions and petitions to the Virgin Mary which arose in the medieval church. Whereas the church on the European continent traditionally incorporated seven or fifteen Joys with some variation, which reflected the medieval interest in number symbolism and enumeration rituals, Great Britain observed only five until the fifteenth century, when the number increased to seven. These often included examples of miracles in the life of Christ, in addition to other references to Christ's divinity as well as the Nativity.

Although the Protestant Reformation essentially obliterated all traces of the Joys as Roman Catholic devotional elements, their sentiment survived in British folk carols which crossed into those of North America during the eighteenth and nineteenth centuries. In the "Joys of Mary" carols found in both regions, the number of Joys is again most frequently seven. Not surprising are the many variant titles befitting these carols: In addition to "The Seven Joys of Mary," there are "The Seven Rejoices of Mary"; "Joys Seven"; "The Seven Good Joys"; and the Appalachian folk carol "The Blessings of Mary," seven– and ten–Joy versions of which have been sung throughout the eastern United States.

Obviously, the subjects of the seven Joys demonstrate some variation and overlapping from carol to carol, with the following as typical examples: first Joy, Mary first sees Jesus as her infant Son; second Joy, Jesus heals the lame; third Joy, Jesus restores sight to the blind; fourth Joy, Jesus reads the "Bible o'er" (refers to Jesus discussing the Scriptures with learned men in the Temple); fifth Joy, Jesus raises the dead; sixth Joy, Jesus "bears the Crucifix" (hangs on the cross); seventh Joy, Jesus ascends into Heaven. A refrain usually follows each Joy, partially repeating the last phrase of the Joy and then praising the Holy Trinity.

"The Seven Joys of Mary" has been sung to various tunes, one of which was that for "God Rest Ye Merry, Gentlemen," once popular with the London Waits. Richard Terry, in his collection *Two Hundred Folk Carols* (London, 1933), provided an arrangement of a traditional tune that has come to be the most frequently used, whereas English churches prefer the variation as published in Henry Bramley and John Stainer's *Christmas Carols New and Old* (London, 1871).

See also **Waits.**

The Seven Rejoices of Mary
See The Seven Joys of Mary

Shepherd, Shake Off Your Drowsy Sleep

("Berger, secoue ton sommeil profond!"). French traditional carol, thought to have arisen during the seventeenth or eighteenth century in the Besançon region. Sometimes the first word in the title is pluralized. Consisting of three verses, the carol urges the shepherd(s) to rouse from slumber and forsake tending mere sheep, for a far greater task is at hand in seeking the Babe, about whom angels are spreading glad tidings. The anonymous English translation appeared in the collection *Christmas Carols New and Old* (London, 1871), edited by Henry Bramley and John Stainer, the latter also having provided a popular musical arrangement of the tune.

Shepherds
See Nativity

Shepherds' Mass
See Christmas Masses

Shepherd's Rocking Carol
See Rocking

Shepherds, What Fragrance All-Perfuming?
See Whence Is That Goodly Fragrance?

Sierra Leone
See Africa

Silent Night
("Stille Nacht"). Christmas carol, reputed to be the world's most popular, composed by Austrians Father Josef Mohr (1792–1848) and Franz Xaver Gruber (1787–1863).

In 1818, Father Mohr served as assistant priest for the Church of St. Nicholas in the then-obscure village of Oberndorf near Salzburg, while Gruber, a school teacher from Arnsdorf, doubled as organist for St. Nicholas. According to popular tradition, frequent floods by the nearby Salzach River had created sufficient rust to incapacitate the church organ by Christmas Eve of that same year; another version holds that mice had destroyed the organ bellows. Facing Midnight Mass with no music, Mohr quickly composed a provocatively simple poem of six stanzas and asked Gruber to furnish a musical setting, whereupon Gruber composed an equally simple tune for two voices, choir, and guitar. The resulting carol beginning with the words "Stille nacht, heilige nacht" ("Silent night, holy night") was presented to the St. Nicholas congregation as Mohr sang tenor and played the guitar while Gruber sang bass. The choir joined in only for the two-line refrain which followed each stanza.

In 1995, the discovery of an authentic, autographed copy of "Silent Night" in Mohr's own hand at the Carolino Augusteum Museum in Salzburg dispelled some of the myths regarding the carol's origin. Titled simply "Weihnachtslied" ("Christmas Song") with lyrics arranged for guitar, this manuscript also bore the inscription "Melodie von Fr. Xav. Gruber" ("Melody by Fr. Xav. Gruber"), confirming Gruber as the musical composer, along with the date of 1816. At that time, Mohr was serving as curate in his first parish, a pilgrimage church in Mariapfarr in southern Austria. Authorities dated the manuscript to 1820, a year after Father Mohr had left Oberndorf. It is now believed to be the oldest surviving copy and likely approximates the version first performed on Christmas Eve, 1818.

While it is now certain that Father Mohr first wrote the lyrics to "Silent Night" in 1816 and requested Gruber's musical setting on Christmas Eve two years later, the exact reasons for presenting a new carol with guitar accompaniment during a traditional Roman Catholic Christmas Mass remain unknown.

While the church organ could have been inoperable, it remains equally likely that Father Mohr, an avid guitar aficionado, chose to present a folk carol in keeping with a common practice of churches in Austria and Germany at that time.

Performing the carol annually after 1818, Gruber freely distributed copies to friends but apparently affixed neither his nor Father Mohr's name nor a specific title. Thus the carol spread through Europe in true folk fashion, popularized particularly by Josef Strasser and his touring family of folk singers from Zillerthal in the Tyrol region of Austria. Strasser may have obtained a copy through Carl Mauracher, an organ builder from Zillerthal who had serviced the St. Nicholas instrument around 1824 (tradition states that Mauracher found a discarded copy of the carol in the organ loft at St. Nicholas). The Strassers performed the carol at a concert in Leipzig in December 1832, and A. R. Friese from Dresden published an arrangement of the carol under the title "Tirolerlied" ("Tyrolean Song") that same year. The 1838 edition of the *Leipziger Gesangbuch* also included an arrangement. Another Austrian touring family, the Rainers, performing for an 1839 exhibition at the Alexander Hamilton Monument outside Trinity Church in New York City, introduced the carol to a most receptive United States under the title "Song from Heaven."

Father Mohr, a chronic alcoholic who was frequently transferred from parish to parish, left Oberndorf in 1819 and died in 1848, never having witnessed the international appeal of his carol. Franz Gruber, who had assumed a new position in Hallein in 1835, also remained ignorant of his carol's success until 1854, when Frederick William IV, King of Prussia, having heard a Strasser rendition of "Silent Night" in 1834, instituted a search for its source. Although Gruber complied by dispatching an explanatory letter and a carol arrangement to the Royal Chapel in Berlin, the world initially refused to credit Father Mohr and Gruber as the songwriters, countering that such a work could only have been the product of a musical genius such as Beethoven, Haydn, or Mozart.

By 1849, English translations of Father Mohr's poem appeared in print, and the translation of verses one, two, and six in 1863 by the Reverend John F. Young, future Episcopal bishop of Florida, has remained the most familiar. Now known by the title of "Silent Night," the carol depicts a scene of holy calm around the sleeping Babe and the gentle Virgin.

A number of Gruber's later orchestral arrangements for his carol still survive, notably those of 1836 and 1845, which remain in the archives of Hallein. The original manuscript of 1816 has long since disappeared, and the Church of St. Nicholas, which first heard "Silent Night" in Oberndorf, no longer stands today. Over the original site stands the Silent Night Memorial Chapel and Museum, where an annual Christmas Eve service traditionally concludes with a rendering of "Silent Night" in its original format. Visitors to Austria may also tour Franz Gruber's schoolhouse-home in Arnsdorf and the Franz Xaver Gruber Museum and grave at his later home in Hallein, or attend Christmas Eve services at the Josef Mohr Birthplace Exhibition in Salzburg. Father Mohr's final resting place is Wagrain, an Alpine ski resort, which hosts the Josef Mohr School.

In addition to German and English, "Silent Night" has been sung in virtually every language of the world, and renditions have sometimes occurred under the most trying of circumstances. The carol especially has been heard along the battlefronts of two world wars during Christmas truces and in prison camps. One account tells how Korean citizens from the bush during the Korean War provided an American soldier on guard duty with a version of "Silent Night" in their native language. One reason the carol has become so popular, particularly during wartime, is because it seems to instill in its singers a yearning for universal peace.

Austria now considers "Silent Night" one of its national treasures, a sentiment reflected in that country's strict protection of the carol against commercialism. For that reason, by tradition, "Silent Night" is neither played, broadcast, nor sung in any form until Christmas Eve.

Silver Bells

Popular American song written in 1950 by New York State native Ray Evans (lyrics) and

Pennsylvania native Jay Livingston (music), both of whom, together with Victor Young, provided the musical score for the Paramount film comedy *The Lemon Drop Kid* (1951), which featured "Silver Bells." Although the song received its screen debut in a duet performance by principal actors Bob Hope and Marilyn Maxwell, Bing Crosby and Carol Richards had first introduced "Silver Bells" in their 1950 duet recording for Decca Records, which became a best-seller. That recording reached position 78 on the *Billboard Hot 100* chart in 1957 and position 22 on the *Billboard Christmas Singles* chart in 1966.

According to Evans, he and Livingston, in seeking a popular yet different Christmas theme apart from the usual scenario of snow and sleigh riding, chose to fashion a tune about bells. He remarked that, at the time, "Silver Bells" was the only song that centered on the atmosphere of a big-city Christmas with its hustle and bustle of holiday shoppers, decorated window displays in department stores, and colorful lights. Evans and Livingston had originally titled their creation "Tinkle Bell," but that name apparently reduced Livingston's wife to such giggles that the title was wisely changed to "Silver Bells."

Of the 25 most frequently performed Christmas songs of the twentieth century listed by the American Society of Composers, Authors and Publishers (ASCAP), "Silver Bells" is ranked number 8.

Together Evans and Livingston produced other notable works for motion pictures, including "Buttons and Bows" for *The Paleface* (1948), "Mona Lisa" for *Captain Carey, U.S.A.* (1950), and "Whatever Will Be, Will Be (Que Sera, Sera)" for *The Man Who Knew Too Much* (1956), all three of which won Academy Awards for Best Song.

The Simpsons

The longest-running prime-time television animated cartoon series, created by Matt Groening. Winner of numerous awards, including the Peabody Award and twelve Emmys, *The Simpsons* originated as a group of fifteen- to twenty-second "shorts" for *The Tracey Ullman Show* in April 1987. The regular cast included Homer Simpson, a nuclear safety technician; wife Marge, who sported a blue beehive hairdo; and their three children: ten-year-old Bart, a hell-raising fourth grader; eight-year-old Lisa, a second grader who played the saxophone; and Margaret, the one-year-old baby. Their success led to a series, the first episode of which was titled "The Simpsons Roasting on an Open Fire," which premiered in December 1989.

"The Simpsons Roasting on an Open Fire" (video title *The Simpsons Christmas Special*) features the Simpsons of Springfield short on cash for the holidays: Bart's acquisition of a tattoo forces Marge to exhaust her savings on laser surgery to have it removed, and Homer's employer decides to forego any Christmas bonuses. Unable to afford even the cheapest of Christmas trees, Homer steals onto private property by night and swipes a tree, barely escaping guard dogs and flying buckshot. Homer's desperation for cash next motivates him to moonlight as a department store Santa, where a net gain of only thirteen dollars after deductions prompts a quick trip to the dog track. There, Homer just as promptly squanders his meager earnings on the entry "Santa's Little Helper." Rejected by its master for losing, the dog retreats to Homer, who brings it home instead of Christmas presents. Marge, however, interprets the dog as the best gift of all, something with which to share their love and frighten away prowlers. This episode introduces Marge's two sisters, twins Patty and Selma; Ned and Todd Flanders, the neighbors next door (all of whom Homer despises); and their pet, "Santa's Little Helper."

The Simpsons Christmas Special received an Emmy Award nomination for Outstanding Nighttime Animated Program, One Hour or Less (1989-90 season).

Voices: Dan Castellaneta, Julie Kavner, Nancy Cartwright, Yeardley Smith, Harry Shearer, Hank Azaria, Jo Ann Harris, Pamela Hayden. Written by Mimi Pond. Produced by Richard Sakai. Directed by David Silverman. A Gracie Films Production in Association with 20th Century–Fox Television. Fox Video. Color. 30 min.

Matt Groening also created the popular comic *Life in Hell*.

The Simpsons Christmas Special
See **The Simpsons**

The Simpsons Roasting on an Open Fire

See **The Simpsons**

Sing We Now of Christmas

("Noël nouvelet!"). French traditional carol, also known as "Noel! A New Noel!" "Christmas Comes Anew," and "Nowell, Sing Nowell." The lyrics are believed to date from the late fifteenth century, the oldest known source being a manuscript from that era that resides in the French National Library in Paris. No definitive version of the lyrics seems to exist, however, for they have varied with subsequent printings over the centuries.

Although no tune accompanied the text in that early manuscript, it is believed that the tune with which the lyrics are now associated was well known at the time and was passed down orally, appearing in written form around the seventeenth century. The tune has been adapted to various hymns, and the celebrated French composer Marcel Dupré (1886–1971) incorporated it in a work for organ, "Variations sur un vieux noël" ("Variations on an Old Carol"). Because the French title "Noël nouvelet!" literally means "New Christmas Song," this carol was also a favorite for the New Year celebration (falling in the midst of the twelve days of Christmas), and signified a new carol for the newborn King in a new year.

In addition to a narrative on the Nativity, one lengthy version (thirteen verses) of "Sing We Now of Christmas," published in Troyes, France (1721), recalls two events not often considered with the traditional Christmas story: Mary's purification forty days after giving birth to Jesus and Simeon's prophecies about Him in the Temple (Gospel of Luke 2:22–35).

See also **The Twelve Days of Christmas.**

Sisters at Heart

See **Bewitched**

Skinflint

See **A Christmas Carol** (Film and Television Versions)

Sleepers, Awake! A Voice Is Calling

("Wachet auf! Ruft uns die Stimme").

German chorale applied to Advent, written in 1598 by Philipp Nicolai (1556–1608), Lutheran pastor of Unna in Westphalia. Nicolai wrote only four chorales, of which this and "How Brightly Shines the Morning Star" are the best known. All four were written following a six-month outbreak of bubonic plague in Unna between July 1597 and January 1598. They were published in Frankfurt in 1599.

The text of "Sleepers, Awake!" is based on Jesus' parable of the five wise and five foolish virgins awaiting the return of the bridegroom, as found in Matthew 25:1–13. The allegorical implications here and in the carol are concerned with the second coming of Christ (the bridegroom). Because He will someday return at an unknown hour (midnight is suggested, not only as an hour of surprise but as the traditional hour of His birth) to claim His brides (the Church, the faithful) and proceed to the marriage feast (Heaven), mankind should watch and be prepared to meet Him and not be left behind, as were the five foolish, unprepared virgins. Thus the carol is considered appropriate for Advent, when Christianity not only celebrates the first coming of Christ, but looks forward to His second coming.

The Unna plague claimed the life of one of Nicolai's former students, fifteen-year-old Wilhelm Ernst, Count of Waldech. According to *The New Oxford Book of Carols*, Nicolai memorialized him in "Sleepers, Awake!" by using the first letter of each of the three verses as a reverse acrostic, creating the initials "G. Z. W.," which stand for *Graf zu Waldech* (Count of Waldech).

The German composer J. S. Bach (1685–1750) based two works on Nicolai's chorale: church Cantata No. 140, *Wachet auf!* (1731), in which the chorale forms the final movement; and an organ chorale prelude of the same title (BWV 645).

The best-known English translation was provided by Great Britain's Catherine Winkworth (1827–1878), a translation specialist.

See also **Advent; How Brightly Shines the Morning Star.**

Sleigh Ride

Popular American song, the music for which was written in 1948 by Massachusetts-born Leroy Anderson (1908–1975) during an

August heat wave. Anderson was an orchestrator for Arthur Fiedler and the Boston Pops Orchestra beginning in 1935. He originally scored "Sleigh Ride" as a purely instrumental work, which clearly conveyed the merriment of gliding over the snow in a horse-drawn sleigh. The Boston Pops first introduced live audiences to the lively piece, which featured a number of colorful sound effects, such as sleigh bells, clip-clops, whip cracks, and even the horse's whinny at the conclusion, imitated by a trumpet. Much like "Jingle Bells," it was an instant success and was quickly absorbed into the Christmas season. Although Mitchell Parish (1900–1993), a lyricist from Shreveport, Louisiana, added a vocal setting in 1950, performances still frequently feature the orchestral version only. Arthur Fiedler and the Boston Pops first recorded "Sleigh Ride" in 1949 on the RCA Victor Red Seal label, and the recording achieved chart status.

Of the 25 most frequently performed Christmas songs of the twentieth century listed by the American Society of Composers, Authors and Publishers (ASCAP), "Sleigh Ride" is ranked number 6.

Respected as a popular and a classical composer, Leroy Anderson contributed other classics, such as "Fiddle Faddle" (1948), "The Syncopated Clock" (1950), "Blue Tango" (1952), "The Typewriter" (1953), and "Bugler's Holiday" (1954). Mitchell Parish also provided lyrics for "Stardust" (1929), "Deep Purple" (1939), and "Moonlight Serenade" (1939), among others.

Slovak Republic

Czechs and Slovaks united in 1918 after World War I to form Czechoslovakia, which Soviet Communists dominated from the end of World War II until 1991, after which Soviet troops withdrew. During the approximately fifty years of Communism's atheistic regime, Christmas was repudiated, the midwinter holiday was moved to New Year's Day with a secular agenda, and St. Nicholas or Baby Jesus, who had brought children's gifts, was replaced by a Soviet "Santa" known as "Grandfather Frost" (*see* **Russia**).

Following the cessation of Soviet occupation, Czechoslovakia split into two independent nations, Czech Republic and Slovak Republic, on January 1, 1993. By then Communism had nearly extinguished the old holiday customs, yet a number of them still survive, primarily in rural areas. These customs revolve around agrarian rituals, romantic matchmaking, the repelling of evil, and forecasts of the future.

The principal Christian faith in the Slovak Republic now is Roman Catholicism. Christmas customs are closely similar to those of the Czech Republic, and minor differences or variations are outlined here.

The Advent season includes observing the feast days of several saints, St. Andrew the Apostle (November 30), St. Barbara (December 4), St. Nicholas (December 6), and St. Lucy (December 13). On the more popular St. Nicholas Day, personages dressed as *Sväty Mikuláš* (St. Nicholas), an angel, and a devil parade about, distributing treats to children and visiting homes to quiz youngsters about their catechism. The devil, in some places known as "Cert," carries a whip and chains and threatens to whisk away naughty children. Children usually set out their shoes by the windowsill on St. Nicholas Eve to receive treats. Superstitions once associated with each feast day, particularly concerning romantic forecasts, are now usually held for Christmas Eve and New Year's Day. During Advent, the entire house and property are thoroughly cleaned, personal disputes and debts are resolved, objects borrowed are returned, and children write letters to Baby Jesus. The Christmas tree is decorated on Christmas Eve with gilded walnuts, candy, fruit, candles, electric lights, colored balls, and gingerbread. All must be in readiness for "Bountiful Evening," Christmas Eve, also known as *Vigilia* (Latin, "watch on the eve of a feast"), the most important and eventful night of the season.

Central to Christmas Eve is Holy Supper, at which all family members gather after having fasted all day. The table is covered with a white tablecloth, under which lies a layer of straw, symbolic of the manger, and straw may be spread on the floor beneath. The table centerpiece often consists of a small crèche or a plate of straw containing *oplatky*, unleavened communion wafers stamped with Nativity scenes. The meal commences upon sighting the first star of the evening, believed to be the Star of Bethlehem, after which the host and hostess bring honey and holy water to the table with ritual greetings. The hostess anoints the table and home with holy water. Grace is said; then the host, taking honey, traces the sign of the cross upon the foreheads of all present. At this point, no one may leave the table (superstition holds that violators will perish in the coming year), for the host now distributes the sacred *oplatky* with honey (considered to be a medicinal) to each person present, along with blessings and wishes for health and happiness. Variations of the ritual include spreading honey in the shape of a cross within a circle on each wafer prior to dispensing it and eating the wafer together with garlic (a talisman against evil and sickness) and honey.

Although the menu prepared for Holy Supper may vary somewhat from region to region and house to house, it traditionally consists of twelve meatless dishes, symbolic of Christ's Twelve Apostles. Along with the obligatory *oplatky* and honey, there may be porridge, *bobalky* (small, baked biscuits with a topping of milk, honey, and poppy seeds), Christmas cake, fruit compote, mushroom soup, sauerkraut soup, *pirohy* (boiled pastries filled with mashed potatoes, cheeses, dried fruit, or sauerkraut), beans, peas, fish (the scales of which are placed under the plates or tablecloth for luck), breads, rolls, and nuts. Mushrooms and fish also symbolize prosperity. Following Holy Supper, the children are escorted out and return only after a bell signals that Baby Jesus has deposited presents beneath the Christmas tree. Children traditionally present their parents with holiday greetings in the form of a song or poem. After livestock receive portions of the meal, the leftovers remain on the table overnight as an oblation to deceased spirits of the family, who are believed to arrive at midnight. Christmas Eve concludes with Midnight Mass.

From Christmas Day to Epiphany, families visit and feast together, while caroling dramatists present traditional Christmas dramas from house to house. This latter tradition, adopted from Germany in the eleventh century, features four shepherds plus an angel character adorned in white with a golden

Painted Slovakian ceramic manger scene, with a wooden X-form manger. Late nineteenth or early twentieth century. From the journal Český Lid *(published in Prague), 1908.*

Early twentieth century Slovakian silhouette of a child and the gift-giver messenger of the Little Jesus holding a small fir tree. From Berta Wegner-Bell, Herzblättchens Beitvertreib *(Berlin: Fleming, 1910).*

crown. The angel bears a wooden crèche or "Bethlehem"; the shepherds perform an *odzemok*, a traditional folk dance; and the household rewards the troupe with food and drink. The cuisine for the remainder of the holidays includes most meats except for New Year's Day, wherein poultry and rabbit are omitted to guarantee lasting happiness and prosperity. The menu on that day includes pork, lentils, and pasta, all symbols of abundance and prosperity.

On Epiphany or *Tri Krále* (Three Kings' Day), which concludes the holiday season, the clergy travel about, blessing the homes and chalking above the entrances the letters "CMB," the initials of the three traditional names of the Wise Men — Caspar, Melchior, and Balthazar, plus the current year. The numerals are evenly divided before and after the letters; thus, the year 2001 would read: "20+C+M+B+01." Groups of "Star Boys" parade about, dressed as the Three Kings (one of whom is blackfaced as Balthazar, the traditional king of Ethiopia). A boy costumed as an angel in white leads them and carries a large paper star on a pole.

• SUPERSTITIONS. A large number of superstitions, now of historical interest, once surrounded the entire Christmas season, and a few popular ones are detailed here. By making a three-legged stool between St. Lucy Day and Christmas Eve, then sitting on that stool during Midnight Mass, one would encounter witches. To escape their clutches while traveling home from church, a person cast either needles or poppy seeds behind him; the witches were compelled either to pass through the needles' eyes or pick up every poppy seed, acts which slowed their pace. Another charm against evil was to rub door hinges with garlic. Following Holy Supper, family members each cracked a nut and sliced an apple. A rotten nut portended bad luck for the new year, as did a cross pattern in the sliced apple; a star pattern predicted good luck. The burning candle wick at the supper table would incline toward any person doomed to die in the coming year. On Christmas Eve, farmers sought predictions about the new year's weather by preparing either twelve nut shells filled with water or twelve onion slices moistened with water. All were labeled for the months of the year and were exposed to air overnight. On Christmas morning, those items remaining wet predicted rain for the corresponding months; for dry items, fair weather or drought. Binding fruit trees with straw, shaking them, or spreading poppy seeds around them on Christmas Eve would yield better crops, and the number of times a rooster crowed on Christmas morning indicated the

number of weeks remaining before spring plowing would commence.

Predictions of romance and marriage were favorite pastimes among young girls on Christmas Eve or New Year's Day. The direction of the first star sighted or the first dog bark heard after supper indicated the direction from which a future spouse would come. In one variation, a girl swept the floor after supper, took the refuse to a crossroads, then listened for the first dog bark. If a girl poured hot lead into water, the shape of the congealed mass provided some hint to a spouse's occupation. Before retiring, a girl placed a ring in one small bag and a piece of bread in another. She put these plus a third, empty bag either under her pillow or at her bedside. If she awoke during the night, she blindly chose one bag but examined it the next morning. The ring predicted an ultimately happy marriage; the bread, a life of hardship; the empty bag, spinsterhood.

"Merry Christmas" in the Slovak Republic is *Vesele Vianoce*.

See also **Croatia; Czech Republic; Poland.**

The Small One: A Story for Those Who Like Christmas and Small Donkeys

Classic children's book written by American author Charles Tazewell (1900–1972), published in 1947. The setting is Old Mexico a few days before Christmas.

When little Pablo scolds Cupido, his seemingly stubborn donkey, an old and gentle Padre explains that, because of a great honor bestowed upon one donkey many years ago, what appears as laziness or a stubborn streak in all donkey descendants is actually pride. Then the Padre tells Pablo the story of Small One:

At his father's bidding, a boy must sell his beloved pet, fourteen-year-old Small One, the oldest and smallest of the family's donkeys, because the animal is no longer useful. Instead of selling him to a tanner for slaughter, as his father had ordered, the boy wanders through the city all day, pleading for someone to buy Small One for one piece of silver. All reject the offer with disdain and deem the donkey as worthless. Yet the boy defends Small One, asserting that his pet is fine enough for a king's stable.

When night falls and Small one has not been sold, the boy is about to resort to the tanner, when Joseph, needing a gentle animal to carry Mary to Bethlehem, purchases him for the piece of silver.

The Padre concludes the story by explaining that Small One, who indeed witnessed the birth of a King in a King's stable along with those who paid homage to his "small Master," fulfilled the destiny of donkeys for all time. And that is why all donkeys, especially at Christmastime, stand and dream of the Small One of Bethlehem.

Bing Crosby provided a narrative recording of the story for Decca Records in 1947.

The Walt Disney Company adapted the story as an animated cartoon short, *The Small One* (1978), which centered only around the Judean boy and Small One. Voices: Sean Marshall, William Woodson, Olan Soule, Hal Smith, Joe Higgins, Gordon Jump. Written by Vance Gerry, Pete Young. Produced and directed by Don Bluth. Walt Disney Productions. Walt Disney Home Video. Color. Approx. 30 minutes.

Disney subsequently published a book version of the cartoon under the same title in 1995, written by Alex Walsh with a foreword by television celebrity Kathie Lee Gifford.

See also **The Littlest Angel; The Littlest Snowman; The Littlest Tree.**

A Smoky Mountain Christmas

(1986). Made-for-television drama loosely based on Grimms' fairy tale "Snow White and the Seven Dwarfs," starring country singer Dolly Parton in her first television movie venture.

As the holidays approach, singing celebrity Lorna Davis (Parton), needing a welcome break from the pressures of Hollywood, retreats to an old friend's remote cabin in the Great Smoky Mountains of Tennessee. There, she discovers that seven runaway orphans have set up residence in the cabin and have become a makeshift family led by an older boy, Jake (Chad Sheets). Not wishing to take any action until after Christmas, Lorna allows the children to remain and soon wins their hearts while acting as their loving foster mother.

In keeping with the "Snow White" sce-nario, Lorna meets her "prince" in Mountain Dan (Lee Majors), who saves her from Jezebel (Anita Morris), a beautiful mountain witch bent on destroying her (Jezebel believes that Lorna is a "white" witch who intends to usurp her domain). Jezebel strikes again after the law, having traced the orphans to the cabin, places them in a local children's home and throws Lorna in jail for obstruction of justice. Baking a spell into an apple pie, Jezebel transforms herself into a sweet-appearing old lady and carries the pie to the jail. Lorna eats the pie and falls into a deep sleep. Dan and Jake stage a jail-break, but instead of Dan's princely kiss, Jake's tears falling on Lorna's cheek break the spell, and she awakens. When Jezebel appears for another coup, Lorna tricks her into eating the pie, thereby dispatching Jezebel.

Now they must rescue the other orphans, who will be split up on Christmas Eve. Posing as Santa and Mrs. Santa, Dan and Lorna create a diversion at the children's home while Jake rounds up his comrades. As they all are about to escape in a one-horse sleigh, the law apprehends them and hauls them into court early on Christmas morning, where a soft-hearted judge (John Ritter) drops all charges and grants Lorna custody of the children.

With Danny Cooksey, Gennie James, Marc D. Robinson, Daryl Bartley, Ashley Bank, Micah Rowe, David Ackroyd, Rene Auberjonois, Douglas Seale, Dan Hedaya, Bo Hopkins. Written by William Bleich. Produced by Robert Lovenheim. Directed by Henry Winkler. Sandollar Productions. Trimark Video. Color. 100 min.

Snow Maiden

See **Russia**

A Snow White Christmas

(1980). Made-for-television animated cartoon, loosely based on the fairy tale by the Brothers Grimm. This version introduces a second Snow White, teenaged daughter of Queen Snow White and King Charming, who rule the kingdom of Noel.

With Christmas drawing nigh, Queen Snow White's stepmother, the Wicked Queen, returns and casts a spell which engulfs all of Noel in ice. Young Snow White and friend

Grunyon escape and are befriended by seven giants, cousins to the seven dwarfs: Thinker, Finicky, Corney, Brawny, Tiny, Hicker, and Weeper.

Failing to eliminate Snow White through fire and flood, the Wicked Queen poses as the giants' aged sister and induces Snow White to fall into a deep sleep by means of poisoned flowers (not an apple). The giants seek revenge, but it is the Wicked Queen's own magic mirror that revolts and destroys her and her castle forever. All spells are broken, except that on Snow White. Only her mother's and father's kisses (not those from a prince) restore her, just in time for Christmas Eve.

Voices: Erika Scheimer, Arte Johnson, Melendy Britt, Diane Pershing, Charlie Dell, Larry Mann, Clinton Sundberg. Written by Marc Richards. Produced by Don Christensen. Directed by Kay Wright. Filmation Associates. Hallmark Home Entertainment Video. Color. 46 min.

The Snowman

(1982). British motion picture animated cartoon short, based on a children's wordless picture book written and illustrated by British author Raymond Briggs, published in 1978. The original book does not feature the subject of Christmas, but its motion picture adaptation alters the story slightly to include holiday sentiment and incorporates only mime and music with a single vocal selection, "Walking in the Air." In 1983 it received an Academy Award nomination for Best Short Animated Film.

Coming to life at midnight on Christmas Eve, a little English boy's snowman frolics with his creator indoors while the household sleeps. After a nocturnal joyride on a motorcycle around the countryside, the snowman lifts the boy, and together they fly to the North Pole, where they join Father Christmas and a host of other snow people (not elves) who are making merry. While touring Father Christmas's domain, the boy visits the reindeer and receives his Christmas gift, a new scarf wrapped in a package labeled with his name, James Brighton.

When James awakens on Christmas morning, nothing is left of the snowman except his old hat, scarf, and pieces of coal, all left in a pile in the front yard. The previous night could have been a dream, yet James's new scarf is proof to the contrary.

Written by Raymond Briggs. Produced by John Coates. Directed by Dianne Jackson. A Snowman Enterprises Production. Columbia/Tristar Home Video. Color. 26 min.

Raymond Briggs (1934–) began a career in advertising but soon switched to illustrating children's books and teaching. Two of his earlier books, *The Mother Goose Treasury* (1966) and *Father Christmas* (1973), both won Great Britain's Kate Greenaway Medal, equivalent to the Caldecott Medal in the United States. Among other honors, *The Snowman* received the Boston Globe–Horn Book Award and the International Reading Association's Children's Choice Award.

See also **Father Christmas**.

Some Children See Him
See **Alfred Burt Carols**

Song of the Bagpipers
See **Carol of the Bagpipers**

South America

Overwhelmingly Roman Catholic because most of the countries on this continent were former Spanish colonies dating to the sixteenth century, Christmas traditions derive from Spain in every country but Brazil, a former Portuguese colony. Therefore, the principal customs common to South American countries include *Nacimientos* or *Pesebres* (respectively, simple or more elaborate Nativity scenes); the Feast of the Immaculate Conception (December 8); the Midnight Mass, termed "Mass of the Rooster" (*Misa del Gallo*, Spanish; *Missa do Galo*, Portuguese), celebrated on *Nochebuena* ("Good Night," Christmas Eve); a large Christmas Eve dinner for the immediate family held either before, or just after, the Midnight Mass; Holy Innocents Day (December 28); New Year's Day (January 1); and *Día de los Reyes* (Kings Day, Epiphany, January 6).

Through foreign influences, predominantly from the United States, Santa Claus and Christmas trees are generally well known, but the Nativity scene remains the most important holiday symbol. It is customary for families to visit the Nativity scenes of friends and relatives and the scene erected in the local cathedral. Traditionally, the crib or manger within each Nativity scene remains empty until midnight on Christmas Eve, at which time each family or church adds a figure of the Christ Child to symbolize that Christ is born.

Pesebres are usually handmade and occupy a large space in the principal room of the home. Consisting of ornate landscapes with perhaps hills and waterfalls, they include figures of the Holy Family; animals, angels and shepherds; the Three Kings; and figures of local familiarity, such as the mayor, police officer, butcher, and carpenter, the latter figures bonding the past with the present.

Formerly, children received gifts only on Epiphany from the Three Kings, but it has become customary for children to receive gifts on Christmas Eve as well, brought either by Santa Claus or the Christ Child. More commonly on Epiphany Eve, children place their shoes upon a window sill, and the Kings fill them with treats by morning.

Religious processions and festive parades with fireworks, music, singing, and dancing abound. Employers in some regions are compelled by law to provide employees with an *aguinaldo* ("gift," Christmas bonus).

The period from December 16 to 24 constitutes a Novena, on each day of which a special mass is held. The first mass is dedicated to the Annunciation; the second, the visit between Mary and her cousin Elizabeth; third, the journey to Bethlehem; fourth, the Nativity; fifth, the shepherds; sixth, the Magi; seventh, the flight into Egypt; eighth, the boy Jesus in the Temple with the scholars; ninth, the boy Jesus' return to Nazareth. The Christmas season generally ends on Epiphany.

The following paragraphs summarize additional customs found in the individual countries. "Merry Christmas" in Spanish is *Feliz Navidad*; in Portuguese, *Feliz Natal*.

• ARGENTINA. Home decorations often consist of red and white garlands, with Father Christmas' boots placed at the door. Following Midnight Mass, the Christmas dinner may consist of roast *lechon* (suckling pig), *niños envueltos* ("children wrapped up," pieces of steak rolled and seasoned with minced meat, hard-boiled eggs, and spices), *sidra* (apple juice with

liquor), *pan dulce* (sweet Christmas bread with dried fruit), and *turron de mani* (Christmas candy). Another drink consisting of different fruits mixed with juice and cider is quaffed for a midnight Christmas toast. Because the holiday falls during the summer, beach activities are common with fireworks on Christmas evening.

• BOLIVIA. Because Christmas is more of a religious celebration here, Christmas decorations and gifts are few, and Christmas trees are absent. Villagers congregate for communal meals, which may feature pork, beef, fresh vegetables, *locotos* (chili), and soup with beef stock and vegetables. Amid the folk dancing and regional music, children attired in assorted costumes also participate in street dancing to the music of drums, whistles, and cymbals. More colorful festivities are reserved for New Year's Eve.

• BRAZIL. Because it is a former colony of Portugal, Brazil's Christmas customs derive from that country, and celebrations vary considerably between urban and rural areas. Generally, the more urban, the more elaborate are the festivities. As in other Latin American countries, the *Presépio* (Nativity scene) remains the chief Christmas symbol, which the Jesuits first introduced in 1583 in Rio de Janeiro. The Christmas Eve dinner often features turkey with *farofa* (stuffing made from manihot meal, butter, hard-boiled eggs, olives, and raisins), suckling pig, assorted fish in northern regions, fresh fruits, nuts, *rabanada* (dessert resembling French toast made with cinnamon, eggs, sugar, and milk or wine), fruit punch, and liquor. Christmas trees generally consist of artificial pines or equivalents, and Santa Claus, termed *Papai Noel*, has supplanted a native equivalent, Grandpa Indian. Christmas Day includes a meal with invited guests, followed by distribution of food and gifts to the needy in public squares, at which governors' ladies and the first lady of Brazil traditionally participate in their respective states.

Traditions are more authentic in rural areas, particularly in the Northeast. In addition to singing and dancing, rural celebrations often feature pageants and traditional Portuguese folk dramas performed on the local church square. These dramas begin around

Christmas Day and extend until Epiphany. Considered to be the most interesting of these is *Bumba-Meu-Boi* ("Whoa, My Ox"), a satire about the death and resurrection of an ox, which is again killed. Its theme reflects elements of black African culture (black slaves were imported to Brazil in the sixteenth century), which are also found in other dramas now in decline. *Pastoris* or *Pastorinhas*, originally sacred Nativity plays with performers attired as shepherds, eventually evolved into burlesques, the final acts of which burned the *Presépio* on stage; today, *Pastoris* assume a purely carnival atmosphere. The name *Pastoris* also refers to Christmas carols sung around Nativity scenes to the accompaniment of tambourines, guitars, and wind instruments. Similar dramas include the *Reisado*, which centers around the Three Kings and which may terminate with a scene from *Bumba-Meu-Boi*, and the related *Folia dos Reis* ("Frolic of the Kings"). Dance festivals at this time include the *Fandango* and the *Chegança* or *Changaca*, both based on maritime plays. A relatively new drama that arose around 1930 is *Guerreiro* ("Warrior"), performed in the State of Alagoas, which features the death and resurrection of a lyre bird and a dancing ox, akin to the *Bumba*. Epiphany features poetry contests, in which participants improvise verses and sing them to instrumental accompaniment. A custom instituted by Protestant missionaries is the "white gift" Christmas collection for the poor. Though many live in poverty, it is customary for those who can to bring gifts to their church. These gifts, often food, are wrapped in white packages and distributed to those who are most destitute. *See also* **Portugal**.

• CHILE. Christmas is more of a secular holiday; while the country remains predominantly Roman Catholic, only some 10 percent of the population practice the faith. The principal gift bringer is *Viejo Pascuero* (Christmas Old Man), who closely resembles Santa Claus and even rides in a reindeer sleigh, despite the summer weather below the equator in December. Children place their shoes in window sills or in corridors on Christmas Eve for Christmas Old Man to fill with treats. Families congregate on Christmas Eve for gift exchanges and a large dinner, which may consist of turkey, seafood, a variety of salads, *azuela de ave* (chicken soup with potatoes and onions), *pan de pasqua* (Christmas bread filled with candied fruit), fruits, cakes, *rompon* (alcoholic beverage similar to eggnog), *cola de mono* (milk and coffee flavored with liquor and cinnamon), and Chilean wine. The Christmas Day dinner itself consists of leftovers plus *choclo* (corn cake) and *chirimoya alegre* (sweet fruit dish). Citywide fiestas are common, and one in particular is that in Andacollo, which honors the Virgin. According to legend, an Indian wood cutter named Collo, obedient to a divine vision, discovered a three-foot statue of the Virgin in the area. Termed the *Virgin del Rosario* (Virgin of the Rosary), the venerated statue is always displayed at the fiesta on a platform of roses. Epiphany is called *La Pascua de Los Negros* ("Holiday of the Black Ones"), paying special tribute to one of the Three Kings who tradition says came from Ethiopia.

• COLOMBIA. Unique to Colombia is the Christmas Eve *Aguinaldos* (gifts), a costume ball held in many cities which resembles an American Halloween party. Clad in elaborate disguises, thousands of merry people flock the streets during the evening and attempt to recognize their friends. If they are successful, they are entitled to claim an *aguinaldo* from the one recognized. The Christmas dinner may include *lechona* (stuffed pork), fowls, salads, vegetables, tamales, *ajiaco* (soup with potatoes), *natilla* (corn-based dessert), *buñuelos* (deep-fried pastries served with powered sugar, cinnamon, and honey), and liquor. In addition to attending mass, families exchange gifts and shoot fireworks at midnight. Those in the North may place gifts under their children's beds early on Christmas morning. From December 26 until New Year's Day, most villages host a Sugar Cane Festival, which sports a carnival atmosphere.

• ECUADOR. The Christmas meal may include *pernil* (baked pork), chicken, *pristiños* (molasses pastries), *canelazo* (spiced, hot liquor with cloves, cinnamon, and sugar), and *anizado* (anise-flavored brandy). Gifts are opened on Christmas Eve, and families often personally donate toys and candy to needy children. The city of Cuenca hosts the most popular of the country's Christmas Eve processions, termed *Pase del Niño Viajero* ("Steps of the Little Traveler"), in which people display their stock of wealth and plenty as they ride in vehicles or on burros.

While the Church observes Holy Innocents Day with religious ritual, the day in Ecuador has become a children's festival akin to the American Halloween, for children dress in costumes and pull pranks and practical jokes. The custom is based on a legend that mothers in Bethlehem saved some children from the Slaughter of the Innocents by disguising them. On New Year's Eve, most people create representations of the "Old Year" by fashioning effigies of objectionable persons or items, which are burned at midnight in a custom known as *La Quema de los Años Viejos* ("Burning of the Old Years"). Shortly into the new year, families remove their images of the Christ Child from their *pesebres* and carry them to church for a mass, which is termed *El Paso del Niño* ("The Step of the Child").

• GUYANA (formerly British Guiana). The majority of the population consists of descendants of slaves from India (50 percent) and black Africa (30 percent). Some 42 percent of the population is Christian, divided between Anglican and Roman Catholic faiths. From the second week of December until Christmas Day, masquerade street bands clad in colorfully ornate costumes dominate festivities with street dancers and dancers on stilts, all of whom perform for profit. Central to the merriment is "Mother Sally" or "Long Lady," a figure costumed as a large doll, which descendants of West African slaves adapted from a protective, matriarchal goddess. Typical musical instruments, vestiges of the British influence, include the fife, kittle, boom, and steel drums (oil drums with indented heads). Guyanese spend Christmas Day with close family, and Boxing Day, December 26, is also a national holiday devoted to a more broad range of fellowship. "Merry Christmas" is said in English, the official language.

• PARAGUAY. The Christmas season begins with the Feast of the Immaculate Conception, and he who brings children their Christmas gifts is a figure similar to Santa Claus, known as *Papa Noel* (Father Christmas). Christmas dinner often features duck, lamb, chicken, and turkey, along with salads, a soup resembling a soufflé, beer, and cider. Paraguay is bilingual with some 90 percent of the population speaking the Guaraní Indian dialect in addition to Spanish. A Guaraní "Merry Christmas" is *V'ya pave mita tupara-pe*.

• PERU. This country's Quechua Indian artisans, Inca descendants, are noted for their Nativity figures carved from wood using techniques dating from the sixteenth century. Open-air markets in this summertime holiday feature all manner of these and other crafts, toys, and delicacies. Such crafts may include the *retablo*, a personal, portable shrine that aids the bearer in giving thanks for spiritual blessings. While *retablos* are known throughout Latin America as principally religious paintings on tin, the Peruvian version consists of a three-dimensional box with triangular top and one or two doors that open outwardly. Overlaid with gesso and brightly painted, *retablos* range from matchbook size to several feet. They are usually divided in half, the top symbolizing heaven, the bottom, earth. At this time of year, figures within the shrine are based on the Nativity. These figures are molded from a potato-based paste, painted, and varnished. The triangle and doors often sport floral patterns.

Children carol from house to house while playing on whistles, small harps, flutes, and bells; their repertoire also features songs dedicated to the *pesebres* passed along their route. Children open gifts on Christmas Eve, and afterwards the family congregates for dinner, which features turkey and stuffing, *panetón* (bread with raisins and glazed fruit), *biblia con pisco* (eggnog made with pomace brandy), hot chocolate, and champagne. On Christmas Day, particularly in Lima, citizens attend a grand bullfight. Then follows an elaborate procession to honor the Virgin, symbolized by a statue held on high. Epiphany is not particularly emphasized, but some families partake of *rosca*, a bread containing a coin or other figure baked inside, similar to the European "Kings' Cakes" of Epiphany.

• URUGUAY. The large majority of the population is of European descent, primarily from Spain, Italy, and France, with Christmas customs reflecting those of the parent countries. Santa Claus is known as *Papa Noel*.

• VENEZUELA. The Christmas season begins with the Novena, called *Misa del Aguinaldo* (Mass of the Gift), which is held each morning around 5 A.M. Church bells pealing and children setting off firecrackers alert villages that the hour of mass has arrived. Holiday music, also called *aguinaldo*, is lively and rich; the specific rhythm is known as the *gaita* ("bagpipe"). Arising in Zulia State, *gaita* has no relationship to a literal bagpipe; instead, typical instruments include a *cuatro* (ukulele), *furruco* and *tambora* (two kinds of drums), *maracas* (rattles), and electronic organs and guitars.

Virtually everyone in Caracas traditionally roller skates to all masses, including the Christmas Eve Midnight Mass. Then follows the Christmas dinner, which usually includes *hallacas* (corn-meal pie stuffed with pork, chicken, olives, raisins, wrapped in banana leaves and boiled), *pan de jamon* (long bread filled with ham and raisins), *pavo* (turkey), *pernil de cochino* (pork dish), *dulce de lechoza* (cold dessert of green papaya and brown sugar), and *ponche crema* (cream punch with or without liquor). Children receive Christmas gifts from *El Niño Jesus* (the Christ Child), who leaves them under their beds.

Holy Innocents Day is spent in performing mischievous pranks, and bands of costumed musicians and singers provide entertainment as they roam about. One notable Innocents' Day festival, termed "On the Loose," is that of Agua Blanca. Attired with swords, ornamental hats, and colored ribbons, the bands first meet in Bolívar Square amid a din of firecrackers. Following mass, they disperse into the neighborhoods with music and dancing.

In some locales on New Year's Eve, children create a life-size effigy of the apostle Judas and solicit money for the poor. At midnight, they burn Judas with fireworks as a sign of burning away the old year and bringing in the new. Another New Year's Eve custom, decidedly Spanish, is to eat twelve grapes for luck within the final minute before midnight. On New Year's Day, the cities of Merida, Tachira, and Trujillo observe the custom of *La Paradura del Niño* ("The Standing Up of the Christ Child"). A figure of the Christ Child is placed in a large handkerchief, the four corners of which are taken up by people holding candles, and the entourage parades around town from house to house. Once peculiar only to Merida, the custom originally involved families removing the Christ Child's figure from its crib in the household *Pesebre* and standing it upright on New Year's Day, where it remained until Candlemas (February 2), which formerly ended the Christmas season in the Catholic Church.

Should a household fail to honor this tradition, neighbors would secretly steal the figure and would return it only after the Christ Child's "godparents" hosted a *paradura* party. Such a gala affair included fireworks, music, traditional carols, youths dressed as Mary, Joseph, and shepherds, and a formal procession to return the statue to the *pesebre*.

See also **Epiphany; Feast of the Immaculate Conception; Holy Innocents Day;** ***Las Posadas*; Mass of the Rooster; Nativity Scene; Spain.**

Spain

As in most Spanish-speaking countries, the Christmas season in Spain begins with the Feast of the Immaculate Conception, traditionally celebrated on December 8, when choirboys costumed in pale blue satin trimmed in lace and with plumed, wide-brimmed hats perform a ritualistic dance called *Los Seises* (Dance of Sixes) before the altar of the cathedral in Seville. The dancers, whose costumes reflect the attire of seventeenth-century pageboys, originally numbered six but have increased to ten. As the boys dance, they sing an Advent hymn invoking the presence of Jesus. From December 16 through 24, villages observe a novena, a devotional period of nine days, in which the Nativity scene, known either as *Nacimiento* ("Birth") or *Belén* ("Bethlehem") is the central figure, although the Christmas tree and Santa Claus are becoming more popular. *Belenistas* are clubs or organizations which sponsor competitions and displays of Nativity scenes. Homes and businesses light small oil lamps which illuminate statues of the Virgin, and the Christmas markets are filled with all manner of fruits, decorations, flowers, sweets, and hand-made gifts. Pageantry, dancing, and Nativity plays abound, as do *tuna*, groups of university students in traditional garb who provide entertainment by singing and playing *villancicos* (traditional carols). Folk instruments commonly providing accompaniment include the tambourine, *sonaja* (round percussion instrument), *zambomba* (hollow, drumlike instrument that produces a rhythmic wail), castanets in the southern regions, and bagpipes in the northwest regions.

Before the *Noche Buena* (literally "Good Night," Christmas Eve) Midnight Mass, known as the *Misa del Gallo* (Mass of the Rooster), the immediate and extended family gathers for a Christmas Eve dinner of multiple courses, the dishes of which vary from region to region. Fairly universal courses, however, include *escudella* (soup with meatballs and grated cheese); turkey stuffed with bacon, ham, or sausage; pork; *paella* (saffron-flavored rice); *flan* (caramel custard); *besugo* (Mediterranean sea bream) or flounder; roasted chestnuts; marzipan; fruit; *turrón* (nougat candy); and assorted wines. In the region of Galicia, the principal courses consist of *bacalao* (codfish) and suckling pig or meat pie; in Aragon, lamb or chicken; in Madrid, turkey with red cabbage. Festivities include dancing and singing traditional carols around the Nativity scene (which receives the figure of the Christ Child only on Christmas Eve), with the merry-making continuing until Epiphany, January 6. Although children may receive gifts on Christmas morning, the traditional gift-giving day is Epiphany (see below).

On Christmas night, citizens gather at the village square to draw from the "Urn of Fate," which contains all participants' names individually written on paper. As the names are drawn out by twos, according to custom, each pair will be friends for the coming year. If an unmarried man and woman pair, fate may precipitate their marriage.

In the Basque folklore, the ancient pagan figure Olentzero, a mountain-dwelling coal miner, descends into villages on Christmas Eve with the good news that Christ is born. Abandoned at birth, Olentzero was raised by a woodland couple after a fairy brought him to them. He grew up a favorite of children and made toys for them, giving his life to save them in a time of calamity. The fairy bestowed immortality on Olentzero, and he returns each year during the time of the winter solstice with gifts for children. Over time, his annual mission acquired a Christmas theme. He is depicted as a plump, straw- or herb-stuffed doll wearing a regional *boine* (cap), woolen socks, and goatskin vest, and carrying a wine flask with frying pan. In Olentzero parades, men dress the part and are carried about on the shoulders of their comrades.

Children in Cádiz often participate in "Swinging in the Sun," competing to swing the highest in conventional swings. The purpose, derived from ancient winter solstice festivals, is to lead the sun back north and encourage the coming of spring. Another solstice custom, common in Granada and Jaén, is *Hogueras* (bonfires), in which it is believed that jumping over fires will provide protection against illness. Although *piñatas* are not commonly seen in Spain as in Mexico, an equivalent activity for Christmas Day exists in the Catalonian "Lucky Strike Game." A *tío* (hollow Yule log) is decorated and filled with small gifts or other treats, and when it is suspended, children hit the log with sticks until the gifts tumble from the trunk. Catalonian boys beat Yule logs with sticks on Christmas Day to bring luck for the new year and drag them from door to door in anticipation of treats.

December 28, Holy Innocents Day or Fools Festival, recalls the Feast of Fools of medieval Europe. Masked men choose a mayor to supervise ludicrous activities. Dressed as clowns or women, the men search out businesses against whom mock charges and fines are levied if their commands are not obeyed. In the evening, citizens convene to hear a litany of "crimes" that were committed. The fines received are used to fund the festivities.

During the final twelve seconds of New Year's Eve, one must swallow twelve grapes to ensure good health and fortune for the coming year. The event is most popularly celebrated at the *Puerta del Sol* (Gate of the Sun) in Madrid, along with festive parties with revelers in costumes and masks. To ensure luck for the new year, Spaniards consume pork, for the pig roots in a forward direction; likewise, fowls are not consumed on New Year's Eve, because they scratch backward for food, a sign of bad luck.

The Christmas season ends on Epiphany, January 6. Tradition holds that the three Wise Men passed through Spain on their journey to Bethlehem, arriving there on Epiphany. Therefore the day is known as *Día de los Tres Reyes* ("Day of the Three Kings"). In the weeks prior to Epiphany, Children write letters to the Magi with requests for gifts and visit them in department stores, much like children do in the United States with Santa Claus. Magi parades, known as *cabalgatas*, along with figures of the Magi and people costumed as the Kings prevail throughout and are usually held on Epiphany Eve. Also on this eve, children fill their shoes with barley or straw and set them on window sills, balconies, or doorsteps for the three Wise Men, particularly the black king Balthasar, to fill with gifts. If children have been good, the Wise Men accept the fodder on behalf of their camels in exchange for the gifts; otherwise, they reject the fodder and leave nothing or a lump of coal. Some parents may mark their children's cheeks with coal or dark ash while they sleep, so that, upon awakening, the children will believe that Balthasar kissed them during the night.

A favorite treat is *roscón*, a fruitcake that contains a small toy, and whoever finds the toy in his slice will receive good luck in the new year.

"Merry Christmas" in Spanish is *Felices Pascuas de Navidad*. In the Basque language it is *Zorionak eta Urte Berri On*, and *Bon Nadal* in Catalan.

See also **Epiphany; Feast of Fools; Holy Innocents Day; Mass of the Rooster; Nativity Scene.**

The Spirit
See **The Waltons**

The Spirit of Christmas
See **A Christmas Carol** (Film and Television Versions)

Sri Lanka
See **Asia and the South Pacific**

The Star Carol
See **Alfred Burt Carols**

Star in the East
See **Brightest and Best of the Sons of the Morning; Nativity**

The Star of Bethlehem

This phenomenon has been the subject of much speculation, with modern explanations for the phenomenon ranging from the purely supernatural to actual astronomical events. Concerning the former, Matthew's Gospel describes the Star as moving ahead of the Wise Men and eventually standing over the site where the Child resided, implying that it had a will of its own. To that end, the Gnostic texts further state that not only did the Star first appear two years prior to Jesus' birth, but that it was a "secret power" which appeared like a star, the actions of which behaved contrary to those of other heavenly bodies. Whereas the paths of the latter normally appeared to move from east to west (from the earth's rotation), the Star coursed "north to south" (Bethlehem lies southwest of Persia), was visible during the day as well as the night, and varied its height in the heavens relative to the other stars. Thus the Gnostic texts imply a supernatural force behind the Star.

On the other hand, the most popular astronomical theory, first proposed by the German astronomer Johannes Kepler (1571–1630), is a conjunction of planets, which would have appeared as a very bright "star." Indeed, by modern calculations, three different conjuctions of Mars, Jupiter, and Saturn occurred in 7 B.C. Other conjunctions include those of Venus and Jupiter in 3 B.C. and in 2 B.C.; and of Jupiter with Regulus, a star of the first magnitude in the constellation Leo, once in 3 B.C. and twice in 2 B.C. These dates all correspond to two time frames proposed for Jesus' birth: between 7 and 4 B.C. (based on scholarly claims that Herod the Great of the Nativity story died in 4 B.C. shortly after Jesus was born), and about 3–2 B.C. (based on other claims that Herod died in 1 B.C). The exact year of Christ's birth remains unknown.

See also **Nativity.**

The Stingiest Man in Town
See **A Christmas Carol** (Film and Television Versions)

Stockings
See **Saint Nicholas; Saint Nicholas Day**

The Story of Holly and Ivy

Classic children's book by British author Margaret Rumer Godden (professional name Rumer Godden), the text for which was first published in the *Ladies' Home Journal* in 1958.

For six-year-old Ivy, a runaway child from St. Agnes Orphanage, having a doll and finding a real grandmother are her fondest Christmas wishes. Holly, a beautiful doll adorned in red in Mr. Blossom's toy shop, wishes not only to find "my Christmas girl"—that is, a little girl who would want her as a Christmas gift—but also to be free of the cantankerous owl, another doll that berates her and all the other toys in the shop. And for Albert Jones and his wife, a middle-aged, childless couple, their wish is to share the love of Christmas with a child. In this wishing story, the magic of Christmas unites Holly, Ivy, and the Joneses together in a special bond of love.

A made-for-television animated cartoon version, titled *The Wish That Changed Christmas* (1991), included only minor alterations from the printed original and featured the voices of Paul Winfield and Jonathan Winters. Written by Romeo Muller. Produced by Nicole Paradis Grindle. Directed by Catherine Margerin. Children's Television Workshop. Republic Pictures Home Video. Color. 23 min.

Author and translator Rumer Godden (1907–1998) centered her fiction principally around foreigners in exotic lands, particularly in India, where she wrote novels for both adults and children. Her children's books, which often featured dolls in worlds of their own, included, among others, *A Doll's House*, *The Rocking Horse Secret*, and *The Mousewife*.

Sugar Bowl

See **New Year's Day**

Sugarplums

Now-archaic term, synonymous with bonbons, describing rich, chocolate confections usually filled with fruit preserves or cream fillings. Hence, the name is a misnomer (implying sugar-coated plums), unless the filling consists of plum preserves. Actually, "plum" is an obscure, generic term for "fruit," as the "plum" in plum pudding (also a misnomer because it contains no plums) is known

Shepherds are awed by the angel announcing the birth of Christ in Bethlehem, over which the brilliant star is shining. From John Fleetwood, The Light in the East *(National Publishing Co. and Jones Brothers, 1874).*

to imply the raisins and other fruits which may be present.

The term "sugarplums" has remained a traditional element of Christmas, at least in concept, and has been perpetuated primarily through two sources: the classic poem "A Visit from St. Nicholas" ("'Twas the Night Before Christmas"), in which the children's Christmas Eve dreams include "visions of sugarplums," and Tchaikovsky's ballet *The Nutcracker* and its "Dance of the Sugar-Plum Fairy," featuring a central character in the Kingdom of Sweets.

Superstitions

Christmas is associated with numerous superstitions derived from pagan European folklore, which has blended with Christian beliefs over two millennia. The sources for many are quite obscure but a few can be traced to specific countries. In the following illustrative compilation — by no means exhaustive — countries or regions of origin, where known, are indicated in parentheses. Other superstitions pertinent to specific countries are listed in the entries for those countries.

The number of happy months a person can expect in the coming year is determined by the number of different homes in which mince pie is eaten during the holidays.

On Christmas Eve, pour melted lead into cold water. The pattern of hardened metal in the water enables an unmarried woman to determine her future husband's initials, looks, or profession. To predict the future in general, Germans carry out this practice, *Bleigiessen*, on New Year's Eve.

Water turns to wine at midnight on Christmas Eve.

Place a branch of a cherry tree in water indoors on the first day of Advent (or on St. Barbara's Day, December 4, or on St. Lucy's Day, December 13). If it flowers by Christmas, good luck is in store.

A child born on Christmas Eve or Christmas Day will have good fortune.

A child born during the twelve nights of Christmas may become a *kallikantzari*, an evil, half-human monster. (Greece)

A child born during the twelve nights of Christmas may become a werewolf. (Germany and Poland)

If an unmarried woman allows a bowl of water to freeze overnight on Christmas Eve, the ice patterns seen on Christmas morning will disclose her heart's desire.

If an unmarried woman lies on the floor on New Year's Eve and tosses her shoe backward over her head, the direction of the toe points in the direction from which her future husband will come.

Eating an apple on Christmas Eve brings good health for the coming year.

Refusing mince pie at Christmas dinner brings bad luck for a year.

Buried treasure reveals itself during the reading of Christ's genealogy at Midnight Mass.

The woman accepting edelweiss at Christmas also accepts the man who presents it. (Switzerland)

On Christmas Eve, if an unmarried woman peels an apple, making sure it remains as a single ribbon, and if she throws it on the floor from above her head, the pattern of the peeling on the floor will disclose her future husband's initials.

Burning old shoes during the Christmas season prevents misfortune in the coming year. (Greece)

A windy Christmas Day brings good luck.

The weather on each of the twelve days of Christmas will determine the weather for the corresponding months in the coming year.

During the twelve days of Christmas, place a blindfolded goose in a circle of unwed girls. The first girl that the goose touches will be the first to wed.

At midnight, cattle kneel facing East on Christmas Eve, and bees hum Psalm 100.

A fire (Yule log) burning all through the twelve days of Christmas brings good luck. Likewise, bad luck is at hand should the fire go out.

The Gates of Paradise are always open on Christmas Eve; those who die at this time may avoid Purgatory. (Ireland)

He whose appetite fails first at Christmas will be the first to die.

On Christmas Eve, if a girl knocks on the hen house door and a rooster crows, she will marry within the year.

Place shoes side-by-side on Christmas Eve to prevent family quarrels. (Scandinavia)

The spouse who first brings holly into the home for Christmas will rule the home in the coming year. Alternative: Prickly holly signifies that the husband will rule; smooth holly, the wife will rule.

Bread baked on Christmas Day never molds.

Leaving a loaf of bread on the table after Christmas Eve dinner assures bread for the coming year.

A clear sky on Christmas Eve promises good crops for the following summer.

From cockcrow until dawn on Christmas Day, trolls roam the land. (Sweden)

Washing an item of clothing before it is given as a Christmas gift spoils the good luck of the gift.

On Christmas Eve, tie a plum cake to a cow's horn and throw cider into her face. If the cake falls off, the harvest will be plentiful. (England)

Wearing new shoes on Christmas Day brings bad luck. (England)

Eating a raw egg before eating anything else on Christmas morning enables one to carry heavy weights.

A cat meowing on Christmas Day predicts bad luck. (American Appalachia)

Any dreams experienced during the twelve nights of Christmas will come true. (Germany)

Discarding evergreen decorations without burning them brings bad luck.

Discarding ashes on Christmas Day is equivalent to throwing them into the face of Christ.

Ashes from the Yule log will protect a household all year from natural disasters; if soaked in water, they form a cure for all manner of illnesses.

Eating plum pudding on Christmas Day assures having a friend for the coming year. (England)

On Christmas Eve, the former priest of a parish conducts Midnight Mass for the dead, who are believed to rise and kneel at the cemetery cross; afterwards, these souls return to their graves. (French Canada)

If a man lies in a coffin during the twelve nights of Christmas, someone from his community will die each month of the coming year. (Germany)

A girl may see an image of her future husband if she approaches a pear tree backwards and walks around it three times on Christmas Eve.

During the twelve days of Christmas, a girl wishing to wed the man of her dreams throws her shoe into a pear tree twelve times. If the shoe remains in the tree at least once, her wish will come true. (Germany)

Suzy Snowflake

Popular American song written in 1951 by New York natives Sid Tepper and Roy Bennett, dedicated to Tepper's baby daughter Susan. A light, generic winter song, its lyrics mirthfully personify a snowflake as a little girl dressed in a white gown who is eager to frolic with anyone in her medium, particularly if one is interested in building a snowman or in taking a sleigh ride. Rosemary Clooney first recorded the song in 1951 on the Columbia label; this recording achieved chart status. Although the song never mentions Christmas, it has found its way into the season though popular association.

Tepper and Bennett also collaborated on a number of other hits, such as "Red Roses for a Blue Lady" (1948), "The Naughty Lady of Shady Lane" (1954), and the novelty tune "Nuttin' for Christmas" (1955).

See also **Nuttin' for Christmas.**

Sweden

This nation has enjoyed Christmas since the ninth and tenth centuries, when Frankish missionaries brought Christianity to Swedish Vikings, and Olaf Skotkonung became the first Swedish King to convert to the new faith. As the Protestant Reformation swept northward from Germany during the sixteenth century, Sweden embraced Lutheranism as its principal faith, which now exists as the Evangelical Lutheran Church of Sweden. Christmas customs blend some traditions of the ancient, winter solstice festival of *Jul* (Yule) with Christian beliefs.

The Advent season features Advent candles; Advent stars fashioned from paper, wood, straw, or metal; and Advent calendars, the latter two decorations having been introduced in the early twentieth century from Germany. During the season, friends gather informally to partake of a custom hosted by virtually every restaurant in the nation during the early weeks of December, the "Christmas Dinner Table." A holiday buffet or *smörgåsbord*, the menu often features pickled herring, liver pâté, hot and cold pork products of every kind, cabbage, "Jansson's Temptation" (creamed potatoes seasoned with onions and anchovies), fried meatballs, rye bread, and schnapps. A custom common in rural areas is to erect a sheaf of wheat on a pole for birds, the so-called "Birds' Christmas Tree."

The Christmas season officially opens on *Luciadagen* (Lucia or Lucy Day, December 13). The name is coincident with that of an Italian (Sicilian) saint martyred around A.D. 304 about whom many legends have circulated, but with whom Sweden shares nothing else in common, except for the Italian folk song "Santa Lucia" (see below). The term "Saint" is not used in reference to Lucia in Sweden. Although some legends hold that Christianized Vikings instituted the celebration after hearing tales that St. Lucia brought gifts of food and light to starving Sicilians, with similar events allegedly transpiring later in Sweden, some scholars contend that Sweden's Lucia derived as a Protestant replacement for St. Nicholas instead. Because the Protestant Reformation forbade the adoration of saints, St. Nicholas was replaced as the bearer of gifts with *Christkindlein*— the little Christ Child or more specifically His "messenger"— who brought gifts on Christmas Day instead of December 6, St. Nicholas' Day. In Germany, this messenger appeared as a young girl clothed in white with wings and a golden crown, carrying a small fir tree, symbolic of eternal life. Sweden also adopted this figure in the seventeenth and eighteenth centuries but transferred her to December 13 (the winter solstice prior to the adoption of the Gregorian calendar), where she presided over the tradition of a large, early morning breakfast served in wealthy establishments. A "Christmas fast," a tradition dating to the Middle Ages, immediately followed this meal and extended until Christmas. This female figure assumed the name "Lucia" based on *lux* (Latin, "light") and the solstice. She kept the white gown, added a red sash, shed the wings and fir tree, and replaced the golden crown with a wreath of ligonberry sprigs containing lighted candles.

By the nineteenth century, Lucia had evolved into a simple household tradition. The youngest daughter would rise at dawn and, attired as Lucia, serve coffee and *lussekatt* ("Lucia cats," saffron buns) to her family. Any sisters or girlfriends would follow, attired in white with halos of tinsel, and each would carry a lighted candle. Any brothers present would assume roles as *stjärn gossar* ("star boys") by donning tall, white, pointed hats adorned with stars, while someone dressed as a *tomten* (elf) formed the last of the procession, and together the entire group would parade through the house singing the Italian folk song "Santa Lucia" as well as Swedish carols.

Today, in addition to the family ritual described above, Sweden celebrates Lucia at the public level with Lucia parades, which date to the 1920s. Virtually all institutions, schools, and offices crown their own Lucia "Queen of Light," as does each city through a series of beauty competitions. Lastly, the winner of the Nobel Prize in Literature crowns a national Lucia in Stockholm, and together she and Lucias from other regions participate in an evening parade, first held in Stockholm in 1927.

Advent continues as homes sport decorations of winter greenery, Nativity scenes, and Christmas trees adorned with candles and sweets. Sweden adopted Christmas trees from Germany during the mid–1800s, while Nativity scenes, initially resisted as Roman Catholic symbols, found their way into Lutheran homes and churches by the early twentieth century.

On *Julafton* (Christmas Eve), families congregate for the traditional midday meal. Prior to this, some families may observe an old custom, "Dipping in the Kettle," commemorative of a long-past famine, by eating pieces of dark bread dipped into a pot that contains the drippings of pork and corned beef. Then dinner is served, which consists of the *smörgåsbord* with its numerous varieties of pork products, along with *lutefisk* (codfish treated with lye and served with a white sauce and seasonings), *pepparkakor* ("pepper cakes," actually gingersnaps), and rice pudding. It is a typically Scandinavian custom to hide one almond in the batch of pudding, and the one finding it in his serving is said to receive luck. In Sweden, the recipient must also compose a "porridge rhyme."

Rhymes continue after the meal with the distribution of *julklapp* ("Christmas knocks"), the term for Christmas presents. This term derives from bygone days when it was customary on Christmas night to knock loudly on doors, then quickly toss in gifts and depart before those inside could identify the giver, who provided a mischievous flare by attaching comical or satirical rhymes about the gifts' contents, the recipient, or the giver. Sometimes the recipient found that he must open a series of empty boxes, each stuffed within another, before finding the gift in the smallest, innermost box. At the extreme, a giver sent the recipient scrambling on a treasure hunt by inserting clues within several boxes strategically hidden about the property. Today, poems still accompany Christmas gifts.

Also on Christmas Eve, Swedish television broadcasts a special service from Turku, Finland. This service formally declares the "Peace of Christmas" in Scandinavia (see **Finland**).

While St. Nicholas has traditionally remained the principal bearer of Christmas gifts in Europe, the gift bringer in Sweden has varied over the centuries. The oldest of these, *Julbock* ("Christmas Goat"), derives from pre–Christian Yule festivals, which paid homage to the gods. At the winter solstice, it was believed that, as he rode through the skies in a chariot pulled by two billy goats named Gnasher and Cracker, Thor distributed gifts to the Vikings, while his father Odin, riding the white, eight-legged steed Sleipner, escorted the souls of slain heroes into Valhalla. Men costumed as goats portrayed this belief by making surprise entrances at Yule parties, and after dancing about, "died," and returned to life. During the Middle Ages, the goat figure symbolized the Devil in Scandinavian Christmas folk revels, and men costumed in goat skins and masks frolicked about, much to the dismay of the Church, which banned such behavior in the sixteenth century. By the eighteenth century, this masked *Julbock* had evolved into the holiday gift bringer, and the figure, now often fashioned from straw, remains as Sweden's oldest Christmas symbol.

In the 1880s, Swedish artist Jenny Nyström created a large series of Christmas cards which combined the traditional physical features of St. Nicholas with those of the *tomten*, a small, aged, mischievous elf, who, according to rural folklore, guarded the home and farm throughout the year. Any mishaps occurring around the house were attributed to his pranks, and he required an annual bowl of rice porridge on Christmas Eve to appease him. Thus emerged the *jultomten* ("Christmas elf") who replaced the *Julbock* as the principal gift bringer. Today on Christmas Eve, someone in each household, disguised as the *jultomten* with white beard, pointed red cap, and toting a sack of gifts, raps loudly on the door and cries, "Are there any good children here?"

Christmas Day is spent with family, who perhaps attend the 7 A.M. *Julottan* (Christmas church service) but people celebrate *Nyårsafton* (New Year's Eve) with friends at parties amid

A little girl flying over the world on a little pig on Christmas Eve. Perhaps the Julgrisen *(Christmas pig) relates not only to the suckling pigs and boar's heads of Christmas feasts, but also to the Norse goddess Freya and her golden boar. Scattered throughout the secular Christmas world history are gift bearers riding unusual steeds, high above the earth, from Odin on his eight-legged horse Sleipner, to Odin's son Thor riding on a chariot pulled by two billy goats, Gnasher and Cracker, to Santa and all his reindeer. From* Harper's Young People, *December 26, 1882.*

noise and fireworks. In former days, noisemaking at this time supposedly kept evil out of the new year, and one may still find those who attempt to peer into the future through such devices as interpreting the shape formed when hot lead is poured into water (see **Superstitions**). Formerly, "star boys" dressed as the Wise Men or other Nativity characters performed dramas among households and collected donations on Epiphany, a custom that became obscure after the nineteenth century. Today, star boys primarily accompany Lucia processions.

The Christmas season terminates twenty days after Christmas Day on *tjugondedag Knut* ("twentieth day Knut," January 13), a day named in honor of the Danish king Knut IV (Canute, Cnut, Knud), who was assassinated in 1086. A strong supporter of the Church through acts of piety and charity, he was canonized in 1100. Sources vary regarding the exact origin of the twenty-day feast. According to one, Knut is said to have made such a decree; in another, because the Vikings feasted and offered human sacrifices on this day, the Church sought to stamp out such practices by extending Christmas through that date. In festivals today, home parties light the Christmas tree one last time, then the decorations are removed, the tree is dismantled and children retrieve its decorative sweets, and trees are often burned in communal bonfires.

"Merry Christmas" is *God Jul.*
See also **Advent.**

Switzerland

Once known as Helvetia to the ancient Romans, the region of Switzerland was conquered through a series of invasions by Germanic tribes from the fourth to the sixth century. The Frankish Empire principally brought Christianity and Christmas to Switzerland by the eighth century, although the Irish monk St. Gall had established a monastery in this land around 613. Lying in proximity to France, Germany, and Italy, Switzerland's twenty-three states or cantons (three of which are divided into half-cantons) reflect considerable cultural diversity, especially during the holiday season. The majority of cantons, those in the northern, eastern, and central regions, speak Swiss-German, a German dialect; the western cantons of Fribourg, Geneva, Jura, Neuchâtel, Valais, and Vaud reflect the French language and customs; and the southern canton of Ticino is predominantly Italian. These cantons mirror those customs of the three bordering countries, the entries for which provide further discussion. The remainder of this entry is concerned with customs unique to several Swiss cities and cantons.

During the Advent season, Christmas markets and bazaars flourish throughout the country, and cities such as Zurich, Bern, and Basel feature decorated *Weihnachtstramer* (Christmas trolleys) operated by conductors in the guise of Santa. Swiss-German cantons are noted for their *Weihnachtsguetzli* (Christmas cookies), especially *Tirggel* from Zurich, flat cookies of flour and honey that take origin from pagan Germanic sacrificial cakes served in the days before sugar was known in Europe. Once fashioned in animal shapes, *Tirggel* now bear religious scenes and figures.

Also favored by many are *Leckerli* from Basel, spiced almond cookies which date to medieval times.

In most cities, carolers parade through the streets. Noted among these are the *Sternsinger* (Star Singers) of Swiss-German cantons, who bear illuminated stars and are accompanied by people dressed as the Wise Men and the Holy Family. Theaters usually feature a production of *D'Zäller Weihnacht* (*A Swiss Nativity*), a play by Swiss composer Paul Burkhard (1911–1977), and those who most appreciate Nativity scenes will enjoy the Bethlehem Diorama in Einsiedeln, Schwyz canton. Consisting of some five hundred carved wooden images, the Diorama stands adjacent to the city's Benedictine monastery founded in the ninth century.

Citizens of Graubünden, the largest and most diverse canton (the languages of Swiss-German, Italian, and Romansh are all spoken here) decorate their homes with evergreens and cover the exteriors with *sgraffito* etchings of the season. After applying whitewash to the dark stucco walls, homeowners create drawings by etching through the dried coating. To Catholic citizens of Graubünden, the Christmas gift bringer remains St. Nicholas; to the Protestants, however, it is *Sontgaclau*, a composite of the saint and a mean-spirited being who bears switches. Christmas trees and *Purseppen* (Nativity scenes) remain the chief holiday symbols, and the Christmas meal is likely to feature *Bündnerfleisch* (dried beef). This canton is famous for its *Churer Zimmetstern* (star-shaped, cinnamon cookies).

To dispel any evil spirits lurking about, loud noises—for example, ringing cow bells, cracking whips, and blowing horns—greet St. Nicholas Day celebrations and parades throughout Switzerland on December 6. Attired in traditional bishop's robes with mitre and staff, a man portraying St. Nicholas parades about on a horse or donkey while distributing treats to children. Accompanying him especially in Swiss-German cantons is an antithetical demon, "Schmutzli," who carries switches and a sack in which to stuff naughty youngsters. On St.

Nicholas Eve, children put out their shoes to be filled with small gifts. The city of Küssnacht in Schwyz canton hosts the *Klausjagen* (Pursuit of St. Nicholas) on St. Nicholas Eve, in which citizens dress as St. Nicholas and wear *Iffele*, gigantic, elaborately decorated mitres illuminated with candles. A related custom, the *Chlauswettchloöpfe* (St. Nicholas Day whip-cracking competition) of Halwill, Aargau canton, selects six young teenage boys to participate in its *Chlausjage* on the following day. There, the six champions portray mischievous spirits who visit homes and distribute gifts or warnings to children as their past behavior warrants. In festivities elsewhere, citizens frequently mimic St. Nicholas in his clerical attire.

Processions also dominate Christmas Eve. Young teenage girls of Halwill form groups of seven, one of whom, veiled in white, poses as the *Wienechtchind* (Christmas Child), the other six as her attendants. As they travel from house to house, the Child greets each family with a silent handshake and distributes treats to any children present; then she and her attendants depart after the attendants have sung a carol. Men in the cities of Rheinfelden and Ziefen don black attire including "stovepipe" hats of great height in preparation for, respectively, *Brunnensingen* (Fountain Singing) and *Nünichlinger* (Ringing of Bells at 9 P.M.). In the former, kept as a memorial to the bubonic plague epidemic of 1348, twelve from the Brotherhood of St. Sebastian proceed to seven different city fountains, at which they sing a carol, removing their hats when the lyrics mention the deity. In the latter, groups of men parade through the streets ringing large bells at the appointed hour and are led by a white-bearded man carrying a sooty rag on a pole. A personification of *Samichlaus* (St. Nicholas), this leader once anointed people with the soot to expel evil spirits.

Noise, commotion, and masquerades continue on New Year's Eve, also known as St. Sylvester's Day (Sylvester I was the first pope to hold office after Constantine the Great accepted Christianity in the fourth century). The most intricate of these celebrations is the *Silvesterkläuse* of Appenzell canton, especially in the city of Urnäsch. Only males participate, donning one of three bizarre costumes known as *Chläuse*: *Schöne* ("pretty," depicting either a man or woman with large, ornate headdresses), *Wüeschti* ("ugly," depicting a demon clad in assorted forest vegetation), or *Schö-Wüeschti* ("less ugly"). All *Chläuse* travel through the streets yodeling and ringing large bells affixed to their costumes. A related custom is the *Achetringele* (Ring Bells Downhill) of Laupen, Bern canton. Groups of boys carrying either large bells, brooms, or pigs' bladders inflated with air, call out New Year wishes as they parade from the hills into town, then hurl the bladders toward young girls in fulfillment of a fertility rite now completely obscure. At 6 P.M. children carrying homemade lanterns parade through the city of Wil and sing carols to the beat of drums, a custom known as the *Silvesterumzug*. By 11:50 P.M., the villagers of Halwill have assembled around a bonfire on the hill above town, at which time eight men commence rhythmic beating on a threshing board. Moments before midnight they cease, but as the New Year arrives, they resume with greater zeal, thus "beating" away evil spirits.

Another pagan ritual most likely derived from an obscure festival anticipating spring forms the theme of *Bärzelitag* (Berthold's Day), January 2. Notably observed in Halwill, the day is filled with pranks and mischief, committed by fifteen young, unmarried people. Five of them must masquerade as the "Green" (symbols of Spring and Life), and five as the "Parched Brown" (symbols of Winter and Death). According to *Christmas in Switzerland*, the other five portray a camel and its drivers.

Epiphany, with its Three Kings pageants and Kings' cakes, concludes the Christmas season. "Merry Christmas" may be said in any one of several languages: *Schöne Weihnachten* (Swiss-German); *Joyeux Noël* (French); *Buone Feste Natalizie* (Italian); *Legreivlas Fiastas da Nadal* (Romansh).

See also **Advent; Epiphany; France; Germany; Italy; Saint Nicholas Day.**

Syria
See **Middle East**

T

There Is No Rose of Such Virtue

English traditional carol dating to an early fifteenth-century manuscript, which resides at Trinity College, Cambridge. Incorporating a typically medieval concept, this anonymous, macaronic (mixture of English and Latin) carol metaphorically depicts the Virgin Mary as a flowering rose, whose young flower is the Infant Jesus. This is also the theme of another popular carol, "Lo, How a Rose E'er Blooming."

Each of the five verses in English terminates with Latin phrases. The first two verses introduce the rose concept, ending respectively with "*Alleluia*" and "*Res miranda*" ("A wonderful thing"). Verse three declares that through the Rose will mankind see God as the Trinity "*Pari forma*" ("Of the same form"). Verse four recalls the angelic chorus to the shepherds and urges, "*Gaudeamus*" ("Let us rejoice"). Verse five urges all to put away earthly pleasure and seek Him who is born, with the admonition "*Transeamus*" ("Let us go").

The carol has enjoyed two other noteworthy musical settings, one by the English composer Benjamin Britten (1913–1976), included in his *A Ceremony of Carols* (1942) for treble voices and harp. The other is by the South African composer John Joubert (1927–) for unaccompanied voices (1954).

See also **A Ceremony of Carols; Lo, How a Rose E'er Blooming.**

This Is Christmas

See **Alfred Burt Carols**

Thou Didst Leave Thy Throne

English carol, the lyrics of which comprise the only poem of note written in 1864 by hymnist Emily E. S. Elliott (1836–1897) of Brighton.

The text for "Thou Didst Leave Thy Throne" is a brief narrative of significant scriptural events in the life of Christ, beginning with the Nativity in the first two verses and concluding with His crucifixion and the hope of redemption at His second coming. Ms. Elliott's approach to the Nativity is unusual in that she elaborates on what Christ left behind in heaven when He came to earth in human form. Matched with an 1876 tune by Anglican clergyman and organist Timothy R. Matthews (1826–1910), this carol often appears in contemporary hymnals.

Three Kings

See **Nativity**

The Three Kings

Poem by American poet Henry Wadsworth Longfellow (1807–1882). A narrative based on the Gospel account of the Wise Men in Matthew 2, its fourteen verses follow the trek of the three traditional Magi, Melchior, Caspar, and Balthasar, on their search for the Child born "King of the Jews." Their gifts, according to Longfellow, are symbolic portents for Christ in later years: the gold is their tribute to a King, the frankincense is for the Priest and Paraclete (Holy Spirit), and the myrrh is to anoint His body for burial.

Longfellow's other works include such narrative poems as *Evangeline* (1847), *The Song of Hiawatha* (1855), and *The Courtship of Miles Standish* (1858).

Three Kings of Orient

See **We Three Kings of Orient Are**

Three Wise Men

See **Nativity**

Thyme

See **Christmas Plants**

'Tis the Season Christmas Trivia

Quiz game distributed by Debco, a division of Anton Enterprises of Downers Grove, Illinois. Designed for playing on *Trivial Pursuit* game boards, *'Tis the Season* consists of 1,800 holiday-oriented, short-answer questions printed on 300, 3½" × 2⅜" cards, each with questions in six categories on one side, the answers on the opposite. The categories are represented by symbols and include "History, Facts, and Figures" (star); "Traditions Around the World" (candy cane); "Cartoons, Animation, Made-for-Television Movies, Specials" (Christmas tree); "Carols and Songs" (Yule log); "Movies on the Silver Screen" (candle); and "Literature and the Performing Arts" (tree ornament). Also included are instructions and score sheets for playing an alternate game, in which individuals or teams receive a successive letter in the word "Christmas" for each correct answer. The winner is the first to spell "Christmas" completely.

To Grandmother's House We Go

(1992). Made-for-television comedy movie featuring the Olsen twins, Ashley and Mary-Kate.

Believing that they are a burden to their single mom, Rhonda Thompson (Cynthia Geary), five-year-old twins Julie and Sarah plan to run away to Great Grandmother Mimi (Florence Patterson) for Christmas. Thinking that mom's friend, parcel truck driver Eddie Popko (J. Eddie Peck), could take them, the twins stow away in Eddie's vehicle. Sarah's full bladder betrays their presence and forces a shocked Eddie to search for a truck stop, where the twins outline their mission.

A cowboy "wannabe" who is far more interested in playing the lottery than in looking after children, Eddie nevertheless treats the girls to lunch and later ice cream, for they must remain with him until his deliveries are completed. Seeing the adorable little girls with Eddie, customers are inspired to give generous tips. By evening, the three have become such good friends that, en route home, the twins are quite satisfied to listen to Eddie's passion: music on the radio by cowboy star Roy Rogers.

Just outside the twins' apartment, husband-and-wife bandits Shirley and dim-witted Harvey (Rhea Perlman and Jerry Van Dyke) overpower Eddie, steal his truck, kidnap the twins, and head for their motor home already laden with stolen Christmas gifts. The bandits, suggesting a $10,000 "reward" for "finding" the twins, set up a meeting with Rhonda in Edgemont, Great Grandma's town, for returning the girls on Christmas Eve. Because Eddie's ulterior motive for finding the twins lies in their holding his winning lottery ticket, which will allow him to spin for a million-dollar jackpot on television's "Win-O-Lotto," he hocks all the recovered Christmas gifts that were aboard his truck to raise the ransom.

At the Christmas Carnival in Edgemont, the twins escape in a horse-drawn wagon, which rapidly becomes a runaway. It's Eddie's big chance to redeem himself and fulfill the role of his dreams, a cowboy rescuing ladies in distress. Racing on a pony, he springs onto the team just as Roy Rogers would have done, and prevents the wagon from plunging off a cliff. With wills of their own, the horses return Eddie and the twins to Great Grandma Mimi's house for a joyous reunion with Rhonda. The police, believing that Rhonda and Eddie robbed the parcel truck, arrive for the arrest, but softhearted Harvey confesses all.

Arriving back home at the television station with moments to spare, the twins spin and win the lottery for Eddie, who replaces the hocked gifts, and together the four make house deliveries late on Christmas Eve to satisfied customers.

With Stuart Margolin, Rick Poltaruk, Venus Terzo. Written by Jeff Franklin and Boyd Hale. Produced by Mark Bacino. Directed by Jeff Franklin. Jeff Franklin Productions in Association with Green/Epstein Productions in Association with Warner Brothers Television. Warner Home Video. Color. 89 min.

Tom and Jerry's Night Before Christmas

(1991). Video collection of four classic, animated cartoon shorts from Metro-Goldwyn-Mayer Studios.

The Captain's Christmas (1938) was part of *The Captain and the Kids* series, based on the United Features Syndicate comic strip *Katzenjammer Kids* by Rudolf Dirk. A crusty pirate and three henchmen usurp Santa's role to bring Christmas and mayhem to the Captain's family.

One Ham's Family (1943) features the Big Bad Wolf impersonating Santa while attempting to make Mama, Papa, and Junior Pig his Christmas dinner. However, he is no match for little Junior.

In *Toyland Broadcast* (1934), toys broadcast a musical revue over the radio from a toyshop. The cartoon was one of the first in the *Happy Harmonies* series, a group of musical cartoons created by former Disney animators Hugh Harman and Rudolph Ising.

The Night Before Christmas (1941) features the Academy Award–winning team of Tom the cat and Jerry the mouse in their first holiday cartoon, as madcap antics reign under the tree on Christmas Eve.

Turner Entertainment Company. Warner Home Video. Color. 45 min.

Tomorrow Shall Be My Dancing Day

English traditional carol, believed to have arisen in the West Country during the fifteenth or sixteenth century. Consisting of eleven verses written in the first person singular, the carol poses Christ presenting a complete narrative of His life, with verse 1 calling for "…my true love… / To see the legend of my play / To call my true love to the dance." Verses 2 and 3 describe the Nativity, verse 4 His baptism, verse 5 His temptation in the wilderness, verse 6 His interactions with Jewish leaders, verse 7 His betrayal, verse 8 His trial before Pilate, verse 9 His crucifixion, verse 10 His descent into hell and His resurrection, and verse 11 His ascension. The last line of each verse makes reference to Christ leading or bringing others to His dance, and a refrain addresses "…my love, / This have I done for my true love."

Whereas the seemingly romantic passages have been interpreted to represent Christ's expressions of love for His Church, the references to dancing and a "play" are believed to place the carol among those written for religious dramas of considerable length. Such dramas often included text which instructed the local musicians to strike up a dance tune either before or after certain segments of the play. In the case of "Tomorrow Shall Be My Dancing Day," the role of Christ in the first verse likely serves to call spectators' attention to the drama at hand. The references to "the dance" or "my dance" in the last line of each verse may signify a life with Christ, filled with joy and dancing.

The text for the carol first appeared in William Sandys' *Christmas Carols, Ancient and Modern* (London, 1833). The musical setting shares opening passages with two other traditional carols, one from Dorset in the West Country, "Rejoice and Be Merry"; the other from Wales, "Wel, dyma'r borau gorau i gyd" ("Behold! The Best of Mornings Is Here"). Russian-American composer Igor Stravinsky (1882–1971) also provided a musical setting in his *Cantata* (1951–1952).

Tournament of Roses
See **New Year's Day**

Toys for Tots
Charitable organization operated by the American Marine Corps Reserve, founded by retired Marine Corps Colonel Bill Hendricks in 1947 in Los Angeles. That year, Hendricks's wife had fashioned a hand-made doll and had desired that an underprivileged child should receive it for Christmas. When Hendricks discovered that no programs existed which distributed toys to needy children, he created Toys for Tots to fill the void. In the first year, 5,000 toys were collected and distributed throughout Los Angeles. The program rapidly evolved into an annual nationwide project and sported the familiar train logo designed by Walt Disney, who also created the first Toys for Tots Christmas poster.

Since its inception, Toys for Tots has brought Christmas joy to more than one hundred million children, and today some two hundred Marine Corps Reserve units across the United States collect an average of eight million toys each Christmas. Public awareness has been achieved through the work of motion picture and television celebrities, professional athletes, entertainers, and thousands of volunteers at the local level, who have donated their time to the cause. Many communities across the United States also sponsor local drives, in addition to those by the Marine Corps Reserve. Toys for Tots is the largest nationwide drive dedicated to collecting new toys for children.

The Trail to Christmas
See **A Christmas Carol** (Film and Television Versions)

Trinidad and Tobago
See **West Indies**

Turkey
See **Middle East**

'Twas in the Moon of Wintertime
See **The Huron Christmas Carol**

'Twas the Night Before Christmas
(Animated cartoon, 1974). Made-for-television production loosely based on the poem "A Visit from St. Nicholas."

When Santa rejects letters from Junctionville because its newspaper published a slanderous letter about him, clockmaker Joshua Trundle builds a clock with magic chimes that will lure Santa to town on Christmas Eve. But a trial run finds the clock inoperative, broken by inquisitive Albert Mouse, who tinkered with its mechanism. Father Mouse also discovers that it was his own son who anonymously wrote the letter against Santa, because he doesn't believe in anything he cannot see.

After learning the degree of sadness there will be if Santa ignores Junctionville, Albert fixes the clock with the aid of a book by Copernicus, and Santa arrives to everyone's happiness.

Narrated and sung by Joel Grey. Voices: Tammy Grimes, John McGiver, George Gobel, Patricia Bright, Scott Firestone, Robert McFadden, Allen Swift, Christine Winter, The Wee Winter Singers. Written by Jerome Coopersmith. Produced and directed by Arthur Rankin, Jr., and Jules Bass. Rankin/Bass Productions. Warner Home Video. Color. 25 min.

'Twas the Night Before Christmas (poem and song)
See **A Visit from St. Nicholas**

'Twas the Night Before Christmas (television episode)
See **The Honeymooners**

Twelfth Day
See **Epiphany**

Twelfth Night
See **Epiphany**

The Twelve Days of Christmas
Time period from Christmas Day, December 25 (Day 0), to Epiphany, January 6 (Day 12); also the title of an English traditional carol (*See* **The Twelve Days of Christmas [Song]**.)

The designation "Twelve Days of Christmas" derives from a decree issued in 567 by the Second Council of Tours, France, which proclaimed the sanctity of those twelve days, preceded by fasting during the Advent season. Alfred the Great (849–899), king of the West Saxons and king of England from 886 until his death, issued a similar decree for England, but instead of sanctity he proclaimed a time for "righteous pleasure" during those twelve days. Thus, Christmas during the Middle Ages evolved from a time of reverence to a time of revelry and licentiousness akin to the pagan Roman Saturnalia, which Christmas particularly Christianized. This was the period not only for the Feast of Fools with its Lord of Misrule, mumming, gaming, gambling, court tournaments with jousting matches, and Twelfth Night — to name a few of the celebrations observed — but also a time when landowners of large estates opened their manor halls to the peasantry with feasts, merriment, and reprieve from labor. In return, the peasants and workers were to bestow gifts upon their masters in the form of fruits and other produce from the fields. In some locales, landowners provided their tenants with holiday meals only as long as the Yule log burned.

During these twelve days, the nobility sought to gain favor with the monarchy through lavish Christmas gifts. King Henry III of England (1207–1272), displeased with the parsimonious merchant class, was once said to have closed their shops for two weeks until they collectively presented him with the expected "gift" of two thousand pounds. Those desiring a more quiet holiday could engage in gambling, which was quite popular among the upper classes. During his reign, King Edward IV of England (1442–1483) permitted gambling only during the twelve days of Christmas, and Queen Elizabeth I (1533–1603) gambled with loaded dice.

Pagans once believed that at the winter solstice, the gates between the physical and spirit worlds stood ajar, enabling communication with and appearances of spirits. This belief carried over into the twelve days of Christmas during the Middle Ages and generated

The Lord of Misrule, masked and done up like a fool, with his small boy page, derived from Saturnalian festivals. Re-enactments of Medieval festivals always include a lord of Misrule. From Robert Chambers, ed., A Book of Days (London and Edinburgh: Chambers, 1879).

A Twelfth-Day scene outside a London Confectioner, early 1800s. "From the taking down of the shutters in the morning, the pastry-cook and his men ... are fully occupied" decorating the window with pastries, baking, taking orders, and at dusk "the gas is turned on ... to illuminate countless cakes of all prices and dimensions, that stand in rows and piles on the counters and in the windows ... Stars, castles, kings, cottages, dragons, trees, fish, palaces, cats, dogs, churches, lions, milkmaids, knights, serpents, and innumerable other forms in snow-white confectionary, painted with variegated colours, glitter by 'excess of light' from mirrors against the walls." From William Hone, Every-Day Book, Vol. 1 (London: 1825–1826).

numerous superstitions to counter the presence of evil or to predict the future (see **Superstitions**). Belief in the supernatural also spawned the tradition of telling ghost stories at this time, a tradition still practiced in some parts of Europe and the United States.

Within the twelve days of Christmas are found five additional observances. Four of these are discussed as separate entries: Boxing Day (also known as St. Stephen's Day, December 26), Holy Innocents Day (December 28), New Year's Day (January 1), and Epiphany (January 6). The fifth, St. John's Day, is discussed below.

• ST. JOHN'S DAY. Falling on December 27, St. John's Day is devoted to St. John the Evangelist (or the Divine), one of Christ's apostles, whom early Christian tradition credits as the author of the Gospel of John. According to St. Irenaeus (140?–202?), John suffered persecution under the Roman emperor Domitian (ruled 81–96), who, around the year 93, sentenced him to exile for life on the island of Patmos in the Aegean Sea. There John, receiving a vision from Christ, wrote the Book of Revelation. Although the Church had established the Feast of St. John by the fifth century, the consumption of blessed wine had punctuated the observance by the sixteenth century. According to legend, St. John suffered no ill effects from having unwittingly consumed tainted or poisoned wine, which led to the belief that blessed wine imbibed on this day would stimulate health.

The feasts of St. Stephen, St. John, and the Holy Innocents, falling consecutively, honor some of the earliest people persecuted for the sake of Christ.

The Twelve Days of Christmas

(Song). English Roman Catholics, whom

the Church of England prohibited from openly practicing their faith from the mid-sixteenth century until the nineteenth century, are said to have created this carol probably during the sixteenth century as an underground memory device for teaching children their catechism. It was patterned after so-called "counting songs," most popular during the Middle Ages, as well as a popular game during that period which was often played on the last night of the twelve-day Christmas season, Twelfth Night (Epiphany Eve, January 5 or Epiphany Night, January 6, depending on the local reckoning). The game consisted of players in turn reciting a list of objects from memory while adding a new one each time. Failure to recite the growing list correctly resulted in a player's elimination from the game. The additional custom among the nobility of exchanging gifts on each of those twelve days probably influenced the gift theme of the carol's lyrics. The following paragraphs discuss the symbolic meanings of the gift numbers and any pagan counterparts.

• FIRST DAY. "On the first day of Christmas, my true love gave to me a partridge in a pear tree." The number "one" represents one God in Jesus Christ, the "true love" of all Christians. "Partridge in a pear tree" has acquired multiple symbols. In one sense, the phrase further likens Jesus to a mother partridge which lures predators away from her young by feigning injury; in another sense, it recalls Jesus' lamentation over Jerusalem (Matthew 23:37). An opposing view likens the partridge to Satan, who, according to legend, told King Herod where the Virgin Mary had hidden herself from his soldiers, who sought to kill the Babe. The pear tree represents the cross, the metonymic "tree" upon which Christ was crucified. In this sense, the partridge and pear tree represent the battle between good and evil. In a secular sense, it has been suggested that, because the gifts come from "my true love," the carol incorporates a pagan superstition regarding pear trees, namely that a girl may see an image of her future husband if she approaches a pear tree backwards and walks around it three times on Christmas Eve (*see* **Superstitions**).

• SECOND DAY. "Two turtle doves" symbolize the Old and New testaments of the Bible as well as the sacrifice of two turtle doves made when the infant Jesus was presented in the Temple (Leviticus 12:8 and Luke 2:24).

• THIRD DAY. "Three French hens" represent the theological virtues of Faith, Hope, and Charity (1 Corinthians 13:13); the gifts of the Nativity, gold, frankincense, and myrrh (Matthew 2:11); and the Holy Trinity of Father, Son, and Holy Ghost.

• FOURTH DAY. "Four calling birds" represent the four Gospels and Evangelists (Matthew, Mark, Luke, and John).

• FIFTH DAY. "Five gold rings" symbolize the first five books of the Old Testament (Genesis, Exodus, Leviticus, Numbers, Deuteronomy), also known as the Pentateuch, the Books of Moses, and the Law of Moses. In a secular sense, the gold rings are thought to imply either the rings of ringed pheasants or a corruption of the Scottish words "goldspinks" (goldfinches) or "gulderer" (turkeys).

• SIXTH DAY. "Six geese a-laying" represent the six days of creation.

• SEVENTH DAY. "Seven swans a-swimming" symbolize the seven gifts of the Holy Spirit (prophecy, ministry, teaching, exhorting, ruling, giving, mercy—Romans 12:6–8) or the seven sacraments of the Catholic faith (baptism, confirmation, Eucharist, penance/reconciliation, anointing of the sick, holy orders, matrimony). Also note that birds comprise the first seven secular gifts.

• EIGHTH DAY. "Eight maids a-milking" represent the eight beatitudes ("Blessed are the poor in spirit ... they that mourn ... the meek ... hunger and thirst after righteousness ... the merciful ... pure in heart ... peacemakers ... persecuted for righteousness' sake"—Matthew 5:3–10).

• NINTH DAY. "Nine ladies dancing" symbolize the nine fruits of the Holy Spirit (love, joy, peace, longsuffering, gentleness, goodness, faith, meekness, temperance—Galatians 5:22–23).

• TENTH DAY. "Ten lords a-leaping" represent the Ten Commandments.

• ELEVENTH DAY. "Eleven pipers piping" represent the eleven faithful apostles who did not betray Jesus as did Judas.

• TWELFTH DAY. "Twelve drummers drumming" symbolize the twelve points of doctrine in the Apostles' Creed:

1. I believe in God the Father, Maker of heaven and earth. 2. I believe in Jesus Christ, His only Son, our Lord, 3. Who was conceived of the Holy Spirit, born of the Virgin Mary. 4. He suffered under Pontius Pilate, was crucified, died, and was buried. 5. He descended into hell; the third day He rose from the dead. 6. He ascended into heaven and sits at the right hand of God, the Father Almighty. 7. He shall return to judge the living and the dead. 8. I believe in the Holy Spirit, 9. The Holy Christian Church, the communion of saints, 10. The forgiveness of sins, 11. The resurrection of the body, 12. And the life everlasting.

Other versions of the lyrics in Great Britain include four colly or cally birds (blackbirds), four canary birds, eight deers (sic) a-running, nine lads a-leaping, ten ladies skipping, eleven bears a-baiting, and twelve parsons preaching. Theoretically, any type of gift could be substituted, but those listed in the previous paragraphs constitute the carol as sung in America.

See also **Boxing Day; Christmas Drama** (MUMMING); **Epiphany; Feast of Fools; Holy Innocents Day; New Year's Day; Saturnalia; Yule.**

U

Uganda
See **Africa**

Ukraine

This nation has enjoyed *Rizdvo* (Christmas) since the tenth century, when Prince Volodymyr accepted Christianity from the Byzantine empire in the year 988. Following the Eastern Orthodox Church, which bases its ecclesiastical (but not secular) events upon the older Julian calendar, Ukraine observes *Rizdvo* (Christmas Day) on January 7 by the Gregorian calendar. Traditions are highly symbolic and blend former pagan agrarian beliefs and harvest symbols from *Koliada*, an ancient winter solstice festival, with those of Christianity. Soviet domination (1922–1991) once suppressed Christmas celebrations, replaced St. Nicholas with *Died Moroz* (Grandfather Frost), and sponsored a non-religious, year-end festival on New Year's Day. Today, Ukraine has rapidly returned to her centuries-old holiday customs.

Preparations for Christmas begin forty days in advance with a meatless and milkless fast, which not only commemorates Christ's fasting in the wilderness for forty days after His baptism, but also honors livestock, since no animals are sacrificed for food during this season. Prior to this cleansing of mind, body, and soul comes the ritual cleaning of homes

and property, the resolution of debts, the return of items borrowed, and the settlement of arguments and disputes, all of which must be completed prior to the days of fasting. During the holy days, marriages and dancing are forbidden, and everyone strives to speak only words of peace.

The Orthodox Church observes six feast days during these holy days prior to Christmas, which are usually accompanied by folk customs and auguries. The Feast of the Presentation (December 4) opens the holy days and commemorates the presentation of the young Virgin Mary in the Temple. On St. Catherine's Day (December 7), girls traditionally place cherry tree branches in water in anticipation that these will bloom flowers by New Year's Eve, a sign of luck. Mischief and pranks reign on St. Andrew the Apostle's Day (December 13), and girls seek predictions about future mates. December 17 honors St. Barbara, and on the eve of St. Nicholas Day (December 19), children set out plates or shoes to be filled with treats by *Sviatyj Mykloaj* (St. Nicholas). Three traditional gifts on this day include an article of clothing, a toy, and a "gift of wonder." Traveling about in the company of an angel and the devil, St. Nicholas makes appearances in public places and at homes to quiz youngsters about their religion, while the devil leaves switches for the naughty. On December 22, the Feast of the Immaculate Conception honors the Virgin Mary as having been born without original sin.

The principal Christmas celebration centers around *Sviata Vecheria* (Christmas Eve and Holy Supper), observed on January 6. The day begins with a total fast, and preparatory rituals include opening the doors of one's home early that morning to receive the blessing of the sun; using blessed logs to light the oven; leading the farm animals past an ax to disperse any evil; and introducing the *didukh* ("Grandfather spirit"), a sheaf of wheat which the head of the household sets in a place of honor after carrying it around the interior of the home three times. The spirits of all family members, living and dead, are believed to reside in the *didukh*, which also symbolizes eternal life through Christ, the fertility of the land, and bread as the staff of life.

After the table is first prepared with a layer of hay on top and beneath to symbolize the earth and the manger, two tablecloths are laid. The first is white, symbolic of deceased family members; the topmost is highly embroidered and symbolizes those living in the present. A band of string or length of chain, symbolic of family ties, binds the table legs, and scattered among the hay on the floor are little treats for the children to discover after dinner. Cloves of garlic placed at each corner of the table ward off illness, and an extra place is set to honor deceased family members as well as any stranger. The centerpiece consists of three loaves of *kolach* (circular, braided Christmas bread) stacked on top of each other, representing the Holy Trinity, and a single white candle in the top loaf represents the sun and Christ as the Light of the world. After these preparations, children search the eastern sky for the first star of the evening, believed to be the Star of Bethlehem, for when the first star appears, *Sviata Vecheria* begins. No family member must ever be late; a violation predicts that someone in the family will die in the next year.

As Holy Supper commences, the host ritually beckons the ancestral spirits and forces of nature to partake of the bounty; a prayer and a *koliadky* (Christmas carol) follow. The menu traditionally consists of twelve meatless dishes,

symbolic of Christ's Twelve Apostles and the moon's twelve phases around the earth. The first and most indispensable dish is *kutia* (believed to have been offered to the sun god Dazhboh at pagan winter solstice festivals), which consists of boiled wheat, poppy seeds, and honey (wheat symbolizes property, poppy seeds the beauty of the earth, and honey the family unity). Holding the bowl of *kutia* in a *rushnyk* (embroidered religious cloth), the host serves this dish to each family member while reciting the greeting "Khrystos Rodyvsya" ("Christ is born"). Upon receiving the *kutia*, each person responds with "Slavim Yoho" ("Let us glorify Him"). Alternatively, the greeting and response may be said in unison before the meal. Next the host tosses a small portion of *kutia* toward the ceiling; the amount that sticks is believed to predict the degree of prosperity in store for the new year. Then follows a toast to the dead, after which the host may, in some regions, offer a piece of bread dipped in honey with garlic to each member at the table (the act symbolizes that life is filled with the sweet as well as the bitter). Although the eleven remaining dishes will vary from region to region, the following are typical examples: *borsch* (beets), baked or fried fish, *osyletsi* (pickled fish), *holubtsi* (stuffed cabbage), *varenyky* (small pies with potato, sauerkraut, or prune fillings), *pyrohy* (dumplings with fruit fillings), beans, *kapusta* (sauerkraut) with peas, fruit compote, and *pompushky* (fried fruit pies). Following the meal, families usually engage in a period of singing carols, portions of food are served to the farm animals, and the remaining food stands on the table overnight in order that family spirits may partake of the feast. Christmas Eve concludes with Midnight Mass, which may extend until dawn.

The week between *Ridzvo* and New Year's Day is filled with visitations, feasting, and *koliadnyky* (carolers), the latter of whom tour neighborhoods attired as shepherds, angels, and Wise Men. Grouped behind an illuminated, eight- or ten-pointed star on a pole, the carolers provide a vast repertoire of ancient songs centering around nature, the Nativity, and matchmaking, for example, which they customize for each person at the homes visited. The carolers may also carry a *vertep* (three-dimensional Nativity scene), and among them a boy may be costumed as a *koza* (goat, a pagan symbol of prosperity and fertility), who dances for the amusement of all. As rewards, the carolers receive food, drink, and donations for charity.

Two additional feast days fall within this week: the Syntaxis of the Blessed Virgin (January 8), which commemorates Mary and Joseph as Jesus' earthly parents, and St. Stephen's Day (January 9), which honors the first Christian martyr.

Shchedryi Vechir (New Year's Eve) is observed either on January 13 (eve of the Feast of St. Basil, an Orthodox patriarch) or on January 18 (eve of the Feast of Jordan — see below), depending on the locale. The customs resemble those of Christmas Eve as families again congregate for a large meal (meat is now permissible), auguries are read, and carolers present a completely different set of tunes, *shchedrivky*, filled with wishes for health and prosperity. Named for a girl in Ukrainian folklore, the popular New Year's Eve tradition of "Malanka" derives from pagan rites that banished evil from the new year. A man dressed as Malanka leads a procession of villagers costumed either as good or evil spirits, who sing carols, present plays, and offer good wishes to households.

New Year's Day brings groups of touring boys who throw wheat and seeds into homes for luck, and many families still observe this as the principal day for gift giving and erecting a *yalynka* (Christmas tree). Others prefer St. Nicholas Day or Christmas Day. Favorite ornaments include spider figures and webs of straw, which derive from legends holding that a spider decorated a poor widow's Christmas tree with its web, and that, while lying in the manger, the Baby Jesus first played with a spider's web. Other ornaments may include apples, candy, cookies, foil, and homemade ornaments such as paper chains.

The Christmas season ends with the Feast of Jordan (January 19), which commemorates Christ's baptism in the River Jordan and is comparable to the Feast of Epiphany in Western (Roman) churches on January 6. People traditionally mark their homes with crosses above windows and doorways. The principal event here is the Blessing of the Waters, in which a priest blesses a river, lake, or other body of water by throwing a small cross into its midst. Traditionally, young men dive for the cross as a display of strength, and the one retrieving it is hailed as a hero. Believers then take samples of the blessed water to sanctify their homes and to repel illness. On this day, the *didukh* is either burned to release the indwelling spirits, or saved for burning in the spring to strengthen orchards. Children traditionally leap through the flames, believing that if they do so, their ancestors will not harm them in the new year. The less superstitious merely retain their *didukh* from year to year.

"Merry Christmas" is *Veseleoho Vam Rizdva*.

See also **Carol of the Bells; Epiphany**.

The Ukraine Carol
See **Carol of the Bells**

United Kingdom
See **Great Britain; Ireland**

United States

Europeans settling in North America brought a diversity of holiday customs which mirrored those of their parent countries and religious faiths. Indeed, Christopher Columbus is credited with first observing Christmas in the New World when, on Christmas Eve, 1492, his flagship *Santa Maria* ran aground off the Caribbean island of Hispaniola, whereupon he erected a fort named *Villa de la Navidad* ("Village of the Nativity").

The first real Christmas celebration in what would become the United States took place in Spanish Florida. Gulevich credits Hernando de Soto's party, which in the fall of 1539 set up a camp of five months' duration near the site of present-day Tallahassee, as probably the first to hold Christmas services. The Spanish conquistador Francisco Coronado, whose party explored the American Southwest in 1540 and wintered near present-day Santa Fe, may also have observed Christmas, though definitive records are lacking.

Through Coronado's exploration, Spanish missionaries spread Christianity and Christmas to the native peoples of the American Southwest and instituted the customs of *Las*

Posadas and the related *Los Pastorelas* as tools for conveying the Christmas story, as they had earlier to the natives of New Spain (Mexico) (*see* **Las Posadas**). The first recorded Christmas service was in 1565 in the city of St. Augustine, Florida, held by a Father Francisco Lopez de Mendoza Grajales.

Although the Spanish Catholics freely celebrated Christmas, differing attitudes prevailed among the English colonists, primarily Protestants settling along the East Coast. The first Christmas in the first permanent English settlement of Jamestown, Virginia (1607), consisted of hardly more than a simple prayer service, as fewer than forty Anglicans struggled against cold and privation. The Pilgrims, Puritans who founded Plymouth Colony, Massachusetts (1620), not only ignored the season completely but ultimately imposed fines of five shillings in 1659 against those acknowledging Christmas in any form; the fine was repealed in 1681 (*see* **Great Britain** for further discussion about Puritans). Other Protestant colonists who denied Christmas for lack of a biblical precedent included Quakers, Presbyterians, and Congregationalists of New England, and Mennonites and Amish of New York and Pennsylvania.

On the other hand, Anglicans, Lutherans, English Catholics, members of the Dutch Reformed Church, and the Moravians brought traditional, Old-World customs to their respective settlements. German immigrants of Pennsylvania, the Dutch of New Amsterdam (New York), and especially the English plantation owners of Virginia and other southern colonies were noted for creating a most festive atmosphere, which included feasting on roasted game birds with stuffing, smoked hams, assorted vegetable dishes, elaborate confections, and liquors (George Washington was particularly noted for concocting a highly potent eggnog spiked with whiskey, brandy, sherry, and rum); elegant balls; gaming; costumed mummers known as "fantasticals"; sporting events; noisemaking with fireworks and shooting of firearms; and open houses among the affluent to which numerous guests flocked without invitation. New Yorkers, who once advertised the hours at which they would receive guests on Christmas Day or New Year's

Day, eventually ceased this practice because of the throngs of strangers who arrived, expecting a free meal. Decorations were simple, consisting of a Yule log, evergreens, flowers, and fruits. Christmas trees and gift-giving to family and friends did not become popular until the mid-nineteenth century (*see* **Christmas Tree**), although the well-off gave obligatory gifts to their inferiors, servants and slaves. A custom among a number of plantation owners was to grant their slaves freedom from work during the holidays as long as the Yule log burned. Therefore, to increase the burning time, slaves commonly chose the greenest logs and soaked them first in water. The custom "Christmas gif'" was a favorite among the slaves of the Old South. Upon meeting anyone, especially a white person, on Christmas Day, the slave would call out "Christmas gif'!" whereupon the one addressed was to supply some coins or other token. Children in the American Southwest continued this practice into the nineteenth century.

With Dutch immigrants came customs that centered around *Sinterklaas* (St. Nicholas), who initially brought gifts to children on December 5, the eve of St. Nicholas Day, and who eventually became known as "Santa Claus" through repeated slurring of his Dutch name (*see* **Saint Nicholas**; **Saint Nicholas Day**). Likewise, German immigrants settling in Pennsylvania (known as Pennsylvania Dutch) brought the concept of the *Christkindlein* ("little Christ Child"), shortened to *Christkindl*, a heavenly messenger who brought Christmas gifts in place of the Infant Jesus (*see* **Germany**). Further corruptions of this name led to "Krish-kinkle" and thence to "Kris (Kriss) Kringle," who merged as an alternate identity with Santa Claus in the nineteenth century (classically portrayed in the 1947 motion picture *Miracle on 34th Street*). A similar corruption changed "Pelz Nicholas" (Furry Nicholas), a combined gift bringer and holiday bogey to the Pennsylvania Dutch, to "Pelsnickel" and "Belsnickel." Originally on St. Nicholas Day, Pennsylvania youths dressed in ragged furs, blackened faces, or masks paraded from house to house with bells and whips, creating comedy and commotion with expectations of food and drink as rewards. This custom, "belsnickeling," incorporated English mumming practices during the eighteenth and nineteenth centuries, then shifted to the twelve days of Christmas and finally to New Year's Day by the turn of the twentieth century, when Philadelphia instituted the annual Mummers Day Parade (*see* **Christmas Drama** [Mumming]).

Another practice, common not only in Pennsylvania but in the South, was known as "barring out the schoolmaster." Derived from a sixteenth-century British custom, this practice was designed to acquire a few days' vacation from the despotic, often harsh methods (floggings) which British schoolmasters frequently employed to maintain discipline. School boys would collect provisions and barricade themselves in their classrooms just prior to Christmas or other holidays. The masters either forced the issue, resulting in violence, bloodshed, and even death, or they relented and granted a few days' reprieve. The practice in America consisted more of mock battles between students and teachers and declined in the nineteenth century as public schools published schedules for vacation days.

John Adams (1735–1826), second president of the United States (1797–1801), became the first chief executive to occupy the White House upon its completion in 1800. The first presidential Christmas celebration there consisted of a party for Adams's four-year-old granddaughter Susanna and her friends. Held in the grand ballroom, the event sported a small orchestra, cake, punch, greenery, carols, and games. Christmas trees did not grace the White House until the presidency of Franklin Pierce in 1853.

As pioneers pushed farther west across America, Christmas observances continued to be rather simple, communal affairs consisting of prayer services, socials, dances, and noisemaking. French descendants living in Louisiana, Missouri, and the Great Lakes regions hosted the Christmas Eve *réveillon* (*see* **France**) after Midnight Mass, and their children customarily received gifts on New Year's Day. Native Americans, observing the white man's Christmas, termed it either the "Big Eating" or "Kissing Day," the latter term deriving from French fur trappers who exchanged gifts with a kiss.

While different cultural and religious communities continued to observe Christmas in ways unique to their traditions, some researchers believe that the mass immigrations of Europeans, accelerated lifestyles, and the cultural and industrial revolutions of the mid-nineteenth century produced a sort of Christmas melting pot, with assimilation of various cultures into a more uniform and widely celebrated holiday in the home with family. This change, most pronounced following the American Civil War, has been attributed to the popularity of three principal traditions: Santa Claus, Christmas trees, and giving of gifts, all of which created a commercial and secular synergy, despite the original religious significance of the holiday.

Through the poem "A Visit from St. Nicholas" (published 1823) and magazine illustrations by political cartoonist Thomas Nast (1840–1902), St. Nicholas–turned–Santa Claus became a sensation as a "jolly old elf" from the North Pole who stuffed gifts into children's stockings on Christmas Eve (*see* **Saint Nicholas**). Francis Church's editorial titled "Is There a Santa Claus?" published in the New York *Sun* (1897) in response to an eight-year-old girl's inquiry, masterfully portrayed this personification of Christmas festivities as a spirit who would "continue to make glad the heart of childhood" (*see* "Yes, Virginia, There Is a Santa Claus"). And where else was the center of childhood than home and family? The German Christmas tree also swept through America in the late nineteenth century and joined the stocking not only as a decoration but as a family medium upon which small gifts were hung until the acquisition of larger gifts required their placement beneath the tree.

Through consumer demand, the 1870s and 1880s saw an increase in commercially produced items which, ironically, shoppers appreciated but initially regarded as too impersonal as Christmas gifts compared with more simple, handmade presents. Retail dealers countered with colorful wrapping paper and ribbons, which concealed the gifts (wrapped gifts were previously unknown), thereby making commercial items more attractive for Christmas. When consumers readily accepted this innovation, retailers saw a means of promoting even

Thomas Nast, a German-born American artist, was noted for the wonderfully tubby, grandfatherly Santas he drew for over 20 years for Harper's Weekly *and* Harper's Young People. *Here he has fun with two sky-borne children's idols: Mother Goose, spilling books, and Santa, whose sack is leaking toys above the world.* Harper's Young People, *December, ca. 1882.*

This complex wood engraving from Peterson's Magazine, *December 1866, shows a group of children gazing devoutly at a small tabletop tree, decorated with the Stars and Stripes (the flag of the Union, which had just won the Civil War), while a society ball takes place in the medallions above, and a loving child feeds hungry birds in the snow below.*

the most mundane of items as gifts through newspaper advertisements, fanciful window displays, and Santa himself, who appeared in person prior to Christmas to promote sales. By the end of the nineteenth century, Americans had begun to place more emphasis on giving presents at Christmastime rather than on New Year's Day as in previous eras.

A heightened urge toward giving to the poor and other charitable causes was especially manifested at Christmastime. As Penne Restad noted, while gift-giving to family members and friends served as a private means of reinforcing attachments and communal bonds, giving to the needy became more of a "cathartic exercise" in unselfishness: in other words, a symbolic escape for the guilt-ridden (*see* **Salvation Army; Toys for Tots**).

Printed Christmas cards, popular from the

post–Civil War era onward, served as substitutes for the former tradition of writing a multitude of Christmas letters or making numerous personal Christmas visits. Cards also conveniently replaced the seemingly obligatory cheap trinkets which families had bestowed upon distant friends and relatives (*see* **Christmas Cards**).

By 1870, 33 states had passed legislation establishing Christmas Day as a legal holiday, which prompted Congress to declare the day as a national holiday that same year. The remainder of what would become the 48 contiguous states had also legally recognized Christmas by the end of the century. The following provides an alphabetical listing of these states and the years in which Christmas became a legal holiday therein: Alabama 1836, Arizona 1881, Arkansas 1838, California 1851, Colorado 1861, Connecticut 1845, Delaware 1855, Florida 1881, Georgia 1850, Idaho 1863, Illinois 1861, Indiana 1875, Iowa 1862, Kansas 1868, Kentucky 1864, Louisiana 1838, Maine 1858, Maryland 1862,

A lithographed trade card from Lissauer & Sond-heim Jewelers shows a young wife, ca. 1880, having "A Christmas Dream" while her pets play and the tabletop tree displays rings, bracelets, and other fine baubles.

A handful of headlines from 1949 pre–Christmas magazine ads shows that everyone had the perfect gift for sale. The most telling of the group is for an aluminum table cooker which "looks many times what it costs"— a valuable asset if you were going to give presents to a lot of people!

Massachusetts 1855, Michigan 1865, Minnesota 1856, Mississippi 1880, Missouri 1877, Montana 1865, Nebraska 1873, Nevada 1861, New Hampshire 1861, New Jersey 1854, New Mexico 1876, New York 1849, North Carolina 1881, North Dakota 1863, Ohio 1857, Oklahoma 1890, Oregon 1862, Pennsylvania 1848, Rhode Island 1852, South Carolina 1875, South Dakota 1877, Tennessee 1857, Texas 1879, Utah 1882, Vermont 1850, Virginia 1849, Washington 1888, West Virginia 1870, Wisconsin 1861, Wyoming 1886. Thus, Alabama and Oklahoma were the first and last of the original 48 states, respectively, to legalize Christmas.

As commercialism soared into the twentieth century, large department stores such as Gimbel's and Macy's in principal Northern cities began sponsoring Thanksgiving Day parades which included Santa Claus as the feature attraction. This grandest of advertising gimmicks, which began in the early 1920s, served to launch the Christmas shopping season from that point. Furthermore, Federated Department Stores of Ohio, seeking to expand the season, convinced President Franklin Roosevelt in 1939 to change Thanksgiving Day from November 30 to November 23, a date that Congress re-established on the fourth Thursday of November in 1941, which ultimately provided four weeks for Christmas shopping. Other midcentury gimmicks featured Santa landing at shopping centers via helicopter. According to the National Retail Federation, holiday sales in 1997 totaled about 160 billion dol-

lars, which comprised about 25 percent of total annual sales, and figures published in 1999 by a major credit card company reflected an average Christmas gift budget of nearly $1,100. To finance such expenses, many Americans partially relied upon Christmas bonuses (more prevalent in the late nineteenth and early twentieth centuries) or "Christmas clubs," which arose in the early twentieth century and consisted of savings accounts into which cash could be deposited and held through the year for Christmas expenses. Otherwise, credit card users required about four months on the average to pay off Christmas debts.

American Christmas music came to the forefront in the nineteenth century as church-affiliated men produced lyrics to the now-familiar carols of "O Little Town of Bethlehem" (Episcopal minister Philips Brooks), "It Came upon the Midnight Clear" (Unitarian minister Edmund Sears), "We Three Kings" (Episcopal minister John Hopkins, Jr.), and "Jingle Bells" (Sunday school teacher James Pierpont). Whereas the former three were reverent Nativity narratives, the latter, completely secular with no mention of Christmas, seemed to pave the way for a large collection of popular, primarily secular songs that extolled the pleasures of a twentieth-century Christmas. Many became best-sellers in the recording industry, and the American Society of Composers, Authors and Publishers (ASCAP) hailed 25 of them as the most frequently performed, with "White Christmas" being number one. (*See* **ASCAP List of Christmas Songs.**)

Santa as secular lord of Christmas dominated numerous motion pictures, television specials, and animated cartoons, the majority of which repetitively presented the following plot: When a disaster or other bogey threatens to prevent Santa from delivering gifts on Christmas Eve, a quick solution must be found, lest Christmas be "canceled." While such pictures were occasionally peppered with holiday sentiment, they still lifted up Santa as the centerpiece of Christmas. They were balanced in part by such classics as *It's a Wonderful Life*, *The Homecoming*, and *Miracle on 34th Street*, all of which interjected home and family values as vital components of a traditional Christmas; and Dr. Seuss's *How the Grinch Stole Christmas*, which clearly sent the message that the joy of Christmas "doesn't come from a store."

At the dawn of the twenty-first century, the American Christmas varies little from that of the late twentieth. Spot groups of carolers tour neighborhoods soliciting donations for charity, though perhaps not as frequently as before. Shopping malls play traditional and contemporary carols as crowds swarm the aisles on the day after Thanksgiving, dubbed "Black Friday" by the retail industry. Because of ongoing controversies over separation of church and state arising in the 1960s, public Nativity scenes and other religious displays are generally absent, as are Nativity pageants in public schools. Sometime during the four weeks before Christmas, most offices will hold one or more parties, where the chief traditions include music, dancing, eating, and drinking.

As Thanksgiving has gradually lost its standing as a separate holiday and become more widely regarded as the opening of the Christmas season, more and more families have begun setting up Christmas trees immediately after Thanksgiving Day. Some families

An American card from 1879 with a seasonal design and a secular greeting with catch-phrases still in use: "cheery glow," "many pleasures bring," and "'Tis the happy time of the year." From "The Story of the Christmas Card," House and Garden, December 1921.

still prefer to wait until the last week or two before Christmas, especially if they are using real trees. Trees are usually decorated with commercially produced ornaments, garlands, tinsel, and electric "minilights," though some families cling to old-fashioned popcorn and cranberry strings, colored paper chains, and strings of electric lights.

Schools usually declare a holiday vacation approximately one week prior to Christmas, and most businesses grant only Christmas Day and New Year's Day as holidays during the season. Children remain out of school until sometime after the new year.

Christmas Eve to many remains a special family night, on which parents may read Christmas stories to their children and the family may attend a midnight service or other church event. Young children generally arise early on Christmas morning to open gifts. Some families attend a church service on Christmas morning. In most American homes a Christmas dinner is served sometime during Christmas Day. Traditional fare includes roast turkey with stuffing or dressing, ham, chicken or goose, cranberry sauce, sweet potatoes, green beans, squash, beets, assorted cakes and pies, coffee, tea, wassail, and eggnog. In the afternoon, families may visit relatives and friends.

Some churches in the United States still

observe special celebrations of Epiphany, but the final celebration of the secular American Christmas season is usually the New Year's Eve party. Traditional for New Year's Eve are fireworks displays at parks and fairgrounds, noisemaking, and kissing and singing "Auld Lang Syne" at midnight. The season ends with New Year's Day.

See also **Moravian Church; New Year's Day.**

Up on the Housetop

American children's song written by Benjamin R. Hanby (1833–1867). A relatively obscure figure and an abolitionist, Hanby also pursued teaching, the ministry, and musical composition. Living in Westerville, Ohio, at least during the latter half of his short life, Hanby wrote some eighty songs, two of which remain familiar today, "Darling Nellie Gray" (based on the story of a runaway slave whom

his father had sheltered in the Underground Railroad) and "Up on the Housetop." According to the Ohio Historical Society, "Up on the Housetop" was first published in October of 1866 under the simple title of "Santa Claus," but it has since come to be known by the first four words of its lyrics. Prior to Hanby, the poem "A Visit from St. Nicholas" ("'Twas the Night Before Christmas"), first published anonymously in 1823, had depicted Santa and his reindeer landing on rooftops; surely this poem inspired Hanby's Christmas tune. That Hanby also wrote another children's Christmas standard, "Jolly Old St. Nicholas," has been suggested but not documented.

See also **Jolly Old St. Nicholas; A Visit from St. Nicholas.**

Uruguay

See **South America**

Venezuela

See **South America**

A Very Merry Cricket

(1973). Made-for-television animated cartoon sequel to *The Cricket in Times Square* (1973), an earlier cartoon that was based on a children's book of the same title by George Selden, published in 1960. In the book, Chester C. Cricket, a most unusual insect from rural Connecticut with the ability to play mesmerizing, violin-like music on his wings, was unwittingly transported via a picnic basket to New York City, where he met friends Tucker Mouse and Harry Cat. There, Chester's music had brought peace and harmony to the harsh environment of the Big Apple.

With the holidays nigh at hand in the sequel, Chester returns to New York — not by accident this time, but as a favor to Tucker and Harry, who desire to bring the true meaning of Christmas back into Manhattan through the cricket's talents. The roar of the streets oblit-

erates Chester's initial strains, however, and the endeavor seems futile, until a massive power outage silences the city. Then from the silence emerge "Silent Night" and other carols, which work their magic of "Peace on Earth."

Voices: Les Tremayne, Mel Blanc. Written, produced, and directed by Chuck Jones. A Chuck Jones Enterprises Production. Family Home Entertainment Video. Color. 30 min.

A Virgin Most Pure

See **A Virgin Unspotted**

A Virgin Unspotted

English traditional carol, thought to have arisen in the Gloucestershire region during the sixteenth century. The text first appeared in *New Carolls for This Merry Time of Christmas* (London, 1661), the sole copy of which currently resides in the Bodleian Library, Oxford. Originally, the carol consisted of thirteen verses, with refrains both before and after each verse exhorting all to rejoice and be merry. The first verse of this Nativity narrative initially began as "In Bethlehem city, in Jewry it was." By the eighteenth century, however, the now-familiar first verse, commencing with "A virgin unspotted, the prophet foretold," had been added. Variations of text exist; notable examples include those published by Davies Gilbert in *Some Ancient Christmas Carols* (London, 1822) and William Sandys in *Christmas Carols, Ancient and Modern* (London, 1833). These versions are believed to derive from West Country broadsides and begin with the phrase "A virgin most pure," which serves as an alternate title. Modern printings of the text feature only one "rejoice and be merry" refrain, which appears after the verses.

The carol has known countless musical settings, the first of which appeared in John Arnold's *The Compleat Psalmodist* (London, 1741). An original setting surfaced in America by the New England composer William Billings (1746–1800), which he published in his *The Singing Master's Assistant* (Boston, 1778).

A Vision of Sugar Plums
See **Bewitched**

A Visit from St. Nicholas

Highly popular American poem, also known as "'Twas the Night Before Christmas" and "The Night Before Christmas." Authorship is controversial. Popular accounts attribute the poem to Clement Clarke Moore (1779–1863), a poet and professor of Greek and Oriental literature at the Episcopal General Theological Seminary in New York City from 1821 to 1850, who supposedly composed his legendary poem during Christmas 1822 to entertain his children. It is said that Harriet Butler, a family friend and daughter of the rector of St. Paul's Episcopal Church in Troy, New York, was visiting the Moore home at the time and copied the poem as Moore first recited it to his children. A year later, Orville Holley, editor for Troy's newspaper, the *Sentinel*, received a copy of the then-anonymous poem from an unnamed woman (possibly Ms. Butler) and published it on December 23 under the heading "Account of a Visit from St. Nicholas" (later

printings shortened the title to "A Visit from St. Nicholas"). The poem was an instant success and became a featured item in the *Sentinel* for several Christmases. In time, children came to know the poem, not by its original title, but by its opening phrase, "'Twas the Night Before Christmas," or simply "The Night Before Christmas."

Although the popularity of the poem spread widely, the author remained anonymous until 1837, when the poem appeared in *The New York Book of Poetry*. This book was the first to credit Clement Moore as the author, apparently at the suggestion of his friend Charles Fenno Hoffman. A sober, religious pedant not inclined to frivolous verse, Moore ultimately claimed authorship when he included "A Visit from St. Nicholas" in his own *Poems*, published in 1844. He later attributed his long silence to embarrassment over his "trifle."

According to the descendants of Henry Livingston, Jr. (1748–1828), however, their ancestor is the poem's true author. Livingston, a painter, cartographer, and amateur poet of Dutch descent from Poughkeepsie, New York, supposedly read his poem to his family and a "guest," after which the latter requested a copy. This guest subsequently became a governess for Moore's children, and it is conceivable that it was she who first delivered the poem to the Troy *Sentinel*. Livingston knew nothing of the dispute, having died long before Moore ever claimed authorship.

Since the latter 1800s, the Livingston family has continued to maintain their claim upon "A Visit from St. Nicholas" based upon circumstantial evidence. According to a *New York Times* article by David D. Kirkpatrick, research published in 2000 by Don Foster, an English professor at Vassar College, supports Livingston as the author. Among the many facts that Foster cites as evidence: Moore's other poems are generally stern, pious, and moralistic, mimicking those of pious poets, and rarely featuring anapestic meter (the meter of "A Visit from St. Nicholas"); Livingston's poems are light, fanciful, and mimic the style of William King and Christopher Anstey, eighteenth-century poets who also wrote popular poems in anapestic meter. Livingston annually wrote anapestic Christmas verses for his family; he preferred the seasonal salutation "Happy Christmas" to "Merry Christmas" (the last line of "A Visit from St. Nicholas" begins "Happy Christmas to all..."); and his favorite expression was "Dunder and Blixem" (Dutch-American words for "thunder and lightning"), which supposedly became the basis for the names of St. Nicholas's last two reindeer, currently known by the German-American equivalent names of Donder and Blitzen (see below). Moore, on the other hand, was conversant in German, not Dutch. In Foster's opinion, Moore simply plagiarized Livingston's poem.

Further controversy surrounds Donder and Blitzen. Popular accounts claiming Moore as author hold that, because of a printer's error, the 1823 publication produced "Dunder and Blixem" and not "Donder and Blitzen" as Moore supposedly intended. Foster contends that the *Sentinel* originally printed "Donder and Blitzen" in error and that Moore perpetuated the error in the four copies of the poem which he produced by hand late in life. Unfortunately, no original manuscript of "Account of a Visit from St. Nicholas" has ever surfaced to lay the matter to rest.

The name "Donner" (German for "thunder") has sometimes replaced "Donder" when the poem has been reproduced in collections of the twentieth century. According to some accounts, "Donner" did not appear in print prior to 1950, the substitution allegedly originating with songwriter John D. (Johnny) Marks, who created the hit tune "Rudolph, the Red-Nosed Reindeer," which cowboy singing star Gene Autry recorded in 1949. Marks's "Rudolph" lyrics included the names of all of the now-famous reindeer and, possibly to improve the flow of the lyrics, supposedly used "Donner" instead. After "Rudolph" became a hit song, the story continues, "Donner" appeared more frequently in printings of "A Visit from St. Nicholas." While Marks may have nurtured the error, he certainly was not responsible for it. Basing his song on Rudolph, a reindeer in a story that his brother-in-law, Robert May, had written in 1939 for the Montgomery Ward Company, Marks was probably influenced by the reindeer names listed therein, which also included "Donner." But one only needs to note "Donner" written in a 1932 Walt Disney animated cartoon short, *Santa's Workshop*, for confirmation that "Donner" existed before the birth of Rudolph, long before 1950. Although the exact origin for the substitution remains obscure, it likely stems from publishers' confusion over two sound-alike words from two foreign languages, both of which mean "thunder."

Ken Darby, a composer noted for having devised the Munchkin voices for *The Wizard of Oz* in 1939, is credited with providing the first musical setting, titled, "'Twas the Night Before Christmas" and published in 1942. Recorded by Fred Waring and the Pennsylvanians on the Decca label that same year, it sold over a million copies. Although similar contributions shortly appeared from other composers such as Frank Klickmann in 1951 and Johnny Marks in 1952, Darby's is considered the definitive version. Nevertheless, neither Darby's tune nor any of the others appeared in the 1974 made-for-television animated cartoon *'Twas the Night Before Christmas*.

Films based on the poem include four silent versions, three titled *The Night Before Christmas* (1906, animation by the Edison Company; 1912; 1926) and *'Twas the Night Before Christmas* (1914, The Edison Company). Sound versions titled *The Night Before Christmas* include two animated cartoon "shorts" (Walt Disney, 1933; Tom and Jerry — MGM, 1941, nominated for an Academy Award, Best Short Subject — Cartoons) and an animated television special with host Art Linkletter and the Norman Luboff Choir (1968).

New York City has held an annual tribute to Clement Moore's memory since 1911. Late in December, the Clement Clarke Moore Commemoration convenes in Manhattan's Church of the Intercession for a candlelight service. After hearing a reading of "A Visit from St. Nicholas," a solemn procession proceeds to Moore's grave in the cemetery at Trinity Church nearby.

Phyllis Siefker's book *Santa Claus, Last of the Wild Men* further contends that the American Santa Claus and the St. Nicholas of "A Visit from St. Nicholas" both derive from "Pelz Nicholas" (Furry Nicholas), a mythical being which migrated with the "Pennsylvania Dutch" to America. The subject is more fully discussed in the entry **Saint Nicholas**.

See also **Rudolph, the Red-Nosed Reindeer** (song); **Saint Nicholas Day**; **'Twas the Night Before Christmas** (animated cartoon).

The Voice of Christmas
See **The Brady Bunch**

Waits

Groups of street minstrels in Great Britain principally noted for providing nocturnal Christmas music. During the eighteenth and nineteenth centuries, waits would go caroling from door to door, soliciting donations from their hosts.

A word with several applications, "waits" first denoted medieval minstrel-pages at court, whose nightly task it was to guard the streets and call out the hours. Their duty was akin to the night watchman's; hence the possible derivation from the German *Wacht* (guard) or even from the Scottish *waith* (roaming about). A company of waits was first known to have been established at Exeter in 1400.

During the seventeenth century, "waits" or "wayghtes" indicated not only hoboys or oboes but also those groups who played wind instruments (other accounts also mention violins) while roaming about at night. By this time, waits were either employed and licensed by cities as watchmen and town criers, or they worked as free-lance minstrels. In the latter case, it became commonplace for men to hire waits to serenade their ladies, sometimes well into the night.

By the eighteenth and nineteenth centuries, the waits' activities included only nocturnal performances of seasonal music for a few weeks prior to Christmas, which terminated on Christmas Eve. In Scotland, performances focused on the new year.

The waits are believed to have performed some of the best-known of English traditional carols, such as "God Rest Ye Merry, Gentlemen," "The Wassail Song," and "We Wish You a Merry Christmas." Apparently "authorized" waits under municipal employment had no monopoly on the profession, for an 1820 dispute that arose in Westminster regarding the legality of itinerant minstrels performing the same functions as waits came to naught.

The late nineteenth century saw a decline not only in the waits but all other British holiday customs which solicited money, such as Boxing Day.

See also **Boxing Day**.

Wales
See **Great Britain**

A Walt Disney Christmas

Video collection of six classic, animated cartoon shorts, including *Once Upon a Wintertime* (1952), sung by Frances Langford; *Santa's Workshop* (1932) and *The Night before Christmas* (1933), both of the *Silly Symphony* musical cartoon series; *Pluto's Christmas Tree* (1952), with Mickey Mouse and chipmunks Chip and Dale; *On Ice* (1935), with Mickey and Minnie Mouse, Goofy, Donald Duck, and Pluto; and *Donald's Snow Fight* (1942), with Donald Duck and nephews Huey, Dewey, and Louie.

Walt Disney Company. Walt Disney Home Video. Color. 46 min.

See also **A Disney Christmas Gift**.

The Waltons

Emmy Award–winning family television series of 210 episodes that ran from 1972 to 1981 on the CBS network, with six specials appearing after that time. Created by novelist and co–executive producer Earl Hamner, Jr., the series depicted the life and adventures of a large, closely knit family living in the Blue Ridge Mountains of Virginia during the Depression years. The regular cast of characters featured John and Olivia Walton (Ralph Waite and Michael Learned); their children, John-Boy (Richard Thomas, who left the series in 1977), Mary-Ellen (Judy Norton-Taylor), Jason (Jon

Walmsley), Erin (Mary McDonough), Ben (Eric Scott), Jim-Bob (David Harper), and Elizabeth (Kami Cotler); and the Walton grandparents, Zebulon (Will Geer, who died in 1978) and Esther (Ellen Corby, died in 1999). *The Waltons* series began on a Christmas note, inspired by Earl Hamner's short, autobiographical novel *The Homecoming: A Novel About Spencer's Mountain.* Hamner, who grew up in Schuyler, Virginia, based this story on that Christmas Eve of 1933 when his father was late coming home from work.

• THE NOVEL. Clay and Olivia Spencer, together with their eight children, Clay-Boy, Becky, Shirley, Matt, Mark, Luke, John, and Pattie-Cake, struggle to make ends meet during lean years. Jobs are scarce, and Clay works all week in a machine shop forty miles away, coming home only on Friday evenings.

Late one Christmas Eve when Clay has not returned, Olivia sends Clay-Boy out on a search. His trek takes him to an African American church, where Clay has been known to gamble at odd hours with his white friends. Instead, a Christmas Eve service is in progress with no sign of his father. Next comes a visit to the home of Emma and Etta Staples, two eccentric, old-maid sisters whose avocation is making bootleg whiskey ("The Recipe"). This visit results in Clay-Boy's near-inebriation from spiked eggnog. The situation looks grim until 1 A.M., when Clay, having missed his bus, finally returns loaded down with gifts. So that his younger children will keep faith in Santa Claus, he explains that he "wrassled" an old burglar dressed in a red suit outside and grabbed an armload of presents before the stranger took off in a reindeer sleigh.

• THE TELEVISION SPECIAL. The next evolutionary step was Hamner's 1971 adaptation of the novel into a two-hour television special, titled *The Homecoming: A Christmas Story,* which introduced the Walton family and was nominated in 1972 for a Golden Globe Award for Best Movie Made for Television. The special starred Andrew Duggan as John and Patricia Neal as Olivia (Neal's performance won a Golden Globe Award in 1972 for Best Actress in a Television Drama), with Edgar Bergen as the grandfather and Ellen Corby as the grandmother. These roles were all recast for the se-

ries, except for Corby, who remained. The Walton children in this special also remained for the series. Although there was no change in "The Recipe," the Staples Sisters (played by Dorothy Stickney and Josephine Hutchinson in the special) became the Baldwin Sisters (Mary Jackson and Helen Kleeb) in the series. Cleavon Little wrapped up the principal cast as the Reverend Hawthorne Dooley. Originally not intended as a pilot for any series, *The Homecoming* nevertheless launched one of the most beloved shows on television.

Memorable scenes from *The Homecoming* include six-year-old Elizabeth's encounter with the overly pious missionary lady who distributes charity gifts on Christmas Eve at Ike Godsey's store in exchange for Bible quotes. As Mary-Ellen prompts them with whispered verses, several children, including Elizabeth, receive presents. But to her horror, the unwrapped doll stares at her through a hideously cracked face; as far as Elizabeth is concerned, someone has "killed" it.

Back at home, Olivia presents John-Boy with his Christmas gift—one of her handknit scarves—as she sends him out to search for his father. John-Boy's trek takes in the children's Christmas Eve pageant at Rev. Dooley's church, after which he and the minister make inquiry at the Baldwin sisters' home. Though John-Boy's efforts prove fruitless, he returns home with a jar. Olivia, of the Baptist persuasion, initially believes this to be "The Recipe," and prepares to rain damnation on all until she realizes that it's merely eggnog, unspiked at that.

About midnight, as the children worry over their father's return and Olivia quietly despairs, John-Boy gathers the family together and tells them about the miracle of cattle kneeling and talking at that time of year. Shortly after, John's safe return brings gifts for all and draws the special to a most happy ending as each family member bids the others good night. But just beforehand, Olivia, seeing that John has exhausted his paycheck on presents, wonders what they will live on in the coming week. John's reply: "Love."

The Homecoming was narrated by Earl Hamner, Jr. With William Windom. Written by Earl Hamner, Jr. Produced by Robert Jacks.

Directed by Fielder Cook. Lorimar Productions. Fox Video. Color. 98 min.

• THE SERIES. Christmas was the subject of only three *Waltons* episodes. In "The Best Christmas" (1976), Olivia believes that this will be the last Christmas with everyone together before World War II calls her boys into military service. A blizzard on Walton's Mountain, however, creates a series of emergencies that keep the family apart until the last moment, Christmas Day. In "The Spirit" (1979), the Waltons on Christmas Eve share the spirit of the season with an escaped German POW (Ned Bellamy), who had been hiding out on Walton's Mountain.

"The Children's Carol" (1977) could be listed as a Christmas special, though it was never billed as such. Set during World War II, the episode features Tess and Pip Wrayburn (Sally Boyden and Jeff Cotler, Kami Cotler's brother), two English children orphaned during the London Blitzkrieg, who come to stay with the Waltons. Their adjustment appears impossible until Allison, an English girl overseas with whom Jim-Bob has been communicating via shortwave radio, locates the children's mother and broadcasts a Christmas reunion with them across the Atlantic. Richard Thomas and Ellen Corby were absent from this telecast, Thomas having left the series earlier in 1977 and Corby having suffered a stroke in 1976, for which she missed eighteen months of the series.

"The Children's Carol" was narrated by Earl Hamner, Jr. With Joe Conley, Ronnie Claire Edwards, Lynn Hamilton, Tom Bower. Written by John McGreevey. Produced by Andy White. Directed by Lawrence Dobkin. Lorimar Productions. Warner Home Video. Color. 97 min.

Wassail

Hot beverage generally consisting of wine, cider, ale, or other liquor with spices such as cloves, ginger, cinnamon, and nutmeg. Other ingredients have included eggs, milk, sugar, molasses, lemon, roasted apples, and thin slices of toast (which yielded the term "toast," a ritualistic salutation of honor). The name "wassail" derives from slurring an old Anglo-Saxon expression "wes hael" ("be well," "be hale," or

"your health"). Wassail was also known as "lamb's wool," so named for the appearance of fleece which the floating, soggy toast or roasted apples imparted to the beverage.

Wassail's association with the drinking or "toasting" of one's health stemmed from a legend surrounding the fifth-century British king, Vortigern. During a feast honoring Vortigern, a group of Saxons offered a bowl of ale to the king, saying, "Louerd king, wes hael" ("Lord king, your health"). They explained the Saxon custom of offering ale to a friend, who, upon receiving the ale, was to respond with "Drinc hael" ("I drink your health"). Then the latter would reciprocate. By the sixteenth century, the liquor as well as the toast itself had acquired the name "wassail," the act of toasting had become "wassailing," and the bowl containing the liquor had become the "wassail bowl." If the toasting became excessive, "wassail" also described a drinking binge.

Toasting became a popular social pastime that eventually played a prominent role during the revelry of holiday feasts, especially at Christmastime. Although guests originally saluted their host by drinking from a single wassail bowl passed from person to person, in due course the wassail was served in individual vessels. In another custom, drawing upon a pagan superstition which held that toasting orchard trees in midwinter would increase the fruit yield, people ceremoniously congregated during the twelve days of Christmas to pour wassail from the wassail bowl over tree roots and trunks. That custom of "wassailing the fruit trees" further evolved into bands of carolers wassailing through the streets and singing from door to door, wishing everyone good health during the holidays. A number of popular "wassailing" songs subsequently emerged, and some of them have survived into the present, such as "We Wish You a Merry Christmas," "Here We Come A-Caroling (Wassail Song)," and "God Rest Ye Merry, Gentlemen." Households almost always rewarded the wassailers with a taste of wassail from the wassail bowl, and the modern party punch bowl is a descendant of that bowl.

A Scandinavian variation of wassail employed slices of a spiced loaf, Yule cake, which floated to the top of the wassail bowl.

See also **God Rest Ye Merry, Gentlemen; Here We Come A-Caroling; The Twelve Days of Christmas; We Wish You a Merry Christmas; Yule.**

Wassail Song

See **Here We Come A-Caroling; Wassail**

Wassail, Wassail All Over the Town

See **Gloucestershire Wassail**

Watchman, Tell Us of the Night

English Advent carol, the lyrics of which were published in 1825 by Sir John Bowring (1792–1872). An author, editor for the *Westminster Review*, member of Parliament, and governor of Hong Kong, Bowring based his carol's lyrics on Isaiah 21:11–12. This otherwise metaphorically grim passage predicts that Dumah, a key oasis in northern Arabia which had fallen to Assyria, will pass through the "morning" or light of relief from this menace, only to fall victim to the "night" or darkness of Babylonian captivity.

Bowring chose to turn the passage around by creating a carol with lyrics promising hope of salvation in Christ, who eradicates the darkness of sin (night) with the glory of eternal life (dawn). Consisting of three verses, the lines alternate between questions from a "Traveler" in anxious expectation and replies from the "Watchman," who, having seen the Eastern Star, heralds the coming joy that the world will experience through the birth of Christ.

No single musical setting for "Watchman" has ever gained general popularity, despite matches with several melodies from Germany, Wales, England, and the United States. The settings most often used include those by Jakob Hintze (1622–1702), a German composer and music editor, and by Welsh music professor Joseph Parry (1841–1903), whose tune has also been used as a setting for the Charles Wesley hymn "Jesus, Lover of My Soul."

We Need a Little Christmas

Song from the 1966 Broadway hit musical *Mame*, written by composer and lyricist Jerry Herman. In this musical, Mame (played in the original production by Angela Lansbury), an eccentric lady with a youthful approach to life, strives to impart her philosophy to nephew Patrick Dennis (Frank Michaels) and husband Beauregard Burnside (Charles Braswell). When Mame and Patrick find themselves destitute in the Great Depression, only Christmas festivities can restore their spirits. Therefore, despite the fact that it's not Yuletide by the calendar, they deck the halls, light the candles, and lift their voices to the tune of "We Need a Little Christmas."

The show has had numerous touring versions, and a 1974 film version starred Lucille Ball and Robert Preston.

Of the 25 most frequently performed Christmas songs of the twentieth century listed by the American Society of Composers, Authors and Publishers (ASCAP), "We Need a Little Christmas" is ranked number 21.

Although *Mame* is considered to be Jerry Herman's best score, that for *Hello, Dolly!* (1964) was also a smash hit, which included the Grammy-winning title number. Herman has been inducted into the Theatre Hall of Fame and the Songwriters Hall of Fame.

We Three Kings of Orient Are

American carol written in 1857 by the Reverend John Henry Hopkins, Jr. (1820–1891). Founder and editor of the *Church Journal* (1853–1868) and an instructor of church music at the Episcopal General Theological Seminary in New York City, Hopkins composed "We Three Kings" as part of an elaborate Nativity drama which he created for the seminary. Other sources state that Hopkins, a bachelor, also wrote the carol as a Christmas drama for his nieces and nephews who lived in Burlington, Vermont, for which he was subsequently dubbed "Vermont's Father Christmas."

The carol first appeared in print under a variant title, "Three Kings of Orient," in Hopkins's collection, *Carols, Hymns, and Songs* (New York, 1865). At the time of its publications, Hopkins was rector of Christ's Church in Williamsport, Pennsylvania. The carol became popular in England and was included in the prestigious collection *Christmas Carols New and Old*, edited by Henry Bramley and John Stainer (London, 1871).

Hopkins originally scored the carol for

three male voices with parts for each of the traditional Three Kings who brought gifts to the manger, Melchior, Gaspar, and Balthasar. The trio were to sing verse 1 together, followed by Gaspar, who sang of bringing gold for a King in verse 2; Melchior, frankincense to worship God in verse 3; and Balthasar, myrrh for Christ's future passion and death in verse 4. The trio together concluded with verse 5. Today, the carol is generally sung without regard for individual solos.

Hopkins contributed the lyrics and music for another, lesser-known carol, "Gather Around the Christmas Tree."

We Wish You a Merry Christmas

Traditional carol thought to have originated in the West Country of England during the sixteenth or seventeenth century. Although it remains today as one of the most popular of the secular carols, little else is known of its history, other than that the Waits included this carol in their repertoire of holiday melodies. The lyrics are preoccupied with "figgy pudding" (plum pudding), demanding that the dish be brought to the carolers awaiting outside as a reward for their musical efforts. This is in keeping with the older wassailing carols as opposed to those of the eighteenth and nineteenth centuries, the lyrics of which often clearly expect the master of the house to invite the troupe indoors for some refreshment.

See also **Waits; Wassail.**

We'll Dress the House
See **Alfred Burt Carols**

West Indies

Following Christopher Columbus's landing in the Bahamas at San Salvador in 1492, a number of European nations laid claim to various islands in the West Indies, including Spain, Portugal, the Netherlands, France, and Great Britain. During the seventeenth and eighteenth centuries, black slaves from West Africa were imported to work on sugar plantations, and in the nineteenth century, following the abolishment of slavery, Muslims and Hindus replaced the blacks on some of the islands. Descendants of these workers now largely occupy the islands, along with people of mixed African-European heritage. Roman Catholicism is prominent, with a number of Christmas traditions reflecting that faith. Also evident are influences from the colonial period as well as the United States, such as Christmas trees, Santa Claus, and traditional carols known well in the United States.

A unique tradition is *Jonkonnu*, which African slaves introduced into the West Indies, Bermuda Islands, the southern United States, and portions of Central America such as Belize and Honduras. It is a tradition perpetuated in the West Indies by their descendants, the black Caribs or Garifuna. Consisting of masked dances, the tradition is thought to have originated early during the eighteenth century as a memorial to John Conny, a celebrated chief on the Guinea coast. Whereas some believe that the name "Jonkonnu" derived from Conny's name, with multiple variations such as "Johnkankus," "John Kooner," "John Kuner," "Junkanoo," and "John Canoe," others hold that these names corrupted the French *gens inconnu* ("unknown people"), a name bestowed because the masks, often skin-covered and imitative of horned beasts, shielded the dancers' identities. The costumes featured colorful strips of paper or cloth attached to the headdresses as well as outfits of dark gunny sack material. To the lively music of gumbay drums, fifes, and triangles (a musical form known as Wanaragua), parades of mostly male dancers sang humorous and often satirical verses. Originally these parades were held on Boxing Day, December 26, and New Year's Day, two days on which slaves were permitted to rest from their work. The dancers often solicited donations of money or liquor, and their repertoire reflected an African-European blend of dance steps and mumming. With the abolition of slavery in the mid–1800s, Jonkonnu essentially vanished in many regions of the Caribbean; it now survives primarily, though not exclusively, in Jamaica, where dancers still perform publicly on December 26.

The following paragraphs summarize additional customs in several of the sovereign islands as well as Puerto Rico.

• BAHAMAS. The Christmas season in this former British colony extends from Christmas Eve until New Year's Day. The Christmas dinner often features a variety of seafood, turkey, ham, pigeon peas, rice, and a soup containing ox tails or pigs' feet. The Garifuna celebrate their festival of "Jonkanoo" between December 26 and New Year's Day. "Merry Christmas" is said in English.

• BARBADOS. Traditions combine those from more than 300 years of former British rule and those from descendants of black African slaves. General revelry dominates the weeks prior to Christmas. Decorations are often fashioned from local shrubs, particularly the casuarina tree. Rural districts sponsor house-to-house caroling events, and churches hold concerts. There are midnight services on Christmas Eve, and many gather in Queen's Park in Bridgetown on Christmas Day for the annual concert performed by the Royal Barbados Police Band.

Family and friends gather together for Christmas dinner, which often consists of turkey and stuffing, ham, pork, spicy sauces, fruitcake, mince pie, plum pudding, rum, and *sorrel*, a traditional drink. The latter is made from the red or white, fleshy portion of sorrel (*Hibiscus sabdariffa*), a shrubby annual originating in the Sudan, and sweetened with sugar or fermented.

"Scrubbers," obsolete since the mid-twentieth century, once consisted of bands of four or five men who traveled about each district, singing carols and delivering poetic speeches at homes early on Christmas morning. In such often humorous and sarcastic poems, the scrubbers clearly made known their desire for a handout, especially liquor. Most households willingly complied, but when some refused, the scrubbers scrawled messages of complaint on the houses. This gave rise to the term "scribes," which became adapted into "scrubbers."

"Merry Christmas" is said in English.

• CUBA. Christmas celebrations ceased in 1961, two years after dictator Fidel Castro and his Communist regime gained control of the island. Although the atheistic government temporarily sanctioned Christmas in 1997 to honor the visit of Pope John-Paul II to Cuba, the only vestige of Christmas now remaining is *Misa del Gallo* ("Mass of the Rooster," Midnight Mass), held on Christmas Eve. Participants attend incognito to avoid arrest. Children do not re-

ceive gifts on Christmas, but on July 26, commemorating the "July 26 Movement," an uprising in 1953 against former President Fulgencio Batista Zaldivar. "Merry Christmas" is covertly said in Spanish, *Feliz Navidad. See also* **Mass of the Rooster**.

• DOMINICAN REPUBLIC. Roman Catholicism predominates in this former Spanish colony, with the population primarily of mixed Spanish and black African descent. A summary of general Latin American Christmas customs is found in the introductions to the entries for Central America and South America.

The holidays are quite noisy with fireworks. In addition, the Dominican Republic observes a period of caroling during the first 25 days of December, in which bands of people arrive at church before dawn to sing. Afterwards, they divide into groups to sing in various homes, where they are usually rewarded with refreshments such as ginger beer and confections. Christmas decorations are similar to those of the United States, along with those fashioned from dried fruits and palm leaves. Employers usually grant an *aguinaldo* (Christmas bonus) in the form of one month's salary to employees, who also engage in gift exchanges known as *angelitos* ("little angels"). Christmas Eve dinner usually features roast pork, turkey, tamales, *pan de huevo* (bread), rice pudding, and fruitcakes. Children generally receive gifts from the Three Kings on Epiphany rather than on Christmas Day, and, since the Kings may have forgotten some poor children, tradition holds that these children receive gifts from the *Vieja Belén* ("Old Woman of Bethlehem"). "Merry Christmas" is said in Spanish, *Feliz Navidad*.

• GRENADA. Roman Catholicism predominates in this former British colony, about 85 percent of which consists of people of black African descent. Christmas customs include caroling groups traveling from house to house during the weeks prior to Christmas; decorations of Nativity scenes, poinsettias, streamers and stars; and community Christmas trees. The Christmas dinner often features turkey, pork, pigeon peas, yams, ginger beer, and *sorrel*, a drink discussed in the Barbados subentry above. The season ends on January 6, when all decorations are removed. "Merry Christmas" is said in English.

• JAMAICA. Today the best known Christmas tradition in Jamaica is Jonkonnu, discussed above.

• PUERTO RICO. A former Spanish colony, this commonwealth of the United States is primarily Roman Catholic. Santa Claus and Christmas trees are well known, but the principal symbol remains the *Belenes* (Nativity scene), known as *Pesebres* in many other parts of Latin America. Each of the early morning masses held during the Novena prior to Christmas is known as *Misa de Aguinaldo* ("Mass of the Gift"). During the weeks of Advent, families and friends hold *Parrandas* ("Sprees," all-night Christmas parties) in different homes, at which groups of carolers known as *Asaltos* ("Assault") traditionally make surprise visits. Each of these groups carries a figure of the Christ Child, which is left at the home of the final *Parranda*, and that family then brings the figure to Midnight Mass.

The Christmas Eve dinner often features baked chicken, turkey, pork, Spanish rice, pigeon peas, cooked greens, yams, *pasteles* (mashed plantains with meat and vegetables wrapped in plantain leaves and boiled), *arroz con dulce* (rice cooked with spices and coconut milk), *tembleque* (custard of cornstarch, sugar, and coconut milk), *turrón* (nougat), nuts, and *coquito* (eggnog made with coconut milk and rum). All festivities include much music and dancing throughout the season.

December 28, *Día de los Inocentes* (Holy Innocents Day), is a time for practical jokes. On this day in Hatillo, citizens engage in comic reenactments of the Slaughter of the Innocents. Men dressed as the evil soldiers of King Herod parade from house to house, "kidnapping" the first-born boys found therein. The families bribe the soldiers with gifts to recover their children, and at the return of them all, the village hosts a gala event to celebrate the return of the "lost boys." Among the festivities of *Año Viejo* ("Old Year," New Year's Eve) are social gatherings where everyone attempts to swallow twelve grapes for luck during the final minute before midnight.

Although children receive gifts on Christmas Day, the traditional, Spanish gift-giving day is Epiphany, better known as *Día de los Tres Reyes* (Three Kings Day), January 6, in which the Three Kings deliver the gifts. On the night before, children prepare for the Kings' visit by placing shoe boxes filled with grass and grain under their beds. The Kings in turn feed the fodder to their camels and replace it with gifts in the boxes. Bethlehem Day, January 12, is closely related, in that children parade through the streets, led by three of their peers dressed as the Three Kings riding horses and bearing gifts for the Christ Child. Also following are those portraying angels and shepherds, along with musicians.

A custom not often practiced today is *Octavas*, observed eight days after Epiphany. In that custom, a person who receives a visit from a friend on Epiphany, must return the favor in eight days, amid festivities. The day is now largely observed as a time for putting away decorations and closing the Christmas season.

"Merry Christmas" is said in Spanish, *Feliz Navidad*.

• SAINT KITTS AND NEVIS. Landing on the islands in 1493, Christopher Columbus named St. Kitts after his patron, St. Christopher. The islands are former British colonies, and their population now consists primarily of descendants of Europeans and West Africans. Aside from Eurocentric customs, the African Christmas traditions date to the days of slavery, when "Christmas Sports," a synergism of African, European, and American Indian elements, appeared throughout these islands from Christmas Eve to New Year's Day, the time period when work on the plantations eased.

Christmas Sports were conducted by lay street dancers in tribal costumes, who performed to the music of the drum, fife, triangle, *quatros* (banjo), *baha* (long, metal pipe that is blown), and shack-shack (tin can containing beans). Their routines usually revolved around various plays based on biblical stories, everyday situations, classic drama, and sketches that often satirized their white overlords, something permissible (to a degree) only at Christmastime. Because of these sketches, it was mandatory that the first performance of the season be held at the local police station for appropriate censorship.

Emigration, players' deaths, lack of an organized program, and white oppression have been cited as causes for a decline in Christmas

Sports. Only six of numerous original varieties primarily remain: "Masquerades," six dances performed by a chief with twelve to fifteen dancers wearing multi-colored shirts, pants, ribbons, handkerchiefs, mirrors, beads, and headpieces of peacock feathers; "Bull," humorous play exaggerating a plantation event of 1917 which revolves around the revival of a wounded bull; "Mocko-Jumbies," stilt dancers wearing long gowns and conical hats; "Mummies," depicting characters from European legends such as St. George and the Dragon, with players wearing colorful short jackets, long white pants, mirrors, and handkerchiefs; "Actors," acrobats from St. Peter's parish performing dangerous feats such as somersaulting over upturned garden forks and having large rocks broken on their chests; and "Clowns," usually fifty players performing whip-swinging dances in loose, two-colored costumes decorated with numerous small bells. These sports usually carry over into the pre–Lenten Carnival Season. Examples of Christmas Sports now virtually extinct include "Niega Business," "Sagwa," "Soldiers," "Cowboys and Indians," "Selassie," "Japanese," and "Millionaires."

Other Christmas customs include caroling by church or civic groups who solicit donations; bands of laborers who serenade comrades all night on Christmas Eve in return for liquor; and street parades of scratch or string bands with throngs of dancing adults and children who are led by a few attired in rags or sack cloth. "Merry Christmas" is said in English, the official language.

• TRINIDAD AND TOBAGO. The islands are former Spanish, French, Dutch, and British colonies. The people are chiefly of African and East Indian descent (about 40 percent each), the remainder consisting of Chinese, West Europeans, and those from the Middle East. Roman Catholicism constitutes the largest single Christian faith. Preparations for Christmas include making plantain wine and sorrel (*see* subentry for Barbados above) as well as black rum cakes, dark fruitcakes soaked in rum. People customarily paint their homes and clean them thoroughly, and performers playing lively Parang music on *quatros* (banjos) serenade their neighbors in the early hours of the morning. The Christmas menu features ham, cakes, yams, pigeon peas, crab, macaroni, rice, and *souse* (broth with pigs' feet). Artificial Christmas trees are the general rule, and children receive gifts from Santa Claus, which they open on Christmas morning. "Merry Christmas" is said in English, the principal language.

See also **Advent**; **Christmas Drama**; **Epiphany**; **Holy Innocents Day**; **Mass of the Rooster**.

Western Australian Christmas Tree
See **Christmas Plants**

We've Been a While A-Wandering
See **Here We Come A-Caroling**

What Are the Signs
See **Alfred Burt Carols**

What Child Is This?

English carol, the verses of which were taken directly from a larger poem, "The Manger Throne," published around 1865 by William Chatterton Dix (1837–1898). The verses were paired with the well-known English folk tune "Greensleeves" and published as "What Child Is This?" in *Christmas Carols New and Old* (London, 1871), edited by Henry Bramley and John Stainer. Although the person who matched the verses with "Greensleeves" remains unknown, it may have been Stainer, for he also harmonized the musical setting. Dix was the manager of a marine insurance company in Bristol; his avocation was poetry and hymnwriting, and he wrote the carol "As with Gladness Men of Old" (1859).

"Greensleeves" is thought to have arisen during the latter half of the sixteenth century, although it could be older. One of the first references to the tune came from a Richard Jones, who registered it in 1580 with a set of somewhat vulgar lyrics. His authorship remains unsubstantiated, however, as is that of Henry VIII, who has also been suggested as the song's author. Elizabeth I, daughter of Henry VIII, danced to it, and by 1600 it had become a well-established piece. The tune has enjoyed extensive utilization. It has been the setting for numerous ballads, an accompaniment for executions, a segment of John Gay's *The Beggar's Opera* (1728), and a Cavalier party song during the British

Civil War (1642–1648). It is twice mentioned in William Shakespeare's *The Merry Wives of Windsor.*

Verse 1 asks a rhetorical question: What Child is this who sleeps on Mary's lap, about whom angels sing while shepherds keep watch? The answer: This is Christ the King, come and praise Him! Verse 2 asks why He lies in base surroundings, then answers that, even as a silent Babe, He pleads for sinners, then predicts His death on the cross. Verse 3 calls for all people, poor and rich, to accept Christ. All verses end with "The Babe, the Son of Mary!"

See also **As with Gladness Men of Old.**

What Is This Fragrance?

See **Whence Is That Goodly Fragrance?**

What Is This Perfume So Appealing?

See **Whence Is That Goodly Fragrance?**

What Perfume This? Oh Shepherds Say

See **Whence Is That Goodly Fragrance?**

When Christ, the Son of Mary

See **Carol of the Bagpipers**

When Joseph Was an Old Man

See **The Cherry Tree Carol**

Whence Is That Goodly Fragrance?

("Quelle est cette odeur agreable?"). French traditional carol, the text of which is believed to have originated in Lorraine during the seventeenth century. Other translations include "What Is This Perfume So Appealing?" "What Is This Fragrance?" "Shepherds, What Fragrance, All-Perfuming?" and "What Perfume This? Oh Shepherds Say."

Based on the annunciation to the shepherds in Luke 2, the first three verses are cast in dialogue between three different shepherds regarding a marvelous fragrance, brilliant light, and soul-stirring singing which herald the coming of the heavenly host. The remaining three verses depict the angels' command to heed their message, Gabriel's tidings of good joy, and the final chorus of "Glory to God in the highest." Although no reference to perfume ex-

ists in Luke's account of the Nativity, it is possible that the carol draws upon a legend which holds that when Christ was born, every tree in the world bloomed and perfumed the earth to welcome Him.

Ironically, the musical setting, also traditional and dating to the eighteenth century, has been used in a number of drinking songs, such as that included in John Gay's *Beggar's Opera* (1728).

While by My Sheep

("Als ich bei meinen Schafen wacht'"). German traditional carol believed to date approximately to 1500. Because phrases in the verses and refrain are repeated, it is also known as the "Echo Carol." Another alternative title is "How Great My Joy."

This echo format suggests that the carol may have been used as an antiphonal song for two or more groups of singers placed in separate locations in the church. It may also have been composed for a Nativity or shepherd folk drama, a traditional art form that was prevalent in Germany and other parts of Europe during the Middle Ages.

The carol first appeared in a Cologne hymnal in 1623 with a Latin echo, "Benedicamus Domino" ("May we bless the Lord"), tacked onto the German refrain. A later setting published in Trier, Germany, in 1871, which became more popular in America, eliminated the Latin, limited the echoes to the refrain, and rephrased the refrain as well: "How great my joy (great my joy!) Joy, joy, joy! (Joy, joy, joy!"). The American music scholar Theodore Baker (1851–1934) provided the best-known English language translation.

While Shepherds Watched Their Flocks

English carol with lyrics by Nahum Tate (1652–1715), the Irish-born poet laureate of England (1692). The lyrics were constructed as a paraphrase of the Nativity story as found in Luke 2:8–14. In 1700 Tate first published this text in his supplement to the *New Version of the Psalms of David* (London, 1696), co-edited by Nicholas Brady. At that time, Tate's text was one of only six hymns legally authorized by the Church of England as suitable for congregational singing (congregational hymns as such in England were remarkably uncommon before the eighteenth century, for the usual music heretofore had comprised the regulation canticles).

Of the scores of musical settings which have been paired with "While Shepherds Watched," two have gained the most popularity. In America, this carol is usually sung to a tune adapted from an aria found in G. F. Handel's opera of 1728, *Cyrus, King of Persia.* Although the person specifically creating the adaptation is not known, speculation includes two Americans, Richard S. Willis (1819–1900), who supplied the musical setting for "It Came Upon the Midnight Clear" (that setting also has been paired with "While Shepherds Watched" on occasion), and hymnist Lowell Mason (1792–1872). The other principal setting is "Winchester Old," an anonymous, sixteenth-century English tune, which a George Kirbye arranged and published in 1592. The Kirbye setting did not appear together with Tate's text, however, until their inclusion in *Hymns Ancient and Modern* (London, 1861), edited by William Clowes.

White Christmas

(Motion picture, 1954). A remake of *Holiday Inn* (1942) and Paramount Pictures' first film photographed in VistaVision, the answer to CinemaScope.

Bob Wallace and Phil Davis (Bing Crosby and Danny Kaye), buddies during World War II, team up after the war to form a musical revue. Auditioning Betty and Judy, the Haynes Sisters (Rosemary Clooney and Vera-Ellen), the enamored lads follow them to the Columbia Inn in Pine Tree, Vermont, where the ladies are booked for a series of holiday performances.

The inn is owned by retired General Tom Waverly (Dean Jagger), Bob's and Phil's former commanding officer. Bob and Phil learn that the inn is foundering, and to rescue their beloved superior, the boys transfer their own New York show to the inn. Learning that the general misses his command, Bob makes a television plea for all members of his former regiment to join him at the inn for a tribute to the general on Christmas Eve. Betty, initially misunderstanding Bob's motives, temporarily

leaves the show for a job in New York but returns after Bob's telecast to resume their budding romance. To Waverly's surprise, hundreds of his former troops salute him during an elaborate show, at which the general, with renewed spirits, takes "command" of his division. Of course, the two leading couples conclude the show and the picture with a memorable rendition of Irving Berlin's "White Christmas."

Fred Astaire, who starred in *Holiday Inn* with Bing Crosby, was Paramount Pictures' first choice for the character Phil Davis in *White Christmas,* but he rejected that role, which then went to Danny Kaye. As in *Holiday Inn,* Crosby sang "White Christmas" twice in *White Christmas,* as a solo at the beginning and as a Crosby/Clooney duet at the finale. Most of the cast actually performed the finale twice, the second time for the benefit of the king and queen of Greece, who visited the *White Christmas* set after the finale's filming was complete. Crosby, however, choosing not to yield to the whims of royalty, refused to return. Crosby also met his future second wife, Kathryn Grant, on this set. Thirty years his junior, Kathryn had auditioned for the part of Susan, Waverly's granddaughter, but was unsuccessful.

Although *White Christmas* received no Academy Awards, it did boast a number of memorable songs by Irving Berlin in addition to "White Christmas": "We'll Follow the Old Man," "Blue Skies," "Sisters," "Snow," "Count Your Blessings Instead of Sheep" (nominated for Best Song), "Choreography," "The Best Things Happen While You're Dancing," "Love, You Didn't Do Right by Me," "What Can You Do with a General?," "Gee, I Wish I Was Back in the Army."

With Mary Wickes, John Brascia, Anne Whitfield. Written by Norman Krasna, Norman Panama, Melvin Frank. Produced by Robert Emmett Dolan. Directed by Michael Curtiz. Paramount Pictures. Paramount Home Video. Color. 120 min.

See also **Holiday Inn**; **White Christmas** (song).

White Christmas

(Song). Highly popular American song written in 1940 by Irving Berlin (1888–1989) and arguably the most popular of American secular Christmas songs. The number was included in the Paramount motion picture *Holiday Inn* (1942), which not only paid tribute in song to the major holidays of the year and boasted Berlin's musical score, but also featured the singing talents of legendary crooner Bing Crosby. Crosby had first introduced the public to "White Christmas" through his Kraft Music Hall radio program on Christmas Day, 1941 (which followed the Japanese attack on Pearl Harbor), and the song achieved even greater fame on film.

It is said that, while he experienced little difficulty in composing songs for most of the other holidays, Berlin, of Jewish heritage, felt that writing a piece about Christmas was a more challenging task and was not sure how "White Christmas" would be accepted. Crosby, after studying the lyrics, eased Berlin's fears with confidence that his masterpiece would certainly become a hit.

"White Christmas" indeed won Berlin an Academy Award for Best Song in 1943, and Crosby's Decca recording in May of 1942 (backed by the John Scott Trotter Orchestra) sold over 30 million copies, making it the largest-selling single Christmas record in the world. By March 1947, because millions of pressings had worn the original master disk, Crosby had to re-record "White Christmas," and it is that version which is most frequently heard. The Crosby recording was the top Christmas song not only for 1942, but also for 1944, 1946, 1947, 1969, and 1983, and it continued to be charted for more than thirty years following its initial release. "White Christmas" was also the top Christmas song for 1963 with Andy Williams's recording on the Columbia label.

During World War II as Crosby toured the world entertaining American troops, hardly a show closed without a request for "White Christmas." Its home-filled sentiment touched the troops deeply, often bringing tears to their eyes. The effect, far greater than either Berlin or Crosby had ever anticipated, prompted a remake of *Holiday Inn* by Paramount, this time appropriately titled *White Christmas* (1954).

Although Berlin's lyrics originally included an introductory passage which expressed a preference for spending Christmas up North rather than in sunny Los Angeles, that passage is rarely sung today, and Crosby also omitted it from the film versions as well as his recordings.

Of the 25 most frequently performed Christmas songs of the twentieth century listed by the American Society of Composers, Authors and Publishers (ASCAP), "White Christmas" is ranked number 1.

Bing Crosby recorded over seventy sacred and secular Christmas songs during his illustrious career. After he signed with Decca Records in 1934, the company president, Jack Kapp, requested that Crosby record "Silent Night" and "Adeste Fideles." Feeling uncomfortable about recording sacred songs for profit, Crosby arranged for charities to receive all proceeds from those recordings, a policy that remained in force for the duration of his career.

See also **Holiday Inn; White Christmas** (motion picture).

Winter Solstice

In the northern hemisphere, that astronomical point in the apparent great-circle annual path of the sun (the ecliptic) at which the sun achieves its lowest position south of the celestial equator. If the heavens are imagined as a great sphere (the celestial sphere), the celestial equator is the great circle produced when the equatorial plane of the Earth intersects the celestial sphere. Because the Earth is tilted on its axis, the plane of the ecliptic intersects the celestial equator at an angle of 23° 27', resulting in four seasons with two annual solstices and two annual equinoxes. The winter solstice in the northern hemisphere occurs around December 21 or 22 and produces the shortest day of the year with the longest night, while the opposite is true for the summer solstice, occurring around June 21 or 22, in which the sun seemingly achieves its highest position north of the celestial equator.

For several days during a solstice, the sun appears to rise from the same position on the horizon, then begins slowly returning in the opposite direction. This apparent solar pause gives rise to the term "solstice," meaning "sun standing still." Twice in the year the ecliptic intersects the celestial equator to produce the vernal and autumnal equinoxes ("equal nights"), occurring around March 21 and September 21, in which the days and nights are of approximately equal length. All seasons, solstices, and equinoxes are simply reversed in the southern hemisphere.

For countless generations prior to the Christian age, the sun's annual declination at the winter solstice had been the source for numerous myths among ancient civilizations regarding the natural cycle of death and rebirth, such as the death of some solar or fertility deities at this time of year and their subsequent rebirth in the spring. Examples include Tammuz, originally a Babylonian sun god who died in winter but revived in the spring, and who later evolved into a god of animal and plant fertility; and Attis, originally a Syrian deity, who in Greek mythology was the son of Cybele, a mother goddess, and whose myth symbolized the death of vegetation in winter with revival in the spring. A similar cycle was known for Dionysus, Greek god of wine and vegetation.

Egyptians, on the other hand, celebrated the winter solstice birth of the sun god Ra at Heliopolis, the chief center for sun worship prior to the Christian age, although by their calendar, the winter solstice fell on January 6. Other Egyptian gods said to have been born on the winter solstice included Osiris, the male productive force in nature, who was murdered by his brother Set, after which Isis, the female productive force and sister-consort to Osiris, resurrected him so that Osiris became ruler of the underworld and a source for renewed life; and Aeon, patron god of Alexandria, born of the virgin goddess Kore (*see* **Epiphany**).

The Persians also observed the birthday of their sun god, Mithras, on the day that coincided with the winter solstice on the Roman or Julian calendar, December 25. Roman soldiers, introduced to the cult of Mithras during their campaigns in the eastern portions of the empire, popularized this new god in the West during the first century A.D. By the third century, this cult, which the Roman emperor Aurelian endorsed as *Sol Invictus* ("the Unconquered Sun"), along with the Saturnalia and a host of other pagan Roman holidays lying in proximity to the winter solstice, became a principal factor which eventually motivated the Church in the fourth century to adopt December 25 as the birthday of Christ (*see* **Christmas Day**; **Saturnalia**).

Ancient civilizations greeted the winter solstice with pomp and circumstance, with feasting, drinking, and considerable merriment. Rituals included the lighting of bonfires (especially in northern regions) to assist the sun in its return, the performance of fertility rites, sacrifices to gods, and the veneration of evergreen vegetation which was believed to hold magical powers because it apparently remained alive through the dead of winter. At the winter solstice, because the barrier between the physical and spirit worlds was said almost to vanish, myths regarding the dead and the supernatural came to the forefront. Divination practices predicted the future and various talismans, such as the bonfires and the creation of as much noise as possible, warded off evil that supposedly lurked just beyond the long darkness. In Norse mythology, the chief god Odin (Woden) descended on Sleipner, his white, eight-legged steed, during the midwinter festival of Yule and transported the souls of warriors who had been slain that year to eternal life in Valhalla, his palace in Asgard, the home of the gods. The spirits of deceased ancestors and family members were also believed to visit their families and former abodes at this time, and food was set aside for their benefit.

Belief in the return of spirits at the winter solstice probably contributed to the concept of the "Wild Hunt," "Furious Hunt," "Furious Host," and other terms for groups of spirits prevalent in northern Europe during the Middle Ages. Appearing most commonly during the twelve days of Christmas, these spirits raced across nocturnal skies to increase the fertility of fields or as messengers of death. Odin's gleaning of warriors' souls was one example of the Wild Hunt, which was also termed "Asgard's Ride." Among the Teutons, Berchta (also known as Bertha, Perchta, Holde, Hertha, and other names), goddess of home and protector of fields, led children's souls on agrarian fertility missions at this time.

Christianized vestiges of many of these ancient winter solstice customs survive in

Christmas celebrations today throughout the world: December 25 as Christmas Day, Christmas dinner, the Christmas tree, the lighting of candles, the adorning of homes with winter greenery, noisemaking, auguries, and ghost stories.

See also **Christmas Tree; The Holly and the Ivy; Mistletoe; Yule.**

Winter Wonderland

Popular American song written in 1934 by lyricist Richard Smith of Pennsylvania and composer Felix Bernard of New York. First introduced that same year by Guy Lombardo and His Royal Canadians, the simple lyrics and bubbly tune outline a couple's romantic interlude of walking through a wonderland of snow, building a snowman, then dreaming cozily by a fire together. The lyrics never mention any specific holiday, yet by popular association, the song has become a pleasant fixture in the repertoire of Christmas music. Two recordings of "Winter Wonderland" became best-sellers in 1946. Lombardo's band provided the backup for the Andrews Sisters' recording on the Decca label which, despite the fact that it never achieved chart status, sold over a million copies. Perry Como's recording on the RCA Victor label was among that year's Top Ten.

Of the 25 most frequently performed Christmas songs of the twentieth century listed by the American Society of Composers, Authors and Publishers (ASCAP), "Winter Wonderland" is ranked number 4.

Bernard also co-wrote the music for a hit of 1919, "Dardanella," recorded by Ben Selvin's Novelty Orchestra. It is believed that this was the first record to sell one million copies in the industry's history.

Wise Men

Aside from a brief account of their visit in the Gospel of Matthew (2:1–12), everything written about this mysterious troupe of gentile sages stems principally from legend. In some stories, the Wise Men's journey to Bethlehem required two years, during which time they miraculously never lacked provisions; in others, they traveled only twelve days, in which they required neither rest nor provisions. In another, Mary gave away the Wise Men's gold,

The three Wise Men, or Magi, are shown in an old engraving of a silver disk, chased in high relief and gilded, said to have formed the center of a large brooch used to fasten the decorated cope of a fourteenth century churchman.

either to the poor or as a temple offering, and the gold later filtered down to Judas Iscariot for betraying Jesus into the hands of the chief priests (Matthew 26:14–16 states that, for his act, Judas received "thirty pieces of silver"). Many years after the death of Christ, the Wise Men allegedly converted to Christianity in India through the evangelism of St. Thomas the Apostle and suffered martyrdom in India for their faith. According to the thirteenth-century journals of Marco Polo, on the other hand, the Italian explorer viewed in the city of Sewa, in what is now Iran, the tombs of three alleged kings with names of Caspar, Melchior, and Balthazar. About three hundred years after their deaths, the legend continues, Empress Helena, mother of Constantine the Great, supposedly carried their remains from the East to Constantinople, and from there they rested at the church of St. Eustorgius in Milan. Then in 1162 or 1164, the German emperor Frederick Barbarossa enshrined their relics in jeweled caskets at the cathedral in Cologne, Germany, where it was believed that anything that touched their skulls was empowered to prevent accidents. In 1903, Cologne returned a portion of the relics to Milan.

A contrarian depiction of Caspar, supposedly the young, beardless King of Tarsus. This fictionalized image, complete with fourteenth century knight's armored footwear, is described as "Caspar, impersonated by a wealthy merchant prince of Rouen" in a miracle play of the Middle Ages. From Harper's New Monthly Magazine, *December 1889.*

fall down before him: all nations shall serve him." Sheba and Seba were once located in what is now the Republic of Yemen, in "the East." The theologian Origen of Alexandria (ca. 185–ca. 254) numbered them at three because of the three gifts named in Matthew, and this number has become traditional. Although no one has ever determined the identities of the Wise Men with any certainty, the now-familiar names of Caspar (or Gaspar), Melchior, and Balthazar (or Balthasar) first surfaced in the sixth century. These names appeared in a Greek manuscript of the same period as well as above a Byzantine mosaic of three Wise Men extant in the nave of the Church of Sant'Apollinare Nuovo (ca. 560) in Ravenna, Italy. St. Bede the Venerable (673–735), the English Benedictine monk and scholar, also mentioned these names.

Even more confusion and uncertainty arise over their ages, their ethnic backgrounds, and the specific gift which each brought, because of variability among different sources. Their proposed countries of origin include Ethiopia, Arabia, Tarsus (in Turkey), Egypt, Mesopotamia, and Persia, and their ages have ranged from sixty to twenty. Despite this diversity, the most common of legends assigns the following identities: Melchior, king of Arabia, fair-skinned, white-bearded and elderly, brought gold; Caspar, king of

Popular tradition during the third century held that the Wise Men were kings, in fulfillment of Psalm 72:10–11: "The kings of Sheba and Seba shall offer gifts. Yea, all kings shall

Tarsus, ruddy, young and beardless, brought frankincense; and Balthazar, king of Ethiopia, middle-aged and black, brought myrrh. The Wise Men portrayed in the Ravenna mosaic above are also of three distinct ages, but an African is not represented. The nearest to Mary is white-bearded and elderly, the second is young and beardless, and the third is middle-aged with dark beard. If the names above the mosaic respectively identify each man, then the eldest is Gaspar, the youngest Melchior, and the third "Balthassar" (sic). Nothing regarding their specific gifts can be ascertained.

As John and Caitlin Matthews discuss in *The Winter Solstice: The Sacred Traditions of Christmas*, so-called Gnostic texts, originating during the second and third centuries and considered heretical by the Roman Catholic Church, further contribute to the enigma. Works such as *The Book of Adam*, *The Book of the Cave of Treasures*, and *The Book of the Bee* number the Wise Men from three to twelve. Additional identities for the traditional three include Hor, King of Persia; Basantar, King of Saba; and Karsundas, King of the East. According to Matthews and Matthews, these books also cite the names of twelve other Persian Wise Men who represented the twelve months of the year and the signs of the zodiac. Four of these allegedly presented gold, the second four myrrh, and the remaining four frankincense.

Another clue about the Wise Men lies in Matthew's Gospel. The phrase "wise men from the east" (2:1) implies the various philosophers, astrologers, and other practitioners of the occult arts at that time. That one or more of the Wise Men came from Persia (presently Iran) is very likely, for the priests, known as Magi (from the Greek *magos*, whence our word "magic"), who belonged to the order of the Persian prophet Zoroaster, dwelt there as master soothsayers and demonologists. By the first century, indeed, the Wise Men were equated with the Magi.

The three gifts which the Wise Men bestowed have been interpreted to be the earliest symbolic portents for the infant Jesus. Gold, a precious metal, has always symbolized royalty; thus the gold represented Jesus as King of Kings and Lord of Lords. Prayers have arisen to

Herod's audience with the three Magi when he learns of the birth of the Messiah. This interview may have taken place as long as two years after Jesus' birth. From Sunday Reading for the Young *(New York: Young & Co., 1903).*

heaven with the burning of sweet incense in ceremonies ancient and modern; thus the frankincense symbolized Jesus as the ultimate High Priest. The ointment myrrh has been used not only as a medicinal balm, but also as an agent in ancient times with which to anoint the deceased prior to burial; thus the myrrh symbolized Jesus as both the Great Physician and as one who would be crucified.

See also **Nativity.**

The Wish That Changed Christmas
See **The Story of Holly and Ivy**

Wooden Soldiers
See **Babes in Toyland**

Works of Art
See **Nativity**

Wreaths
See **Saturnalia**

Wren Hunt
See **Hunting the Wren**

X

Xmas

Abbreviation for "Christmas," derived by combining the Greek letter "Chi" and a contracted form of "Mass" in the Roman Catholic usage. Chi, which resembles an "X," is the first letter in the Greek word for Christ, *Xristos*. Although this abbreviation for Christmas has been in common usage since the twelfth century, over hundreds of years the significance of the letter Chi has been lost among the general public. As a result, people have often protested that using "Xmas" instead of "Christmas" cheapens the season by eliminating Christ or crossing out Christ. This was never the intent of the early Christians who originally developed the abbreviation.

See also **Christmas Day.**

Now old XMAS has come once more,
And boys bring holly to the door.
Now let me hope you'll always find,
Christmas bring gifts of choicest kind.

From an alphabet in American Chatterbox *(New York: Worthington, 1884).*

Y

The Year Without a Santa Claus

Classic children's book (actually a narrative poem) published in 1956 by Phyllis McGinley, subsequently adapted for television as an animated special. In the book, Santa, suffering from a cold and other ailments, announces that he will take a vacation from the hassle of delivering Christmas gifts. At first the news is devastating to children around the world, but six-year-old Ignatius Thistlewhite argues that it is time for Santa to have his own Christmas holiday for a change. Rallying behind Ignatius, children forward millions of gifts to the North Pole, an act which touches Santa beyond measure. With gifts filling his abode, there's no place for the toys except in his sleigh. Seeing his sleigh packed with gifts, Santa declares that he doesn't need a holiday after all.

Not only does he make his usual rounds; he also leaves a special gift and a note of thanks for Ignatius.

In the 1974 animated special featuring stop-motion puppets (Animagic), Santa's belief that the world cares nothing for Christmas prompts Mrs. Claus to send two elves, Jingle and Jangle Bells, out into the world to find some remnant of Christmas spirit. They find it in Ignatius, and together the three experience a whirlwind of adventure with Snowmiser, Heatmiser, Mother Nature, and the mayor of Southtown, USA. Featured songs: "Blue Christmas" and "Here Comes Santa Claus." Narrated and sung by Shirley Booth. Voices: Mickey Rooney, Dick Shawn, George Irving, Robert McFadden, Rhoda Mann, Bradley Bolke, Ron Marshall, Colin Duffy, Christine

Winter, The Wee Winter Singers. Written by William Keenan. Produced and directed by Arthur Rankin, Jr., and Jules Bass. Rankin/Bass Productions. Warner Home Video. Color. 51 min.

Yes, Virginia, There Is a Santa Claus

Title now applied to an editorial by Francis P. Church that appeared in the *New York Sun* on September 21, 1897. Originally headed "Is There a Santa Claus?," the editorial was published in response to a letter written by eight-year-old Virginia O'Hanlon of 115 West 95th Street. Virginia had always believed in Santa but began to have doubts when her friends scoffed at her notions. Well acquainted with the *Sun* because her family often submitted queries to its question-and-answer column regarding matters of historical fact, Virginia wrote, "Papa says, 'If you see it in the *Sun*, it's so.' Please tell me the truth, is there a Santa Claus?" Church's editorial, a masterful and sensitive appeal for Virginia to have faith in what she could not always see, answered with an emphatic "Yes, Virginia, there is a Santa Claus." It became an instant success and was published annually thereafter in the *Sun* until 1949, when the newspaper folded.

Virginia O'Hanlon received numerous inquiries about her letter, to which she always replied with an attractive, printed copy of Church's editorial. Receiving her education at Hunter College and Columbia University, she taught in the New York City school system and also became a principal, retiring after 47 years of service. Virginia O'Hanlon Douglas died in 1971 at the age of 81.

Francis P. Church covered the Civil War for the *New York Times* and spent 20 years as an editorial writer for the *Sun*. His literary interests included controversial issues, especially theology.

Two television versions of the story remain holiday favorites. The animated cartoon *Yes, Virginia, There Is a Santa Claus* (1974), featuring actual photographs of Virginia, Church, and Virginia's father, Dr. Philip O'Hanlon, won an Emmy Award for Outstanding Children's Special for the 1974-75 season. Narrated by Jim Backus. Vocalist: Jimmy Osmond. Voices: Courtney Lemmon, Susan Silo, Billie Green, Sean Manning, Tracy Belland, Christopher Wong, Vickey Ricketts, Jennifer Green, Herb Armstrong, Arnold Ross. Written by Mort Green. Produced by Bill Melendez, Mort Green. Directed by Bill Melendez. A Burt Rosen Company Production in Association with Wolper Productions and Bill Melendez Productions. Paramount Home Video. Color. 30 min.

The live-action drama *Yes, Virginia, There Is a Santa Claus* (1991) is a more fictionalized account of the lives of Virginia (Katherine Isobel), her poverty-stricken father (Richard Thomas), Church (Charles Bronson), and Church's editor (Ed Asner). There, a cynical Church, broken by his wife's death, battles alcoholism amid the holidays. Written by Val De Crowl, Andrew J. Fenady. Produced by Duke Fenady. Directed by Charles Jarrott. Color. Video N/A.

Yogi's First Christmas

(1980). Made-for-television animated cartoon. Ordinarily hibernating in Jellystone National Park at Christmastime, Yogi Bear and pal Boo Boo are awakened by the revelry of other Hanna-Barbera cartoon characters, Huckleberry Hound, Snagglepuss, Augie Doggie, and Doggie Daddy, who are attending Christmas Carnival Week at Jellystone Lodge. The week is fraught with a series of mishaps created by Herman the Hermit in an attempt to get Mrs. Throckmorton, the owner, to sell the lodge. Collaborating with Herman is Snively, Mrs. Throckmorton's young brat of a nephew, who despises Christmas as much as Herman does. Barred from the Christmas Eve tree trimming party because of his attitude, Snively finds Herman poor company compared to the gaiety at the lodge.

At the party Mrs. Throckmorton also hosts a group of orphans, to whom Yogi and Boo Boo (respectively disguised as Santa and elf) distribute gifts. Eventually she takes pity on the two culprits outside and shares Christmas cheer with them as well. When they both receive unexpected and undeserved gifts, Christmas means something more to them than before. Mrs. Throckmorton donates the lodge as a year-round vacation spot for the orphans, and Santa himself arrives with the ideal gift for Yogi: a picnic basket.

Voices: Sue Allen, John Bolks, Daws Butler, Paul DeKorte, Darlene Lawrence, Edie Lehman, Ida Sue McCune, Don Messick, Marilyn Powell, Michael Redman, Andrea Robinson, Marilyn Schreffler, Hal Smith, John Stephenson, Janet Waldo. Written by Willie Gilbert. Produced by Lew Marshall. Directed by Ray Patterson. Hanna-Barbera Productions. World Vision Home Video. Color. Half-hour.

Yule

Midwinter celebration observed by pre–Christian Celtic and Germanic tribes of northern Europe. Yule is thought to have extended from mid–November until the end of January, although sources are not in total agreement regarding the exact time period. Some believe these midwinter festivals originally commenced in November but switched to the time of the winter solstice through contact with, and influence from, the Roman Empire. Others hold that the festival originally centered around the winter solstice.

"Yule" derives from *Jul*, which in turn is thought to derive from several sources, including the Germanic *Giul* and the Saxon *hweol* (both meaning "wheel"); the Germanic *Geola* ("feast"); and "Jolnir," an alternative name for Odin or Woden, king of the Norse gods, to whom sacrifices of boars were made at this time (a boar symbolized Freya, Norse fertility goddess, who rode in a chariot pulled by a boar). Yule celebrated fertility and the rebirth of life and the sun, the latter visualized as a return of the "burning wheel" at the winter solstice.

Yule was a time for bonfires— a symbol of the returning sun in the heavens and the promise of spring — and for revelry and clamor to repel evil spirits which were believed to inhabit the winter darkness. It was a time for divination and magic; a time when Odin, riding upon his white, eight-footed steed Sleipner, descended to collect the souls of Viking warriors slain in battle to his palace, Valhalla; a time when Odin's son Thor rode through the skies in a chariot pulled by two billy goats, Gnasher and Cracker; and a time for feasting. Because heavy November snows barred livestock from grazing, large numbers of cattle were slaugh-

tered for feasts and for sacrifices to Odin. Hence the Venerable Bede (673?–735), the English Benedictine monk and historian, referred to November as *Blotmonath* (Blood Month), and the entire season paralleled the abandon of the Roman Saturnalia.

From the fifth century onward, the Christianization of northern Europe gradually witnessed local Yule customs merging with those of Christmas. By the eleventh century, Yule and Christmas had become synonymous holidays. The formerly venerated gods had fallen away, but other vestiges of Yule remained, which included boisterous revelry and the Yule log with its associated superstitions.

The Yule log is thought to have evolved from the Zagmuk, a New Year festival of ancient Sumer. According to Sumerian mythology, the supreme god, Marduk, annually saved the world from dying at year's end by defeating the monsters of chaos in the underworld. The burning of wooden effigies of those monsters was believed to assist Marduk in his task; hence, primitive Yule logs.

Recalling those midwinter bonfires of past ages, the Yule log of the Middle Ages slowly burned all during the twelve days of Christmas, lest evil befall the house or hall wherein the flame prematurely died. To burn a log for this duration generally required an entire tree trunk, which was placed headlong into the fireplace with the remainder occupying a large portion of the room. Traditionally, each family selected its own Yule log for the following season on Candlemas, February 2, a day that, until the Second Vatican Council (1962–1965), had officially ended the Christmas season in the Roman Catholic Church. Logs often were of ash wood in memory of a legend which held that the Christ Child was first washed and dressed by an ash wood fire; alternatively, logs cut from fruit trees became tokens of the fertility of the land. Logs could also be of oak, olive, or birch wood. The log was never bought. It was laid up to dry during the spring, and a piece of the previous year's log was saved to light the new log, the latter act symbolically cycling the light of life from one year to the next.

Because of the belief that spirits of family ancestors became manifest in the glowing embers, a libation of wine poured over the log

A relatively short Yule log is being dragged to the fire in an Elizabethan-era scene in Harper's New Monthly Magazine, *December 1884.*

beforehand honored their memories, and all who touched the log first purified themselves by washing their hands. A ceremony invoking blessings for Christmas and the coming new year customarily preceded the lighting. In medieval England, tenants often presented Yule logs to their landlords, who in turn furnished their meals for as long as the log burned. On the same note, slaves in the antebellum United States were granted rest from their work for this duration; to prolong the burning, slaves first soaked the log in water.

A number of other customs and superstitions surrounded the Yule log, including the following:

A person casting a headless shadow from the light of the fire would die within one year.

In certain parts of England, the log was banded or hooped with strips of the same tree. As each band snapped, the master of the house was expected to furnish his guests with a fresh bowl of cider or liquor. The bands were often associated with pairs of lovers, and the order of the snapping bands predicted the sequence of their weddings.

Upon beating the log, one could see evil spirits departing in a shower of sparks.

A barefoot person, squinting person, or a

A Victorian Yule scene, with a very big Yule log (obviously the bottom of a pollarded tree like those still standing). From Robert Chambers, ed., A Book of Days *(London and Edinburgh: Chambers, 1879).*

flat-footed woman approaching the log brought bad luck.

Ashes from the log, if placed in fruit trees, improved the crop yield, and if placed under the bed, prevented lightning from striking the house.

Today, the custom of burning a Yule log still exists in Europe and the United States, albeit on a much smaller scale than in earlier days. Instead of a continuous, twelve-day burning, the trend is to burn the log only during Christmas Eve and Christmas Day; alternatively, some prefer to burn their log for a brief period on each of those twelve days. In France, the Yule log survives only as log-shaped cake, the *bûche de Noël* ("Christmas log").

See also **Saturnalia; Superstitions; The Twelve Days of Christmas; Winter Solstice.**

Yule Log
See **Yule**

Z

Ziggy's Gift

(1982). Made-for-television animated cartoon based on the popular comic strip *Ziggy*, created by Tom Wilson.

Responding to an ad recruiting street Santas for charity, Ziggy unwittingly peddles for a fraudulent ring run by the Fly-By-Nite Loan Company. Dogged by a petty thief as well as a policeman intent on arresting Ziggy as one of the ring, Ziggy still manages to perform good deeds, such as miraculously pulling cash from his empty kettle for donations, liberating live Christmas turkeys, and befriending a homeless man. Ziggy's greatest gift is to the children at Mrs. Ostblom's Foster Home, in which the thief and cop also become unsuspecting instruments of Christmas magic for the little ones. This program, Ziggy's first prime-time special, won an Emmy Award for Outstanding Animated Program (1982-83 season).

Voices: Richard Williams, Tom Mc-Greevey, Tony Giorgio, John Gibbons, Harry Nillson, David Arias, Perry Botkin, Katrina Fried, Natasha Fried, Jack Hanrahan, Linda Harmon, Anna Ostblom, Latoya Prescod, Gloria Prosper, Andy Raub, Terry Stillwell-Harriton, Lena Tabori, Holly Williams, Tim Williams, Tom Wilson, Tom Wilson, Jr. Written by Tom Wilson. Produced by Tom Wilson, Richard Williams, and Lena Tabori. Directed by Richard Williams. A Welcome Production in Association with Universal Press Syndicate. Vestron Video. Color. 30 min.

Zimbabwe

See **Africa**

References

Abate, Frank R., ed. *Omni Gazetteer of the United States of America*. 9 vols. Detroit: Omnigraphics, 1991.

Alcott, Louisa May. *Little Women*. New York: Pocket Books, 1994.

Alston, G. Cyprian. "Boy-Bishop." In *The Catholic Encyclopedia*, 1913. New Advent, Inc. www.knight.org/advent/cathen/02725a.htm

"American Express Retail Index Finds More Consumers Planning to Begin Their Holiday Shopping on the Day after Thanksgiving." American Express Company. home3.americanexpress.c...rp/latestnews/black-friday.asp

Andersen, Hans Christian. *The Complete Illustrated Stories of Hans Christian Andersen*. Translated from the Danish by H. W. Dulcken. Illustrations by A. W. Bayes. London: Chancellor Press, 1982.

Andrews, Bart. *The "I Love Lucy" Book*. New York: Doubleday, 1985.

Armenta, Martin A. "Las Posadas: Christmas in Mexico." The Mining Company Guide to Mexican Culture. mexicanculture.tqn.com/library/weekly/aa121397.htm

"ASCAP Announces Top 25 Holiday Songs of the Century." American Society of Composers, Authors and Publishers. www.ascap.com/press/holiday-121598.html

Ashe, Geoffery. "Magical Glastonbury." Britannia, Gateway to the British Isles. www.britannia.com/history/glaston1.html

Auld, William Muir. *Christmas Traditions*. New York: Macmillan, 1931.

"Auld Lang Syne." In *The Burns Encyclopedia*. The Official Robert Burns Site. www.robertburns.org/encyclopedia

"Australian Christmas Plants." Australian National Botanic Gardens. www.anbg.gov.au/christmas/christmas.html

Autry, Gene. *Back in the Saddle Again*. Garden City, New York: Doubleday, 1978.

"*Babes in Toyland*: The 1934 Classic Film Starring Stan Laurel and Oliver Hardy." Way Out West Tent. www.wayoutwest.org/toyland

Baggelaar, Kristin, and Donald Milton. "John Jacob Niles." In *Folk Music: More Than a Song*. New York: Thomas Y. Crowell, 1976.

Barrett, John. *The Bear Who Slept Through Christmas*. Illustrations by Rick Reinert Productions. Developed by the LeFave Company. Chicago: Children's Press, 1980.

Barth, Edna. *Holly, Reindeer, and Colored Lights: The Story of the Christmas Symbols*. New York: Seabury Press, 1971.

Bartlett, Clifford. Program notes for George Frideric Handel, *Messiah*. Bavarian Radio Symphony Orchestra and Chorus. Sir Colin Davis. Philips compact disc set 412 538-2, 1985.

Basinger, Jeanine. *The "It's a Wonderful Life" Book*. New York: Alfred A. Knopf, 1986.

Baum, L. Frank. *The Life and Adventures of Santa Claus*. Illustrated edition with pictures by Mary Cowles Clark. New York: Greenwich House, 1983.

Baxter, Batsell Barrett, and Harold Hazelip. *A Devotional Guide to Bible Lands*. Grand Rapids, Michigan: Baker Book House, 1979.

Beck, Denis P., Sr. "History of the King Cake." home.sprynet.com/~dpbeck/kingcake/kingcake.htm

Bemelmans, Ludwig. *Madeline's Christmas*. New York: Viking Kestrel, 1985.

Berenstain, Stan, and Jan Berenstain. *The Berenstain Bears' Christmas Tree*. New York: Random House, 1980.

Bertrin, Georges, and Arthur F. J. Remy. "Miracle Plays and Mysteries." In *The Catholic Encyclopedia*, 1911. New Advent, Inc. www.newadvent.org/cathen/10348a.htm

Bindokiene, Danute Brazyte. *Lithuanian Customs and Traditions*. Translated from the Lithuanian by Vita Matusaitis. Chicago: Lithuanian World Community, 1989.

Black, Naomi, Nancy Kalish, and Loretta Mowat, eds. *The Whole Christmas Catalogue: The Complete Compendium of Christmas Traditions, Recipes, Crafts, Carols, Lore, and More*. Philadelphia: Running Press, 1994.

Briggs, Raymond. *Father Christmas*. New York: Coward, McCann, and Geoghegan, 1973.

_____. *The Snowman*. New York: Random House, 1978.

Brown, Les. *Les Brown's Encyclopedia of Television*. New Expanded Edition. New York: Zoetrope, 1982.

Brunhoff, Jean de. *Babar and Father Christmas*. Translated from the French by Merle Haas. New York: Random House, 1940.

Campbell, Kathleen. "Notes on the English Mystery Plays." Medieval Images and Biblical Interpretation, Austin College, Sherman, Texas. artemis.austinc.edu/acad/hwc22/medieval/index.html

Capote, Truman. *A Christmas Memory*. New York: Random House, 1956.

_____. *One Christmas*. New York: Random House, 1983.

Carpenter, Humphrey. *Benjamin Britten: A Biography*. New York: Charles Scribner's Sons, 1992.

Cathcart, Rex. "Festive Capers? Barring Out the Schoolmaster." *History Today*. (December 1988).

Cayetano, Sebastian R. "Garifuna Music." Garifuna World. www.garifuna-world.com/musigari.htm

Chalmers, Irena. *The Great American Christmas Almanac*. New York: Viking Penguin, 1988.

Chambers, E. K. *The English Folk-Play*, 1933. Reprint. New York: Haskell House, 1966.

"Christmas and New Year's Eve in Denmark." The Royal Danish Embassy, Washington, D.C. www.denmarkemb.org/danskjul.html

"Christmas Around the World." From Christmas.com, Inc. Christmas Information Services. christmas.com/worldview

Christmas in Australia. Chicago: World Book, 1998.

"Christmas in Austria." Austrian Press and Information Service, Washington, D.C. www.austria.org/ausmas.html

Christmas in Brazil. Chicago: World Book, 1991.

Christmas in Britain. Chicago: World Book, 1996

Christmas in Canada. Chicago: World Book, 1994.

Christmas in Colonial and Early America. Chicago: World Book, 1996.

Christmas in Denmark. Chicago: World Book, 1986.

Christmas in France. Chicago: World Book, 1996.

Christmas in Ireland. Chicago: World Book, 1996.

Christmas in Italy. Chicago: World Book, 1996.

"Christmas in Luxembourg." The Grand Duchy of Luxembourg. ourworld.compuserve.com...ges/hotel_claravallis/xmas.htm

Christmas in Mexico. Chicago: World Book, 1996.

"Christmas in Norway." The Royal Norwegian Ministry of Foreign Affairs, Washington, D.C. odin.dep.no/ud/publ/x-mas/engelsk/velkommen.html

Christmas in Poland. Chicago: World Book, 1989.

Christmas in Russia. Chicago: World Book, 1997.

Christmas in Spain. Chicago: World Book, 1996.

Christmas in Switzerland. Chicago: World Book, 1995.

Christmas in the American Southwest. Chicago: World Book, 1996.

Christmas in the Holy Land. Chicago. World Book, 1987.

Christmas in the Philippines. Chicago: World Book, 1990.

Christmas in Today's Germany. Chicago: World Book, 1993.

Christmas in Ukraine. Chicago: World Book, 1997.

"The Christmas Pageant of Peace and National Christmas Tree." The National Park Service. www.nps.gov/ncro/PublicAffairs/NationalChristmasTree.htm

The Christmas Story Told Through Paintings. Commentary by Richard Mühlberger. New York: The Metropolitan Museum of Art and GulliverBooks/Harcourt Brace Jovanovich, 1990.

"Christmas Traditions in France and in Canada." French Ministry of Culture and Canadian Heritage. www.culture.fr:80/culture/noel/angl/noel.htm

"Christmas Trees." The National Christmas Tree Association. www.itschristmas.com/tree.htm

Crowley, T. J. "Feast of Asses." In *The Catholic Encyclopedia*, 1913. New Advent, Inc. www.knight.org/advent/cathen/01798b.htm

Crowther, Stuart. "Hogmanay! The Scots at New Year." Essential Scotland.www.caithnessmm.co.uk/discover/essential/esshogm.html

Czech, Beata. "Christmas Eve Superstitions." Internet Polska. www.polishworld.com/christmas/

"Czech Christmas 1999." Radio Prague. www.radio.cz/christmas

Davies, Valentine. *Miracle on 34th Street*. Text, 20th Century–Fox Film Corporation, 1947. Illustrated edition, with an introduction by Elizabeth Davies and paintings

by Tomie dePaola, New York: Harcourt Brace Jovanovich, 1984.

Dearmer, Percy, R. Vaughn Williams, and Martin Shaw. *The Oxford Book of Carols*. New York: Oxford University Press, 1964.

"December 24, 25, 26." *In The Book of Days*, edited by Robert Chambers. Vol. 2, 1862–1864. Reprint, Detroit: Gale Research, 1967.

Del Re, Gerard, and Patricia Del Re. *The Christmas Almanac*. Garden City, New York: Doubleday, 1979.

Dickens, Charles. *A Christmas Carol and Other Christmas Books*. Everyman's Library. New York: E. P. Dutton, 1961.

_____. *Christmas Stories*. The Oxford Illustrated Dickens. New York: Oxford University Press, 1956.

_____. "A Good-Humored Christmas Chapter" and "The Story of the Goblins Who Stole a Sexton." Chaps. 28 and 29 in *The Pickwick Papers*. New York: Penguin Books United States, 1964.

"Dr. Elmo's Biography Page." Laughing Stock Records. www.picklehead.com/elmo/bio.html

Dr. Seuss. *How the Grinch Stole Christmas*. New York: Random House, 1957.

Donovan, Stephen M. "Crib." In *The Catholic Encyclopedia*, 1908. New Advent, Inc. www.newadvent.org/cathen/04488c.htm

Drum, Walter. "Magi." In *The Catholic Encyclopedia*, 1910. New Advent, Inc. www.newadvent.org/cathen/09527a.htm

Dumitru, Petru, and students. "Romanian Customs and Traditions." The Duiliu Zamfirescu School, Focsani, Romania.festivals. projects.eun.org/Romania

Dumois, Luis. "Inside Mexico, the Series: Posadas, Pastorelas and Nacimientos." Mexico Connect. www.mexconnect.com

Duris, Joseph, ed. *Slovak Christmas: A Symposium of Songs, Customs and Plays*. Cleveland, Ohio: Slovak Institute, 1960.

Edelstein, Andrew J., and Frank Lovece. *"The Brady Bunch" Book*. New York: Warner Books, 1990.

Egan, Bill. "Oldest Known 'Silent Night' Manuscript Discovered." *Austrian Information*. www.austria.org/dec96/silent.html

_____. "The Song Heard 'Round the World." *Austrian Information* (December 1999).

Elliott, Sara. *Italian Renaissance Painting*. London: Phaidon Press, 1993.

Esselman, Mary. "Remembering Christmas in Belize." www.companysj.com/v162/remembering.html

"Estonia's Folk Traditions: Christmas and Christmas Customs." Estonian Foreign Ministry. www.mfa.ee/eng/comesee/christmas.html

Evans, Richard Paul. *The Christmas Box*. New York: Simon and Schuster, 1995.

"A Festival of Nine Lessons and Carols." King's College, Cambridge, England. bear.kings.cam.ac.uk/chapel/9lessons/history.html

"Folklore Traditions of the Winter Months in Austria." Austrian National Tourist Office. www.anto.com/artikel3.htm

Frankel, Stanley A. "The Story Behind 'Rudolph, the Red-Nosed Reindeer.'" *Good Housekeeping* (December 1989).

Fries, Adelaide L. *Customs and Practices of the Moravian Church*. Revised Edition. Winston-Salem, North Carolina: Moravian Board of Christian Education and Evangelism, 1973.

Frost, Robert. *Christmas Trees*. Text, New York: Holt, Rinehart and Winston, 1916. Illustrated edition by Ted Rand, New York: Henry Holt and Company, 1990.

Gardner, Martin, ed. *The Annotated Night Before Christmas: A Collection of Sequels, Parodies, and Imitations of Clement Moore's Immortal Ballad About Santa Claus.* New York: Summit Books, 1991.

Garrison, Webb. *Treasury of Christmas Stories.* Nashville: Rutledge Hill Press, 1990.

Gilson, Nancy. "A Trunk Show: Son Carries on Father's Legacy of an Elephant." *Dispatch Arts Reporter.* Pertains to *Babar and Father Christmas.* www.cd.columbus.oh.us/news/newsfea98/jan98/babar0119.html

Godden, Rumer. *The Story of Holly and Ivy.* 1957. Illustrated edition by Barbara Cooney, New York: Viking Penguin, 1985.

Greene, Richard Leighton, ed. *The Early English Carols,* Second Edition. Oxford, England: Clarendon Press, 1977.

Griffith, Alison B. "Mithraism." The Ecole Initiative. Hosted by The University of Evansville, Evansville, Indiana. cedar.evansville.edu/~ecoleweb/articles/mithraism.html

Grubb, Nancy. *Angels in Art.* New York: Artabras, 1995.

Gulevich, Tanya. *Encyclopedia of Christmas.* Illustrated by Mary Ann Stavros-Lanning. Detroit: Omnigraphics, 2000.

Hamilton, James. "Paintings." In *Christmas,* edited by Jacqueline Ridley. Poole, Dorset, Great Britain: Blandford Press, 1978.

Hamner, Earl, Jr. *The Homecoming: A Novel About Spencer's Mountain.* New York: Random House, 1970.

"Hanby House" (regarding Benjamin R. Hanby). Ohio Historical Society. www.ohiohistory.org/places/hanby

Hardy, Thomas. "The Oxen." In *The Complete Poems of Thomas Hardy,* edited by James Gibson. New York: Macmillan, 1976.

Harrison, Jim. *American Christmas.* Atlanta: Longstreet Press, 1994.

Hartman, Tom, ed. *Guinness Book of Christmas.* Enfield, Middlesex, England: Guinness Books, 1984.

Haynes, Page. "Beautiful Star Rises from Rutherford County Barn." Tennessee Farmers Cooperative. www.ourcoop.com/News_Features/Feat_archive/beth-star.htm

Haynie, Elizabeth. *The Christmas Book of Lists.* Downers Grove, Illinois: Anton Enterprises, 1994.

Henry, O. *The Gift of the Magi.* 1905. Reprint, Mankato, Minnesota: Creative Education, 1984.

Hicks, Anthony. Program notes for George Frideric Handel, *Messiah: A Sacred Oratorio.* Choir of Christ Church Cathedral, Oxford, and The Academy of Ancient Music. Christopher Hogwood. Decca Records *Editions de L'oiseau-Lyre* box set SD189D 3, 1980. Long-playing records.

Hill, Richard S. "Not So Far Away in a Manger: Forty-One Settings of an American Carol." *Notes,* Vol. 3 (December 1945).

"History of Medford" (information regarding Lydia Maria Child and James Pierpont). In *Over the River and Through the Wood,* an on-line project of Hobbs Middle School (Class of 1996) and the Medford Historical Society, Massachusetts. www.medford.org/fHistoryX.htm

"History of the Cracker." Absolutely Crackers. www.absolutelycrackers.com/historynew.html

"History of the Declaration of Christmas Peace in Turku, Finland." City of Turku, Finland. www.christmas-city.com/eng/historica.html

"History of *The Nutcracker Ballet.*" The Kirov Ballet Home Page. www.webcom.com/shownet/kirov/nuthist.html

Hoffmann, E. T. A. *Nutcracker.* Translation of *Nussknacker und Mausekönig* from the German by Ralph Manheim. Pictures by Maurice Sendak. New York: Crown, 1984.

"Holiday Sales Data." National Retail Federation. www.nrf.com/hot/holiday/dec98.htm

Holme, Reginald. "Christmas Around the World." In *Christmas,* edited by Jacqueline Ridley. Poole, Dorset, Great Britain: Blandford Press, 1978.

Holweck, Frederick G. "Candlemas." In *The Catholic Encyclopedia,* 1913. New Advent, Inc. www.knight.org/advent/cathen/03245b.htm

_____. "Holy Innocents." In *The Catholic Encyclopedia,* 1913. New Advent, Inc. www.knight.org/advent/cathen/07419a.htm

Hottes, Alfred Carl. *1001 Christmas Facts and Fancies.* New York: Dodd, Mead, 1944.

Howells, W. D. "Christmas Every Day." In *Christmas Every Day and Other Stories Told for Children.* New York: Harper and Brothers, 1892.

Hughes, Langston. *Carol of the Brown King: Nativity Poems.* Illustrated by Ashley Bryan. New York: Atheneum, 1998.

Irving, Washington. *History, Tales, and Sketches.* Edited by James W. Tuttleton. The Library of America. New York: Literary Classics of the United States, 1983.

_____. *The Sketch Book of Geoffrey Crayon, Gent.* Everyman's Library. New York: Dutton, 1963.

The Japan of Today. Third edition. Tokyo: The International Society for Educational Information, 1996.

"Jean Shepherd Page." Provided by Bob Kaye. www.spacelab.net/~bkaye/Shep.html

"Jean Shepherd Web Site." Provided by Jim Sadur. www.intercall.net/~jsadur/shep.htm

Jesko, Mark. "Christmas in Eastern Slovakia." The Baltimore Czech and Slovak Heritage Association. www.iarelative.com/xmas/jesko.htm

"John Wesley Work, Jr." In "Hymnuts Web Site." Luther Seminary, St. Paul, MN. hymnuts.luthersem.edu

Jones, Nick. Program Notes for Handel's *Messiah.* Atlanta Symphony Orchestra and Chamber Chorus. Robert Shaw. Telarc compact disc set CD-80093, 1984.

Jonson, Ben. *Christmas His Masque.* In *Ben Jonson: The Complete Masques,* edited by Stephen Orgel. The Yale Ben Jonson, 4. New Haven, Connecticut: Yale University Press, 1969.

Kaufman, Joanne. "Life in Hell's Matt Groening Goes Overboard to Make *The Simpsons* the First Family of TV 'Toons." *People Weekly* (December 18, 1989).

Keyte, Hugh, and Andrew Parrott, eds. *The New Oxford Book of Carols.* New York: Oxford University Press, 1992.

Kiesewetter, John. "'Grandma' Novelty Song Keeps Dr. Elmo in the Christmas Green." *The Tennessean* (December 10, 1997).

Kightly, Charles. *The Customs and Ceremonies of Britain: An Encyclopedia of Living Traditions.* New York: Thames and Hudson, 1986.

Kirkpatrick, David D. "Whose Jolly Old Elf Is That, Anyway?" *The New York Times* (October 26, 2000).

Lamb, Peter. Program Notes for Benjamin Britten, *A Ceremony of Carols.* Westminster Cathedral Choir. David Hill. Hyperion compact disc CDA66220, 1986.

"Langston Hughes: The Poet Laureate of Harlem." Queens Borough Public Library. mickey.queens.lib.ny.us/special/langston.bio.html

Lankford, Mary D. *Christmas Around the World.* New York: Morrow Junior Books, 1995.

Lawrence, Robert Means. "Horses' Heads as Talismans." *The Magic of the Horse-Shoe* (1898). conjurefolk.tripod.com/horsehead.html

Lenburg, Jeff. *The Encyclopedia of Animated Cartoons.* Second Edition. New York: Checkmark Books, 1999.

Libby, Jennifer. "Five Good Reasons to Spend Christmas in Costa Rica." *Guide Magazine.* www.cocori.com/guide/old96/articles/xmas.htm

Linder, Vladimir. "Slovak Christmas Traditions." The Slovak Heritage and Cultural Society of British Columbia. www.iarelative.com/xmas/bc_xmas.htm

Lishtar. "Akitu: The Babylonian New Year's Festival." Gateways to Babylon. www.angelfire.com/tx/gatestobabylon/Akitu.html

"Lithuanian Customs and Traditions: Christmas Eve." Lithuanian-American Community, Inc. avlb.org/educat/tradicijos/kucios.html

"Llangollen International Eisteddfod: How It Started." Llangollen International Musical Eisteddfod. www.llangollen.com/eist3.html

Longfellow, Henry Wadsworth. "The Three Kings." In *The Complete Poetical Works of Henry Wadsworth Longfellow,* edited by Horace E. Scudder. Student's Cambridge Edition. Boston: Houghton Mifflin, 1922.

Margetson, Stella. "Medieval Nativity Plays." *History Today* (December 1972).

"Mari Lwyd: The Magic of the Mari." Celfyddydau Mari Arts. www.folkwales.org.uk/mari.html

Marston, Elsa. *Lebanon: A New Light in an Ancient Land.* New York: Macmillan, 1994.

Martindale, Cyril. "Christmas." In *The Catholic Encyclopedia,* 1913. New Advent, Inc. www.knight.org/advent/cathen/03724b.htm

_____. "Epiphany." In *The Catholic Encyclopedia,* 1913. New Advent, Inc. www.knight.org/advent/cathen/05504c.htm

"Masque." In *The Cambridge Guide to Theatre,* edited by Martin Banham. Revised edition. Cambridge, England: Cambridge University Press, 1995.

"Masque." In *The Oxford Companion to the Theatre,* edited by Phyllis Hartnoll. Third edition. New York: Oxford University Press, 1967.

Mastrantonis, Rev. George. "The Feast of Epiphany: The Feast of Lights." The Greek Orthodox Archdiocese of America. www.goarch.org/access/orthodoxfaith/ epiphany.html

Matthews, John, and Caitlin Matthews. *The Winter Solstice: The Sacred Traditions of Christmas.* Wheaton, Illinois: Quest Books, 1998.

May, Robert L. *Rudolph, the Red-Nosed Reindeer.* Illustrated by Denver Gillen. Chicago: Montgomery Ward, 1939.

_____. *Rudolph, the Red-Nosed Reindeer, Shines Again.* Chicago: Follett, 1954. Reprinted as *Rudolph Shines Again,* illustrated by Diana Magnuson. Chicago: Follett, 1981.

_____. *Rudolph's Second Christmas.* Illustrated by Michael Emberley. Bedford, Massachusetts: Applewood Books, 1992.

Mayell, Hillary. "The Evolution of the Christmas Flower." Environmental News Network. www.enn.com/features/1998/12/120498/poinsettia.asp

McCloud, Barry, et al. *Definitive Country: The Ultimate Encyclopedia of Country Music and Its Performers.* New York: Berkley, 1995.

McCrohan, Donna, and Peter Crescenti. The Honeymooners Lost Episodes. New York: Workman, 1986.

McGinley, Phyllis. *The Year Without a Santa Claus.* Pictures by Kurt Werth. New York: J. B. Lippincott, 1957.

"Medieval Drama in Europe." In *The Cambridge Guide to Theatre,* edited by Martin Banham. Revised edition. Cambridge, England: Cambridge University Press, 1995.

Menotti, Gian Carlo. *Amahl and the Night Visitors.* New York: G. Schirmer, 1951. Adaptation, New York: William Morrow, 1986.

_____. *Amahl and the Night Visitors: Original Cast of the NBC Telecast, Christmas Eve, 1951.* RCA Gold Seal compact disc 6485-2-RG, 1987.

Mershman, Francis. "Advent." In *The Catholic Encyclopedia,* 1913. New Advent, Inc. www. knight.org/advent

Mikkelson, Barbara. "Origin of the Candy Cane." Urban Legends Reference Pages. www.snopes.com/holidays/xmas/cndycane.htm

_____, and David Mikkelson. "Rudolph, the Red-Nosed Reindeer." Urban Legends Reference Pages. www.snopes.com/holidays/xmas/rudolph.htm

Milton, John. "On the Morning of Christ's Nativity." In *The Complete Poetical Works of John Milton,* edited by Douglas Bush. Cambridge Edition. Boston: Houghton Mifflin, 1965.

"Mummers Parade." The Philadelphia Recreation Department. www.phila.gov/departments/recreation/mummers.htm

"Mummers' Play." In *Cassell Companion to Theatre.* Revised edition. London: Market House Books, 1997.

"Mumming." Medieval Images and Biblical Interpretation, Austin College, Sherman, Texas. artemis.austinc.edu/acad/hwc22/medieval/index.html

"Mumming Play." In *The Oxford Companion to the Theatre,* edited by Phyllis Hartnoll. Third edition. New York: Oxford University Press, 1967.

Nosal, Salomea. "The Polish Christmas Tradition." The Polish American Journal. www. polamjournal.com/library/christmas.html#Tradition

Ola, Per, and Emily D'Aulaire. "Glorious Gift from Christmas Past." *Reader's Digest* (December 1993).

"Our Nation's Christmas Tree." The National Park Service. www.nps.gov/seki/xmastree.htm

Palfrey, Dale Hoyt. "Feliz Navidad: Making Merry in Mexico." Mexico Connect. www.mexconnect.com

"Pantomime, English." In *The Cambridge Guide to Theatre,* edited by Martin Banham. Revised edition. Cambridge, England: Cambridge University Press, 1995.

"Pantomime." In *The Oxford Companion to the Theatre,* edited by Phyllis Hartnoll. Third edition. New York: Oxford University Press, 1967.

"Pasadena Tournament of Roses." The City of Pasadena, California. www.tournamentofroses.com/index.html

"Patsy Trigg (of Elmo & Patsy)." *Chicago Tribune.* (December 16, 1990).

Pattillo, Craig W. *Christmas on Record: Best Selling Xmas Singles and Albums of the Past 40 Years.* Portland, Oregon: Braemer Books, 1983.

Perry, Leonard. "Herbs with a Holiday History." The University of Vermont Extension, Department of Plant and Soil Science. pss.uvm.edu/ppp/articles/xmasherb.html

Perton, Marvin H. "Celebrating Christmas in Mexico." Mexico Online. www.mexonline.com/xmas.htm

Pilato, Herbie J. *Bewitched Forever: The Immortal Companion to Television's Most Magical Supernatural Situation Comedy.* Arlington, Texas: Summit, 1996.

The Postal Service Guide to U.S. Stamps. 25th Special Edition, 1999 Stamp Values. Washington, D.C.: United States Postal Service, 1998.

Prescott, Dorothy. "Saints." In *Christmas,* edited by Jacqueline Ridley. Poole, Dorset, Great Britain: Blandford Press, 1978.

Restad, Penne. "Christmas in Nineteenth-Century America." *History Today* (December 1995).

Ridley, Michael. "Cards." In *Christmas*, edited by Jacqueline Ridley. Poole, Dorset, Great Britain: Blandford Press, 1978.

"Riga at Yuletide." Riga in Your Pocket. www.inyourpocket.com/Latvia/Riga_christmas.htm

Rihtman-Auguštin, Dunja. *Christmas in Croatia*. Translated from the Croatian by Nina H. Antoljak. Zagreb, Croatia: Golden Marketing, 1997.

Robinson, Barbara. *The Best Christmas Pageant Ever*. Pictures by Judith Gwyn Brown. New York: HarperCollins, 1972.

Robinson, Dale, and David Fernandes. *The Definitive "Andy Griffith Show" Reference: Episode-by-Episode, with Cast and Production Biographies and a Guide to Collectibles*. Jefferson, North Carolina: McFarland, 1996.

Robinson, James Harvey, ed. "Willibald's Life of Boniface." In *Readings in European History*. Vol. 1. Boston: Ginn, 1904.

Robinson, Paschal. "St. Francis of Assisi." In *The Catholic Encyclopedia*, 1909. New Advent, Inc. www.newadvent.org/cathen/06221a.htm

Rock, Gail. *The House Without a Christmas Tree*. New York: Alfred A. Knopf, 1974.

"The Salvation Army." The Salvation Army United States. www.salvationarmyusa.org

Sammon, Paul. *The "Christmas Carol" Trivia Book: Everything You Ever Wanted to Know About Every Version of the Dickens Classic*. New York: Citadel Press, 1994.

Sansom, William. *A Book of Christmas*. New York: McGraw-Hill, 1968.

Sawyer, Edwin A. *All About the Moravians: History, Beliefs, and Practices of a Worldwide Church*. Bethlehem, Pennsylvania: The Moravian Church, Northern Province, 1990.

Schug-Wille, Christa. *Art of the Byzantine World*. Translated from the German by E. M. Hatt. Panorama of World Art. New York: Harry N. Abrams, 1969.

Scott, Sir Walter. *Poetical Works: With the Author's Introduction and Notes*, edited by J. Logie Robertson. London: Oxford University Press, 1904.

Shakespeare, William. *The Complete Works of William Shakespeare with Themes of the Plays*. New York: Walter J. Black, 1937.

Sheler, Jeffery L. "In Search of Christmas." *U.S. News and World Report*. www.usnews.com/usnews/issue/23xmas.htm

"Shetland Islands Norse a Hangover and Torch a Longship, Too." Cable News Network. www.cnn.com/world/9801/29/norse.festival

Siefker, Phyllis. *Santa Claus, Last of the Wild Men*. Jefferson, North Carolina: McFarland, 1997.

Simon, William L., ed. *The Reader's Digest Merry Christmas Songbook*. Pleasantville, New York: The Reader's Digest Association, 1981.

Smalls, Irene. "Johnkankus: Roots of an African-American Christmas." new.melanet.com/Johnkankus/roots.html

Smith, Brian. "History of Up-Helly-Aa." *The Shetland Times Ltd*. www.up-helly-aa.org.uk/history.htm

Smith, Jon Guyot. "Liner notes for Gene Autry, *Sing, Cowboy, Sing! The Gene Autry Collection*." Rhino Records. www.rhino.com/ features/liners/72630lin.html#track

Smith, Richard Norton. *Christmas Around the World*. West Branch, Iowa: Herbert Hoover Presidential Library Association, 1993.

Snodgrass, Denise. "The Zagmuk" and "Saturnalia." In *Heathen Holidays*. www.prime.org/holiday/xmas2.html

Snyder, Phillip V. *The Christmas Tree Book: The History of the Christmas Tree and Antique Christmas Ornaments*. New York: Viking, 1976.

"Sports History." HickokSports.com. www.hickoksports.com/history

Staufer, Countess Maria Hubert von. "The Great British Christmas." The Christmas Archives. people.delphi.com/mariachristm/gbx.html

Stockert, Father Hal. "Origin of 'The Twelve Days of Christmas': An Underground Catechism." Catholic Information Network. www.cin.org /twelvday.html

Stradley, Linda. "History and Legends of Famous Foods." What's Cooking America. www.geocities.com/familysecrets/History/HistoryIndex.htm

Strassfeld, Michael. *The Jewish Holidays: A Guide and Commentary*. New York: HarperCollins, 1985.

Studwell, William. *The Christmas Carol Reader*. Binghamton, New York: Harrington Park Press, 1995.

_____. *Christmas Carols: A Reference Guide*. New York: Garland, 1985.

Swahn, Jan-Öjvind. *Maypoles, Crayfish and Lucia: Swedish Holidays and Traditions*. Stockholm: The Swedish Institute, 1999.

Swiney, Cathleen. "Grandma's Hit." *The Tennessee Magazine* (December 1995).

Tazewell, Charles. *The Littlest Angel*. Chicago: Children's Press, 1946. Illustrated Edition by Paul Micich, Nashville: Ideals, 1991.

_____. *The Littlest Snowman*. Pictures by George De Santis. New York: Grosset and Dunlap, 1958.

_____. *The Littlest Tree*. Illustrated by Karen A. Jerome. Nashville: Ideals, 1997.

_____. *The Small One: A Story for Those Who Like Christmas and Small Donkeys*. Illustrated by Franklin Whitman. Philadelphia: John C. Winston Company, 1947.

Thomas, Dylan. *A Child's Christmas in Wales*. Text, New Directions, 1954. Illustrated edition by Trina Schart Hyman. New York: Holiday House, 1985.

Thompson, Charles. *Bing: The Authorized Biography*. New York: David McKay, 1975.

Thompson, Jack. "Ha Ha! Look at Rudolph." Michigan State University. www.hfs.msu.edu/~thomps34/ rudolph.html

Thompson, Sue Ellen, ed. *Holiday Symbols 1998*. Detroit: Omnigraphics, 1998.

Thurston, Herbert. "Feast of Fools." In *The Catholic Encyclopedia*, 1913. New Advent, Inc. www.knight.org/advent/cathen/06132a.htm

Tierney, John J. "Feast of the Circumcision." In *The Catholic Encyclopedia*, 1908. New Advent, Inc. www.newadvent.org/cathen/03779a. htm

_____. "New Year's Day." In *The Catholic Encyclopedia*, 1911. New Advent, Inc. www.newadvent.org/cathen /11019a.htm

"Toys for Tots." Kitsap Community Network. www.kitsap.net/toysfortots/history.html

Van Allsburg, Chris. *The Polar Express*. Boston: Houghton Mifflin, 1985.

Van Ausdall, Clair W. Program notes for *Joy to the World*. Reader's Digest compact disc set RC7-103, 1994.

Van Dyke, Henry. *The First Christmas Tree: A Story of the Forest*. Marietta, Georgia: The Larlin Corporation, 1987.

_____. *The Other Wise Man*. Fort Worth, Texas: Brownlow, 1989.

Vuolio, Kaisu. "Christmas in Finland." Virtual Finland. virtual.finland.fi/finfo/english/joulueng.html

Wakefield, Charito Calvachi. *Navidad Latinoamericana: Latin American Christmas*. Lancaster, Pennsylvania: Latin American Creations, 1997.

Walburg, Lori. *The Legend of the Candy Cane.* Illustrated by James Bernardin. Grand Rapids, Michigan: Zondervan, 1997.

Waldron, Vince. *The Official "Dick Van Dyke Show" Book.* New York: Hyperion, 1994.

Walkup, Nancy. "The Retablo and Beyond: A Cross-Cultural View of Personal Shrines." North Texas Institute for Educators on the Visual Arts. www.art.unt.edu/ntieva/artcurr/latino/retablo.htm

Wallace, Lew. *Ben-Hur: A Tale of the Christ.* New York: Harper and Row, 1880.

Walsh, Alex. *Disney's "The Small One."* Illustrated by Jesse Clay. New York: Disney, 1995.

The Waltons. Blue Ridge Publications. www.the-waltons.com/home-b.html

Wernecke, Herbert H. *Christmas Customs Around the World.* Philadelphia: Westminster Press, 1959.

West, Ewan. Program notes for Peter Ilyich Tchaikovsky, *The Nutcracker.* Royal Philharmonic Orchestra. Andre Previn. EMI compact disc set CDS 7472678, 1986.

Whitburn, Joel. *The Billboard Book of Top 40 Hits.* Sixth Edition. New York: Billboard, 1996.

_____. Program notes for *Billboard Greatest Christmas Hits: 1935–1954.* Rhino compact disc DPC1 0884, 1989.

_____. Program notes for *Billboard Greatest Christmas Hits: 1955–Present.* Rhino compact disc DPC1 0885, 1989.

"White Christmas." In *Steven Lewis' Bing Crosby Internet Museum.* www.kcmetro.cc.mo.us/pennvalley/biology/lewis/crosby/bing.htm

Wilkins, Edward. *The 10 Greatest Christmas Movies Ever Made: Fun Facts, Quizzes, and Behind-the-Scenes Trivia About Your Holiday Favorites.* Downers Grove, Illinois: Anton Enterprises, 1994.

Williams, Peter. "Welsh Cultural Traditions." Wales on Britannia. www.britannia.com/wales/culture2.html

Wilson, John. "The Origins of the Tune 'Antioch.'" *Bulletin of the Hymn Society of Great Britain and Ireland*, No. 166 (June 1986).

Wolfe, Charles K., and Neil V. Rosenberg. Program notes for Bill Monroe, *Bluegrass: 1950–1958.* Vollersode, Germany: Bear Family Records box set BFB 10013, 1989. Long-playing records.

"Yes, Virginia, There Is a Santa Claus." Ascension Research Center. www.ascension-research.org/yes.html

"Yule in Iceland." Islandia-Internet. www.islandia.is/~gardarj/

Index